DATE DUE

MY 6'			
AP 7 00			
MY 1 6 '01			
JE 1 1 '01			
NO 2 02			

DEMCO 38-296

THE SACRED FIRE OF LIBERTY

The Sacred Fire of Liberty

JAMES MADISON AND THE FOUNDING OF THE FEDERAL REPUBLIC

Lance Banning

CORNELL UNIVERSITY PRESS

ITHACA AND LONDON

PUBLICATION OF THIS BOOK WAS ASSISTED BY A GRANT FROM
THE PUBLICATIONS PROGRAM OF THE NATIONAL ENDOWMENT
FOR THE HUMANITIES, AN INDEPENDENT FEDERAL AGENCY.

Copyright © 1995 by Cornell University

First published 1995 by Cornell University Press

Library of Congress Cataloging-in-Publication Data
Banning, Lance, 1942-
   The sacred fire of liberty : James Madison and the founding of
the federal republic / Lance Banning.
      p.   cm.
   Includes bibliographical references and index.
   ISBN0-8014-3152-2 (cloth: alk. paper)
   1. Madison, James, 1751-1836.   2. United States—Politics and
government—1775-1783.   3. United States—Politics and
government—1783-1789.   4. United States—Politics and
government—1789-1797.   5. United States—Constitutional history.
I. Title.
E342.B245 1995
973.5'1'092–dc20   95-14369

Printed in the United States of America

⊗ The paper in this book meets the minimum requirements
of the American National Standard for Information Sciences—
Permanence of Paper for Printed Library Materials,
ANSI Z39-48-1984.

TO LANA

"The preservation of the sacred fire of liberty, and the destiny of the republican model of government, are justly considered as *deeply*, perhaps as *finally* staked, on the experiment entrusted to the hands of the American people."

WASHINGTON'S INAUGURAL ADDRESS *(drafted by James Madison)*

Contents

Acknowledgments

SO MANY FRIENDS have listened to these arguments or read a portion of this work that I will not attempt to name them. A comprehensive list would necessarily include anonymous reviewers, editors of various collections, antagonists who forced a change of mind, and—most especially—the several dozen scholars from a range of disciplines with whom I shared the broadening and interchange of thoughts encouraged by the conferences sponsored by Liberty Fund of Indianapolis. A few, however, volunteered extraordinary effort and deserve a very special thanks. Kenneth Bowling deployed his unrivaled knowledge to correct a number of mistakes in the chapters on the First Federal Congress. Peter Onuf, Drew McCoy, Paul Rahe, Michael Zuckert, and Alan Gibson carefully reviewed the whole. Collectively, they pointed me to sources I had overlooked, caught most (I hope) of the remaining gaffes, and noted many points at which the manuscript required more work. I am deeply grateful for their help and for the editorial advice of Andrew Lewis and Kay Scheuer.

The book draws freely on some articles and essays that appeared originally in other works. "James Madison and the Nationalists, 1780–1783," *William and Mary Quarterly*, 3rd ser., 40 (1983), 237–55, served as a preliminary draft for Chapter 1. Chapter 7 incorporates much of my essays, "1787 and 1776: Patrick Henry, James Madison, the Constitution, and the Revolution," originally published in *Toward a More Perfect Union: Six Essays on the Constitution*, ed. Neil L. York (Provo, Utah: Brigham Young University Scholarly Publications, 1988), 59–89, and "Virginia: Sectionalism and the General Good," which appeared in *Ratifying the Constitution: Ideas and Interests in the Several American States*, ed. Michael Allen Gillespie and Michael Lienesch (Lawrence: University Press of Kansas, 1989), © 1989 by the University Press of Kansas, 261–99. Chapter 3 draws on parts of "James Madison, the Statute for Religious Freedom, and the Crisis of

Republican Convictions," in *The Virginia Statute for Religious Freedom*, ed. Merrill D. Peterson and Robert C. Vaughn (New York: Cambridge University Press, 1988), 109–38. Part III draws freely on "The Practicable Sphere of a Republic: James Madison, the Constitutional Convention, and the Emergence of Revolutionary Federalism," in *Beyond Confederation: Origins of the Constitution and American National Identity*, ed. Richard Beeman, Stephen Botein, and Edward C. Carter II (Chapel Hill: University of North Carolina Press, 1987), 162–87, and on "The Constitutional Convention," in *The Framing and Ratification of the Constitution*, ed. Leonard W. Levy and Dennis J. Mahoney (New York: Macmillan, 1987), 112–31. Bits of "The Hamiltonian Madison: A Reconsideration," *Virginia Magazine of History and Biography* 92 (1984): 3–28, appear throughout. I am grateful to the publishers who granted me permission for this use and to the funding agencies that made it possible to complete the work during the current century. Time for research and writing was provided by the John Simon Guggenheim Foundation, the National Humanities Center, the University of Kentucky, and a talented, efficient wife. To her the book is dedicated, with appreciation and with love.

LANCE BANNING

Lexington, Kentucky

THE SACRED FIRE OF LIBERTY

The Madisonian Madison
An Introduction

IN 1834, WHEN HE WAS EIGHTY-THREE and many years into a vigorous
retirement from a brilliant public life, a correspondent called James Madison the "author" of the Constitution. This was a "credit" that the sole
surviving framer quite deliberately disclaimed, protesting that the federal
charter had not sprung, full blown, from any single brain.[1] Perhaps the
least vainglorious of all the famous founders, Madison was conscious, also,
that the nation's veneration for the Constitution rested partly on the memory that it had not been framed in anybody's study and had not become
the law at all until it was adopted by the people in a solemn act of national
deliberation and decision. Contemporaries, nonetheless, were far from
wrong when they accorded Madison a special place among the Founding
Fathers. The writing of the Constitution was indeed, as he reminded this
admirer, a summer's work of many heads and hands. The founding of the
federal republic was a larger labor still, which started long before and
stretched for years beyond the Constitutional Convention. Yet even after
full allowance has been made for all of the achievements of his colleagues,
Madison's centrality at every step in the creation of the federal republic
marks him as preeminent among the men who shaped, explained, and
won an overwhelming mandate for the nation's fundamental law.[2]

Madison led Virginia, which led the other states, in organizing a successful federal convention. He was principally responsible for the preliminary resolutions used as the initial outline for reform. By general
agreement of the other framers, no one took a larger part in the proceedings of the Constitutional Convention; and after it adjourned, he
joined with Alexander Hamilton to write the most important commentary
on the plan, defeated Patrick Henry in Virginia's narrowly divided state
convention, and assumed a leading role again as the First Federal Congress launched the infant government and wrote the Bill of Rights. Only

Washington, it has been said, was truly indispensable to the experiment's success. Hamilton and Thomas Jefferson, at least, proved equally important in establishing its early character and tone. But it is Madison on whom we unavoidably depend to comprehend its intellectual foundations. Madison was so essential at so many points in the creation and conceptualization of the new republic that we necessarily perceive the product partly through his eyes. If we have misinterpreted his conduct or mistaken his ideas, we have misunderstood the Founding. If we can reach a better understanding of the major architect and most compelling advocate of constitutional reform, we cannot fail to gain a fuller knowledge of the new republic's purposes and nature.

There is, in fact, a good deal more to learn. Because his words and deeds were obviously vital to the writing and interpretation of the Constitution, Madison has been a central subject for a host of brilliant scholars. There are four superb biographies of nicely varied scope.[3] The articles and essays number many score, as do the lengthy portions of impressive longer works that focus on the framer. Surprisingly, however, there has never been a book about the evolution of his founding vision; and this will be the subject of these pages.[4] The story to be told is that of Madison's participation in the reconstruction of the federal system: his effort to identify the nation's needs, to meet them in accord with its ideals, to first conceive and then defend a governmental form and practice that would shelter and perfect the Revolution. The argument, anticipated briefly in this introduction, is that a careful reexamination of the founder's course, accompanied by close analysis of the progression of his thoughts, suggests substantial alterations of prevailing views about the nature of his vision.

"Prevailing views," I know, may seem a problematic subject. There are few unchallenged understandings of a man so often studied. It would be entirely feasible, in fact, to write a book devoted solely to conflicting readings of his best known essay, *Federalist* number 10. On top of this, prevailing understandings may be changing even as I write.[5] For all of this, however, most disputes about the meaning of the founder's words occur within the framework of some widely shared impressions of his course and contributions. Commonly accepted by authorities who sharply disagree at more specific levels of interpretation, these impressions shape the questions scholars ask and form the image that persists when subtle differences among the answers are forgotten. By calling them to mind, I hope to summarize some central themes from which I partially dissent and sketch the structure that can be improved by the developmental study offered in this volume.

Explanations vary, for example, yet nearly all authorities discern a radical discontinuity between the Madison of the 1780s and the Madison of the 1790s. As a member of the Continental Congress, it is universally agreed, the young Virginian won a national reputation as an early advocate of federal reform. Then, like many of his allies of the war years, he returned to local politics to grapple with the economic difficulties and political disputes that followed on the peace, becoming legislative leader of Virginians who resisted debtor-oriented state responses to the postwar slump and advocated the amendment of the Articles of Confederation. Increasingly alarmed by both the problems of the Union and commotions in the states, repeatedly defeated by the Articles' requirement of unanimous consent to any alterations of the current federal system, the young reformer next embarked, with other continentalists, on extra-legal action. From the Annapolis Convention through the drafting of the Bill of Rights, Madison was more responsible than any other individual for bringing a successful federal convention into being, for turning the attention of this meeting to a thoroughgoing reconstruction of the federal system, for defending the completed Constitution as consistent with the principles of 1776, and for securing the amendments that destroyed the movement for substantial changes in the plan. The Bill of Rights was barely ratified, however, when its major author joined with Thomas Jefferson to launch a systematic opposition to the new administration. Within three years of Washington's inauguration, the archetypal Federalist of 1788 was metamorphosing into the party leader whose Virginia Resolutions, ten years later, would be seized upon by the succeeding generation to construct a theoretical foundation for secession.

Most political histories of the new American Republic attribute Madison's reversal to the pressures of the moment, as did most of his contemporary critics.[6] Most of Madison's biographers deny that he was moved exclusively, or even mainly, by political considerations. "In order to *preserve* consistency" in the defense of freedom, one biographer insists, Madison revised his views about the powers that could safely be confided to the new regime.[7] Consistently associating liberty with the perpetuation of the Union, another analyst suggests, Madison detected different dangers under different conditions and changed his mind about the policies and constitutional constructions most consistent with his fundamental ends.[8] But even authors who insist that the Virginian's course was deeply principled throughout agree that it was curiously twisted. Admirers and detractors both describe a statesman whose determination to enlarge the powers of the central government gave way to a determination to restrict them. Both inquire how Madison, the theorist of Federalism in 1787 and 1788, could also have become a shaper of the Jeffersonian resistance.

Politicians switch positions when confronted by new situations. Statesmen change their minds if they are capable of growing, and historians have little reason to admire a leader who maintains a rigid philosophical consistency in the face of changing circumstances and requirements. Everyone agrees, of course, that Madison was capable of learning, that he was, in fact, one of the most inventive and constructive thinkers of his age. Similarly, few interpreters believe that he was totally without a compass to direct him through the many turnings of his long career. Yet there has never been a scholarly agreement on the workings of that compass, and Madison's consistency—not day by day and not on every great and little point, but on the most important fundamentals—is anything except an academic issue. If the Founding did not end with Washington's inauguration—and few would any longer say it did—then it is possible to write about a Madisonian perspective only in so far as we can reconcile the founder with himself, identifying what was fixed beneath the flux. And even on the fundamentals, this is not, with Madison, an easy thing to do.

Throughout the 1780s, nearly all authorities agree, Madison believed in "easy discovery" of federal powers where none were explicitly granted, conducting a deliberate campaign to expand the boundaries of federal authority by way of a doctrine of implied congressional powers; he switched abruptly to a strict construction of the Constitution only when confronted with Hamilton's proposal for a national bank.[9] Although most scholars have concluded that Madison's construction of the federal charter was dependent on the ends he wanted to pursue, this hardly solves the puzzle. For, demanding new securities against majority oppressions, as well as greater power for the Union, the Madison of 1787 and 1788 envisioned an enlarged republic in which dangerous majorities would seldom form and complicated governmental checks and balances, by counterbalancing ambition with ambition, might protect the nation's liberties when all else failed. The Madison of 1792 not only feared that institutional and constitutional protections were collapsing; he was already working to create a party that would bring the will of the majority to bear to rescue liberty from governmental policies and constitutional constructions that appeared to him to threaten its destruction. The gulf between the pluralistic foe of faction and the advocate of party as an "instrument of democratic choice" seems so profound that one interpreter has recently suggested that we do not find one Madisonian legacy, but two.[10] And coming little more than three years after the inauguration of the new regime, the second legacy suggests disturbing challenges, to say the least, to dominant interpretations of the first.

It is, of course, the legacy of 1787 and 1788 that has attracted much the most intensive scholarly investigation. Here, as well, some serious disputes occur within the confines of some general agreements. Contemporary critics of the Constitution found it inconsistent with the democratic spirit of the Revolution. Led by Charles A. Beard, historians of the "Progressive" school, which was the dominant interpretation through the first half of the twentieth century, agreed that the reform was counterrevolutionary in intention and effects.[11] "Progressive" views were strongly challenged after World War II, but they have never been entirely overturned. In more sophisticated form, they strongly influenced Gordon Wood, whose masterful discussion of the background of the Constitution argues that it was, at once, an effort to restrain "the democratic tendencies of the period" and a logical development of revolutionary thinking.[12] Thus, conflicting explications of *The Federalist* and of the movement for reform continue to affect, and be affected by, a classic controversy over the relationship between the Constitution and the Declaration of Independence, a dispute compounded by a running disagreement over the degree to which the public writings of the framers actually reflect their private judgments of the Constitution. Still, none of the disputants would deny that understanding Madison is indispensable to understanding Federalist opinion, and there is little argument about the points at which he made his greatest contributions.

During the 1780s, no one doubts, a very large proportion of the national elite became increasingly alarmed by both the weaknesses of the Confederation and conditions in the states. Early in the Revolution, a majority of states had written democratic constitutions that delivered overbearing power to the most immediate representatives of the majority of voters. Composed, to a significant degree, of men whose relatively modest social rank might have excluded them from higher office under the colonial regimes, and chosen annually by an expanded, more demanding electorate, several of the lower legislative houses responded to the postwar slump with policies that favored debtors over creditors or postponed public obligations in order to provide relief. Growing numbers of conservative, established men, contemptuous of newly minted politicians, considered many of these measures—postponements of taxation, paper money, or laws impeding private suits for the recovery of debts—as violations of the fundamental liberties that Independence was intended to protect. Even as they blamed the nation's economic troubles on the impotence of the Confederation, even as they realized that arguments among the states could culminate in fragmentation of the Union, many of these well- established leaders grew increasingly disgruntled with the revolutionary constitutions. Growing numbers of the nation's influential citizens began to wonder whether individual rights were really as secure in democratic polities as they had once believed.[13]

Madison, according to prevailing views, completed the connections and provided the creative spark that made it possible to diagnose and treat this national malaise. To him, the weaknesses of the Confederation and the rising discontent with populistic policies and democratic constitutions seemed related aspects of a single crisis of the Revolution, which could not be overcome except by a complete reorganization of the Union. *Both* dimensions of the illness must be treated, he insisted, and the proper remedy for both was to reconstitute the central government as a republic. A large republic could be trusted with the powers necessary to invigorate the union, and a well-constructed large republic, by providing new securities for private rights, might also reinvigorate the revolutionary faith. This was the reasoning behind the plan that the Virginians offered to the Constitutional Convention. It was the reasoning, historians agree, by which the most important author of that plan directed the convention toward a sweeping reconstruction of the federal system and a thoroughgoing reconsideration of the proper structure of a sound republican regime.[14]

Madison's defense of the enlarged republic, elaborated in *The Federalist*, is generally considered to be little less significant than the ideas that led to its construction. The centerpiece, again, was his insistence that a large republic would incorporate so many different interests that majorities would seldom violate essential rights or sacrifice the long-term public good to more immediate considerations. Perhaps the most effective answer to the Antifederalist concern that liberty would be endangered by the Constitution, this reversal of the ordinary supposition that republics should be small and founded on a homogeneous population was itself conditioned by a new analysis of the societal foundations of the state. Conceiving of the people as dividing naturally into a congeries of overlapping interest groups, not into a many and a few, Madison did not believe that liberty could be protected only by establishing a governmental equilibrium between distinctive social groups. Rather, severing the preference for a balanced form of government from its traditional association with a mixture of estates, he cut the strings that tied republican philosophy to theories rooted in the classics and led the Federalists in the construction of a new political science.[15]

The new political science, according to the finest recent work, was largely, though not wholly, Madison's creation. It was a politics of "interest," not of "virtue."[16] Starting with a realistic view of human nature, it did not assume that a republic must or could depend upon a superhuman readiness to sacrifice self-interest to the common good. Taking humans for the interested, opinionated creatures that they are, it nevertheless affirmed that public needs and private rights could both be reconciled with governments deriving wholly from consent. In the pluralistic, large republic, Madison asserted, partial interests would be counterbalanced by competing interests, tyrannical majorities would be restrained, and popular desires would be refined and rendered more consistent with the long-term needs of the community by filtering opinion through superior officials, who would have to have the stature necessary to secure election in expanded districts. Should the best men fail to find their way to office, liberty and public good would still be guaranteed by institutional arrangements that would check ambition with ambition. The interests of the officeholder would defend the powers of his office, and the constitutional machinery for managing competing interests would be safe, as well, from managers who might be tempted to manipulate it in their own behalf.

With these ideas and others, it is generally agreed, Madison and other Federalists accomplished more than a defense and exegesis of the Constitution. Building on the lessons of the past ten years and pushing forward with the theoretical revisions started by the Revolution, they left the intellectual landscape thoroughly transformed. Redefining terms like "sovereignty," "democracy," and "federation," they speeded the American departure from a neo-classical conception of political society and moved republican philosophy decisively toward the adoption of a modern, liberal perspective. They left us both the polity and the political vocabulary that have lasted to this day.

These seem to me the leading features, briefly stated, of the current view of Madison's position at the Founding: the understanding of his course and contributions commonly accepted as the framework for interpretive debates. As is often true of a prevailing understanding, much of it is genuinely wise. Most of it I shared when I decided to begin a study of my own. But as I probed more deeply into Madison's career and thought, intending a biography, it seemed increasingly impossible to reconcile my findings with the views with which I had begun. Two difficulties were especially disturbing and especially responsible for my conclusion that a full biography should be postponed in favor of a systematic reconsideration of the actions and ideas connected most directly with the launching of the Constitution.

In the first place, it became increasingly apparent that some of our impressions would have pained and puzzled Madison himself. During his retirement, when contemporaries asked why he had switched directions after 1789, he quarreled with the question.[17] In his own opinion, no contemporary statesman had pursued a more consistent course.[18] He would have been especially, though not exclusively, perplexed by modern scholarly agreement that he changed from an expansive to a strict construction of the Constitution, from a centralizing to a states' rights stance.

By itself, of course, the founder's own dissent from dominant interpretations hardly seemed an insurmountable objection. Historians are used to taking autobiographical reflections with a healthy dose of salt, and Madison himself had thoroughly distrusted anyone who acted as a judge in his own cause. And yet, at least about the framer's attitude toward the construction of a written constitution, it became increasingly apparent that modern scholarship was simply wrong. Even when the federal charter was the Articles of Confederation, Madison had normally assumed a strict-constructionist position, and the implications of this fact seemed more and more important as I followed them into related stands or actions that did not make sense in terms of my original assumptions. The point was not that Madison deserved more praise for philosophical consistency than he was currently receiving, and it was definitely not that he had never changed his mind at all. The problem was that our interpretive container simply would not hold the founder's understanding of himself. It leaked important evidence at several vital seams and twisted his opinions into shapes that seriously distorted his position, shapes entirely inconsistent with the way in which his viewpoint had emerged.

The reconsideration offered in these chapters follows Madison from his appearance on the national scene until his understanding of the Constitution and his definition of the nation's needs solidified into the vision that would guide him through the rest of his career. It concentrates throughout on the emergence or construction of that vision, suggesting that our understanding of the founder's thought can be significantly improved by reexamination of the way that it developed. Examining the process by which Madison became the major theorist of federal reform, attempting to recover the Virginian's understanding of himself, I argue first that analysts since Irving Brant, whose great biography still serves as the essential starting point for modern studies, have generally mistaken Madison's position during the early 1780s. A different view of Madison's initial stand compels a fresh interpretation of the train of thought that led him to the Constitutional Convention. This, in turn, suggests that we have not completely understood his conduct and intentions at this meeting.

Studies of the Constitutional Convention rightly stress the powerful effects of Madison's original proposals. It may be equally important, though, to ask how Madison was influenced *by* the framing of the Constitution. Pursuing this neglected question, I submit that Madison's participation in the Constitutional Convention affected him more deeply and in different ways than standard studies have revealed. Tracing the resulting changes through the ratification contest and the drafting of the Bill of Rights, I finish with a reconsideration of the essays for the *National Gazette*, which publicly explained his reasons for determined opposition to the new administration. Not till then, I argue, did the framer systematically relate his settled understanding of the Constitution to the fundamental objects he had had in mind throughout its writing and adoption. Not until we can successfully relate these essays to *The Federalist* and to the Constitutional Convention can we firmly grasp his underlying vision.

Careful reexamination of the evolution of the founder's thought convinces me that modern scholarship has generally misjudged the hopes and fears he brought into the Constitutional Convention, that analysts have misinterpreted a major change of mind which started while the meeting was in process, and that we therefore hold a poorly balanced view of what he said and what he was attempting in *The Federalist*. Moreover, efforts to explain the framer's contributions to the explanation and success of constitutional reform have usually concluded with his drafting of the Bill of Rights, though Madison was still attempting, at this point, to come to terms with the convention's work and to define the policies that he believed the Constitution was intended to permit. The Madison who wrote the platform for an opposition party was not as inconsistent with the "father of the Constitution" as is usually believed. Not only does the opposition leader help explain the Federalist of 1788, he is essential to a fuller understanding of the ways in which the father meant to guarantee his progeny's success.

James Madison did more to shape the early nation's comprehension of its governmental institutions than any other member of his generation. A reinterpretation of his contribution to the Founding, concentrating on the fundamental constancies suggested by the evolution of his thought, has much to say about this fascinating era. It urges reconsideration of the tensions present in the Constitutional Convention and among the men who led the way toward federal reform, challenging the habit of conceiving of the Federalists as members of a single movement, sharing common goals. Compelling a reemphasis on Madison's commitment to the people's active and continuing participation in the system, together with a reassertion of his genuine acceptance of the novel, compound features of a partly national, but also partly *federal* Constitution, it reminds us of the genuinely revolutionary sources of the new regime.[19]

Perhaps because we think of Madison so often as one of those who brought stability to the Confederation and prepared the institutional and theoretical foundations for today's United States, we seldom fully recognize how constantly and consciously he was himself intent on the protection and perfection of a democratic Revolution. Yet, in the end, the thing that most distinguished Madison from all the other framers was his early, firm, and intimate association of the continental union with a great, republican experiment that he consistently conceived, in insufficiently acknowledged ways, in early-revolutionary terms. The "liberty" he wished to save—and spoke of in the passage written for the first inaugural address—was not just liberty defined as the inherent rights of individuals, but also liberty defined as popular control. Convinced that neither sort of liberty could be secure without the other, temperamentally unable to decide between his "liberal" and his "republican" convictions, Madison set out to rescue *both* of the ideals enunciated in the Declaration at a time when growing numbers of Americans believed that they might have to choose. If he had not rebelled so fiercely at this prospect, the Confederation might have solved its problems in a different way, but the United States would not have framed or ratified the kind of Constitution that emerged. If he had not continued to insist so stubbornly on the republican and federal features of that Constitution, the infant federal government might either have collapsed within his lifetime or taken on a character quite different from the one it actually assumed. By following his struggle and recovering his mode of thought, it may be possible to gain new insight into the completed Constitution and to reach a different understanding of the revolutionary federalism that he meant as his bequest.[20]

PART ONE

The Crisis of the Revolution

MADISON IN 1783.
Miniature by Charles Wilson Peale.
Courtesy of the Photoduplication Service,
Library of Congress

CHAPTER ONE

James Madison
and the Nationalists,
1780–1783

JAMES MADISON PRESENTED HIS CREDENTIALS to the Continental Congress on March 20, 1780. He was barely twenty-nine and almost totally unknown outside his native state, so youthful in his mannerisms and appearance that an older delegate mistook him for a youngster fresh from college.[1] Graceless and retiring at social events, slight and unassuming, Madison did not impress a casual acquaintance as a likely candidate for greatness. Virginia's legislators, who had sent him to this body, knew that he had labored faithfully, although obscurely, for the past two years as a member of the Council of State. They counted on his single-minded dedication to his duty when General Washington and others begged for able men who might revivify a delegation decimated by internal bickering and midterm resignations.[2] Some Virginians may have glimpsed the power of his mind, but even they had little reason to suspect his aptitude for legislative business.

Within two years, the awkward freshman had become the most effective man in Congress. Another nineteen months, and he was able to return to local politics a skillful legislative rival of the Old Dominion's revolutionary giants, Patrick Henry and Richard Henry Lee. The years in Congress gave him national stature. They permitted him to hone the talents that would make him preeminent in every subsequent deliberative assembly he attended.[3] They are the years about which there is least dispute among the scholars, and perhaps the most significant mistake.

In the Continental and Confederation Congresses, according to the great biography that has profoundly influenced every later work, Madison "endeavored to establish . . . national supremacy—first by a return to the original authority Congress lost when it stopped printing money and became financially dependent upon the states, next by recognition of implied powers in the Articles of Confederation, then by the vigorous exercise of powers whose validity could not be challenged, finally by amendment of the Articles to confer new powers upon Congress." Before his term was over, Irving Brant declared, Madison was "the acknowledged leader in every activity that bulwarked independence and pointed toward a strong, firm national union of the states."[4] Subsequent biographers have challenged Brant on lesser points, but they and other students of Confederation politics have generally affirmed his central theme. Current scholarship portrays the young Virginian as an eager advocate of centralizing change throughout his years in Congress, a leader of "the nationalists of 1781–1783."[5]

Several elements of this familiar portrait are enormously misleading. More, perhaps, than any other influence, they erect imposing obstacles to better understanding of the nature and development of Madison's ideas. They also interfere in a variety of ways with recognition of some fundamental differences among the continentalists of the early 1780s— differences with major implications for the more successful effort for reform that came at the decade's end.

Standard works do not explain that Madison first rose to prominence in Congress as a capable defender of Virginia's special interests. For months, those interests reinforced his inclination to *resist* unauthorized extensions of congressional authority—an inclination deeply rooted in his revolutionary creed. And this was so however loudly a commitment to Virginia and the Revolution also called for greater power for the Confederation. Day by day, as British forces overran the Carolinas and then turned toward Virginia, Congress groped for one expedient after another to keep an army in the field. The victory at Yorktown ended the danger that the South might be torn from the Confederation, but the agonizing crawl toward peace brought difficulties nearly as severe. Although Madison continued to defend his state's distinctive interests, he came increasingly to favor larger federal powers—as, indeed, did nearly everyone in Congress.

Still, Madison's acceptance of the need for radical reform was limited and halting. Until the fall of 1782, he supported centralizing measures with demonstrable reluctance, often as a product of his deep alarm about Virginia and the revolutionary cause. Even in his final months of service, when he joined with Robert Morris to support a centralizing change, he proved unable to accept the ultimate objectives of his allies. Madison, in short, was simply not a "nationalist" during the early 1780s—not, at least, in several of the senses commonly suggested by that term. He was not an early or enthusiastic friend of radical reforms. His cooperation with the Morrisites did not reflect a concord of opinion. On the contrary, the course of the cooperation suggestively prefigured the confrontation with

Alexander Hamilton that eventually divided the Federalists of 1789 into the warring parties of the 1790s.

When Madison retired from Congress, he intended to reenter the Virginia legislature to advocate compliance with Confederation treaties and acceptance of the congressional recommendations of 1783, which he had largely written. But he did not, as yet, support a thoroughgoing reconsideration of the Articles of Confederation, and his enthusiasm for reform was tempered by his doubts about the program and intentions of his allies. Developments pushed him further in the years ahead. By 1787, he was ready to propose a nationalizing program of his own. And yet the doubts he carried with him from the early 1780s would also help to shape his subsequent career. At the Constitutional Convention, as before, Madison's assumptions and desires were not just different from, but incompatible with, the centralizing vision of the more determined nationalists who gathered, first, around the old Confederation's superintendent of finance and, after 1789, around the new republic's secretary of the treasury. This incompatibility had quite important consequences, mostly overlooked, during the crisis of 1783. It would become explicit after a new federal government had been approved.[6]

Madison became a delegate to Congress at a gloomy juncture in the history of the Confederation. North America was near the end of the most severe winter in a generation. At Morristown, where continental soldiers were enduring hardships more extreme than they had suffered in the winter camp at Valley Forge, Washington found it hard to see how he could keep his hungry, unpaid troops together when their three-year enlistments began to expire. The Massachusetts Line had mutinied at West Point on January 1. Charleston was besieged, and its surrender later in the spring would bring the largest American losses of the war. In December 1779, Congress had been forced to turn to requisitions of specific goods in order to supply the northern army. On March 18, 1780, as Madison was riding into town, Congress had agreed to devalue the continental dollar and approved a new financial plan that threw responsibility for generating new bills of credit on the states. Desperate as these decisions were, the long delay in reaching them had shattered congressional prestige. During 1779, while precipitate inflation threatened to destroy the army, Congress had been paralyzed by bitter public controversy over peace terms and arguments among its diplomats abroad.[7]

Though Madison was well informed about these problems and had labored in particular to organize his thoughts on the financial crisis, the desperate condition of affairs impressed him with redoubled force as soon as he began to view it from the central government's perspective. Soon after reaching Philadelphia, he warned Thomas Jefferson, then governor of Virginia, that "the course of the Revolution" had seen no moment "more truly critical than the present." The army was "threatened with an immediate alternative of disbanding or living on free quarter." The treasury was empty. Public credit was exhausted. Congress complained "of the extortion of the people, the people of the improvidence of Congress, and the army of both." Congress recommended measures to the states, and the states individually decided whether it was expedient to comply. "Believe me, Sir, as things now stand, if the states do not vigorously proceed in collecting the old money and establishing funds for the credit of the new, . . . we are undone."[8]

The shock that seems apparent in the congressman's first letters to Virginia is a critically important clue to understanding his career.[9] Forced to grapple daily with the nation's problems through the Confederation's most difficult years, he never forgot the desperation of those times. Having occupied the station that he did, he could not see American affairs in the manner that he might have had he never left Virginia. His later letters comment often on the different perspectives of those who comprehended problems from a national vantage and those who were immersed in local concerns.[10] Nevertheless, these early letters may also easily mislead. They do not justify the view that Madison was bent on aggrandizement of congressional authority from the beginning of his term.

The youngest man in Congress, Madison was shy, thin-voiced, and diffident. Through his first six months of service, he made no motions and probably never entered a debate. Surviving public records tell us little more about these months than that his colleagues seldom chose him for important duties and that he must have been primarily concerned with the exigencies of war, especially through his assignments to the Board of Admiralty and the committee to correspond with General Greene, on both of which he was the junior member. Authorities agree, however, that Congress was preoccupied with the war and relatively free of factional disputes during the spring and summer of 1780, months marked by military disaster in the Carolinas, continuing depreciation of the currency, and the failure of the system of specific requisitions to meet the needs of the northern army, in which mutinies again erupted in May and June. The optimism sparked by the financial plan of March eventually gave way to virtually unanimous alarm about conditions in the army and to a general conclusion that dependence on the states might have to be abandoned in favor of a strengthening of Congress.[11]

Madison seems clearly to have shared the general sense of crisis and national humiliation. Writing Jefferson again, he characterized the "public situation" as fully as "alarming as when I lately gave you a sketch." Drafts on the states for unpaid requisitions had kept the army from starvation, but according to the new plan of finance, these drafts must shortly cease. When they did, he warned, "we must depend wholly on the [new] emissions," which Congress could not make until the states collected and destroyed the older continental paper. As long as Congress "exercised the indefinite power of emitting money," Madison observed, "they had the whole wealth and resources of the continent within their command." Now that the presses had been stopped, they were "as dependent on the states as the King of England is on the Parliament. They can neither enlist, pay, nor feed a single soldier, nor execute any other purpose, but as the means are first put into their hands. Unless the [local] legislatures are sufficiently attentive to this change of circumstances and act in conformity to it, everything must necessarily go wrong, or rather must come to a total stop."[12]

Plainly, Madison agreed with Joseph Jones, his senior colleague in Virginia's delegation, that Congress had surrendered too much power to the states.[13] He certainly agreed that circumstances called for prompt ratification of the Articles of Confederation, which Congress had submitted to the states in 1777.[14] Perhaps he was prepared for more significant reforms, but there is nothing in the public records or in Madison's surviving papers to support the usual suggestion that the young Virginian was ahead of other delegates in accepting the necessity for centralizing change. Rather, there are several hints that he persisted somewhat longer than most in hoping that such change would not be needed. The want of money, he protested, "is the source of all our public difficulties." One or two million guineas "would expel the enemy from every part of the United States" and "reconcile the army and everybody else to our republican forms of governments, the principal inconveniences which are imputed to these being really the fruit of defective revenues." The troops, he thought, could be as well equipped "by our governments as by any other if they possessed money enough."[15]

By the time he wrote these words, the modest freshman had been pushed into a larger role in Congress, though hardly as an advocate of larger federal powers. On September 6, he seconded a motion in which Joseph Jones, to whom the delegation had deferred on this outstanding matter, offered terms on which Virginia might agree to cede to the Confederation its impressive claim to all the lands northwest of the Ohio—a concession Maryland had long demanded as a precondition for its ratification of the Articles of Union. Soon thereafter, Jones departed for Virginia to attend his ailing wife and to persuade the legislature to complete the cession. Appointed to a committee to consider Jones's motion, Madison was prominent from this point on in all congressional deliberations concerning the West—not least because he feared that his remaining colleagues in the delegation, John Walker and Theodorick Bland, were not sufficiently attentive to Virginia's long-term interests. In mid-September, with Kentucky much in mind, he thrust himself into the argument about Vermont, whose independence Bland supported, with a set of resolutions asking Congress to declare that the New Hampshire grants were "within the limits of some one or more of the United States; [and] that every attempt by force to set up a separate and independent jurisdiction within the limits of any one of the United States is a direct violation of the rights of such state and subversive of the Union."[16] Then, when Congress received the committee's report on the Virginia cession and agreed to strike a clause that would have voided private purchases from the Indians, Madison opposed the change, though Bland and Walker voted for the altered resolution.[17]

Anxious as he was for Maryland to approve the Articles of Confederation—Cornwallis had destroyed the tiny southern army under General Gates and crossed into North Carolina on September 8—Madison continued to oppose congressional attempts to force Virginia to relent from its demand that any act of cession must refuse to recognize the claims of the great land companies, which had concluded private contracts with the natives. Congressional acceptance of these speculative claims, in his opinion, would transfer an enormous treasure "from the public to a few land mongers."[18] It would also—and improperly—imply that Congress had a legal jurisdiction over the Northwest. Through all the months ahead, while British forces terrorized the South and terms for the completion of the cession periodically divided Congress, Madison denied that the Confederation had a valid, independent claim to lands northwest of the Ohio. He repeatedly insisted that Virginia's sovereignty was absolute within the whole of its chartered bounds. Although he urged Virginia to complete its western cession and would later prove an early advocate of independence for Kentucky, he was rigidly determined that Virginia would control the timing and conditions of both acts.[19]

Meanwhile, Madison's determination to defend Virginia's claims, as well as the essential interests of the westerners themselves, encouraged him to take a major role in congressional deliberations over the terms of a projected treaty with Spain. Like other frightened delegates from the invaded South, Madison supported close cooperation with America's French allies, who had a separate treaty with the Spanish. He soon established close relationships with both the Chevalier de La Luzerne and with the secretary of the French legation, François de Barbé-Marbois.[20] He has often been identified as a member of a "French party" in Congress, and French agents described him as "devoted to us"—"devoted," yet, according to La Luzerne, "not free from prejudices in favor of the various claims of Virginia, however exaggerated they may be."[21] Certainly, Virginia's claims made Madison a problematic friend of France on the issue of America's relationship with Spain.

Aware that Spain would not complete a treaty of alliance with the new United States on terms that might endanger its position in Louisiana, French emissaries urged their friends in Congress to be flexible about a western boundary and about American pretensions to a right to navigate the Mississippi River through the Spanish enclave at its mouth. No congressman was *less* inclined to make concessions on such matters than the young Virginian. The original instructions for a Spanish treaty, which Congress had assigned him to explain, were wholly to his liking.[22] But when desperate delegates from Georgia and South Carolina moved to abandon the original insistence on free navigation of the Mississippi, Madison succeeded in having the motion postponed even though his stand embroiled him in another disagreement with his colleague Theodorick Bland. He trusted, he explained to the departed Jones, "that Congress will see the impropriety of sacrificing the acknowledged limits and claims of any state" without that state's consent.[23] And when he wrote to Jefferson to seek a legislative resolution of his difference with Bland, he made it clear that desperate conditions in the South were not sufficient to convince him that Virginia should accept a Spanish treaty at the price of free navigation of the Mississippi or the state's extensive western claims. He also asked for specific instructions concerning what the delegates should do if Congress made concessions on either of these matters without Virginia's consent.[24]

By the end of his initial year in Congress, Madison was being chosen with increasing regularity for service on the critical committees. Early in 1781 he was mentioned as a candidate for the position of secretary for foreign affairs.[25] Created just a month before, this post was the first of four executive offices established by Congress while Virginia and Maryland were acting to complete the Confederation. Congress made these important administrative changes, culminating in the appointment of Robert Morris as superintendent of finance, without a serious division. Madison supported them, although his papers are entirely silent on the subject. In the years ahead, the young Virginian often served as the administrators' man in Congress. He was willing to accept a good deal of executive initiative, normally supported the secretaries' recommendations, and often guided their proposals through the Congress.[26]

Madison's approval of executive efficiency should not, however, be confused with a desire, much less with a consistent effort, to encourage the centralization of power. In close conjunction with the creation of executive departments, Congress asked the states for the authority to levy a 5 percent duty on foreign imports and launched into a broad consideration of the adequacy of the newly ratified Articles. Analyzing these deliberations of the first six months of 1781, most students of Confederation politics have identified the young Virginian as a leader of a nationalistic push. Failing, it is said, to win congressional endorsement of a federal power to coerce delinquent states, Madison conducted a deliberate campaign to expand federal authority by means of a doctrine of implied congressional powers.[27] This interpretation comes quite close to standing the Virginian on his head. It rests on partial reading of the evidence and smothers a profound ambivalence in his position. It also raises an unnecessary barrier to understanding how he would arrive at the position he occupied by 1793.

What we know of the decisions of 1781 can be reduced to a few essentials. On February 3, John Witherspoon, Madison's former teacher at the College of New Jersey, moved to ask the states for an amendment granting Congress the authority to regulate trade. This motion was defeated, four states to three. Then, by the same margin, Congress recommended an amendment authorizing it to levy a 5 percent duty on foreign imports (the impost amendment). Madison and Jones overrode Bland to cast Virginia's vote *against* both motions.[28] At some point in the business, Madison prepared a substitute proposal, which we can take as the clearest indication of his wishes: "That it be earnestly recommended to the states, as indispensably necessary to the support of public credit and the prosecution of the war, immediately to pass laws" levying a 5 percent duty on foreign imports and vesting Congress with the power to collect these funds and to employ them to discharge the principal and interest of its debts.[29] The language shows that although he wanted both the impost and congressional collection of the duties, Madison did not support an independent federal power to impose the tax or to employ the funds for any other purpose than to make provision for the debt. On this issue, as on the related question of congressional superintendence of commerce, he was plainly not prepared to extend congressional authority as far as many of his fellows would have liked.

Similar conclusions can be reached about the episode that may appear to offer the strongest evidence for Madison's early participation in a nationalistic thrust. During the spring and summer of 1781, three congressional committees considered ways to strengthen the Articles of Confederation. Madison served on the first of these committees and wrote its report, which recommended an amendment authorizing Congress "to employ the force of the United States" to compel delinquent states to fulfill their "federal obligations."[30] Madison's biographers have rightly stressed that he regarded this coercive power as implicit in the Articles without amendment and was deeply serious about employing this forbidding tool. Virginians were complaining bitterly about inadequate support, and Madison shared fully in their anger, writing that coercion was required because of the "shameful deficiency" of some of the "most capable" states and the "military exactions" to which others, "already exhausted," were consequently exposed.[31] He not only wondered whether Congress, by proposing an amendment, ought to risk denial of a power it already had by implication; he also mentioned a "collateral reason" why Virginians should support a federal navy, which would be the most convenient instrument of federal force. "Without it," he inquired, "what is to protect the southern states for many years to come against the insults and aggressions of their northern brethren?"[32]

Every part of this is worth remarking. If Madison was thinking of coercion of delinquent states, this was not because he was intent, in abstract fashion, on increasing federal powers, but because New England's failure to respond more vigorously to the invasion of the South had put Virginia in peril. Moreover, desperate as he was, he still decided in the end to favor an amendment rather than to rely on implicit federal powers. Why he did is crucial to our understanding of his thought, and his report for the committee was explicit on this point. Although the power of coercion *was* implicit in the Articles, he wrote, the absence of a more "determinate and particular provision" could lead to challenges by recalcitrant states. Moreover, it was "most consonant to the spirit of a free constitution that . . . all exercise of power should be explicitly and precisely warranted." This preference for explicit grants of power was a theme to which he would return repeatedly in the months—and years—ahead.[33]

Madison insisted, in the early months of 1781, on an implied congressional authority to coerce delinquent states. He presupposed implied powers—logically at least—when he proposed to tighten the restrictions on illegal trade or when he moved to authorize the forces under General Wayne to impress supplies on their march to Virginia. So, however, did virtually the whole of Congress, for neither of these motions generated constitutional debate, and neither of them advocated anything except renewal or extension of the sort of measures Congress had traditionally

employed. Apart from the coercion of the states, the actions usually enumerated to support the view that Madison was consciously campaigning
to enlarge congressional authority were uniformly based on the undoubted federal power to carry on the war. They do not suggest a conscious effort to increase the powers of Congress, and no one had to offer
forced constructions of the Articles in order to support them. Madison
demonstrably did not. Ordinarily, in fact, he was extremely wary of the
doctrine of implied congressional authority. His respect for written limitations of authority and charter boundaries between the powers of the
nation and the states did not develop after 1789. It was apparent during
the Confederation's darkest years.[34]

Madison's position on a national bank is one of many illustrations.
Like nearly all his colleagues, he favored Robert Morris's appointment as
superintendent of finance, approved the financier's conditions for accepting the appointment, and supported his attempts to rescue public
credit. The bank was a partial exception. Morris urged creation of this
institution on May 17, 1781, three days after his appointment, two weeks
after the Virginia delegates reported the final collapse of the currency,
and one week after the Virginia legislature had been forced to flee from
Richmond. On May 26, Madison nevertheless distinguished himself as one
of only four congressmen to oppose a resolution endorsing the superintendent's plan, objecting that the Articles conferred no federal power to
create a corporation. On December 31, he evidently acquiesced in the
ordinance of incorporation itself, but not without explicit reservations. To
Edmund Pendleton he wrote, "You will conceive the dilemma in which
. . . circumstances placed the members who felt on the one side the *importance* of the institution, and on the other a want of power and an aver-
sion to assume it." Unwilling to frustrate the financier, disappoint the
army, or break an implicit promise to subscribers, worried congressmen
had been obliged to settle for a resolution recommending actions by the
states to give the charter for the bank validity within their several bounds.
"As this is a tacit admission of a defect of [federal] power, I hope," Madison explained, "it will be an antidote against the poisonous tendency of
precedents of usurpation."[35]

The bank was not the only issue on which Madison revealed the limits
of his continentalism and his inclination to insist on strict construction of
the federal charter. On May 28, with Austria and Russia hinting that they
might compel a mediated peace, French minister La Luzerne asked Congress to define its terms for a treaty. Through the summer and into the
fall, opposed at every turn by Witherspoon, the French, and frightened
delegates from Georgia and the Carolinas (who feared a peace that would
leave them to the British), Madison fought a stubborn, losing battle to

make the western claims of the United States—or, at minimum, the western claims of Virginia—one of the conditions of a peace. Failing that, he tried to make these claims a necessary part of any commercial treaty with Great Britain.[36] He worried, too, about increasing sentiment in favor of independence for Vermont, not least because he feared that "some of the little states . . . hope that such a precedent may engender a division of some of the large ones."[37]

Through these months, though Maryland had ratified the Articles of Confederation, the smaller states (and members with a speculative interest in the matter) continued to resist Virginia's terms for cession of the northwest lands. On June 27, 1781, a committee recommended that all state acts of cession be rejected and that a line be drawn beyond which Congress would not guarantee the states' remaining western claims. This was rejected, and the issue was referred to a new committee, before which the Virginia delegates maintained that Congress should accept the western cessions without inquiring into the validity of titles and that, under the Articles of Confederation, Congress had no jurisdiction over conflicting state claims. On October 6, still clinging to this ground, the delegates protested the committee's willingness to receive land company petitions. Nevertheless, on November 3, the new committee recommended accepting the New York cession, rejecting those of Connecticut and Virginia, and validating the claims of the Indiana Company.[38] On November 7, Edmund Randolph, now a member of the delegation, reported to Governor Thomas Nelson that its members were "almost worn down with motions respecting your cession." Virginia, he protested, was "not merely destitute of friends but surrounded by those who labor to retrench her territory."[39]

Before the year was over, Madison was thoroughly embittered over these proceedings. They "clearly speak the hostile machinations of some of the states against our territorial claims," he complained to Jefferson, "and afford suspicions that the predominant temper of Congress may coincide with them." Madison did not advise despair. Congress, he explained, had not adopted "the obnoxious doctrine of an inherent right in the United States to the territory in question." He therefore hoped that Jefferson would try to counteract "any intemperate measures that may be urged in the legislature." He admitted, nonetheless, that the congressional proceedings were "ample justification" for a legislative revocation of the cession and for a remonstrance by the state against congressional interference in Virginia's jurisdiction. The proceedings offered ample warning, too, he said, that the Virginia legislature should "in all their provisions for their future security, importance, and interest, . . . presume that the present Union will but little survive the present war."[40]

Through the spring of 1782, as he completed his second year in Congress, Madison remained preoccupied with independence for Vermont and with the western cessions. He still preferred to block Vermont's admission as a state. He questioned whether Congress had authority for such an act, he feared the precedent that might be used against Virginia, and he worried that admitting Vermont would add another state to the landless and New England blocs in Congress.[41] He also tried repeatedly to force a favorable decision on Virginia's cession, which he considered intimately tied to the dispute about Vermont.[42] When Congress stalled, he suggested to Arthur Lee, another new arrival in the delegation, that it would not be "consistent with the respect we owe to our own public characters nor with the dignity of those we serve to persist longer in fruitless applications." Instead, he thought, the delegation should request new instructions from the legislature, "who will certainly be fully justified in taking any course . . . which the interest of the state shall prescribe."[43] He hoped the legislature would stand firm. The delegation even gave some thought to making its support for measures pressuring reluctant states to ratify the impost "subservient to an honorable" decision on the cession.[44]

Madison still hoped, in time, to see the transfer of the northwest lands from Virginia to the Confederation, which would be greatly strengthened by the acquisition. Here, as almost always, he considered the distinctive rights and interests of his state to be consistent with the long-term general good. Nonetheless, he was determined to delay this act—together, naturally, with any revenues that might accrue from sales of western lands—until the cession was accepted on Virginia's terms. He still maintained, as always, that Congress had no valid, independent claim to the Northwest, no legal jurisdiction there. And he could be so irritated by assertions that it did, so thoroughly disgusted by the speculators' greedy grasping for this treasure, and so profoundly angered by the jealous jibes of members from the "landless" states that he could privately suggest that the Old Dominion, anticipating dissolution of the Union soon after Independence was secured, should be prepared to "defy" her insulters "from whatever quarter" they appeared.[45]

Madison's positions on the West, the impost, commerce, and the bank should caution us against identifying him with a cohesive group of nationalist reformers through his first two years and more in Congress. The more one questions this interpretation, the more apparent are the problems. In his standard study of congressional divisions, for example, H.

James Henderson explicitly endorses Brant's portrayal of Madison as an energetic and consistent member of a nationalistic coalition.[46] Henderson's analyses of voting patterns in Congress do not support his text. The cluster bloc analysis for 1780 places Madison in a New England-Virginia group on the fringes of an "Eastern Party," which included most of the "Old Revolutionaries" still in Congress and which voted quite differently from the Southern and New York blocs, whose members Henderson identifies with a nationalistic thrust.[47] The table for 1781 places Madison in a separate Virginia bloc, which was the most loosely attached of the four groupings within a dominant "Middle-Southern Coalition."[48] The quantitative study for 1782, when Congress was preoccupied by the issues of Vermont and the western cessions, associates Madison with a separate Virginia group within a "Southern Party," which opposed a "Northern Party," which itself was divided into distinct New England and Middle States blocs.[49] Only during 1783 does the analysis of roll calls identify the young Virginian firmly with a nationalistic coalition.

For the months between the spring of 1780 and the fall of 1782, the scanty evidence permits few generalizations about Madison's congressional position, and these must differ markedly from the conclusions that have usually been drawn.[50] Madison did consistently advocate a harmonious relationship between the United States and France, though no one was a more persistent or effective foe of French attempts to win American concessions on the matters of a western boundary or navigation of the Mississippi River. By the summer of 1782, as several scholars have observed, his wish for close relationships with France had put him bitterly at odds with yet another colleague in his delegation, Arthur Lee, whose enmity toward Benjamin Franklin and suspicion of the French Madison denounced as portending a revival of the party controversies of 1779.[51] Madison's dislike of Lee was compounded by the latter's vendetta against Robert Morris, whom Madison normally supported. "My charity," he wrote,

> cannot invent an excuse for the prepense malice with which the character and services of this gentleman are murdered. I am persuaded that he accepted his office from motives which were honorable and patriotic. I have seen no proof of misfeasance. . . . Every member of Congress must be sensible of the benefit which has accrued to the public from his administration. . . . The same fidelity to the public interest which obliges . . . its supporters to pursue with vigor a perfidious or dishonest servant . . . requires them to confront the imputations of malice against the good and faithful one.[52]

Through the fall of 1782, however, Madison did not conceive of Congress as divided into parties over Morris. Neither does the body of the evidence support attempts to link him with a group intent on national aggrandizement. He did not vote that way across a range of issues. On the impost, commerce, and the national bank, he sided with the members most resistant to reform. Moreover, one may search in vain through Madison's surviving papers for any indication that he was even aware of a reformist push toward greater national authority, much less identified with one. Far from seeking subtle means to extend the constitutional boundaries of congressional power, Madison was usually a strict constructionist of sorts. Exceptions can be found, together with occasions when he consciously departed from the principle to meet a pressing need, but it is clear that he transgressed the Articles with obvious reluctance and concern. His ordinary inclination was to start with charter definitions of the boundaries between the central government and the states and to insist on *both* the full assertion of the powers granted Congress *and* a genuine regard for the authority remaining with the states. If this could lead him to support coercion of delinquents, it could also—and more often—lead him to defend states' rights.[53]

Nowhere was this plainer than in Madison's determined struggle to defend the Old Dominion's western claims, the issue that distinguished him most clearly in the minds of the majority in Congress. Historians have emphasized his role in the creation of a national domain, and it is fair to stress that he repeatedly wrote home to advocate completion of the cession, adoption of the impost, and compliance with other congressional recommendations. Madison was never a particularist in his essential inclinations. Even in the matter of the western claims, he was defending, as he saw it, both states' rights and an important national interest. Contemporaries nonetheless saw him correctly as a dedicated servant of his state, a continentalist whose vision of the nation's needs was unmistakably Virginian. He was willing to delay the impost or the cession in order to exclude the speculators from the West and to defend Virginia's jurisdiction. He opposed congressional control of commerce. He shared with most Virginians a visceral suspicion of New England and a fierce resentment of the jealousy that smaller states repeatedly displayed in confrontations with the large ones. When he wrote about congressional divisions, he identified his foes as easterners, as mid-states speculators, and as members from the landless states. He could not commit himself consistently to centralizing change while these remained his dominant preoccupations. He would not be unaffected by these feelings when his thinking changed.

During the fall of 1782, as Congress anxiously awaited news from its peace commissioners in Paris, changing circumstances altered Madison's preoccupations. Deliberations on Vermont and on the western cessions both took turns that he approved.[54] Meanwhile, the Confederation government drew ever nearer to financial desperation. Robert Morris had successfully supplied the army's victory at Yorktown. He had instituted valuable administrative changes at the Office of Finance, initiated operations at the national bank, and urged a settlement of the accounts between the central government and the states as an initial step toward funding the public debt. Still, peace was not yet certain, and the states were increasingly in arrears on their congressional requisitions (Virginia notoriously so). Rhode Island had not approved the impost, and the public creditors and soldiers were growing ever more impatient for their pay. In July, the superintendent of finance had seized on the occasion of a memorial from civilian creditors to deliver an important paper on the state of public credit, insisting that a whole new set of federal taxes would have to be combined with the receipts anticipated from the impost and from sales of western lands in order to meet current expenses and pay the interest on the debt. By fall, however, Congress had been able to agree on nothing more than further requisitions on the states.[55]

Through the fall of 1782, Madison still acted frequently as the superintendent's advocate in Congress. He agreed wholeheartedly with Morris when the clamors of civilian creditors and soldiers led two states to contemplate assuming portions of the Confederation's financial obligations. Reporting on New Jersey's warning that it might be forced to pay its continental line out of funds intended for its annual quota, Madison insisted, in language borrowed partly from Morris's July report, that "the federal constitution" provided that costs for the common defense be paid from the common treasury.[56] He also served with John Rutledge and Alexander Hamilton on another committee which managed to dissuade the Pennsylvania assembly from adopting a plan to pay its civilian federal creditors from state funds.[57] As before, he was as ready to defend the powers clearly granted to the general government as to insist on their limitations. As before, he conscientiously protected the distinctive interests of his state, not only in continuing deliberations on the cession and Vermont, but also in debates on the adjustment of the state accounts.[58]

Then, all at once, the budding crisis burst, and Madison was hurled into the center of the war years' most important effort to enlarge the powers of Congress. In December 1782, a deputation from the army came to Philadelphia from its winter camp at Newburgh, demanding an immediate provision for the unpaid private soldiers and firm assurances from Congress that the continental officers would actually receive the half-pay pensions promised them two years before. Congress hurriedly appointed a committee to travel to Rhode Island to make a personal appeal for ratification of the impost. They were barely on the road, on Christmas Eve, when a humiliated Madison was forced to tell the fundless Congress that his own Virginia had rescinded its approval of the measure, destroying all remaining hope that this amendment might provide an answer to the army's pleas.[59] Soon thereafter, fearing that the final weeks of war might also prove the final opportunity for doing justice to the army, restoring public credit, and securing revenues that could promote the nation's post-war economic growth, Robert Morris launched a formidable campaign to win approval of the taxes he had recommended in July. As rumors grew that terms for a preliminary peace had been agreed upon in Paris, the murmurs from the army steadily became more ominous in tone, and a "movement for uniting" all the public creditors, military and civilian, "emanated . . . from the Office of Finance."[60]

On January 6, Congress received the memorial from the army. On January 7, a congressional committee met with Morris, who informed them that the treasury could neither pay the soldiers now nor offer firm assurances of future pay until new funds had been established for the purpose. On January 9, the financier informed another committee that accounts abroad were overdrawn and won permission for a final draft on foreign funds despite this fact. On January 17, he told the deputation from the army that one month's pay could be provided from this draft, but that additional provisions were impossible without congressional approval, advising Congress simultaneously against further applications for foreign loans. Finally, on January 24, without preliminary warning, he announced that he would resign his office at the end of May if no provision had been made by then for managing the debt. Morris refused to serve as "the minister of injustice."[61]

The letter from the financier severely jolted Congress, which immediately turned its full attention to provisions for the debt. Moreover, some of Morris's supporters evidently took his threat as a signal for a concentrated effort to enlist the public creditors and soldiers in the push for independent federal taxes. Through the next two months, as news from Europe gradually confirmed reports of a preliminary peace, Congress battled over revenues and commutation of the half-pay pensions in the midst of growing rumors that the army might refuse to disband. At camp, the agitation culminated in the Newburgh Addresses of March 10 and 12, 1783.

The basic elements of Madison's response are clear.[62] Through most of February, as he served on all the key committees to confer with Morris and the deputation from the army, he agreed with Morris on the measures necessary to resolve the crisis. Despite Virginia's opposition to an alteration in the current mode of apportioning state requisitions (which required an assessment of land values), Madison joined with Hamilton and James Wilson, Morris's closest supporters in Congress, to argue that the constitutional rule for apportioning requisitions was unworkable and must be changed.[63] And although he shared the general resentment of the threatened resignation,[64] he agreed with Morris, too, that Congress must be granted both an impost and additional general revenues in order to meet its constitutional responsibilities. "Justice, gratitude, our reputation abroad, and our tranquility at home require provision for a debt of not less than fifty millions," he explained to Edmund Randolph. "If there are not revenue laws which operate at the same time through all the states and are exempt from the control of each, the mutual jealousies which already begin to appear among them will assuredly defraud both our foreign and domestic creditors."[65]

With Madison restrained by his instructions from Virginia, Hamilton and Wilson took the early lead in advocating independent federal taxes. Theodorick Bland and Arthur Lee insisted on a first recourse to further requisitions. By January 28, however, circumstances called imperatively for action, and Madison delivered what was possibly the most impressive speech of his congressional career. It was unnecessary, he remarked, to argue the necessity of paying the public debt, since "the idea of erecting our national independence on the ruins of public faith and national honor must be horrid to every mind which retained either honesty or pride." No one, though, could still suppose that Congress could continue to rely on "a punctual and unfailing compliance by thirteen separate and independent governments with periodical demands of money." Neither could the members reasonably depend on all the states to make separate, permanent provisions for the debt. Innumerable occasions would arise for the diversion of these individual appropriations to state uses. With every state convinced that others would default, such funds would soon dry up entirely. Payment of the debt could be assured only by "the plan of a general revenue operating throughout the United States under the superintendence of Congress." The alternative, as Pennsylvania's recent conduct showed, would be an individual assumption by the states of portions of the federal obligations. "What then," he asked, "would become of the Confederation?" What would happen to the army? "The patience of the army has been equal to their bravery, but that patience must have its limits."

Madison denied that general revenues, as Lee and Bland contended, would contravene the principles of the Confederation. Strictly speaking, Congress was already vested with the power of the purse: "A requisition of Congress on the states for money is as much a law to them as their revenue acts, when passed, are laws to their respective citizens." In addition, he observed, the Articles explicitly gave Congress the authority to borrow money. If adequate provision for its debt could not be made in any other way, "a general revenue is within the spirit of the Confederation." It was true, of course, that several states resisted even an impost. Virginia's recent recision of its earlier approval of this measure

> could not but produce some embarrassment in a representative advocating the scheme—one, too, whose principles were extremely unfavorable to a disregard of the sense of constituents. But it ought not to deter him from listening to considerations which in the present case ought to prevail. . . . Although . . . the declared sense of constituents . . . were to be a law in general to these representatives, still there were occasions on which the latter ought to hazard personal consequences from a respect to what his clear conviction determines to be the true interest of the former.

This was certainly the case, he finished, when the representative believed that his constituents would take the same position given equal knowledge of the public situation, a situation in which only the plan of general revenues could fulfill the intention of "the federal constitution" by making it "efficient."[66]

With this speech of January 28, Madison seized the leading role in the attempt to win congressional approval of independent federal taxes. He became, indeed, floor general of the effort, as Hamilton began deferring to his parliamentary talents. The advocates of independent funds had been trying to secure agreement on the principle itself. Madison believed that they must first convince opponents that their fears were groundless by suggesting a specific mix of taxes that would distribute the burden evenly on every state and section. And viewing the congressional support for requisitions based on land assessments as a stubborn obstacle to the approval of new taxes, he backed a motion to consider a procedure for completing this assessment before resuming the consideration of new federal funds. Hamilton, who realized that Madison was trying every means to bridge the gap between the congressional majority and Morris, quickly fell in line with his attempts to cut the procedural knots.

The strategy misfired. By the end of January, even Bland and Lee were moving toward support of a modified impost. Madison argued quietly for commutation of the army's half-pay pensions, a compromise the officers were willing to accept in light of fixed republican hostility to lifetime grants. Still, the members from New England and New Jersey continued to resist, provoking him to say that he was "astonished to hear objections against a commutation come from states in compliance with whose objections against the half-pay itself this expedient had been substituted."[67] Even worse, the members managed, to Madison's surprise, to agree on a method for assessing lands, although he voted to the last against the plan that was eventually approved.[68] He had anticipated that a full discussion of a plan for an assessment would convince the other members, as he was now convinced, that the current rule for apportioning requisitions could never be put into practice. Instead, Congress agreed on a method of assessment, and the faith of many members in requisitions based on such assessments remained a major obstacle to other federal taxes.

This problem was immediately apparent when John Rutledge and Virginia's John Francis Mercer moved to apply the proceeds from a new impost exclusively to the debt due to the army, assuming that civilian creditors would ultimately get their dues from requisitions and the sale of public lands. Madison helped to defeat this proposal on February 18, only to be startled by a motion in which Hamilton and Wilson urged that Congress open its deliberations to the public when debating matters of finance. Sharing in the general dislike of this surprising motion, which was greeted with a quick adjournment, he approached the Pennsylvanians privately for explanation. They said that they had put themselves in a delicate position with their legislature by persuading it to drop its plans to assume a portion of the federal debt and only wanted their constituents to see that they were doing everything they could. "Perhaps the true reason," Madison suspected, was that the Pennsylvania delegates anticipated that "the presence of public creditors, numerous and weighty in Philadelphia, would have an influence" from the galleries on the congressional proceedings.[69]

Congress had already heard one speech in which the brilliant but incautious Hamilton had urged a general revenue on grounds that worried several members. "As the energy of the federal government was evidently short of the degree necessary for pervading and uniting the states," the New Yorker had argued, "it was expedient to introduce the influence of officers deriving their emoluments from and consequently interested in supporting the power of Congress."[70] "This remark," wrote Madison, "was imprudent and injurious to the cause which it was meant to serve," since fears of just this sort of influence were among the most important reasons why the states resisted revenues that were to be collected by the officers of Congress. All the members most opposed to independent federal revenues had "smiled," he thought, "at the disclosure"; Bland and Lee said privately that Hamilton "had let out the secret."[71] Now, with

Hamilton's new motion, the obvious attempt to throw the doors of Congress open to a potent lobby reinforced the gathering impression that the advocates of general funds were hoping that the army and the public creditors would pressure both the state and federal governments into a grant of independent taxes.[72] Madison himself was patently uneasy over what his allies seemed to have in mind.

At just this point, the agitation in the army neared its peak, encouraged, if not deliberately provoked, by some of the Philadelphia advocates of independent federal taxes. On February 13, Congress had received firm news of a preliminary peace. Its joy, wrote Madison, was tempered by a fear "that the cloud which has been some time lowering on the North River will not be dispelled by the rays of peace. The opinion seems to be well founded that the arms which have secured the liberties of this country will not be laid down until justice is secured."[73]

Six days later, on the morning after Hamilton's attempt to open the congressional debates and with some congressmen referring openly to pressure from the army,[74] Rutledge renewed the motion to appropriate the impost exclusively to the soldiers' needs. Hamilton again denounced "such a partial dispensation of justice," suggesting that "it was impolitic to divide the interests of the civil and military creditors, whose joint efforts in the states would be necessary to prevail on them to adopt a general revenue." Wilson seconded the young New Yorker, adding that "by dividing the interest of the civil from that of the military creditors provision for the latter would be frustrated." Nevertheless, Virginia's Mercer still opposed "a permanent debt supported by a permanent and general revenue." He believed that "it would be good policy to separate instead of cementing the interest of the army and the other public creditors."[75]

On the following evening, February 20—after another day of angry debates—Madison joined Hamilton, Nathaniel Gorham, Richard Peters, and Daniel Carroll for dinner at the home of Congressman Thomas FitzSimons. Here, Hamilton and Peters, former officers whose military contacts kept them well informed about conditions in the camp, told the gathering that it was certain that the army had decided not to put away its arms until its just demands were met. A public manifesto, they revealed, would be forthcoming soon, and "plans had been agitated if not formed for subsisting themselves after such a declaration." Washington, the two ex-officers announced, had come to be "extremely unpopular among almost all ranks from his known dislike to any unlawful proceeding," and "many leading characters" were working to replace him with the more compliant Horatio Gates. Hamilton had written the commander, he reported, in order to alert him to these schemes, urging Washington to lead the army in any plans for redress, "that they might be moderated."[76]

Why Hamilton and Peters chose to make these revelations at this moment is impossible to know. Perhaps the conversation simply led them to
divulge their latest information. For, certainly, if the disclosures were intended to intensify the pressure for new taxes, the stategy could not have
been more misconceived. With only Hamilton dissenting, the gathering
agreed that Congress was unlikely to approve any general revenues except
the impost, and several of the diners seem to have concluded that the
temper of the army would permit no more delay.[77]

For Madison, there is no doubt, the dinner party was a critical event.
The next day he was on his feet again in Congress to defend general
revenues as consistent with "the principles of liberty and the spirit of the
constitution." Now, however, he "particularly disclaimed the idea of perpetuating a public debt," and he conceded that the Congress would be
forced to limit its recommendations to the impost and a "call for the
deficiency in the most permanent way that could be reconciled with a
revenue established within each state separately and appropriated to the
common treasury."[78] Before this speech of February 21, Madison had
worked in close cooperation with Morris and his congressional spokesmen. From this point forward, he was bent upon a compromise of which
they disapproved. On February 26, he outlined a proposal that he hoped
would end the crisis, together with a list of the responses he expected
from each state.[79] By early April he believed that his proposals would be
passed. They were, indeed, accepted in amended form on April 18, 1783,
and Madison was asked to draft an explanation to the states. Already, on
March 17, Congress had received George Washington's report that he had
defeated the conspiracy at camp.[80]

Madison's separation from the other advocates of general revenues has
commonly been seen, when it is mentioned, as a simple consequence of
his conclusion that nothing but a compromise could end an urgent crisis.[81] More was certainly involved. To start with, the Virginian's plan of
February 26 was not intended merely to provide as permanent a fund for
managing the debt as Congress and the states seemed likely to approve.
Madison intended something much more comprehensive. Congress would
renew its call for power to impose an impost, although the impost would
be limited, this time, to a term of twenty-five years, applied exclusively to
payment of the principal and interest of the debt, and collected by officers
appointed by the states (although removable by Congress). This amendment to the Articles, together with additional, though individual, state
appropriations for the debt, would be combined with the completion of

the western cessions, a federal assumption of state debts, abatement of
the portions owed by states most damaged by the war, and alteration of
the rule for apportioning congressional requisitions from a standard
based on land assessments to a formula based on population (counting
slaves as three-fifths of their numbers). By making every part of this proposal contingent on approval of the others, Madison hoped to put an end
to nearly all of the recurrent conflicts that had characterized the Continental Congress through his first three years, ranging landless states
against the landed, small against the large, the South against New England. This was not the quickest or the simplest way to counteract the
pressure from the army, but Madison believed that it might be the surest
way to guarantee that both the military and civilian creditors would actually receive their dues. Moreover, he was seeking, now, not only to avert
a national disgrace, not only to conciliate the soldiers, but also to repair
the fundamental fractures that appeared increasingly to threaten the very
survival of the union.[82]

The long and often bitter argument about the funding of the debt
had sharpened nearly all of the persistent controversies that had troubled
Madison throughout his years in Congress. Sectional disputes about apportioning the obligations of the states were older than the separation
from Great Britain. Any general tax—and almost any mixture of a set of
general taxes with an impost—still appeared to threaten unequal burdens.
In addition, jealousies between the landed and the landless states had
recently been heightened once again by news of the preliminary peace,
in which America had won the West and a potential treasurehouse of
future revenues before Virginia and the other states had completed their
western cessions. For Madison, who had so often warned that the Confederation might collapse soon after Independence was secured, that moment seemed more imminent than it had ever seemed before. Compelled
to look it squarely in the face, he never afterward, from this point to his
death, spoke boldly of preparing to "defy" Virginia's rivals "from whatever quarter" they appeared. The Newburgh crisis sealed a dedication to
the Union that the young Virginian congressman had sometimes seemed
to make contingent, in preceding years, on the continuation of the war
or on a resolution of outstanding disagreements on the terms his state
desired.

A second train of thought was little less compelling. For, beginning
with his speech of February 21, Madison deliberately attempted to disassociate himself from Hamilton's suggestion that a funded debt could be
a useful tool for strengthening the Union. Although he was convinced
that funding and a commutation of the half-pay pensions could not be
more at odds with "our republican character and constitutions than a

violation of good faith and common honesty," he declared himself "as much opposed to perpetuating the public burdens as anyone" in Congress.[83] He was willing, he insisted, to concur "in every arrangement that should appear necessary for an honorable and just fulfillment of the public engagements and in no measure tending to augment the power of Congress which should appear unnecessary."[84] Madison was out of sympathy by now, not only with the tactics, but also with the ultimate objectives of Hamilton, Wilson, and Morris. He was, indeed, no longer certain of the patriotism and republicanism of some of his fellow advocates of general funds, though it is most unlikely that he doubted any of these three.

Robert Morris's July report had advocated general revenues that would be adequate to meet the ordinary operating costs of Congress, as well as to ensure the steady payment of the interest on the debt. These revenues would be collected by the officers of Congress, and they would be coterminous with the existence of the federal obligations. Though Madison, as has been seen, insisted that such measures were "within the spirit" of the present constitution, no one had expressed a clearer understanding that independent federal taxes of this sort would mean a fundamental change in the relationship between the central government and states.[85] This alteration of the federal balance was precisely what opponents disapproved, and it was just what Morris, Hamilton, and Wilson found so difficult to relinquish. It was this that Madison first favored, then abandoned in his speech of February 21—not because he was inherently more pliable than many of his allies, but because it did not seem to him, as it did to many of them, an object worth the risks it now entailed. He gave it up because it had become apparent that several of the advocates of independent general funds had motives and objectives he had never fully shared.

All of the original supporters of independent general funds regarded a dependable federal revenue as essential to the restoration of public credit and possibly to the continuation of the Union. All of them regarded steady payment of the interest on the debt as a critical test of national character and an indispensable security against the day when it might be necessary to borrow again. Not all of them, however, actually wished to see the debt retired, nor did the superintendent's plan provide for payment of the principal as well as of the interest on the public obligations. Contemporary critics noticed this when they condemned a "permanent" or "perpetual" debt, and historians increasingly agree that several of the advocates of general funds were looking consciously beyond the reestablishment of public credit toward a funding plan that would promote the nation's postwar economic growth and advance a particular variety of political centralization. Properly funded, as Morris said in his July report, the mass of "dead" certificates of debt (that is, of paper promises too poorly backed to trade on private markets) would appreciate in value, become "a sufficient circulating medium" for the country, and provide the capital for more intensive economic development.[86] Simultaneously—to use the current metaphor—the obligations of the federal government would become a new "cement" of Union. Looking to Congress rather than the states for their salaries, pensions, or other claims, civilian creditors, the discharged soldiers, and the officers appointed to collect federal taxes, along with merchants doing business with the national bank, would "unite the several states more closely together in one general money connection" and "give stability to government" by combining in its support.[87]

Hamilton, like Morris, had been thinking in this fashion since the beginning of the decade. His private correspondence and his anonymous newspaper series, "The Continentalist," had repeatedly insisted on the need to create among the nation's leadership an influential class tied to the federal government and capable of counterbalancing the many influential figures currently tied to the states. As Hamilton conceived it, an enduring and effective central government required the union of the general government's resources with those of a monied and officeholding class directly dependent on that government for the promotion of its economic interests.[88]

The implications of this thinking can be understood more clearly, in the light of recent scholarship, than was the case as recently as 1980. So can its opponents' reasons for alarm. Remembering their histories of England in the decade following the Glorious Revolution of 1689, Hamilton and Morris and perhaps some other economic nationalists were thinking of replicating Great Britain's path to national greatness. They were thinking of combining certain segments of America's elite into a single interest intimately tied by fortune and ambition to the infant federal regime, much as standard histories said that the ministers of William III had once successfully created a "monied interest" loyal to the new succession and capable of counterbalancing the Tory gentry. It is not, in fact, a gross exaggeration to suggest that these reformers hoped to use the national debt to build a single nation—or at least to forge a single national elite—where none was really present in 1783. They wanted to encourage the emergence in America of a facsimile of those related interests—government, the military, commerce, and finance—that ordinarily united in support of British ministries and lent stability to that familiar system: interests that the English had in mind when they referred in general terms to the forces supporting the "court." Envisioning a national greatness predicated on an imitation of the economic and political strengths of England, Hamilton and Morris were prepared to risk some further clamors from

the army, if not to feed the agitation for the sake of general funds.[89] But
Madison, who was preoccupied with the defense of a republican revolution (and who would never see Great Britain as a proper model for the
new United States), was not. Although he did not quarrel with the financier's supporters or join with Rutledge, Lee, and Mercer, he knew what
he implied when he deliberately disclaimed a desire to perpetuate the
national debt.[90]

Aware that his abandonment of Morris would defeat the latter's plans,
Madison added to his private record of his speech of February 21 a
lengthy footnote explaining why he had earlier favored the general revenues that he had now decided to forgo. This should be read with care,
for it suggests the gulf between his motives and those of the other reformers, as well as the extent of his discomfort with their views. "Many of the
most respectable people of America," he wrote—and it is hard to see
whom he intended if these "respectable people" did not include the circle of public creditors, army officers, and congressmen that radiated from
the Office of Finance—"supposed the preservation of the Confederacy
essential to secure the blessings of the Revolution and permanent funds
for discharging debts essential to the preservation of Union." If they were
disappointed, he imagined, their ardor in the revolutionary cause might
cool and, in a "critical emergence," they might "prefer some political
connection with Great Britain as a necessary cure for our internal instability." Madison himself, as he recalled it, had not been able to see how
"the danger of convulsions from the army" could be halted without general funds, which also seemed required in order to avert "the calamities"
sure to follow from continuing disputes among the states. Without general
funds

> it was not likely the balances would ever be discharged. . . . The conse-
> quence would be a rupture of the Confederacy. The eastern states would
> at sea be powerful and rapacious, the southern opulent and weak. This
> would be a temptation. The demands on the southern states would be an
> occasion. Reprisals would be instituted. Foreign aid would be called in by
> first the weaker, then the stronger side, and finally both be made subser-
> vient to the wars and politics of Europe.[91]

Collapse of the Confederation, Madison believed, would soon expose the
southern states to depredations by the northern. It might eventually entail
the failure of the republican revolution.[92]

Concern for the republican experiment, distrust of the New Englanders, and doubts about the loyalty of some of the most eager advocates of
general funds may all, as Madison suggested in this note, have entered

into his original decision to support this strengthening of Congress. What is certain from the February memorandum is that all these fears contributed to his decision to *abandon* general revenues in favor of a complex compromise designed to satisfy the army and to put an end to the recurrent disagreements that had periodically disrupted Congress *without* so large an alteration of the federal system. Madison did not simply conclude that it was inexpedient to delay a resolution of the crisis. Rather, as he saw more clearly the directions that the economic nationalists hoped to take, as Morris's opponents developed their objections, and as he gave increasing credence to the rumors of intrigues between the capital and the camp, Madison deliberately drew back.[93] He believed, as Washington believed, that it was dangerous to use the army as a tool. But he had also come to be uneasy with the corollaries of his allies' plans, and he was more profoundly worried now than he had ever been before about the peacetime implications of persistent conflicts in the Congress. Thus, in his "Address to the States" of April 26, 1783, Madison urged the legislatures to approve his compromise financial plan because it was "as small" an alteration of "the federal constitution . . . as could be reconciled" with the necessity of paying the public debt, "as small" a change as seemed consistent with the preservation of the Union.[94]

This was not just special pleading. Throughout his years in Congress, Madison had shown a genuine reluctance to transgress the Articles of Confederation. He was not an unreserved enthusiast for altering them now, representing his proposals (much as he had earlier defended general funds) more as a regrettable necessity than as a positive advantage for the nation.[95] But although sincere respect for written limitations of authority was near the center of his creed, so was his regard for national honor; and he saw with growing clarity how the disruption of the Union might imperil both Virginia and the Revolution. At the climax of the crisis, it is clear, Madison stood between the economic nationalists and his Virginia colleagues, genuinely swayed by what he heard from both, thinking of the distribution of authority between the general government and states in a manner that distinguished him from either group.

By 1783, the most determined nationalists were already advocating a convention that would thoroughly transform the federal system.[96] Madison was not prepared for a solution so extreme.[97] He was willing, unlike Lee or Mercer, to accept a more powerful central government. But this was not, for Madison, a principal objective in itself. He would approve a tilting of the federal balance only to the point that he conceived it necessary for the preservation of the Union, and he was not immune to Lee's or Mercer's fears that certain federal measures might prove incompatible with what he called the "spirit" or the "principles" of a republican revolution.

Therefore, he specifically denied a wish for the sort of political centralization that other advocates of funding seemed to have in mind. In January, he had thoroughly agreed with Hamilton and Morris that greater federal powers were required in order to defend the nation's honor and to guarantee the preservation of the Union. By April, he had changed his mind about how far this shift should go. Although he shared the economic nationalists' desire to reestablish public credit, he could not accept a program meant, as one historian has put it, "to achieve political centralization by fiscal reform."[98] He did not articulate a systematic explanation of his discontent. This would await developments after 1789, when Hamilton's desires assumed a more substantial form. It would require a further evolution of Madison's own thinking. By 1783, experience had taught him that relying on the states for revenues endangered both the character and harmony of the Confederation. But he was not yet ready to conclude, with Hamilton, that the Confederation government was irredeemably defective in its fundamental structure. He had yet to formulate a truly nationalizing program of his own.

In 1783 Madison was not less continental-minded than the other advocates of funding. Educated at the College of New Jersey, he had been accustomed since his youth to thinking of the Revolution as a national movement, and the years in Congress had intensified this habit. By 1783, he was convinced that even after Independence had been won, the Revolution would be insecure without the Union. Still, Madison was inescapably Virginian, and he had come to Congress deeply influenced by the thinking of the early Revolution, which itself was deeply influenced by a hundred years of strident criticism of the modern British system of administration and finance. These criticisms strongly influenced his and other delegates' reactions to Hamilton's and Morris's ideas.

Originating in the 1670s, but building on ideas that had appeared in England thirty years before, condemnations of Britain's system of administration and finance—a Country criticism of the Court—had served from that point forward, both for Tories and for radical Old Whigs, as an essential strategy for reconciling a determined opposition to the Modern Whig regime with a commitment to the mixed and balanced constitution.[99] At the center of this opposition language was a charge that modern ministries—where we might say "the Cabinet"," contemporaries said "the Court"—were using governmental influence in elections and executive control of offices and pensions to subvert the legislature's independence. Through the years, however, accusation after accusation had been added to this charge until the threat to British freedom seemed of diabolical proportions: a grasping monster with its head at court and tentacles in every pocket in the kingdom, reaching out voraciously to eat away the governmental balance and the social fabric on which liberty was taken to depend. By 1765, when trouble with the colonies erupted, this opposition image of a cancerous conspiracy was a conventional device for understanding an enormous range of national ills. And many of the most destructive of these evils seemed to have been born with the financial innovations introduced by the creators of the Modern Whig regime.

Beginning in the middle 1690s, England had developed an unprecedented method of financing its involvement in recurring European wars. Central to this system was a firm commitment of specific revenues for steady payment of the interest on the national debt, together with a sinking fund, which could be used for the debt's retirement during peacetime. Tightly interwoven with this funding system were the Bank of England and the other chartered corporations, which purchased vast amounts of government certificates of debt in exchange for their monopolies in certain sorts of trade. An active private market in these corporations' stocks and in the government's own bonds appeared as an essential adjunct of the system.[100]

The new financial structure made it possible for tiny England to compete successfully with France in four great wars for empire. Thus, to Modern Whigs, defenders of such great prime ministers as Robert Walpole, the new financial system seemed the very crux of national stability and international prestige.[101] But to the critics of its managers and builders, Walpole's system seemed a vast, deliberate addition to the instruments of influence and corruption which were driving England rapidly to ruin.

Critics of the new finance were not invariably opposed to commerce, manufacturing, or liquid forms of wealth. Several of the greatest opposition writers, including "Cato" and James Burgh, were spokesmen for the city and its interests.[102] Nevertheless, most eighteenth-century thinkers were as conscious of the new finance as of the growth of commerce strictly speaking, and opposition thinking started from a set of neoclassical assumptions that had been imported into English thought by Harrington and other thinkers of the Interregnum: that power follows property, that great extremes of poverty and wealth are incompatible with freedom, and that only those who do not owe their livelihoods to others are the masters of themselves and capable of virtuous participation in a healthy public life.[103] On all these counts, the new financial system and its creatures seemed inherently corrupt. Like parliamentary placemen, public pensioners, or representatives of rotten boroughs, dealers in the public funds or owners of the stock of chartered corporations seemed dependent on the treasury for their support. Their economic interests chained them to the will of an executive whose aims were always different from, and often hostile to, the will and interests of the body of the freemen. In Parliament, the placemen, pensioners, and other tools of grasping ministers enabled the executive to undermine the balanced constitution. Out of Parliament, the unearned wealth of creatures of the new finance spread habits of dishonesty, subservience, and waste to every corner of the kingdom. And while the placemen and the "monied interests" fattened on the public spoils, independent farmers, artisans, and tradesmen were impoverished by high taxation and demoralized by the example of the great. Under such conditions, the survival of the nation's ancient freedom seemed increasingly in doubt.

For American colonials, it now seems clear, British opposition thinking offered a compelling explanation of the crisis that impelled them into Independence. Understood in opposition terms, the British measures the Americans resisted did not seem mistaken or misguided. Rather, they appeared to flow from a deliberate conspiracy against the nation's freedoms, a conspiracy that had already undermined the virtue of the English and was working now to undermine their own. Separation from a grasping and decaying Britain thus emerged as both a necessary flight from this devouring monster and a revolutionary opportunity for making liberty complete. Indeed, to a remarkable extent, the early revolutionaries tended to define their hopes and character as a distinctive people by contrasting their republican experiments with what the opposition writers said was wrong with eighteenth-century Britain. "America" *meant* virtue rather than corruption, vigor rather than decay. It meant a pleasing mediocrity of fortunes, citizens who lived upon their own resources, freemen who could fight or vote according to their own autonomous desires. It meant, in short, whatever seemed to have been lost with the appearance of the eighteenth-century system of administration and finance.[104]

Experience, of course, produced a certain disenchantment. Profiteering, hoarding, and a growing weariness of war reminded everyone that even staunch republicans were human. In order to defeat the British, the militia had to be supported by a continental army. By the time the war was won, the powers of the central government were widely recognized to be unequal to its tasks. Still, the dream was stronger than the disenchantment, and of the evils of the old regime were still too vivid in the national recollection for many to be willing to abide its reconstruction, even in the most attenuated form. Resistance surfaced most explicitly in 1783 when Lee or Mercer warned that Morris's proposals would "perpetuate a monied interest," which "would gain the ascendance over the landed interest . . . and by their example and influence become dangerous to our republican constitutions."[105] Nevertheless, for Madison as well, the lengthy battle to defend Virginia's claims, hostility to privilege, contempt for speculative greed, respect for written constitutions, and dread of the corrupting possibilities of long-term public debts united to create a revolutionary continentalism that was more at odds with Hamilton's or Morris's objectives than any of them presently perceived.[106]

In his "Address to the States" of April 26, Madison appealed to all the legislatures to remember why the national debt had been incurred, to whom it would be paid, and why the several states must keep their "plighted faith." The rights for which America contended, he explained, "were the rights of human nature."

> In this view, the Citizens of the United States are responsible for the greatest trust ever confided to a political society. If justice, good faith, honor, gratitude, and all the other qualities which ennoble the character of a nation and fulfill the ends of government, be the fruits of our establishments, the cause of liberty will acquire a dignity and luster which it has never yet enjoyed; and an example will be set which cannot but have the most favorable influence on the rights of mankind. If, on the other side, our governments should be unfortunately blotted with the reverse of these cardinal and essential virtues, the great cause which we have engaged to vindicate will be dishonored and betrayed; the last and fairest experiment in favor of the rights of human nature will be turned against them; and their patrons and friends exposed to be insulted and silenced by the votaries of tyranny and usurpation.[107]

James Madison, in 1783, was a Virginia continentalist. He was a dedicated revolutionary statesman. He was a nationalist, however, mostly in his eloquent conception of the mission in which all Americans were joined. He was a nationalist, that is, at certain times, on certain issues, and within the limits of his revolutionary hopes. Thus, when he retired from the Confederation Congress, he intended to reenter the Virginia House of Delegates to advocate compliance with the Treaty of Paris and acceptance of the financial recommendations of 1783. But there had been few signs, as yet, that he would favor, much less author, any plan for sweeping constitutional reform. Before he could do that, the road to the Convention had to take him through a serious rethinking of his revolutionary suppositions, and the difficulties of the Union had to reach a point at which he would be able to imagine that the positive advantages of centralizing change might outweigh its undoubted risks.[108]

CHAPTER TWO

The Crisis of
Confederation Government,
1783–1787

MADISON HAD ENTERED CONGRESS looking younger than his years, a shy, unprepossessing, slightly anxious youth from whom extraordinary contributions might have been expected only by a few Virginia politicians. He left it, three years later, still appearing barely half his thirty-two, but as a deeply self-possessed and highly practiced continental leader. Few citizens, as yet, had ever heard his name, but politicians from throughout the Union knew him as the most effective legislator in the Congress and the draftsman of its most comprehensive plan for federal reform. By the spring of 1783, informed Virginians saw him as the commonwealth's most knowledgeable authority on federal affairs. By the time his term expired, everyone—including Madison himself—expected him to take command of continental-minded forces in the legislature of the Union's largest state, which he would lead, some four years later, to the Constitutional Convention.

But let us not rely too much on hindsight, for hindsight at this point has proved a potent enemy of understanding. Knowing that the weaknesses of the Confederation would become increasingly apparent through the next few years, granting Madison's acuity, and recognizing his unquestionable commitment to reform, authorities have commonly assumed that he returned to local politics already dedicated to a sweeping reconstruction of the current federal system, though aware that national opinion was unready for the project.[1] While he waited for opinion to mature, this would suggest, his own ideas developed mainly in response to his revulsion at the populistic policies permitted by the early revolutionary constitutions. Twentieth-century scholarship has always been more interested in the elite's increasing disenchantment with conditions in the states than in the growing, general recognition of the need to strengthen the Confederation, and it is customary to insist that Madison's most striking contributions issued from his growing discontent with local legislation.[2]

Significant misunderstandings are embedded in this view. The dominant interpretation does not merely err in its dating of a major change in the Virginian's thinking. It is not misleading merely in its flawed analysis of his congressional career. Rather, by inaccurately depicting his positions in the Continental Congress, then identifying his digust with popular abuses in the states as the essential impetus behind his later actions, it encourages a serious misjudgment of his thinking later in the decade. It is true, of course, that Madison's proposals at the Constitutional Convention were intended to restrain majority abuses. But it is also true—and not inconsequential—that his planning *started* with a fresh assessment of the crisis of the Union.

In 1783, as has been shown, a small minority in Congress might have voted for a resolution to convene a federal convention. Madison opposed it, and he did not do so just because he thought it premature. During the preceding years, he had identified himself with the proponents of a more effective union. Always much inclined to link the nation's well-considered needs with the essential interests of Virginia, he had set his sights from the beginning of his term on the creation of a national domain that would be free from private, speculative claims. He had appealed repeatedly to his Virginia friends for full compliance with congressional requests and patience in the face of irritating jealousies of the Old Dominion, taking national humiliations almost as a form of personal disgrace. For all of this, however, he had never been a centralist by instinct. Neither did he share the admiration shown by some of his reformist allies for an English model of administration and finance. Eloquent about the bonds that made Americans a single people—undeniably a leading unionist in this respect—he advocated centralizing measures only in so far as they appeared compatible with the essential interests of Virginia and the fundamental character of the emerging, revolutionary nation. This is not to say that he subordinated national needs to local interests, but it does describe a continentalism that was very much a product of his revolutionary aspirations and of the distinctive geographical and cultural perspective of a young Virginia statesman. Conditioned in this way, Madison's approval of a sweeping transformation of the federal system did not date from his initial years in Congress, and it would never take a form consistent with the plans envisioned from that time by Hamilton and Morris.

Throughout his years in Congress, Madison attributed the difficulties of the central government to the conflicting interests of the several states and to the devastation all the states had suffered in the Revolution. He hoped that peace would ameliorate these problems, that renewed prosperity "would give to the Confederacy in practice the efficiency [implicit in] its theory." During his initial years in Congress, he objected neither to the concept of a purely federal union nor to the republican regimes established by the early revolutionary constitutions. Only after he returned from Congress to struggle year after year in the Virginia House of Delegates against the advocates of paper money, tax abatements, and assessments for religion—and only as the states persisted during peacetime in "omissions and in measures incompatible with their relations to the federal government and with those among themselves"—did he begin to think of far more radical reforms. Only then did he conclude that accusations he had once dismissed as "calumnies" on republican government—charges of inconstancy, weakness, and oppression of minorities—were true of small republics and would have to be corrected in the course of federal reform. Not till then, morever, did he reason that the continental union that protected these republics could only be preserved by a complete rewriting of the Articles of Confederation. Not, in short, until he was compelled to reexamine suppositions that had guided him throughout the years in Congress did Madison commit himself wholeheartedly to a complete reconstitution of the Union. Even then, his revolutionary ardor and his long, determined effort to protect Virginia's interests shaped a plan that was as incompatible as his desires had always been with a consolidated national system.[3]

Shortly after delivering his "Address to the States," Madison left Philadelphia for a trip into New Jersey with the family of New York congressman William Floyd, to whose daughter he had recently become engaged. From the time of his return, thinking now of marriage and retirement from the national scene, he was no longer such a paragon of conscientious service.[4] On June 21, rebellious soldiers of the Pennsylvania Line besieged the Pennsylvania State House, where Congress and the state executive were sitting. Angered by the state authorities' reluctance to confront the mutineers, Congress moved its seat to Princeton on June 24.[5] Madison decided to commute, suffering the packed accommodations at the temporary seat of Congress only when his presence seemed essential, planning but repeatedly postponing a preliminary visit to Virginia. Kitty Floyd had barely reached New York before her letters hinted second thoughts about the marriage. She sealed her final one, according to tradition, with a piece of dough; and Madison decided to remain in Philadelphia until his term expired, probably because Virginia's western cession and a permanent location for the seat of federal government were once again the central subjects of attention.[6]

Through his final months in Congress, with peace at hand and the financial plan awaiting the decision of the states, Madison resumed his familiar role of servant of Virginia. He favored Congress's return to Philadelphia until a permanent location could be readied, less because it suited his convenience than because he calculated that a different temporary seat would make it harder to secure a permanent location at the falls of the Potomac River, where Congress would be closer to (and more profoundly influenced by) the South and West. Most southerners, however, bitterly opposed returning to a large, commercial city, and the enemies of Robert Morris hoped to speed his resignation by refusing to accommodate his needs. With Madison outvoted in his delegation, New England and the South combined against the middle states and reached agreement on a plan for alternating temporary seats of government at Trenton and Annapolis. The falls of the Potomac were selected, though only briefly it proved, as an alternate permanent location.[7]

On the cession, Madison's success was much less mixed, his adamance at last rewarded. Although the act was not completed until after his retirement, he was present in September when deliberations opened on a compromise in which his old opponents finally decided to concede Virginia's principal conditions. Maryland, together with New Jersey, dissented to the end. Virginia failed to win a guarantee of its remaining territory south of the Ohio River. Still, the speculators were defeated, and the federal government secured undisputed title to a western empire where a host of agricultural republics might eventually appear. Madison and Joseph Jones were pleased, and their cooperative endeavors helped secure the state's agreement on December 22, 1783.[8]

Unhappily, Virginia would agree to little more. Madison's delight with the successful resolution of the old dispute about the cession was severely tempered by the legislature's quick rejection of the impost and the other congressional recommendations of 1783. "I wish," he wrote to Edmund Randolph, "that those who abuse Congress and baffle their measures may as much promote the public good as they profess to intend. I am sure they will not do it more effectually than is intended by some at least of those who promote the measures of Congress."[9]

When Madison retired from Congress, he intended to reenter the Virginia legislature to work for two great ends: the state reforms initiated by Thomas Jefferson, who had replaced him in Congress, and compliance by the Old Dominion with the Treaty of Paris and the financial recommendations of the spring. Madison and Jefferson had been together intermittently through many weeks in 1783, lodging at the same establishment when Jefferson was in the city, their old acquaintanceship developing into the intimate political collaboration that would characterize the rest of their careers. In countless hours of unrecorded conversations, the two Virginians analyzed the state and federal situations, discovered a complete accord on major issues, and reached a broad agreement on objectives each would seek as they exchanged positions. They parted at Annapolis on November 27, and, as planned, the younger partner visited George Mason on his journey home. He found the major author of Virginia's constitution more inclined than he expected to favor measures he and Jefferson desired. "His heterodoxy," Madison reported, "lay chiefly in being too little impressed with either the necessity or the proper means of preserving the Confederacy."[10]

The "proper means" of bolstering the Union had very recently expanded, in Madison's own mind, to include another, critically significant addition to the powers of its Congress. Indeed, it was his wish for this reform that set him on the path he was to follow to the Constitutional Convention.

Throughout his years in Congress, Madison had been reluctant to accept extensive federal powers over commerce. As recently as May 1783, he had resisted even a commercial treaty with Great Britain, believing that a pact, though eagerly desired by northern shippers, could be purchased only with concessions that would sacrifice the vital interests of the planting states. Commercial treaties, he admitted, might become "a new bond to the federal compact." On the other hand, commercial treaties could distort the natural course of economic growth; and ill-advised provisions in such treaties could provoke the disadvantaged states to actions that might "first involve the whole confederacy in controversies with foreign nations and then in contests with one another." The current interest of America, he wrote to Edmund Randolph—a clear example of his tendency to generalize from the Virginia context—was to favor agricultural production and the importation of the other "objects of consumption." "The wider, therefore, our ports be opened . . . , the more likely we shall be to buy at cheap and sell at profitable rates." In time, of course, America would grow more crowded, and it *might* (his emphasis) prove necessary to adopt a policy designed to favor native manufacturing and shipping. But whether one considered current needs or future prospects, it did not seem prudent to conclude the sort of treaty being talked of in congressional committees.

Under such a treaty, Madison explained, British merchants would be granted equal privileges with natives in American ports. In exchange, Americans would be admitted to the trade between the United States and the British West Indies and to the carrying trade between the islands and the rest of the world, Great Britain itself excepted. But it was certainly unnecessary, Madison believed, for the United States to grant the British equal privileges with its own merchants (and forgo the possibility of an exclusive place for natives) in order to secure admission to direct trade

with the islands, which Britain would be forced to open anyway in order
to obtain American supplies. And if participation in the islands' other
trade would be a valuable concession, it would be a valuable concession
"only to those states which abound in maritime resources," paid for principally by states which would "share least" in the advantages received.
Virginia's interest in particular, he thought, was "to reserve her right as
unfettered as possible over her own commerce." Virginia's farmers had a
present interest in encouraging an open competition for their trade, and
looking toward the future, it could not be in the interest of the state "to
preclude it from any regulations which experience may recommend for
its thorough emancipation" from "the monopoly which formerly tyran-
nized over it."[11]

Before he reached Virginia, Madison's opinions had begun to change.
In August, as he neared conclusion of his term in Congress, he read the
earl of Sheffield's *Observations on the Commerce of the American States*, which
argued that Great Britain could maintain its dominant position in the
trade of the United States without dismantling its restrictive navigation
laws.[12] By autumn, he had seen the British proclamation of July, which
confined most American commerce with the West Indies to British bottoms and barred the importation there of all except enumerated American goods.[13] Congress, he now told Randolph, "will probably recommend
some defensive plan to the states. . . . If it fails . . . it will prove such an
inefficacy in the Union as will extinguish all respect."[14]

Madison returned from Congress deeply troubled by the Old Dominion's economic situation. In the same letter to Jefferson in which he
reported on his visit with George Mason, he described Virginia's economic
plight as "even more deplorable than I had conceived." British traders,
he remarked, were rushing to resume their dominance of its external
commerce. Currency was pouring from the state to pay for British imports.
Without a Philadelphia or Baltimore to concentrate and regulate this
trade, Virginia was forgoing revenues that, paid into its treasury, "would
more than supply all its wants."[15] The anger present in these lines is reminiscent of the letters written when the freshman congressman began to
see the War for Independence from a national perspective. Detection of
this note is equally important to our understanding of his thought.

To Madison, as Drew McCoy has capably explained, the viability of the
American experiment in popular self-government depended on the moral
fiber of the people. This, in turn, depended heavily on the conditions of
their economic life, which would be prosperous or poor in close relationship to their ability to find sufficient outlets for the products of their work.
Most Americans—and almost all Virginians—were agricultural producers;
and as long as this was so, they had to trade their surpluses for foreign

goods, stop buying foreign imports (and lapse into a primitive, subsistence mode of life), or risk their personal and even national independence by going ever deeper into debt. Lacking markets for their products, citizens could be demoralized by idleness, indebtedness, or want, and a demoralized majority could mean no end of trouble for a fragile, new republic. "Most of our political evils," Madison was soon remarking, "may be traced up to our commercial ones, as most of our moral may to our political."[16] A healthy public life had economic preconditions, and a sound political economy for the United States demanded demolition of the mercantilist barriers that all the European powers—and Britain most injuriously of all—had placed around themselves and their possessions.[17] When Madison reentered the Virginia House of Delegates, refreshed by a winter's reading, he was hopeful that this goal, along with other changes, could be gained within the framework of the current federal system. The failure to achieve it, together with the implications that this failure seemed to hold for both Virginia and the Union, would become the single strongest impetus for his conclusion that a strictly federal government was not just self-destructive, but a peril to the revolutionary order. From this thought, in turn, would come his dedication to a thoroughgoing structural reform.

Virginians who expected much from Madison on his return from Congress were by no means disappointed. During 1782 and 1783, while he was winning growing recognition as the Old Dominion's leading expert on the business of the Union, legislative politics at home had centered on the rivalry between the revolutionary giants Richard Henry Lee and Patrick Henry. The Virginia constitution vested legislative initiative in the lower house, and members of the House of Delegates were jealous of their independence, spurning factions as dishonorable and dangerous to a republic yet deferring to the finest speakers and tacticians. In this antiparty culture, the arrival of another able "general" profoundly changed the legislative mix. Recognizing Madison as such a man, Henry wrote to him in April to welcome his return, closing with affection and anticipating his assistance on a range of pressing problems.[18]

There was nothing disingenuous in Patrick Henry's welcome. Jefferson despised the former governor, but Madison had always been on cordial terms with Henry, who had always been more "federal" in his politics than Richard Henry Lee, the older brother of the colleague Madison had battled with continually in Congress.[19] As he travelled down to Richmond in the spring of 1784, Madison was no one's protégé. Although he sometimes sided with Lee on local matters and often pushed for Jeffer-

sonian reforms that neither of the older revolutionaries favored, he expected Patrick Henry's help on federal issues.[20] For several months, he
got it, and the two together proved a potent combination. Early in the
session, at a coffee house in Richmond, Henry met with Madison and
Joseph Jones and offered to support them on the floor if they would
recommend a plan for strengthening the federal system. Like Madison
and Jones, the three-term former governor was conscious that Virginia's
leadership could set a valuable example for the other states. Favoring a
federal power to coerce delinquents, as well as action to comply with various congressional requests, he told the former congressmen that he had
entered the assembly solely to prevent the "ruin" that he anticipated from
the weaknesses of Congress.[21]

    After its initial hesitation, Virginia had approved the impost. Now, with
Henry's valuable support, Madison was influential in securing several
other measures urged by the congressional reformers. The assembly ratified the alteration in the method of apportioning congressional requisitions, which was part of his financial plan of 1783. It set aside a portion
of the land tax and Virginia's local impost to comply with federal demands, and it endorsed a federal power to retaliate against European
trade regulations.[22] With Henry against him, Madison could not prevent
the spring assembly from declaring that Virginia would remove impediments to British creditors attempting to collect their prewar debts only if
the British first made restitution for the slaves they had removed in violation of the terms of peace. But he renewed the effort at the fall assembly
session, where he was equally successful with his federal agenda. Still seeking full compliance with the terms of peace, he drafted an important law
prohibiting further confiscations of loyalist property; and only a last-
minute accident, he thought, prevented the enrollment of an act providing for installment payments of the British debts. A flood had trapped
some legislators on a trip across the James, blocking their return before
adjournment of the session.[23]

    Setting an example for the other states was only one of Madison's
objectives at the 1784 assemblies, and granting Congress power to retaliate against the British was a single front in his determined war against
Virginia's economic woes. At the spring assembly session, he initiated legislation to restrict the state's external commerce to Alexandria and Norfolk, though he was forced to add three other ports and to exempt
Virginia traders in the final bill. The fundamental purpose, he explained
to Jefferson, was not to favor native merchants at the price of raising
planters' costs (and definitely not to put the state's own traders on a better
footing than the citizens of other states). The port bill was intended to
combat the insurmountable advantages that British vessels would enjoy as

long as they could come directly to the planters' wharves, monopolizing trade, evading taxes, and extracting more on both ends of the commerce than they could in mid-states ports, where there was greater competition.[24]

Evasion of the customs duties was a problem, too, on the Potomac, which could not be opened past the falls or regulated properly without cooperation with Virginia's neighbors. As chairman of the Committee on Commerce, Madison was principally responsible for the appointment by the spring assembly of commissioners to meet with delegates from Maryland on better regulation of the river, the resolutions that resulted in the Mount Vernon Conference of March 1785.[25] In the fall, he and his committee turned in earnest to a broader program of improvements, working closely now with General Washington, who was the linchpin of Virginia's drive to open the Potomac and construct a better system of internal routes of commerce.[26] As Madison put it in a letter to Jefferson in January 1785,

> A mind like his, capable of great views and which has long been occupied with them, cannot bear a vacancy, and surely he could not have chosen an occupation more worthy of succeeding to that of establishing the political rights of his country than the patronage of works for the extensive and lasting improvement of its natural advantages; works which will double the value of half the lands within the Commonwealth, will extend its commerces, link with its interests those of the western states, and lessen the emigration of its citizens by enhancing the profitableness of situations which they now desert in search of better.[27]

Madison's assessment of the general may have said what modesty would never have permitted Madison to say about himself. It certainly identified a major focus of his labors in the fall assembly. Although a cold prevented him from managing the act for improving the Potomac, he drafted a related bill for opening the James, moved a resolution to construct a road between the Cheat and the Potomac, untangled disagreements that were snarling surveys for additional improvements, and managed bills intended to reward the general and keep him at the head of this important work by granting him 150 shares of Potomac and James River stock.

When the fall assembly rose, Madison had ample reason to be pleased with Virginia's compliance with its federal responsibilities and its progress with a program of improvements. Other states, regrettably, had been less "federal" in their conduct. Through all of 1784, the news from Congress had been uniformly disappointing. In the spring, before departing for his ministry to France, Jefferson had kept his friend abreast of what was happening in Congress, but Jefferson was able to report substantial action only on his plans for managing the national domain.[28] As many of the continentalists had feared, the needs of the Confederation seemed less urgent with the Union now at peace—even to its own officials. Congress took advantage of the Articles in June to pass its first adjournment since the summer of 1775, leaving federal business in the hands of a Committee of the States. By August, Madison lamented, this committee had itself dissolved for failure to maintain a quorum, leaving "an entire interregnum of the federal government" until November 1, when Congress reassembled at its temporary seat in Trenton only to discover only seven delegates on hand.[29] "Great and effectual repairs" were needed, Virginia delegate John Francis Mercer wrote to Madison on November 26, just to keep the federal machinery in motion, yet Mercer saw no prospect of "decisive" measures from the Congress. "For my part," he confided, "I have no hopes but in a convocation of the states."[30] Letters from the other delegates confirmed that many congressmen were talking once again of a federal convention, and Richard Henry Lee, who had returned to Congress in the fall, requested Madison's opinion on the subject.[31]

Madison's response was cautious, yet it did suggest that he was willing now, if not yet eager, to support a special meeting. "In general," he replied on Christmas Day, "I hold it for a maxim that the Union . . . is essential to . . . safety against foreign danger and internal contention, and that the perpetuity and efficacy of the present system cannot be confided on." Without a better knowledge of the dispositions of the other states, he felt unable to decide whether Congress should suggest a general convention or request the necessary powers on its own. Even in Virginia, with its "excellent disposition toward the Confederacy," the fate of any proposition seemed uncertain. Still, he finished, "Should a view of the other states present no objections against the expedient, individually I would wish none to be presupposed here."[32]

The dispositions of the other states, unhappily, presented numerous objections, not only to a federal convention but even to the measures that Virginia had already passed. As Madison returned to his Orange County home in the fall of 1784, Congress dropped its talk about a meeting of the states and failed to reach agreement on important lesser measures. Through the spring of 1785, Madison bombarded James Monroe, who had begun a correspondence in November, with reiterated questions. Had Congress taken further action toward the sale of western lands? "What other measures are [on] foot or in contemplation for paying off the public debts? What payments have been made of late into the public treasury?" And was it really true that Massachusetts meant to press Rhode Island to approve the impost?[33]

The answers were discouraging, to say the least. Congress had received no revenues, as yet, from sales of public lands, and many states were lagging badly in the payment of their ordinary requisitions. Several states had not approved the impost, passed the other laws required for managing the debt, or ratified a federal power to retaliate against British trade policies. During 1785, a sharp depression spread across the country. Several northern states attempted independent action to discriminate against the flood of British goods, but it was clear from the beginning that these measures could be baffled by the rival laws or sheer inaction of their neighbors. With public meetings all along the coast demanding federal action, a congressional committee headed by Monroe proposed a new amendment granting Congress limited authority to regulate the country's trade. By July, the measure had been dropped for lack of adequate support, and Madison responded to Monroe's report on the congressional deliberations with what amounted to an outburst on the desperate condition of affairs.[34]

Madison's emotions had been building through the spring as he complained of isolation at his family's plantation; yet he kept himself thoroughly informed on state and federal affairs. In addition to the worrisome accounts in newspapers and letters from the north, local information hinted that his port bill might be overturned before it ever took effect. "Our trade was never more monopolized by Great Britain . . . than it is at this moment," he told Monroe in June. "But as our merchants are almost all connected with that country and that only, and as we have neither ships nor seamen of our own, nor likely to have any in the present course of things, no mercantile complaints are heard." The planters were dissatisfied, he thought. Selling low and buying high, they probably did not receive a half of what they should be making on their staple. But it was difficult "to make them sensible of the utility of establishing a Philadelphia or Baltimore among ourselves," the more so over merchant opposition and the readiness of politicians such as Arthur Lee to appeal to "local views."[35] In these conditions, with Virginia's efforts holding no more promise than the separate regulations of her sisters to the north, Monroe's request for Madison's opinion on a federal power over commerce prompted an unusually impassioned letter, one in which his thoughts as well as feelings struggled unsuccessfully with his habitual restraint.

Ideally, he wrote, he favored "perfect freedom" of commerce. "But before such a system will be eligible perhaps for the United States, they must be out of debt" and "all the other nations must concur." As long as other powers favored their own merchants, "we must either retort the distinction or renounce not merely a just profit, but our only defense against the danger which may most easily beset us." British policy especially, he pointed out, excluded U.S. merchants from "the channels without which our trade with them must be a losing one." But how was a redress to be "extorted?" "Only by harmony in the measures of the states." Acting individually, the states could not compel the Europeans, any more than they could "separately carry on war or separately form treaties of alliance or commerce." Like war and peace, he now maintained, the regulation of external trade was "within the reason of the federal constitution."

Madison doubted that a federal power over trade "would be relished" in Virginia. He had hardly relished it himself, he did not add, two years before, and southerners were often warned (as he had warned them then) against a hasty concurrence with the carrying states in action against the British. "But will the present system of Great Britain ever give the southern states bottoms" of their own, he now inquired. And "if they are not their own carriers I should suppose it . . . no folly . . . to give our custom to our brethren rather than to those who have not yet entitled themselves to the name of friends." Though Madison had balked at a relinquishment of state authority in 1783, the pressures of the past two years had taught him that "the interests of the states . . . meet in more points than they differ." He had not abandoned every caution. But no one, at this point, was talking of a plenary authority for a majority in Congress, and Madison insisted that "a case can scarcely be imagined in which it would be the interest of any two-thirds of the states to oppress the remaining one-third." The common interest of the states in forcing freer trade with the West Indies by itself outweighed "all the inequalities which may result from any probable regulation by nine states."

There remained, of course, the natural reluctance of the local legislatures to relinquish portions of their power, and the last two years had brought new proofs that many individuals were so suspicious of the Congress that they treated every new proposal as a further proof of a design for federal aggrandizement. Madison's awareness of this self-defeating aspect of congressional requests, together with his rising fear of the conflicting measures of the several states, may have elicited his most revealing passage:

> If Congress as they are now constituted cannot be trusted with the power, . . . let them be chosen oftener and let their period of service be shortened; or, if any better medium than Congress can be proposed by which the will of the states may be concentered, let it be substituted. . . . But let us not . . . rush on certain ruin in order to avoid a possible danger [of concentrated power]. I conceive it to be of great importance that the defects of the federal system should be amended, not only because such amendments will make it better answer the purpose for which it was instituted, but

because I apprehend danger to its very existence from a continuance of defects which expose a part if not the whole of the empire to severe distress. The suffering part . . . cannot long respect a government which is too feeble to protect their interest.[36]

The "ruin" that Madison imagined, as before, was the collapse of the Confederation, but this passage in the letter to Monroe not only linked that danger with the inability of the confederated states to grapple separately with costly and demeaning British domination of their trade. It was the earliest in all of his surviving papers to suggest that mutual hostilities resulting from the separate regulations of the states and from repeated failures to achieve unanimous agreement to amendments of the present system might require complete reconstitution of the current federal Congress or replacement of that Congress altogether by a "medium" that would elicit greater trust.

Before he went to Richmond in the fall of 1785—the state had dropped its spring assembly sessions—Madison escaped his isolation much as in the autumn of 1784, by mixing business with pleasure on a trip through Philadelphia and on into New York.[37] Stopping by Mount Vernon, he found the general well and sanguine on the prospects for improving the Potomac. In New York, however, to which Congress had removed, several conversations with the delegates on hand suggested slight improvement in the federal situation. "Congress have kept the vessel from sinking," he reported to Jefferson in October, "but it has been by standing constantly at the pump, not by stopping the leaks which have endangered her. All their efforts for the latter purpose have been frustrated by the selfishness or perverseness" of some of the states.[38]

In Madison's opinion, the current situation urgently demanded settlement of the accounts between the central government and the states, apportionment of federal obligations, recognition of a federal power to compel the states to pay their requisitions, and a federal power over trade. By now, however, Madison doubted that a settlement of the accounts could ever be effected by the Congress, whose members seemed incapable of acting as "impartial judges" rather than as "advocates for the respective interests of their constituents." And without a federal power to coerce delinquent states, requisitions would continue, he complained, "to be mere calls for voluntary contributions, which every state will be tempted to evade by the uniform experience that those states have come off best which have done so most." Madison continued to believe that federal coercion—or provisions that would make the threat of force sufficient—would be wholly practicable and safe. "A single frigate under the orders of Congress could make it the interest of any one of the Atlantic states to pay its just quota," he remarked. Yet even the congressional authority to regulate the country's trade was currently "suspended," and states attempting separate action to obtain relief were "less likely to obtain it than to drive their trade into other channels and to kindle heart burnings on all sides."[39]

At the 1785 assembly session, as before, Madison pressed hard for measures he considered necessary to maintain the federal vessel. This time, he was uniformly disappointed. He introduced another bill providing for installment payments of the British debts. The bill was so disfigured by amendments that he preferred to let it die.[40] And although the House of Delegates turned back a move to remit the land tax for the year—a "narrow escape," said Madison, from a "severe attack" on public credit—the defeat of the remittance was accomplished only by a compromise that once again postponed the actual collection of the tax. "The wisdom of seven sessions," he complained, "will be unable to repair the mischiefs of this single act," which would make it impossible to pay "a shilling" on Virginia's federal requisitions.[41]

Of all of Madison's defeats, the most disheartening, however, was the failure of a resolution to instruct Virginia's delegates to move again in Congress for a federal power over trade. Early in the session, a majority of members had appeared to favor federal action rather than a state response to the petitions of Virginia merchants. Madison was principally responsible for a committee draft of a set of resolutions asking Congress to request authority to levy duties on the ships of nations having no commercial treaty with the United States or to prohibit entry of such vessels altogether. Working from an outline, he delivered an unusually elaborate defense of federal regulation, arguing from the examples of Connecticut and Massachusetts, Delaware and Pennsylvania, New Jersey and New York, and even from the lessons of the Swiss and Dutch confederacies that uniformity was absolutely necessary to encourage native manufacturing and shipping, to counter foreign regulations, and to check the rising animosities among the states attempting action on their own. As in his letter to Monroe, he argued that a federal power over commerce was "within [the] reason" of a federal constitution that confided to the general Congress powers that could not be exercised effectively by separate states; and he maintained that the distinctive situation of the smaller northern states would join with southern interests to prevent abuses of the federal power, which was carefully confined. Above all, he insisted, the federal power might be necessary to prevent the dissolution of the Union, and he pleaded with the House of Delegates to recognize what the collapse of continental union would entail. It would be followed, he believed, by wars between the states, peacetime military forces, foreign interference, endless debts—by nothing short of the complete destruction of "the glorious prospects of [the] Revolution."[42]

Eloquence and careful argument were not enough. On November 30, the House amended the committee's resolutions to dilute the grant to Congress and to limit any federal act to a term of thirteen years. On December 1, believing that this faulty measure might impede a better one, Madison reluctantly agreed with the majority, which voted to postpone it.[43] As a substitute, John Tyler quickly introduced a resolution to appoint commissioners to meet with delegates from other states to recommend a federal plan for regulating commerce. On the last day of the session, with the grant to Congress dead, Tyler's resolution was extracted from the table and approved without significant dissent, initiating the Annapolis Convention.[44] As Madison reported to Monroe, a meeting of the states was "no doubt liable to objections and will probably miscarry." Still, it now seemed better than continuing inaction, and he hoped that it might lead to an effectual proposal for "additional powers to Congress."[45]

Was Madison responsible for launching the Annapolis Convention? Did he hope from the beginning that the meeting might be made "a step to a more comprehensive and adequate provision for the wants of the Confederacy"?[46] Neither question can be answered with assurance. Plainly, Madison preferred to act through Congress rather than a meeting of the states. Still, when he reluctantly decided to abandon an imperfect grant to Congress, he may already have arranged for Tyler to propose the resolution of December 1; and he was probably responsible, at minimum, for the revival of the latter's motion on the session's final day.[47] Though he was dubious about the workability and wisdom of conventions, he was more and more convinced that something must be done to circumvent the blockage in the ordinary channels of reform; and he may well have hoped that a meeting on commercial problems might become a means toward even larger ends.[48] Only three assertions seem beyond dispute. When he accepted his commission to attend this meeting, Madison was intent on altering the existing federal system, not on constructing a new one.[49] As the new year began, however, he was thoroughly persuaded that the inability to act on the nation's economic problems was endangering the Union, and that the dissolution of the Union could destroy the revolutionary dream. And finally, before he reached Annapolis, the animosities resulting from these problems would erupt in an explosion that appeared to threaten the Confederation's imminent collapse. For Madison, with the Annapolis Convention, the crisis of the continental union was at hand.

∼

Tiring from his winter's reading, Madison must frequently have gazed up from his books and fixed his vision on the Blue Ridge Mountains, which could usually be seen on the horizon. Beyond them, he was conscious, lay the West, the Mississippi River, and a providential opportunity for the emerging nation to fulfill its revolutionary dream. Many continental statesmen calculated that the vast reserves of western lands might someday pay the costs of Independence.[50] Most Virginia politicians hoped that the Potomac could be linked with the Ohio and become the natural entrepôt for European imports to the West, which would assure the Old Dominion's economic future. But Madison's conception of the West subsumed such calculations in a larger vision that associated the Confederation's western growth with nothing less than the emergence of a common nationality for the United States and even with the durability of happy, sound republics in the East.[51]

Reared in the Virginia piedmont, Madison had never seen the West as vastly distant or the westerners as a distinct and vaguely foreign people. Dozens of Virginia's landed families, including his own, had purchased tracts beyond the mountains or had said goodbye to kin and neighbors moving to Kentucky.[52] Like Kentucky, he believed, the whole Virginia cession would eventually be settled by the progeny of eastern families. There, indeed, a flow of immigrants from all of the Atlantic states would meet and mingle and become a single people, forming new communities to which the older ones would each be bound more tightly, by "the ties of friendship, of marriage and consanguinity," than any of them were to one another. "On the branches of the Mississippi," he explained to Lafayette, there would develop, not "distinct societies" but "only an expansion of the same . . . one," not "a hostile or a foreign people" but a people who would be more and more be seen as "bone of our bones, and flesh of our flesh," a people whose essential interests merited the same consideration as those of any other portion of the Union.[53]

A special, virtually paternal, feeling for this people had been present even during Madison's congressional career, when he had often shown as much concern for the westerners themselves as for Virginia's territorial pretensions. Thus when British armies threatened Richmond and controlled two southern states, many delegates were willing to relinquish some of the Confederation's western claims in order to avoid a peace based on the *uti possidetis* (in which belligerents retain the territories currently controlled). Madison had doggedly resisted, opposing even southern motions to forgo American insistence on a right to navigate the Mississippi River if the Spanish proved unwilling to ally themselves with the United States on any other terms. Knowing that the westerners depended on an open Mississippi as an outlet for their produce, Madison resented the congressional decision to reward the "selfish" Spanish with a "cession" that would "sacrifice the value of the finest part of America."[54] Not surprisingly, when he returned from Congress, the Kentuckians considered him their friend, solicited his aid in managing their separation from Virginia, and requested his advice on framing a Kentucky constitution. Madison was happy to oblige, though he was also careful to incorporate a clause providing that the separation from Virginia must be linked with federal action to admit Kentucky to the Union.[55]

Happily, as he conceived it, the United States did not complete a wartime pact with Spain, and Congress reinserted its insistence on a right to navigate the Mississippi in its new instructions for a Spanish treaty. Madison maintained an anxious watch on subsequent negotiations. As Kentucky moved toward separation from Virginia and depression deepened in the East, the West loomed ever larger in his vision. When the masters of Louisiana closed the river to Americans in 1784, he wrote at once to Jefferson and Lafayette to ask them to request the French to intercede with their Spanish allies. The stakes, as he explained them to these friends, will help us understand the depth of his alarm when a majority in Congress, with the wartime dangers past, proved willing once again to bow to Spanish pressure.

Madison had formed a special bond with Lafayette soon after learning of the Spanish closure of the river, crossing paths with the marquis as he began his annual "ramble" to the north and joining him again for an adventure to the Iroquois negotiations on the Mohawk.[56] From Philadelphia, where he and Lafayette were parting temporarily before rejoining at New York, Madison explained to Jefferson that he had lost no time in urging the marquis to seek French mediation on the Mississippi, warning him "emphatically" that Spanish conduct could produce a "rupture" of the wartime coalition and permit the British to insert themselves between the wartime allies. France would have to reason with her European partner, he insisted, since America could never be "diverted from her object."[57]

If Madison spoke freely to the Frenchman, as he claimed, he probably repeated much of what he told Jefferson on August 20, 1784, in a letter drafted before he left Virginia. Spain, he thought, could hardly "be so mad as to persist" in policies that might "delay" the navigation of the Mississippi but could no more stop it, finally, "than she can stop [the current of] the river itself." The law of nations, human rights, and natural justice—all of which were "every day deriving weight from the progress of philosophy and civilization"—all suggested that the owners of a river's mouth might levy tolls on the inhabitants above, but had no right to bar their trade completely. Carefully considered, Madison maintained, Spanish interests should themselves suggest the benefits of opening the navigation. "A free trade down the Mississippi would make New Orleans one of the richest and most flourishing emporiums in the world." It would secure the city's shaky loyalty to Spain and seal "a lasting peace" with the United States. "The U.S. are already," Madison observed, "a power not to be despised by Spain; the time cannot be distant when in spite of all her precautions, the safety of her possessions in this quarter of the globe must depend more on our peaceableness than her own power." But if the Spanish thought that they could count on "the pacific temper of republics, unjust irritations" on their part would quickly teach them "that republics have like passions with other governments." The only "*permanent* security" for Spain's possessions in Louisiana lay in

> the complexity of our federal government and the diversity of interests among the members of it, which render offensive measures improbable in council and difficult in execution. If such be the case when 13 states compose the system, ought she not to wish to see the number enlarged to three and twenty? A source of *temporary* security to her is our want of naval strength. Ought she not then to favor those emigrations to the western lands, which as long as they continue will leave no supernumerary hands for the sea?

Similar considerations, Madison continued, should encourage France—and all of Europe—to support an open Mississippi. Here, indeed, his reasoning revealed how indispensable the westward movement was to all his own ambitions for the nation. "By this expansion of our people," he believed, the growth of native manufactures would be long postponed, American demand for European imports would continually increase, and the production of the agricultural commodities that the United States would trade for European manufactures would continually expand. "Reverse the case," he argued,

> and suppose the use of the Mississippi denied to us, and the consequence is that many of our supernumerary hands who in the former case would [be] husbandmen on the waters of the Mississippi will on this other supposition be manufacturers on this [side] of the Atlantic; and even those who may not be discouraged from seating the vacant lands will be obliged by the want of vent for the produce of the soil and of the means of purchasing foreign manufactures, to manufacture in a great measure for themselves.[58]

Many easterners, it should be noted, *feared* the emigration to the West for just the reasons Madison touched on in this passage. He was thoroughly familiar with their thinking. Perhaps because he did not want to make their case, perhaps because he was uncertain how his correspondent felt about the subject, he deleted from the finished letter an admission that "the only sufferers by the encouragement of the western settlements will be those [who] remain in the Atlantic states." Although the latter's taxes would decrease with the increasing value of the western lands, "this advantage," he conceded, would be greatly overweighed "by the danger to the Confederacy from multiplying the parts of the machine, by the depopulation of the [eastern] country, by the depreciation of their lands, and by the delay of that maritime strength which must be their only safety in case of war." Pennsylvania, New York, and Virginia would "lose the advantage of being merchants for the western states in proportion as their trade has a ready passage through the Mississippi. Virginia will, moreover, suffer a loss of her staple, though she may be thought to have an equivalent for this in being disburdened of the slaves who will follow the culture of that plant."[59]

Madison was fully conscious of the costs of westward emigration, which was strengthening developments he feared: depopulation of the eastern states, depreciation of their lands, delay in the emergence of a navy, and the chronic inability of the Confederation to agree on common goals. Still, he never wavered in his course. When Lafayette returned to France and wrote that many of his correspondents in Virginia (including Washington himself) seemed far from eager for an open Mississippi, Madison replied that Lafayette was right to count him "out" of those whose interest had relaxed and who were reasoning on "very narrow and very delusive foundations." Repeating all the major arguments that he had given Jefferson some months before and adding his insistence that the westerners were not a foreign people, he reminded the marquis that France had joined the War for Independence "chiefly" for the "revolution" it appeared to promise in the trade between the new world and the old. He emphasized again that Europe had a choice between a maritime and manufacturing United States and growing commerce with its farmers. He warned again that the American affection for its major European ally could be threatened if it seemed that France supported Spain.[60] Knowing that Virginia and the Union could be weakened by the westward movement, he persisted nonetheless in doing everything he could to help promote it. Given his analysis of its effects, this unrelenting effort is a striking testimony to the depth of his commitment, and the strength of that commitment calls for close attention to its central place within his thought.

Something very like a sense of providential purpose was involved. Mentioning the eighteenth century's hopes for human progress, Madison included in these letters lengthy calculations showing that the westward movement would increase the numbers and prosperity of all mankind. He saw the West as a frontier for all of Western Europe, as well as for the seaboard states, and he suggested that the Mississippi River was the outlet "nature" had intended for its products, much as nature "gave to the United States their independence." It mattered, to his mind, that acquiescence in the closure of the river would be "treason" to these natural "laws."[61] It mattered, too, that the ability of the Confederation to retire the public debt depended heavily on the value of the western lands. By themselves, however, none of these considerations seems entirely to account for the intensity of Madison's commitment. A fuller explanation must return to the profundity of his fraternal feelings for the westerners themselves, which deepened his conviction that betrayal of their needs would be a form of treason, *and* to his repeated warnings that the closure of the river could compel the West and East alike to turn from agriculture to intensive manufactures.

Madison's implicit condemnation of a turn toward manufactures may appear surprising, given the extent to which so many modern writings hammer the assertion that his vision advocated "multiplying interests" in a "large, commercial republic."[62] Not, it seems apparent, if we are to judge by his position on the Mississippi. Here, in fact, he quite deliberately rejected much of what this language usually implies.[63] During the depression of the middle 1780s, native manufacturing was winning vocal new support; and many of its advocates were capable opponents of the westward movement, which was thought to be attracting workers who were needed in the shops. Domestic manufacturing, its advocates maintained, would mean new jobs for idle workers in the seaboard towns, together with internal markets for the food and raw materials that lacked sufficient outlets overseas. Domestic markets would increase the value of depreciated eastern farms, and native manufacturing would strengthen the Confederation, both by easing its dependence on expensive foreign imports and by offering alternative employment (many said) to citizens who were reverting to a barbarous existence in the West. Madison agreed that rapid emigration was retarding more intensive economic change, but he supported it, in part, *for just this reason.* As Drew McCoy has argued, Madison preferred that the United States would long continue at a "middle level" of development. He dreaded the progression to the "higher" economic stage that others wanted to encourage.[64]

The advocates of manufacturing, it should be recognized, could draw on many of the best political economists of their time. Scottish economic thought, culminating in the celebrated works of David Hume and Adam

Smith, suggested that humanity had moved from savagery to comfort by means of an increasing specialization of labor. Modern, specialized economies, the Scots maintained, were able to support a greater number of mankind in greater comfort than the purely agricultural societies of Greece or Rome because a more efficient allocation of their economic tasks produced a growing surplus for exchange.[65]

Madison, it should be clear, was not an enemy of commerce—not if "commerce" meant the civilizing, comfort-raising benefits of trade, which he was doing everything within his power to encourage. But "commerce" had a second set of implications in contemporary thinking. It could also mean intensive economic change: the transformation of a largely agricultural economy into an urban, manufacturing society that could produce and even export many of the niceties and luxuries of life. And in so far as modern economic thinking could be taken to suggest that the United States should move as rapidly as possible in this direction, Madison, and Jefferson, responded with alarm. In the first place, these Virginians knew that most Americans enjoyed a level of material prosperity that was the envy of the most "advanced" economies in Europe. In the second, they were deeply influenced by some countervailing strands in eighteenth-century thought which warned that the transition to a manufacturing or heavily commercialized economy could render a society incapable of freedom. Even Adam Smith conceded that as nations move from savagery through agriculture to the most advanced commercialization, the benefits prove dangerously unequal. Idleness and ennervating luxury appear among the rich, and independent craftsmen are replaced, as work is subdivided to its most productive point, by laborers whose narrow lives and straitened circumstances render them unfit as citizens and soldiers.[66] To Madison and Jefferson, these consequences of intensive economic change were critical considerations.

It was Jefferson, of course, with his supreme ability to dress received ideas in gifted prose, who had reduced the argument to memorable phrases:

Those who labor in the earth are the chosen people of God, if ever he had a chosen people, whose breasts he has made his peculiar deposit for substantial and genuine virtue.... Corruption of morals in the mass of cultivators is a phenomenon of which no age nor nation has furnished an example. It is the mark set on those who, not looking up to heaven, to their own soil and industry, as does the husbandman, for their subsistence, depend for it on the casualties and caprice of customers. Dependence begets subservience and venality, suffocates the germ of virtue, and prepares fit tools for the designs of ambition.... Generally speaking, the proportion which the aggregate of the other classes of citizens bears in any state to that of its husbandmen is the proportion of its unsound to its healthy parts, and is a good enough barometer whereby to measure its degree of corruption. While we have land to labor then, let us never wish to see our citizens occupied at a workbench or twirling a distaff. Carpenters, masons, smiths are wanted in husbandry; but for the general operations of manufacture, let our workshops remain in Europe. . . . The loss by the transportation of commodities across the Atlantic will be made up in happiness and permanence of government. The mobs of great cities add just so much to the support of pure government as sores do to the strength of the human body. It is the manners and spirit of a people which preserve a republic in vigor.[67]

Not until the early months of 1792 would Madison prepare a very similar discussion of the proper population for republics.[68] If there is any doubt, however, that the thoughts expressed in 1792 already influenced his position of the middle eighties, this should be dispelled by the reflections he articulated in response to Jefferson's emotional denunciation of the poverty that he had witnessed on a trip through rural France.

Jefferson attributed the "wretchedness" of the majority in France to the excessive concentration of its landed property in great estates. Remarking that "the earth is given as a common stock for man" and that the combination of uncultivated lands and massive unemployment was a violation of this natural law, the diplomat suggested legislation like his own attacks on primogeniture and entail in Virginia, laws that would work gradually to level the inequities so evident in Europe.[69] Madison's response probed deeper. "I have no doubt," he wrote, "that the misery of the lower classes will be found to abate wherever the government assumes a freer aspect and the laws favor a subdivision of property." Still, the greater comfort of the mass of people in the new American republics seemed to him as much a product of their smaller populations as it did of the "political advantages" they all enjoyed. "A certain degree of misery," he feared, might be inevitable in countries "fully peopled," for wherever this was so, a fraction of the people would suffice to raise a mighty surfeit of "subsistence," and there would still remain a greater number of inhabitants "by far" than would be necessary to provide for all the other needs and even comforts of existence. How could surplus people be employed? "Hitherto," he answered, they had been divided into "manufacturers of superfluities, idle proprietors of productive funds, domestics, soldiers, merchants, mariners," and such. Yet all of these employments had been insufficient to absorb the surplus, and "most" of them would be reduced by the republican reforms that he and Jefferson desired. A better government would have less need for soldiers. "From a

more equal partition of property must result a greater simplicity of manners, consequently a less consumption of manufactured superfluities and
a less proportion of idle proprietors and domestics." There would thus
be no exemption for republics from the pressures rising from the pro-
ductivity of laborers and land. Republican ideals could speed developments that good republicans must fear.[70]

For the long run, Madison confessed, he had no answer to the problem
of "a country fully peopled." Even North America would one day be as
crowded as contemporary Europe, perhaps with all the misery that this
implied. But this, he knew, was looking far into the future. For the present—and for years to come—the westward movement promised an escape. As long as it continued freely, the United States would not be forced
to hurry toward intensive economic change, and its republics would be
shielded from the inequalities and misery that more intensive changes
would entail. Expansion to the west would multiply the agricultural societies that were the best foundations for republics. It would also, and continually, relieve the crowding that would otherwise propel the East into
conditions that would threaten these foundations there.

But none of this would work without an open Mississippi. None of it
would work without free trade between the old world and the new. Already
at a middle level of development, Americans would never be content, as
Madison explicitly admitted, to return to mere subsistence. If western
farmers were unable to exchange their surplus for the comforts and con-
veniences of life, then westerners would either choose to manufacture for
themselves or else potential migrants would remain in the Atlantic states,
where growing population and a lack of foreign markets were already
urging this solution. The clock could only run one way, and in that way,
in some respects, lay genuine improvement. Madison, accordingly, did not
propose to turn it back, or even to arrest its progress. He wanted only to
prevent its speeding uncontrollably toward social circumstances undesir-
able for liberal republics.[71] This, however, he desired more desperately
with every passing year. Afflicted by depression, all of the Atlantic states
were being pressured into legislation he condemned. And with conditions
in the East already changing, Spanish closure of the Mississippi threatened
to accelerate precipitous decline.

In 1786, developments propelled the country into crisis. Madison had
helped to manage the Virginia act for statehood for Kentucky in December 1785. On January 21, profoundly troubled by repeated state and federal failures to retaliate effectively against the Europeans, he had voted
for a general convention to consider better regulation of the nation's
foreign trade. By April, as he planned a journey to New York and on to
the Annapolis Convention, correspondents told him of another notable

revival of the old congressional discussion of a broader general convention.[72] This time, he discouraged the idea.[73] By now, the prospects for a
good attendance at Annapolis seemed bright, and he was hopeful that the
gathering would prove a useful step toward necessary changes. At the same
time, he increasingly despaired that anything effective could be done
through Congress.[74] On March 19, Monroe had told him that New Jersey
had deliberately refused to pay its annual requisition. "Is it possible,"
asked Madison, to have a clearer proof of "impotency in the federal system?" "A government cannot long stand which is obliged . . . to court a
compliance with its *constitutional* acts from a member not of the most
powerful order, situated within the immediate verge of authority, and ap-
prized of every circumstance which should remonstrate against disobedience."[75]

Unhappily, clearer proof of federal impotence was soon forthcoming.
On May 31, Monroe him that the Union's secretary for foreign affairs,
John Jay, who was responsible for the negotiations with the Spanish, had
moved to get himself relieved of the instruction to insist on navigation of
the Mississippi. Opening the letter on the verge of his departure for the
north, Madison was outraged and astounded. There was little need to
think about the distant implications of the news. He knew at once that
the Confederation faced the most divisive confrontation of its short existence. The promise of Annapolis diminished. The need to act assumed
the urgency of an alternative to national disintegration.

The sectional collision sparked by John Jay's effort to conclude a treaty
with Spain is described in every standard study of the background of the
Constitutional Convention.[76] Instructed to resolve outstanding boundary
disputes, secure a recognition of the right to navigate the Mississippi, and
obtain a freer trade with Spain and its dominions, Jay had been immersed
in tedious negotiations with Diego de Gardoqui since the early summer
of 1785. The Spanish envoy was prepared to recognize the borders
claimed by the Confederation since the peace, especially if he could win
a mutual guarantee of territorial possessions. He offered valuable concessions in the monarch's European ports, Spanish purchases of naval masts
in the United States, and Spanish aid against the troublesome North Af-
rican corsairs—all, however, only if the Union would accept the closure
of the Mississippi. After months of talk, the most that Jay could manage
to extract from his opponent was a tentative agreement that the Union
need not sacrifice its abstract claim, but must forgo the navigation for a
period of twenty-five or thirty years. Finally, believing that these terms

demanded only that the Union should forebear a while from pressing a claim of no great present consequence to the United States—a claim, in any case, that it was hopelessly unable to enforce—Jay initiated a request for new congressional instructions. Led by Massachusetts, whose representatives were eager to assist their struggling fishermen and shippers, seven northern states were willing to approve the change. But nine states were required to ratify a treaty (if not, indeed, to alter the instructions nine had earlier approved); and marshaled by Virginia, all the planting states were bitterly opposed. Cultural and economic differences between New England and the South had long accounted for the most persistent coalitions in the Continental Congress.[77] With Jay's request for new instructions, these antagonisms spewed. As Congress deadlocked on the issue, leaders on both sides began to talk about a fracture of the Union with an earnestness that they had never shown before.

New Englanders were understandably infuriated by the stubborn southern stand on Jay-Gardoqui. The people of the northern ports desperately needed markets and employment, but the selfish southerners, it seemed, were more concerned about protecting their investments in the West.[78] Privately, some eastern politicians wondered whether it would make more sense to form a smaller, regional confederation homogeneous enough to have a set of common interests.[79]

To southerners, of course, the selfishness seemed altogether on the other side. As Virginia's William Grayson put it, "the occlusion of the river" would indeed "destroy the hopes of the principal men in the southern states in establishing the future fortunes of their families." But this would hardly be the only consequence of a denial to the westerners of a convenient outlet for their produce. Agreement with the Spanish would destroy the value of the western lands, depriving the Confederation of the fund on which it counted to discharge the debt. Westerners and southerners alike would be profoundly disaffected from the Union "when they saw dearest interests sacrificed and given up [in order] to obtain a trivial commercial advantage for their brethren in the East."[80] The proper policy for the United States, as Grayson saw it, was to grant an independent revenue to Congress, together with the right to regulate the country's trade, and then to force a Spanish recognition of the right to navigate the Mississippi. But the southern states would never grant these necessary powers, Grayson warned, if easterners persisted in their present conduct.[81]

Eastern talk of separate regional confederations was abundantly repaid by Grayson and Monroe, both of whom suspected that the whole attempt to alter Jay's instructions was an eastern plot to either dominate the Union or destroy it. In 1786, the West was everywhere perceived as an extension of the South. Western settlement was still almost exclusively on lands southwest of the Ohio, and as population moved increasingly into the Old Southwest, it was becoming ever more apparent that admission to the Union of new southwestern states could fundamentally affect the federal balance.[82] James Monroe, who took a leading part in the congressional proceedings, probed these implications in a deeply troubled missive to Governor Patrick Henry on August 12. After blasting Jay's intrigues with eastern congressmen, Monroe warned Henry that creation of a separate northern confederacy was talked of "familiarly" in Massachusetts. Massachusetts congressmen, he warned, might have no other object than to further such a scheme, calculating that the southern opposition would inflame the shipping states. On the other hand, he added, a Spanish treaty on these terms might be a calculated eastern ploy for permanent ascendancy within the Union. A lengthy closure of the Mississippi would destroy the western settlements and either "prevent any in future" or ensure that the westerners would find it in their interest to separate from the Confederation. Emigration from the older states would be abruptly checked, new states would not be added to the Union, and "the vacant lands of New York and Massachusetts" would appreciate in value and desirability. "In short," Monroe concluded, the Jay-Gardoqui project was designed to keep "the weight of government and population" in the East; and if the men behind it could not succeed at that, they would not hesitate to use their failure to destroy the Union.[83]

There is nothing to suggest that Madison accepted Grayson's or Monroe's analysis of Jay's maneuvers. There is every evidence, however, that he fully shared their anger and alarm. Although he knew that he would soon be leaving for New York and promised a complete communication once they were together, he could not restrain the fury and amazement prompted by Monroe's original report, delivering a lengthy, livid blast as soon as he received it. Congress, he insisted, had no better right to bar Virginia's western citizens from passing down the Mississippi "than to say that her eastern citizens shall not pass through the capes of Henry and Charles." He had forgiven Congress, he suggested, for considering this measure under the duress of war. But to adopt it now

would be a voluntary barter in time of profound peace of the *rights* of one part of the empire to the *interests* of another part. What would Massachusetts say to a proposition for ceding to Britain her right of fishery as the price of some stipulations in favor of tobacco?

Again, can there be a more shortsighted or dishonorable policy than to concur with Spain in frustrating the benevolent views of nature, to sell the affections of our ultramontane brethren, to depreciate the richest fund we possess, . . . [and] to court by the most precious sacrifices the alliance of a nation whose impotency is notorious, who has given no proof of regard for us, and the genius of whose government, religion, and manners unfit them of all the nations in Christendom for a coalition with this country?

Madison could hope that Grayson and Monroe exaggerated the support for Jay's proposal, that Congress would reject it "with becoming indignation." Still, with the Annapolis Convention heavy on his mind, he found it "mortifying" that the eastern states should be pursuing policies that would invigorate the southern enemies of federal reform. "God knows," he finished, remembering the last assembly, "that they are formidable enough in this state without such an advantage."[84]

Leaving Orange County on June 25 or 26 and stopping for ten days in Philadelphia, Madison arrived in New York City early in the fourth week of July. He was just in time for some of the most serious strategic preparations of the summer. On August 4, a grand committee on the state of the Confederation handed in the period's most sweeping recommendations for amendments of the Articles of Union.[85] On August 3, however, Jay's address to Congress had initiated the deliberations that soon foreclosed congressional attention to any other subject. At the seat of Congress, Madison was thoroughly immersed in private talks on both these topics. What advice he gave, if any, is uncertain.[86] What he learned is more apparent—and would deeply influence the decisions he would soon be called upon to make.

By early August 1786, eight of thirteen states had chosen delegates to the Annapolis Convention. While Madison was in New York, he learned that "many gentlemen both within and without Congress wish to make this meeting subservient to a plenipotentiary convention for amending the Confederation." By now, he wrote to Jefferson, he shared this wish, "yet I despair so much of its accomplishment at the present crisis that I do not extend my views beyond a commercial reform. To speak the truth, I almost despair even of this." The reason was the furor over Jay-Gardoqui, which overshadowed every other subject through his fortnight in New York. Madison did not believe that nine states would consent to Jay's proposal, yet the very effort by a lesser number could be "fatal," he suspected, "to an augmentation of the federal authority, if not to the little now existing." Like Grayson, he believed that thoughts of regional confederations should be countered by empowering the Union to relieve the economic suffering that lay behind them. But even while the current crisis showed how urgent action had become, it also threatened to defeat it. He had listened to the bitter talk in Congress. "Figure to yourself," he wailed, the consequences in Virginia, among them the extreme embarrassment the project threatened for himself. "Ever since I have been out of Congress I have been inculcating on our assembly a confidence in the equal attention of Congress to the rights and interests of every part of the republic and on the western members in particular the necessity of making the Union respectable by new powers to Congress if they wished Congress to negotiate with effect for the Mississippi." The Jay-Gardoqui crisis threatened to discredit years of patient work.[87]

Madison returned to Philadelphia on August 10, stopping briefly on the way at Princeton, where he urged John Witherspoon to help reverse New Jersey's stance on Jay's proposal.[88] As the argument in Congress neared a temporary resolution, Monroe continued to report on every new maneuver. Sure that seven states would vote for Jay's proposal unless some new arrivals in the Pennsylvania delegation altered its position, he wanted Madison to talk to absent members, probe their views, and "send them up" if they were likely to assist.[89] Three days later, he requested Madison's advice about a compromise designed to keep the Mississippi open as an avenue for western exports in exchange for an agreement that would close it to their imports for a time. Most of all, perhaps, he wanted Madison to understand that "Jay and his party are determined to pursue this business as far as possible, either as the means of throwing the western people and territory without the government of the U.S. and keeping the weight of population and government here or of dismembering the government itself for the purpose of a separate confederacy."[90]

On August 17, Madison advised Monroe not to introduce his compromise proposal, warning that its probable defeat would force the delegation to continue "under the disadvantage of having forsaken your first ground."[91] The warning came too late. On August 30, Monroe reported that a seven-state majority, from Pennsylvania north without a break to Massachusetts, had swept aside the southern opposition and instructed Jay to yield the right of navigation if the claim would otherwise prevent conclusion of a treaty.[92] On September 3, he added that Jay was determined to pursue his talks despite the dubious legality of these instructions. Everything, he wrote, would now depend on Pennsylvania and New Jersey, where the pro-Jay forces were already working to solidify their following or to prepare for a dismemberment of the Confederation on the line of the Potomac if they could not keep these states in line. Monroe expected Madison to counter these intrigues, especially among the Pennsylvanians. "If a dismemberment takes place, that state must not be added to the eastern scale. It were as well to use force to prevent it as to defend ourselves afterwards."[93] Written on the eve of Madison's departure for Annapolis, Monroe's alarmist letter reached him in that town, where he and several others had been waiting for a week for the remaining delegations to arrive.[94] It was a vivid, late reminder of the circumstances of their meeting.

Several mounting problems had conjoined by 1786 to highlight the debility of the Confederation and to prompt the strong support for a revision of the Articles that Madison had learned of in New York. Violations of the Peace of Paris by a number of the states were being used by Britain to defend her own refusal to evacuate a string of forts in the American Northwest. Pirate raids had nearly closed the Mediterranean to U.S. merchant ships. But Congress had no navy, only seven hundred unpaid soldiers, and insufficient funds to even buy a treaty with the pirates.[95] In every year since the conclusion of the peace, payments on the federal requisitions had been smaller than the ordinary, annual expenses of the tiny central government, and total federal revenues had never been remotely equal to the interest charges on its debt. In a minority of states, domestic creditors could trade their federal notes for state certificates of debt, but state assumptions of the federal obligations were a dubious advantage for the Union. Meanwhile, Congress had suspended interest payments on its debt to France and Spain and was approaching an exhaustion of its credit with Dutch bankers.[96] To dramatize the wreck of federal finances, New Jersey had resolved that it would pay its federal requisitions only when the three remaining states approved the impost. In fact, however, every effort to amend the Articles had come to ground on the requirement for unanimous consent, and Congress was itself increasingly unable to agree on new proposals for reform. Early in the year, as members talked about a grand convention, Congress took an inventory of the state of the proposed amendments. Nine states had ratified the impost, but only three had made provision for the other funds required by the proposals of 1783. Only ten had ratified the limited commercial powers requested in 1784.[97] This was the context that had taken Madison to the Annapolis Convention and had prompted a revival of congressional discussions of a plenipotentiary meeting of the states. And in this context, the addition of the bitter schism over Jay's negotiations with Gardoqui was an urgent warning that the federal paralysis was now almost complete.

On March 18, 1786, before Monroe alerted him to Jay's proposal, Madison had written Jefferson about his reasons for supporting the Annapolis Convention. In 1783, another crisis had convinced him that a dissolution of the Union would compel its fragments to adopt defensive measures incompatible with their continuation as republics. The durabil-

ity of these republican experiments, as he conceived it, also had a set of
economic preconditions, none of them more vital than a free exchange
of agricultural commodities for foreign manufactures. Yet during the depression of the middle 1780s, every year had brought new proof that state
attempts to force an opening of European markets simply set the members
of the Union "by the ears." When Massachusetts tried retaliation, he reminded Jefferson, Connecticut declared its own ports free. New Jersey
served New York the same, and Delaware was likely to defeat the laws of
Pennsylvania.[98]

Of all the nation's needs, a federal power over trade now seemed to
Madison the most essential, especially as such a grant would carry with it
the assurance of a steady source of independent general funds. Continental measures were the only ones that might compel the Europeans to
accept the sort of world that would sustain America's new order. In their
absence, ineffective separate regulations were producing rising animosities
among the states and general discontent with a Confederation helpless to
provide relief. In their absence, too, the inability to trade commodities
for European imports drained the country of its scarce supply of precious
metals and provided "pretexts for the pernicious substitution of paper
money, for indulgences for debtors, for postponements of taxes," and for
other unjust legislation in the states. Thus, before Monroe informed him
of the threat that Jay was ready to trade the navigation of the Mississippi
for a partial opening of Spanish ports, Madison already thought that
nearly all of the Confederation's most distressing problems could be
traced to its commercial crisis.[99] The Jay-Gardoqui conflict was another—
and incalculably pernicious—consequence of these commercial ills. "An
alarming proof of the predominance of temporary and partial interests
over . . . just and extended maxims," it even helped the anxious Madison
to give expression to his growing discontent with what was happening
within the several states. As he told Monroe, if nine—or even all thirteen—of the confederated states approved the closing of the Mississippi,

I shall never be convinced that it is expedient, because I cannot conceive
it to be just. There is no maxim in my opinion which is more liable to be
misapplied and which therefore more needs elucidation than the current
one that the interest of the majority is the political standard of right and
wrong. Taking the word "interest" as synonomous with "ultimate happiness," in which sense it is qualified with every necessary moral ingredient,
the proposition is no doubt true. But taking it in the popular sense, as
referring to immediate augmentation of property and wealth, nothing can
be more false. In the latter sense, it would be the interest of the majority
in every community to despoil and enslave the minority. . . . In fact, it is

only reestablishing under another name and a more specious form, force as a measure of right.[100]

If the Virginia legislature had been willing to support a forceful move in Congress, Madison would not have favored a convention on commercial problems. As it was, however, the assembly had been less supportive of his federal measures during 1785 than during 1784. Peace had not produced the better times and stronger state support for the Confederation that he had hoped for on retiring from the Congress. Peace had been succeeded by depression, desperate local legislation, and increasing state suspicions of a central government that might infringe their separate interests. Convinced that something must be done to get around this impasse—that the failure to relieve the nation's economic problems was at once an urgent danger to the Union and the leading cause of vicious legislation in the states—Madison had reasoned that a special meeting of the states, if not the "best expedient" of all, was yet the best that could be carried in Virginia.[101] Had it worked—that is, if the Annapolis Convention had been capable of an effective call for a congressional authority to regulate the nation's commerce—perhaps he would have been content with further efforts at a piecemeal process of reform. But in the context of the dreadful prospects opened by the furor over Jay-Gardoqui, he could not accept inaction. And, indeed, he may have feared that circumstances had been changed so radically by sectional collision and betrayal at the seat of the Confederation Congress that extraordinary measures had become the only ones that now held any prospect for success.

Madison obtained a room at George Mann's tavern in Annapolis on September 4, the day appointed for the meeting to convene.[102] Only two commissioners, besides himself, were present in the city.[103] After seven days, when he responded to Monroe's frantic letter of September 3, several other delegates had trickled into town, but prospects for a large enough attendance "to make the meeting respectable" continued to be glum. Only Delaware, New Jersey, and Virginia were fully represented, joined by one commissioner from Pennsylvania and two more from New York.[104]

We do not know exactly what transpired among the dozen members present. But even with a few additions, they must surely have perceived, the meeting would have seemed an ineffective rump of the respectable assemblage hoped for in the spring; and those on hand were nearly of a single mind about the "delicate and critical" conditions under which they met. Thus, confronted with the possibility of total failure and aware that the commission of the members from New Jersey mentioned "other important matters" in addition to the nation's trade, the delegates unani-

mously agreed to turn their disappointment into yet another evidence of
the necessity for bolder action. They called on their states to seek concurrence by the others

> in the appointment of commissioners to meet at Philadelphia on the sec-
> ond Monday in May next to take into consideration the situation of the
> United States, to devise such further provisions as shall appear to them
> necessary to render the constitution of the federal government adequate
> to the exigencies of the Union, and to report such an act for that purpose
> to the United States in Congress assembled as, when agreed to by them
> and afterwards confirmed by the legislatures of every state, will effectually
> provide for the same.[105]

Signed by John Dickinson and drafted by Alexander Hamilton, an address
appealing for a second general convention, empowered to consider *all*
the defects of the federal constitution, was the most decisive action that
the delegates could take. Hamilton, of course, had favored this expedient
since the beginning of the decade. Madison had come to Maryland with
little hope that any such proposal could emerge, but ready, after years of
hesitation, to concur wholeheartedly in the idea.[106]

The shift in Madison's attitude was striking. As he left Annapolis for
Philadelphia, Mount Vernon, and the annual session of the state assembly,
he was probably as skeptical about the prospects for a full and efficacious
constitutional convention as he once had been about Annapolis itself.
From this point forward, nonetheless, his own commitment to extraordinary measures would be wholly free from all the other doubts with which
he had been troubled through the winter. In January, he had been apologetic in supporting the Annapolis Convention, leading the assembly from
behind the scenes and advocating a commercial meeting with open reservations. Respectful of legalities and mindful of the danger to the van-
ishing authority of Congress, he had never been a ready friend of
supralegal action. But beginning in September, he hurled himself unhes-
itatingly into the busiest and most productive months of his career, doubting neither the propriety nor the wisdom of a constitutional convention,
acting as a principal director of something very like a second revolution.
He did so, it seems certain, in the literal conviction that the first one was
immediately at risk.

It is unlikely, to be sure, that Madison was thinking in September 1786
of anything resembling the proposals he would make in Philadelphia in
May. And yet the crisis of the summer had convinced him that the peril
to the Union was immediate and sharp, the sort of peril that demanded
revolutionary measures. The Jay-Gardoqui crisis warned him that the pow-

ers necessary to preserve the Union might never be confided to the present Congress. And finally—what may have been the most important consequence of all—the sectional collision over Jay's instructions strengthened his conviction that the weaknesses of the Confederation were the major reason why majorities in all the states were passing economic legislation incompatible with his ideas of fundamental justice. Between the two conventions, this association of the failings of the Union with the growing tendency of state majorities to sacrifice the general good to pressing, temporary interests would tighten in his mind into a vision of a full-blown crisis of the Revolution. The conviction that these threats were linked—and so completely intertwined that they could not be countered separately—would be the crux of his proposals for sweeping constitutional reform.[107]

CHAPTER THREE

The Crisis of
Republican Convictions

JAMES MADISON, "THE FATHER OF THE CONSTITUTION," was a child of the republican revolution. The fact is obvious, but when we state it in these terms and let the implications permeate our thinking, valuable new insights can result. Previous analyses have taught us that his most important contributions started when he linked his discontent with the Confederation with his rising fear of what was happening within the several states and urged the Constitutional Convention to approve a plan that would address both problems. But previous analyses have only partially recaptured the intensity and nature of his revolutionary vision. Madison matured with the American rebellion, coming to adulthood just as the colonial resistance was beginning to transform itself into a democratic revolution.[1] A full appreciation of his absolute immersion in the spirit of this time is vital to an understanding of the sort of revolution he would later seek to save.

The eldest son of Orange County's leading planter, Madison was in his middle teens, learning Greek and Latin at Donald Robertson's tidewater boarding school, when Patrick Henry opened the revolt against the Stamp Act. Although his father was a vestryman of the established church and James received additional instruction from the local rector, climate, politics, and educational superiority outweighed denominational considerations when the three of them decided on a college, choosing Presbyterian but fiercely patriotic Princeton. There, the young Virginian got a thorough grounding in Scottish moral-sense philosophy and in the major classics of the English libertarian tradition. There, as well, he dressed in homespun, joined in student demonstrations to protest the Townshend Acts, and listened to commencement speeches on religious toleration, public spirit, and such topics as "The Rising Glory of America." Completing three years' work in two (and damaging his health so badly that he felt unable to complete the journey home), he stayed in Princeton through the early months of 1772, reading law and Hebrew with President John Witherspoon. When he returned to the plantation, he was still in feeble health and still unwilling to commit himself to a profession. But he was only twenty-one, and two years later an infuriated Parliament responded to events in Boston with the infamous Coercive Acts. As Orange County mobilized behind the recommendations of the Continental Congress, the young man joined his father on the county committee of safety, practiced with a rifle, and drilled with the local minute company. In October 1775, he was commissioned colonel of the Orange militia. As he phrased it in a late-life sketch, "On the commencement of the dispute with Great Britain, he entered with the prevailing zeal into the American cause, being under very early and strong impressions in favor of liberty both civil and religious."[2]

In Madison's career and thinking civil and religious liberty were intimately linked. The zeal with which he gave himself to both, together with the content of his "early," "strong" impressions in their favor, call insistently for more attention than they ordinarily receive. Recent scholarship has rediscovered the profoundly revolutionary spirit of years surrounding Independence. Prevailing understandings of the Revolution's character and sources have been thoroughly revised. And yet perhaps because the scholarly tradition was so long inclined to see the framing of the Constitution as a counterrevolutionary act—and to identify Madison so completely with the movement to control majority abuses—modern writings seldom give sufficient emphasis to the intensity and scope of his original commitments. In consequence, although it is conventional to note that the Virginia Plan for constitutional reform envisioned a republican corrective for republican excesses, analysts have never fully recognized the very great degree to which its major author still defined "republican" in early revolutionary terms. And in remarking that his most original ideas were predicated on his rising fear of popular abuses, scholars have been tempted to forget that it was not the fear itself, but Madison's conviction that it must and could be overcome—and overcome without surrendering the revolutionary faith—on which his contributions ultimately hinged. To put it in the language of a recent scholarly debate, modern analysts have emphasized the "liberal" to the neglect of the "republican" dimensions of his thought. A fresh insistence on the latter is essential to a fuller understanding of his views.[3]

During the depression of the middle 1780s, as he became increasingly convinced that the debilities of the Confederation were endangering the Union, Madison became no less alarmed about conditions in the states. Everywhere, as he conceived it, private rights and public good were being sacrificed to the apparent interests and immediate desires of the majority of voters. Year by year, his personal revulsion deepened. Year by year, there seemed to be new signs of general restlessness among the people and, at least among an influential few, of growing disenchantment with the revolutionary cause. In the interlude between the Jay-Gardoqui crisis and the Constitutional Convention, his anxiety was stretched unbearably by Shays's Rebellion, which struck him as a final warning of imminent collapse.

Modern scholarship has not exaggerated Madison's disgust with local politics and local legislation. It has not mistaken the enormous consequences for the course of constitutional reform. By 1787, most informed Americans discerned an urgent crisis of the Union. Hundreds, maybe thousands, were alarmed about conditions in the states. To Madison, however, these distinctive worries seemed related aspects of a single, general crisis of the Revolution. On this thought, he built a plan that was intended to address both sets of ills, and he insisted that the crisis could not be resolved within the framework of the current federal system. If he had not proposed so radical a reconstruction, federal reform might not have gone beyond amendments to the Articles of Confederation. If he had not been so determined to correct the ills within the states, both the institutions and the theory of the modern liberal republic might have taken different forms.

More, however, needs to be explained, and much of it cannot be well explained without a shift of focus. Preoccupied with Madison's alarm about abuses in the states, most interpreters have overlooked his claim that many of the most distressing of these evils could be traced to the debilities of the Confederation. Conscious of his deep revulsion from majority abuses, many modern analysts have heavily discounted his abiding faith in "liberty" defined as governments depending wholly and continually upon the body of a democratic people—which, in fact, is how he almost always used this term. In short, though it is true that Madison's proposals to the Constitutional Convention cannot be explained without a close consideration of his rising discontent with early revolutionary institutions, neither can they be explained exclusively, primarily, or even properly as consequences of a personal rejection of the revolutionary faith. In the fullest flush of youthful ardor, Madison immersed himself entirely in the revolutionary dream, and not until we recognize how conscientiously he set his course according to an early revolutionary compass can we fully understand how deeply he was challenged by the local legislation of the middle 1780s, how he linked the failings of the Union with the problems of the states, or what he hoped a constitutional revision could accomplish. Madison's alarm about majority abuses initiated a dramatic reexamination of his earlier assumptions, but the fear itself, as well as his solution, took the forms they did because there was so little in his early faith that he was willing to abandon.

In the years preceding Independence, many of the Federalists of 1787 may have been reluctant to commit themselves to a transforming revolution.[4] Madison, however, was a revolutionary militant from the beginning of our records. With his earliest surviving letter, written to his former tutor shortly after his arrival at the College of New Jersey, he enclosed a recent publication praising and defending London's celebrated pro-American and radical, John Wilkes.[5] Letters to his father also vividly suggest the whiggish atmosphere at both the college and his home. Knowing that his father will approve, he tells him that the college has awarded honorary degrees to John Dickinson and John Hancock. He denounces New York merchants for abandoning nonimportation and describes the ritual in which the Princeton students, dressed in black and tolling the college bell, had gathered in the yard to burn the New York letter asking businessmen in Philadelphia to join in this "base conduct."[6] From our earliest acquaintance to the eve of Independence, all of the surviving evidence suggests that Madison moved always and at every step with radical colonial opinion. Thus, although he questioned the Bostonians' "discretion" in the dumping of the tea, he heartily endorsed their "boldness" and condemned the "obduracy and ministerialism" of Governor Thomas Hutchinson. An early advocate of military preparations and a total economic boycott, he criticized the moderates in Pennsylvania and the Continental Congress. In the spring of 1775, he may have mustered with the Orange militia for one or both of the abortive marches prompted by Lord Dunmore's seizure of Virginia's military stores; and when hostilities began, he probably both drafted and delivered an address approving Patrick Henry's march on Williamsburg and calling Lexington and Concord "a hostile attack on this and every other colony," fully justifying "violence and reprisal."[7]

Information on the youthful Madison is spotty, making it impossible to answer all the questions we might ask. We cannot say exactly when he set his sights on Independence. His surviving letters tell us nothing of significance about the sort of revolutionary constitution he initially preferred. What the records do contain are many little indications of the very great extent to which he shared the values, expectations, and assumptions that were leading militants throughout the colonies to hope that liberty could be secured and made complete by basing governments entirely on the people. Convinced that private rights and public liberty were mutually dependent and that both were being guarded by a zealous public spirit, he believed that both could be perfected by a revolutionary transformation that would make America a model for the world. A radical commitment to the natural rights proclaimed at Independence was accompanied from the beginning by a radical commitment to the people's rule.[8]

When Madison came home from college, he was deeply moralistic and determined to enroll his name in the "Annals of Heaven."[9] The texture of his stern morality is clear: its British-oppositionist and Protestant-dissenting flavor tinged by youthful preachiness and hardened by a physical debilitation so prolonged and so severe that he did not expect "a long or healthy life."[10] His doctrinal convictions are, by contrast, an enduring scholarly enigma. Reared in the established church, he would prefer its services throughout his life, and yet he never entered full communion or identified himself as an Episcopalian. It is possible, of course, that Presbyterian objections to religious hierarchy influenced him at college, along with Witherspoon's defense of toleration. It is certain only that he disapproved of both enthusiasm and the skepticism of the radical Enlightenment.[11] In the years preceding Independence, he studied Hebrew and the Bible, read theology, condemned the irreligion of the popular reviews, and wrote so favorably of those who testified their disapproval of the worldly vanities "by becoming fervent advocates in the cause of Christ" that there is room to wonder if he gave some thought to entering the ministry himself.[12] And yet his more mature opinions are a matter for conjecture, for religious topics simply disappear from his surviving writings after 1776.[13]

This was not the case with the intense morality demanded in his early writings. Honesty, frugality, simplicity, and plainness—the serious, reforming ethic advocated with a new assertiveness by patriots as well as by dissenters—was the youthful Madison's ideal.[14] If he condemned frivolity, he feared and hated greed, yearning for a calling rather than for wealth or fame.[15] Law, he thought, was second only to divinity among the "honorable" professions.[16] He studied it for years, yet never formed an "absolute determination" to make it his career.[17] Perhaps, when he returned from college, he was simply too demoralized by his "discouraging" debilitation to fix his mind on any occupation, having "little spirit and alacrity to set about anything that is difficult in acquiring and useless in possessing after one has exchanged Time for Eternity."[18] But it is likely, too, that his demanding, service-oriented ethic, together with an unadmitted craving for excitement, played a role in his reluctance to decide on a career. Lawbooks were "a barren desert." An attorney's life seemed difficult to reconcile with a continual respect for "probity and truth." His lively conscience may already have been troubled by the family's dependence on the labor of its slaves.[19] Madison, in brief, was very much the sort of youth who needed a challenge and a cause, and there was little to engage him during the deceptive cooling of imperial relations between his graduation and the fall of 1773. Happily, his health was mending rapidly when Boston's "Mohawks" dumped the tea into their harbor; and if his disability was partly psychological in nature, this may not have been coincidence alone. The news from Boston reached him shortly after he had hurled himself into his first great cause—the same one, as it happens, that later played perhaps the central part in leading him to the distinctive insights of his middle thirties.[20]

"Is an ecclesiastical establishment absolutely necessary to support civil society?" Madison asked a Pennsylvania classmate, through whom he ordered copies of the latest treatises on toleration.[21] Northern opposition to the Tea Act and to other parliamentary encroachments suggested different conclusions, for "dependent states" at least.

> If the Church of England had been the established and general religion in all the Northern colonies as it has been among us here . . . , it is clear to me that slavery and subjection might and would have been gradually insinuated among us. Union of religious sentiments begets a surprising confidence [in rulers] and ecclesiastical establishments tend to great ignorance and corruption, all of of which facilitate the execution of mischievous projects.[22]

A broad comparison of Pennsylvania with Virginia reinforced the lesson. Pennsylvania's "liberal, catholic, and equitable way of thinking as to the rights of conscience," Madison believed, encouraged commerce, immigration, virtue, industry, the arts, and a productive love of fame and knowledge. "Religious bondage shackles and debilitates the mind and unfits it for every noble enterprise, every expanded project."[23] "I have . . . nothing to brag of," he complained,

> as to the state and liberty of my country. Poverty and luxury prevail among all sorts: pride, ignorance, and knavery among the priesthood, and vice and wickedness among the laity. This is bad enough, but it is not the worst I have to tell you. That diabolical, Hell-conceived principle of persecution rages among some, and to their eternal infamy, the clergy can furnish their quota of imps for such business. This vexes me the most of anything whatever. There are . . . in the adjacent county not less than five or six well-meaning men in close jail for publishing their religious sentiments, which in the main are very orthodox. I have neither patience to hear, talk, or think of anything relative to this matter, for I have squabbled and scolded,

abused and ridiculed so long about it . . . that I am without common patience.[24]

As Virginia mobilized to meet the latest threat from Britain, Madison found more to brag of. "The proceedings of the Congress are universally approved of in this province," he reported at the end of 1774; "a spirit of liberty and patriotism animates all degrees and denominations of men."[25] Thrilling to this spirit, he was positively boastful of the unity and dedication of his neighbors. In Orange County, as in hundreds of localities that winter, a committee of enforcement purchased military stores and pressured everyone to sign a copy of the Continental Association, which was a method of distinguishing the friends of the resistance from its foes. By January, Madison was buried in this work and buoyant on its progress. Throughout the county, he insisted, only Quakers were refusing to subscribe to the Association. An independent rifle company had formed. "By the spring," he thought, there would be "thousands of well-trained, high-spirited men ready to meet danger whenever it appears, who are influenced by no mercenary principles, bearing their own expenses, and having the prospect of no recompense but the honor and safety of their country."[26] As the fighting started, Madison anticipated that Virginia's strength would rest primarily on independent riflemen from Orange and other "upland counties," and he was confident about their skills and public spirit. "The most inexpert hands reckon it an indifferent shot to miss the bigness of a man's face at the distance of 100 yards. I am far from being among the best and should not often miss it on a fair trial at that distance."[27]

Some of this, no doubt, was youthful innocence and bluster, like the young committeeman's desire to have the Tory publisher, James Rivington, in Orange County for a day.[28] But even the ferocity with which he boasted of the county's vigilance against the enemies of the resistance is another unmistakable reminder of the breadth and depth to which he shared the hopes that linked Independence with the possibility of a regenerating revolution. Although it seems romantic to suggest that Madison experienced the final crisis of the empire as a personal rebirth from the malaise of the preceding years, it does not seem extravagant at all to emphasize that he discerned a striking transformation in his neighbors. "Vice and wickedness among the laity" had given way to vigilance against a common danger. The "insolence" and "pride" of local parsons, which had prompted him to intervene against the jailing of dissenters, had been humbled by a recognition that their power rested on "the favor of the people." Self-indulgence had been swept away as men of sturdy independence gathered at their own expense in military uniforms with "Liberty or Death" emblazoned on their shirts.[29] Ten years later, as he agonized about majority abuses, Madison did not forget that "liberty and property" had been protected from a graver threat, as he conceived it, by this brilliant burst of patriotic fervor.[30] Ten years later, in the midst of many signs that public spirit was endangered, he remained convinced that it was still sufficient to support a people's government and that it could be animated once again by constitutional reforms that would restore its preconditions.

Eighteenth-century Orange County may appear a most unlikely training ground for democratic revolution. Certainly, its most distinguished son never totally transcended its limitations. His father owned three thousand acres and perhaps a hundred slaves. Madison was fully conscious of the wickedness of slavery, probably from the beginning of the war. Throughout his life—and with increasing guilt—he thought of it as an abomination absolutely incompatible with his ideals. Nevertheless, through forty years of active public service, he refused to risk his usefulness in other urgent causes by identifying with the more outspoken, active critics of the institution; and he never freed himself from daily, intimate involvement with the evil. Attended by a body servant even when he traveled to the North, he willed his chattels to his wife and hoped in his retirement that a voluntary, gradual emancipation could be speeded by permitting slavery's diffusion to the West. Trapped by his belief that whites would not permit equality for blacks and that the former slaves would be impoverished and dangerous in a state of partial freedom, he could do no more, in his old age, than to commit his waning energies and great prestige to the leadership of the American Colonization Society. Slavery clamped its fetters even on his mind.[31]

But there were other facts about the context in which Madison matured, and these would also leave a lasting imprint on his mind. When the militia mustered in the aftermath of Lexington and Concord, Orange County held about 550 free, white families. Nearly all of its 1100 male adults, with the exception of dependent sons, owned more than fifty acres of productive land, which qualified them for the franchise. This they exercised, traditionally, to send the ablest, most distinguished of their number to guard their common interests in the world beyond the county. Among the holders of the great estates, in turn, there were a host in late-colonial Virginia who conceived themselves as obligated to employ their great advantages in public service. The most impressive of these local worthies understood themselves, in consciousness of all the implications of the phrase, as fathers of their counties; and the senior Madison was evidently just this sort of man. A justice of the peace, a vestryman, and head of the county militia, he was careful to provide his namesake with a formal education much beyond his own, and he appears to have conducted the plantation as a family business to which everyone contributed according to their talents and could draw on in accordance with their needs. As his sons attained maturity, the father acted as a loving first of equals. As the eldest son assumed his obligations in the county, he inherited a favored station in a wider family in which political authority already rested on the deferential, but conditional, consent of equal, independent owners. As these independent owners mustered with their arms, Orange County was an archetype of the republican community idealized in early revolutionary thought, and there was every reason to believe that property as well as liberty was safest in these freemen's hands.[32]

Perfect liberty, of course, did not imply that independent freemen were to rule directly or without restraint. None of the republicans of revolutionary times envisioned anything except a representative, contractual, and limited regime.[33] In 1776, however, many revolutionaries did suppose that private rights and the public good could be protected quite completely by eradicating the remains of monarchy and aristocracy, purging their existing governments of all of the familiar means by which executives could influence and corrupt their other parts, and binding representatives more closely to the will of citizens who seemed to be ideally suited for the preservation and perfection of their freedom.

These, of course, were just the suppositions that would be severely tested in the decade after Independence. The challenge came in a variety of forms, for there were many instances by then in which experience suggested that the people as a body might not be the best protectors of the private rights that individuals had not surrendered when a lawful government was formed.[34] For Madison himself, however, what we now regard as an enduring tension in the effort to combine republican with liberal convictions reached a climax—and began to find a resolution—only when his early, strong commitment to religious freedom was at first directly threatened, then abundantly supported, by the body of the people. There were many sources for the reconstruction of his youthful thinking. But none was more instructive than Virginia's revolutionary settlement of conflicts over church and state.

Among the rights that Madison believed could be protected more completely in republics, none was literally more sacred than the liberty of conscience. He first involved himself in local politics, in 1773, in order to protest the persecution of dissenters in neighboring Culpeper County. When shaky health defeated his determination to defend the cause of liberty in arms, the gratitude of Baptist neighbors may have helped him win election to the state convention of 1776, which framed one of the earliest, most widely imitated revolutionary constitutions.[35] Here, despite his modesty and youth, he made his next important contribution to a lifelong battle for religious freedom, standing on a set of principles that placed him from the start among the most advanced reformers of his age. Ten years later, the renewal of this battle became perhaps the single greatest test of his original convictions and the single most important catalyst for the distinctive insights that revitalized his revolutionary faith.

When the Virginia constitution came to the convention from committee, George Mason's draft of a Declaration of Rights contained a generous, though basically conventional, protection for dissenters:

> That religion, or the duty which we owe to our Creator, and the manner of discharging it, can be directed only by reason and conviction, not by force or violence; and therefore, that all men should enjoy the fullest toleration in the exercise of religion, according to the dictates of conscience, unpunished and unrestrained by the magistrate unless, under color of religion, any man disturb the peace, the happiness, or safety of society. And that it is the mutual duty of all to practice Christian forbearance, love, and charity towards each other.

Madison was not content. The language of the article, like the language of the preface to the Declaration, suggested the enormous influence of John Locke, whose famous *Letter Concerning Toleration* grounded freedom of religious conscience on the character of human understanding and the separate origins and purposes of church and state, yet listed several opinions that the magistrates should punish.[36] On his copy of the printed draft of the religious article, Madison prepared a change that pressed Locke's premises to logical conclusions from which Locke himself had shied. In place of Mason's "all men should enjoy the fullest toleration," Madison's amendment, which was introduced by Patrick Henry, said:

> All men are equally entitled to the full and free exercise of [their religion] according to the dictates of conscience; and therefore that no man or class of men ought, on account of religion, to be invested with peculiar emoluments or privileges; nor subjected to any penalties or disabilities unless, under color of religion, any man disturb the peace, the happiness, or safety of society.[37]

Someone asked if Henry really meant to disestablish the Anglican Church. He denied it, the amendment failed, and Madison wrote out a substitute, this time asking Edmund Pendleton to introduce it. The new proposal altered Mason's "All men should enjoy the fullest toleration . . . unpunished and unrestrained by the magistrate" to "All men are equally entitled to enjoy the free exercise of religion unless the preservation of equal liberty and the existence of the state are manifestly endangered." As approved by the convention, Article 16 incorporated Madison's replacement of the reference to "toleration" with recognition of an equal right and simply dropped the clause referring to the state's authority to keep the peace.[38]

Momentous implications were contained in what might seem a minor change of wording. However broadly it extended, Madison perceived, "toleration" was a privilege permitted by the state, and it implied a state authority to set a standard from which some degree of deviation, but perhaps no more, might be allowed. An equal right, not just to hold, but also to express and freely exercise the differing demands of conscience, placed religious freedom on entirely different grounds. Although the failure of his first amendment left the question of a state establishment unsettled, the logic of his second still demanded equal treatment for competing faiths and urged withdrawal of the state from the entirety of the distinctive sphere which Locke had carefully defined but not consistently defended. In its final phrasing, Article 16 erected an ideal that no society had ever written into law and spurred the commonwealth at once toward its achievement. Dissenters seized on it immediately to call for equal treatment. Among Virginia's legislative leaders, it identified the shy, young representative from Orange as one from whom extraordinary deeds might be expected.[39]

Madison's mature position on religious freedom was probably complete in its essentials when he drafted these amendments. He seems from that point forward, with unwavering consistency, to have envisioned total freedom of opinion, absolute equality for various denominations, and an end to the prevailing intermixture of the logically distinctive spheres of politics and religion, this world and the next.[40] He probably agreed with the dissenters that despite the failure of his first amendment, Article 16 implied a speedy disestablishment of the Anglican Church, together with the revocation of a panoply of statutes punishing dissent, providing tax support for the established church, and licensing or regulating both dissenting preachers and the regular parishes and clergy. When the General Assembly met again for its October session, Thomas Jefferson, who had been busy in the Continental Congress in the spring, assumed direction of a legislative drive for most of these reforms. Madison, who served on the Committee for Religion, gave Jefferson his full support.[41]

The effort met with only limited success. Though Madison and Jefferson, who called the fight the hardest of his life, already looked toward disestablishment, repeal of all restrictions on opinion, and a wholly voluntary system of support for all denominations, the majority of delegates was not prepared for such a large departure from tradition. The assembly did revoke all parliamentary statutes concerning religion. It did suspend collection of religious taxes, from which dissenters now received exemption. Nevertheless, the state retained the power to license dissenting preachers and meetings as well as to supervise the established church, whose parishes continued to perform several civil functions. Although the gains were great, many fundamental issues continued unresolved. In order to address them, Jefferson secured appointment of a small committee charged to undertake a general republican revision of Virginia's laws.

Among the many bills that Jefferson prepared for the committee of revisors was the famous Statute for Establishing Religious Freedom, one of three accomplishments that he would have inscribed on his tombstone.[42] Number 82 of the revised code, this bill was introduced to the assembly in 1779, as was a rival bill providing for a general tax for the support of the Christian religion. Neither was enacted. Except for the repeal of the suspended law providing salaries for the Episcopal clergy, the legislature passed no major bills relating to religion for the duration of the war.[43] Jefferson's ability to press his program of reforms was ended when the legislature chose him to be governor in 1779 and Congress followed by selecting him as minister to France. Madison was not a member of the General Assembly after 1776. Alarmed about the customary practice of "corrupting" voters by providing them with alchohol and other treats, he "trusted" that in the next election his neighbors would approve a new example more consistent "with the purity of moral and of republican principles." Regrettably, competitors adhered to custom (as he would himself in future), and the county's freeholders insisted on a due "respect" for habit and their palates. The disappointment surely deepened Madison's distaste for popular electioneering. Still, it was the only election he ever lost, and even as he lost it, he was reinforcing his emerging reputation as a man of principle and virtue.[44]

Defeated in the spring election of 1777, Madison was promptly chosen by the legislature as a member of the Council of State, where he served with Governors Henry and Jefferson. Two years later, in December 1779, the legislature saved him from this "grave of useful talents" and sent him on to Congress. There, as has been seen, he gradually acquired the stature and experience that permitted him to renew the legislative efforts that had been deflected by the vagaries of politics and the necessities of war.[45]

When Madison returned to the Virginia General Assembly in the spring of 1784, he was primarily concerned about the needs of the Confederation and the economic future of his state. In the long run, he believed, prosperity depended on a more effective Union, and the viability of the American experiment in popular self-government depended on the economic underpinnings of a healthy civic life. Since liberty and Independence would be judged according to their fruits, he also hoped, however, to revitalize the Jeffersonian agenda for reform. In 1783, Jefferson had urged him to consider a revision of the revolutionary constitution, which both of them considered poorly balanced and without an adequate foundation in authoritative action by the people.[46] Madison was also eager to encourage legislative action on his friend's revision of the laws.

In all of these objectives, Madison was persevering, highly capable, and seldom more than partially successful. In the spring of 1784, as has been seen, the legislature passed his act restricting foreign traders to specific ports. With Patrick Henry's valuable support, he won approval of a federal power to retaliate against the British. On May 29, he also moved successfully to fund a public printing of the stalled revision of the laws. Nevertheless, he was severely disappointed by the session. Encouraged by support from Richard Henry Lee, he urged a state convention to amend Virginia's constitution. But Lee and Patrick Henry were traditional opponents, and Henry's disapproval crushed the move and carried resolutions that prevented its revival.[47] Later, Madison and Lee were checked again when they attempted to defeat a resolution that postponed collection of the land tax for 1784, without which the assembly could not fulfill its earlier resolution to meet its congressional requisitions. Madison was thoroughly disgusted by the postponement of the tax, the miserable condition of the state's accounts, and bills that seemed to him so poorly drafted that they threatened to reduce the legislature to contempt. He also noted with distaste that several petitions had arrived requesting an assessment to support religion and that supporters of the clergy had concocted an objectionable proposal to incorporate the Episcopal Church. "Extraordinary" as the latter project was, he wrote, it was held over for the fall, "preserved from a dishonorable death by the talents of Mr. Henry."[48]

Madison was fully as successful in the fall assembly session as he had been in the spring. The legislature passed his bill prohibiting additional confiscations of loyalist property. As chairman of the Committee for Courts of Justice as well as the Committee on Commerce, he successfully prepared an assize bill, establishing a system of circuit courts; and he was instrumental, as we saw, in passing an ambitious program of improvements.[49] Once again, however, he was scarcely able to enjoy his triumphs.

Long and tedious, the session was preoccupied from the beginning with religious issues, and Madison was heavily afflicted by a sudden (temporary) turn in Presbyterian opinion. Outvoted in the House of Delegates, he felt compelled to sacrifice his opposition to the Episcopal Incorporation Act in order to postpone the final passage of a measure even more at odds with his and Jefferson's ideals. Indeed, this bill, Establishing a Provision for Teachers of the Christian Religion, could have pressed Virginia's—and perhaps America's—relationship of church and state into a mold profoundly different from his and Jefferson's desires.[50]

The House of Delegates had found a quorum for its autumn session on October 29, 1784. Already in its hands were numerous petitions calling for a general assessment to support religion and the bill providing for incorporation of the church, held over from the spring. Although the Presbyterians and Baptists still objected to the legislature's special treatment of Episcopalians, neither group had reaffirmed its customary preference for a voluntary system of church finance. The silence of dissenters, the continuing decline of the Episcopalians, and mounting fears of immorality and inattention to the public good encouraged yet another effort to support the Christian churches. In the eighteenth century, almost everyone believed that virtue rested on religion, and many thought that an assessment which made it possible for every individual to designate which church received his portion of the tax was an acceptable security for the morality without which no republic could endure.[51]

Making many of these points, Patrick Henry quickly moved for an assessment act, and over Madison's objections, by a vote of 47 to 32, the Committee of the Whole approved the preparation of a bill. Madison was not immediately alarmed. When Henry was elected governor again and left the House to take his new position, Madison was hopeful that a bill would never issue from the select committee, which Henry had chaired, or that a bill would be defeated in the absence of the orator's support.[52] By the beginning of December, though, when an assessment bill appeared, he recognized the danger. On November 12, the House of Delegates had received its annual petition from the Hanover Presbytery. In a remarkable reversal of its previous position—"shameful," Madison described it—the Presbytery dropped its customary opposition to religious taxes, providing that the act was fair to all denominations. With this important portion of the clergy "as ready to set up an establishment which is to take them in as they were to pull down that which shut them out," with the overwhelming weight of an increasing number of petitions favoring a bill, and with the pro-assessment forces willing to revise the marriage law and the incorporation bill to satisfy the main objections of dissenters, the prospect for successful legislation was growing day by day.[53]

While the assessment bill was on the table, the House directed its attention to the new incorporation act, which carried on December 22 by a vote of 47 to 38. Although he still considered it "exceptionable" in several respects, Madison abandoned his objections and voted with the majority. Some such act was clearly necessary to permit the church to hold and manage property, he wrote, and this one seemed as harmless as the circumstances would permit. Moreover, its defeat, he reasoned, might have doubled its supporters' "eagerness" for the "much greater evil" of the general assessment, to which the House immediately proceeded.[54]

To Madison's dismay, support for the assessment showed few signs of cooling. The bill completed its preliminary readings by a vote of 44 to 42, and there was nothing left to do except to argue that a measure so important should be printed for the public's consideration before its final passage. In support of this appeal for a delay, Madison prepared one of the most elaborate speeches of his career. Sometime during the debates, in fact, he drafted outlines for at least two major speeches.[55]

If he followed the surviving outlines, the shorter speech observed that the assessment bill required the courts to determine what was "Christian." How, he asked, were they to do so? Which Bible would they use, "Hebrew, Septuagint, or Vulgate?" Which translation? How were judges to decide which books were canonical and which apocryphal when Catholics, Lutherans, and other Protestants disagreed? How should the courts interpret scripture? "What clue" could guide them through the "labyrinth" of Christian doctrine?

The longer speech placed state support in broader context. The tendency of the assessment bill, it opened, was to establish Christianity as a state religion, although religion was "not within [the] purview of civil authority." The fundamental issue, Madison insisted, was not whether religion was necessary, but whether an establishment was necessary for religion. Human beings were naturally religious, he maintained, but history showed that state establishments "corrupted" the religious impulse. Contemporary Pennsylvania, other middle states, and early Christianity all showed that religion could thrive without state support, which would discourage immigration and might even lead Virginia's own dissenters to seek a freer climate. Patrick Henry, it was true, had warned that immorality had led to the collapse of several mighty states. But most such states had had established churches, Madison observed. So did most of the New England states, which were as troubled as Virginia. Rising immorality was not a product of the absence of a state-supported church; it was a consequence of wartime dislocations and "bad laws." The proper cures, accordingly, were peace, a better administration of justice, education, the personal example of leaders, laws that would "cherish virtue," and an end to the hope for a general assessment instead of voluntary support for religious bodies. The assessment bill, he finished, would "dishonor Christianity." The "progress of religious liberty" was inconsistent with the resurrection of a state religion.

Madison was seldom a "forensic" member of a legislative body (in his own disdainful phrase), but he could be uncommonly effective when he was. He was undoubtedly an able parliamentary tactician. On Christmas Eve, eight other delegates who had supported the incorporation act changed sides and voted with him to postpone the final reading of the assessment bill until November 1785. The vote was 45 to 38, almost exactly a reversal of the numbers that had carried the Episcopal incorporation.[56]

Madison's appeals and legislative stategy were not, of course, the only influence on this outcome. By itself, moreover, the postponement of the final reading of the bill did not assure defeat of the assessment. Yet Madison had plainly served as legislative leader of his side, and his defense of freedom left a memorable impression on his colleagues. Two of them, the brothers George and Wilson Cary Nicholas, immediately appealed for his continued leadership in a campaign to muster public opposition. They urged him to prepare a form for a petition, which could be circulated in the counties in the months before the next assembly as an instrument for shaping and expressing popular opinion.[57] The product, his anonymous "Memorial and Remonstrance against Religious Assessments," became a cornerstone in the American tradition of religious freedom.[58] It also proved perhaps its author's clearest and most eloquent enunciation of a set of fundamental principles that guided him throughout his public life.

The "Memorial against Assessments" was eclectic rather than inventive, an effort reminiscent of Jefferson's attempt, when drafting the Declaration of Independence, to express the general understandings of the age. Drawing on the body of his knowledge rather than on a few specific sources, and recalling all the arguments that moved his own emotions, Madison appealed to many different segments of Virginia's varied public: evangelicals as well as Deists, Baptist ministers as well as the enlightened members of the vestries, all who shared (or could be taught to share) his libertarian convictions. The comprehensive reach of the appeal, together with its unfeigned fervor, may explain its lasting impact. Madison was not a man of ready, strong emotions, but religious freedom was a topic on which he was quickly and repeatedly aroused.[59]

Like Jefferson, if Madison was specially indebted to a single source for his remonstrance, this indebtedness was principally to Locke.[60] As before, however, he carried Locke's contractual philosophy to rigorous extremes, admitting none of the exceptions Locke himself had made to his original insistence on the separate spheres of church and state, politics and religion, this world and the next. Beginning from the point where Locke had started and quoting Article 16 of the Declaration of Rights, Madison called religious liberty "unalienable" in its essential nature. Because opinion, by its nature, could not be coerced, it was the right of every man to hold and exercise his own convictions. Moreover,

> what is here a right toward men is a duty toward the Creator. It is the duty of every man to render to the Creator such homage and such only as he believes to be acceptable to Him. This duty is precedent, both in order of time and in degree of obligation, to the claims of civil society. Before any man can be considered as a member of civil society, he must be considered as a subject of the Governor of the Universe: And . . . every man who becomes a member of any particular civil society [does] it with a saving of his allegiance to the Universal Sovereign.

"In matters of religion," Madison insisted, "no man's right is abridged by the institution of civil society, and . . . religion is wholly exempt from its cognizance."[61]

But if society itself had no legitimate authority to intervene in the sphere of conscience, "still less" could any such authority devolve on the "legislative body."

> The latter are but the creatures and vicegerents of the former. Their jurisdiction is both derivative and limited: it is limited with regard to the coordinate departments, more necessarily is it limited with regard to the constituents. The preservation of a free government requires not merely that the metes and bounds which separate each department of power be invariably maintained, but more especially that neither of them be suffered to overleap the great barrier which defends the rights of the people. The rulers who are guilty of such an encroachment exceed the commission from which they derive their authority, and are tyrants. The people who submit to it are governed by laws made neither by themselves nor by an authority derived from them, and are slaves.[62]

Having hinted the regard for fundamental charters that had guided him throughout the 1780s—the profound respect for fundamental law that would become the starting point for his and Jefferson's strict construction of the Federal Constitution—Madison implied that no one should be tempted to conceive of the assessment as a valid compromise between the rights of conscience and the requirements of the state, as only an inconsequential deviation from pure doctrine. The proper time to "take alarm" for liberty, he cautioned, was the moment it was first endangered, much as patriots had done at the beginning of the Revolution (or as he and Jefferson would do when Hamilton presented his proposal for a national bank).

> The free men of America did not wait till usurped power had strengthened itself by exercise and entangled the question in precedents. They saw all the consequences in the principle, and they avoided the consequences by denying the principle. . . . Who does not see that the same authority which can establish Christianity, in exclusion of all other religions, may establish with the same ease any particular sect of Christians in exclusion of all other sects? that the same authority which can force a citizen to contribute three pence only of his property . . . may force him to conform to any . . . establishment in all cases whatsoever?[63]

Equal rights were yet another test of the validity of every republican law. Quoting once again from Mason's Declaration, Madison reminded legislators that "all men are to be considered as entering into society on equal conditions, as relinquishing no more, and therefore retaining no less, one than another, of their natural rights." Like Jefferson, therefore, and unlike Locke, he forcefully maintained that there could be no logical exceptions to the rule. Even atheists must be accorded full protection:

> Whilst we assert for ourselves a freedom to embrace, to profess, and to observe the religion which we believe to be of divine origin, we cannot deny an equal freedom to those whose minds have not yet yielded to the evidence which has convinced us. If this freedom be abused, it is an offence against God, not against man: To God, therefore, not to man, must an account of it be rendered.

Any breach of this essential principle, even one that afforded an equal preference to every Christian, must imply either that the civil authority is competent to judge religious truth or that the state may legitimately "employ religion as an engine of civil policy. The first is an arrogant pretension falsified by the contradictory opinions of rulers in all ages; . . . the second an unhallowed perversion of the means of salvation."[64]

What logic taught, experience confirmed; and Madison could transit neatly to a series of historical and practical objections to the general assessment. He argued first, as he had in the assembly, that Christianity did not require state aid, "for it is known that this religion both existed and flourished, not only without the support of human laws, but in spite of every opposition from them, and not only during the period of miraculous aid, but long after it had been left to its own evidence and the ordinary care of Providence." State support had several consequences, the Memorial suggested, just the opposite from those its advocates intended. It weakened Christians' confidence in the intrinsic excellence of their religion and encouraged nonbelievers to suspect that Christians were "too conscious of its fallacies to trust it to its own merits." Instead of bolstering the purity and power of the faith, ecclesiastical establishments had always had the opposite effect. What were the fruits of nearly fifteen centuries of state support? "More or less, in all places, pride and indolence in the clergy, ignorance and servility in the laity, in both, superstition, bigotry, and persecution." Every Christian teacher knew that Christianity was purest and had reached "its greatest luster" in the "ages prior to its incorporation with civil policy," when its ministers "depended on the voluntary rewards of their flocks."[65]

If Christianity required no help from government, but prospered best without it, neither did the needs of government demand establishments or general assessments.

> What influence in fact have ecclesiastical establishments had on civil society? In some instances they have been seen to erect a spiritual tyranny on the ruins of the civil authority; in many instances they have been seen upholding the thrones of political tyranny; in no instance have they been seen the guardians of the liberties of the people. . . . A just government . . . will be best supported by protecting every citizen in the enjoyment of his religion with the same equal hand which protects his person and his property, by neither invading the equal rights of any sect, nor suffering any sect to invade those of another.

"What a melancholy mark" the general assessment would appear, Madison warned, of "sudden degeneracy" from the policy of "offering an asylum to the persecuted and oppressed of every nation and religion": "It degrades from the equal rank of citizens all those whose opinions in religion do not bend to those of the legislative authority. Distant as it may be in its present form from the Inquisition, it differs from it only in degree. The one is the first step, the other the last in the career of intolerance." The foreign sufferer could only see a general assessment "as a beacon on our coast, warning him to seek some other haven." The bill would add another motive to the many presently existing for emigration from the state. It would destroy the harmony and moderation that had prevailed among the different denominations while the laws forbore to "intermeddle" with religion. "Torrents of blood have been spilt in the old world by vain attempts of the secular arm to extinguish religious discord by proscribing all difference in religious opinion." Such differences were best assuaged, and Christianity most generally diffused, "by leveling as far as possible every [artificial] obstacle to the victorious progress of truth," not by "ignoble and unchristian" efforts to defend the faith from error.[66]

Returning once again to the words of the Virginia constitution, words that he himself had written, Madison completed the Memorial by powerfully restating its main theme. "The equal right of every citizen to the free exercise of his religion," he concluded, "is held by the same tenure with all our other rights."

> Either then, we must say that the will of the legislature is the only measure of their authority and that, in the plenitude of this authority, they may sweep away all our fundamental rights, or that they are bound to leave this particular right untouched and sacred. Either we must say that they may control the freedom of the press, may abolish the trial by jury, may swallow up the executive and judiciary powers of the state, nay that they may despoil us of our very right of suffrage and erect themselves into an independent and hereditary assembly, or we must say that they have no authority to enact into law the bill under consideration.[67]

Nowhere else, in any of his writings, was Madison more eloquent or more explicit in explaining the consistent core of fundamental principle that guided him through all the turns of his career. In its brief but clear elucidation of the origins of governmental power, its insistence on inherent, equal rights, which individuals do not surrender when they enter a society, its fear of even slight transgressions of the chartered bounds of power, and even in its ultimate concern with rulers who might free themselves entirely from dependence on the people, the Memorial is indispensable for understanding why the leader of the Federalists of 1787 would also be the future captain of the Jeffersonian resistance. In its sincere regard for both the purity of faith and the protection of the state from bigots, the petition nicely balanced Christian and republican preoccupations.[68] In its insistence on the total separation of these spheres, it linked the youth of 1776 to the distinguished elder statesman who worried during his retirement that he might have missed an implication of the principle before the War of 1812 when he gave in to Congress and issued a presidential proclamation for a day of prayer.[69] In its conviction that the truth requires no artificial aids and that religious freedom is the litmus test of freedom of the intellect in all its forms, the powerful remonstrance was in full accord with Jefferson's great bill, which it elaborated and would shortly help to pass.

Completed by the end of June, Madison's anonymous Memorial was circulated widely through the state.[70] By the time of its appearance, as he hoped, opinion was already shifting noticeably against the general assessment. Lay and clerical Episcopalians were increasingly at odds over governance and doctrine. The dissenters were returning to their customary stance. In August, the Virginia Presbyterians agreed on a long petition that rejected the assessment, disapproved of several features of the late incorporation act, and called for the approval of the Bill Establishing Religious Freedom. The General Committee of the Baptists also roundly and specifically condemned a general tax.[71] During its 1785 session, the General Assembly received more than a hundred religious petitions, only eleven of which supported the assessment. Among the ninety that condemned the measure, signed by nearly 11,000 Virginians, thirteen were copies of Madison's remonstrance. So plainly did the people speak that no one tried to resurrect the bill providing for religious taxes, and Madison took full advantage of the situation.[72]

Chairman of the Committee for Courts of Justice, as before, Madison decided early in the session to force the laggard House of Delegates to act on the proposed revision of the laws, which had been printed at his instigation in 1784. On October 31, he introduced more than a hundred bills, virtually the whole of the revision except for portions that had been enacted in preceding years.[73] It was a huge commitment for the busy House and for its legislative leader, yet the Delegates agreed to set aside three days per week until the work was finished. Holding faithfully to this agreement, they labored systematically through the revision, amending and enacting thirty-five proposals. But with the opposition steadily increasing and supporters growing tired, progress stalled completely when the members reached the bill on crimes and punishments, number 64 of the new code. The session had already stretched into December, and it was clear that there was insufficient patience to complete the task. From the remainder of the code, therefore, Madison extracted number 82, the Bill Establishing Religious Freedom. Despite significant, "warm" opposition on the floor, it passed the House of Delegates on December 17 essentially unchanged. Opponents in the Senate carried an amendment that would have devastated Jefferson and robbed the bill of much of its importance by striking its impressive preamble and substituting Article 16 of the Declaration of Rights. The Delegates refused the change. Tedious maneuvering continued nearly to adjournment of the session, but Madison's tenacity and legislative skills were equal to the challenge. The act was signed by Speaker Harrison on January 19, 1786, with its preamble fundamentally unmarred.[74]

Although he never bragged about his legislative feats and did not change his custom of reporting the assembly's actions in a style that never mentioned his personal role, Madison did not disguise his exultation over the defeat of the assessment and the passage of the Statute for Religious Freedom. Sending the news to Jefferson in France, he reported that an argument between the houses had "defaced the composition" of the act. Delegates who favored Jefferson's original language, he explained, had thought it "better to agree" with minor Senate changes "than to run further risks, especially as it was getting late in the session and the House was growing thin." Nevertheless, the enacting clauses of the bill had passed unchanged "and I flatter myself have in this country extinguished forever the ambitious hope of making laws for the human mind."[75] Passage of the statute was a proud achievement. It was also an important moment in the evolution of the legislator's thought.

To many of his legislative colleagues, Madison had never seemed more formidable than in 1785. "Can you suppose it possible that Madison should shine with more than usual splendor this assembly?" one delegate inquired. "It is, sir, not only possible but a fact. He has astonished mankind and has by means perfectly constitutional become almost a dictator upon all subjects."[76] With Patrick Henry serving as the governor again and Richard Henry Lee in Congress, Madison had no competitor for domination of the lower house and took a leading role on nearly every issue.[77]

From his own perspective, nevertheless, the 1785 assembly was the most distressing he had seen.[78] One of his persistent worries was alleviated for a time. "Not a word has passed in the House as to a paper emission," he told Monroe.[79] Nevertheless, he still discerned a danger. "A considerable itch for paper money" was apparent, he reported to Jefferson at the session's end, and "the partizans of the measure . . . flatter themselves, and I fear upon too good ground, that it will be among the measures of the next."[80] Even his success with the revision of the laws was tempered in his mind by the reflection that "it might have been finished at one session with great ease if the time spent on motions to put it off and other dilatory tactics had been employed on its merits."[81] It is clear that Madison's determination to hold impatient colleagues to the work on the revision cost him much good will and influence as the session lengthened. The colleague who had been astonished with his influence early in the session later wrote that the House "was upon the whole the most stupid, knavish, and designing Assembly that ever sat, . . . and as . . . proof of this

I need urge no other argument . . . but that Madison after the first three weeks lost all weight in the House, and the general observation was that those who had a favorite scheme ought to get Madison to oppose it, by which means it would certainly be carried."[82] The resentment of his colleagues may have been responsible in part for a succession of defeats that left him powerfully disheartened.

As always, federal measures had been high on Madison's agenda. During the preceding year, he had secured the state's support for several congressional proposals. In 1785, by contrast, he was forced to settle for the resolutions that initiated the Annapolis Convention.[83] Uniformly checked in every effort to support the dignity and needs of Congress, he was hardly more successful on domestic matters. No one raised the cry for paper money, but his assize act of 1784 was subjected to strong attacks.[84] The port bill, too, was nearly overturned, and he anticipated its repeal at the succeeding session. "It would have been repealed at this," he wrote, "if its adversaries had known their strength in time and exerted it with judgment."[85] From all these points of view—despite the passage of his friend's historic bill—the 1785 assembly seemed to Madison the nadir of his legislative service. The threats and disappointments suffered in its course bore no small part of the responsibility for what can fairly be described as the most important intellectual crisis of his life.

"True it is," Madison's Memorial had said, that the majority must rule in a republic, "but it is also true that the majority may trespass on the rights of the minority."[86] True it also seemed to be—and never more apparently than in the 1785 assembly—that the will of the majority could be repeatedly at odds with honor or the public good. With every legislative session, Madison had felt increasingly dishonored and revolted by poorly drafted, fluctuating laws. Since his return from Congress, he had struggled unsuccessfully for a revision of Virginia's constitution, lost as often as he won on federal issues, and crafted several state reforms to see them gutted in succeeding sessions. By the spring of 1786, as his attention turned toward the Annapolis Convention, his disgust was equaled only by his fears. For every year had also seen a tide of legislative measures, threatened or enacted, that attempted to combat the current economic troubles by preventing creditors from pressing for their dues or by depriving both the state and federal governments of revenues required in order to perform their duties.

Virginia, it is true, had managed to avoid the most objectionable measures of the postwar years: paper money, postwar confiscations, and laws preventing citizens (though not their British creditors) from suing for recovery of debts.[87] To Madison, however, the escape seemed narrow and increasingly in doubt, nor was it any consolation to a man of continental vision that the malady seemed national in scope. Throughout America, he was beginning to conclude, the "multiplicity," the "mutability," and the "injustice" of provincial laws were calling into question "the fundamental principle of republican government, that the majority who rule in such governments are the safest guardians both of public good and of private rights."[88] The framers of the early revolutionary constitutions, he soon observed, had thought that "a provision for the rights of persons" (that is, for republican self-government) would "include of itself" protection for the rights of property and for the other liberties that individuals had not surrendered to the state.[89] Every year, however, was producing rising doubts that this assumption was correct. "What we once thought the calumny of the enemies of republican governments," he would tell the Constitutional Convention, "is undoubtably true": wherever "a majority are united by a common interest or passion, the rights of the minority are in danger"; the rule of the majority was not assuring a consistent preference for the well-considered interest of the public as a whole.[90]

For Madison, it must be recognized, this was a painful, difficult admission: an insight reached in sorrow, not in triumph. Indeed, whenever he discussed the errors of the early Revolution, Madison consistently referred to the mistakes that "we" had made, to misconceptions he had shared. It was not, he knew, that early revolutionary thinkers had naively thought that a majority could do no wrong. Educated in a culture that idealized the English constitution, revolutionaries had expected individuals to differ, clash, and take advantage of one another, especially if they were rulers. Heirs to British thinking, which insisted on a balanced mixture of the powers of the one, the many, and the few, most early revolutionaries had conceded that a sound and lasting government demanded qualities that they could not associate with representative assemblies: unity, consistency, and wisdom, as well as a reflection of majority desires. Therefore, all the states had instituted complex governments, and most of them had tried, by various expedients, to make the upper house of legislature balance the lower. Many revolutionary leaders still expected that a second legislative house would act as the protector of the few against the many. Bills of rights and written constitutions—most of them insisting on a rigid separation of executive and legislative powers—were intended to assure additional protection for the rights of all.[91]

Nevertheless, in all the early revolutionary constitutions, overwhelming power had been trusted to the lower houses—and thus to the majorities who chose them. When the new state governments were formed, a decade of confrontation with the British had resulted in a revolutionary new insistence on an active and continuous relationship between legitimate authority and popular consent, as well as in a newly literal insistence on inherent, equal rights.[92] The confrontation with a central government that the colonials could not control had taught them that the wielders of authority respond primarily to those to whom they owe their places, those with whom they share a fundamental unity of interests. Throughout the colonies, the governmental branches most immediately responsive to the people had been valiant in the defense of liberty, as had the people "out of doors." Meanwhile, the persistent threat from Britain had destroyed the former trust in English institutions, laying the essential groundwork for the democratic argument that liberation from the tyranny of lords and kings would free America to institute new governments that would be free from the enduring differences and unavoidable corruptions that now appeared inherent in a mixed regime.[93] Even in democracies, of course, individuals would still be equal *only* in their rights, not in their material possessions or their talents. Differences of interest or opinion would continue to result in disagreements and collisions. Nevertheless, the very crux of the republican departure from the English or colonial tradition was the bold new faith that in societies without hereditary ranks, no individual or group could have an interest *permanently* different from the well-considered interest of the whole. By 1776, theory and experience had joined to make it easy to conclude that governments derived entirely from the people, governments reconstituted in a manner that would make the rulers continuously responsible to the ruled, would necessarily pursue the people's interests and defend the people's private rights. Theory and experience had joined to make it difficult to see how the majority—the greater number of the equals who composed republican societies—could wish for anything expect the public good, which was their own. Therefore, all the revolutionary states provided for an annual election of the lower house, and most provided for the annual election of their senates and executives as well. Massachusetts, followed by New Hampshire after 1784, was the only state to grant its governor a legislative veto (although New York provided for a governor who was to be a member of a council with this power). And in all the states the upper houses were invariably inclined—or, like Virginia's, constitutionally obliged—to let the lower houses take the lead in writing legislation. In other words, in all the states but two, a relatively ineffective senate was the only institutional restraint on lower houses, chosen yearly by the people.

In the circumstances of the middle eighties, as the people struggled with depression, these arrangements proved a recipe for conflict and a formula for fluctuating laws. Yet only long experience with a disturbing train of measures could compel convinced republicans to reexamine the assumptions that were at their base, for the idea that the majority itself could constitute a faction—"a number of citizens . . . who are united and actuated by some common impulse of passion, or of interest, adverse to the rights of other citizens, or to the permanent and aggregate interests of the community"—could force consistent thinkers to conclude that they might have to choose between their liberal and their republican commitments, neither one of which could be relinquished.[94]

For Madison, the troubling legislative measures and repeated disappointments of the postwar years precipitated just this sort of crisis. With many others, he had come to be increasingly concerned with legislation that infringed the rights of contract or prevented governments from meeting contracts of their own: paper money, stay laws, moratoriums on taxes, and the rest. More than many others, Madison was troubled also by the "multiplicity" and "mutability" of laws. Not only did his ordered mind rebel against these constant fluctuations, but he also sensed that constant changes, like repeated interferences with private contracts, undermined the certainty and trust that bound societies together.[95] In all of his experience, moreover, nothing had disturbed him quite so much as the demand for an assessment to support religion. He had always known that individuals are selfish, that majorities can be mistaken, and that people may pursue their personal, immediate desires at the expense of other people's interests or a more enlightened understanding of their own. Still, the threat of the assessment showed him with a clarity that nothing else had shown that declarations of inherent rights were flimsy barriers to rulers who could fairly claim to speak for the majority itself. And none of his preceding disappointments had presented him with such compelling proof that his convictions could not tolerate a democratic version of the rule that might makes right.[96]

Thus, as he departed for Annapolis, Virginia's legislative leader was entrapped in a profoundly agonizing reexamination of his early revolutionary suppositions. Madison was deeply dedicated to the revolutionary principle that governments derive their just authority from popular consent and must remain responsive to the people. He was deeply dedicated, too, to "justice," by which he meant equality before the laws, security for every individual in what was properly his own, and scrupulous respect by governments for the inherent rights that governments were instituted to preserve. But in the aftermath of recent struggles in the state assembly, he was finding it extremely difficult to reconcile his libertarian with his majoritarian commitments, though he could not abandon either. Though there were many signs that popular majorities were threatening inherent rights, he still believed that rulers who escaped from their dependence on the people were a greater danger still.

The seed of a solution, hindsight may suggest, was present in a corner of his mind. The rights of conscience, his Memorial had said, are "held by the same tenure with all our other rights"; the power that could threaten these could threaten all the others. If this was so, however, then it might be so, as well, that the conditions which had guarded liberty of conscience might protect all other liberties as well. Indeed, in every free society, he soon would write, "the security for civil rights must be the same as for religious rights. It consists in the one case in the multiplicity of interests and, in the other, in the multiplicity of sects."[97] If the Presbyterians and the Episcopalians had been able to cement their tentative alliance, nothing, Madison observed, could have defeated the general assessment.[98] Jealousies between the sects had done what no appeal to principle could have accomplished by itself. And differences among the many more denominations of a vastly larger, federal republic might afford increased security for other rights as well.

This, however, carries us significantly beyond the mental linkages that Madison had forged in 1786. When he returned from the Annapolis Convention in the autumn of that year, he was convinced that a successful meeting of a constitutional convention might prove the final opportunity to prevent the imminent disintegration of the Union. By itself, I hope to show, his fear of national disintegration can account for his proposal of a revolutionary reconstruction of the federal system, for he had long been certain that a fragmentation of the Union would endanger the republican experiment itself, and he had probably decided that the Union's problems were insoluble within the current federal framework. By itself, however, Madison's determination to preserve the Union only partially accounts for the specific shape of his proposals to the Constitutional Convention. The intervening months were crucial. When the state assembly reconvened in the fall, Madison was still imprisoned in a mental trap from which he saw no obvious escape. And before the session closed, his agony would be intensified to such a point that he would fear that a collapse of the Union was the least of the catastrophes that might result if the proposed convention proved abortive. Between October and the meeting of the federal convention, the pressure mounted so unbearably that it could only find a vent in the imaginative leap that marks authentic genius.

The legislative session, in this case, was not the problem. As soon as he returned to Richmond, Madison drove forcefully to win Virginia's backing for the meeting recommended by the Annapolis Convention. By November 6, he had prepared a bill that gave Virginia's approval "a very solemn dress and all the weight" that could be given it by any "single state."[99] Exceeding all his hopes, the House approved the bill unanimously on November 9 and followed by appointing Washington himself to head a delegation whose distinguished reputations were a vivid signal to the other states of its profound commitment to the meeting. Eventually, both Richard Henry Lee and Patrick Henry declined to serve, but Washington's attendance was essential. Madison immediately joined in efforts to persuade the general that circumstances were so "menacing as to supersede every consideration but that of our national existence or safety."[100]

From the beginning of the session, Madison took every step with the convention much in mind. His first concern was to secure a powerful endorsement of the gathering before "the business of the Mississippi" could begin to "ferment" in the members' minds.[101] His second was to seize direction of the anger over Jay's proposals and to channel it into support for federal reform. Sharing in that anger, he had warned his friends outside the state that prospects for reform would certainly be blasted in Virginia unless the Jay-Gardoqui project could be squelched. At Richmond, he immediately discovered that the fury was as fierce as he had feared. The members from Kentucky could barely be restrained, and "many of our most federal leading men," he cautioned Washington, "are extremely soured with what has already passed. Mr. Henry, who has been hitherto the champion of the federal cause, has become a cold advocate and, in the event of an actual sacrifice of the Mississippi by Congress, will unquestionably go over to the opposite side."[102] Still, Madison succeeded in securing resolutions ordering Virginia's delegates in Congress to oppose the closing of the river, yet referring also to the legislature's "confidence in the wisdom, justice, and liberality of the federal councils, which is so necessary at this crisis to a proper enlargement of their authority." Working closely with the western members, he molded the Virginia protest nicely to his goals.[103]

Compared to the 1785 session, the 1786 assembly was a ringing triumph for the delegate from Orange. The Senate "saved [Virginia's] commerce from a dreadful blow which it would have sustained from a bill . . . imposing enormous duties without waiting for the concurrence of the other states or even of Maryland."[104] A petition to retire the state's securities at their deflated, current value was unanimously rejected.[105] On November 1, by a majority of 85 to 17, the House of Delegates resolved that paper money was "unjust, impolitic, destructive of public and private confidence, and of that virtue which is the basis of republican governments."[106] Edmund Randolph, Madison's old friend, was elected governor when Patrick Henry opted not to serve another term, and Madison himself was easily selected for another term in Congress as well as for the Constitutional Convention.

Despite these great successes, Madison felt anything except triumphant as the session closed. As he rushed to New York City to resume his seat

in Congress, Jay was still negotiating with Gardoqui. There was no assurance, yet, that other states would join Virginia for a full and capable convention.[107] Much as was the case the year before, he felt as though he had
been wedged throughout the 1786 session, shoulder to the door, and
barely able to withstand the daily hammering from measures that he
dreaded. He wrote to Edmund Pendleton that the legislature's "merit on
the score of justice was entirely of the negative kind." Although "sufficient
to reject violations of this cardinal virtue"—paper money, a repudiation
of a portion of the public obligations, and a measure for installment payments of private as well as public debts—it had not sufficed "to make any
positive provisions in its behalf."[108] Moreover, by the time the session
closed, disturbances in western Massachusetts had ignited into open insurrection. And in Shays's Rebellion and its aftermath, a troubled Madison
discerned conclusive evidence that popular commotions were combining
with the failures of the Union to create a full-blown crisis of the Revolution.

Madison had doubtless followed the reports of growing trouble in New
England as he traveled in September from Annapolis through Philadelphia to Richmond. Reaching the Virginia capital, he had been greeted by
alarming letters from his correspondents in New York, and as the session
lengthened, all his information from the north prepared him for the
worst. At this point, he was taking his correspondents at their word. On
November 1, repeating language from a frightening report from Henry
Lee, he told his father that the rebels were "as numerous" as the supporters of the Massachusetts government "and more decided in their
measures. . . . They profess to aim only at a reform of their constitution
and of certain abuses in the public administration, but an abolition of
debts public and private and a new division of property are strongly suspected to be in contemplation."[109] On November 5, Washington reported
that a frantic letter from Henry Knox, who had just returned from Massachusetts to New York, informed him that the rebels' "creed is that the
property of the United States has been protected from confiscation of
Britain by the joint exertions of *all* and therefore ought to be the *common
property* of all." Knox suggested, Washington continued, that the Massachusetts rebels could be joined by discontented farmers from Rhode Island, Connecticut, and New Hampshire "so as to constitute a body of
twelve or fifteen thousand desperate and unprincipled men, . . . chiefly of
the young and active part of the country."[110] Other correspondents
warned him that the Shaysites might be leagued with the Vermonters and

that British agents were encouraging the insurrection,[111] Madison was primed to credit that as well.[112]

Shortly after his arrival in New York, to which he rushed as soon as the assembly had adjourned, Madison was able to report that Shays's Rebellion had been crushed.[113] In the meantime, though, as he had said, an armed revolt against the government that many thought of as the best in the United States had been "distressing beyond measure to the zealous friends of the Revolution."[114] Little less distressing, he shortly found, was the reaction the rebellion had provoked. On one hand, it was soon apparent that the troubles had persuaded Massachusetts, which had been reluctant to this point, to send a delegation to the federal convention. In the end, it convinced all the states except Rhode Island "of the necessity of such a vigor in the general government as will be able to restore health to any diseased part of the federal body."[115] On the other hand, however, there were soon disturbing rumors of a rapid spread of deeply counter-revolutionary sentiments among New England's leading men.[116] Six months before, the Jay-Gardoqui conflict had persuaded Madison that the collapse of the Confederation could be close at hand. Now, Shays's Rebellion struck him as the final evidence of a related—and, for him, an even more appalling—crisis of republican convictions.

At the seat of Congress, as at Richmond, Madison considered every action in the light of its potential contribution toward a well-attended and successful federal convention. During the preceding fall, with Shaysites threatening the federal arsenal at Springfield, Congress had approved a loan to raise a special force for use in Massachusetts, covering its lack of an explicit constitutional authority to act with references to hostile natives.[117] In February, with the rebels shattered, Charles Pinckney moved to put a stop to these enlistments. Although Madison confessed that he was less than comfortable with the original congressional decision, admitting that he found it hard to reconcile with candor, with the powers delegated by the federal charter, and even with the principle that force and right were on the same side in republics, he deferred to Rufus King's appeal for a continuation of congressional support until the consequences of the Massachusetts legislature's punishments were clear. Congress had sufficient warrant for its actions, Madison maintained, in the suspicion that Great Britain was involved in the rebellion. "Every state," he argued, should "submit to such indulgences to others as itself may in a little time be in need of."[118] He did not exempt Virginia. Current letters from its governor reported local incidents too like the ones that had preceded the rebellion in the Bay State.[119]

As he readied colleagues for the federal convention, Madison was tempted to indulge New York as well as Massachusetts. Thus, he voted for a New York substitute for a committee's motion to endorse the federal meeting even though he knew that many members thought that the New Yorkers really wanted to impede the convention.[120] And much as he preferred to see the seat of Congress moved from New York City, he voted to remain there in dread of the effect departure would have on New York's attitude toward the convention.[121] Still, with letters pouring in from correspondents in Kentucky, Madison remained determined to confront the easterners about the project that could quash Virginia's interest in reform.[122] After talking twice to Don Diego de Gardoqui, who refused to budge,[123] he set about a series of maneuvers meant to give the Jay-Gardoqui business the decisive check that might be needed to appease Patrick Henry and the others.[124] He first demanded a report from Jay on the negotiations.[125] When this appeared, and showed that Jay had pressed his talks but doubted that a concord could or should be reached, Madison proposed that the negotiations should be transferred to Madrid and trusted to Jefferson, currently serving as the minister to France.[126] Thus far, as he explained in an April 23 letter to Jefferson, he was attempting to revoke the steps that had been taken under the "usurped authority" of a vote by seven states, but in a manner that would "least offend" the Spanish and congressional opponents.[127] Defeated in this effort—and aware, by now, that all the states except Rhode Island would attend the Constitutional Convention—he moved directly to declare that Jay's instructions were invalid, along with the congressional resolution barring a renewed discussion of the matter. On April 26, this motion was postponed. Madison was now convinced that the attempt to close the Mississippi had been stopped and could not be successfully revived, but the attendance at the session had remained too thin for a definitive decision.[128]

From February to the end of April, for that matter, Congress had been barely able to maintain a quorum, and Madison had kept a very fragmentary record of its work. The present government, he had complained to Randolph "is tottering to its foundations."[129]

> No money is paid into the public treasury; no respect is paid to the federal authority. Not a single state complies with the requisitions, several pass them over in silence, and some positively reject them. The payments ever since the peace have been decreasing and of late fall short even of the pittance necessary for the civil list.[130]

Thus, from his arrival in the city, Madison had followed an "unsocial plan" of giving every moment he could spare to preparations for the great convention.[131] Now, in an April 15 letter to Randolph, he urged his colleagues in Virginia's delegation to arrive in Philadelphia some days before the time appointed for the meeting, suggesting that the Old Dominion ought to be "prepared with some materials for the work."[132] He left New York May 2. Most of the materials the delegation would require were in his head and on the papers he had drafted during his "unsocial" stay.

PART TWO

The Framing of the Constitution

CHAPTER FOUR

The Virginia Plan

STUDIES OF THE CONSTITUTIONAL CONVENTION almost always emphasize its numerous divisions: small states against large, "pure" federalists against proponents of a large republic, planting states against commercial interests, the South against the North. There is no denying the importance of these conflicts. The convention *was* a battleground for disagreeing politicians and competing state and sectional concerns. It succeeded, as the textbooks say, because the delegates discovered ways to compromise their disagreements. Analyses of its divisions, sometimes with the aid of the computer, have taught us much of what we know about how the document emerged.[1]

For all its benefits, however, there are also ways in which a fascination with conflicting coalitions can leave us with misleading images of how the meeting worked. In many cases, an excessive emphasis on conflicts and divisions has encouraged a neglect of the cooperative dimensions of the meeting.[2] In every case, the application of a static method of analysis to a dynamic situation misses certain aspects of the story. This can happen even when the votes in the convention are analyzed in series, showing that the coalitional configurations shifted over time as compromises settled certain issues and new disputes arose.[3] It can happen even when the ideologies of delegates or the specific interests of their states are invoked to help explain the quantitative findings.[4] The most sophisticated studies of conflicting coalitions still do not allow for the continual necessity of every state and every member to adjust to the dynamics of the *process*, one in which the general character of the emerging constitution could be changed with each new vote and every individual could be compelled to readjust repeatedly to a collective effort to resolve a common set of problems.[5]

Madison was a Virginian. He had represented the Confederation's largest state for years in the Confederation Congress, where majorities were often fiercely jealous of Virginia's claims. He was a southerner, a continentalist, and a defender of the West. He was a scholar, a republican, and an effective legislative politician. All these facts are necessary to comprehend his stands at the convention. All of them together offer only a beginning toward an understanding of his course and contributions.

This is so, of course, in part because James Madison was too complex a figure to be neatly typed, because he can be fitted only loosely into categories that could pull him several ways at once. But it is so, as well, because the Constitutional Convention forced his active mind into a fluid interchange with others, all of whom were struggling day by day to understand a changing plan, and most of whom were listening to (as well as battling with) the other members. Long after the convention had adjourned, Madison insisted that there were few delegates "who did not change in the progress of the discussions the opinions on important points which they carried into the convention, . . . few who, at the close of the convention, were not ready to admit this change as the enlightening effect of the discussions."[6] This was plainly true of Madison himself, whose essays in *The Federalist* were partly a confession of what (and how much) he had learned. And yet most studies seldom make full allowance for changes of this kind.

The following discussion stresses Madison's *experience* of the convention. This has at least two uses. First, by general agreement, no one came to the convention with his thoughts more thoroughly in order than "the father of the Constitution." If he was influenced by the meeting, changing his original opinions on several consequential points, others surely changed their minds as well. Madison's experience may therefore help to highlight the dynamics of the meeting, the process of deliberation. In addition, I believe, there is a sense in which a "theory" of the Constitution started to emerge in course of the proceedings, a theory we might try to see as immanent in the decisions and debates. When Madison and other delegates completed the construction of this theory, they accomplished this in part by sorting back in memory through every stage in the convention's work, comparing its decisions to the thoughts with which they had begun, and building on the lessons they had learned. From this perspective, the convention proved the most important episode in Madison's lifelong education. His participation in the framing of the Constitution was the challenge he required in order to become the most sophisticated constitutional thinker of his time.

∾

Madison is often called "the father of the Constitution" partly for his leading role in the drafting of the Virginia Plan. These fifteen resolutions, introduced by Edmund Randolph on May 29, as soon as the convention had agreed on its rules, captured the initiative for radical reform. Though greatly modified before the work was through, they set the meeting's early course and served throughout the summer as the starting point for the deliberations. They succeeded so impressively in setting forth some general guidelines for the meeting that interpreters have sometimes overlooked the critical consensual parameters within which many of the arguments occurred. A close examination of these resolutions is essential to a reconstruction of Madison's preliminary views. A close examination shows, moreover, that his first ideas and contributions were significantly different than has often been supposed.

The resolutions of May 29 did not propose to make the Articles of Confederation "adequate to the exigencies of the Union," though this is probably what a majority of states expected the convention to consider. Instead, they offered to reconstitute the current, single-chamber central government on lines suggested by the constitutions of the states, and then to vest this national republic with the right "to legislate in all cases to which the separate states are incompetent, or in which the harmony of the United States may be interrupted by the exercise of individual legislation." To guarantee the central government's supremacy wherever common measures were required, the reconstructed articles of union would be ratified by state conventions of the sovereign people, and federal powers would include authority to veto local legislation inconsistent with the Constitution or "to call forth the force of the Union against any member of the Union failing to fulfill its duty."[7]

Several delegates were rudely jolted by the daring scope of these "preliminary propositions." Few were thoroughly prepared for a solution so extreme. Leaders of a democratic Revolution, including thirty veterans of the war, the delegates had not forgotten the experiences that had compelled them to seek Independence; they were not about to risk a central tyranny again. Still, Madison and his Virginia colleagues had correctly sensed, as other delegations trickled into town, that early sentiment was overwhelmingly opposed to patchwork efforts to repair the tottering Confederation. The members of the Constitutional Convention overwhelmingly agreed that an effective central government required, at minimum, an independent source of revenue, authority to regulate the country's trade, and power to compel obedience to its legitimate commands, though nearly everyone agreed, as well, that powers that the colonies had stubbornly denied to England would have to be accompanied by firm securities against their possible abuse.[8] The first essential contribution of the resolutions of May 29 was to suggest that this conundrum might be solved by trusting necessary powers to a well-constructed representative republic. The Virginia Plan proposed a revolutionary answer to the revolutionary fear of grasping central power.

And before the hesitant could catch their breath, they found that the agenda for the meeting had been radically transformed. The Virginia Plan not only sketched a radical solution to the problems of the Union. It also drew the delegates inexorably into a reconsideration of the fundamental nature of republics, seizing here, as well, on an original consensus of the meeting. For although they recognized—and mostly shared—the people's fierce commitment to a democratic revolution, nearly all the delegates were as alarmed by popular abuses in the states as by the ineffectiveness of the Confederation Congress. Everywhere, as Elbridge Gerry phrased it, the country seemed to suffer from "an excess of democracy."[9] Local violations of inherent rights, as Madison would say, "were evils which had more perhaps than anything else produced this convention." If the members failed to come to grips with these abuses, Madison believed, "republican liberty could [not] long exist."[10] The second contribution of the resolutions of May 29 was their attempt to shape a national republic that would not repeat the oversights and errors of the constitutions of the states.

Sound republics, the Virginia Plan suggested, should incorporate two legislative houses: one elected by the people; the other chosen in a manner that would shield its members from the whims of the majority and thus assure continuing protection for the rights of the minority and other public goods. The legislature should be balanced by a separate executive, and the judiciary should be independent of them both. Through almost four months of sometimes-bitter quarrels, there was little serious dispute about these fundamental principles of governmental structure. Even members who resisted the creation of a national republic were determined not to replicate the errors they believed had been committed in the states. Thus the plan not only forced the meeting to consider a republican solution to the revolutionary fear of concentrated central power, which had resulted in a general government unable to advance the nation's interests or even to fulfill its legal obligations. It also both elicited and guided a collective search for principles and structural devices that could guarantee a place for governmental energy and wisdom, as well as for responsiveness to popular demands. And this cooperative endeavor was as real a part of the proceedings as the contest of specific interests— as real and as responsible for its success.

Madison was not, and never claimed to be, *the* author of Virginia's Resolutions. The whole Virginia delegation had arrived in Philadelphia by May 13. Its seven members caucused daily while the great convention waited for a quorum, harmonizing their opinions and anticipating that the other states would be receptive to some propositions from their larger sister, which had taken the initiative in bringing a successful meeting into being. There are no surviving records from these talks, and the participants agreed that all of them would be as free as any other member to dissent from the proposals, which they prevailed on their governor to introduce. Madison, however, was the man to whom Virginia politicians customarily deferred on federal issues. He had suggested all the key provisions of the plan in preconvention writings. Contemporaries understood that it was principally his work, and there is nothing to suggest that any of its major points were inconsistent with his wishes.[11]

Madison had come to Philadelphia the best prepared of all who gathered for the Federal Convention. Recognized since early in the decade as a leading advocate of federal reform, he had initiated more specific preparations for the meeting sometime just before or shortly after the Annapolis Convention. He first prepared elaborate research notes on the histories and structures of other ancient and modern confederacies, each entry summarizing the authority confided to the general government of a confederation or denied to its component states, each adding some remarks about the weaknesses or "vices" of this distribution.[12] Next, in letters to his friends, written during his "unsocial" service in New York, he analyzed the ills of the American Confederation and elaborated the essentials of a cure.[13] Finally, in April, just before the gathering convened, he wrote a formal memorandum entitled "Vices of the Political System of the United States," which Randolph may have read before the speech in which he introduced the delegation's resolutions.[14] The evolution of the plan and Madison's initial purposes and thinking can be confidently reconstructed from these sources.

They suggest—and it is seldom emphasized enough by modern scholars—that Madison began with an analysis of the relationship between the central government and states, though he was also much alarmed by what was happening *within* the thirteen "members" of the Union. He began, moreover, with a basically *conventional* conception of the proper spheres of state and federal action. Close attention to this fact and to the course of his considerations is absolutely vital to a proper understanding of his purposes and contributions. Many of the most persistent misinterpretations of his conduct start when we discount his early concentration on the federal relationship and jump immediately to how his plan would have enlarged the sphere of federal action or addressed conditions in the states. The Virginia Plan did certainly address these other objects, which were not less dear to Madison than dominant interpretations would suggest. But the Virginian's first and most important contribution to the framing did not lie in his objections to contemporary definitions of the proper business of the Union or in radical suggestions for additions to its duties. It lay in his conclusion that the fundamental flaw of the Confederation was its irredeemably defective structure.[15]

As he thought his way toward the convention, Madison concerned himself from the beginning less with the necessity of redistributing responsibilities between the central government and states than with the inability of the existing central government to do the tasks that everyone admitted were its proper business. "Positive" additions of authority were needed, his earliest reflections ran, so that the powers of the general government would reach all cases in which "uniformity is proper," "as in trade, etc., etc."[16] These additions, he was quick to see, held sweeping implications, which I shall come to shortly. But the striking fact about his earliest, brief comments on reform is that he gave so little space to "positive" additions of this kind, and that he plainly said that such additions ought to be confined to instances where uniformity was needed.

Little space was space enough for Madison's initial comments on additions to the Union's duties—partly, we shall see, because his thoughts were not extremely novel on this subject, but primarily because he was extremely eager to proceed to the essential point, which was that *no* additions to the positive responsibilities of the existing central government could possibly suffice. "However ample the federal powers may be made," he wrote to Jefferson, "or however clearly their boundaries may be delineated on paper, they will be easily and continually baffled by the . . . states" unless accompanied by further changes rendering the general government "clearly paramount" to the state legislatures and capable of acting without their "intervention."[17]

With the exception of the power over trade, Madison had long believed, the current Articles of Union granted Congress positive authority to do most of the things a general government should do—power even to require the states to raise the revenues it needed.[18] Nevertheless, the Union was in peril of collapse and the republican experiment itself in deadly danger. The fatal failing, then, was less a faulty definition of the objects of the Union than the inability of the existing central government to execute its acts without cooperation from the states. State governments, he wrote, were necessary instruments of federal action, but the states were not amenable to federal commands. They could "rejudge" and countermand congressional decisions, take conflicting actions of their own, or frustrate federal measures simply by neglecting to fulfill their legal obligations. The Confederation had the "form," but lacked the "vital prin-

ciples," of a political constitution. It was a government on paper, but a
league of sovereign states in structure and in operation.[19]

Probing for essentials and placing the American Confederation in historical perspective, Madison identified three fundamental ills: the inability
of Congress to enforce decisions that were plainly in its province; the
inability of the entire Confederation to achieve unanimous agreement on
amendments favored by a huge majority of states; and consequent attempts by several of its members to secure by separate legislation ends
that called imperatively for common action, especially the regulation of
their trade. How, he asked, could uniformity actually be secured within
that relatively small but vitally important sphere where nearly everyone
agreed that uniformity was needed? Not, he answered, simply by extending the authority of Congress, which was unable to perform its present
duties. Although new grants of power were required in order to perfect
the definition of decisions that belonged in federal hands, the most complete authority would still prove "nominal" unless the general government was actually obeyed. Constitutional reform, to be effective, would
thus require two further changes. First, the people, from whom all authority derived, would have to ratify the work of the convention. Next, the
general government would have to be empowered with a right to veto all
state laws. The sovereign people were the only agents capable of ordering
the states' submission where the general interest was involved, the only
agents with the right to make the necessary alterations in the state as well
as federal constitutions. Federal reform "would make essential inroads on
the state constitutions," he would tell the Constitutional Convention,
"and it would be a novel and dangerous doctrine that a [state] legislature
could change the constitution under which it held its existence." Popular
approval was essential, too, to make the fundamental law more than just
a treaty between the states and to oblige the courts to treat transgressions
of the federal compact as "null and void."[20] A federal veto on local legislation, formerly a power of the crown, was equally essential to ensure
that the Confederation would be able to protect its limited preserve
against encroachments by the states, as well as "to restrain the states from
thwarting and molesting each other, and even from oppressing the minority within themselves by paper money and other unrighteous measures
which favor the interest of the majority."[21]

Madison's insistence on a federal right to veto *all* state laws has usually
been taken as an indication of how far he wished to go toward a consolidation of authority in central hands.[22] This is a serious mistake. In context, the idea emerged from Madison's attempt to find a constitutional
device that could secure the general government's supremacy *within a*

system where the overwhelming burden of political responsibilities would still be carried by the states.[23] The federal veto was an effort to create a "sovereign" central government by one who still imagined at this point that there must be a governmental sovereign somewhere in a system of divided powers, but who still assumed, as well, that the United States was to remain a federation of republics, whose general government would be responsible exclusively for only certain common duties. The fundamental problem, Madison believed, was to prevent the states from "baffling" federal measures and from "intervening" in the federal sphere.[24] Far from thinking of the veto as an instrument of central aggrandizement, he conceived of it initially as necessary to protect the weaker central government from the encroachments of the states. Indeed, it is extremely difficult to see how he could ever have arrived at the idea if he had not thought so habitually in terms of separate state and federal duties, which he was trying not to intermix (though with imperfect mental tools). Thus he carefully distinguished this "defensive power" from the "positive" responsibilities the central government should have, and he insisted that he favored it because it struck him as the *minimal* "abridgement" of the local "sovereignties" consistent with a lasting union and a system of divided powers.[25]

My object here is not to palliate a bad idea or to deemphasize its central role in Madison's preliminary thinking. As will be seen below, the federal negative on local acts became the very hinge of Madison's solution to the central riddle of a liberal republic. Nevertheless, I think it crucial to distinguish Madison's intentions in proposing this forbidding power from how a universal federal veto might in fact have worked. This power might, in operation, have resulted in enormous central intermeddling in the business of the states. The great majority in the convention thought it would and, in the end, defeated even the Virginia Plan's proposal to confine the federal negative to local laws that violated the federal charter. But whatever we might think about this question, it is critical to understand that central aggrandizement was by no means what Madison had in mind when he arrived at the idea, nor did he think that this would be its probable effect.

Thomas Jefferson saw all of this at once when he objected to the federal veto on grounds that the "patch" was not commensurate with the "hole." Not more than one in every hundred local acts, he cautioned, would concern the Confederation as a whole, "but this would give Congress a power they ought not have over the 99" in order to get at the one, "upon a presumption that they will not exercise the 99."[26] Madison was, indeed, *presuming* that the former royal prerogative would not be abused if placed in responsible hands—and this was not a wise presumption from his own perspective. Still, the federal negative, as he envisioned it, was never meant to concentrate decision-making in the hands of federal officials. He thought of it consistently as a defensive power: as a tool that might create a legislative power rather comparable in operation to the modern workings of judicial review (complete, we might remark, with modern readings of the Fourteenth Amendment). Grasping this is critical if we are, first, to understand the insights Madison achieved before most delegates were even on the scene, and then to recognize how different his original proposals were from the document he signed.

The point is subject to a different formulation. At the opening of the convention, I suggest, Madison had analyzed the failings of the old Confederation with a critical acuity that proved unanswerable by the opponents of his plan.[27] That plan itself—and not the author's eagerness to remedy injustices within the states—was thus the first and most important step toward the decision to reconstruct the federal system completely, for it was premised on a studied argument that the debilities of the existing Union were *untreatable* unless the very nature of the Union could be changed. Still, Madison's analysis had overreached his great, though limited, ability to think his way to a solution of the problems he perceived. At the beginning of the meeting, he identified the fundamental problem as state "intervention" in the federal sphere, and so he planned to solve it mainly by suggesting how the states might be excluded from their current role in choosing federal officials, compelled to execute the federal government's commands, and blocked from taking independent actions that could damage other states or vital national interests. But because he thought of the confederation as an instrument for doing what the states could not accomplish on their own, because he was determined to define a "middle ground" between state sovereignty and a consolidated national government, he did not immediately see that a reconstituted central government might never need to call on the states at all for actions necessary to the execution of its laws.[28] Thus, his preconvention letters advocated both the federal veto and a federal power to coerce delinquent states, as did the resolutions of May 29. He understood, by then, how problematic it would be to operate "by force on the collective will of a state"; and yet he still assumed that the reconstituted central government would still depend on the states for requisitions and for other actions necessary to enforce its laws.[29] The preconvention letters demonstrate, in short, that Madison did not, as yet, consistently envision a regime that would derive entirely from and act exclusively on the individual members of society. Though he was moving toward this thought—and moved the whole convention in the same direction—the Virginia Plan proposed to place a great republic at the head of a confederation of republics. It was still a partly federal, and not a wholly national, solution to the Union's problems—in this sense *and* in its major author's wish to constitute a central government whose powers would be "paramount," yet limited to matters that the states were individually incompetent to handle. When the Constitutional Convention opened, neither Madison nor anybody else possessed a well-developed, thoroughly coherent concept of concurrent state and general governments, none of which would actually be "sovereign."[30]

Still, Madison's peculiar genius carried him habitually to the relationships between political phenomena that others thought of as discrete. He was instinctively inclined to press relentlessly to basics, to grapple with complexity by slicing through the issues to the principles involved. These qualities were part of what contemporaries had in mind when praising him as a distinctive mixture of the scholar and the politician (or in condemning him as an impractical theorist). Because of them, the resolutions of May 29—and the completed Constitution—were indeed a good deal more than an attempt to solve the federal problem.

When Madison assessed the nation's ills, he found two perils, not just one. Much earlier, he had concluded that the Union would disintegrate in time if it continually failed to meet its members' expectations; and for years, he had been deeply fearful that the revolutionary enterprise could not survive a fragmentation of the continental union. If the Union should collapse or fragment into several confederations, every part would fear the others, each might be compelled to seek out foreign allies, and all would either lose their independence or would find themselves eventually with standing military forces, powerful executives, swollen taxes, and persistent public debts. European intervention or a replication of conditions similar to those of Europe would entail the end of liberty itself. Of all the states and sections, none would lose their liberty more quickly than Virginia and the South.[31]

By 1787, Madison and many others thought that fragmentation of the Union might be close at hand, and Madison was deeply fearful that collapse of the republican experiment could follow quite closely behind. The inability of the confederation government to pay its debts, enforce its treaties, or relieve the economic difficulties of the postwar years contributed directly, he perceived, to arguments between the states and rising talk about a dissolution of the Union. But the weaknesses of the Confederation, he believed, were also more responsible than any other fact for popular abuses in the states and thus for growing doubts about the benefits of the republican experiment itself. This twofold crisis of commitment—to the Union *and* to the revolutionary state experiments in popular self-governance, which depended both on the Union and on their own consistency with "justice"—was the illness he proposed to treat.

Modern scholarship, of course, has clearly recognized that Madison intended to correct both sets of ills: to use the Constitutional Convention to redress conditions in the states as well the debilities of the Confederation. Modern scholarship, in fact, has often focused *too* exclusively on the Virginian's eagerness to counter popular abuses or on his conviction that the local legislatures were persistently inclined to sacrifice the interests of the Union to temporary, partial interests of their own. Neither of these points is wrong. The emphasis, however, is misplaced, and this misplacement of the emphasis has broader consequences than may be immediately apparent. For Madison was less peculiar in his recognition that the local governments were selfish and abusive than he was in his conviction that the failings of the Union were the leading *source* of many of the most disturbing measures of the states. Madison was most distinctive, not in his alarm about majority abuses, but in his unswerving dedication to a change that would correct these evils and resolve the problems of the Union *without* "infringing fundamental principles" that seemed to him the essence of the revolutionary faith.[32] It is not his quest for national supremacy that needs new stress, but his unwavering determination to achieve a more effective Union at acceptable expense to the residual authority of the states. It was not his fear of the majority that set him off most clearly from a number of the continentalists who joined him in this search. It was his fierce commitment to preserving popular control.

The members of the Constitutional Convention gathered with a solemn sense of high responsibility and urgent common purpose, none of them more consciously than Madison himself. Eight months before, the bitter conflict over Jay's negotiations with Gardoqui had given rise to serious talk about dividing the Union into smaller, regional confederations whose members might possess a clearer commonality of interests.[33] And even as the states were choosing delegates to the convention, economic suffering had flamed into an armed revolt in western Massachusetts. The terrified response of an important portion of the continental leadership was yet another aspect of Madison's concerns. Greatly as he feared the fragmentation of the Union, the elite's response to Shays's Rebellion warned him that the Revolution faced another threat, which might be no less deadly if it grew. As he wrote the letters leading up to the Virginia Plan, he worked against a background that convinced him that the whole republican experiment was urgently at risk.

Shays's Rebellion was itself, of course, a frightening concern. At the beginning of the year, before he left Virginia, Madison had credited the most alarming tales about the Shaysites and their prospects: that the rebels were as powerful as their opponents; that British agents were among them; that the insurrection threatened to engulf all of New England. In February, after he had settled in New York, fuller information gradually corrected some of these misapprehensions. Throughout the spring, however, as he sketched his earliest ideas about reform, he kept a worried eye on Massachusetts. He was anxious, first, about reactions to the Massachusetts legislature's "rigorous" response to the rebellion, next about successes by the Shaysites in the spring elections.[34] When he left New York for the convention, he was still concerned that Massachusetts was a tinderbox of violent discontents. Throughout the spring, moreover—and continuing into the summer—letters from Virginia warned that much the same materials were on the verge of conflagration in the Old Dominion. Edmund Randolph wrote of new support for paper money and reported that "inflammatory summonses" had recently been posted on the roads in Hanover and Henrico Counties.[35] John Dawson, an assembly ally, noted that in Caroline, the people had "entered into an association and are determined to purchase no property sold by auction." "In most of the counties," Dawson added, "petitions to the next assembly will be handed about for the payment of debts either in property or by installments, and should both be refused and the scarcity of money continue, I know not what may be the consequence, as I am informed that in some of the low counties they talk boldly of following the example of the insurgents in Massachusetts and preventing the courts proceeding to business."[36]

Madison undoubtedly anticipated further popular commotions. He unquestionably shared the fear of leveling designs among the Shaysites. Greatly as he feared these things, however, they were not the worries he brought up time and time again in letters written in the weeks immediately before the Constitutional Convention. What those letters stressed was growing talk of small confederations vigorous enough to deal effectively with civl unrest and—more disturbing still—increasing evidence of serious support for a solution even more extreme. As he remembered it much later in his life, "the unstable and unjust career of the states had . . . forfeited the respect and confidence essential to order and good government," and "individuals who had betrayed a bias toward monarchy . . . were yielding to anticipations that, from an increase of the confusion, a government might result more congenial to their tastes."[37]

Evidence of an alarming rise of deeply counterrevolutionary sentiments had come to Madison before he reached New York. There, the city was alive with rumors, as was Congress. On February 21, a worried Madison weighed the prospects for the federal convention in the pages of his record of congressional debates. "Members from the southern and middle states," he jotted, "seemed generally anxious" for a change "which

would preserve the Union and give due energy to the government of it";
only one of them had openly avowed a preference for separate confederations, an idea that had been broached for the first time in the
newspapers that day. Members from New England, on the other hand,
"were suspected by some of leaning toward some antirepublican establishment (the effect of their late confusions) or of being less desirous or
hopeful of preserving the unity of the empire."[38] He hoped, he wrote to
Washington, that the desires of "leading characters" in Congress would

> gradually be concentered in the plan of a thorough reform of the existing
> system. Those who may lean towards a monarchical government and who,
> I suspect, are swayed by very indigested ideas will of course abandon an
> unattainable object whenever a prospect opens of rendering the republican
> form competent to its purposes. Those who remain attached to the latter
> form must soon perceive that it cannot be preserved at all under any mod-
> ification which does not redress the ills experienced from our present es-
> tablishments.[39]

Washington's March 31 reply was not well calculated to relieve his
correspondent's mind: "Those who lean to a monarchical government
have either not consulted the public mind or . . . live in a region where
the leveling principles in which they were bred" were "more productive
of monarchical ideas" than were conditions in the South. "Even admitting
the utility—nay necessity—of the form," Washington insisted, "the period
is not arrived for adopting the change without shaking the peace of this
country to its foundations." No one could deny the indispensability of a
complete reform of the existing system, which he hoped the Constitutional Convention would attempt. But only if complete reform were tried,
and the resulting system still proved inefficient, would a belief in the necessity of greater change begin to spread "among all classes of the people.
Then, and not till then in my opinion, can it be attempted without involving all the evils of civil discord."[40]

Washington and Madison were of a single mind about the indispensability of thoroughgoing changes in the present system—and about the
consequences should this fail. On March 19, well before he could have
opened Washington's response, with its suggestion that the general himself could contemplate a drastic remedy if the convention failed to check
the national deterioration, Madison was warning Thomas Jefferson that
the diseases of the current system had "tainted the faith of the most or-
thodox republicans." The symptoms were so serious, he said, as to convince "the votaries of liberty" that great concessions to stability were now

"the only safeguard against an opposite extreme of our present situation."[41]

Like Washington, Madison was confident that even in New England, the majority would not "submit to any antirepublican innovations."[42] As he wrote to Edmund Pendleton, however, there was growing reason to believe that if the federal convention failed to find a remedy for current ills, "some very different arrangement will ensue":

> The late turbulent scenes in Massachusetts and the infamous ones in Rhode Island have done inexpressible injury to the republican character in that part of the United States, and a propensity toward monarchy is said to have been produced by it in some leading minds. The bulk of the people will probably prefer the lesser evil of a partition of the Union into three more practicable and energetic governments.

But although a fragmentation of the Union was undoubtedly a lesser evil than rejection of the revolutionary faith, it was, withal, "so great a one" that it should "rouse all the real friends to the Revolution to exert themselves" to head it off.[43] "Many individuals of weight," he wrote to Randolph, were leaning toward an unrepublican solution. Others were predicting a partition into two or more confederations. "It is pretty certain that if some radical amendment of the single one cannot be devised and introduced, that one or other of these revolutions—the latter no doubt—will take place."[44]

Madison undoubtedly exaggerated the extent of promonarchical opinion, and probably of sentiment for separate confederacies as well.[45] But we can hardly doubt that both these fears were near the forefront of his mind, and that they troubled him increasingly just when he was sketching his preliminary thoughts about reform. A searching probe of federal weaknesses, he cautioned Edmund Randolph on April 8, showed that an effectual reform could not assume the character of an amendment of the "old Confederation"; the basic structure of the federal system was inherently defective. On top of that, a sensitivity to other dangers warned that an effectual reform could not be limited to the necessities of the Confederation Congress; it must confront the panoply of evils threatening the revolutionary faith. "Unless the Union [can] be organized efficiently *and on republican principles*, innovations of a much more objectionable form may be intruded, or in the most favorable event, the partition of the empire into rival and hostile confederacies will ensue."[46]

Madison approached the Constitutional Convention literally convinced that revolutionary fundamentals were at stake. He outlined his initial plans in circumstances that persuaded him that partial measures could not possibly suffice. A rigorous analysis of the defective structure of the current federal system told him that a strengthening of the Confederation Congress would at best delay, but could not stop, the fragmentation of the continental union. The states would still find ways to frustrate federal measures and encroach on federal rights. Their rival, separate regulations would continue to contribute to a rising, mutual ill will. Within each state, inconsistent, ill-considered, and unjust legislation would continue to promote the insecurities and doubts that were beginning to produce nostalgia for a king. Such sentiments, he thought, were limited thus far to a minority of (highly influential) men, but the conditions that were at their root were capable of spreading the support for drastic remedies through growing numbers of the people. And if the disillusionment should ever take root there, the sole remaining question would be which of the diseases would destroy the patient first. Liberty could die, in no great time, from the destruction of the Union. It could die more quickly from a general despair with its abuses. Some Americans were coming to believe that the republican experiment had failed, that there was insufficient virtue in the nation to sustain a governmental system that demanded a subordination of conflicting interests to the general good.[47] Madison was not among these doubters (though the opposite has often been asserted).[48] He did, however, take these doubts as symptoms of a malady that could prove fatal if allowed to run its course untreated.

A second line of thought was not less influential, though it is largely overlooked by scholars who have emphasized a growing fear of a collapse of public virtue. If amendments to the current constitution would not work, neither would a strengthening of the existing Congress be consistent with the "fundamental principles" that Madison intended to preserve; and he was thoroughly in earnest when he said that he would make "concessions" only to the point at which "stability" and governmental vigor still appeared consistent with the precepts of the Revolution.[49] Two specific, new responsibilities, his early thinking ran, were critical to the success of constitutional reform: federal authority to regulate the country's trade, and federal power to collect at least a portion of the necessary federal taxes. These additions, though, together with a federal negative on local legislation, would produce a general government whose "positive" authority would equal or exceed the British claims that had provoked the Revolution. As a Virginian, Madison refused to contemplate a change that would destroy his state's capacity to "rejudge" federal measures unless the change included a transition to proportional representation, which would assure the Old Dominion power equal to its size and contributions.[50] As a dedicated revolutionary, he insisted, too, that such extensive powers could be trusted only to a well-constructed, representative republic.[51]

Revolutionary principles and a determination to preserve the revolutionary order linked all of Madison's ideas into a complex chain. Because he saw the crisis of the Union as intrinsically a crisis of the Revolution, his thinking flowed without a pause into a systematic reconsideration of the other ways that liberty was threatened and the other ways in which republican commitments might be reinvigorated and secured. Thus a federal veto on local legislation occurred to him, initially, as he was groping for a means to keep the states from countermanding federal measures and from injuring one another. But as soon as he concluded that a federal veto was a necessary instrument of national supremacy, he saw immediately that this revival of the former royal power might permit the general government to intervene as guardian of private rights whenever these were threatened by majorities within the states:

> The great desideratum which has not yet been found for republican governments seems to be some disinterested and dispassionate umpire in disputes between different passions and interests in the state. The majority who alone have the right of decision, have frequently an interest real or supposed in abusing it. In monarchies the sovereign is more neutral to the interests and views of different parties, but unfortunately he too often forms interests of his own repugnant to those of the whole. Might not the national prerogative here suggested be found sufficiently disinterested for the decision of local questions of policy, whilst it would itself be sufficiently restrained from the pursuit of interests adverse to those of the whole society?[52]

Vicious legislation, Madison observed, could issue either from a government whose officers pursued partial interests of their own or, in republics, from a popular majority that acted as the judge in its own cause.[53] The former danger was the one that led him to propose the reconstruction of the central government as a republic. A republican reconstitution of the central government was necessary to prevent it from abusing just those powers which had once been noxiously abused by Parliament and the king: taxation, regulation of the nation's commerce, and the like. Having reasoned to this point, however, Madison was naturally induced to take account of evils that were undermining the republican commitment in the states; and it was here that genius truly intervened. Or should we say that it was here that an imaginative leap of genius was suggested by the very structure of his thought? For it is stunning to remark how clearly he was thinking, at this point, of a republican replacement for the old imperial regime, complete with the prerogative to overturn provincial legislation that was incompatible with the requirements of the "empire" as a whole. Before the Revolution, of course, the exercise of this prerogative by the British monarch had been a grievance mightily resented. But in the hands of rulers who would not be able to escape a due dependence on the people, the power might create exactly that impartial referee whose absence was the central problem in the states.

This, it seems to me, is how the federal veto on local legislation, very much Madison's own original proposal, became the very hinge of his initial plan for constitutional reform (and, very soon, the starting point for his defense of the superiority of large republics).[54] Acting as an umpire over the contentions of provincial factions, acting also as a check on the "vicissitudes" of fluctuating local laws, the reconstructed central government, he hoped, might rescue democratic rule from its excesses and revivify the faith that popular self-government could be combined with fundamental justice. If revolutionary principles proclaimed that such enormous powers were unsafe when trusted to a monarchy or an indirectly chosen, single-chamber Congress, revolutionary precepts also said that the sovereign people could distribute power as they pleased—and were, in fact, the only agents with authority to reduce the powers of the states. To Madison, in short, a principled consideration of the crisis of the Union argued, on the one hand, that liberty would not endure unless the central government was granted powers that required its reconstruction as a sound republic. A principled consideration also argued that the general government, if thus transformed, could safely be entrusted with the powers necessary to correct the economic suffering responsible for vicious local legislation, could be given taxing powers equal to its needs, and thus could work in a variety of ways to reconcile the few who had already faltered while the body of the people was still firm.

None of these remarks, it might be emphasized again, should be regarded as an effort to deny that Madison participated fully in the rising fear of popular abuses. None of them suggests that his proposals constituted anything except a sharply radical—and therefore a profoundly challenging—assessment of the national malaise. My purposes are two. First, to utterly deny—in face of very old and very influential emphases on the reactionary character of constitutional reform—that there was any hint of such a counterrevolutionary attitude in Madison himself. However widely and however firmly opposite impressions may have spread—however fairly these impressions may describe some other framers—Madison himself cannot be fairly cited even as suggesting that the fundamental problem for the nation was an insufficiency of public virtue. Second, which may

not be possible until the ghost of counterrevolutionary sentiments is finally laid to rest, the object is to raise a framework that permits a fuller,
more precise appreciation of the founder's most distinctive contributions.

Madison's republican convictions had, indeed, been gravely tested as
he battled schemes for tax support for teachers of religion, struggled unsuccessfully for a revision of Virginia's constitution, and became increasingly revolted by poorly drafted, inconsistent legislation, especially by
measures (passed or threatened) that were meant to shield majorities
from economic troubles by infringing private rights or by postponing taxes
necessary for the states to keep their promises and meet their federal
obligations. These experiences, as I have said, had carried him into the
sharpest, deepest crisis of his life. They did so not because he often lost,
and plainly not because his personal investments were immediately at risk.
They did so principally because they challenged the convictions on which
he had based his whole career, forcing him to reconsider the very viability
of the commitments he had undertaken early in the Revolution. In his
words, the authors of the early revolutionary constitutions had assumed—
and so had he—that the majority of people are "the safest guardian both
of public good and of private rights."[55] Experience had shown, however,
that this early revolutionary maxim was imperfect. Private rights could
certainly be threatened by a government that sacrificed the interests of
the people to an independent interest of its own. But private rights were
being threatened most repeatedly, in the American republics, by *majorities*
who had a partial interest of their own, and who were sacrificing the
considered interests of the whole community to an apparent, temporary
object of its larger part.[56]

Nonetheless, there seems to me no greater error than to think that
Madison's republican convictions had not passed this test, or even that he
thought that some of the ideals of 1776 would have to be severely compromised in order to preserve the rest. Others were inclined by the experiences of the 1780s to reject the revolutionary maxim altogether—to
Madison's intense alarm. He never was. That is, he never came to think
that any agency except a government depending solely on the people
could be trusted with the public good. He never came to doubt that liberty
defined as firm security for private rights (or "justice") is inseparable
from liberty defined as majority control, nor did he ever see the body of
the people (as contrasted with majorities of *factious* people) as the fundamental problem for republics. He certainly participated far enough in
the alarm about majority abuses to be fully conscious of how dangerous
it was, and yet he entered not at all into the counterrevolutionary sentiments that fear of state majorities provoked. Though he was tortured to
the point of bursting many of the usual constraints on federal reform, the

agony was not enough to force him to recant the fundamentals of his faith. And his refusal to recant them, not the agony alone, was at the crux of his creative daring.

By 1787, much of the American elite shared Madison's alarm about majority excesses in the states. Many, maybe most, of these articulate Americans identified the problem as a classic crisis of relationships between the many and the few: a textbook illustration of the dangers either of these "natural" social groups could face if unprotected from the other. Among these gentlemen of property and status, a few were so disturbed that they could look nostalgically toward England, where the independent powers of the lords and king imposed a more effective check on popular desires. Many more might have conceded privately that gentlemen in England were more secure in their investments and estates than gentlemen in Massachusetts or Rhode Island.

Madison's distinctive contribution was to understand these discontents in slightly different terms, to link them in a different way with the debilities of the Confederation, and boldly to proclaim that all the ills were curable *without abandoning the Revolution.* Even in societies without hereditary ranks, he readily agreed, there were indeed persistent differences of interest and opinion between the

> rich and poor, debtors and creditors, the landed, the manufacturing, the commercial interests, the inhabitants of this district or that district, the followers of this political leader or that political leader, the disciples of this religious sect or that religious sect. . . . Debtors have defrauded their creditors. The landed interest has borne hard on the mercantile interest. The holders of one species of property have thrown a disproportion of taxes on the holders of another species.[57]

The lesson to be drawn from these collisions and injustices was not, however, that experience disproved the ultimate superiority of polities that rested wholly on elections. The lesson was that the convention should "enlarge the sphere" of republican government "and thereby divide the community into so great a number of interests and parties that, in the first place, a majority will not be likely at the same moment to have a common interest separate from that of the whole or of the minority, and in the second place, that in case they should have such an interest, they may not be apt to unite in the pursuit of it." This, he argued, was "the only defense against the inconveniences of democracy consistent with the democratic form of government."[58] A large republic would be far less subject to majority abuses than the small republics in the states. A large republic, by that fact, could be entrusted with the powers it would need to save those small republics from themselves.

In urging this reform, it should be noted, Madison did not condemn the architects of the Confederation. He did not attempt to disassociate himself from early revolutionary errors, but spoke instead of the defective reasoning that most Americans had shared. From the beginning of the Revolution, he believed, most Americans had been committed to the principles that governments derive their just authority from popular consent, but are created to protect the natural liberties of all. Like himself, however, few of the republicans of 1776 had then foreseen the regularity or the severity with which these two commitments could collide. Circumstances, he suggested, had misled them all. The circumstances of the early Revolution had misled the architects of the Confederation into "a mistaken confidence that the justice, the good faith, the honor, the sound policy of the several legislative assemblies would render superfluous any appeal to the ordinary motives by which the laws secure the obedience of individuals: a confidence which does honor to the enthusiastic virtue of the compilers, as much as the inexperience of the crisis apologizes for their errors."[59] The historical conditions of the early Revolution had likewise led the patriots of 1776 to underestimate the difficulty of combining their majoritarian convictions with their nearly universal wish to fix some limits on what governments could do. It had been easy to assume that governments depending wholly on the people would instinctively respect the rights for which the people were at war.[60]

Time had taught new lessons, and, for Madison, experience had forced a reexamination of original assumptions. All of his experience and all of his extensive reading must have played some part. In all of his experience, however, nothing had been more instructive than Virginia's recent struggle over church and state. The movement for a general assessment had elicited his earliest explicit recognition that majorities could be, not just mistaken or unfair, but deeply threatening to rights that no political authority could be permitted to infringe. More obvious still, the *failure* of the general assessment, followed by the relatively easy passage of the Statute for Religious Freedom, had become the single most important catalyst for his conclusion that a multiplicity of interests in a large, diverse republic might afford a more effective safeguard for inherent rights than any of the institutional protections that the framers of the early revolutionary constitutions—not excluding Madison himself—had then thought necessary to impose.

In all of his experience, moreover, Madison had never been involved in a dispute that made it more apparent that the body of the people did not naturally divide into two polar pairs, such as the many and the few, but into a plurality of different groups whose great variety could pose a stubborn obstacle to the success of any partial interest. On this insight, which was strongly reinforced by his awareness of the pluralistic nature of divisions in the Continental Congress, he was able to erect a new conception of the character of democratic factions. Moreover, in the outcome of the struggle over the assessment, he began to see how the recurring clash between his liberal and his republican commitments might be overcome.

All Madison's most famous presentations of the case for an extension of the sphere of republican government list differing opinions in religion as a "latent cause" of faction, often as the first of several potential sources of majority oppression.[61] On several occasions, he was quite explicit in suggesting that the struggle for religious freedom was the model he had had most centrally in mind when he envisioned how the great republic would "control the violence of faction."[62] The best example may have come in 1788, when he explained to Jefferson why he was not initially concerned that the recently completed Constitution did not include a bill of rights:

> Repeated violations of these parchment barriers have been committed by overbearing majorities in every state. In Virginia I have seen the bill of rights violated in every instance where it has been opposed to a popular current. Notwithstanding the explicit provision contained in that instrument for the rights of conscience, it is well known that a religious establishment would have taken place in that state if the legislative majority had found, as they expected, a majority of the people in favor of the measure; and I am persuaded that if a majority of the people were now of one sect, the measure would still take place and on narrower ground than was then proposed, notwithstanding the additional obstacle which the law [establishing religious freedom] has since created. Wherever the real power in a government lies, there is the danger of oppression. In our governments the real power lies in the majority of the community, and the invasion of private rights is *chiefly* to be apprehended, not from acts of government contrary to the sense of its constituents, but from acts in which the government is the mere instrument of the major number of the constituents.[63]

In every free society, he now believed,

> the security for civil rights must be the same as for religious rights. It consists in the one case in the multiplicity of interests and, in the other, in the multiplicity of sects. The degree of security in both cases will depend on the number of interests and sects, and this may be presumed to depend on the extent of country and number of people comprehended under the same government.[64]

Once he had arrived at his commitment to a federal negative on local legislation, Madison was obligated to explain why a prerogative that had been harshly criticized in the Declaration of Independence should be voluntarily confided to a central government again. His famous argument for the advantages of an "extension of the sphere" began as a defense of this and other powers that he planned to vest in the enlarged republic.[65] As I hope to show, however, there was never any point at which the major author of the resolutions of May 29 believed that *any sort* of large republic would suffice. He was always conscious, on the one side, of the dangers of excessive central power. On the other, he was adamant from the beginning that the large republic must not reproduce the radical infirmities that had been built into the constitutions of the small.

Early in the decade, during his initial years in Congress, Madison may not have had the time or inclination for a penetrating criticism of the constitutions of the states. There is nothing in his papers from those years that suggests that he was greatly discontented or, indeed, that he had thought about the matter much at all. Technically, he was himself a framer of Virginia's revolutionary constitution, having served in 1776 as a very junior member of the large committee charged with its initial drafting. All authorities agree, however, that he made slight contribution to this work and left no current comments on the finished constitution. Apparently, he turned his thoughts in earnest to the subject only toward the end of 1783, when Jefferson suggested that he ought to make a constitutional revision part of his agenda after he returned from Congress to the state assembly.[66]

In the spring of 1784, with Richard Henry Lee's support, Madison did seek a resolution calling for a constitutional convention for Virginia.[67] An outline for a speech supporting this proposal is virtually the only evidence we have about his constitutional opinions at this time, which seem to have been strongly Jeffersonian in flavor.[68] Two-thirds of the surviving outline is concerned to demonstrate the current constitution's lack of an authoritative grounding in explicit popular consent and to suggest that this could be corrected safely by recurring to the people. The Virginia constitution had been instituted much like any piece of ordinary legislation: drafted by a body charged with many other tasks and put into effect like any other law. Revolutionary thinking since that time had moved increasingly toward an insistence on procedures that would recognize the people's power to create a government and would distinguish fundamental law from ordinary statutes. Jefferson demanded the election of a separate convention charged exclusively with writing an organic law. Madison insisted also that the people ought to ratify the constitution after it was drafted. Massachusetts, which was widely thought of as a model, had combined these two techniques to institute a constitution that appeared to be a vivid illustration of a social compact.[69]

The remaining third of Madison's appeal to the assembly was a condemnation of the current constitution's "union of powers." Citing Montesquieu, it pointed to the many ways in which the other branches of Virginia's government depended on the lower house: the judges for their salaries, and the executive for both its salaries and reelection. In the absence of alternative provisions, Madison objected, even the interpretation of the constitution rested with the General Assembly. Like Jefferson, who advocated indirect election of the upper house, Madison went on to criticize Virginia's senate as "badly constituted" and improperly forbidden from initiating legislation. Like Jefferson, he also criticized the equal representation of the counties in the lower house. Sketchy as it is, the outline tells us less than we would like to know. It does, however, powerfully suggest that Madison agreed wholeheartedly with Jefferson in the desire to alter the Virginia constitution so that it would be, at once, more democratic in its derivation, more equal in its principles of representation, but *less* responsive to the will of the majority as expressed by its immediate representatives in the lower house.

Another year's experience in the Virginia House of Delegates confirmed and deepened all of these desires. Patrick Henry crushed the move of 1784 and carried resolutions barring its revival. But Madison was asked for his opinions once again as his Kentucky friends began to move toward separation from Virginia. In August 1785, as his "Memorial Against Assessments" was circulating through the counties, he replied at length to a request for his advice about a constitution for Kentucky. Drawing on a comprehensive knowledge of the constitutions of the other states, he brought his thoughts together as completely as he ever would before preparing the Virginia Plan. As before, he borrowed heavily from Jefferson's proposals for a new Virginia constitution. As was often true, however, he diverged significantly from Jefferson whenever his reflections prompted new ideas.[70]

This was not the case on many of the fundamentals. As in 1784, Madison insisted in the strongest terms on a clear and firm division of the "three great departments," roundly criticizing the Virginia constitution for its violation of this maxim. "Our executive," he wrote, "is the worst part of a ba[d] constitution." Dependent on the legislature for their salaries and reappointments, the governor and members of the council were unable to withstand the "usurpations of that branch," and council members could conceivably continue there for life. Judicial independence was of comparable importance, but judicial independence was impossible unless provisions for a fixed and liberal salary were added to the judges' good-behavior tenure in their office. The reputation of the British constitution, Madison opined, depended wholly on the independence of this branch, which made it possible for British judges to protect the rights of individuals "against all the corruptions of the other two departments." Therefore, even in an "infant country" like Kentucky, where talents and experience might be in short supply, a mixture of the personnel or powers of the three departments should be carefully avoided. "Temporary deviations from fundamental principles are always more or less dangerous. . . . The first precedent . . . familiarizes the people to the irregularity, lessens their veneration for those fundamental principles, and makes them a more easy prey to ambition and self interest."[71]

Since early in the Revolution, bills of rights and written constitutions had been understood as indispensable for keeping governments within the limits fixed by natural rights and for maintaining an identity of interests between the rulers and the ruled. But early in the Revolution, an insistence on a rigid separation of the three departments had been pointed most especially, though not exclusively, against the possibility that the executive might undermine the independence of the other branches. Madison, like Jefferson, continued to be sharply conscious of this danger. Neither man, for instance, recommended an enlargement of the governor's appointive powers. Neither, for that matter, was inclined to free the chief executive from the advice of an executive council or to trust him with a legislative veto, though Madison was willing to consider popular election.[72] Like Jefferson, however, Madison had learned that the excessive influence of executives was not the pressing problem in the new American republics. Both of them were now concerned primarily about the overbearing power of the lower houses and, in consequence, as Madison expressed it, of "the want" of "steadiness" and "wisdom" in the laws. "The want of *fidelity* in the administration of power," he explained, had been the "grievance" felt most sharply in the years preceding Independence. Thus it had been "natural" for the framers of the early constitutions "to give too exclusive an attention to this primary attribute," strengthening the branch that would be most responsive to the people. In consequence, however, the absence of stability was now "the grievance complained of in all our republics."[73]

Madison continued to be troubled by Virginia's failure to establish any mechanism for resolving constitutional disputes or for preserving the organic law and governmental equilibrium from legislative usurpations. Like Jefferson, he was unwilling to confide a final power to construe the constitution to the judges. (Indeed, he would resist this concept even in his final years.)[74] Realizing, though, that written constitutions were an ineffective barrier when their interpretation rested with an overbearing lower house, he followed Jefferson in recommending a provision that would make it possible for a majority in any two of the three great branches "to call a plenipotentiary convention whenever they may think their constitutional powers have been violated by the other department or that any part of the constitution needs amendments." Like Jefferson, he also much approved of New York's Council of Revision, which combined the governor and several members of the higher courts into a body with a power to compel a reconsideration of improper legislation and a two-thirds vote for its repassage. Calling this provisional veto "a valuable safeguard both to public interests and to private rights," he also saw it as a needed check on "fluctuating and indigested laws." Poorly drafted, fluctuating laws seemed so pervasive and obnoxious that he also recommended a provision for a "standing committee" of "a few select and skillful individuals" to draft all legislation.[75]

Inconsistencies and errors in the laws could be reduced by skillful draftsmen. Steadiness and wisdom could be aided by a council of revision, which would also give the weaker branches of the government a means to guard their own preserves from legislative usurpations. Still, the legislature was to make the laws; and given their insistence on a separation of the three great branches, it was logical for Madison and Jefferson to look for steadiness and wisdom mostly from a better constituted upper house. In classic theories of mixed government, the second house was always thought of both as the essential locus of these missing virtues and as the part of government that would protect the few against the power of the many. Revolutionary thought had broken only partially with these conventions. For republicans, of course, the few were not to be distinguished from the many by their birth, and they were not to be accorded different legal rights. Even for republicans, however, it was common to assume that every aggregate of individuals would naturally contain a few who could be readily distinguished from the rest by their superior experience, their greater property, their leisure, or their wisdom. This distinction was a heritage as old as ancient Greece, and it was strongly reinforced for many revolutionary thinkers by the circumstances of the middle 1780s. Thus for Madison and Jefferson alike, the great desideratum was to constitute an upper house that could impart the steadiness and wisdom missing from the early revolutionary constitutions, but without infringing the equality of rights to which they were committed.[76] For Madison, at least, this wish was deepened by a growing recognition that the rights of propertied minorities were just the rights that were endangered most repeatedly by overbearing lower houses. It was here, in fact, that his ideas diverged most clearly from his friend's; and it was here, as well, that he was least successful in resolving the increasing conflict of his liberal with his majoritarian commitments.

As in 1784, Madison agreed with Jefferson in recommending Maryland's provision for the indirect election of the upper house. (Virginia's was directly chosen by the voters.) Whereas Jefferson, however, now proposed to change Virginia's three-year term for senators to two, Madison proposed to lengthen it to four or five.[77] Moreover, Caleb Wallace's request for recommendations on the suffrage prompted some additional suggestions for ways to make the upper house distinctly different from the lower and, in consequence, more capable of counterbalancing the will of the majority with other qualities required by an enduring constitution. To restrict the suffrage to the landholders, he wrote—which was the practice in Virginia—would "in time" exclude too many from the franchise. "To extend it to all citizens without regard to property, or even to all who possess a pittance, may throw too much power into hands which will either abuse it themselves or sell it to the rich who will abuse it." Therefore, Madison proposed a "middle course": "narrow the right in the choice of the least popular and . . . enlarge it in that of the most popular branch of the legislature," as was the practice in North Carolina and New York. This solution, he admitted, might "offend the sense of equality which re[i]gns in a free country" (and which he himself had said in his Memorial was a fundamental feature of republics). Still, he saw "no reason why the rights of property, which chiefly bears the burden of government and is so much an object of legislation, should not be respected as well as personal rights in the choice of rulers."[78]

When Madison elaborated his ideas about a constitution for Kentucky, the Virginia struggle over an assessment to support religion had not yet been resolved. The Jay-Gardoqui crisis and the prospect of a federal convention lay ahead. Over the succeeding months, as he prepared for this convention, Madison concerned himself initially with the debilities of the Confederation, and it was this analysis that led him to propose a sweeping reconstruction of the federal system. But once he had concluded that the needs of the Confederation demanded its reordering as a republic, all of his ideas about the constitutions of the states were relevant to his proposals. All his discontents—and all the deeper discontents of many of his colleagues—had to be considered.

In his proposals for Virginia and Kentucky, Madison did not abandon any of his revolutionary maxims. He still believed that power can corrupt, that governmental officers will always be inclined to free themselves from their dependence on the people, and that the "fidelity" of rulers to the ruled was the essential, first requirement for a proper constitution. By "fidelity," it seems apparent, much of what he had in mind was the responsiveness and faithfulness of rulers to the body of the people, not to any smaller part thereof. Thus, he thought Virginia's freehold franchise was too narrow. He insisted, too, on annual elections of the lower house, on secret ballots, and on constitutional provisions for maintaining a proportionality of representatives to population.[79]

By itself, however, as the states' experience had shown, a prompt response by government to the majority's immediate demands was not the only quality to be desired. "Fidelity" meant something more. In the circumstances of the middle 1780s, Madison was more and more inclined to favor measures that would temper the majority's demands with wisdom, steadiness, and new protections for the rights of the propertied few (who were the most conspicuous minority until the struggle for religious freedom led to new ideas about this problem). Fearing the executive, as revolutionaries always had, he pinned his hopes primarily on the part of government that classic theories of the balanced constitution had conventionally associated with stability and wisdom, favoring an upper house that would be chosen indirectly or by freehold suffrage. A differential suffrage, to be sure, accorded poorly with his dedication to equality as well as private rights, which helps explain his great enthusiasm for a large republic armed with the capacity to intervene when state majorities insisted on injustice and thus to solve this problem in a different way. For just this reason, though, the concept of a differential suffrage graphically suggests the lengths to which he had been driven by the conflict of his two commitments and his consciousness that this intrinsic tension would be troublesome however much the size of the republic was enlarged. For years, he had been thinking of a range of constitutional devices meant to reconcile his liberal and his republican commitments, and most of his ideas were interwoven in the resolutions of May 29. Under the Virginia Plan, one house would be elected by the people. The second house would be elected by the first from persons nominated by the states. The resolutions did not merely aim to make the powers of the central government coequal with its duties. They proposed, as Madison expressed it, "to perpetuate the Union and redeem the honor of the republican name."[80]

CHAPTER FIVE

To Perpetuate the Union

MADISON MADE THREE DISTINCTIVE CONTRIBUTIONS to the framing
of the Constitution. First, he was primarily responsible for the preliminary
propositions that initiated the creation of a federal republic and served
throughout the summer as the outline for reform. Second, in the early
weeks of the deliberations, he persuasively explained why lesser changes
would not work, an enterprise in which he was impressively assisted but
never overshadowed by a handful of like-minded men. Finally, he forcefully maintained that the convention could not limit its attention to the
crisis of the Union, but must also come to terms with a crisis of republican
convictions, both by placing limitations on the states and by creating an
enlarged republic free from the structural errors of the state constitutions
and capable of restoring the damaged reputation of the revolutionary
cause. With the latter plea particularly, he led the Constitutional Convention to a thoroughgoing reconsideration of the proper structure of a
sound republic. Meanwhile, with his famous argument that private rights
could be protected more completely in a large republic, he helped instill
a confidence that the completed Constitution might accomplish most of
what he had in mind.

All these contributions have been widely recognized by scholars. All,
it might be noted, came early in the course of the proceedings. Madison
was first among the framers, by general agreement of historians and his
peers, in part because he came to Philadelphia the best prepared. Of all
the delegates, he seemed to have the most precise and comprehensive
knowledge of American affairs, together with a masterful ability to place
the country's situation in historical and philosophical perspective. He had
thought things through to a degree that no one else had done, and it was
therefore his ideas that set the course, his proposals to which other delegates initially responded.[1] Throughout the summer, he spoke as often

and as influentially as any. He served on most of the convention's key
committees. But he was not responsible for any of the famous compromises or for any of the late additions that reshaped the resolutions of May
29 into the document completed on September 17. He earned his reputation as the father of the Constitution principally because of what he
did at the beginning of the work and after the convention had adjourned,
by which time his own ideas had been significantly remolded.[2]

My discussion focuses on that remolding. For, although the finest modern scholarship has clearly recognized his most important contributions,
it has seldom asked how Madison was influenced *by* the framing of the
Constitution—except to say that he was gravely disappointed.[3] Analysts are
well aware that the convention thoroughly revised the resolutions of May
29 and that the finished plan reflected great defeats as well as stunning
triumphs for Madison's original proposals. They have carefully assessed
his victories and disappointments. But they have yet to realize how much
he *learned*, how greatly he was changed by his participation in the meeting.
Thus, a careful effort to approach the framing of the Constitution as an
episode in the development of his ideas can cast new light on the convention, on Madison's most fundamental objects, and even on his understanding of the product.

The Constitutional Convention, as Madison put it later, proposed a
form of government that had no precedent in history. Neither "wholly
national" nor "purely federal" in the prevailing usage of those terms, this
novel scheme divided political responsibilities between concurrent and
interlocking state and central governments, each of which would act directly on the individuals composing the political societies from which they
rose. The people of the thirteen states could be conceived as granting
portions of their sovereign power to the different parts of both the state
and general governments while reserving their remaining rights, together
with the ultimate authority to alter or abolish any of these governments,
for themselves. The structure thus established, Madison maintained, could
make the central government effective without endangering the people
or the states. It constituted a republican solution to the characteristic
problems of republics.[4]

This solution to the nation's problems was significantly different from
the one that Madison envisioned when the great convention opened. It
differed even more, though this has not been noticed, from the proposals
he supported midway through the work. Madison resisted some of its distinctive features through the greater part of the convention, and he worried when the gathering adjourned that they would vitiate the system.[5]
Nevertheless, his contributions to *The Federalist* did not defend a system
that he privately regarded as severely flawed, although this seems the dom-

inant impression. Rather, these impressive essays, building on ideas that first occurred in course of the convention and representing his more settled views, confessed his reconciliation to decisions he had earlier opposed and outlined a position he defended through the rest of his career.

Between May 30 and June 13, sitting in the character of a Committee of the Whole, the Constitutional Convention conducted a complete consideration of the resolutions of May 29, which the Virginians had proposed as a preliminary basis for discussions. During these two weeks, a brilliant group of delegates from Pennsylvania and Virginia developed a compelling case for radical reform, building on, but moving rapidly beyond, the insights Madison had reached before the meeting opened. Thus, from the beginning of debates, the major architect of the Virginian Plan was led into a first—and heretofore neglected—reexamination of his earliest opinions.

Madison had come to Philadelphia convinced that no extension of the central government's authority could overcome the crisis of the Union if the execution of congressional decisions continued to depend on intermediary actions by the states. The fundamental flaw of the Confederation, he believed, was in its basic structure. States were necessary instruments of federal action, but they were not amenable to federal commands. The current Articles of Union took the form of a "political constitution," but the Confederation Congress lacked the independent means required to carry out the tasks with which it was entrusted. It was thus as ineffectual in practice as the states themselves would be if every citizen were free to follow or ignore their laws.[6] This insight was the starting point for the Virginia Resolutions, which sought to free the general government from secondary, state decisions capable of baffling all its measures. It was Madison's first major contribution to the framing.

When the Constitutional Convention opened, nonetheless, the major author of the resolutions of May 29 had not yet formed a clear conception of fully concurrent state and general governments, each possessed of all the means required to carry out its tasks and neither having the capacity to intermeddle in the business properly belonging to the other. Although he recognized the need to end the states' capacity to intervene between the making and the execution of federal decisions, he did not yet see how they could be denied all agency in executing federal commands, nor did he see how it was possible to keep the lesser legislatures from "molesting" one another or infringing private rights unless the general government could act directly *on* the states. On the eve of the convention, he had written Washington of his hope that positive additions to the powers of the general government—authority to regulate and tax the country's trade, together with at least a partial power of direct taxation—would render it unnecessary, *for the most part,* for Congress to coerce the states.[7] He evidently still imagined, then, that on occasion, the central government would still rely on the states for requisitions or for other actions necessary to enforce its laws. And he was equally concerned to vest the central government with power to defend itself, the private rights of citizens, and peaceable relationships between the states from independent, countervailing state decisions. Accordingly, though the Virginia Resolutions sought to solve the federal problem partly by removing the state governments from their direct and equal role in making federal decisions—by basing Congress on the people rather than the legislatures of the states—they also sought to guarantee the faithful execution of the central government's decisions by *compelling* the confederated states to follow federal directives. The resolutions recommended both a federal power of coercion and a federal veto on state laws.

As deliberations started, to put this point in language that the delegates themselves employed, Madison had not entirely freed himself from the assumption that the Union would remain confederal in some of its essential principles of action. He had not yet firmly grasped the concept that rapidly became the key to the convention's ultimate solution to the problems he defined. Although his thinking had been moving him in this direction—had, indeed, approached the point so closely that his colleagues seized on it at once—the concept that the central government should act *exclusively* on the people, not on the states, is nowhere to be found in his preconvention writings.

Language of this sort was introduced to the convention on May 30, when Gouverneur Morris contrasted a "national" government with one "merely federal," and George Mason distinguished a government acting on individuals from one acting on states. Madison, suggestively, was not as quick as others to adopt this language, which soon was heard on every side. Given his intense commitment to a federal negative on local acts, it was by no means wholly consonant with his ideas.[8] Nevertheless, as early as May 31, he moved for the deletion of the federal power of coercion, referring to the inadvisability of applying force "to people collectively and not individually,"[9] and it was quickly clear that he was powerfully attracted to the concept. It strengthened and improved his earlier analysis of the Confederation's ills. It rendered more explicit what was probably the most important thrust of the Virginia Resolutions, a thrust that he had neither followed to its logical conclusion nor separated from proposals based on different ideas. And yet, from the beginning of the meeting, it became increasingly apparent that the concept of a central government that would compel obedience directly from the people, if more consistently applied, might become the central premise of reform. Day by day, the delegates could see more clearly that immediate connection with the people could permit the general government to wield effective power without relying on or trying to coerce the states at all.

Seizing on this thought, the Pennsylvanians and Virginians, who had met together once, at least, before the full convention found a quorum,[10] speedily developed a compelling case for comprehensive reconstruction of the federal system. Elaborating on the differences between a "national" government and a purely "federal" one, Madison, James Wilson, Edmund Randolph, George Mason, Gouverneur Morris, and others argued that the fatal weakness of the old Confederation was its unavoidable dependence on the thirteen states for revenues and for a host of intermediary actions necessary to enforce its laws and treaties. Lacking independent means to carry its decisions into action, they explained, Congress had been baffled by the states even when its measures were supported by a huge majority and undeniably within its proper province. The central government could never prove effective, they insisted, if the states retained the power to ignore or countermand its acts; and yet a federal power to coerce the states might introduce a constant threat of war between the Union and its members. The inescapable necessity, these "nationalists" maintained, was to abandon the unworkable idea of a government over governments, a sovereignty over sovereignties, and give the central government the means to act directly on the individual members of society. Revolutionary principles required, however, that a central government with direct authority to reach the people's lives and purses would have to represent its citizens immediately and fairly. Given the necessity for larger, more effective federal powers, the traditional equality between the several states would have to be abandoned in order to preserve equality among the people and majority control.[11]

Under the Virginia Plan, both houses of the legislature were to be apportioned according to the numbers of the free inhabitants or to the contributions of the states. Madison regarded this provision as obviously "just," by which he meant consistent with equality and standard rules of representation. He reasoned that the northern states would readily approve, because they had the larger current population, whereas the southern states would be attracted to the concept by the rapid shift of population to the South and West. He considered the provision absolutely necessary to persuade Virginia and the other larger states to part with portions of their power, and he was certain that the smaller states would be compelled to go along if all the large ones were agreed.[12] He discovered, as we know, that members from the smaller states adamantly opposed the change, which they believed was certain to subject them to a total domination. Their dissent would quickly generate the most enduring conflict of the meeting.

One of the finest modern studies of the Constitutional Convention, Clinton Rossiter's *1787*, calls its early weeks a period of "nationalist assault."[13] Certainly, the members from the smaller states *felt* powerfully assaulted by a plan that offered to apportion legislative seats according to this rule. George Read immediately protested that the delegates from Delaware, who were specifically instructed to insist on the equal vote that every state had always had in Congress, might have to leave the meeting if the larger states insisted on this change.[14] Neither Read nor any of his fellows really planned to quit before the business had begun. Yet it was clear from the beginning that the smaller states anticipated absolute subjection, even loss of their identities as states, in a republic grounded wholly on proportional representation. Nor were theirs the only worries prompted by Virginia's original proposals. No sooner was the first one taken up than Elbridge Gerry of Massachusetts and Charles C. Pinckney of South Carolina, both representing larger states, questioned whether the convention could or should propose so radical a reconstruction.[15] The Virginia Plan not only frightened delegations from the smallest states, it also seemed to many other members to depart too far from the essential spirit of a limited confederation and to call for more participation by the people than the people were equipped to make to national affairs.[16] The framing of the Constitution thus became a complicated story of a conflict so complex that it is easy to neglect the members' early sense of vital common purpose. Still, the "miracle" at Philadelphia resulted from a complicated interplay of disputation and consensus, during which the delegates collectively developed a conception of a form of government so novel that it lacked a name. To understand this process, it is necessary both to simplify a set of disagreements so complex that they defy brief description and to recognize that these disputes were only one dimension of the story.

From this perspective, the convention's first two weeks are best described as an initial exploration during which a complicated pattern of divisions rapidly emerged within a framework of evolving general agreements. Madison provided some important early guidance, intervening in the earliest proceedings mainly to prevent disputes about specific issues until the meeting could define some common ground. The major architect of the Virginia Plan had come to Philadelphia convinced that clearer definition of the central government's responsibilities, though needed, was not the most important task. Therefore, he refused to let the members be distracted by this issue. On May 31, two delegates proposed an immediate enumeration of the legislative powers. Madison opposed the motion—not, as will be shown, because he was opposed to an enumeration, but because he was determined that the delegates should focus, first, on structural and operational reform.[17] Similarly, when the members reached the resolution recommending the apportionment of representatives according to the free inhabitants *or* to the contributions of the states, Madison suggested thay they drop the reference to "free" inhabitants for now, warning that an argument about this point "might divert the Committee from the general question whether the principle of representation should be changed."[18] During the initial days, the members quickly recognized the benefits of Madison's approach, moving through the fifteen resolutions rapidly by simply passing over any that provoked or threatened to provoke serious contention.

The strategy was quite successful. The Virginia Plan was only a preliminary outline of a finished constitution. It did not specifically define which powers were beyond the competence of individual states. It embodied inconsistencies that Madison had carried with him to the meeting. It barely sketched some of the leading features of a sound republic—not even indicating, for example, whether the executive should be a council or a single man. Still, Madison, James Wilson, and their allies quickly made it clear that what they wanted was to build a wise and energetic central government on a broadly popular foundation, blending a responsibility to the majority with multiple securities against an overbearing, popularly elected lower house. Impressed by their analysis of the debilities of the existing system, the convention speedily agreed to substitute a complex and authoritative central government for the present, feeble, unicameral regime.[19] Sharing their dissatisfaction with the constitutions of the states, the members also worked from the beginning to establish genuinely independent, fully countervailing branches. The outline introduced at the beginning speedily assumed a more substantial shape, for the most part as the democratic nationalists desired.

The Virginia Plan survived its first examination fundamentally intact. During the convention's early days, Madison and Wilson towered over the proceedings. Two days into the deliberations, with only South Carolina and New Jersey dissenting, the members overwhelmingly approved the popular election of the lower house, a decision reaffirmed a few days later with the two dissenting delegations taking opposite positions. With Madison resisting a divisive argument about the scope of federal powers until some structural decisions could be made, the meeting easily decided on a three-year term for representatives and seven years for the executive and senators. As the Pennsylvanians helped elaborate the concept that the general government might act consistently on the people, the Virginians dropped the resolution calling for a federal power to coerce the states. Wilson led a winning struggle for a single chief executive, though he could not prevent the fearful delegates from ruling that this magistrate could only serve a single term and was to be elected by the legislature, not the people. Madison and Wilson would have liked to reinforce the legislative veto granted to this branch by involving the judiciary in the process (as the initial resolutions recommended), but Madison approved of the majority's decision that the veto was to be reversible instead of absolute.[20]

Intellectually outclassed by men like Madison and Wilson, lacking an alternative to the Virginia Plan, most members from the smaller states squirmed silently through the convention's early days. Nevertheless, as the Virginia Plan acquired some flesh and as it grew increasingly more difficult to settle lesser questions with the greater ones unanswered, the confrontation that had loomed from the beginning could no longer be contained. On June 9, New Jersey's delegates demanded a decision on apportioning the Congress. William Paterson insisted that proportional representation would destroy the smaller states and place the whole confederation at the mercy of a coalition of its larger members: Massachusetts, Pennsylvania, and Virginia. Ten of thirteen states, he warned, would certainly reject this scheme. If he could not defeat it in the hall, he would oppose it in his state. New Jersey would "never confederate on the plan before the convention."[21]

Sunday intervened and tempers cooled, but not before James Wilson answered Paterson in kind. "If the small states will not confederate on this plan," he assured them, Pennsylvania and some others "would not confederate on any other."[22] The division that would dominate proceedings for the next five weeks had burst into the open. It would prove the clearest, most dramatic, most persistent argument of the convention—the single conflict over which the gathering repeatedly approached collapse.

Nevertheless, for all its threatening potential, the clash between the small states and the large cannot account entirely for developments between May 30 and June 13. It was not the only conflict that emerged, nor can a single-minded emphasis on conflicts and divisions properly illuminate the course of the proceedings. The Constitutional Convention was successful, in the end, because its battles almost always raged in multiple dimensions, because the push-and-pull that marked its course was never simply a result of clashing interests, and because the men involved were more than merely clever brokers for their states. We need not resurrect old myths to recognize that the convention was, at once, a battleground for contending politicians and a theater for one of the most brilliant exercises in creative statesmanship that history has ever witnessed. The famous compromises that reshaped the resolutions of May 29 into the document completed on September 17 *were* necessary consequences of conflicting state and sectional desires, capably advanced by representatives who were acutely conscious of competing interests. But each decision was a product, too, of a *cooperative* endeavor to achieve a better understanding of the nation's needs and to resolve its problems in accord with its ideals. Moreover, this was not the sort of meeting at which everyone arrived inflexibly committed to a set of clear objectives, and compromised no more than he was forced to. It was the sort in which not even the Virginians knew exactly what they wanted at the outset, the sort from which the great majority departed rather awed by what they had achieved and with their thinking greatly changed by the collective effort.

Thus "the nationalist assault" by no means carried everything before it. Instead, the fierce resistance vocalized by Paterson and Read became increasingly imposing as it coalesced with opposition based on different concerns. Three delegates—no more—were rigidly committed to a "merely federal" system, but Robert Yates and John Lansing could control New York, and Luther Martin, who was present from June 9, often managed to divide the Maryland contingent. For each of these obstructionists, moreover, there were several other members whose reluctance to surrender local powers to majorities in Congress was compounded by the general distrust of popular misrule. Although the delegations from Connecticut and South Carolina were especially inclined to distrust a scheme that would erect a stronger central government on greater popular involvement, almost every delegation was composed of men who differed widely in their judgments of the people's competence as well as in their willingness to shift additional responsibilities to federal hands. As the smaller states discovered partial allies, sometimes here and sometimes there, the democratic nationalists encountered mounting opposition and suffered two significant defeats.

The Virginia Plan provided for election of the senate by the lower house from persons nominated by the states. On June 7, over loud complaints from Madison and Wilson, majorities in every delegation overturned this proposition in favor of election of the senate by the legislatures of the states. Nearly everyone agreed that the selection of the senate by the lower house might give the people's representatives an overweaning influence, but few were willing to entrust election of the upper house directly to the people, as Wilson recommended. Doubting that the people were equipped to make a fit selection or insisting that a senate chosen in that way would prove unable to defend minorities against majority demands, many members saw election by the local legislatures simply as a lesser evil. Many others, though, including several members from the larger states, were forcefully impressed by the insistence of John Dickinson (Delaware) and Roger Sherman (Connecticut) that selection by the local legislatures would ensure the regular expression of the views of the states as states, assure a federal harmony, and offer firm securities against potential federal usurpations.[23]

Madison was deeply disappointed. Before the meeting opened, he had seen that the pernicious "interventions" of the states in federal affairs could be defeated partly by excluding them from direct participation in the choice of federal officials. In the earliest deliberations, he had heard James Wilson say that he preferred "to derive not only both branches of the legislature from the people, without the intervention of the state legislatures, but the executive also, in order to make them as independent as possible of each other as well as of the states."[24] Madison could not agree, as yet, to popular election of the other branches, sharing the majority's opinion that this might render them unable to defend minorities or to resist the people's passing whims. But he decidedly concurred with Wilson that he wanted to avoid "too great an agency of the state governments in the general one."[25] Fearing that selection of the senate by the states could build into the system just the flaw that was destroying the Confederation, he also saw that it must either reinforce demands for equal voting, which would be an "inadmissable" inequity, or else produce an upper house whose membership would be too large to give the government the "coolness," "wisdom," and "stability" expected from a senate.[26]

This defeat, however, was immediately followed by another, which was equally severe. On June 8, Madison supported a proposal to extend the federal negative to cover *all* state laws, which is what he had preferred from the beginning.[27] He would, in fact, appeal repeatedly for this provision through the weeks ahead, believing even at the close of the convention that such a veto was a better instrument for overturning local legislation harmful to the Union than federal courts could be—and, of course, the *only* tool with which the federal government could intervene directly in the states in order to protect minorities against majority transgressions of their rights.[28] From early in the meeting, Madison had pleaded with the other delegates to recognize that they were not assembled merely to repair the defects of the Union. It was necessary also, he insisted, to provide more certainly "for the security of private rights and the steady dispensation of justice." "Interferences with these," he said, "were evils which had more perhaps than anything else produced this convention."[29] The argument was powerfully effective. In the end, it won the war, for the convention did propose a democratic remedy for democratic ills, both by designing an enlarged republic consciously intended to avoid the errors of the early revolutionary constitutions and by placing

prohibitions on the sorts of local legislation that Madison especially condemned. But although the great majority appproved of the Virginian's
objects, they disapproved his means. He lost the battle to extend the veto,
7 states to 3, and the convention later voted to dispense with it entirely,
preferring to rely on the federal courts to overturn state legislation inconsistent with the Constitution or with federal laws.[30]

The easy part was over. On June 11, even in the aftermath of Paterson's impassioned protest, the Committee voted 7 states to 3, with Maryland divided and New Hampshire not yet present, for proportional
representation in the lower house. Only tiny Delaware and antinational
New York, where Alexander Hamilton was regularly outvoted by his colleagues, sided with New Jersey on the question. As Madison had feared,
however, the increasing protests from the smaller states and the decision
for election of the senate by the legislatures of the states had strengthened
advocates for an equality between them. Just before the crucial ballot on
the lower house, Roger Sherman had suggested that the lower house
should be apportioned according to the states' free populations, but that
every state should keep its equal suffrage in the senate. By moving to revive
the old Confederation formula, which counted slaves as three-fifths of a
person for the purposes of requisitions, Wilson headed off an argument
that might have split the large-state coalition. Nevertheless, the nationalists' impressive triumph on the lower house was followed by a very close
decision on the Senate, where Sherman's motion for equality was narrowly
rejected, 6 to 5: Connecticut, New York, New Jersey, Delaware, and Maryland approving the motion, Massachusetts, Pennsylvania, Virginia, North
Carolina, South Carolina, and Georgia voting no.

A combination of concerns had joined to check the nationalist momentum. On June 13, the Committee of the Whole reported its amended
resolutions to the House, but the convention then immediately adjourned
in order to permit opponents to prepare alternatives to the Virginia Plan.
In his record of debates, Madison reported that John Dickinson approached him privately and said, "You see the consequence of pushing
things too far. Some of the members from the small states . . . are friends
to a good national government, but we would sooner submit to a foreign
power than submit to be deprived of an equality of suffrage in both
branches of the legislature and thereby be thrown under the domination
of the large states."[31] Madison, however, had insisted from the first that
the convention ought to recommend a plan that would be "right and
necessary in itself," trusting that the reputation of its members and the
influence of "enlightened" citizens throughout the Union could secure
its ratification.[32] In addition, he had listened carefully to two weeks of
debates, during which his several allies had improved considerably on the

reasoning that he had brought to the convention. In consequence, in some respects, he had become a more consistent "nationalist" than he had been at the beginning of the meeting. He could now envision a re-formed regime in which the states would have no role at all in making or in executing federal decisions. Accordingly, as he conceived it, the convention had already gone too far toward meeting the demand that "the citizens of the states [should] be represented both *individually* and *collectively*" in the new Congress, too far toward recognizing that election of the senate by the states was necessary to provide them with a "means of defending themselves against encroachments of the national government."[33] And so, as the convention entered on the great debate that culminated in the famous compromise between the large states and the small states, Madison resisted with increasing stubbornness and passion. He would be among the last to come to terms with Dickinson's appeal.

William Paterson's New Jersey Resolutions, introduced on June 15, were thrown together quickly by the coalition that had voted for an equal senate days before. This coalition was united only by its opposition to the plan of June 13, and its proposals did not represent the real desires of any of their framers. As Dickinson had said, many of the members from the smaller states were not opposed to an effective "national" system. In order to protect themselves from large-state domination, they were willing to ally themselves with those who were. But if the large-state nationalists would bend a bit, the Delawaran had hinted, both his own state and New Jersey would support a vigorous, bicameral regime. To them, the contest with the larger states was not a controversy over *how much* power should be granted to the central government, nor was it a debate about the merits of a complex system. On both these points, their sympathies were closer to the nationalists' than to their temporary allies', and Paterson's proposals did not hide that fact. Under the New Jersey Plan, the general government would still have had the power to impose a stamp tax, postal duties, and an impost, to compel compliance with its requisitions, and to regulate the country's interstate and foreign commerce. Federal laws would still have overridden local legislation. A separate executive and independent federal courts would still have shared authority with Congress. For Luther Martin and the two New Yorkers, this was plainly rather much. For Dickinson and others, just as clearly, Paterson's proposal that the legislature should remain a single house, in which each state would keep its equal vote, was mainly an attempt to force concessions from the other side.[34]

Switching back into Committee of the Whole, the delegates compared the Virginia and New Jersey Plans on Saturday, June 16. Paterson and Lansing argued that the resolutions of the first two weeks could never win approval from the states. The nationalists refused to budge. In a brilliant exposition of the two proposals, Wilson argued that the gathering was free to *recommend* whatever changes it considered proper and should not consent to an enlargement of the powers of an indirectly chosen, single-chamber Congress. In his finest speech of the convention, Edmund Randolph reasoned that the members had to choose between a power to coerce the states, which could not work, and power to command the people, for which the present, single-chamber Congress was unfit.

Hamilton monopolized the floor on Monday, June 18, for a speech that would be talked about for years. Paterson's proposals, he insisted, were totally inadequate to the "exigences" that had produced the meeting; "two sovereignties cannot coexist." Even the Virginia Plan, he argued, was "but pork still, with a little change of the sauce." It could neither counteract the power of the many to oppress the few nor the variety of forces that would lead most individuals to favor their provincial governments in any contest with the general one. What should the convention do? Opinion would not tolerate an abolition of the states, although he saw "no *other*" reason for rejecting such a proposition. But for himself, he said, "he had no scruple in declaring . . . that the British government was the best in the world, and that he doubted much whether anything short of it would do in America." He certainly believed that the convention "ought to go as far in order to attain stability and permanency as republican principles will admit." How far that ought to be he illustrated with a third plan of his own, calling for a senate and executive to serve for life, greater powers for the latter branch, and the appointment of provincial governors by Congress.[35]

Madison completed the comparison of the Virginia and New Jersey Plans on Tuesday morning, June 19. Ignoring Hamilton, he argued in his longest speech to date that the New Jersey Plan would neither "preserve the Union" nor remedy the ills "which prevail within the states individually as well as those which affect them collectively." It would not prevent the states from injuring each other, from violating federal treaties, or from encroaching on the federal authority in other ways. It offered no corrective for "the dreadful class of evils" flowing from the "multiplicity," "injustices," and "impotence" of the states' internal legislation. Drawing on his preconvention writings, Madison insisted that the histories of all confederations showed that they were far more likely to be ruined by "the tendency of the particular members to usurp" the general powers than by any danger from the opposite extreme. Paterson's proposals still ignored this fundamental lesson. Making no provision for a popular ratification of the plan, they failed to make the federal authority even legally superior to local legislation. They depended, rather, on a federal power of coercion, which could never be effectively employed except against the smallest members of the Union. "He begged the smaller states . . . to consider the situation" that would actually result if they insisted on these resolutions. He asked them to consider their condition if their adamance should end in dissolution of the Union. If the Union should dissolve, the smaller states would either find themselves entirely at the mercy of their larger neighbors or compelled to enter small confederations, which their larger neighbors still would not approve on principles of equal suffrage. In neither case would they be safer than "under a general government pervading with equal energy every part of the empire and having an equal interest in protecting every part."[36]

As soon as Madison completed his remarks, the meeting voted 7 states to 3, with Maryland again divided, to adhere to the Virginia Plan. The delegates had needed less than three full days to reconfirm their general agreement that a strictly federal reform, however thorough, simply could not meet the needs of Union.

Little else, however, was decided by the vote of June 19, on which Connecticut, by siding with the larger states, had merely signaled its commitment to accommodation. As soon as the convention turned again to the amended resolutions of May 29, Lansing moved to vest the legislative power in a single house. Connecticut switched sides again to reproduce the characteristic 6-4-1 division: Massachusetts, Pennsylvania, and the four states to the south of the Potomac facing Connecticut, New York, New Jersey, and Delaware, with Maryland divided. Indeed, it soon became apparent that the conflict over representation overshadowed and impinged on every lesser disagreement. The convention managed, with increasing difficulty, to confirm its preference for a bicameral system. It voted once again for popular election of the lower house and state election of the upper. It reached agreement on a two-year term for representatives and six years for senators. At every step, however, members fearful of a wholly national reform attempted to insert provisions that would give the states a larger role in paying or selecting federal officials. Small-state delegates attempted a variety of schemes that might disrupt the large-state coalition. Though Madison and Hamilton insisted that the little states had no real reason to expect a combination of the large ones, because the most important differences within the Union were between the North and the South, William Samuel Johnson of Connecticut replied that the convention had to form a government for states as well as people and that even Mason had admitted that the states should have some means to guarantee their rights and place within the federal system.[37]

By the end of June, when the convention voted 6-4-1 (as usual) for proportional representation in the lower house, the meeting was approaching dissolution, and the coalition of the larger states was showing patent signs of serious internal stress.[38] At this point, Connecticut again proposed the compromise that Dickinson and Sherman had suggested weeks before, putting the proposal now in the language of an ultimatum. Remarking that the reconstructed system could be "partly national" in nature, but should continue "partly federal" as well, Oliver Ellsworth said that he was not entirely disappointed that the meeting had approved proportional representation in the lower house, which would conform to national ideas and offer safety to the larger states. But he could see no ground for compromise and no alternative to the collapse of the convention and the Union if the larger states would not concede an equal senate.[39]

Madison and Wilson still refused to blink. "If the minority of the people of America refuse to coalesce with the majority on just and proper principles," the Pennsylvanian said, "a separation . . . could never happen on better grounds."[40] Madison was less choleric only in his phrasing. "He was much disposed," he said, "to concur in any expedient not inconsistent with fundamental principles that would remove the difficulty concerning the rule of representation. But he could neither be convinced that the rule contended for was just, nor necessary for the safety of the small states against the large."[41] "He admitted that every peculiar interest, whether in any class of citizens or any description of states, ought to be secured as far as possible." He had even been considering a rule that would assure the North and the South that each would dominate one house of Congress, for "wherever there is danger of attack, there ought to be given a constitutional power of defense."[42] But the smaller states, he said, had no distinctive interests simply as a consequence of being small, no reason to expect a combination of the larger. Massachusetts, Pennsylvania, and Virginia were as different as could possibly be wished "by the most jealous citizen of the most jealous state. In point of manners, religion, and . . . staple productions, they were as dissimilar as any three other states in the Union."[43]

State equality, moreover, *would* infringe the "fundamental principles" of equity and majority control. Accordingly, although Madison agreed with Dr. Johnson "that the mixed nature of the government ought to be kept in view," that state preserves should be protected, he denied that this required that the states be represented equally—or even directly—in either house of Congress. To give "*unequal* portions of the people" equal voices in the upper house would be to give a small minority the power to defeat legitimate majority desires. It would enable this minority to use its power to extort concessions on a host of other matters. Madison insisted that an equal senate was "confessedly unjust." It would exaggerate the North's superiority of population and perhaps perpetuate a sectional imbalance that was tending otherwise toward equilibrium with every passing day. It would "infuse mortality into a Constitution which we wished to last forever," for the upper house, on such a plan, would be no better than "another edition of [the Confederation] Congress," "absolutely dependent on the states." "I would compromise on this question if I could do it on correct principles," Madison repeated, "but otherwise not. If the old fabric of the Confederation must be the groundwork of the new, we must fail."[44]

On the final day of June, with the convention nearly at a deadlock, Wilson said that he could go so far as to concede that every state should have one senator, and that each state should get another for each 100,000 of their people, which would make a membership of twenty-six. Madison announced that he could go that far as well, provided that the Senate was selected in a manner that would give its members a due independence of the states. But Rufus King of Massachusetts spoke for all three men when he declared that "he could never listen to an equality of votes." "A government founded in a vicious principle of representation," all of them believed, "must be as shortlived as it would be unjust."

Gunning Bedford's sharp reply suggested that the next few days could settle the convention's fate. "*I do not, gentlemen, trust you,*" the Delaware attorney said.[45] The coalition of the large states during the convention seemed to Bedford a sufficient warning of the consequences that could follow if the smaller states submitted to the "degredation" of the Virginia Plan, and he refused to be intimidated by the prospect that the large states would permit the Union to collapse. "If they do," he warned, "the small ones will find some foreign ally . . . who will take them by the hand."[46]

Bedford soon apologized for this remark, but his apology did not diminish its effects. Adjourning over Sunday, the convention moved without additional debate on Monday, July 2, to a decision on Connecticut's proposal. The motion for an equal senate failed on an even division: Connecticut, New York, New Jersey, Delaware, and Maryland in favor of the measure; Massachusetts, Pennsylvania, Virginia, North Carolina, and South Carolina opposed; Georgia now divided.[47] With the meeting at an impasse, C. C. Pinckney recommended the appointment of a grand committee to devise a resolution. Only Madison and Wilson disapproved, sensing that the tide was turning irreversibly toward the construction of a bargain—as, indeed, it was. Voting for a member from each state, the delegates constructed a committee that included Martin, Ellsworth, Bedford, Paterson, and Yates, but not a single member from the larger states who had not hinted at an interest in conciliation. The convention then adjourned till Thursday to celebrate the anniversary of Independence and permit the grand committee to prepare a plan.

To Madison and Wilson, the result was not a compromise at all, but a surrender to the smaller states—and one that seriously marred the symmetry of the evolving system. In exchange for equal representation in the upper house, the smaller states accepted proportional representation in the lower *and* agreed to bar the senate from initiating or amending money bills. Two of Madison's Virginia colleagues, Randolph and George Mason, saw the clause concerning money bills as a valuable concession, since an equal senate would be dominated by the smaller northern states and, therefore, in contemporary thinking, by the shipping interests rather than the agricultural majority of people.[48] Madison and Wilson, on the other hand, regarded this "concession" as worse than none at all. The clause might keep the senate from contributing consistency and wisdom to a vital class of legislation, but it would not prevent minorities from blocking necessary measures or from using their position in the senate to compel majority concessions on a host of other things.[49] Throughout the next two weeks, the leading nationalists persisted stubbornly in trying to reverse the swelling current favoring the Connecticut scheme.

Madison was clearer now than he had been when the convention opened on how to solve the problems he perceived. He had intended from the start to build a more effective system by removing the state legislatures from their current, equal role in making federal decisions, as well as by destroying their capacity to rejudge federal acts. But neither he nor any of his fellows had been able from the start to think consistently in terms of fully concurrent state and general governments, each of which would rise entirely from and act directly on the individual members of society. Madison had entered the discussions willing to concede the states a role in nominating members of the upper house, and he had entered them anticipating that the states would have a larger part in executing federal commands. At the beginning of July, he still desired a federal negative on local legislation, which would operate directly on the states as states and even make the national government "a branch of the state legislatures" in this respect.[50] But although he still believed that there should be a federal power to prevent the states from taking actions inconsistent with their federal duties or infringing private rights, the concept of concurrent governments was clear enough by now that he no longer thought the states' cooperation would be necessary for enforcement of federal laws. As early as May 31, he had abandoned the provision for a federal power of coercion, and he had grown increasingly determined to exclude the states from any role whatever in the choice of federal officials. In this sense, he had become a more consistent "nationalist" than he had been at the beginning of the meeting. Therefore, he denounced the earlier decision for election of the senate by the states and drew the line inflexibly on an equality of voting.

Madison's rigidity on this important issue was not as inconsistent as it may appear with his conviction that the future of humanity might be determined by the Philadelphia Convention, or even with his reputation as a skillful parliamentary tactician. He was as dedicated to a thoroughly republican regime as to a lasting federal union, and nearly all of his concerns were vitally affected by this issue. An equal senate violated democratic principles, endangered the "perpetuation" of the Union, and threatened the essential interests of Virginia. Moreover, Madison was not the weak-kneed politician of the myth. He knew that legislative victories occasionally called for a successful game of "chicken," and he still believed, not only that the smaller states would blink if their opponents could maintain a solid front, but also that the larger ones might *have* to stare them down in order to complete a plan that would be ratified by states that were essential to its ultimate adoption.[51]

In fact, however, fissures in the large-state coalition were becoming wider every day. The two weeks after the committee's introduction of the compromise proposal saw a jumble of confusing motions. Regional considerations, which had lurked below the early 6-4-1 divisions—in which all the southern states had voted with the large-state block—now bubbled to the surface. In arguments about a periodic census and admission of new states, as well as in maneuvers over allocation of the seats in the first house of representatives, members hostile to the three-fifths rule or fearful of the West confronted southerners who realized that they would be outnumbered 8 to 5 in the projected senate and insisted on provisions that would guarantee a speedy reinforcement by new, southwestern states.[52] The smaller northern states proved willing to concede a little on these points in order to secure their principal objective; and as this happened, it became increasingly apparent that several influential members from the larger states were less and less inclined toward a continued confrontation. Not only did they realize that the convention's work would surely be rejected if the smaller states walked out, but some of them conceded that a senate that would represent the states as states might help maintain a federal equilibrium while standing at a proper distance from the people. Mason, who was anything but moderate in his instinctive inclinations, said that he would "bury his bones in this city rather than expose his country to the consequences of a dissolution of the convention without anything being done."[53]

Madison was less inclined to a surrender. Lansing and Yates left the meeting on July 11, depriving New York of its vote. (Hamilton had left some days before and would return, as a nonvoting member, only to be present at the end.) Three days later, Madison delivered a final plea. It had been said, he opened, that the reconstructed Union should be "partly national" but also "partly federal" in structure, that this suggested that the states should have an equal vote in one branch of the Congress. "If there was any solidity in this distinction, he was ready to abide by it." But Madison had changed his views sufficiently since the beginning of the meeting that he now saw *no* solidity in this distinction. As modified by the convention to this point, the plan he was supporting now would operate in every instance "on the people individually." "The practicability of making laws, with coercive sanctions, for the states as political bodies, had been exploded on all hands."[54]

Madison was willing, he had said, to violate proportionality sufficiently to concede each state at least a single member in the senate.[55] He was willing, now, to talk of other measures that might temper members' fears for the specific interests of their states.[56] If this was not enough, however, he believed that the convention was compelled to choose between "departing from justice in order to conciliate the smaller states and the minority of the people of the U.S. or . . . displeasing these by justly gratifying the larger states and the majority of the people." For himself, he had no doubts about the proper option. "It was in vain to purchase concord in the convention on terms which would perpetuate discord among their constituents." The convention, he insisted, should "pursue a plan which would bear the test of examination" on its merits. It should put aside the fear "that the people of the small states would obstinately refuse to accede to a government founded on just principles and promising them substantial protection." "If the principal states, comprehending a majority of the people of the U.S., should concur in a just and judicious plan, he had the firmest hopes that all the other states would by degrees accede."[57]

Despite the absence of New York, the final pleas of Madison and Wilson for a compromise that would have minimized disparities between the states, although without conceding equal voting, were defeated 6 to 4. On July 16, the convention voted 5-4-1 for the committee's compromise proposal: Connecticut, New Jersey, Delaware, Maryland, and North Carolina in favor; Pennsylvania, Virginia, South Carolina, and Georgia opposed; Massachusetts now divided. It was not as close as the roll call might suggest. New York, New Hampshire, and Rhode Island were all unrepresented at the time. All would probably have favored equal representation in at least one house. In addition, several moderates from Georgia, Pennsylvania, and Virginia sympathized to a considerable degree with those in Massachusetts, Maryland, and North Carolina, who voted for the Connecticut plan. Madison, nevertheless, opposed it to the end. Indeed, when the large states caucused in the aftermath of their defeat, he was undoubedly among the number who "supposing that no good government could or would be built on that foundation, . . . would have concurred in a firm opposition to the smaller states and in a separate recommendation, if eventually necessary." Few large-state delegates, however, were willing to continue with this game. "The time was wasted," Madison complained, "in vague conversation on the subject." All the members from the larger states returned to the convention, and the little states were satisfied from that point on that there would be no serious attempt to overturn the critical decision.[58]

The bargain of July 16 assured that the convention would succeed. This is not to say that the completion of the work proved quick or easy. Several complicated passages remained, and more than one debate became quite heated. Other compromises were required in order to produce a document that every delegation could consent to sign. Still, none of the remaining difficulties blocked the members' progress as completely as the conflict over representation; and nearly all the delegates appear to have assumed, from that point on, that they would finish what they had begun.

In hindsight, it is clear, the delegates' decision that the general government would represent both individuals and states did more than just resolve a single conflict. Both the large states and the small, the North together with the South, could now anticipate that each would soon control one house of Congress. With each assured of a capacity to counter threats to its essential interests, every delegate felt freer to address the national ills that none of them denied. Almost all the delegates had made it clear by now that they intended to define a middle ground between the ineffectuality of the Confederation and excessive concentration of authority in central hands. Nearly all agreed, as well, that what they wanted in a senate was a body that would stand at a sufficient distance from the people and the lower house to check majority oppression, but one that would be chosen in a manner that would not offend the democratic precepts of the Revolution. With the decision that the upper house would represent the states, whose legislatures would select its members, the delegates had satisfied demands for more protection for states' rights. They had also reconfirmed a mode of indirect election that promised to secure the senate's independence from the lower house without provoking popular suspicions. Cutting through a thicket of entangled problems, the compromise permitted the convention to resume a path along which arguments among its members could be guided by their general agreements.

For Madison, the bargain of July 16 was nonetheless a devastating blow. It tempted him to risk a walkout by the smaller states and the completion of a constitution by a rump of large-state delegations. Along with the excision of the federal negative on local acts, it was undoubtedly the major reason why he wrote, at the conclusion of the meeting, that he feared that the completed plan would "neither effectually answer its national object nor prevent the local mischiefs which everywhere excite disgusts."[59] Indeed, his discontent was so profound that many analysts have followed Irving Brant in seeing it as possibly the most important watershed in his career. The small-state triumph, they have said, initiated a retreat from an expansive view of federal powers which originated in the second half of the convention, gathered new momentum during Washington's administration, and culminated in the strict-constructionist and states'-rights stance of the Virginia Resolutions of 1798. The dominant impression of the framer's whole career is grounded in important ways on this interpretation, as are many of the best- known explications of his founding vision.[60]

The evidence for this interpretation is impressive; and given the importance of the question, it demands a close consideration. Nevertheless, I am convinced that careful reexamination shows that the prevailing view is badly off the mark. It opens with a misinterpretation of the framer's purposes and politics in the years before the meeting and ends in a misunderstanding of the 1790s. It rests on a flawed analysis of how he changed as a result of his defeat. And it contributes heavily to a mistaken, very partial comprehension of his role and contributions during both halves of the Constitutional Convention.

Madison did certainly initiate and help to lead a "nationalist" offensive at the Philadelphia Convention—providing that we use this word as the delegates themselves employed it *for the purposes of this particular debate.* Madison, that is to say, embarked on the deliberations seeking national supremacy wherever national interests were involved. Influenced by his allies in the battle with the smaller states, he came to be convinced that such authority demanded the complete exclusion of the local legislatures from a role in choosing federal officials or in executing federal commands. With other leading "nationalists," he bitterly opposed the critical decisions on the senate, both because they seemed unfair *and* because he knew that they were consciously intended, by many on the other side, to build "state agency" into a "partly federal" system. During this initial phase of the convention, Madison expressed almost no fear of concentrated central power. Some of his proposals and remarks can easily suggest that he was willing to pursue consolidation nearly to the point of turning

states into the counties of a great republic. It is not surprising, then, that
it is often said that his desires seem very similar to Hamilton's at this point
in the work.[61]

Later in his life, however, Madison repeatedly objected to the supposition "that the term *national*," as applied "in the early stages of the convention, particularly in the propositions of Mr. Randolph, was equivalent
to *unlimited* or consolidated." The term was used, he wrote, in order to
distinguish the Virginia Plan and the emerging constitution from the existing "*federal* government," which rested on the states instead of on the
people. "Not more than two or three members," he added, "and they
rather theoretically than practically, were in favor of an unlimited government founded on a consolidation of the states."[62] During his retirement,
the framer also had occasion to deny that the Virginia Plan's initial, vague
description of the reach of national powers was ever "meant to be inserted
in . . . the text of the Constitution." A definition or enumeration of these
powers, he insisted, "was to be the task of the convention." "If there
could be any doubt that this was intended and so understood by the convention, it would be removed by the course of the proceedings."[63]

Madison was absolutely right on both these points—so plainly so, it
seems to me, that serious attention to his warnings might have saved some
of the finest studies of the Constitutional Convention from some evident
mistakes. For example, many of the major studies of the gathering suggest
that the convention saw a serious division—often understood as an important part of bigger battles pitting nationalists against localists, large
states against small, or advocates of a large republic against defenders of
a small republic—over whether there should be a general grant of legislative powers or a constitutional enumeration.[64] In fact, however, there
was never any serious division at the Constitutional Convention over
whether, as opposed to *when*, the meeting should attempt a clearer limitation of the legislative powers. Like Madison himself, the overpowering
majority of members intended, from the first, "to draw a line of demar-
cation which would give to the general government every power requisite
for general purposes, and leave to the states every power which might be
most beneficially administered by them."[65]

The Virginia Plan initially suggested that the reconstructed Congress
should be vested with the legislative rights already granted by the Articles
of Confederation, together with the right to legislate "in all [other] cases
to which the separate states are incompetent, or in which the harmony of
the United States may be interrupted by the exercise of individual legislation." On May 31, when the convention reached this clause, Charles
Pinckney and John Rutledge objected to its vagueness, saying that they
"could not well decide how to vote until they should see an exact enu-

meration." Pierce Butler called on Edmund Randolph, who had introduced the plan, to clarify its meaning. The Virginia governor "disclaimed any intention to give indefinite powers to the national legislature." Madison then said

> that he had brought with him into the convention a strong bias in favor of an enumeration and definition of the powers necessary to be exercised by the national legislature; but had also brought doubts concerning its practicability. His wishes remained unaltered; but his doubts had become stronger. What his opinion might ultimately be, he could not yet tell. But he should shrink from nothing which should be found essential.

The convention voted 9 to 0 to retain the original clause.[66]

Several observations may be made about this episode. Although most analysts have stressed his growing doubts about the workability of an enumeration (in part because most analysts believe that he had been a broad constructionist throughout the 1780s), Madison did say that his original desire for an enumeration "remained unaltered."[67] He did *not* express a preference for a broad grant of power. What he said, when his remarks are studied in the context of the Carolinians' request for an immediate enumeration, is that he did not think that he or the convention were prepared at this conjuncture even to decide that an enumeration would be workable, much less to get into an argument about its contents. As was pointed out above, Madison's objective in the early days of the convention was to keep the delegates from getting sidetracked into other issues until they could define some common ground. And this is just what they agreed on. The 9 to 0 vote was not a *choice between* enumeration and a general grant of powers (although the latter might itself, of course, have been so phrased as to impose strict limits on the Congress). It was simply a decision to postpone a full discussion.[68]

The full discussion was held on July 16, soon after the decision on the senate. The result virtually recapitulated the earlier proceedings. Butler called again for explanation of the hazy wording. Gorham answered that "the vagueness of the terms constitutes the propriety of them. We are now establishing general principles, to be extended hereafter into details which will be precise and explicit." Rutledge moved again to commit the clause immediately to a committee, but the motion failed on an even division (with Virginia voting *in favor* of the commital). The matter was resumed quite briefly on the following morning, when Sherman moved an alteration of the language of the clause and read a sketch of an enumeration as an illustration of his thinking. A brief discussion made it clear that Sherman wanted to exclude direct taxation from the legislature's powers, and his motion was defeated 8 to 2. The members satisfied themselves at this conjuncture with approval of a different, minor change of phrasing in the clause.[69] And this is where the business stood on July 26, when they appointed a Committee of Detail. No one had suggested that the language of May 29 could be incorporated in a finished constitution. There had never been an argument or vote about the merits of a general grant *instead* of an enumeration. The discussions had been overwhelmingly concerned with *when*, not whether, the convention should attempt to clarify the resolution. And, indeed, when the Committee of Detail included an enumeration in its report, no one even asked why it had done so.

Clearly, Madison himself, as he insisted later in his life, had no intention of confiding an indefinite extent of legislative power to the reconstructed Congress. After the report of the Committee of Detail, he proved, in fact, to be the meeting's most consistent advocate of strict, though full, enumeration. On August 18, he moved successfully to refer a lengthy list of additional enumerated powers to the Committee of Detail. On September 14, Benjamin Franklin moved to add a congressional power to cut canals, and Madison urged extending this to include a power to create corporations. Like his early effort to prevent a premature attempt at an enumeration, both of these proposals have been misinterpreted as evidence of the enormous reach of his "nationalism" during the convention. Carefully considered, I submit, they are in fact among the clearest indications of its limits. The powers he proposed to add in August were far from extensive. Several were so obviously required—powers over a seat of national government, to dispose of western lands, to organize western governments, and so forth—that his attempt to add them can be seen more reasonably as one of many indications that he wished to leave as little as he could to implication. The motion of September 14 was plainly prompted by this motive. In moving that a power of incorporation should be added to the power to construct canals, Madison was thinking mainly of internal improvements such as those by the Potomac Company in Virginia. He may conceivably have had another national bank in mind, for he had agonized about the absence of a constitutional authority to incorporate a bank in 1781. Suggestively, however, Rufus King maintained that a power to charter corporations was unnecessary, probably suggesting that he thought it already implicit. Similarly, Gouverneur Morris argued that the power to create a university, another of Madison's desires, was implicit in the power over a seat of government.[70] All of these maneuvers, I suggest, should be interpreted in light of Madison's insistence in *The Federalist* that every omission from the Constitution of grants of necessary powers would become a ground for "necessary usurpations of power, every precedent of which is a germ of unnecessary and multiplied repetitions."[71]

After the convention, Madison repeatedly insisted that the Constitution should be understood less as a grant of new authority than as a means of rendering effective the powers that the central government had always had (at least on paper).[72] Usually dismissed as an expedient response to Antifederalist objections, these statements might instead remind us of the reasoning behind the resolutions of May 29, which tells us much about the limits of their author's wishes. Other than the power over trade, as I have argued, Madison believed that the existing Articles of Union granted Congress positive authority to do most of the things a general government should do. It was the inability of the Confederation government to carry out these tasks—the structural and operational deficiencies of the existing system, not the definition of its business—with which his preconvention thinking had been principally concerned. From the beginning of the meeting, he advocated an *effective* central government, not a vastly swollen one. Madison had never been an unreserved enthusiast for centralizing change, and he did not become an advocate of concentrated power at the Constitutional Convention. He wanted a reform that would impinge on state authority only when the clear necessities of union or the fundamental liberties intended by the Revolution seemed to be endangered.

The very speeches always cited to support the view that Madison "shared Hamilton's quest for a unitary central government,"[73] also say in passing that he sought a "mixed" regime, that he intended to "preserve the state rights, as carefully as the trials by jury."[74] Two speeches have been singled out most often for quotation. Closely studied, neither actually confirms the usual interpretation—least of all when often-quoted passages are put into their context.

On June 21, William Samuel Johnson of Connecticut remarked that Madison and Wilson, unlike their ally from New York, "wished to leave the states in possession of a considerable, though a subordinate, jurisdiction." Johnson challenged them, however, to explain how "the individuality of the states" could be preserved, their rights effectually secured, if the states were not to be able to defend themselves with "a distinct and equal vote."[75] Madison answered that the histories of all confederations showed that state encroachments on the general government were actually the greater danger. But suppose, he said, for purposes of argument, "that indefinite power should be given to the general legislature and the states reduced to corporations dependent on the general legislature; why should it follow that the general government would take from the states any branch of their power as far as its operation was beneficial and its contintiance desirable to the people?" The national legislators would be the representatives of the people. Insofar as the general government could practicably "extend its care to all the minute objects . . . of the local jurisdictions," its powers would not be improper or the people less free. Insofar as it could not attend to matters of this sort, the general government itself would wish to maintain the subordinate ones. "Supposing therefore a tendency in the general government to absorb the state governments"—a supposition he had just disputed—"no fatal consequence could result."[76] In context, it is clear, Madison was not *advocating* an unlimited central government, which he plainly thought impracticable. He was suggesting, rather, that even the fulfillment of the deepest fears of his opponents would prove less fatal to the people's liberty than a continuation of the present "independence" of the states.[77]

The second speech that has been quoted endlessly to bolster the old interpretation is his longer one of June 28:

> The two extremes before us are a perfect separation [or independence] and a perfect incorporation of the 13 states. . . . In the first case the smaller states would have everything to fear from the larger. In the last they would have nothing to fear. The true policy of the small states therefore lies in promoting those principles and that form of government which will most approximate the states to the condition of counties.

Again, Madison was not defending either of the two extremes he mentioned, and he was not suggesting that the modified Virginia Plan would change the states into administrative districts. He was suggesting that the smaller states mistook their own best interests in insisting on a strictly "federal" system. He was trying yet again, as he so often did, to turn to the fears of his opponents to his own advantage.[78]

Early in his preconvention thinking, Madison had written Edmund Randolph that the possibilities before the country extended, theoretically, from total independence for the thirteen states to their complete consolidation into a single, national republic. In that letter, he rejected both of these extremes, as he was doing now, in favor of a "middle ground" that would provide for national supremacy where common measures were required, but would preserve the states' authority where uniformity was not essential. He sought this "middle ground," not just because he thought a more complete consolidation could not be achieved, but because he never doubted that a fragmentation of the Union *or* excessive concentration of authority in federal hands would eventually betray the Revolution.

Another chapter will be necessary to explain how Madison defined "excessive"—and thus to reach a balanced view of all of his distinctive

contributions to the framing. But even for the early weeks of the proceedings, if we fail to recognize how firmly he rejected any option other
than the "middle ground," we will mistake his purposes, misread his
words, and end with an imperfect grasp of what he taught and what he
learned at the convention. This, indeed, has happened with distressing
regularity as analysts have studied Madison's conduct at the meeting, usually in light of an imperfect or mistaken understanding of his stands
throughout the decade. During the extended conflict with the smaller
states, Madison was fierce in his determination to create a general government that would suffice for all the nation's common needs; he was so
fixed in this intention that an analyst can easily forget those early references to "middle ground." Phrases lifted from their qualifying context
then may be combined with Madison's insistence on the federal negative
on local legislation, with an entirely proper emphasis on his determination
to exclude the states from federal decisions, and with an undue fascination with his argument for an extension of the sphere of the republic to
build a case that simply contradicts his early and repeated statements that
he meant to find a middle way between state sovereignty and a consolidated national system, that he meant to guard states' rights as well as to
invigorate the Union. But even on July 16, Madison was a determined
"nationalist" only in his view of how the new regime should work, not in
his opinion of the work it ought to do. It is impossible to place him at a
single point on any single spectrum of opinion. On the matter of "state
agency" within the federal structure, he was a radical extremist, standing
at the end of one specific spectrum. On the matter of the quantum of
responsibilities that should be placed in federal hands, he stood much
closer to the middle of a different spectrum of opinion. And in his firm
commitment to a government that would accord entirely with republican
ideals, he cannot be identified at all with many of his closest allies in the
battle with the smaller states. From first to last, he was a "nationalist" who
thought that too much power, placed in hands too distant from the people, might endanger revolutionary ends. And not until we place an equal
emphasis on all of his commitments can we clearly see the whole of his
position at the meeting, the major lessons that he learned, or how he was
in fact affected by his most severe defeats.

CHAPTER SIX

To Redeem the Republican Name

AT TIMES, THE STANDARD VIEW OF MADISON is only slightly out of focus. At other times, however, it distorts a major portion of the subject or leaves it wholly out of view. Certainly, a clear appreciation of his course and contributions has been badly blurred by failure to distinguish his commitment to a general government whose powers would be sovereign within its sphere from his opinion of the reach of the authority, the nature of the duties, that ought to be confided to its hands. Numerous interpretative difficulties can be traced to this confusion. When these difficulties are combined, they can produce an image bearing little real resemblance to Madison himself.

Studies that do not distinguish Madison's desire for an effective central government from a desire for an unlimited or unitary national system underestimate—and sometimes altogether miss—a critical dimension of the tensions he was grappling with at the convention. Genuine consolidationists, though few, were present at the meeting. Their attendance reinforced a potent fear of an excessive concentration of authority in central hands, as did the literally antidemocratic sentiments of several of the framers. Madison was bent on sweeping structural and operational reforms. He was unquestionably a leading "nationalist" in this respect. But Madison was also as committed a republican as any member of the great convention, and even as he battled for a central government that would be wholly "national" in structure, he shared the fears aroused by several of his allies. Thus if we confuse his purposes with theirs, failing to remark how frequently he stood between the higher-flying nationalists and their opponents, we are certain to neglect some of the most significant dimensions of his contributions. If we misjudge his purposes at the beginning of the meeting, we will unavoidably misunderstand the changes that began with his defeats. In the second half of the convention, he struggled constantly to readjust his thoughts to the demands of previous decisions: to identify the novel system that was starting to emerge and to adjust to its peculiar logic. He struggled constantly, as well, to guarantee that the reform would be consistently republican in nature and compatible with the essential interests of his state. Much of this is missed in most examinations of his conduct. Much of it is as essential to a balanced understanding of his vision as a full appreciation of his quarrel with the smaller states.[1]

As Edmund Randolph said before the session of July 16 adjourned, the small-state victory on the construction of the senate threw everything into confusion. Every previous decision, Randolph noted, had been influenced by the expectation that "a proportional representation was to prevail in both branches of the legislature"; all would have to be rethought in light of this new ruling.[2] Every delegate was forced to reconsider how the actions of the central government were likely to affect his state. Madison, who had opposed not merely state equality, but *any* role for the provincial legislatures in selecting federal officials, was also forced to come to terms with the convention's ruling that the reconstructed government was not to be entirely national in structure, that the senate was to represent the states. Few delegates were more profoundly disappointed by this ruling. Few, if any, saw the implications more completely. Nevertheless, a careful reexamination of his course through the remainder of the meeting shows that the Virginian turned in quite a different direction than is usually believed.

Madison did not "reverse his course" as a consequence of the decision of July 16. He did not become "less nationalistic" than he had been while it had appeared that the convention might approve proportional representation in both houses. It is true that he had warned that a surrender to the smaller states could rob the reconstructed government of "every effectual prerogative," making it "as impotent and short lived as the old."[3] Here, however, he predicted the effect that compromise might have on other members from the larger states, not the course he would himself pursue. After the decision on the senate, several members from the smaller middle states began to favor ample federal powers, much as Dickinson had predicted. Many southerners, by contrast, suddenly became more wary. Madison demonstrably did not.

Madison had sought from the beginning of the meeting to create a general government whose powers would extend effectively to all those great and national matters that the states were individually incompetent to handle, together with a federal power to protect minorities from local violations of their rights. Through the second half of the convention, he remained intent on these objectives. He continued to support a federal negative on all state legislation.[4] Unlike other southerners, he powerfully endorsed a federal power to impose a tax on exports.[5] He opposed insertion of provisions limiting the senate's role in making money bills or requiring more than a majority of Congress for the passage of commercial legislation.[6] Near the close of the convention, he moved to place additional specifics on the list of the enumerated powers. I cannot, indeed, identify a single power that he wanted to withhold from Congress after the Great Compromise but had favored before it. He did not reverse his course or change his mind in any fundamental way about the quantum of authority that should be placed in federal hands, the business that the general government should do. He still intended, as he always had, to make that government supreme *within its proper sphere.*[7]

But although the compromise did not significantly change his vision of the proper *scope* of federal powers, it did almost immediately affect his views about how this power should be shared among the different branches of the reconstructed system.[8] At the start of the convention, Madison had seen the indirectly chosen upper house as the branch best suited to control the passions of the people, to secure a place for wisdom and stability in the enlarged republic, and to guard against the mutability, injustices, and multiplicity of laws which he identified as major weaknesses of democratic rule.[9] Through the early weeks of the proceedings, the enormous role that he envisioned for the upper house contrasted sharply with his evident uncertainty about the character and powers of a national executive. His preconvention letters all confessed that he had yet to form a clear opinion on the latter subject. His advice about a constitution for Kentucky had been strongly marked by early revolutionary fears of executive influence and ambitions. Through the early weeks of the convention, he (and the majority of members) planned to give the senate many of the powers that, to us, appear intrinsically executive in nature: to appoint ambassadors and judges, to negotiate with foreign nations, and the like.

The Virginia Plan itself did little more than to suggest the need for a separate executive, and the records of the earliest deliberations on this branch are quite confusing. Edmund Randolph, who had introduced the resolutions, argued earnestly from the beginning against "a unity in the executive department," fearing even a resemblance to a king. George Mason also voted for a plural executive, fearing that a single person would in time become a monarch.[10] According to his own report, Madison involved himself in this preliminary skirmish only to suggest that a decision on the powers of the office should precede a choice between a council and a single man. Rufus King and William Pierce, however, wrote that on

June 1 Madison, together with his colleagues, expressed a fear that great executive authority could end in an "elective monarchy," preferring the construction of a council whose advice could be ignored only at the peril of its head.[11] This was the provision of Virginia's constitution, and it seems entirely likely that Madison agreed with his Virginia colleagues, too, on legislative choice of the executive and on a clause that would exclude its chief from serving two successive terms.[12] On June 4, he spoke against a move by Hamilton and Wilson to make the executive veto absolute, then seconded Wilson's motion to associate the judges in this power, as in New York's Council of Revision. Madison and Wilson both believed that the participation of the judges would make the veto more effective, but Madison also hoped that their participation would restrain the executive branch and favor "consistency, conciseness, perspicuity, and technical propriety in the laws, qualities peculiarly necessary and yet shamefully wanting in our republican codes."[13] The different wishes of these allies was apparent also, on June 5, when Madison agreed with Wilson that it was not a good idea to have the legislature choose the judges, but favored appointment by the senate over Wilson's wish to vest the power in the chief executive alone. In the early going, the convention voted for a single chief executive, to be elected by the legislature for a single term of seven years, and vested powers over treaties and appointments in the senate. It left the matter there until the great debate about the legislature could be settled.

The decision for an equal senate on July 16 struck Madison as inconsistent with majority control, a barrier to the pursuit of general interests, and a potential peril to the South. By this time, moreover, he was forcefully impressed by Wilson's argument that a responsible executive could only be secured by concentrating the authority in the hands of a single accountable official, who would be independent of the legislature for his office.[14] Together, these considerations moved him steadily toward strengthening this branch at the expense of the improperly constructed senate. As early as July 18, he favored an attempt to shift the power to appoint the federal judiciary from the senate to the head of the executive, acting with concurrence of a portion of the upper house. Three days later, he was frank about his reasons:

> The principle of [the great] compromise . . . required . . . that there should should be a concurrence of two authorities, in one of which the people, in the other the states, should be represented. The executive magistrate would be considered as a national official, acting for and equally sympathizing with every part of the United States. If the second [house] alone

should have this power, the judges might be appointed by a minority of the people, [though they would act directly *on* the people rather than the states]. As it would, moreover, throw the appointments entirely into the hands of the Northern states, a perpetual ground of jealousy and discontent would be furnished to the Southern states.[15]

Similarly, on August 23, he argued that the chief executive should have a role in making treaties, as "the senate represented the states alone."[16]

Despite the rulings on the senate, Madison remained committed to an upper house that could effectively restrain the lower.[17] Similarly, he did not become a leading advocate of great executive vigor. For example, he proposed to make it possible to make a peace without executive consent.[18] As late as September 7, he supported Mason's motion to revive an executive council.[19] Nevertheless, as he attempted to adjust his thinking to the ruling that the government would still be "partly federal" in structure, Madison was plainly more inclined to transfer more responsibilities to truly "national" hands, as well as to imagine the executive as a completely equal, fully countervailing branch. Near the end of the proceedings, he opposed a motion to substitute two-thirds of Congress for the three-quarters currently required to override a presidential veto, observing that he wished to arm the president against encroachments on his powers as well as to erect a barrier against "factious injustice."[20] As early as July 19, discontent with state equality, a fear of legislative domination, and a wish to make it possible for an experienced executive to succeed himself (which seemed impossible to reconcile with an election by the Congress) had influenced him to switch decisively to popular election of the head of this department. These changes were the most apparent, most immediate effects of the Connecticut Compromise on his thinking.[21]

A second consequence, unnoticed in the standard literature, was fully as important. By July 14, as has been seen, Madison had come to be completely dedicated to the prospect that the great republic might be made entirely national in structure. The decision of July 16 completely wrecked this hope, compelling him and all the other delegates to form an image of a system neither wholly national nor purely federal in nature, but a novelty compounded of some elements of both—a government in which the upper house, elected by the legislatures of the states and granting each an equal vote, was still to represent the states as states, although the lower house would represent the people. Madison, in fact, was probably the first to make this point explicit, when he argued that the compromise suggested that important powers should be shared "by two authorities, in one of which the people, in the other the states, should be represented." On August 31, he even proposed a complex formula by which the Constitution was to go into effect only after it had won approval both from a majority of people *and* from a majority of states.

Madison said nothing during the convention to suggest that he approved of this unprecedented hybrid; he only talked about its logic and employed that logic to advance specific objects of the moment. Even at the close of the convention, he remained unhappy with how state agency had been retained to constitute a partly federal system, referring to the product as "a feudal system of republics."[22] Nevertheless, there obviously echoed in his mind the earlier insistence of John Dickinson, George Mason, Roger Sherman, and the rest that it was *proper* for the states to be directly represented in the central government, if only to protect their proper share of power in a "mixed" regime. For when he came to write *The Federalist,* he persuasively defended exactly this position—in language very like the language he had heard from his opponents during the convention. He still objected to the *equal* representation of the states, excusing this provision only as a compromise that the convention "must have been" unable to avoid. And yet he now defended the participation of the states as states in the workings of the reconstructed system.[23] Indeed, at the Virginia state convention he said, "If the general government were wholly independent of the governments of the particular states, then, indeed, usurpations might be expected to the fullest extent"; but as the central government "derives its authority from [the state] governments, and from the same source from which their authority is derived," no usurpations need be feared. Far from threatening a gradual absorption of the powers of the states, adoption of the Constitution would "increase the security of liberty more than any government that ever was," since in America the powers ordinarily confided to a single government—and sometimes even to a single branch—would be entrusted to two sets of governments, each of which would watch the other at the same time as its several branches served as an internal check against abuse.[24] This acceptance of a federal role for states as states—and not a change of mind about the powers that should be entrusted to the new regime—was Madison's real reversal in the aftermath of the convention's famous bargain. Before the meeting closed, he had adjusted grudgingly to its peculiar logic. Within nine months, he had become its most effective spokesman.

What had caused this change of mind (assuming, for the moment, that the change was real and not a difference between his public and his private views)? The mounting opposition to the Constitution is an influence not to be denied. *The Federalist* was written to defend the Constitution from its critics, and their criticisms surely forced its advocates to see advantages in clauses they had not especially regarded or had even disapproved.[25] It seems entirely likely that Madison adopted arguments that he had disagreed with during the convention in part because he saw that they might ease the critics' minds. Some interpreters, indeed, would argue that his new position was advanced exclusively for such a purpose, that he was using constitutional provisions he privately despised to further his immediate objectives.[26] This possibility, it seems to me, can be decisively rejected. Madison *was* trying to convince the Constitution's critics, but it is equally apparent that he had managed to convince himself that these provisions were a valuable security against consolidation. From 1788 until his death, he defended a Constitution that was only partly national in nature, and I can see no better way to judge the fit between his public and his private views than by his stances after (not before) his public views had been developed.

That Madison was genuinely influenced by the Antifederalist critiques—and by the arguments of his opponents of the summer—seems all the likelier if we insist on a developmental understanding of the framing of the Constitution, which challenges a very common, deep, and usually unrecognized assumption that Madison and other framers entered the convention with their thoughts essentially in order, struggled with opponents representing different interests and ideas, and compromised no more than they were forced to. Studies of the meeting seldom make a full allowance for truly fundamental changes of opinion. But even founding fathers can experience the same fluidity of shifting, jarring, dawning thoughts that we ourselves experience in any group endeavor. The Constitutional Convention was a learning process, an interchange of thoughts, for every member present. Early in the work, the course of the deliberations forced the major author of the Virginia Resolutions to begin rethinking his original proposals, which themselves were very far from a completed constitution. The decision of July 16 compelled another wrenching readjustment. From then until adjournment, like every other delegate, he struggled constantly to understand a plan whose shape was changing day by day. These changes outraced even Madison's ability to fully comprehend what was emerging. Not until he wrote *The Federalist* did he attempt a systematic rationalization of the summer's work, and his defense of the completed Constitution led him to articulate ideas that first began to jell only in the course of the deliberations or even after they were through.

For Madison, moreover, Antifederalist objections to the Constitution were more than merely arguments that he was obligated to rebut. They were worries worthy of concerned reflection, worries to which he himself was not immune. Like most supporters of the Constitution, he occasionally condemned most Antifederalists as men of little intellect and impure motives, but he did not regard all doubters in this way. Some of them were colleagues he had long esteemed, colleagues whose anxieties he shared to a significant degree, even colleagues he had listened to and learned from through the Philadelphia summer. Indeed, if we insist on a renewed attention to the limits of his nationalism during the convention, if we recognize that he was seldom simply on a single side of its divisions, it becomes apparent that the framing of the Constitution may have influenced Madison in ways that modern scholarship has wholly overlooked. It may have taught him that among his allies in the battle with the smaller states, were some who wished to carry centralizing changes to objectionable extremes, some whose sentiments were deeply antidemocratic, and some who were inclined to treat the document completed by the meeting more flexibly than he considered safe. If so, as he prepared to write *The Federalist*, as he reflected on the course of the convention and anticipated the important role that many of the framers would continue to perform, he may have recognized that his opponents at the meeting had been more correct than he had then been willing to admit to seek additional assurances that the general government would stay within its proper bounds. In short, his post-convention reconciliation to a partly federal system may have started *during* the proceedings, prompted by his constant recognition that centralization could go too far and by what he learned from delegates on both extremes. Certainly, on any spectrum that would take into account *all* issues faced by the convention, Madison stood almost equidistant from Alexander Hamilton and Edmund Randolph, from George Mason and Gouverneur Morris. If we are willing to explore the possibility that standing in between, he was affected and occasionally alarmed by what he heard from both extremes, his later conduct may appear less puzzling. Madison's Virginia continentalism meshed imperfectly with the intentions of a number of his allies in the quest for an effectual reform. A fresh and firm insistence on the great disparity between his purposes and theirs may help reveal that he had grown uneasy with their views before the framing of the Constitution was complete and that the discomfort which would sharpen into open conflict in the years immediately ahead can be detected in the course of the proceedings. More attention to his other objects at the meeting is, at all events, essential to a rounded understanding of his contributions.[27]

On September 17, three delegates refused to sign the finished Constitution. Two of them were prominent Virginians, allies and associates of Madison since 1776. Edmund Randolph, former congressman, long-time attorney general of the state, and heir to one of its premier family names, had recently succeeded Patrick Henry in its highest office. Through the past ten years, not even Jefferson had worked with Madison more closely or more often.[28] George Mason, planter-statesman, was the major architect of the Virginia Constitution and the author of its widely influential Declaration of Rights. Though he had seldom served with Madison in the Virginia state assembly and had never deigned to take an extra-local office, Mason was a venerated elder statesman and had joined wholeheartedly with Madison in the Virginia struggle for religious freedom.[29] At the opening of the convention, both of these eventual non-signers had advocated the replacement of the old Confederation with a republican government of national extent.[30] During the extended battle with the smaller states, both spoke repeatedly and often quite effectively for large-state, "nationalist" positions.[31] For both, the process culminating in decisions not to sign originated with the small-state triumph of July 16 and flowed from mounting fears about the future of self-government, Virginia, and the South within a system dominated by the smaller, northern states.[32] One of the surest ways to come to grips with Madison's distinct position at the meeting is to compare his stands with theirs.

The sectional considerations that were near the heart of Mason's and Randolph's discontent became apparent in the days immediately preceding the decision to accept the Connecticut Compromise. With several delegations seeking to increase their representation in the lower house or to reduce the seats allotted rivals, remarks by several members made it clear that North-South issues were involved. The members of the Constitutional Convention generally assumed, as most contemporaries did, that growth was fastest in the South and West, which would in no great time possess more people than the North and East. Randolph's motion for a periodic census, which would force the legislature to adjust apportionment in Congress to the movement of the population, therefore led to sharp exchanges on the previous decision for a partial representation of the southern slaves, as well as on the terms on which new states might be admitted to the Union.[33] Mason summarized the southern point of view, delivering one of the earliest of the convention's several ultimatums. The northern states, he said on July 11, were undeniably entitled to dominate at present, but without provisions that would guarantee that this would change as population shifted, "he could neither vote for the system here nor support it in his state."[34]

The northern attitude toward slavery was not the major worry. Mason was concerned, as grew increasingly apparent, with familiar economic differences between the planting and commercial states, with the position of Virginia, and with the prospect of minority control. With passage of a compromise between the large and small states, the South would be out-numbered slightly in the lower house, but much more so in the senate. In order to preserve the Union, Mason would accept a [temporary] dis-advantage in the lower house, and yet he knew that an equality of voting in the senate would exaggerate and probably prolong the northern dom-ination of that branch. A periodic census, liberal admission of new states, and an exclusion of the senate from the power of the purse thus struck him as the minimal securities required to shield the planting states from the resulting risks to their essential interests, as well as to assure majority control.

Minimal securities, moreover, were not, on further thought, enough; and by the time that the Committee of Detail delivered its report, both Mason and Randolph had become extremely anxious. For both, a pow-erful, reeligible executive had been a constant worry. For both, however, the construction of the senate, together with the powers contemplated over commerce and taxation, were undoubtedly the principal concerns.

The Committee of Detail (Randolph, Rutledge, Ellsworth, Wilson, and Nathaniel Gorham of Massachusetts) delivered their report on Monday, August 6, following a ten-day recess. Without objection from the rest of the convention, its members took responsibility for more than just a care-ful ordering of the convention's previous decisions. Among their many contributions, they incorporated several provisions that a number of the delegates had warned would be conditions for their states' consent. South-erners had been especially insistent on this subject, and the committee made provision for all of their demands: requirement of a two-thirds vote in Congress for the passage of commercial regulations; prohibition of a tax on exports; and a ban on any federal interference with the slave trade. Northerners were outraged, and the numerous concessions to the South became the focus for a sectional dispute that raged through much of August. This was finally resolved by the convention's second famous com-promise—between the Deep South and New England. In exchange for confirmation of the ban on export taxes and a temporary prohibition of restrictions on the slave trade, South Carolina voted to forgo the two-thirds rule on commerce. Though this was not the only source of Ran-dolph's or Mason's discontent, it was unquestionably the act, when linked with the convention's alteration of the clause concerning money bills, that prompted them to declare their refusal to sign. From their distinctive point of view, almost every part of the agreement was profoundly wrong.

On August 8, soon after the committee had reported, Charles Pinck-ney moved to strike the clause prohibiting the senate from originating or amending money bills, which Madison and many of the leading nation-alists had never seen as a significant concession. Mason forcefully objected. To give the senate equal power over revenues, he said, could only tend toward aristocracy. This branch, whose powers over treaties and appointments already made it stronger than the lower house, was not to be elected by the people. Its members' terms would be of long duration. He and Randolph had insisted since July that denying the senate a part in raising taxes was a valuable protection for the larger (southern) states. On August 8, despite this protest, the two dissenters were outvoted in their delegation by Madison, Washington, and John Blair, who cast Virginia's vote with the majority opposing the prohibition. On August 9, Randolph moved to reconsider. Both he and Mason warned that their support for the Connecticut Compromise had been contingent on this clause. Correctly estimating their increasing discontent, Washington changed sides on August 13, and Virginia voted for Randolph's motion, which was nonetheless defeated once again. In the end, a firm majority of states proved willing to do no more than stipulate that all money bills must be *originated* in the lower house, which struck the two Virginians as no security at all. By that time, Randolph and Mason were on the verge of an explosion, which erupted as the meeting sealed its North-South bargain.

On August 22, Mason angrily denounced the slave trade, insisting that the common interests and security of all the states were threatened by the practice, and that the efforts of the Upper South to halt it would be futile if the Lower South continued to import new slaves and supply them to the West. Although he favored prohibition of a tax on exports, which was certain to be levied mainly on the southern staples, Mason also bitterly condemned the other half of the convention's second bargain, protesting that majority control of commerce would deliver southerners, "bound hand and foot," into the mercies of the "Eastern States."[35] Randolph fervently agreed. "There were features so odious in the Constitution as it now stands," he insisted, "that he doubted whether he should be able to agree." Rejection of the two-thirds rule on commerce, he complained, "would complete the deformity of the system."[36] Mason seconded this warning two days later, "declaring that he would sooner chop off his right hand than put it to the Constitution as it now stands."[37]

These declarations, together with the final motions of the two Virginians, leave no doubt that it was the conjunction of their sectional concerns with their republican convictions that led to their decisions not to sign. On September 7, Mason urged revival of a privy council as an instrument to aid and check the single national executive. He was unwilling to confide extensive powers of appointment to the president alone, already fearing an elective monarch, yet neither was he willing to accept so many links between the chief executive and an objectionable senate, whose members' lengthy terms would make them relatively independent of the people.[38] For Randolph, too, it was the combination of a powerful, reeligible executive, a malapportioned senate, and the sometimes-hazy grant to a majority in Congress of powers that could be manipulated to the disadvantage of the planting states that touched the quick of his dissent. Convinced that nothing less than radical reform could meet the Union's needs, he had, he said, "brought forward a set of republican propositions as the basis and outline of reform. These republican propositions had, however, . . . been widely and . . . irreconcilably departed from." Thus he declared on September 10, he could no longer lend his aid to "a plan which he verily believed would end in tyranny."[39]

The convention made a series of attempts to reconcile its three dissenters (Randolph, Mason, and Elbridge Gerry). It conceded that money bills must originate in the lower house, whose ratio of members to the people it decreased. It ruled that two-thirds of the legislature, rather than three-fourths, would be enough to override a presidential veto. It transferred from the senate to the lower house the power to select the president whenever an electoral majority failed to appear. Still, the delegates would not reinstitute the two-thirds rule on navigation laws or listen seriously to Mason's argument that two-thirds should be necessary to adopt commercial regulations until 1808 (by which time, he may have hoped, the South would have its reinforcements from the West).[40] The delegations also brusquely and unanimously declined to add a bill of rights.[41] All three dissenters, in return, rejected the majority's appeals to leave their doubts within the hall. Mason wrote at once to Richard Henry Lee, who mounted a resistance in the Confederation Congress and soon was writing letters of his own, several of them meant for publication. The veteran congressman explicitly concurred in Mason's published explanation of his views.[42]

Mason's pamphlet, which became a starting point for Antifederalists throughout the country, put his fears succinctly. The crusty author powerfully denounced the failure to include a bill of rights. He emphasized his principled objections to a government that seemed profoundly flawed in its essential structure, not his sectional concerns. Still, no power troubled Mason more than the majority's ability to regulate the country's trade, through which "the five Southern States (whose produce and circumstances are totally different from that of the eight Northern and Eastern States) will be ruined." And it was hardly incidental that he placed such heavy stress on the faulty character and swollen powers of the senate, where the sectional imbalance would be greatest. The upper house, he pointed out, would share the power of the purse, although the senators were "not the representatives of the people." This violation of a basic revolutionary maxim, together with the numerous, "alarming" links between "that branch . . . and the supreme Executive," had always struck him as a fundamental danger, possibly because this was the point at which his revolutionary principles fused most completely with his sectional concerns. "This government," said Mason, "will commence a moderate aristocracy," and it would irresistably become more thoroughly aristocratic or monarchical with time. And though he did not say it, it is plain that Mason thought that this "corrupt, oppressive aristocracy" would prove the more "tyrannical" because it would commence a northern one.[43]

The contrast with the views of the Virginia signers of the Constitution could hardly be more striking. Mason feared that constitutional reform would in the end revive hereditary rule and in the meantime ruin Virginia and the South. Madison believed, no less sincerely, that the Constitution was a necessary, wholly "democratic" remedy for democratic ills. He also thought that it was in the interests of Virginia. Why he did—and why first Randolph, then a slight majority in the Virginia state convention, took his side—can tell us much about his course throughout the summer. And this will be more certainly the case if we begin by recognizing that Madison and Mason, who had often been close allies, were by no means as opposed as may at first appear.[44]

Madison was not insensitive to the concerns that troubled his dissenting colleagues. At the peak of the collision with the smaller states, in fact, he had been more inclined than either of his friends to risk a small-state walkout from the Constitutional Convention rather than accept state equality in the Senate, which all of them condemned for sectional as well as other reasons. No delegate protested more insistently than Madison that the essential differences within the nation were between the North and the South, the carrying and the producing states, not between the small states and the large.[45] Like Mason, Madison did not expect or fear a sectional collision over slavery itself, and he did not disguise his personal revulsion from the institution and the slave trade, though he was less outspoken than his colleague.[46] Like Mason, nevertheless, he was acutely conscious of the economic differences that followed from the circumstance of having slaves or not.[47] Throughout the Constitutional Convention, Madison's Virginia background and perspective strongly influenced his positions. On balance, these distinguished him as clearly from his northern allies as they did from the dissenters in his delegation. Along with his republican concerns, their influence is as necessary to an understanding of his conduct as an emphasis on his dedication to the Union.[48]

Madison's initial attitudes toward the executive, as has been shown, are one instructive illustration. His original opinions on this branch were quite Virginian in their flavor, changing only as he listened to the other members' views and thought about the consequences of decisions on the senate. But Madison's continuing attempt to balance his residual concern about an overpowerful executive with his awareness that the upper house would be controlled by the smaller, northern states was never more apparent than it was when he proposed to give a simple majority in the senate, acting in the absence of executive concurrence, power to conclude a peace. Madison's intentions were transparent here, as were the reasons for his speedy second thoughts. War, he reasoned, was a certain and familiar instrument of magisterial ambition. He therefore wished to make it possible to end a war without executive consent, and the convention followed him at first by making a majority of senators sufficient for such treaties. Two southerners, however, quickly moved a clause providing that a two-thirds vote should still be necessary whenever territory was involved. Doubtless recollecting his determined wartime efforts to protect Virginia's claims, and with the Jay-Gardoqui battle surely also in his mind, Madison confessed that it had proved too easy to agree on treaties despite the Article's requirement of concurrence by nine states. He therefore joined with the majority to overturn his own proposal and followed with an unsuccessful motion that a quorum of the Senate should consist of two-thirds of all its members.[49]

Madison was not less conscious of the differences between the North and South than his Virginia colleagues. He was by no means inattentive to Virginia's special interests. He certainly had no intention of delivering the planting states into the hands of a commercial faction. Nevertheless, he did define Virginia's interests in a manner quite his own, and nothing throws a brighter light on his unique position at the Constitutional Convention.

Consider his position on a tax on exports, where he stood at odds with every other speaking member from the South. Export taxes, he contended, had been fertile sources of contention when levied by the several states, since states with major ports could levy them, in practice, on the products of their neighbors. Under the Confederation government, Connecticut, North Carolina, and New Jersey were compelled to carry portions of the revenue requirements of Rhode Island, Virginia, Pennsylvania, and New York. But if the power to impose such taxes were confided to the general Congress, he observed, this constant source of animosity between the landlocked states and their commercial neighbors would be ended. In federal hands, moreover, export taxes would be more than a convenient, painless source of needed revenues. Export taxes could be used both to encourage native manufacturing and shipping and to force the European powers to concede more "equitable" commercial regulations. "The Southern States," he said, "being most in danger and most needing naval protection," which might be paid for by these taxes, "could the less complain if the burden should be somewhat heaviest on them." "Time," in any case, would "equalize the situation of the states."[50]

Madison, it needs to be recalled, had not decided firmly to support a sweeping constitutional reform until he came to be convinced that separate regulations by the states were not just futile, but a twofold danger to the Union: while the "interfering" efforts of the several states engendered bitterness between them, all grew more disgusted with a general government that could do nothing to relieve their plight. By the time of the convention, Madison was absolutely dedicated to a general power over commerce, which he planned to use to force the British to relax their navigation laws. As he conceived it, this was necessary both in order to preserve the Union and in order to create the economic basis for a sound republican society in the United States: one in which American producers would have outlets for their agricultural commodities and could avoid the unjust legislation, overcrowding, and intensive economic growth that might endanger their ability to sustain a healthy civic life. He therefore struggled to the last to save a federal tax on exports, moving to permit them on a two-thirds vote as "a lesser evil than a total prohibition"; and he parted from most southerners again to argue strongly for majority control of commerce.[51]

Madison's political economy, as has been said, should not be seen as narrowly and strictly southern. In the first place, he anticipated western growth that would transform Virginia into a shipping as well as a planting state. Natural development, he thought, would render all of the Atlantic states more homogeneous in time. In the second place, he reasoned that abuse of the commercial power would be made improbable by the complexity of the federal government, the presence of an agricultural majority in inland regions of even the most commercial states, and the rapid admission of new states from the West.[52] Nevertheless, Virginia's economic difficulties in the postwar years did enter heavily into his thinking, as did the Old Dominion's military situation. Madison conceded that the price of an American navigation act would be a temporary rise in southern shipping costs, but he insisted that this cost would be a fair exchange for benefits received. As before, he emphasized above all else the southern need for the protection that would be afforded by an increase in the Union's maritime capacities. "He stated the vulnerable situation of all [the southern states] and of Virginia in particular."[53]

Even as a revolutionary youth, when bragging of his neighbors' prowess with their rifles, Madison had been acutely conscious of Virginia's vulnerability to foreign and domestic dangers. "If America and Britain should come to an hostile rupture," he had told a college classmate, "I am afraid an insurrection among the slaves may and will be promoted."[54]

"To say the truth," he added, slavery was "the only part in which this colony is vulnerable; if we should be subdued, we shall fall like Achilles by the hand of one that knows that secret"[55]—one, he might have added, who could use that secret in conjunction with a domination of the state's great rivers.

The War for Independence, Madison believed, held patent lessons for the South. Penetrated everywhere by navigable rivers, having no ships of their own, and always faced with the potential danger of a slave uprising, the southern states were desperately exposed to British naval power and could look for succor only to their stronger, northern sisters. Postwar British dominance of their external trade and postwar conflicts with the northern states, to which the South's extensive commerce would be easy prey in case of a collapse of the Confederation, were other indications of the region's inability to stand alone. Of all essential southern interests, then, as Madison conceived it, none was dearer than the Union. Of all potential perils to Virginia's or America's commitment to the democratic Revolution, none thrust deeper than the danger that the Union might collapse and every state or every small confederation would have to treat its neighbors as potential foes. If the United States should ever replicate the fractured politics of Europe, then all its states or all its small confederations would eventually be governed in the European way. None would lose their liberties more quickly than Virginia and the South.[56] Thus the sectional disputes and regional considerations that affected all of the Virginia framers pulled in two directions, not just one, intensifying an awareness of the indispensability of union at the same time that they heightened the suspicion of the North. Thus, as well, a dedication to republican ideals could argue as insistently for an effective general government as for additional securities against the possibility of sectional abuses.[57]

In urging an effective, lasting Union, Madison did not believe that he was risking the submission of Virginia's vital interests to a northern and commercial faction in the Congress. New Jersey and Connecticut, he reasoned, were "agricultural, not commercial states," as were the inland parts of Massachusetts, Pennsylvania, and New York. Accordingly, the House of Representatives, at least, would have an agricultural majority from the beginning and would become more agricultural as population moved increasingly into the West.[58] That, to Madison, was ample guarantee that the "producing interests" would be safe within a well-constructed federal republic, and Madison was not less dedicated to protecting the producing interests than was Mason. Rather, he identified the fundamental interests of the planters with the fundamental interests of the vast majority of farmers, and he analyzed their current situation and their long-term needs in different, deeper terms.

Moreover—what at first may seem less plausible in light of his enthusiasm for a multiplicity of interests—Madison was not, in actuality, more fearful of majorities than Mason, nor any less committed to their rule. Both of them believed that private rights and the public good can be endangered by majority desires—especially if that majority is not composed of independent farmer/owners. Both of them believed, as well, not merely in a government derived entirely from elections, but in a government unable to escape from a continuing dependence on the people. Both of them, in short, were liberal republicans from a distinctively Virginian mold, and their perspective as Virginia revolutionaries distanced both of them from less committed democrats and more determined centralists at the convention. A firm insistence on this point is critical to fuller understanding of Madison's objectives at the meeting and to better insight into what he learned.[59]

In modern commentaries on Madison's special role at the convention, nothing has been emphasized more properly or more consistently than his determination to protect minorities against majority infringements of their rights. His fear of unrestrained majorities stares out at modern democrats from page after page of his account of the debates, and it is absolutely clear that he was most especially concerned for propertied minorities among the people: creditors who had been cheated by Rhode Island's legal-tender laws, who were prevented from pursuing private suits for debt, or who were forced by moratoriums on taxes to forgo the payments promised them on public obligations. All such legislation, he believed, was morally repulsive, incompatible with civilized society, inconsistent with the rights that Independence was intended to secure, and thus increasingly subversive of the revolutionary faith. Holding these convictions, Madison was not content to hope that an enlargement of the sphere of republican government would render it less likely that a factional majority would form. He also wanted to create a federal watchdog over local legislation and to raise imposing obstacles to national majorities as well, so clearly so that many modern analysts regard the Constitution as a system of redundant checks, too often working to defeat all action.[60]

Time and time again, in course of the proceedings, Madison spoke forcefully for measures that would check majority desires. He opposed the popular election of the senate and, at first, of the executive as well. Notes by King and Lansing quote him as suggesting that "the senate ought to come from and represent the wealth of the nation."[61] His own notes leave no doubt that he desired, at minimum, an upper house that would be small enough and firm enough and far enough removed from popular demands to "interpose against tempestuous councils," whether in the lower house or among the body of the people.[62] "What we wished," he said, "was to give to the government that stability which was everywhere called for and which the enemies of the republican form alledged to be inconsistent with its nature." To secure it, he was not afraid that seven years would be too long a tenure for the senate. "His fear was that the popular branch would still be too great an overmatch for it."[63] At one conjuncture, he was even willing to support a nine-year term, although he would have linked this with a perpetual ineligibility for reelection.[64]

King and Lansing may not have quoted Madison precisely. Some of his positions changed before the meeting closed or as a consequence of later, more mature reflection. As he said much later, the context of the meeting "made it natural" for the convention to be more concerned for national vigor and for new restraints on populistic legislation "than was perhaps in strictness warranted by a proper distinction" between temporary evils and problems "permanently inherent in popular forms of government." "I was among those most anxious to rescue [the principle of self-government] from the danger which seemed to threaten it," he recollected, "and with that view, was willing to give . . . as much energy as would ensure the requisite stability and efficacy. It is possible that in some instances this consideration may have been allowed a weight greater than subsequent reflections within the convention or the actual operation of the government would sanction." It sometimes happened also "that opinions as to a particular modification or a particular power of the government had a conditional reference to others which, combined therewith, would vary the character of the whole."[65] A nine-year tenure for the senate was probably an illustration of this final observation. Madison supported this extended term soon after the convention had decided on election by the legislatures of the states and at the peak of his concern that such a senate might be dangerously subservient to state desires.

Still, Madison's determination to protect the propertied minority was not a temporary deviation from his normal course. Neither was the thought that unrestrained majorities could threaten both the rights of property and the community's enduring interests, which he did not identify with the majority's immediate desires. To modern democrats, in fact, some of his least attractive statements are the ones that seem to have been motivated more by his concern about the distant future than by his alarm about the current situation:

> An increase of population will of necessity increase the proportion of those who will labor under all the hardships of life and secretly sigh for a more

equal distribution of its blessings. These may in time outnumber those who are placed above the feelings of indigence. . . . No agrarian attempts have yet been made in this country, but symptoms of a levelling spirit . . . have sufficiently appeared in a certain quarters [sic] to give warning of the future danger.[66]

The proper time to make provision for this danger, he believed, was now—while ownership was so widespread that the majority was as attached to property as to their other rights. Therefore, he was greatly tempted by the concept of a freehold franchise. "Viewing the subject on its merits alone, the freeholders of the country would be the safest depositories of republican liberty. In future times a great majority of the people will not only be without landed but any other sort of property." This propertyless majority might then combine against the rights of property "or, which is more probable, they will become the tools of opulence and ambition."[67]

This speech embarrassed Madison when he reread it later in his life. It was the only one, in fact, on which he later wrote two notes disclaiming his position at the meeting. "Men cannot be justly bound," he wrote, "by laws in [the] making of which they have no part. Persons and property being both essential objects of government, the most that either can claim is such a structure of it as will leave a reasonable security for the other."[68]

As this later comment shows, however, Madison was not embarrassed by his view that property deserved protection, only by the thought that this concern had led him to neglect another fundamental precept of the Revolution. Even in the aftermath of Shays's Rebellion, he had not in fact forgotten that "the rich may oppress the poor," that "property may oppress liberty." At no point in his life did he believe that the protection of the rights of property was *more* important than the people's right to rule. This was, indeed, the very point on which he may have differed most profoundly from some others at the meeting. What he did believe, however—and believed throughout the rest of his career—was that "in a just and a free government the rights both of property and of persons ought to be effectually guarded," that the former had been gravely violated during the preceding years, and that transgressions of these rights were likely to become more threatening as ownership decreased.[69] All of these considerations—and the last not least—were fundamental to his thought about the purposes and necessary character of constitutional reform.[70]

Passage after passage from the records of the meeting strikes the reader once again with the intensity of Madison's revulsion from conditions in the states. Everywhere, he was convinced, experience had shown that all effective power tended to be sucked into "the legislative vortex," that legislative power tended to be concentrated in the lower house, and that the lower houses, when unchecked, were dangerous custodians of private rights and public good.[71] He plainly wanted multiple impediments against a federal replication of this problem. Accordingly, when urging that a legislative veto should be vested in a council of revision, he observed that even the combined resistance of the president and judges might prove insufficient to defeat the legislature's tendency "to absorb all power." "This was the real source of danger to the American constitutions," he insisted, and it "suggested the necessity of giving every defensive authority to the other departments that was consistent with republican principles."[72] Again, when he opposed the substitution of two-thirds for the three-fourths currently required to override a presidential veto, he argued that experience had shown that all the checks attempted in the states were insufficient to defeat "legislative injustice and encroachments."[73] In August, he observed that the convention planned to frustrate legislative usurpations by employing two devices borrowed from the constitutions of the states: a senate modeled on the Maryland provision for an indirect election, and a veto modeled on New York's. "Separately," he argued, these devices "had been found insufficient." Whether they would prove effective when combined was still unclear, but he preferred to take additional precautions.[74] For example, near the close of the convention, in order to avoid a legislative choice when there was no majority in the electoral college, he moved to make the electoral decision final even if as few as a third of the electors were agreed.[75]

Here, however, it is crucial to revert again to Madison's original intentions and to call insistently for equal emphasis on the other side of his distinctive role at the convention, which was evident, indeed, in several of the passages just quoted. For, by focusing excessively on his undoubted fear of unrestrained majorities, as well as by confusing his determination to erect a "national" system with a wish for a consolidated one, many studies leave a false impression of his overall position. But passage after passage from the records of the Federal Convention also show that Madison intended to restrain the legislature and the people only to the point that this appeared consistent with republican commitments. Although he was convinced that "the preservation of republican government" required effective checks on instability and legislative usurpations, he was also certain that it "required evidently at the same time that in devising [these], the genuine principles of that form should be kept in view."[76] In emphasizing his determination to restrain majority excesses, we should never let ourselves forget that it was popular self-governance that he was working to preserve.

In 1787, Madison was every bit as worried as was Mason about a gradual revival of hereditary rule. For years, he had been bent on the perpetuation of the Union because he was convinced that the republican experiments that had been started in the states could not endure without this continental shield. And what is more—although it seldom gets the notice it deserves—for all of his revulsion from conditions in the states, he still defined the principles of a republic much as Congress had defined them early in the Revolution. Liberty, as he conceived it, did require additional securities for private rights and public good. But "liberty," as he employed this word, more often denoted governments that derived entirely from, and remained responsive to, the body of the people. Thus, the same considerations that committed him to an effective general government committed him, as well, *against* excessive concentration of authority in hands too distant from the people or imperfectly familiar with their needs.

From the beginning of the Constitutional Convention, Madison had insisted on the popular election of the lower house, and this was not exclusively because he wanted to prevent the states from making national decisions. If the lower house were chosen by the states and other branches built on that—a second option in his preconvention letters or in Randolph's speech presenting the Virginia Plan—"the people," Madison observed, "would be lost sight of altogether and the necessary sympathy between them and their rulers and officers too little felt." "He was an advocate," he said, "of refining the popular appointments by successive filtrations" (that is, of indirect elections) "but thought it could be pushed too far." In order to be durable and safe, the central government would have to "rest on the solid foundation of the people themselves."[77] Early in July, therefore, he moved to double the membership of the lower house, concerned that sixty-five would be too few to win the people's confidence or "to bring with them all the local information which would be frequently wanted."[78] On September 8, he seconded another motion to enlarge this house.[79] And he was adamant throughout the meeting that the Constitution must be ratified in state conventions of the sovereign people.

These motions and remarks are worthy of renewed attention, the more so when we recollect that Madison and the majority of the convention reasoned from assumptions that are not immediately apparent from a twentieth-century perspective. One of these assumptions was that in a national republic, as in all the states, the lower house would take the lead in writing legislation. On domestic matters in particular, the House of Representatives would be the sails, the other parts the anchors, of the ship of state. The lower house would be the branch with which the people would especially identify, the branch they would instinctively support in any confrontation with the others.

Multiple securities aginst encroachments by the lower house were nec-essary, Madison believed, in part because he never doubted that the House of Representatives *would* be continually responsive to the people, and because he knew that an enlargement of the size of the republic could not possibly, in every case, prevent a factional majority from forming or the people's representatives from advocating the majority's desires.[80] Checks and balances were necessary, then, as an additional security against majority abuse. But checks and balances were necessary, too, because ma-jority excess had *never* seemed to Madison the only danger to republics— not even in the revolutionary states. Popular abuses, at this moment, were undoubtedly his principal concern, yet he did not forget that rulers can betray the people, that power can corrupt, that legislators may prefer their personal ambitions to the people's needs, and that elected representatives might someday try to free themselves entirely from their due dependence on the people in order to pursue distinctive interests of their own.[81]

The Constitutional Convention was not the proper time or place for Madison to emphasize his fierce allegiance to early revolutionary maxims. He was in the midst of other former congressmen who knew his ways of thought and often saw him as a bit too doctrinaire.[82] In order to secure the governmental vigor he desired, he was compelled to form a temporary alliance with several individuals with whom he differed hugely on the other fundamentals. For all of this, however, Madison reiterated time and time again—first in private, pre-convention letters, then in several of his speeches—that he was willing to concede no more to governmental vigor and stability than revolutionary precepts would permit. He opened the convention with a plan that was as conscientiously republican as it was national in nature, and he was conscientiously concerned from the begin-ning to the close of the proceedings to see that the emerging system would remain consistent with *both* goals.

Two episodes, I think, especially illuminate the special combination of republican and national concerns that Madison imparted to the meeting. In the first, he stood with other southerners, as he had done so often in the Continental Congress, as a dedicated spokesman for the West. As it became apparent that the smaller, northern states would win their battle for an equal senate, Madison's Virginia colleagues pushed insistently for constitutional provision for a periodic census and for clauses guaranteeing quick admission of, and equal treatment for, new western states, which everyone assumed would help the South reverse the North's initial dom-ination of the Congress. Madison, moreover, had a very special interest in issues of this sort, for his conception of an integrated nation was more western than southern in its flavor. The best security for the essential interests of the planting states, as he conceived it, would be found in the agrarian majority that would preponderate in nearly every region, would constitute the bedrock of a sound republican society, and would be steadily renewed by western growth.[83]

Many eastern delegates contemplated the eventual predominance of the South and West with horror, none of them more vocally than Gouverneur Morris. On July 11, Morris urged the gathering to leave the legislature free to apportion representation on a standard that would take account of wealth as well as numbers, warning that a flood of poorer western states could ruin the more developed East. Madison replied that he "was not a little surprised to hear this implicit confidence [in representatives] urged by a member who on all occasions had inculcated so strongly the political depravity of men and the necessity of checking one vice and interest by opposing to them another vice and interest." Even while Morris, he remarked, was recommending "this implicit confidence to the Southern states in the Northern majority [in Congress], he was still more zealous in exhorting all to a jealousy of a Western majority. To reconcile the gentleman with himself it must be imagined that he determined the human character by the points of the compass." "All men having power," Madison insisted, "ought to be distrusted to a certain degree."[84] And this was nowhere more essential than when fixing the requirements for the suffrage. "A gradual abridgment of this right has been the mode in which aristocracies have been built on the ruins of popular forms."[85]

Madison, contemporaries said, was notable for his remarkably good temper. He never lost control. He often answered his opponents in debate much as a friend responds in private to another friend's mistakes. But Madison demolished Morris with a stinging wit that he would not have loosed on others because he was disgusted by the Pennsylvanian's jaundiced view of human nature and had had his fill of this urbane aristocrat's unhidden antidemocratic inclinations.[86] Madison's revulsion from popular misrule was every bit as deep as any other member's, but so were his convictions that the people still possessed sufficient virtue to sustain a totally elective system and that a people's government demands abiding vigilance against the irrepressible ambitions of even democratic rulers.

Time and time again, in course of the convention, Madison condemned implicit confidence in rulers.[87] Though he was willing to impose the most elaborate restraints on the immediate desires of popular majorities, he nevertheless assumed that once these checks had been applied, the product of successive distillations of the people's will must still reflect the wishes of the greater number. And although he feared that unrestrained majorities could undermine democracy itself, he was determined that the government would always be responsive to the body of the people.

The constitutional machinery of checks and balances was meant, from his perspective, as a needed check against majority abuses, but it was also meant—and not less firmly—as an added guarantee that representatives would not be able to pursue distinctive interests of their own.[88] "In all cases where the representatives of the people will have a personal interest distinct from that of their constituents," he argued, "there was the same reason for being jealous of them as for relying on them with full confidence when they had a common interest."[89] Popular election was the first and most important guarantee of an enduring bond between the rulers and the ruled, but the convention also needed to be sure that rulers, once elected, could never free themselves from their dependence on the people or from the community of interests with the people that elections were supposed to forge.[90] On these considerations, Madison had privately denounced John Adams' view that the American and English constitutions were variations on the same idea, and he decidedly did not agree with Hamilton that good-behavior tenures for the senate and executive would be republican as long as they were based on indirect elections.[91]

A second incident was even more revealing of this other, deeply revolutionary side of Madison's distinctive role at the convention. Of all his speeches, I believe, the most impassioned was his final, eloquent appeal on June 29 against John Lansing's motion to restore the states' equality of voting in the lower house. Madison

> entreated the gentlemen representing the small states to renounce a principle which was confessedly unjust, which could never be admitted, and if admitted must infuse mortality into a Constitution which we wished to last forever. He prayed them to ponder well the consequences of suffering the Confederacy to go to pieces. . . . Let each state depend on itself for its security, and let apprehensions arise of danger from distant powers or from neighboring states, and the languishing condition of all the states, large as well as small, would soon be transformed into vigorous and high-toned governments. . . . The same causes which have rendered the Old World the theatre of incessant wars and have banished liberty from the face of it would soon produce the same effects here. [The smaller states would] quickly introduce some regular military force against sudden danger from their powerful neighbors. The example . . . would soon become universal. [Great powers would be granted to executives.] A standing military force, with an overgrown executive, will not long be safe companions to liberty. The means of defense against foreign danger have always been the instruments of tyranny at home. Among the Romans it was a standing maxim to excite a war whenever a revolt was apprehended. Throughout all Europe the armies kept up under the pretext of defending have enslaved the people.[92]

This was not a new idea for Madison, nor did the higher-flying nationalists at the convention miss the implications of the thought that standing armies and an overpowerful executive were incompatible with freedom. It is seldom noted, but a fact, that Hamilton was on his feet immediately to second Madison's appeal against equality of voting, but also to remark that "no government could give us tranquility and happiness at home which did not possess sufficient stability and strength to make us respectable abroad."[93]

James Madison had come to Philadelphia in May a dedicated revolutionary statesman. He believed that liberty depended on the continental union and that neither would endure unless the general government was reconstructed as a great republic, which would make it possible to trust it with effectual authority to rule. In order to preserve the Union and to foster an environment in which the revolutionary enterprise could thrive, he insisted on a new regime with power to fulfill the general government's financial obligations, to enforce its laws, and to create the proper economic context for a healthy public life. Positive additions to the Union's powers were essential, he believed, in order to persuade the Spanish to reopen the Mississippi River, to retaliate against the British for their crippling navigation laws, and thus to alter the conditions that had given rise to legislation which endangered both the Union and the revolutionary faith that justice could be realized most fully in republics. New defensive powers were required, as well, in order to permit the general government to guard itself against encroachments by the states and to protect minorities against majority injustice. From first to last, however, Madison assumed that powers would be granted by the people only to perform the *common* business of the nation, that the great republic ought to be constructed to ensure that its elected rulers could not develop independent interests of their own, and that excessive governmental vigor was as incompatible with revolutionary purposes as any of the state abuses he condemned. On June 26 Hamilton confessed that he himself did not "think favorably of republican government," but he appealed to those who did to "tone their government as high as possible" lest it be "lost among ourselves, disgraced and lost to mankind forever."[94] Madison, of course, concurred entirely with this view of what was fundamentally at stake, but Madison was also one of those to whom the New York delegate addressed *both* parts of his appeal. Madison was not only an admirer of republics, he was one of those whose underlying definition of a sound republic was considerably at odds with Hamilton's desires. Hamilton believed that if a totally elective system was to work at all, it would be necessary to concentrate power in the Union and the Union's powers in the branches least immediately responsive to the people, that a vigorous executive and even an established military force were necessary means to national greatness. Madison, by contrast, consciously intended to invigorate the Union in order to *protect* the Revolution from persistent public debts, swollen military forces, overpowerful executives, and legislation incompatible with justice. He intended to invigorate the Union, we could say, in order to assure that it would *not* be necessary for the disunited states to tone their governments so high that their republican regimes would be endangered. It followed, naturally, that he did not intend to tone the central government itself so high that it would reproduce the European evils he was trying to avoid.

The Constitutional Convention debated an enormous range of issues—many more than can be handled at convenient length. On many of these issues, it is clear, Madison stood between the fearful foes of radical departures from the early revolutionary order and men who sympathized more fully with his centralizing means than with his revolutionary ends: Hamilton, both Gouverneur and Robert Morris, Rufus King, and—after the Connecticut Compromise had been adopted—several other members from the smaller middle states. This moderation calls for more attention than it often gets, and it is not to be confused with pliability or lack of underlying passion. The Constitution would have been a different document (if any Constitution had emerged) if Madison had not contributed republican as well as unionist commitments to its framing. And Madison might never have defended it in quite the terms he did if he had not, throughout the summer, been affected more than the convention's records may immediately reveal by what he heard from delegates on either side of his unique position.

As the meeting closed, Madison and many others were exhausted by the work, conscious that the Constitution had been shaped by their disputes, and temporarily depressed by their defeats. The major architect of the Virginia Plan was very much aware that the completed document did not propose as radical a cure for current ailments as the scheme he had originally proposed. Without a veto on state laws, the federal government possessed imperfect tools with which to guard itself against encroachments by the states or to prevent the states from harming one another; the system still involved "the evil of imperia in imperio" in this respect. Rejection of the federal negative in favor of specific limitations on the states (even when combined with the judiciary's power to review the constitutionality of local legislation) had also robbed the central government of its capacity to intervene if the provincial legislatures should discover new and different ways to threaten private rights. And finally, of course, the constitution of the Senate was a serious departure from the national and democratic maxims he preferred.[95]

But Madison's attempt to understand the Constitution did not end with the adjournment of the great convention, and the discontents expressed at the convention's close are not a certain guide to his mature convictions. Very soon, his willingness to undertake a systematic exposition of the plan induced him to review the course of the convention and to think again about the sentiments expressed by "allies" such as Hamilton or Morris or "opponents" such as Dickinson and Sherman (as well as by the Antifederalists whom he was now compelled to answer). As he did so, he implicitly confessed that his opponents in the battle with the smaller states had been more nearly right than he had then been willing to admit. Borrowing from their ideas, he set about to answer both the critics who believed that the convention had departed dangerously from revolutionary maxims and supporters of the Constitution who believed that it had not departed far enough. At times, as will be seen, he answered even his collaborator on the series.

Scholars know that in a major writing project (or in any process of deliberation) insights come when we exchange ideas with others, and conclusions change again as we attempt to put them onto paper. The most extraordinary minds are not so very different from our own. Madison's was changed considerably by his experience at the convention. It was changed again as he attempted to encompass and explain what the convention had accomplished, for there was little of the propagandist in his makeup. The more he thought and wrote about the finished Constitution, the more he managed to convince himself, as well as others, that the Constitutional Convention had indeed prepared a viable corrective for the nation's ills—in fact, the best solution to the central riddle of a liberal republic that human ingenuity had ever yet devised. The Constitution did specifically forbid the types of local legislation that had challenged even his abiding faith that popular self-governance could be combined with justice. In this way—and in the structure of the central government itself—the document did promise to perpetuate the Union and redeem the revolutionary faith. Internal checks and balances, together with the size of the compound republic, offered every safeguard for minorities consistent with a totally elective system. The role and powers of the states would serve—together with the people's vigilance, of course—as an effective, final check on the ambitions of the national rulers. This solution was a fragile settlement, no doubt, and not the one he had originally intended. But there was also little vanity in this Virginian's makeup. As he concluded that the finished Constitution might be better than the plan he had concocted in his closet, he was making a commitment, too, to keep a careful watch on policies or constitutional constructions that could overturn the summer's work. The father of the Constitution did not have to travel quite so far as it is sometimes thought in order to become coauthor of the Jeffersonian persuasion.

PART THREE

Revolutionary Federalism

"The Practicable Sphere of a Republic": Madison, The Federalist, *and the* Republican Interpretation of *the Constitution*

THE SIGNING OF THE CONSTITUTION should have brought some rest for the convention's hardest-working member. The final weeks at Philadelphia were packed with unrelenting labor. Rushing toward a finish, the convention sat six days a week from ten till three (and briefly until four). Committees met before and after the convention's formal sessions. In the evenings, Madison returned to his familiar room at Mrs. House's boarding house to transcribe his shorthand notes of the proceedings. The effort must have drained his last reserves. Years later, he confessed that it had nearly killed him. Still, the signing brought him only brief relief. Seven days from the adjournment of the Constitutional Convention, Madison was back in the Confederation Congress at New York, where Richard Henry Lee and Nathan Dane were trying to amend the plan or, failing that, to pass a resolution criticizing the convention's radical departure from the current Articles of Union.[1] The next nine months proved little less demanding than the four just passed, and they were nearly as important to the shaping of the Constitution.

Opposition in the Congress proved the least of Madison's concerns. The supporters of the Constitution overwhelmed and outmaneuvered its opponents, contriving a "unanimous" agreement (from the delegations, not the members) to a resolution that did not endorse the plan, but did provide its advocates with everything that really seemed required. On September 28, Congress forwarded the Constitution to the legislatures of the states, "to be submitted," as its framers had proposed, to state conventions chosen by the people.[2] And at this time, though not for long, the popular reception of the Constitution seemed as favorable as any of its architects had ever really hoped.[3]

The seat of Congress was a natural clearinghouse for national information, and the framers who resumed their stations there slipped naturally into the role of leading the struggle for adoption. As the other members of the great convention traveled home, they reported local sentiments to colleagues in New York; and Madison and others passed this news along, forging the beginnings of a continental network. As the opposition gathered strength, the framers still in Congress also started to arrange for the reprinting of defenses of the Constitution, which were being published, now, in newspapers throughout the country.[4] By the middle of October, it was obvious that a concerted effort would be needed. Already, Madison complained, the local papers teemed "with vehement and virulent calumniations" of the Constitution, "chiefly borrowed" from the newspapers in Pennsylvania.[5] Of all of these, however, the Virginian seems to have been genuinely troubled only by a local series signed by "Brutus";[6] and within a week, he may have felt that even "Brutus" would be handled. On October 27, *the Independent Journal* published the initial number of another local series, signed by "Publius," directed "To the People of the State of New York," but obviously fit for wide republication. When the introduction to *The Federalist* appeared, this may be all that the Virginian knew. But certainly the elevated style and contents of the first installment promised an outstanding run, and Madison was well informed, at minimum, about the author's other efforts in the state. Satisfied, in any case, that the decision in New York depended on the outcome in New England and New Jersey, he was less alarmed about the situation there than by increasing evidence of potent opposition in Virginia.[7] Accordingly, he turned his thoughts toward home, and history nearly missed his contributions to a classic.

The Federalist was Hamilton's idea, planned, begun, and probably continued through its first few weeks with no intention of enlisting Madison's participation.[8] Though Hamilton and Madison had worked together intermittently for years, their common dedication to a stronger Union flowed from quite contrasting visions of the nation's needs, and their political relationship had never warmed into a friendship. Thus when Hamilton decided that a major project would be necessary to combat the opposition in New York—a larger enterprise than even he could manage while he carried on a busy practice at the bar—he sought assistance, first, from local allies whose political ideas were more consistent with his own. John Jay agreed at once, and wrote the next four numbers (published on October 31, November 3, November 7, and November 10). William Duer, a merchant friend, composed three essays. But Duer's attempts were judged unsuitable for publication in the series, Gouverneur Morris rejected Hamilton's appeals, and Jay's ability to carry on may soon have been in doubt. (Sometime after writing number 5, Jay was disabled altogether by severe rheumatic pains and would prove able to complete only one additional essay). The evidence is so extremely sparse that nothing can be said with certainty about the sequence of events, but all of the surviving hints seem strongly to suggest that Madison was drawn into the project only as the other options failed and very nearly at the final moment for securing his assistance.[9]

On September 28, eleven delegations had approved transmission of the Constitution to the states. By November 8, shortly after the conclusion of the federal year and just as Jay was finishing his essays, there were probably five congressmen in town.[10] On that date, his bags already packed, Madison responded to a query from his brother. He had not originally intended, he explained, to seek a seat in the Virginia state convention, "supposing that it would be as well that the final decision . . . should proceed from men who had no hand in proposing and preparing" the Constitution. "As I find, however, that in all the states the members of the general convention are becoming members of the state conventions, as I have been applied to on the subject by sundry very respectable friends," and as a personal attendance might correct some misconceptions of the plan, "I shall not decline" to represent the county "if I should be honored with its appointment. You may let this be known in such way as my father and yourself may judge best." Signing with affection and conveying "dutiful regards," as always, to his parents, he sealed the letter, caught the stage, and traveled down to Philadelphia again, undecided whether to return to Congress or to continue on to Orange (where the elections had been scheduled for the spring).[11] Obviously, he had not decided at this point to join with Hamilton and Jay. And yet there must have been a consultation of some sort before he left Manhattan, possibly a desperate appeal.

Something turned him round—and much more quickly than he seems to have intended. Perhaps there was a message, oral or discarded, although the records do not even hint of something quite so urgent. If not, however, then the atmosphere in Philadelphia must have resulted in a sudden change of mind about an invitation issued just before he left. This, at least, is certain: Madison could not have reached the Pennsylvania capital before November 10 and had no cause for hurry; Congress might not ever find another quorum. Six days later, he was back aboard the eighteenth-century version of the New York shuttle. Arriving in the city sometime on the seventeenth, he did not sleep a second night before committing all his talents to Hamilton's impressive project.[12] He still had not agreed to carry half the load. In fact, it seems more probable than not that the original intention was for him to fill a gap until a fourth

collaborator could be found.[13] But failure here, combined with Jay's debility, proved fateful for the project, for himself, and for the country. *The
Federalist* may not have been essential to adoption of the Constitution
(though it was, at least, extremely helpful). But with Madison's assumption
of a larger role, the series certainly assumed a greater part in shaping
what the Constitution was to mean, and this was no less true for Madison
himself than for the readers whom he reached.[14]

For Madison, as clearly as for Hamilton, *The Federalist* was not a natural
and not a wholly comfortable collaboration. Thus when he explained the
project to Jefferson, his closest friend, he carefully included one significant disclaimer: "The writers are not mutually answerable for all the ideas
of each other."[15] Later in his life, he emphasized the point again. In the
beginning, he remembered, he and Hamilton had shown their essays to
each other before they sent them to the press. Haste obliged them to
dispense with such a close collaboration. In the struggle to produce four
articles per week (or something like a thousand words per day), it
sometimes happened that an author was still composing the conclusion
of an essay while the printer was putting its early pages into type. "Another
reason," he recalled, "was that it was found most agreeable to each not
to give a positive sanction to all the doctrines and sentiments of the other,
there being a known difference in the general complexion of their political theories."[16] The different attitudes and different theoretical concerns
that Madison imparted to the series were essential for establishing its
quick and lasting reputation, not only as the most authoritative commentary on the Constitution, but also as the most important contribution to
political philosophy that the United States has ever produced.[17] A due
attention to these differences, which have been heavily discounted by the
dominant interpretative tendencies of recent years, is equally essential to
the effort to recover Madison's founding vision.

In the 1950s, many of the most respected experts on *The Federalist*
stressed the underlying differences between its major authors.[18] Since
then, the great majority of writers has emphasized the fundamental unity
and overall coherence of the text.[19] *Both* of these positions are correct,
when carefully explained, but not to the exclusion of the other. Which of
them deserves the stronger emphasis depends on the questions being
asked.

The Federalist is not a house divided. Hamilton and Madison were one
in their conviction that the Constitution was a safe and necessary remedy
for pressing national ills. Both of them believed that proper governments

originate in the consent of the society they serve and are intended to secure the people's happiness and rights. Both maintained that private rights and popular consent could be successfully combined only by establishing effective checks and balances between distinctive governmental parts. Writing with a common purpose, to a common audience, and in a similar prose style, the two collaborators were, indeed, so thoroughly in concord on so many of the fundamentals that a hundred years of argument was necessary to achieve a general agreement on the authorship of a few disputed essays.[20] Thus, from the perspective of a theorist who wants to place *The Federalist* within the long tradition of Western political philosophy, the series *is* essentially coherent. The differences between the authors can elude attentive readers even on a close examination.

Nevertheless, on Madison's authority, these differences were real, and they were serious enough that neither author wished to sanction all the other's views. Many of the points on which Hamilton and Madison differed most profoundly lay beyond the subject of the series. Others tended to be hidden by the instrumental manner in which Hamilton approached the work, writing brilliant briefs for a reform which he approved wholeheartedly because he calculated that it would permit a vigorous administration to reshape the system gradually in ways that would accord more closely with his private understanding of its needs.[21] For all of this, however, there were reasons why Madison did not want to be identified with all of Hamilton's ideas and may have known that Hamilton did not approve of all of his. Underlying differences, though seldom readily apparent, did intrude into the essays. On the matter of a peacetime army, for example, close consideration may suggest that Madison deliberately attempted to revise and moderate his colleague's stance. On several other topics, there is ample reason to suspect that he cannot have felt entirely comfortable with Hamilton's opinions.[22] Accordingly, the scholars who have emphasized important differences between the authors have been no less right than those who have insisted on the harmony of their positions. Although it is entirely possible (and may be quite appropriate in certain cases) to decide what "Publius" believed, it is by no means safe, in face of Madison's explicit cautions, to attribute the ideas of "Publius" to either of the authors taken singly. And although their differences may pale if placed within a broader context, these differences are nearly as important to the *story* of the Founding as the commonalities that made it possible for Hamilton and Madison to join.

Certainly, for present purposes, these differences demand the most elaborate attention. For in any search for Madison's position at the Founding, *The Federalist* presents enormous problems. Many modern readers are familiar with his thinking only through this work, or only from selected portions of the work, or even mainly from the many modern commentaries on it. *The Federalist* comes down to us today with what must surely be the thickest overlay of scholarly interpretation ever lavished on a set of essays written with astounding speed and for a quite specific purpose. And much of this interpretative overlay is deeply problematic as an exposition and analysis of Madison's distinctive views. In much of it, despite his warnings, Madison has not escaped association with a Hamiltonian position. In more of it, *The Federalist* has been approached as though it were a full, authoritative explication of his vision, though every scholar knows that it was not, in fact, a philosophical treatise. Most important, perhaps, in nearly all of the imposing corpus of this secondary work, modern commentators have neglected some revealing facets of the spirit in which Madison was writing: a state of mind so different from his colleague's and so foreign to the attitude with which most modern publicists would come to such a task that twentieth-century analysts can hardly take it earnestly for what it really was.

At the Constitutional Convention, during the comparison of the Virginia and New Jersey Plans, James Wilson said that he considered the convention free to *recommend* whatever it considered right, but utterly unable to *enact* a single measure.[23] Wilson's simple statement of this general understanding was the view that Madison would cling to all his life. As signed by the convention, Madison maintained, the Constitution could be likened to a bill prepared by a committee for a legislative body. It was nothing but a "draft"—ineffective, unauthoritative, even "dead"—"until life and validity were breathed into it by the voice of the people, speaking through the several state conventions."[24] From this fact, he would insist, it followed that the *people's* understanding of the Constitution, as expressed in the proceedings of the state conventions and in the extensive arguments surrounding its adoption, was a more authoritative guide to the authentic meaning of the charter than "the opinions or intentions of the body which planned and prepared" it. The people, not the framers, "gave it all the validity and authority it possesses."[25]

Madison's opinion on this point may offer little help (and smaller comfort) if we hope to find the clear, original, definitive intentions of the founders.[26] It does, however, offer some invaluable assistance in the search for his own ideas. The Constitution was, indeed, a lifeless instrument until it was explained, approved, and put into effect. Madison's outstanding role through all of this extended drama, not merely his commanding part in several of its scenes, is why he seems so central to the Founding. But if this is so, his comments ought to warn, we cannot simply freeze a single frame from the extended process of his thinking and present it as the essence of his understanding.[27] Only gradually, he seems to caution, did his own conception of the Constitution assume its finished shape. Only gradually, he certainly maintained, was the convention's piece of parchment actually defined, its meaning changing and emerging only in the course of national action and debate. Moreover, when he thought about this process, Madison did not portray himself and other framers as the givers and definers of the law, guiding and instructing a passive nation. He pictured them, instead, as having been involved in a communicative interchange with a superior—the body of the people—who played a very active role.

All of these considerations, I submit, are useful, even indispensable, to an informed examination of his greatest text. When Madison agreed to join with Hamilton and Jay, he knew that he was taking an important part in shaping national opinion. He obviously hoped to shape it in ways consistent with his own. And yet he did not understand himself to be exclusively a teacher. He understood himself, as well, to be participating in a still-unfinished effort to create a fundamental law that was to be the nation's act, emerging from a national process of deliberation. As he wrote, he therefore also meant to listen and to learn. He was determined to discover what the people wanted from their fundamental law and how *they* understood the document that the convention had prepared. This was not because he meant to tell the people only what he thought might help promote his cause.[28] It was because he really did consider it his "duty" to adjust his own opinions, in important measure, to the nation's will.[29] It was because not even he had left the Constitutional Convention with a perfect understanding of its work.[30]

The Federalist has been the subject for a literature so vast that it is risky to approach it in a single chapter (and would not be possible at all if it were less available or less well known). Yet Madison himself, together with the circumstances under which he wrote, can offer some essential guidance. *The Federalist* was certainly his earliest and most elaborate discussion of the Constitution. Written with a national audience (if not posterity) in mind, it is entitled to its customary status as the single most important source for understanding his political and constitutional ideas. *The Federalist* is nonetheless a snapshot of his changing vision, not a thorough, full, or finished exposition of his views. To comprehend the latter, it is necessary, first, to peel away some widely shared and deeply seated misconceptions of these essays. This is critical, it proves, merely to avoid mistaking certain portions of the snapshot for the whole. But even this, it will emerge, is not sufficient. The frozen frame must still be fitted back into the film. For Madison did not embark on *The Federalist* with his conception of the Constitution firmly fixed, nor did he use these essays to explain the whole of the philosophy from which he wrote. Rather, taking many things for granted and declining to explore important topics that were not immediately at issue, he set about to answer questions that were as important to himself as to the Constitution's critics, striving toward the settled understanding he had yet to reach. As he wrote, he was, indeed, still trying to define that "middle ground" that he had sought throughout the Constitutional Convention and would not discover, finally, for many months to come.

When Madison assumed the cloak of "Publius," he may have been especially concerned to answer "Brutus," whose series he had recently described as striking plausibly "at the foundation" of the great convention's plan by arguing that any government which was to operate directly on the people was impractical and dangerous for the United States.[31] When Madison took up his pen, Hamilton and Jay were well along with the first section of Hamilton's original prospectus: an examination of the benefits of union.[32] For both these reasons, Madison launched immediately into a fuller exposition of the novel argument that he had first advanced as he prepared himself for the convention:

> Among the numerous advantages promised by a well-constructed Union, none deserves to be more accurately developed than its tendency to break and control the violence of faction. The friend of popular governments never finds himself so much alarmed for their character and fate as when he contemplates their propensity to this dangerous vice. He will not fail, therefore, to set a due value on any plan which, without violating the principles to which he is attached, provides a proper cure for it. The instability, injustice, and confusion introduced into the public councils have in truth been the mortal diseases under which popular governments have everywhere perished. . . . Complaints are everywhere heard from our most considerate and virtuous citizens, equally the friends of public and private faith and of public and personal liberty, that our governments are too unstable; that the public good is disregarded in the conflicts of rival parties; and that measures are too often decided, not according to the rules of justice and the rights of the minor party, but by the superior force of an interested and overbearing majority. . . . Many of our heaviest misfortunes, and particularly . . . that prevailing and increasing distrust of public engagements and alarm for private rights which are echoed from one end of the continent to the other, . . . must be chiefly, if not wholly, effects of the unsteadiness and injustice with which a factious spirit has tainted our public administrations. . . . To secure the public good and private rights against the danger of such a faction, and at the same time to preserve the spirit

and form of popular government, is then the great object to which our enquiries are directed. Let me add that it is the great desideratum, by which alone this form of government can be rescued from the opprobrium under which it has so long labored, and be recommended to the esteem and adoption of mankind.

Having limned the problem, Madison proceeded step by step toward its solution. In all democracies, he argued, the corrective for a factious spirit in a minority of the people was inherent in majority control, which would defeat the faction's "sinister designs." In "pure" democracies, however—city-states like ancient Athens—there could be no cure for the injustices or errors of a majority of voters, "who assemble and administer the government in person." "Hence it is that such democracies have ever been spectacles of turbulence and contention, have ever been found incompatible with personal security or the rights of property, and have in general been as short in their lives as they have been violent in their deaths." Against the "mischiefs" of majorities (in governments deriving wholly from the people), a corrective could be hoped for only in republics, "by which I mean a government in which the scheme of representation takes place." Here, "the public views" could be "refine[d] and enlarge[d] . . . by passing them through the medium of a chosen body of citizens, whose wisdom may best discern the true interests of their country, and whose patriotism and love of justice will be least likely to sacrifice it to temporary or partial considerations."

Yet even in republics, as recent history showed, this remedy was not sufficient. Only in a well-constructed, large republic, Madison concluded, might the cure approach perfection. In a large republic, in the first place, it would be less likely that the advantages of representation would be "inverted" by corrupt, designing men, who "first obtain the suffrages, and then betray the interests of the people." In a large republic, too, there would be fewer times when even patriotic representatives would find a factious majority to represent;

and it is this circumstance principally which renders factious combinations less to be dreaded. . . . Extend the sphere, and you take in a greater variety of parties and interests; you make it less probable that a majority of the whole will have a common motive to invade the rights of other citizens; or, if such a common motive exists, it will be more difficult for all who feel it to discover their own strength and to act in unison with each other. . . . In the extent and proper structure of the Union, therefore, we behold a republican remedy for the diseases most incident to republican government."[33]

The many contributions of this famous essay, *Federalist* no. 10, are so well known that they should not require elaborate discussion. On the authority of Montesquieu, opponents of the Constitution endlessly repeated that republican self-government was inappropriate for polities of great extent.[34] Madison's inversion of this powerful convention was the most impressive answer to the most profound objection to the Constitution. Drawing silently on David Hume, but mostly on the lessons of the last ten years, he argued that the truth about a people's government was nearly the reverse of what some "theoretic politicians" had supposed; popular regimes were likely to be stablest, longest-lived, and freest from a factious spirit in direct proportion to their size.[35] To make this argument complete, he carefully distinguished modern representative republics from the classical democracies that Montesquieu had used as archetypes of popular regimes.[36] And in the character of the United States, he found materials to challenge suppositions that had been embedded in the theory of the mixed republic since the days of ancient Greece. From Aristotle forward, advocates of mixed or balanced governments had focused on the need to counterpoise the wishes and to blend the virtues of the many and the few. Madison was still determined to secure the virtues that this long tradition had associated with these "natural" social groups; his condemnation of majority injustices still emphasized the danger to minorities (especially to propertied minorities) whenever overbearing power rested with the many. But in America, as he conceived it, people did not naturally divide into two social groups; and in the cultural and regional variety of the United States, he saw a prospect that the multiplicity of social differences would control their tendency to do so. The classic conflict of the many and the few could be contained in the United States without confiding portions of political authority to officers who would be independent of majority control.[37]

This summary does not do justice to the essay's many contributions. No speedy summary could capture these in full or in a language that would long withstand critical scrutiny. My purpose, though, is not to make a final statement at this point, but only to suggest some reasons why the essay is so often seen as an epitome of Madison's conceptual achievements. It was, in truth, a major watershed in western governmental theory, so much so that it is always given a distinctive place in scholarly discussions of how the Federalists departed from the old conventions and constructed new foundations for modern democratic thought. But for these very reasons, *Federalist* no. 10 has also proved a sturdy groundwork for persistent misconceptions of its author's meaning and intentions.

Three related themes of modern scholarship, each resonating nicely with the others, are responsible for many of the gravest flaws in most analyses of Madison's position at the Founding. The first, which can be traced to Irving Brant, is the ubiquitous belief that Madison had been an eager centralist throughout the 1780s. The second, which has been enormously encouraged by the first, is an inaccurate depiction of his purposes and conduct at the Federal Convention: a depiction that mistakes the character and overestimates the reach of his determination to consolidate the Union. The third, supporting and supported by the other two, is a reductionist fixation on the absolute centrality of *Federalist* no. 10 to proper understanding of its author's purposes and contributions. Despite repeated warnings that this single essay cannot be regarded as the sum of Madison's thinking,[38] a compulsive fascination with its themes has captivated modern scholarship since Charles A. Beard. Culminating in the work of Martin Diamond, the persistent inclination to permit the essay's arguments to overwhelm and overshadow every other facet of the founder's thought continues to exert a powerful attraction. Hugely misdirecting in itself, this fascination with this single number has been rendered all the more misleading by a flood of misinterpretations, among which Diamond's own has exercised the most enduring influence.[39]

The history of modern scholarly analysis of *Federalist* no. 10 has been notorious for the repeated overthrow of one compelling misinterpretation by another. At its publication and throughout the nineteenth century, number 10 was seldom singled out for special notice. Modern interest started, as did so much else, with Beard, who thought that it anticipated and confirmed his economic interpretation of political behavior.[40] In the 1950s, Beard's misreading was persuasively rebutted, yet the essay held an equal fascination for many of his critics. The economic misinterpretation was succeeded by a pluralist misreading, which attained its widest influence through the work of Robert A. Dahl.[41]

In cruder forms, which would suggest that Madison delighted in the clash of special interests and identified the outcome of such clashes with the public good, the pluralist interpretation, too, is now quite generally rejected. As Daniel Walker Howe has recently remarked, the public good was not for Hamilton or Madison whatever was agreed on by bargaining among competing interests: " 'Faction' was not a value-free concept for Publius; a faction was by definition evil."[42] Nevertheless, in versions that associate *Federalist* no. 10 with the culmination of a long-term trend toward the acceptance of interest-group politics and an ideology of pluralistic individualism, echoes of the pluralist interpretation still resound. And it is almost universally the case that even scholars who condemn the tendency to take this single number as the key to Madison's entire position find it difficult to free themselves from Beard's original mistake.[43] To see why this is so, it may be useful to explain more fully how an undue fas-

cination with the essay resonates with the predominant interpretation of
the founder's earlier intentions to construct a perfect circle, though a
circle that does not in fact describe his founding vision.

Studies of the Constitutional Convention strongly emphasize Madison's leadership of the attempt to reconstruct the central government as
a republic. This is wholly proper; it identifies his most important contribution and accords entirely with his own description of the major premise
of reform.[44] But Madison's determination to create a great republic can
be greatly misconstrued when it is studied at a distance of two hundred
years, and misconceptions fostered by our own location in the modern
great republic can be deepened and confirmed by a preoccupation with
the thoughts developed in this essay. However great the effort, it is nonetheless extremely difficult for scholars living in today's republic to remain
continually conscious of the very limited responsibilities that members of
the founding generation generally regarded as the proper field for federal
action; and *Federalist* no. 10 is a profound distraction from this task. To
minds accustomed to the modern scope of federal action, number 10 can
hardly fail to summon up a set of mental images profoundly different
from those which Madison could possibly have had in mind. Our images,
not his, may then profoundly color all our questions and conclusions.
Partly for this reason, a correct and necessary stress on Madison's commitment to a "nationalist" solution to the problems of the Union has
almost always been accompanied by inattention to the limits of his
wishes—limits that reveal important differences within the nationalist coalition, alert us to a secondary struggle that engaged him even as he
battled for this change, and highlight other objects that, to him, were no
less dear. Supported by an overbearing emphasis on Madison's determination to control majority abuses, an imprecise description of his stand
at the convention, blurring his desires with those of truly dedicated centralists among the members, necessarily suggests that Madison preferred
a more consolidated system than he did. And this impression can be reinforced again—the circle can be closed—by commentaries that inflate
his argument that private rights are safer in a large republic into the very
essence of his vision.

This was plainly Martin Diamond's inclination, and he followed it with
consequences that have shaped prevailing views from 1959 until the present. "Madison's whole scheme," says Diamond's memorable critique of
Beardian interpretations,

> essentially comes down to this. The struggle of classes is to be replaced by
> a struggle of interests ... a safe, even energizing, struggle which is com-
> patible with, or even promotes, the safety and stability of society ... In a

large commercial society the interests of the many can be fragmented . . . into relatively small groups, seeking small immediate advantages. . . . The mass will not unite as a mass to make extreme demands upon the few. . . . The Madisonian solution involved a fundamental reliance on ceaseless striving after immediate interest. . . . It is a system that has no necessary place and makes no provision for men of the founding kind. . . . Its perpetuation requires nothing like the wisdom and virtue necessary for its creation.[45]

From this beginning, Diamond built an argument that Madison, like Hamilton, preferred a unitary national government, pursued this preference at the Constitutional Convention, and defended the completed Constitution in the hope that it would gradually evolve into a wholly national system, changing his position only after 1789.[46] I have disputed several aspects of this argument in the preceding chapters; but in this passage Diamond also introduced the influential concept that the soul of Madison's solution to the fundamental problem of a liberal democracy was the idea of *multiplying interests in an extended commercial republic.* This formulation will require careful scrutiny as well, for there is surely not another phrase that tends to be employed so universally to summarize Madison's vision—and almost every connotation of the phrase is radically misleading. First, however, let me offer some preliminary comments on the essay's words and place, for it is not so much one reading or another as it is the universal tendency to generalize so broadly from its themes that is the crux of the interpretative problem.

Federalist no. 10 *is* indispensable to understanding the concerns and hopes that generated the Virginia Resolutions and inspired James Madison's defense of the completed Constitution. Agonized by his perception that the rule of state majorities had been persistently at odds with private rights and long-term public needs, unable to relinquish either his commitment to a people's government or to a wise and limited regime, Madison attempted to escape the trap by generalizing lessons drawn from his familiarity with multiplex divisions in the Continental Congress and, especially, from his experience of the Virginia struggle over state support for teachers of religion. If a single sect had dominated his society, he thought—or even if the largest sects had managed to maintain their brief alliance—no considerations could have blocked this measure. The multiplicity of jealous, disagreeing sects had done what no appeal to revolutionary principles and public good could have accomplished by itself. From this and other lessons, in the manner earlier described, he leaped to the conclusion—in the face of the prevailing wisdom—that private liberties and public good might both be safer in a large than in a small republic.[47] A large enough republic would incorporate so many sects and economic interests that majorities would seldom have a common interest in pursuing policies inimical to private rights or long-term public needs (or, at a minimum, would find it harder to discover and unite behind a common purpose of this sort). The large electoral districts of a large republic would also help to "break . . . the violence of faction," favoring the choice of representatives who would be less inclined to sacrifice the rights of the minority or the enduring public good to "temporary or partial considerations."[48]

This train of reasoning was basically complete when Madison prepared his "Vices of the Political System of the United States." He pressed it at the Constitutional Convention. It became a cornerstone of his assertion that the finished Constitution promised a republican solution to the vices most endemic to republics. Taken by itself, however, Madison's defense of an extension of the sphere by no means offers the sufficient, single key that can unlock his whole position. Taken by itself, it leads almost inevitably to serious distortion of his views.

This is true, to start, because the argument for the superiority of large republics seems to have no limits. Its logic seems to march unswervingly to the conclusion that almost all decision-making should be concentrated at the national level and in representatives elected in expanded districts. This, indeed, is how it often has been read. Seizing on his discontent with state assemblies and on his hope that the enlarged electoral districts of the great republic would encourage the selection of wiser, better leaders, analysts since Gordon Wood have often taken an improvement in the quality of representatives to be the crux of Madison's desires.[49] And yet, to see the concept of a filtration of talent as the centerpiece of Madison's solution is as problematic as the pluralist interpretation, which commonly insisted that the federal representatives envisioned in the essay would be little more than spokesmen for contending interest groups.

For Alexander Hamilton, perhaps for several others, the critical necessity of the 1780s and 1790s was, indeed, a massive transfer of authority from state to federal hands—and even to the hands of federal officials least responsive to the people. Madison's desires were different. Thus he did not even mention the idea of a filtration of the people's will in his letter to Thomas Jefferson of October 24, 1787, which sketched an early version of the essay. The possibility of an improvement in the quality of representation is mentioned only briefly, as an "auxiliary desideratum" of good government, in the "Vices of the Political System of the United States." And it is clearly identified as a secondary consideration in the tenth *Federalist* itself.[50] Madison did hope that the enlarged electoral districts of the great republic would favor better men. Nevertheless, he neither wanted nor expected federal representatives who would not truly represent the character and interests of their constituencies.[51] The *major* argument of the tenth *Federalist* is that the large republic will incorporate so many different interests as to make a factious majority unlikely. This reasoning immediately collapses if the representatives do not mirror the variety among the people. Laws that threaten people's rights are passed by legislatures, not directly by the people, and only if the legislators actually reflect the plural interests of the people will a multiplicity of interests check a combination for improper ends.[52]

Like the pluralist misreading, an interpretation overemphasizing Madison's desire for wiser, more impartial legislators carries with it the assumption that he wanted and expected an increasing concentration of decision-making at the federal level, although a radical consolidation of this sort was not what he supported at the Constitutional Convention, not what the convention recommended, and not what his contemporaries (as opposed to modern scholars) thought he was defending. Advocates of both interpretations have been swept too far by their preoccupation with his effort to defeat majority abuses and his bold insistence on the evident superiority of large republics for accomplishing this task.

But how could a mistake be easier to make? The fact, I think, is that the argument for the advantages of large republics did, indeed, have few if any limits—even in the founder's own imagination—*when he was concentrating only on the need for new securities for "justice,"* which helps account for his determined struggle for a federal negative on local laws. But it may also be a fact—a fact of absolutely critical importance—that Madison was simply not as single-mindedly concerned with added guarantees for private liberties as modern scholarship has taken him to be.[53]

Certainly, distortions rising inescapably from an excessive emphasis on this concern can be exaggerated wildly if, as often happens, scholars disregard the qualifications that Madison himself was careful to insert in every presentation of his thesis. For example, as he carefully explained to Jefferson, a single month before he wrote the famous essay, the general government created by the Constitution might safely have been trusted even with a veto on state laws because the national representatives, who (*as a group*) would be impartial judges of contentions in a single state, would at the same time have no interests separate from the interests of the body of the states or from the body of the people.[54] Not just one, but two considerations had been present in his mind throughout the shaping of the federal republic. Vicious, fluctuating legislation, he repeatedly observed, could issue *either* from the passions of an interested majority *or* from rulers who were able to pursue distinct ambitions of their own.[55] Enlargement of the size of the republic would make it harder for a dangerous majority to form, protecting the minority from popular abuses. But this was only one of the requirements of a sound republic, and Madison was as aware as any Antifederalist that an extension of the sphere entailed a heightened risk that representatives would not reflect the people's needs and will. Therefore, he emphatically did not believe that *any sort* of large republic would suffice. "There is a mean," he warned, "on both sides of which inconveniences will be found." Though small electorates may favor representatives so close to their constituents that they may be unable or unwilling to pursue the general good, large electorates may favor men who may be insufficiently "acquainted with all their local circumstances and lesser interests."[56] Extension of the sphere of the republic will therefore prove a truly democratic remedy for democratic ills "only . . . within a sphere of a mean extent," only when the local interests and the general ones are properly divided. "In too extensive" a republic, "a defensive concert may be rendered too difficult against the oppression of those entrusted with the administration."[57]

Though it was not his habit, Madison allowed himself to get entangled in his metaphors in passages like these, damaging the clarity of what he was attempting to convey. Still, the central points seem clear. Extension of the sphere of a republic was a geographic concept, suggested by the regional configuration of the multiplicity of economic interests and religious sects in the United States. The limits to this possibility, however—what he called the "mean extent"—were not imposed by size, but by the character of an appropriate relationship between the people and their rulers. Madison had *never* considered majority excess the only problem for republics; and even when he was preoccupied primarily with the majority's excesses, he did not forget that power can corrupt, that representatives will always have an interest in escaping their dependence on the people, and that power independent of the people was exactly what the Revolution had opposed. Therefore, he was always careful to insist that framers of a constitution "must first enable the government to control the governed; and . . . next . . . oblige it to control itself."[58] Neither need was more essential than the other, and dependence on the people for election never seemed to Madison an absolute assurance that the rulers would remain responsive to the needs and wishes of the people (although it always seemed the most important guarantee). Accordingly, his numbers of *The Federalist* were quite particular about the special sort of large republic he defended. *Federalist* no. 10 is full of references to *well-constructed* great republics, and Madison prepared two dozen other essays to explain what "well-constructed" means. Among the most important was number 51, whose most suggestive passage reads: "The larger the society, provided it lie within a practicable sphere, the more duly capable it will be of self-government. And happily for the *republican cause*, the practicable sphere may be carried to a very great extent, by a judicious modification and mixture of the *federal principle*."[59]

The Constitution, number 10 itself insists, had managed to achieve a "happy combination" of the relevant concerns of statesmen who were deeply dedicated to providing new securities for private rights, but only in a manner that would faithfully "preserve the spirit and form of popular government." Thus, according to their plan, state and national representatives were each to be entrusted with the duties for which each was properly equipped. Both were to be denied authority to act on matters poorly suited to their character or knowledge. Local representatives were not to participate in national decisions, which demanded less-constricted vision. Federal representatives were not to act on matters that required familiarity with local situations.[60]

There are many keys—not just one—to understanding Madison's participation in the Founding. Among the most important is to see it as a *process* in which Madison's initial preparations, the Philadelphia Convention, and the effort to secure adoption of the Constitution may be understood as acts in one extended drama. Every act is necessary to explain the others and the whole. Through all its course, this view of his participation would suggest, he had been searching for "the practicable sphere" of a republic, the "middle ground" between destructive localism (and the tyranny of unrestrained majorities) and undue concentration of authority in distant, unresponsive rulers. He found this "middle ground" only when he felt compelled to make a systematic, public effort to relate the Constitution to the principles of the republican revolution: only as he reconstructed the collective reasoning of the convention, compared the Constitution to the hopes with which he had begun, and listened to the views of its opponents. He found it in the document itself: in the compound, partly federal features of the system. A proper allocation of responsibilities between the state and general governments had always been an integral component of his thoughts about reform. The maintenance of this division, he continued to believe, was fully as essential to the preservation of the Revolution as a remedy for popular abuses. Indeed, the practicable limits of the sphere of a *republic* could be pushed to continental scope *only* by relying on the partly federal features of the system.

The essential points, to draw these thoughts together, may be summarized as follows. Even on its face, when it is read with serious attention to its cautions, *Federalist* no. 10 is absolutely not an unequivocal endorsement of the absolute superiority of large republics. It is quite explicitly an argument that large republics offer more security than small republics *from majority abuses and mistakes*. Moreover, even in this essay, Madison explicitly conceded that enlargement of the sphere of a republic could endanger popular control, and he was adamant in his insistence that the framers had provided for this danger. They had done so, he maintained, by weaving federal as well as national elements into their plan. Madison's increasing admiration for these federal elements has been explained away by Diamond, Brant, and others. It has been ignored in many of the finest commentaries on the famous essay.[61] The fact remains, however, that even in the essay which is overemphasized so much, it was a large, *compound* republic, not a large, consolidated one, that Madison was seeking to defend. Circumvention of this fact can be accomplished only by a tortuous construction of his statements and at heavy cost to understanding what he aimed at in the years surrounding the creation of the Constitution.[62]

Further observations might be made. Thus if *Federalist* no. 10 was not an unequivocal endorsement of a large republic, neither was it actually an argument for "multiplying" the variety of interests in the nation. Madison explicitly repudiated such a reading, insisting that a critical distinction should be made between *increasing* the variety of differences among the people and relying on existing differences that were inseparable from freedom.[63] Similarly, *Federalist* no. 10 was not, in fact, an argument for a "commercial" great republic. This expression is as clear a case as any we could find of forcing Madison into a Hamiltonian position. Thoughtlessly employed, it puts the great Virginian squarely in the opposite position from the one he actually assumed on one of the contemporary issues on which he and Hamilton most consistently disagreed. When Hamilton took up the pen, "Publius" was undeniably an eloquent proponent of the benefits of an expanding commerce.[64] When Madison was writing, nothing like this language can be found. Madison was quite aware, of course, that he was living in a "civilized" society, which commerce helped define;[65] but it is no exaggeration to insist, as has perhaps been shown, that he regarded sweeping constitutional reform as an *alternative* to excessive commercialization. And nowhere in *The Federalist* or in his other writings does Madison refer to the United States as a "commercial society" or a "commercial republic," as Hamilton does in *Federalist* no. 6.[66]

Admittedly, the careful reader will discover nothing in his best-remembered essay to support the argument that Madison regarded constitutional reform as an alternative to intensive economic development, but that should only serve to warn us once again against mistaking a distorted fragment of a frozen frame for the film in which it fits. Although it was a marvelous discussion of a palliative for faction, *Federalist* no. 10 was not intended as a comprehensive exploration of the nature of a sound republic. It did not elaborate Madison's rounded and considered view of human nature.[67] It barely hinted at other deep concerns. Madison included some internal cautions in the essay, which should help us to avoid confusing his assumptions with our own. Still, in terms suggested by the piece itself, this vice is so endemic to the modern exegesis of the essay that the only sure corrective is to read the number only in the light afforded by the other essays in the series and the other acts and writings of the years immediately surrounding Madison's participation in this project. Far too often, *Federalist* no. 10 has been accepted as the framework into which its context must be twisted. But if things are done the other way around, the essay will itself assume a different aspect. Examined in its context, *Federalist* no. 10 is not a summary of Madison's desires. It is a brilliant preface to a lengthy effort to defend the Constitution from objections that if valid, would have been as devastating to its author as they seemed to many of his foes.

Which brings us, once again, to the distinctive personality and attitudes that Madison brought to his participation in the project. For him, *The Federalist* was more than an attempt to justify what the convention had concocted. It was also part of an extended effort to define and comprehend a governmental system so peculiar that it lacked a name: a novel plan that he was temperamentally unable to support unless he was convinced that it was thoroughly consistent with the Revolution. Revolutionary principles, for Madison, had always meant *both* firm securities for private rights *and* the perpetuation of a form of government that derived entirely from, and remained responsive to, the body of an equal people. Pressed by circumstances, other members of his generation could be tempted to conclude that one of these two principles might have to be severely compromised in order to preserve the other. But Madison had something in his makeup that rebelled against this choice, and this rebellion was the crux of his distinctive contribution to the Founding. At the Constitutional Convention, he had advocated a reform that would repair the defects of the Union and restrain majority abuses without denying the majority its right to rule. "The practicable sphere of a republic," he had even then believed, would be that sphere which would be large enough to "break . . . the violence of faction," but not *so* large (or misshapen) that it would also break the democratic bond between the rulers and the ruled: the "communion of interests and sympathy of sentiments" that joins the legislators to the people.[68]

At the moment of its signing, to be sure, Madison did not consider the completed Constitution free from major defects; but he did believe that it preserved the democratic bond, and that it did define a better "middle ground" than had the old Confederation.[69] Then, in face of numerous and serious denials, he was forced to think again; and reconsideration told him that the Constitution was an even better instrument than he had first believed. "The practicable sphere of a republic," he was now prepared to hope, had actually emerged—and not by accident alone—from the collective wisdom of the Constitutional Convention, which he was not too proud to think might be superior to the ideas that he had thrown together on his own. Carefully respected, he was now prepared to think, the Constitution could provide as much security for *all* the objects of the Revolution as the nation's ingenuity could offer. Liberty, democracy, and union would be safer in a federal system of republics than in any simpler structure.[70] This is what his contributions to *The Federalist*— twenty-nine in all—were most concerned to show.

"Justice is the end of government," says *Federalist* no. 51. "It is the end of civil society. It ever has been and ever will be pursued until it be obtained or until liberty be lost in the pursuit."[71] Few of Madison's remarks have been so widely quoted, usually in efforts to suggest that he was speaking for a "modern liberal" philosophy in which protection of the rights of individuals is understood to be the purpose of political society, and individual participation in the popular direction of affairs, which "classical-republican" philosophers had valued much more highly, is understood as merely instrumental to this end.[72] Parts of several other numbers—and, of course, the whole of number 10—are often seen as further evidence that Madison's contributions to *The Federalist* were a landmark in the triumph of a modern politics of interest over an older politics of virtue, of a modern emphasis on freedom *from* societal constraints over a received insistence on a freedom *to* participate with equals in an active public life.[73] Since the early 1970s a movement from a "classical-republican" toward more completely modern modes of thought has been an organizing theme of revolutionary studies, and Madison's participation in the making and defense of the new government has been identified as pivotal in this transition.[74]

The benefits of this approach are not to be denied. The rediscovery of the compelling influence of a "classical-republican" or "civic-humanist" tradition has transformed our understanding of the early Revolution. A different understanding of the early Revolution has, in turn, produced a more precise appreciation of the changes introduced by constitutional reform. More recently, however, there has also been a gathering awareness that the terminology and content of this "classical to modern" or "republican to liberal" interpretation have themselves resulted in confusion and dispute. Several years of scholarly debate about the "modern liberal" and "classical-republican" dimensions of the Revolution have resulted in a growing recognition of the flaws embedded in the newer formulation. There is now a promise of some new agreements, and these new agreements may permit (and be promoted by) a clearer understanding of Madison's distinctive contributions. For, despite its benefits, the argument that Madison repudiated early revolutionary thought and moved America decisively toward modern, liberal assumptions can be nearly as misleading as overemphasizing his idea that an extension of the sphere of the republic would help control majority abuses.[75]

"Classical republican," it now appears, has proved a deeply troubling term for the collection of ideas whose influence on the Revolution scholars have been emphasizing since the publication of Wood's *Creation of the American Republic.* Over time, that term, which was originally employed for sensible and solid reasons, has encouraged an impression that the thinking of the early Revolution was considerably less modern than it was—less modern, at a minimum, than "modern" ordinarily implies for scholars trained in political theory.[76] For much of the 1970s and 1980s—partly as a consequence of this confusion over terms—historians and theorists alike described the "classical" and "liberal" traditions in a fashion that suggests that philosophically or analytically distinctive modes of thought, traditions whose development and implications may be separated for important objects of our own, were also separate and competing in the minds of those we study. But early revolutionary thinking, we may now be coming to agree, was always an amalgam of republican and liberal ideas, and these traditions did not stand in some objective sense as separate and competing choices. Rather, they were linked and blended in the minds of early-modern individuals whose thinking changed as they attempted to assimilate and manage new phenomena and new events, but who were neither truly classical nor fully modern in their thinking. Efforts to distinguish classical and liberal traditions have contributed importantly to understanding. More of them will doubtless be forthcoming. Nevertheless, these efforts, by their nature, have encouraged us to sever what the revolutionaries joined—and joined without a consciousness of contradiction. Attempts to stress the growing triumph or hegemony of liberal ideas have clarified some changes at a heavy cost to clearer understanding of some others. With Madison, at least, the habit of imagining a clash between the two traditions has resulted all too often in a portrait that is more a construct of our own interpretative models than a faithful image of our subject.

The Madison who set about to advocate the Constitution was, of course, quite unmistakably a liberal and a modern—provided that we use these words with care. Madison, that is, was deeply dedicated to the principle that governments originate from compacts and exist in order to protect individuals in what is properly their own. In his conception of the origins and limits of the state, his definition of the individual's domain, Madison, in fact, was as consistently Lockean as any of the Founding Fathers.[77] In other ways, as well, he was unquestionably a "modern." Certainly, his argument with Montesquieu's insistence that republics should be homogeneous and small—that classical republics rested on "heroic virtues which we admire in the ancients, and to us are known only by tradition"[78]—unequivocally insisted on a modern representative regime. The contest over the adoption of the Constitution was one of history's most fundamental reexaminations of the nature of republics. Hamilton and Madison were leaders of this effort, and both of them pursued the reexamination partly by contrasting the United States with truly classical regimes, the values of their countrymen with those of ancient Greece and Rome. In course of doing this, as Gordon Wood has best explained, they severed the defense of balanced government from its traditional association with a mixture of estates and placed it firmly on a new foundation.

Still, in recognizing that he was, in all these ways, a liberal and a modern, we need not conclude—it simply did not follow in his mind, however much the modern analyst believes that logic should have forced it—that Madison was breaking absolutely with the neoclassical tradition, which connected revolutionary thinking to the English Interregnum. He never thought of his rejection of classical democracy, together with the way of life and moral values of the ancient city-states, as a rejection of the thinking of the early Revolution. He did not even think that he was separating from the eighteenth-century sources of this thinking any more decisively than early revolutionaries had themselves already done. Moreover, Madison was justified in this conviction. He was fully as correct as scholars who have reached the opposite conclusion. At minimum, it can be shown conclusively that he was not so modern that he thought that countervailing institutions and a multiplicity of interests comprised a sufficient basis for a republic—and that many of his most distinctive contributions will be missed if we assume that he was choosing modern liberty in place of early revolutionary precepts and the neoclassical or British commonwealth tradition, which had influenced them so much.[79]

The fourteenth *Federalist* is an important illustration. In his second contribution to the series, which concluded the discussion of the benefits of union, Madison again distinguished classical democracies from modern representative republics, in which the people do *not* "meet and exercise the government in person." This remark has often been described as an amazing feat of verbal magic and a clear example of the Federalists' departure from tradition, since it turned the classical or Montesquieuan image of "republics," which emphasized direct, immediate participation by the people, squarely on its head.[80] Moreover, later in the essay, Madison insisted that the Constitution should not be rejected merely because it was new. "Is it not the glory of the people of America," he asked, that "they have not suffered a blind veneration for antiquity . . . to overrule the suggestions of their own good sense, the knowledge of their own situation, and the lessons of their own experience?" These comments, too, are often seen as challenging the neoclassical tradition, which is often said to have been fundamentally inimical to innovation. And yet, what seems to have been wholly overlooked in emphasizing Madison's departures from the "classical" conventions, is that he was not departing in the least from early revolutionary thinking on this subject. The English-speaking peoples, after all, had made their peace with representation a hundred years before the American Revolution, whose leaders *never* planned on anything except a representative regime. Madison was hardly casting off the eighteenth-century mode of thought when he insisted on the value of this modern innovation. He was hardly challenging original assumptions when he praised the leaders of the early Revolution for refusing to confine themselves to precedent and building "governments which have no model on the face of the globe." If modern Europe had invented representation, he exulted, America could "claim the merit of making the discovery the basis of unmixed and extensive republics." The early revolutionaries' critical departure from tradition, he believed, was not a sudden break with practices or theories rooted (only distantly) in the direct democracies of ancient Greece. The radical departure from the really relevant conventions was America's rejection of hereditary privilege and the American determination to erect new governments that would derive entirely from an equal people.[81]

It is not my point that there is nothing to be learned by analyzing Madison's dispute with Montesquieu or noticing his claim that "had every Athenian citizen been a Socrates, every Athenian assembly would still have been a mob."[82] It is not an error to insist that Madison was pioneering new ideas. The errors start when our interpretative model leads us to believe that early revolutionary thought was *ever* literally classical or Montesquieuan in its image of the citizen and the republic—or when we fail to see that Madison, like most of his opponents in the argument about the Constitution, had by no means broken free entirely from thinking that continued to be far from *wholly* modern in its values, patterns, or assumptions.[83] As he wrote his essays, Madison was not attempting to dissociate revolutionary thought from its original (and only partly classical) foundations, for which he said that Montesquieu was not, in fact, a sympathetic spokesman.[84] He was not attempting to depreciate the value or reduce the *current* scope of popular political participation, and he did not believe that "public liberty" (or popular self-governance) was viable without a certain virtue in the people. He was trying, as he saw it, to identify the constitutional mistakes that had originated in a faulty effort to combine the modern with the neoclassical variety of freedom. This required an effort to restate original assumptions with sobriety and care. It demanded clearer recognition of the tensions that would always be inherent in this combination. It did not, however, force a *choice between* the two traditions that the revolutionaries and their most important British sources had conventionally blended and combined.[85]

The often-quoted sentences from *Federalist* no. 51, with which this section opened, will support a set of inferences quite different from the ones usually drawn. On close consideration, I believe, these sentences by no means privilege private rights over the people's rule. They grant a nearly equal—and supreme—priority to both. "Liberty," the passage says—and "liberty" is unmistakably a synonym for popular control—*will* certainly be lost (however highly it is valued) if it renders private rights unsafe, for "justice" and protection of inherent rights are certainly the needs that lead to a society's creation. But "liberty" itself is also greatly to be valued, *both* as a security for other rights *and* for its own sake. Indeed, it was in order to prevent the loss of this great good, as I have argued all along, that Madison had hurled himself into the movement for reform. Yes, he was revolted by injustice. Certainly, he thought that many of the worst injustices were consequences of majority demands. Still, if he was deeply moved by his alarm about majority abuses, this was not the least because he was ferociously determined to preserve majority control.

The point has implications deeper than may be immediately apparent, and thus is worth making in a slightly different form. At the Constitutional Convention, Alexander Hamilton had candidly admitted that his own commitment to a perfectly republican regime had been severely shaken by his doubt that governments without hereditary parts could ever prove consistent with security for private rights or with a requisite consistency and vigor. Hamilton had not abandoned hope. Here and elsewhere, he repeatedly insisted that a number of expedients could still be tried before surrendering the revolutionary dream. Still, Hamilton's priorities seem clear. If forced to choose between a totally elective government and firm security for private rights, Hamilton would clearly opt for the latter.[86]

Would Madison have made the same decision? There is at least more room for doubt than modern analysts have usually conceded.[87] All that can be said for certain is that he consistently refused to choose, that his determination to escape this choice is the phenomenon that ought to seem most striking, and that these are facts which may suggest how poorly he is often represented. In effect, the modern emphasis on Madison's alarm about majority abuses has distracted us from his consistent dedication to republican solutions. It has covered over many of the ways in which the fears and aspirations of the British republican tradition continued to be central in his thought. Captivated by his search for new restraints on the immediate expression of the people's will, too many scholars have been inattentive to his underlying trust in popular control. But in the last analysis, it is his faith and not his fear that cries most loudly for attention. Faith, not fear, was in the end the element that set him off most clearly from many of the other signers of the Constitution and infused his effort to defend it.[88]

According to his late-life memorandum, Madison and Hamilton did not decide on any firm division of responsibilities for their collaboration on *The Federalist*.[89] Each, however, naturally pursued his own distinctive interests, so that there is much to learn by noticing the subjects with which each was principally concerned. Hamilton wrote most of sections 1 through 3 of his original prospectus (an examination of the benefits of union, the failure of the old Confederation, and the principal requirements of a more effective constitution), placing special emphasis throughout on the military needs and the commercial and financial benefits of an enduring union. At this point, he passed the pen to Madison, who was more concerned with theory and had kept the most extensive record of the Federal Convention.

Madison had entered the collaboration earlier with numbers 10, 14, and 18 through 20, which drew on his "Notes on Ancient and Modern Confederacies," to reinforce the argument "that a sovereignty over sovereigns, a government over governments, a legislation for communities as contradistinguished from individuals" had always proved as insupportable in practice as it now appeared in theory.[90] For his central subject, though, he picked the fundamental principles of the reform and the arrangement and extent of legislative powers (article 1 of the new Constitution). On these topics, he completed an unbroken stream of twenty-two essays (numbers 37–58), published between January 11 and February 20, 1788. Before he could complete them, he was under mounting pressure from his friends and family in Orange, who mailed him letter after letter warning that his presence at the state elections was essential to assure his seat in the Virginia state convention. Still, he stayed until the final moment to complete two essays on the Senate (numbers 62 and 63). Only then, he evidently felt, had he arrived at a convenient point at which to pass the article-by-article discussion back to Hamilton, who was, in any case, better suited for a long defense of the executive and judicial powers.

Knowing Madison, we can be sure that he absorbed a large proportion of the most important criticisms of the Constitution, many of the best of which were published or reprinted in New York. From these, from correspondence, and from recollections of the arguments in the convention, he was thoroughly familiar with the fears of his opponents. Realizing that their worries often flowed from principles he shared, he set about to meet them squarely and forthrightly.

Where did he begin? After an appeal for understanding of the difficulties the convention had confronted, he introduced the "first," most fundamental question: "whether the general form and aspect of the government be strictly republican?" "No other form," he wrote,

> would be reconcileable with the genius of the people of America, with the fundamental principles of the Revolution, or with that honorable determination which animates every votary of freedom to rest all our political experiments on the capacity of mankind for self-government. If the plan of the Convention therefore be found to depart from the republican character, its advocates must abandon it as no longer defensible.[91]

As an organizing theme for the substantial body of his essays, he undertook to show that the convention's plan was perfectly consistent, in the words of number 10, with "the spirit" as well as with the form "of popular government." The central government created by the Constitution, he maintained, was in itself the best-constructed representative republic that humanity had ever devised; and in the federal features of the system, every votary of freedom would discover all the new securities for liberty that good republicans could reasonably demand.

Opposition to the Constitution flowed from many sources and assumed a wide variety of forms, yet Antifederalists of every stripe, from every section of the country, chorused two related fears. These were the alarms to which the Federalists were most alert. For Madison, they were the worries that provoked his most extensive reexamination of the work of the convention and his most complete articulation of his own assumptions. The first was that the effort to concentrate greater power in a national majority would threaten local interests. The second was that this attempt, in practice, would subvert the people's rule by shifting an unlimited discretion into hands that they would not be able to control. *Federalist* no. 10, though seldom read this way, was in itself a partial answer to the fear that local liberties and local interests would be threatened by the national will. Here and in number 14, Madison introduced one critical component of his answer: "The general government is not to be charged with the whole power of making and administering laws. Its jurisdiction is limited to certain enumerated objects which concern all the members of the republic but which are not to be attained by the separate provisions of any."[92] A more elaborate discussion of the partly federal features of the system would become a central thread of his discussion. "First," however, he intended to dispel the fear of loss of popular control, which he admitted would, if justified, compel a Federalist capitulation. First, he meant to show that, under this new government, America was still to be a genuinely revolutionary nation.

Few critics of the Constitution could have faulted Madison for insufficient rigor in his definition of a popular republic. The fundamental problem for the Constitutional Convention, he began, had been the difficulty of "combining the requisite stability and energy in government with the inviolable attachment due to liberty and to the republican form." Experience had driven home the dangers of an ineffective system, not the least of which was growing discontent among the people. But stability and energy demanded lengthy terms of office and the execution of the laws "by a single hand." "The genius of republican liberty," by contrast, demanded "not only that all power should be derived from the people, but that those entrusted with it should be kept in dependence on the people by a short duration of their appointments, and that even during this short period, the trust should be placed not in a few but in a number of hands."[93] A republic, he continued, could be defined as "a government which derives all its powers directly or indirectly from the great body of the people, and is administered by persons holding their offices during pleasure, for a limited period, or during good behavior." But in America at least, it was agreed that "it is *essential* to such a government that it be derived from the great body of the society, not from an inconsiderable proportion or a favored class of it."[94]

By all of these criteria, as Madison conceived it, the central government created by the Constitution was unimpeachably republican in nature. Unlike the old Confederation, it was not to go into effect without explicit popular consent, nor could it operate without direct elections by the people, which would forge a closer link between the voters and Congress.[95] Critics charged, of course, that even the directly chosen lower house would "be taken from that class of citizens which will have least sympathy with the mass of the people and be most likely to aim at an ambitious sacrifice of the many to the aggrandizement of the few." But Madison did not believe that the defenders of the Constitution should defer to critics who professed a "flaming zeal for republican government yet boldly impeach the fundamental principle of it," who championed the people's rights yet seemed to be assuming that the people would elect "those only who will immediately and infallibly betray the trust committed to them." Of all objections, he maintained, this was the most astounding for republicans to make.[96]

"The aim of every political constitution," Madison maintained, "is or ought to be first to obtain for rulers men who possess most wisdom to discern and most virtue to pursue the common good of the society, and in the next place to take the most effectual precautions for keeping them virtuous whilst they continue to hold their public trust."[97] The plan of the convention met both tests, incorporating every safeguard that sincere republicans could wish. The House of Representatives would be elected by the body of the people: "not the rich more than the poor, not the learned more than the ignorant, not the haughty heirs of distinguished names more than the humble sons of obscure and unpropitious fortune," but all who had the right to vote in state elections. Any citizen who satisfied requirements of residence and age might be elected as a member, and the plan included every rational precaution for maintaining their dependence on the people. The representatives would enter office with affection for the voters: "There is in every breast a sensibility to marks of honor, of favor, of esteem, and of confidence which, apart from all considerations of interest, is some pledge for grateful and benevolent returns." Selfish motives would combine with these affections to encourage faithful discharge of the public trust. "Before the sentiments impressed on their minds by the mode of their elevation can be effaced . . . , they will be compelled to anticipate the moment [two years hence] when their power is to cease, . . . when they must descend to the level from which they were raised, there forever to remain unless" their conduct earned them reelection. In the meantime, representatives could pass no law which would not be as binding on themselves, their families, and their connections as on any other person—not, at least, so long as the electors still possessed "the vigilant and manly spirit which actuates the people of America, a spirit which nourishes freedom and in return is nourished by it."[98] These securities for faithfulness were all that human prudence could devise, and all that could be found in any of the states. They were as much as any genuine republican could wish.

> As there is a degree of depravity in mankind which requires a certain degree of circumspection and distrust, so there are other qualities in human nature which justify a certain portion of esteem and confidence. Republican government presupposes the existence of these qualities in a

higher degree than any other form. Were the pictures which have been drawn by the political jealousy of some among us faithful likenesses of the human character, the inference would be that there is not sufficient virtue among men for self-government, and that nothing less than the chains of despotism can restrain them from destroying and devouring one another.[99]

Madison preferred republican presuppositions.

Of course, the other branches of the central government were not to rest directly on the voters. The longer terms and indirect election of the president and senate represented the convention's recognition of the need for more stability and vigor. Again, however, Madison denied that these provisions were departures from the fundamental precepts of the Revolution. Stability and vigor were required to check the people's growing disaffection. They were qualities that every solid government required. Moreover, though dependence on the people for elections was unquestionably the foremost guarantee that rulers would be faithful to their charge, "experience has taught mankind the necessity of auxiliary precautions": "It may be a reflection on human nature that such devices should be necessary to control the abuses of government. But what is government itself but the greatest reflection of all on human nature? If men were angels, no government would be necessary. If angels were to govern men, neither external nor internal controls on government would be necessary." Since, however, men were neither beasts nor angels, "rival interests" had to be relied on to supply "the defect of better motives." (Not the "absence" of such motives, we should note, but yet their "defect"—in the representatives as well as in the voters.) As further guards against betrayal of the people's trust—and even as a check on momentary passions of their own—power had to be distributed among distinctive governmental branches, "standing on as different foundations as republican principles will well admit." And to maintain this distribution, each department had to have the means and motives to resist encroachments by the others: "Ambition must be made to counteract ambition. The interests of the man must be connected with the constitutional rights of the place."[100]

Madison's discussion of the constitutional division of responsibilities has always been considered one of his outstanding contributions. On this point, moreover, he was sharply conscious of the framers' disagreements with the writers of the early revolutionary constitutions, as well as of those early leaders' own departures from the eighteenth-century advocates of mixed and balanced constitutions. Once again, however, he insisted that the Constitutional Convention had departed from the early Revolution only to correct its oversights and misconceptions, only to incorporate the lessons of a lengthening experience into an effort to secure the fundamental objects on which all republicans agreed.

In order to defend the Constitution, Madison had little need to justify a bicameral Congress, and none at all to write a full defense of a division of authority between the great departments. Of all the revolutionary constitutions, only Pennsylvania's (followed for a time by Georgia's and Vermont's) had trusted legislative powers to a unicameral assembly. All, without exception, had assumed, as Madison now put it, that "the accumulation of all powers, legislative, executive, and judiciary, in the same hands, whether of one, a few, or many and whether hereditary, self-appointed, or elective, may justly be pronounced the very definition of tyranny."[101] But many of the most persuasive critics of the Constitution argued that its framers had repeatedly and dangerously violated just this maxim, blending powers that they should have kept distinct and doing so in ways that seemed entirely likely to expose the House of Representatives—still widely thought of as the popular or "democratic" branch—"to the danger of being crushed by the disproportionate weight of the other parts."[102] In order to rebut these criticisms, Madison attempted first to clarify the concept of a separation of powers, then to demonstrate that there was no substantial danger to the lower house.

Montesquieu, "the oracle who is always consulted and cited on this subject," was once again his foil. But Montesquieu himself, said Madison, had used the British constitution "as the perfect model" for his rules, a system in which "the legislative, executive, and judiciary departments are by no means totally separate and distinct." Thus, the Frenchman "did not mean that these departments ought to have no *partial agency* in or no *control* over the acts of each other." He meant "no more than this: that where the *whole* power of one department is exercised by the same hands which possess the *whole* power of another department, the fundamental principles of a free constitution are subverted."[103] Indeed, Madison continued, unless the three departments "be so far connected and blended as to give to each a constitutional control over the others, the degree of separation which the maxim requires . . . can never in practice be duly maintained." The clearest effort to divide the three great powers would inevitably fail unless each branch was given a sufficient check on the essential operations of the others as to arm it with a "practical security . . . against the invasion of the others."[104]

A faulty understanding of these precepts, Madison maintained, had been encouraged by the circumstances of the early Revolution. In fact, this faulty understanding was primarily responsible for many of the evils that the Federal Convention had confronted. The writers of the early constitutions

> seem never for a moment to have turned their eyes from the danger to liberty from the overgrown and all-grasping prerogative of an hereditary magistrate, supported and fortified by an hereditary branch of the legislative authority. They seem never to have recollected the danger from legislative usurpations; which, by assembling all powers in the same branch, must lead to the same tyranny as is threatened by executive usurpations.[105]

In order to maintain a firm division of the three departments, Madison insisted, the members of each branch "should have as little agency as possible in the appointment of the members of the others," as little power as is practicable to alter "the emoluments annexed to their offices," and "the necessary constitutional means and personal motives to resist encroachments" on their own domain.[106] Fearing the executive and upper house, the writers of the early constitutions had been insufficiently concerned to guard the other branches from encroachments by the popular assemblies. "Everywhere," in consequence, the legislative branch had been "extending the sphere of its activity and drawing all power into its impetuous vortex."[107] Recognizing this, but still assuming that the legislature must and would predominate in a republic, the framers of the Federal Constitution had attempted to avoid a replication of the problem by giving the executive a veto, instituting a division of the single-chamber Congress, and rendering the legislative houses "by different modes of election and different principles of action as little connected with each other as the nature of their common functions and their common dependence on society will admit."[108]

In none of this, however, was there any violation of the maxim that the branches should remain distinct, any danger that the House of Representatives would be unable to resist a combination of the other branches, or any violation of the democratic precepts of the Revolution. The reference to the "common dependence on society" of both the Senate and the House followed shortly after Madison's insistence that there were two ways "to guard one part of the society against the injustice of the other," the minority against majorities "united by a common interest":

> The one by creating a will in the community independent of the majority, that is, of the society itself; the other by comprehending in the society so many separate descriptions of citizens as will render an unjust combination

of a majority of the whole very improbable, if not impracticable. The first method prevails in all governments possessing an hereditary or self-appointed authority. This, at best, is but a precarious security, because a power independent of the society may as well espouse the unjust views of the major as the rightful interests of the minor party, and may possibly be turned against both. The second method will be exemplified in the federal republic of the United States.[109]

Madison's discussion of the senate was consistent with this effort to distinguish the American solution from the British. To the argument that such a body would degenerate into an aristocracy, it could be answered, he remarked, "that liberty may be endangered by the abuses of liberty as well as by the abuses of power . . . and that the former rather than the latter is apparently most to be apprehended by the United States."[110] Moreover, legislators "may forget their obligations to their constituents and prove unfaithful to their important trust." The institution of a second legislative house "doubles the security to the people by requiring the concurrence of two distinct bodies in schemes of usurpation or perfidy where the ambition or corruption of one would otherwise be sufficient." In addition, the existence of a smaller legislative body, holding office for a longer term, would check "the propensity of all single and numerous assemblies to yield to the impulse of sudden and violent passions." Chosen in the manner "most congenial with the public opinion" and without regard to property or birth, the senators could be expected to impart the qualities of wisdom and stability traditionally hoped for from an upper house, but they could not become an aristocracy without corrupting first themselves and then the other branches of the state and general governments, together with "the people at large."[111]

The House of Representatives was large enough, in Madison's opinion, "for the purposes of safety, of local information, and of diffusive sympathy with the whole society."[112] And once these vital qualities had been assured, every increase in its size would work against the objects that critics wanted to secure. Not only would a further increase make it harder to secure the ablest men, it would in practice make it easier for eloquent, ambitious leaders to dominate proceedings. With a very large assembly, "the countenance of the government may become more democratic, but the soul that animates it will be more oligarchic."[113] Here, again, the Constitution would assure a happy balance. Chosen by the people, for brief terms, the members of lower house *would* faithfully reflect the voters' interests, character, and will—at least on all those great and general subjects which would be the constitutional responsibilities of Congress. And the character and powers of this house were ample to defend it from encroachments.

In any confrontation with the other branches, which did not possess the means to undermine its independence, the House of Representatives was certain to be favored by the people. "The utmost degree of firmness that can be displayed by the federal senate or president will not be more than equal" to defending them against the power of the lower house, even on occasions when the indirectly chosen branches "will be supported by constitutional and patriotic principles."[114]

In one respect, of course, the constitution of the senate did depart from democratic precepts. It provided for an equal vote for states instead of people. Madison did not deny it. He did not disguise his lingering dissatisfaction. "It is superfluous," he wrote, "to try by the standards of theory" a provision that was "evidently the result of compromise between the opposite pretensions of the large and the small states," a provision that would have been "more rational" if the smaller states had actually possessed distinctive interests of their own. Nevertheless, he added, state equality assumed a certain rationality in terms of the peculiar logic of the system, and it was "not impossible" that the provision might prove "more convenient in practice than it appears to many in contemplation." "In a compound republic partaking both of the national and federal character, the government ought to be founded on a mixture of the principles of proportional and equal representation." The mixture would assure that no law could be passed "without the concurrence first of a majority of the people, and then of a majority of the states." The equally apportioned senate was "at once a constitutional recognition of the portion of sovereignty remaining in the individual states and an instrument for preserving that residuary sovereignty."[115] Thus, Madison employed his essays on the senate to complete a long discussion of the federal division of responsibilities, which was another of his most distinctive contributions to contemporary thinking—and an aspect far more crucial to his central argument than many commentaries may suggest.

Not infrequently, the controversy over the adoption of the Constitution has been represented as, at heart, an argument between the advocates of small and large republics: between Americans whose principal commitment was to small, self-governing communities and those who hoped to move the theater of politics onto a broader stage, where popular desires could be refined and filtered, countervailing interests could become a substitute for public virtue as a mechanism for protecting private rights and public good, and an efficient conduct of affairs would bind the people to the system.[116] Without denying that important insights have resulted from this view, it may be useful to reflect that even its most capable proponent recognized its limitations. For there were few Americans in 1788 who really thought that small republics (or even states as large as Massa-

chusetts or Virginia) could endure without the Union; and there were
also few who really advocated a consolidated system in which countervailing institutions, better leadership, and clashing private interests would
provide a substitute for virtue. Madison was not among the latter group,
although, of course, he has been frequently portrayed as probably its leading spokesman. To represent him in this way demands a resolute dismissal
of the many passages in which he says that liberty depends on vigilant,
continuing participation by the people. It also calls for a determined disregard for the essential role in guaranteeing liberty that he explicity ascribed to federal features of the Constitution. The latter argument, in fact,
is probably the clearest instance of how the Antifederalist critique affected
his conception of the charter.

Opponents of the Constitution knew, as Madison had said in his initial
essays, that the plan of the convention did not grant a comprehensive
jurisdiction to the federal Congress, president, or courts. Had it done so,
he conceded, critics would have been on better ground for their objection
that the Union was too large to be administered as a republic.[117] Thus,
although he opened his discussion of the reconstructed system with a
comprehensive demonstration that the plan was only partly national in
nature, Madison was more concerned to show that it could not *become*
entirely national in time.[118] This was what the critics really feared. This
was the anxiety that he was most concerned to ease. This, indeed, may
well have been the single point on which he disagreed most clearly with
the critics—not about the incompatibility of liberty with a complete consolidation, not about the proper distribution of responsibilities between
the central government and states, but over whether any such division of
authority could actually endure.

Madison insisted that it could, that governmental sovereignty—whatever "theoretic politicians" said—*could* be successfully and lastingly divided, provided that the state and general governments were both the
creatures of a common master, who was ultimately sovereign over both.[119]
More specifically, he argued that the central government could not absorb
the powers of the states as long as both depended on a people capable
of freedom.

In numbers 41 through 44, Madison attempted clause by clause to
show that every power granted to the general Congress was "absolutely
necessary" for a government "commensurate to the exigencies of the
Union."[120] If this was so, he reasoned, was it not "preposterous" to argue
that the mass of this authority might "derogate from the importance" of
the states? "Was the precious blood of thousands spilt . . . not that the
people of America should enjoy peace, liberty, and safety, but that . . .
particular municipal establishments might . . . be arrayed with certain dig-

nities and attributes of sovereignty?" To say so, he believed, amounted to reviving "the impious doctrine in the old world that the people were made for kings, not kings for the people.... As far as the sovereignty of the states cannot be reconciled to the happiness of the people, ... let the former be sacrificed to the latter." The only question worthy of discussion was whether the remaining powers of the states would be endangered by the mass that had been transferred, and reason and experience alike suggested that the federal balance was unlikely to be threatened from this side. In case of conflict, "the state governments will have the advantage of the federal government whether we compare them in respect to the immediate dependence of the one on the other, to the weight of personal influence which each side will possess, to the powers immediately vested in them, ... [or to] the probable support of the people."[121]

"The state governments," Madison pointed out, "may be regarded as constituent and essential parts of the federal government, whilst the latter is nowise essential to the operation or organization of the former." The president would usually be elected by the legislatures of the states. The senate always would. The dependence of these federal branches on the states would be "more likely to beget a disposition too obsequious than too overbearing." In addition, the federal government would appoint fewer officers than the states (even if, as seemed unlikely, it decided to appoint its own collectors of internal revenue). "There will consequently be less of personal influence" on its side. No less important, "the powers delegated ... to the federal government are few and defined. Those which are to remain in the state government are numerous and indefinite. The former will be exercised principally on external objects, as war, peace, negotiation, and foreign commerce." State powers, on the other hand would extend "to all the objects which ... concern the lives, liberties, and properties of the people and the internal order, improvement, and prosperity of the state."

Nowhere in the series did Madison suggest more clearly how restricted was his concept of the sphere of federal action. Such passages, of course, have often been dismissed as instances of special pleading: examples of suppressing private views in order to promote adoption of the Constitution. The soundness of this judgment must depend, however, on the strengths and weaknesses of differing assessments of Madison's objects and position in the years before and after he expressed them. The evidence from the convention and its background, I believe, supports the view that he was not dissembling either his convictions or his wishes when he argued that the Constitution "proposes ... much less ... the addition of NEW POWERS to the Union than ... the invigoration of its ORIGINAL POWERS." For the most part, he insisted, the Constitution only "substitutes a more effectual mode of administering" powers that, in theory, were already vested in the Confederation Congress. These powers were by no means as extensive as the powers still residing in the states. They did not amount to a "consolidation." Neither was it likely that they would inexorably expand.[122]

Critics of the Constitution, Madison implied, had not adjusted fully to the implications of the Revolution. When opponents of the plan envisioned the inevitable subversion of the states, they were forgetting that the state and central governments were both to be "substantially dependent" on the people, controlled by a "common superior" who would ultimately guide them both. "The federal and state governments are in fact but different agents and trustees of the people, instituted with different powers and designated for different purposes." Whether either would be able "to enlarge its sphere of jurisdiction" would depend on their common master, whose "first and most natural attachment" would "beyond doubt" be to the respective states. Indeed, the members of the central government itself would carry state attachments with them into office. "Measures will too often be decided according to their probable effect, not on the national prosperity and happiness, but on the prejudices, interests, and pursuits of the . . . individual states." The Constitution would encourage broader views, but federal representatives would certainly retain sufficient local spirit to be "disinclined to invade the rights of individual states."

Suppose, however, that a different disposition should appear. Federal encroachments, Madison concluded, would produce a general alarm. "Plans of resistance would be concerted," as they were against Great Britain. A handful of ambitious federal usurpers would be faced with "thirteen sets of representatives" and "the whole body of their common constituents." "The only refuge left for those who prophecy the downfall of the state governments is the visionary supposition that the federal government may previously accumulate a military force for the projects of ambition." But this involved the supposition that the people and the states would first elect a succession of plotting traitors and then sit idly by, supplying the materials, until the storm should burst. No sober patriot would make this supposition, Madison believed. Neither would a sober patriot conclude that federal plotters could succeed if they were somehow able to create as large a standing army as the country could support. Twenty-five or thirty thousand regulars could never conquer half a million citizens in arms, "officered by men chosen from among themselves, fighting for their common liberties, and united and conducted by [state] governments possessing their affections and confidence." If these American advantages were universally enjoyed, "the throne of every tyranny in Europe would be speedily overturned in spite of the legions which surround it."[123]

In *Federalist* no. 41, Madison had laid down basic guidelines for a rational consideration of the Constitution. A dispassionate examination, he had argued, should first review the "sum or quantity of power" vested in the general government, and then assess its distribution. Recognizing that "a power to advance the public happiness" might always be abused, a careful analyst should ask two fundamental questions: "whether any part of the powers transferred to the general government be unnecessary or improper, [and] whether the entire mass of them be dangerous to the portion of jurisdiction left in the several states." Pursuing both of these inquiries through the body of his essays, Madison believed that he had shown that every power granted to the general Congress was at once required and guarded "as effectually as possible against a perversion."[124] Accordingly, he did not argue merely that the people's liberty was not endangered by the Constitution. He insisted that the people's rights, both private and collective, would be safer in this complicated system than in any other government that history had seen. "In the compound republic of America," he wrote, the will of the majority would be refined and purified by passing it successively through several different filters. "The power surrendered by the people is first divided between two distinct governments and then the portion alloted to each, subdivided among distinct and separate departments." Within each set of governments, the different branches would be chosen sometimes more and sometimes less directly by the people, which would guarantee a due concern for both their short- and long-term needs. The state and general governments would each be charged with the responsibilities that each was best equipped to handle. Each would help control the other "at the same time that each will be controlled by itself." Thus the product of successive distillations of the people's will would be, withal, the well-considered wishes of the people. No single branch of any part of the compound republic—indeed, no likely combination of a number of the branches—would be able to pursue distinctive interests its own; and future generations would continue to enjoy as much self-government as human nature would allow.[125]

Shortly after reading *Federalist* no. 1 and weeks before his own initial contribution to the series, Madison had written to an old Virginia friend, one of many who reported that the state's most influential men were thoroughly divided by the Constitution. He was "truly sorry," he remarked, "to find so many respectable names on your list of adversaries." The division of opinion on so critical a question struck him as "a melancholy proof of the fallibility of the human judgment and of the imperfect progress yet made in the science of government." He hoped, however, that the people and their leaders would in time conclude "that if any Constitution is to be established by deliberation and choice, it must be examined with many allowances and must be compared, not with the theory which each individual may frame in his own mind, but with the system which it is meant to take the place of and with any other which there might be a probability of obtaining."[126]

The writing of *The Federalist* enormously enriched its authors' understanding of the Constitution. Like any project of this sort, it also changed their minds—not just because it forced a fresh and closer study of the text, but also because it forced them to be conscious of their own assumptions, to articulate their thoughts, and to construct coherent explanations of their own political positions. For Madison, I think, the effort to rebut the critics, which was very like a many-sided confrontation with himself, completed yet another stage of personal, political, and mental maturation. His was a capacious mind, inherently respectful of the complications of an issue, deeply conscious of the strengths on every side, insistent on conclusions that took complexities into account. *The Federalist* was very much the challenge he required to bring his thoughts to focus, bind them into new configurations, and construct an unexampled synthesis of revolutionary thought. The effort shaped him into greatness as a thinker and, together with his contributions to the framing of the Constitution, gave him influence few could match. Judging from how this influence would be used, it also greatly strengthened his commitment to the plan, settling underlying doubts and leaving him convinced that the reform was better than he had originally believed. Nevertheless, as he approached completion of the project, his appeal to his opponents asked them to apply the same criteria that he had written of in private after reading Hamilton's first essay.

A general recognition of a crisis, Madison observed, had led to the appointment of the Federal Convention. Given the inherent difficulties of the task, it should not seem surprising if the Constitution showed

some deviations from that artificial structure and regular symmetry which an abstract view of the subject might lead an ingenious theorist to bestow on a Constitution planned in his closet. . . . The real wonder is that so many difficulties should have been surmounted, and surmounted with a unanimity almost as unprecedented as it must have been unexpected. It is impossible for any man of candor to reflect on this circumstance without

partaking of the astonishment. It is impossible for the man of pious reflection not to perceive in it a finger of that Almighty hand which has been
so frequently and signally extended to our relief in the critical stages of
the Revolution.[127]

Opponents of the Constitution recognized the crisis, he continued, yet
they were so divided in their reasons for resistance that if they could be
assembled in a second general convention, they would never reach a positive agreement. Moreover, as they often failed to see, most of their objections to the Constitution could be leveled even more effectively against
the Articles of Confederation. Therefore, why not test the new against the
old? "It is not necessary that the former should be perfect; it is sufficient
that the latter is more imperfect. No man would refuse to give brass for
silver or gold because the latter had some alloy in it."[128]

As Madison put down his pen, he still may not have judged the Constitution to be perfect, but he did believe that there was nothing in it that
debased its revolutionary metal. He believed that its rejection could entail
the failure of reform and, with this failure, the collapse of the Confederation. And he was thoroughly convinced—it was, as always, his supreme
consideration—that a cataclysm of the Union would be catastrophic for
the Revolution. Accordingly, although he was never very good at putting
passion onto paper (and was probably embarrassed in the trying), he reserved perhaps his strongest language for this point:

We have seen the necessity of union as a bulwark against foreign danger,
as the conservator of peace among ourselves, as the guardian of our commerce and other common interests, as the only substitute for those military
establishments which have subverted the liberties of the old world, and as
the proper antidote for the diseases of faction, which have proved fatal to
other popular governments and of which alarming symptoms have been
betrayed by our own. . . . Hearken not to the unnatural voice which tells
you that the people of America, knit together as they are by so many chords
of affection, can no longer live together as members of the same family.
. . . Shut your ears against the poison which it conveys; the kindred blood
which flows in the veins of American citizens, the mingled bood which they
have shed in defense of their sacred rights, consecrate their union and
excite horror at the idea of their becoming aliens, rivals, enemies. And if
novelties are to be shunned, believe me the most alarming of all novelties,
the most wild of all projects, the most rash of all attempts, is that of rending
us in pieces in order to preserve our liberties and promote our happiness.[129]

Fortified in this position, weapons freshly honed, the author girded for
the battle in Virginia.

CHAPTER EIGHT

The Virginia
Ratifying Convention

FROM TIME TO TIME, REALITY SURPASSES ANY DRAMA we could reasonably believe. It did so in the Old Dominion in 1788. Eight states had ratified the Constitution when Virginia's state convention met; nine were needed for adoption. No one doubted that the national decision was at stake, for all of the remaining states had potent oppositions, and everyone assumed that they would follow Virginia's lead in ratifying the reform or in insisting on conditions that were likely to defeat it. Yet everyone agreed, as well, that the elections had resulted in a gathering too evenly divided to predict. Thomas Jefferson was still in France, his sentiments so mixed that both sides tried to claim him. George Washington did not attend, knowing that his presence might have smacked of personal ambition while his absence would not diminish his influence. With these exceptions, though, the meeting brought together nearly every public man of major stature in the commonwealth that occupied about a fifth of the United States in 1788: Madison, John Marshall, Edmund Pendleton, George Mason, Patrick Henry, James Monroe, and many others who were overshadowed only by these giants.[1] Perhaps no other state—at this or any other time—could have assembled such a cast, and nowhere were such towering abilities so evenly divided. As the meeting came to order, Madison was marginally more optimistic than his foes, estimating a majority of three or four among the 160 present. But many delegates were wavering or undecided, and the Antifederalists believed that most of them could be persuaded to demand amendments. The circumstances favored Patrick Henry, who needed only to provoke more doubts than Federalists could put to rest, and who was every bit as capable of dominating a Virginia public meeting as his legend would suggest.[2]

In Virginia, as throughout the country, popular reception of the Constitution had at first been overwhelmingly enthusiastic. Fairfax County voters ordered Mason to support a state convention and made it clear that he would not be representing them when it assembled.[3] Edmund Randolph fretted over mounting pressure to explain why he had not united with the signers.[4] On October 31, 1787, the legislature scheduled March elections and called a state convention to convene in Richmond on the first Monday in June.[5] As Madison had feared, however, opposition quickly jelled; and by November, under Patrick Henry's influence, the Assembly was debating resolutions to finance a delegation to a second federal convention if such should be required.[6] Dismayed by the division of the state's great men, on which he blamed the growing popular resistance, Madison abandoned his initial hope that he could skip the state convention.[7] He was anything but eager for the contest, foreseeing that a public confrontation with "several very respectable characters whose esteem and friendship I greatly prize may unintentionally endanger the subsisting connection." But Washington and others argued that his presence was essential, and he realized that "every private inclination" should be "sacrificed" on this occasion. "If I am informed that my presence at the [county] election . . . be indispensable," he promised Washington, "[I] shall submit to that condition also, though it is my particular wish to decline it."[8]

Madison despised political campaigning and had never really "run" for an election. As the winter passed, however, letter after letter from his family and friends insisted that the Antifederalists were stronger and more scheming than he had anticipated and that he would have to be in Orange County by early March to guarantee his seat in the convention.[9] Perhaps because he dreaded it so much, perhaps because he wanted to complete his essays on the Senate, he delayed until the final moment. He left New York about March 1, spent several days in Philadelphia and at Mount Vernon, and did not reach home until the very eve of the election.[10] At the Orange County Courthouse on March 24, he was compelled "to mount . . . the rostrum" for the first time in his life and "launch into a [long] harangue" in order to correct "the most absurd and groundless prejudices against the federal Constitution."[11]

Orange County was secure (if it was ever really threatened); Madison and James Gordon Jr. defeated their Antifederalist opponents by a margin of 4 to 1.[12] The state returns, however, offered no such cheer. Though there were numerous exceptions, the division in Virginia followed a familiar pattern: the least commercial portions of the state, most clearly Patrick Henry's Southside, tended to oppose the Constitution; the most commercial portions, especially the Northern Neck, overwhelmingly endorsed it; the central Piedmont was divided.[13] Overall, the vote was inconclusive; several delegates were little known, and many more could not be fitted neatly into either camp. As Madison explained, the Constitution split Virginians into Federalists and Antifederalists *and* Federalists who favored some amendments.[14] If the latter, as expected, supported the strategy that Federalists had pioneered in Massachusetts—to ratify the plan while recommending changes to the first new Congress—the supporters of the Constitution probably comprised a small majority east of the Appalachian Mountains. But many thought the outcome might depend on the Kentucky members, who were generally assumed to be embittered by the northern readiness to close the Mississippi River—the same consideration to which most attributed Patrick Henry's opposition.[15]

In the weeks between the March elections and the June convention, Madison did everything he could. He wrote repeatedly to Federalists in Maryland, South Carolina, and New York to urge the speediest delivery of any news that might improve the outlook in Virginia. He peppered his Kentucky friends with reassurances about the Mississippi.[16] Most important, perhaps, he pressed his effort, carefully pursued through months of correspondence, to persuade his old friend Randolph to get off the fence he had been straddling since they had parted at the Constitutional Convention. At last, he got the opening he needed. When Randolph admitted that he now believed that only "a coalition of the high and low Federalists" could "save the federal government," Madison responded that he would be pleased "to see a coalition among all the real Federalists." But such a coalition, he was quick to add, could only happen on the Massachusetts plan of "recommendatory alterations," not on Governor Randolph's plan for previous amendments and a second general convention. "A conditional ratification or a second convention appears to me utterly irreconcilable . . . with the dictates of prudence and safety," Madison explained. In the first place, this idea could only work if six or eight approving states would first rescind their unconditional ratifications. Even then, upon the meeting of a second federal convention, it would be extremely easy for a few designing men to wreck it by insisting on amendments that could never be approved in other sections of the Union. "Desperate measures," Madison reminded Randolph, were Patrick Henry's "game." Mason, too, was "ripening fast for going every length." Indeed, the latter's ire, he none too subtly added, "no longer spares even the *moderate opponents* of the Constitution."[17] When Randolph answered that he realized that any plan for previous amendments might indeed provide a cover for a "higher game," Madison could hope that he had gained an influential convert.[18] Unhappily, his other efforts met with less success. As he was packing for the trip to Richmond, he received the first reports on the elections in Kentucky. The Constitution, he lamented, now appeared to have "a very minute" majority on its side.[19]

At the Massachusetts state convention, according to reports from Rufus King, supporters of the Constitution had been able to command a huge preponderance of talent. There, indeed, the very eloquence of its supporters proved a problem. Specifically expressed objections to the Constitution could be answered, King complained. The really baffling difficulty was the opposition's fixed "distrust of men of property or education." Every effort to respond to that served only to confirm that all the lawyers, judges, clergymen, and merchants favored the reform, that it was "the production of the rich and ambitious."[20]

Madison, to whom King wrote, may have recalled his letter wryly when the Richmond gathering convened. In all the ratifying states, the overwhelming weight of social and political prestige had favored the reform. At the Virginia state convention, Federalists were neither certain that they had sufficient votes nor confident that they could hold the votes they had in face of the forensic talents and the backstage stratagems of their opponents. Most of all, they feared the mesmerizing might of Patrick Henry's tongue, together with concerted efforts, in the hall and out, to play on the members' "local interests"—especially the western interest in an open Mississippi.[21] From one perspective, then, the meeting brought together nearly every man of major influence in the country's largest state for a dramatic recapitulation of the larger national debate—an argument in which the Antifederalists would have the oratorical and tactical advantage. From another angle, it would not suffice for Madison and his supporters to rebut a moving argument that constitutional reform might undermine the democratic Revolution. Somehow, they would also have to show that it would not endanger the essential interests of Virginia. No wonder Jefferson remarked that Madison would be the Constitution's main support, "but though [he is] an immensely powerful one, it is questionable whether he can bear the weight of such a host."[22] It was to be his greatest test, and he would meet it with perhaps his most revealing explication of his early understanding of the Constitution.

On June 3, 1788, as soon as the convention had completed its preliminary business, George Mason moved for full discussion of the Constitution, clause by clause, before a question should be taken. Suspecting that the Federalists might have a small majority, Mason feared that they might force a decision before the opposition could develop its appeal for previous amendments. Madison immediately agreed to Mason's motion, less because he doubted that he had the votes than because he was determined to avoid alienating his opponents.[23]

Mason's motion, it is sometimes said, was a severe strategic blunder, since no one could match Madison in a clause-by-clause examination of the Constitution. In fact, however, the convention followed this procedure very loosely through its first few days. Patrick Henry raised repeated, often devastating objections, directed less at particular provisions of the proposed Constitution than at its fundamental thrust and nature. The Federalists were forced to meet him on his own terrain. With help from Madison, George Nicholas, and Henry "Light Horse Harry" Lee, Edmund Randolph took the point, stunning the convention by immediately announcing that he still retained the reservations that had led him to withhold his name, but that the unconditional approval of the eight adopting states had simplified the question. Virginians, Randolph said, had only to decide between the Union and disunion, to which he never would agree.[24]

Under Henry's inescapable direction, the debates went quickly to the fundamentals. "The people," Henry opened, "are exceedingly uneasy and disquieted" with this "alarming" plan "to change our government." Delegated to prepare amendments to the Articles of Confederation, the members of the Philadelphia Convention had instead proposed a change "as radical as that which separated us from Great Britain," a plan of government that would transform the United States from a confederation into a national republic. "You ought to be extremely cautious," Henry warned. All "our privileges and rights are [once again] in danger." "A wrong step . . . now will plunge us into misery, and our republic will be lost."[25]

Patrick Henry gloried in his role of revolutionary tribune of the people, and he played it to the full in this assembly. Yet language of this sort was not adopted merely for theatrical effect. When the convention met, the nation's republican experiment was barely twelve years old. It was by no means inconceivable that it could fail. The standard wisdom taught that a republic should be small enough and homogeneous enough that all its citizens would share a set of common interests and could keep a jealous watch on the ambitions of their rulers. Now, suddenly, the Constitution offered to create a national republic larger than the largest European state. It sketched a central government whose powers would be greater than the British Parliament had claimed—a government, moreover, strikingly similar to the hated British form, where only the lower house of legislature would be chosen in direct elections by the people. "I may be thought suspicious," Henry said, "but, sir, suspicion is a virtue [when] its object is the preservation of the public good."[26]

Having spent so much of his career resisting an encroaching, unresponsive central government, the aging firebrand was unmoved by Federalist insistence that rejection of the Constitution might destroy the

Union. He was unimpressed by Federalist descriptions of the benefits the nation could expect. Supporters of the Constitution, one of Henry's allies scoffed, would like the delegates to think

> that we shall have wars and rumors of wars, that every calamity is to attend us, and that we shall be ruined and disunited forever, unless we adopt this Constitution. Pennsylvania and Maryland are to fall upon us from the north, like the Goths and Vandals of old; the Algerines . . . are to fill the Chesapeake with mighty fleets, and to attack us on our front; the Indians are to invade us with numerous armies on our rear, in order to convert our cleared lands into hunting grounds; and the Carolinians, from the south, (mounted on alligators, I presume) are to come and destroy our cornfields, and eat up our little children![27]

These were the mighty terrors, Henry sarcastically agreed, that would await Virginia if the Constitution was defeated. The nation was at peace, rapidly recovering from devastation and depression. He would not be terrified into an irreversible mistake when it was in Virginia's power to insist, at minimum, on alterations that might make the Constitution safer for the states and people.[28] Neither was he willing to concede that so much governmental power would produce the blessings some expected. "Those nations who have gone in search of grandeur, power, and splendor, have . . . been the victims of their own folly," he declaimed. "While they acquired those visionary blessings, they lost their freedom."[29] "You are not to inquire how your trade may be increased, nor how you are to become a great and powerful people, but how your liberties can be secured; for liberty ought to be the direct end of your government."[30]

Here the venerated hero loosed the whole of his impressive prowess. "Whither is the spirit of America gone?" he asked, the spirit that had checked the "pompous armaments" of mighty Britain. "It has gone," he feared,

> in search of a splendid government—a strong, energetic government. Shall we imitate the example of those nations who have gone from a simple to a splendid government? Are those nations more worthy of our imitation? What can make an adequate satisfaction to them for the loss they have suffered in attaining such a government—for the loss of their liberty? If we admit this consolidated government, it will be because we like a great, splendid one. Some way or other we must be a great and mighty empire; we must have an army, and a navy, and a number of things. When the American spirit was in its youth, the language of America was different: liberty, sir, was then the primary object.

"Consider what you are about to do," Henry pleaded. History was full of cautionary lessons, "instances of the people losing their liberty by their own carelessness and the ambition of a few." "A powerful and mighty empire," he insisted, "is incompatible with the genius of republicanism."[31]

Obviously, Henry was indulging in some verbal terrorism of his own. Yet this was not the language of an intellect that we can readily dismiss, and it does not suggest a thoughtless fear of extralocal power. Henry's sentiments had not been "anti-federal" through most of his career, and they were anti-federal now for well-considered reasons. Federalists believed that recent sectional collisions in the Continental Congress had predisposed the former governor to oppose whatever issued from the Constitutional Convention, and there can be no doubt that he did oppose the Constitution partly from a fear that vital local interests might be threatened by a stronger federal system. Nevertheless, the presence of these state and regional considerations, which were shared by Federalists and Antifederalists alike, does not suggest that either side was insincere when they addressed more theoretical concerns; and it does not permit us to conclude that local interests were "really" what the argument was all about.

As a speaker, Patrick Henry used a shotgun, not a rapier, demolishing his target with scattershots that intermixed the trivial with the profound, sectional complaints with fundamental revolutionary theory. But Henry's oratory rose to inspiring heights because it rested on a base of penetrating, substantive objections, which were shared by Antifederalists throughout the country and persuaded hundreds to conclude that this unprecedented plan of government was unacceptably at odds with the principles of 1776.[32] For the majority of people, Henry warned, national glory is a poor exchange for liberty and comfort; and whatever benefits the Constitution might appear to hold, it ought to be rejected—or at least substantially amended—if it would also prove oppressive for the body of the people. There was ample reason for anticipating that it would.

When Henry warned that liberty was once again at risk, he meant, most obviously, that the new Constitution incorporated no specific guarantees of freedom of religious conscience, trial by jury, freedom of the press, or other privileges protected by the constitutions of the states.[33] The absence of a bill of rights was certainly the commonest and probably the most persuasive reason for opposition to the Constitution. The standard Federalist response—that it had not been necessary to deny the federal government powers it had not been granted in the first place—was entirely unconvincing, given the supremacy clause and the power to employ whatever measures might seem "necessary" to achieve enumerated ends. In

Virginia, as in other states, the clamor for explicit guarantees was so widespread that Federalists were forced to promise that a bill of rights would be prepared by the first new Congress once the Constitution was approved (which means, of course, that their descendents owe this fundamental charter of their freedoms, perhaps the plainest link between the Constitution and the Declaration, more to its opponents than its framers).[34]

For many Antifederalists, however, the promise of a bill of rights was not enough. I should think that man "a lunatic," Henry exclaimed, "who should tell me to [adopt] a government avowedly defective, in hopes of having it amended afterwards. . . . Do you enter into a compact first, and afterwards settle the terms?"[35] Henry wanted his additional security while sovereignty still rested wholly in the people and the states, not least because addition of a bill of rights would not alleviate his deeper worries. Liberty, as every revolutionary knew, was simply not reducible to any list of privileges on which a government would be forbidden to intrude. Liberty also meant a government directed and controlled by the body of a democratic people, which seemed, in any case, the only kind of government that would be likely to abide by written limitations on its power. This sort of liberty as well appeared to be profoundly threatened by the Constitution, which is why the fiery patriot initiated his attacks by warning that the "republic" might be lost. He did not believe that this new government would stay within the limits of its charter or, even if it did, that this would be sufficient to assure that it would prove responsive to the people's needs and will.

"This government is so new, it wants a name," Henry complained. Madison might say that "it is national in this part, and federal in that part, etc. We may be amused, if we please, by a treatise of political anatomy," but for ordinary purposes of legislation the central government would act directly on the people, not the states.[36] It was to be a single, national government in this respect, and it would irresistibly become more national in time. Antifederalists were not persuaded by the Constitution's novel effort to divide what all the best-regarded theorists maintained could not be workably divided. Madison, of course, had recently maintained that sovereignty resided only in the people, who could certainly distribute portions of it to the states, portions to the general government, or even a concurrent jurisdiction to them both. But holding to the standard view, which stated that there had to be some agency in every governmental system that would have the final power of decision, Antifederalists could not believe that neither government would really have the final say. In its attempt to balance state and federal powers, they insisted, the Constitutional Convention had created a notorious monster: an *imperium in imperio*. "I never heard of two supreme coordinate powers in one and the same country," William Grayson said. "I cannot conceive how it can happen."[37] Both the state and general governments, George Mason pointed out, would possess a power of direct taxation, and they would necessarily compete for the same sources of revenue. "These two concurrent powers cannot exist long together; the one will destroy the other; the general government being paramount to, and in every respect more powerful than the state governments, the latter must give way."[38] Sooner or later, all power would be sucked into the mighty vortex of the general government. It would be little consolation to posterity, said Henry, to know that this consolidated, unitary system had been a "mixed" one at the start.[39]

It would be little consolation, Henry thought, because consolidated central power would inevitably be unresponsive to the people. To many revolutionaries this was both the clearest lesson of the colonies' rebellion against Great Britain and the irresistible conclusion of democratic logic. The size and pluralistic character of the United States were simply inconsistent with the concept of a single, national republic. George Mason, the most important framer of Virginia's revolutionary constitution, made the point in no uncertain terms. Can anyone suppose, he asked,

> that one national government will suit so extensive a country, embracing so many climates, and containing inhabitants so very different in manners, habits, and customs? . . . There never was a government over a very extensive country without destroying the liberties of the people; . . . popular government can only exist in small territories. Is there a single example, on the face of the earth, to support a contrary opinion?

"Sixty-five members," Mason reasoned, referring to the number who would sit in the first House of Representatives, "cannot possibly know the situation and circumstances of all the inhabitants of this immense continent." But "representatives ought to . . . mix with the people, think as they think, feel as they feel—ought to be . . . thoroughly acquainted with their interest and condition." If this were not the case, the government would not be really representative at all.[40]

Antifederalists throughout the country stressed this theme, which was nearly as ubiquitous as the demand for a bill of rights. "A full and equal representation," one of their finest writers said, "is that which possesses the same interests, feelings, opinions, and views the people themselves would were they all assembled. A fair representation, therefore, should be so regulated that every order of men in the community . . . can have a share in it." And yet this federal House of Representatives would be so small that only men of great distinction could be chosen. "If we make the proper distinction between the few men of wealth and abilities and consider them . . . as the natural aristocracy of the country and the great body of the people, the middle and lower classes, as the democracy, this federal representative branch will have but very little democracy in it." With great men in the House and even greater men in the presidency and Senate, which would be chosen indirectly, all of the important powers of the nation would be lodged in "one order of men"; the many would be committed to the mercies of the few.[41]

To many Antifederalists, in short, a government was either sovereign or it was not, and genuine democracy was more than just a matter of popular elections. If the Constitution concentrated undue power in the central government (or threatened to in time), and if the powers of that government would be controlled by "representatives" unsympathetic to the needs of ordinary people, then the Constitution was profoundly flawed in its essential spirit. Insufficiently republican to start with, the structure of the general government, together with the hazy wording of its charter, would operate in practice to make it even less republican in time. First in substance, then perhaps in form as well, the system would become entirely undemocratic; the Revolution might result in nothing more than the replacement of a foreign tyranny by a domestic one. Mason had already made the point in print:

> This government will commence in a moderate aristocracy; it is at present impossible to foresee whether it will, in its operation, produce a monarchy or a corrupt, oppressive aristocracy; it will most probably vibrate some years between the two and then terminate in the one or the other.[42]

Grayson reinforced the argument in the convention:

> What, sir, is the present Constitution? A republican government founded on the principles of . . . the British monarchy. . . . A democratic branch marked with the strong features of aristocracy, and an aristocratic branch [the senate] with all the impurities and imperfections of the British House of Commons, arising from the inequality of representation and want of responsibility [to the people].[43]

These were the features Henry had in mind when he denounced "that paper" as "the most fatal plan that could possibly be conceived to enslave a free people."[44]

"Plan," he said, and "plan" he meant. Through all these Antifederalist remarks there courses a profound distrust of Federalist intentions. And, indeed, in several states, the natural aristocracy had been so solidly in favor of the Constitution that their uniform support had strengthened the suspicions prompted by the superficial similarity between the reconstructed government and Britain's mixed regime. The Massachusetts state convention, where virtually the whole elite supported ratification, had elicited a memorable expression of the underlying fear:

> These lawyers, and men of learning and moneyed men, that talk so finely, and gloss over matters so smoothly, to make us poor illiterate people swallow down the pill, expect to get into Congress themselves; they expect to be managers of this Constitution, and get all the power and all the money into their own hands, and then they will swallow all us little folks like the great *Leviathan*; yes, just as the whale swallowed up Jonah![45]

Even in Virginia, whose greatest public men were rather evenly divided by the Constitution and usually avoided charging one another with conspiratorial intentions, Antifederalists occasionally expressed distaste for some of the elitist phalanx who seemed so eager for the change. Speaking as a member of the Constitutional Convention—one of three who had refused to sign—Mason made a telling thrust:

> I have some acquaintance with a great many characters who favor this government, their connections, their conduct, their political principles. . . . There are a great many wise and good men among them. But when I look round . . . and observe who are the warmest and the most zealous friends to this new government, it makes me think of the story of the cat transformed into a fine lady; forgetting her transformation, and happening to see a rat, she could not restrain herself, but sprang upon it out of the chair.[46]

Who would fill the powerful and lucrative positions created by the Constitution? What did its supporters really want? These were the questions Henry posed when he warned of the ambitions of the few, when he insisted that "a powerful and mighty empire is incompatible with the genius of republicanism." They were at the heart of his demand for the "real, actual, existing danger which should lead us to . . . so dangerous" a step.[47]

The challenge was in earnest, and none of these suspicions can any longer be dismissed as groundless fantasies of fearful local politicians. Henry and his allies knew the country's situation. Nearly all of them conceded that the powers of the central government should be enlarged. But this did not compel them to agree that there was no alternative between the unamended Constitution and anarchy or economic ruin. Neither were they wholly wrong about the motives of a number of the advocates of constitutional reform. Since Charles Beard demythologized the making of the Constitution, twentieth-century scholarship has overwhelmingly con-

firmed two leading tenets of the Antifederalist position: (1) a dispassionate consideration of the social, cultural, and economic condition of the
United States during the middle 1780s does not suggest a *general* crisis
from which it was necessary for the country to be rescued; but (2) even
cursory examination of the movement for reform *does* reveal that it derived important impetus from some of the American elite's increasing
disenchantment with democracy.[48] "The Constitution," according to the
leading modern student of its sources, "was intrinsically an aristocratic
document designed to check the democratic tendencies of the period."
Many Federalists, Wood writes, supported the reform for the same reasons
that Antifederalists opposed it: because it would forbid the sort of populistic measures that many states had taken in response to economic troubles; because it might deliver power to a "better sort" of people; "because
its very structure and detachment from the people would work to exclude
. . . those who were not rich, well born, or prominent from exercising
political power."[49]

Among these Federalists, moreover, were several influential individuals
and groups whose discontent with democratic politics as practiced in the
states was accompanied by dreams of national grandeur very like the ones
that Henry denounced. Particularly conspicuous among the latter were
the economic nationalists, who had been seeking since early in the decade
to reshape the central government into an instrument of economic progress, and former continental officers, who associated sovereignty, stability, and national prowess with a small professional army.[50] Rapidly
emerging as the most effective spokesman for these groups was Alexander
Hamilton of New York, who had spoken at the Constitutional Convention
in favor of consolidated central power and lifetime terms of office for the
president and senate, who hoped to help create a thriving, imperial republic, and who did undoubtedly believe that national greatness would
require a close alliance between the country's men of capital and national
rulers capable of guiding and resisting the majority's demands.

Mason's cat was real. Henry's dreamers of ambitious schemes of national might and splendor were entirely real—and likely to hold important offices if the Constitution was approved. Virginia ratified the
Constitution, then, in spite of rational misgivings about the antidemocratic inclinations of some of its supporters. It ratified the Constitution in
the face of deeply held and well-considered theoretical objections to its
tendencies and structure, objections capably developed by several of the
state's most honored revolutionary heroes. It ratified the Constitution, I
believe, in part because the state convention's most impressive spokesmen
for reform were men who did *not* share the vision Henry feared: men who
were as conscientiously concerned with revolutionary principles as any of

their foes, men who advocated the reform because they thought it was the only way to safeguard and perfect the nation's revolutionary gains. To understand the Constitution's triumph in Virginia (and the nation), it is necessary to begin with a renewed attention to the differences among its friends. We need to recognize that some of these were fully as alert as Henry to the dangers he denounced, and not at all inclined to sacrifice democracy to national greatness and prestige.[51]

At Richmond, Henry's principal opponents were Madison and Edmund Randolph. Randolph's stand and story, to which we shall return, offers unexampled insight into why the Constitution was approved despite a potent fear of counterrevolution. But it was Madison, of course, who had been more responsible than any other individual for the distinctive shape of constitutional reform, and it was Madison to whom the members looked for a response to his opponents' most profound concerns.

Like Randolph, Madison replied to Henry's condemnation of the quest for national grandeur by *agreeing* that "national splendor and glory are not our [proper] objects."[52] And when Mason said that certain clauses of the Constitution were *intended* to prepare the way for gradual subversion of the powers of the states, Madison immediately broke in, demanding "an unequivocal explanation" of an insinuation that all the signers of the Constitution preferred a consolidated national system.[53] "If the general government were wholly independent of the governments of the particular states," he had already said, "then, indeed, usurpations might be expected to the fullest extent." But the general government "derives its authority from [the state] governments and from the same sources from which their authority derives," from their sovereign peoples, who would certainly resist attempted usurpations.[54] "The sum of the powers given up by the people of Virginia is divided into two classes—one to the federal and the other to the state government," Madison explained. "Each is subdivided into three branches."[55] In addition, "the powers of the federal government are enumerated; it can only operate in certain cases."[56] Far from threatening a gradual absorption of the proper powers of the people and the states, adoption of the Constitution would "increase the security of liberty more than any government that ever was," since powers ordinarily entrusted to a single government—and sometimes even to a single branch—would be distributed by the reform between two sets of governments, each of which would watch the other at the same time as its several branches served as an internal check against abuse.[57]

It is impossible to place excessive emphasis on Madison's denial that the Constitution would result in a consolidated system *or* on his disclaimer of a wish for national splendor. For him, as plainly as for Henry, liberty and comfort, not riches or the might to rival European powers, were the proper tests of national happiness and greatness. And liberty, to Madison as well as his opponents, meant governments that would be genuinely responsive to the people, not merely governments that would derive from popular elections and protect the people's private rights.[58] This is why he placed such stress on the enumerated powers and the complicated federal structure of the system. He did not deny that too much power, placed in hands too distant from the people, would imperil republican liberty. He even spoke occasionally of the "concessions" federal reform demanded from the people and the states.[59] He understood as well as his opponents did that national representatives would be less sympathetic to the people's local needs and better shielded from their wrath or clamors than the members of the state assemblies. Therefore, he insisted, local interests had been left in local hands, and federal representatives would be responsible only for those great and national matters—few and carefully defined—on which they *could* be trusted to reflect the people's needs and will.[60] "As long as this is the case," he reasoned, "we have no danger to apprehend."[61]

"Where power can be *safely* lodged, if it be *necessary*," Madison maintained, "reason commands its cession."[62] It was true, of course, that every grant of power carried with it the potential for abuse, and it was true as well that revolutionary principles demanded constant scrutiny of rulers. Yet it was also possible to carry an appropriate distrust of power to extremes that would deny the very feasibility of a republic:

> Gentlemen suppose that the general legislature will do everything mischievous they possibly can and that they will omit to do everything good which they are authorized to do. If this were a reasonable supposition, their objections would be good. I consider it reasonable to conclude that they will as readily do their duty as deviate from it; nor do I go on the grounds mentioned by gentlemen on the other side—that we are to place unlimited confidence in [national officials] and expect nothing but the most exalted integrity and sublime virtue. But I go on this great republican principle: that the people will have virtue and intelligence to select men of virtue and wisdom. Is there no virtue among us? If there be not, we are in a wretched situation. No theoretical checks, no form of government, can render us secure. To suppose that any form of government will secure liberty or happiness without any virtue in the people is a chimerical idea.[63]

No American ever thought more deeply about the machinery of government than Madison, yet none has ever said more clearly that mechanical contrivances are not enough. Intelligent, attentive voters, Madison repeatedly maintained, are in the end the necessary precondition for any democratic state; and the assumption that the people will repeatedly elect only those who will betray them is really an objection to self-government itself.[64]

Apart from Mason's charge that many signers of the Constitution actually preferred a unitary system, nothing angered Madison so much as Henry's hints that only men of unsound principles or dangerous ambitions could support the proposed reform. "I profess myself," he awkwardly exclaimed, "to have had a uniform zeal for a republican government. If the honorable member, or any other person, conceives that my attachment to this system arises from a different source, he is mistaken. From the first moment that my mind was capable of contemplating political subjects, I never, till this moment, ceased wishing success to a well-regulated republican government."[65] The outburst did him little credit. He ordinarily had little use for "flaming protestations of patriotic zeal." Still, Madison was understandably infuriated by aspersions that suggested motives nearly opposite to those he felt. For he not only thought the Constitution perfectly consistent with republican philosophy, he doubted whether there was any other way to save the Revolution.

Henry challenged his opponents to explain the "actual, existing danger" that compelled so great a change. No one, then or later, could explain it more completely than the major architect of the reform. The history of the Confederation, Madison insisted, offered "repeated unequivocal proofs . . . of the utter inutility and inefficacy" of a central government that depended on thirteen other governments for revenues and for enforcement of its laws, proofs confirmed by the experiences of other historical confederacies.[66] "The Confederation is so notoriously feeble," he continued, "that foreign nations are unwilling to form any treaties with us," for these had been "violated at pleasure by the states." Congress was "obliged to borrow money even to pay the interest of our debts," although these debts had been incurred in the sacred cause of Independence.[67] It was evident, accordingly, when delegates assembled for the Constitutional Convention, that the nation could no longer trust its "happiness" and "safety" to "a government totally destitute of the means of protecting itself or its members."[68] And revolutionary principles themselves required that independent taxing powers and independent means of compelling obedience to federal laws should rest directly on the people, not the states. In these circumstances, a complete reconstitution of the old confederation was the only means by which consistent revolutionaries could have solved the problems the convention faced.[69]

But national humiliation and dishonor, disgraceful though these were, were only part of the impending peril as Madison explained it. Members of a union were entitled to expect the general government to defend their happiness and safety, which were gravely damaged by the economic dislocations caused by British restrictions on American commerce. Neverthe-less, the Union's Congress had been checked in every effort to secure a power to retaliate against the British, and states attempting independent actions had been checked by the conflicting laws of neighbors. The re-sulting discontent with the Confederation and hostility between the states had led to open talk of the replacement of the general union by several smaller confederacies, and Madison did not believe that the republican experiment could long outlive the continental union. At the Philadelphia Convention he had said:

> Let each state depend on itself for its security, and let apprehensions arise of danger from distant powers or from neighboring states, and the lan-guishing condition of all the states, large as well as small, would soon be transformed into vigorous and high toned governments. . . . The same causes which have rendered the old world the theatre of incessant wars and have banished liberty from the face of it, would soon produce the same effects here.[70]

Writing in *The Federalist*, he had again affirmed the warning. "Nothing short of a Constitution fully adequate to the national defense and the preservation of the Union can save America from as many standing ar-mies" as there are states or separate confederacies, he had insisted, "and from such a progressive augmentation of these establishments in each as will render them . . . burdensome to the properties and ominous to the liberties of the people." Without the general union, liberty would every-where be "crushed between standing armies and perpetual taxes." The revolutionary order would collapse.[71]

Henry "tells us the affairs of our country are not alarming," Madison complained. "I wish this assertion was well founded."[72] In fact, however, both the federal and state conventions had assembled in the midst of an immediate crisis of American union, and the Union was the necessary shield for the republican experiment that Henry wanted to preserve. Nor was even this the sum of current dangers. The nation also faced a second crisis, which Henry failed to recognize in his repeated condemnations of "the tyranny of rulers." In republics, Madison suggested, "turbulence, violence, and abuse of power by the majority trampling on the rights of the minority . . . have, more frequently than any other cause, produced despotism." In the United States—and even in Virginia—it was not the acts of unresponsive rulers, but the follies and transgressions of the sym-pathetic representatives of state majorities that tempted growing numbers of the people to abandon their revolutionary convictions. "The only pos-sible remedy for those evils," he protested, the only one consistent with "preserving and protecting the principles of republicanism, will be found in that very system which is now exclaimed against as the parent of oppression."[73]

With these words the framer introduced the train of reasoning that had produced another of his crucial contributions to the Founding. In every state the lower houses had struggled to protect their citizens from the economic difficulties of the middle 1780s. Many of their measures—paper money, laws suspending private suits for debt, postponements of taxation, or continued confiscations of the property of former loyalists—had interfered with private contracts, endangered people's right to hold their property secure, or robbed the states of the resources necessary to fulfill their individual and federal obligations. Essentially unchecked by the other parts of government, the lower houses had ignored state bills of rights and sacrificed the long-term interests of the whole community to more immediate considerations. As this happened, Madison believed, a disenchantment with democracy was threatening to spread through growing numbers of the people, who might eventually prefer a despotism or hereditary rule to governments unable to secure their happiness or even to protect their fundamental rights. The crisis of confederation government, as he conceived it, was compounded by a crisis of republican convictions, and the Constitution was the only instrument that promised an escape from all the interlocking dangers with which liberty was faced.

Madison assumed a very special place among the founders—more special, I would argue, even than is commonly believed—because he personally bridged so much of the abyss between the revolutionary tribunes such as Henry and the aspiring consuls such as Hamilton, with whom he formed a brief and less than wholly comfortable alliance. He fully shared with higher-flying Federalists not only the determination to invigorate the Union, but also the emotional revulsion from the populistic politics facilitated by the early revolutionary constitutions—from conditions Elbridge Gerry called "an excess of democracy." Madison believed, as Hamilton believed, that revolutionary governments were *so* responsive to the wishes of unhampered, temporary state majorities that they endangered the unalienable rights that Independence was intended to protect. He agreed with other Federalists as well that just, enduring governments demanded qualities not found in popular assemblies: protection for the propertied minority (and others); the wisdom to discern the long-term general good; and power to defend both against more partial, more immediate considerations.

No more than Henry, though, did Madison approve the vision of a splendid, mighty future; and whatever was the case with other Federalists, *his* fear of the majority had always been accompanied by a continuing awareness of the dangers posed by unresponsive rulers or excessive central power. Hamilton intended to employ a stronger central government to speed developments that would prepare the groundwork for successful competition with the great Atlantic empires. Madison intended to "perpetuate the Union" in order to *protect* the Revolution from the European curses of professional armed forces, persistent public debts, powerful executives, and swollen taxes, as well as to invest the general government with the ability to counteract the European trading policies that seemed to him to threaten the social foundations of American democracy. *Some* members of the Constitutional Convention may have wanted to create a system that would place as much authority as possible in rulers only distantly dependent on the people. But Madison had never shared this wish. Although he did anticipate that large electoral districts would encourage the selection of representatives who would be less inclined to sacrifice the general good to more immediate demands, he had been equally concerned, throughout the Constitutional Convention, to control potentially ambitious rulers and assure that they could never free themselves from their dependence on the people. In *The Federalist*—and, now, in the Virginia state convention—the Constitution *he* defended would protect minorities against majority abuses, would ensure superior attention to the long-term good, and yet would *not* produce a government unresponsive to the people's needs or will. Responsibility would be secured, as always, by popular elections and internal checks and balances. For the first time in the history of representative democracy, it would be further guaranteed by the enumerated limits and the compound, federal features of the reconstructed system.

Recent scholarship has not placed equal emphasis on every part of Madison's attempt to understand and justify the Constitution. It credits him, of course, with an essential role in the creation of a central government whose branches would derive entirely from elections, as well as with the most elaborate defense of its republican characteristics. It devotes elaborate attention to his argument that private rights are safer in a large than in a small republic. It leans on him, indeed—more heavily than on any other individual—for its recognition that "the Constitution presented no simple choice between accepting or rejecting the principles of 1776," since the Federalists could "intelligibly picture themselves as the true defenders of the libertarian tradition."[74] In doing so, however, recent scholarship has melded Madison's desires too fully with the movement's, emphasized his fears more strongly than his faith, and thus obscured some differences that had important consequences in Virginia and the country as a whole.

"There is something decidedly disingenuous," writes Gordon S.

Wood, "about the democratic radicalism" of Federalist defenses of the Constitution, for behind this language lay an evident desire "for a high-toned government filled with better sorts of people, . . . partisan and aristocratic purposes that belied the Federalists' democratic language."[75] For some, perhaps for many Federalists this characterization may be apt, and yet a careful effort to distinguish Madison's position from that of other key reformers—one that gives full weight to his insistence on the complicated federal structure and enumerated powers of the central government, his fear of independent rulers, and his conviction that the Constitution was a wholly democratic remedy for democratic ills—both qualifies and clarifies Wood's generalization. The Federalists did generally believe that private rights and public happiness were threatened in the states by populistic politics and poorly balanced constitutions. They looked to federal reform not only to correct the weaknesses of the Confederation, but also to remedy those other ills; and they believed a proper remedy required both limitations on the states and the establishment of a general government better able to resist immediate majority demands. Madison not only shared these wishes, he was more responsible than any other thinker for defining problems in these terms and sketching leading features of the Federalist solution. But this was only part—and maybe not the most important part—of Madison's peculiar contribution.

If Madison was not unique, he was at least distinguishable from many other Federalists by his emotional determination to preserve a genuinely revolutionary order. Anxious as he was for a reform that would restrain tyrannical majorities, he never doubted that majorities should rule—or that the people *would* control the complicated structure raised by the completed Constitution. It is possible, of course, to question the sincerity or depth of his convictions on these points. Indeed, it is quite common to deemphasize their role, if only by devoting nearly all attention to his other objects and assumptions. But it is also possible—and seems to me a better explanation of the facts—that Madison's republican convictions were as central to his thinking as he claimed: the hub on which his other contributions turned. And, certainly, if we acknowledge the centrality and depth of these convictions, if we accord them more than fleeting recognition as we hurry on to other things, it will be easier to see why he repeatedly denied that he approved of a consolidated system, placed increasing emphasis on federal aspects of the structure, and heatedly insisted that he had no other object than the people's liberty and comfort. He was advocating a reform that he had always understood—and was still trying to define—as an attempt to rescue *both* of the ideals adopted early in the Revolution: private rights, but also governments that would be based on the people's active and continuing consent. Madison's commitment to a people's government — albeit to a wise one — was every bit as deep as Patrick Henry's. His ability to justify the Constitution on these grounds was indispensible to Federalist success in the Virginia state convention.

Madison's republican response to Antifederalist concerns, seconded by capable lieutenants and delivered to an audience that was familiar (in a general way) with his outstanding role in shaping the reform, was an effective answer to the most impressive criticisms of the Constitution. It answered basic questions, reassured supporters, and alleviated the anxieties provoked by serious objections.[76] For all of this, however, it was not sufficient, by itself, to carry the convention. Few, if any, of Virginia's revolutionary leaders questioned Madison's republican credentials. All, no doubt, were comforted by their awareness that George Washington would head the federal government if it were put into effect. In 1788, however, quite unlike today, few believed that the executive would set the federal government's directions; and few considered Madison the coldly realistic founder of a modern governmental theory. As Patrick Henry hinted, many saw the leading spokesman for the Constitution as impossibly naive: a brilliant, well-intentioned spinner of a cobweb. And in any case, as Mason indicated, many feared that principled republicans like Washington or Madison would not, in practice, set the nation's course. Thus, in order to persuade the unpersuaded, Madison was forced to move beyond an "anatomical" discussion of the plan and to combat the Antifederalists with a compelling demonstration that the Constitution was consistent with the interests of their state. The theoretical discussion was essential to the Federalists' success, but it would not be enough unless it could be forcefully applied to more specific worries.

When Mason recognized the wise and good supporters of the Constitution, he was complimenting Washington and Madison and others in the hall; and when the leading spokesman for the Constitution interrupted Mason with a sharp demand that he explain his charge that signers of the Constitution *wanted* a consolidated system, Mason readily admitted that none of his Virginia colleagues had been members of that group.[77] Still, Mason spied the cat within the lady; and when Mason spoke of looking further round at the supporters of the Constitution, few mistook his meaning. His and Randolph's refusal to sign the proposed Constitution can be traced beyond dispute to state and regional considerations,[78] and the Federalists believed that Patrick Henry had been so alarmed by recent sectional aggressions that he really aimed at dissolution of the Union.[79] Without exception, the Virginia Antifederalists condemned the Constitution as a threat to their constituents and region.

An appeal to "local interests" was the stategy that Madison had dreaded most at the beginning of the meeting; and as the deliberations turned from generalities to more specific issues, his initial optimism cooled.[80] On the fourth day of debates, Henry interjected the alarming issue of the Jay-Gardoqui treaty.[81] Hampered by a "bilious attack," Madison had struggled from the start to dam the flood of theoretical objections. Now, he also had to face the opposition on perhaps its strongest ground.[82]

Fear of northern domination of the South, which had assumed so critical a role at Philadelphia, was naturally expressed with even less restraint at Richmond. Antifederalists returned time after time to the inadequate securities against a gradual "annihilation" of the states, to their conviction that a unitary government could not care fairly for the great diversity of interests in the country, and to the likelihood that, from the first, Virginia's interests would be sacrificed to the demands of the majority in Congress. "I hope my fears are groundless," William Grayson said, "but I believe it as I do my creed, that this government will operate as a faction of seven states to oppress the rest of the union."[83]

Commercial regulations seemed an obvious example. "The interest of the carrying states," Grayson hardly needed to remark, "is strikingly different from that of the productive states." The former would "assuredly unite," and the condition of the latter would be "wretched." Virginia's agricultural commodities would be carried only on the northerners' conditions. "Every measure will have for its object their particular interest."[84]

Direct taxation posed another danger. Suppose, suggested Grayson, that the northerners should lay a tax on slaves. They would neither help to pay this tax nor be accountable to southern voters for their conduct. "This total want of responsibility and fellow-feeling," Grayson said, "will destroy the benefits of representation."[85]

Mason fervently agreed. Though it had been the power over commerce that had most alarmed him at the Philadelphia convention, it was now the "ruinous" potential of direct taxation that troubled him the most. The federal government, he reasoned, would undoubtably impose such taxes as would be the most productive and the easiest to gather, probably the kinds of taxes that Robert Morris had recommended in 1783. Poll taxes would appear an obvious recourse, although no tax was more oppressive to the poor. Land taxes were another, though any tax on land could only operate unequally within a nation where assessments varied so enormously by region. Madison had argued, it was true, that population changes were already working to remove the federal majority into the South and West. Several Antifederalist speakers had agreed. Mason mocked that reassurance: "A very sound argument indeed, that we should cheerfully burn ourselves to death in hopes of a joyful and happy resurrection."[86]

Death might certainly result, Henry felt obliged to add, from yet another difference between the North and South. Federal authorities would obviously construe the Constitution as they pleased, and they would readily discover an implicit power, in time of war, to "liberate every one of your slaves." Much as he deplored this institution, Henry said, he recognized "that prudence forbids its abolition." But "the majority of Congress is to the north, and the slaves are to the south." Let urgent national necessity combine with antislavery feelings, and a sectional majority, "who have no feeling of your interests," would "certainly exercise" this power.[87]

Fantastical imaginings, the Federalists responded—and, in truth, this was the politician speaking, not the prophet. Henry was himself a good deal more concerned about the hazy powers of the new regime than with the force of antislavery opinion, and there is nothing in the record to suggest that worries which would dominate a later generation had significant effects in 1788. Not slavery, but the Mississippi, was the issue that transfixed contemporary minds and seemed to demonstrate most graphically why sectional aggressions would undoubtedly result from differences between the regions.[88]

Virginia Antifederalists were eager, not simply to contrast the voting strengths of North and South, not merely to remind the delegates of inconsistent regional desires, but to produce persuasive evidence of a prevailing northern *disposition* to take advantage of their numbers. For this purpose—and because both sides believed that westerners might hold the balance in the meeting—the critics of the Constitution turned repeatedly to the congressional proceedings of 1786, emphasizing that the Constitution's alteration of the rule requiring an agreement by nine states in order to approve a treaty offered just the sort of opening that easterners would seize. Federalists replied with evident alarm, insisting that the larger powers of the reconstructed government would guarantee that southern senators would always be alert and present in their seats, so that the two-thirds rule would still require nine states for the conclusion of a treaty. But the anxious tone of Federalist replies suggests that Antifederalists were gaining, and Henry probably expected to assure his triumph when he called directly on the former members of the Continental Congress for a full discussion of proceedings on the Mississippi. Hugh Blair Grigsby tells us that the hall was overflowing when the congressmen delivered their replies, with many thinking that the Antifederalists might move immediately for a decision as soon as this discussion was complete.[89]

Henry Lee led off, satisfied to stress that the majority in Congress had never planned a *permanent* surrender of the right to navigate the river.[90] Monroe and Grayson followed with fuller narratives of the congressional transactions, emphasizing that a seven-state majority had certainly (and, in their view, unconstitutionally) approved a change in Jay's instructions that would bind the nation to forgo the navigation of the Mississippi for a generation's time. This "temporary" sacrifice of southern interests, they insisted, would devastate the West as certainly as a complete surrender of the claim, and neither congressman saw any indication that the northern states were willing to abandon the disgraceful project. Both believed that northerners intended, not only to advance their economic interests, but also to "depress the western country, and prevent the southern interest from preponderating." Both maintained that a surrender of the Mississippi would be likelier if two-thirds of a quorum of the senate was sufficient to conclude a treaty.[91] The Federalists were in a desperate position by the time Monroe concluded his remarks, and Madison responded with a brilliant demonstration of the legislative talents that so often made him first in any public meeting he attended.

Madison did not dispute the facts that Grayson and Monroe had just presented, nor did he deny that southerners were right about the critical importance of the Mississippi (which he knew that no one had a better reputation for defending). Rather, he disputed Antifederalist impressions of the "disposition" of the North, together with their judgments of the relative positions of commercial and producing interests in the Union. On both these scores, he roundly disagreed with Grayson's and Monroe's assessments of the nature of the most important threats to western interests or the interests of Virginia.

If economic interests were the sole consideration, Madison maintained, the eastern states would shortly recognize that none had more to gain than they themselves from opening the Mississippi, for the carrying trade would rise or fall with the productions of the West.[92] These kinds of interest, though, were simply not the sole consideration. Emigration to the West was rapidly increasing from New England as well as from the South, and this would quickly have the same effects on northern sentiments as it already had on southern.[93] Individuals might still be hostile to the West, but once the Constitution went into effect, "the sense of the people at large," not the sentiments of northern business interests, would "direct the public measures." Commercial needs would have *less* influence in the new regime than in the old. Sending representatives from the interior of northern states, as well as from the South, the "landed interest" would control the House of Representatives from the inauguration of the new regime, would dominate elections of the chief executive, and

thus would make the general government more western in its character
and sentiments with every passing year.[91]

The Mississippi, Madison concluded, could not be more endangered
if the Constitution was approved. If senators attended to their duty, nine
states would still be necessary to conclude a treaty, which would also need
the president's consent. The president's dependence on the agricultural
majority for his election would assure *additional* protection for the South
and West. Moreover, it should never be forgotten, Madison reminded the
convention, that the weaknesses of the Confederation had "produced"
the Jay-Gardoqui "project." Resolutions that the nation had a *right* to
navigate the Mississippi had "re-echoed," he declared, "from every part
of the United States," but resolutions of this sort would prove as "fruitless" in the future as they had in past until "a change takes place which
will give energy to the acts of the government." A stronger system would
remove temptations to exchange the nation's general interests for temporary, partial ones. It would permit a stronger stance in the negotiations.
Only by adopting such a system could "the people of [the western] country" win "an actual possession of the right, and protection in its enjoyment."[95]

If there was one decisive day at Richmond, June 13 was probably that
day. Madison's rebuttal of Grayson and Monroe was quickly seconded by
Nicholas, whose repetition of its central points was all the more effective
because he spoke as one who was already planning a removal to Kentucky.
The two of them did not decisively defeat the opposition. There is no
conclusive evidence that any votes were changed.[96] Yet subsequent proceedings do suggest that Madison and Nicholas successfully defused the
issue, robbing it of much of its potential to impinge on other matters or
to occupy the members out of doors. On June 14 the convention turned
with a renewed determination to a clause-by-clause discussion, and Madison began to dominate proceedings much as Henry had been able to
direct the earlier debates. During the convention's final days, the Antifederalists increasingly despaired.

It was not sufficient, to be sure, for Federalists to argue that the right
to navigate the Mississippi had been threatened by the weaknesses of the
existing system and might be most effectively asserted by a stronger, new
regime. Federal powers over commerce and taxation also seemed compelling threats, and it is clear that Madison did not convince most delegates that the "producing" interests would control the reconstructed
system.[97] But Madison and Nicholas accomplished something hardly less
important in the argument about the Mississippi. They showed the wavering and undecided members why Virginians might conclude that even
local interests might be best advanced within a stronger federal system.

They did so by advancing arguments that Madison had offered in *The Federalist* and at the Constitutional Convention: arguments that clearly seem responsible for Edmund Randolph's change of course; and arguments that may have seemed decisive, now, to others in the state convention.

Newly sensitized to fundamental differences between New England and the South, which had erupted in so frightening a form when Jay requested new instructions, *all* Virginia leaders read the Constitution partly for how it would affect their state and region. Never more distrustful of the North, *most* of them concluded that it held inadequate securities against manipulation of the great and hazy powers of the new regime by northern politicians who had given recent warning of their sectional designs, and who were commonly suspected of being disillusioned with the Revolution. The structure of the senate seemed unduly advantageous to the smaller, northern states, as did the senate's special powers over treaties and appointments. The federal government was granted several powers that were subject to abuse and likely to result in sectional collisions. Accordingly, though most Virginia politicians readily conceded the necessity for federal reform, most also wanted constitutional amendments that would guarantee additional protection for their state, together with additional protection for the people's unsurrendered rights. The central question for the state convention, then, was whether such amendments would be made conditions for Virginia's ratification or trusted to the action of the first federal Congress.

Antifederalists advanced a simple, yet compelling, case for previous amendments. As Patrick Henry put it, it was senseless to adopt "a government avowedly defective" in the hope that its deficiencies and dangers would be speedily repaired.[98] Virginia was at peace, as Henry saw it, confronted by no dangers more apparent than the perils to its vital interests and to liberty itself inherent in the unamended Constitution. Time was on the Old Dominion's side. The need for constitutional reform was felt most urgently in the commercial North and East, although the South and West, which were becoming stronger year by year, were being asked to shoulder all the risks. Given these conditions, Henry argued, Virginia could afford a year or two's delay in putting a reform into effect. The ratifying states would be compelled to grant the safeguards it required.[99]

Several serious miscalculations, Federalists replied, were hidden in the Antifederalist position. Wherever there was power, Madison admitted, there was always the potential for abuse. And yet, wherever power could be safely granted (if necessity required it), "reason commands its cession." "We are reduced to the dilemma of either submitting to the inconvenience or losing the Union."[100] Through the second half of the convention, Madison and his assistants countered Antifederalist objections clause by clause, always arguing that every delegated power was at once *essential* and invariably accompanied by multiple securities against misuse. The central government created by the Constitution, they repeated, was carefully restricted to responsibilities that separate states could not effectively discharge. The powers of the states, internal checks and balances, and the predominating influence of the agricultural majority would all combine to guard against a dangerous consolidation or against misuse of governmental powers by the North. Federal powers would be delegated, Madison insisted, to representatives "chosen for short terms, . . . responsible to the people, and whose situation is perfectly similar to their own. As long as this is the case," he reasoned—and it would be the case as long as the people retained sufficient virtue "to select men of virtue and wisdom"—"we have no danger to apprehend."[101] Virginia's special interests, like liberty itself, would actually be less at risk in an enlarged, compound republic than in the current, feebler system.

Of all the Antifederalist miscalculations, though, none seemed more apparent to supporters of the Constitution than the confidence with which the opposition talked of previous amendments and denied the urgency of the existing moment. The ratifying states, the Federalists maintained, would not reverse their stands "to gratify Virginia."[102] If the Old Dominion did succeed in blocking the reform, opponents of the Constitution in the different regions of the country would never reach agreement on the changes they desired.[103] The present moment, then, might really be the last for making needed changes in the context of a general confederation; and a general union of the states was simply not less necessary for the South than for New England.

The old confederation, Edmund Randolph cried, was gone. "It is gone, whether this house says so or not. It is gone, sir, by its own weakness."[104] "Could I . . . believe," the governor continued, "that there . . . was no storm gathering," that previous amendments could really be secured, "I would concur" with Henry's plan for previous amendments, "for nothing but the fear of inevitable destruction would lead me to vote for the Constitution in spite of the objections I have."[105] But to insist on previous amendments at this point could only prove "another name for rejection." "If, in this situation, we reject the Constitution, the Union will be dissolved, the dogs of war will break loose, and anarchy and discord will complete the ruin of this country."[106]

"Is this government necessary for the safety of Virginia?" Randolph asked. He was willing for the outcome to depend on a considered answer to this question, and he answered it himself as Madison had answered fellow southerners at Philadelphia or earlier within the current meeting.

Vulnerable to Indians or foreign enemies by land and sea, internally endangered by its large slave population, Virginia had no navy, Randolph said, no military stores. All her patriotic efforts in the War for Independence would have been without avail without assistance from her sisters. But if the Union should collapse, "those states, then our friends, brothers, and supporters, will . . . be our bitterest enemies."

> The other states have upwards of 330,000 men capable of bearing arms. . . . In case of an attack, what defense can we make? . . . Our export trade is entirely in the hands of foreigners. We have no manufactures. . . . Shall we form a partial confederacy? . . . Partial confederacies will require such a degree of force and expense as will destroy every feature of republicanism.[107]

"I believe that, as sure as there is a God in heaven, our safety, our political happiness and existence, depend on the union of the states," Randolph concluded. "In union alone safety consists."[108]

At the Constitutional Convention, Edmund Randolph had been first to plead for a procedure under which the Constitution would be offered to the people of the states, the state conventions would propose amendments, and a second general convention would complete the plan of constitutional reform. What had happened in the intervening months to change his mind? Henry pressed him with this question to the point of personal exchanges that provided the dramatic highlight of the meeting.[109] The answer was uncomplicated, but revealing. "I refused to sign," he answered, and if the circumstances were the same today, would still insist on alterations that would satisfy some serious objections. Now, however, eight states had approved the unamended Constitution. In these circumstances, to continue to insist on previous amendments was impossible "without inevitable ruin to the Union, . . . and I will assent to the lopping of this limb (meaning his arm) before I assent to the dissolution of the Union."[110]

Henry feared the Revolution would be lost if the convention ratified the unamended Constitution. "I am a child of the Revolution," Randolph replied. "I would join heart and hand in rejecting the system did I not conceive it would promote our happiness." But the Constitution offered new securities against "injustice, licentiousness, insecurity, and oppression,"[111] and Virginia could not "exist without a union with her neighbors"—not, at least, as a republic. "*I went to the federal Convention,*" Randolph repeated. "*I refused to subscribe, because I had, as I still have, objections to the Constitution,* and wished a free inquiry into its merits." But "the accession of eight states reduced our deliberations to the single question of *Union or no Union.*" "When I see safety on my right, and destruction on my left, . . . I cannot hesitate to decide in favor of the former."[112] In the Old Dominion, as in other evenly divided states, a crucial handful of the silent, backbench delegates may have agreed. A motion to insist on previous amendments was defeated 88 to 80. Virginia ratified the Constitution by a margin of ten votes, recommending numerous amendments to the first new Congress.[113]

Supporters of the Constitution surely would have lost at Richmond if the opposition had been able to convince a scattering of doubtful delegates that the reform would undermine the democratic Revolution. They would have lost as certainly if Antifederalists had managed a superior analysis of state and southern interests, for the records of the state convention show that these considerations entered heavily into the views of every speaking member. But the interests of Virginia were a complicated matter, and a dedication to republican ideals could call as plainly for immediate approval of the Constitution as it could for previous amendments. Thus, on both essential points, the Federalists debated their opponents to, at worst, a draw. They seem to have preserved and may have slightly widened the narrow margin they began with.

This result does not suggest that the proceedings of the meeting offer little insight into the opinions of the silent delegates and voters, whose reasoning determined the decision. If the arguments at Richmond changed few minds, they do permit a number of instructive inferences about the patterns of Virginia thinking, and they do suggest some further observations on the reasons for, and the conditions of, the triumph of the Constitution.

Virginia's close division on the Constitution does not lend itself convincingly to any of the most familiar explanations of the ratification contest. It was not essentially a function of conflicting economic interests, class divisions, or contrasting localist and cosmopolitan perspectives.[114] It did not range radicals against conservatives or younger men against their seniors. Among the state's most influential men, it pitted unionists against particularists only in a complicated sense, and one that only partly overrode their shared commitments and agreements.

Among Virginians whose ideas we can directly reconstruct, from private correspondence, public writings, and the records of the state and federal conventions, *none* disputed the necessity for constitutional reform. Just as clearly, *none* believed that constitutional reform was worth the sacrifice of liberty or the essential interests of Virginia. Rather, men of com-

parable experience and intellect, responding to the same alarms and
sharing many common values, were compelled to work a very difficult
equation when presented with the Constitution. Regional disparities, the
history of sectional disputes, the current disposition of the North, and
even the condition of the revolutionary enterprise itself in both the Old
Dominion and the nation—all had to be considered in order to determine where Virginia's interests lay. Several speakers at the state convention candidly confessed that they could see no easy answer and could
judge the Constitution neither altogether good nor altogether bad. Many
silent delegates and many voters, I suspect, were swayed by all of the concerns the speakers voiced and made their individual decisions in related
ways.[115]

Virginia's leaders had reacted with intense and virtually unanimous
alarm to the sectional crisis of 1786. (Patrick Henry may have been the
only one who silently resisted the conclusion that the Union must be
strengthened or who flirted later with the thought that separate regional
confederations might be preferable to a proposal that appeared to
strengthen it too much).[116] And yet, confronted with the unamended Constitution, William Grayson, James Monroe, and several others who had
always been regarded as among the state's most "federal" politicians were
seized by much the same anxieties as Henry. Commercial regulations
could be made, they saw, and federal taxes could be levied, by congressional majorities whose sympathies and interests seemed as incompatible
with theirs as Parliament's had been. Recent history showed, they thought,
that sectional temptations would result in sectional abuses. It even seemed
to warn that many influential easterners were eager to employ the great
and often dangerously ambiguous authority of the new government in
ways deliberately intended to produce additional consolidation and a permanent subjection of the South and West. Virginia's liberties and interests,
they concluded, simply could not be entrusted, even temporarily, to northern politicians.

On the other side, James Madison was certainly exceptional in his conviction that Virginia's economic interests would be safe because an agricultural, republican majority would use the Constitution to dismantle
European regulations and construct a national economy in which the interests of the shipping and producing states would harmonize and gradually converge. But Madison and other Federalists could offer a persuasive
case that the debilities of the Confederation were themselves the leading
cause of closure of the Mississippi and the economic suffering that had
produced the recent sectional collision. They could argue that opponents
of the Constitution, even in Virginia's own convention, would never agree
on the changes they required. And finally—what may have been the mar-

gin—they could make a potent case that both Virginia and republican self government, as most Virginians tended to define it, were incalculably more vulnerable to a collapse of the confederation than the Antifederalists were willing to admit. They carried the convention and the state, I would suggest, because the calculations that persuaded Edmund Randolph influenced others too. Virginians did not vote to sacrifice their liberties or local interests to larger, national needs. Rather, a majority may have decided that the interests of Virginia, which included its survival as a liberal republic, were inseparable from the perpetuation of the Union. Randolph clearly did, and Randolph's tortured course may have epitomized the ratification contest in the state.

If this was so, however, there are grounds for yet another, final observation. The majority at Richmond voted, as their governor preferred, for subsequent amendments that would guarantee additional protection for Virginia's special interests, as well as for a bill of rights to guarantee the private liberties protected by the Old Dominion's revolutionary charters. Madison, as Patrick Henry feared, would nevertheless do everything within his power to prevent reductions in the commerce and taxation powers of the new regime, even as he kept his promise to support a bill of rights. The state convention's leading advocate of federal reform continued to believe that federal navigation laws, together with a federal power of direct taxation, were essential to the document's success. He also thought—and his positions at the state and federal conventions should suggest that this had never seemed to him a merely incidental point—that they were in the interests of his state.[117] Madison transcended local interests in a manner that exposed him to the deep distrust of some Virginians. Still, his concept of the Union was indelibly conditioned, as was theirs, by his Virginia background and perspective. He supported constitutional reform in part because he was more fearful than the Antifederalists about Virginia's fate outside the Union. But he supported it, as well, because he was more confident than they that a majority of agricultural producers would direct the new regime and keep the central government within its chartered limits. When that faith was tested, it is not surprising that his vision was to prove as incompatible as theirs with a consolidated system or with eastern domination of the reconstructed Union.

The Constitution split Virginians sharply and in truly fundamental ways. Though he was not a vengeful man, Patrick Henry died without forgiving Madison for the defeat of 1788, and Edmund Randolph's promising career was wrecked by his reversal of that year.[118] In hindsight, nonetheless, the record of the ratifying contest speaks as clearly of the commonalities among Virginians as it does of their differences. They disagreed about Virginia's interests (or, at least, about the most effective way

that these could be secured). But in their general association of the interests of producers with the interests of republics, their shared commitment to the West, their uniform denunciations of consolidation, their
dislike of government "splendor," and their settled, common fears of
standing armies, public debts, and magisterial ambitions, it is easy to de-
tect the themes that would unite the great majority again behind the
Resolutions of 1798 and the distinctively "Virginian" policies of the "Dy-
nasty" years. In these agreements, too, it may be possible to see that it
was not expediency alone, or even mainly, that explains why Madison
continued at their head.

The victory at Richmond was conditional and incomplete. Many chil-
dren of the Revolution entered on the federal experiment with reservations much like Randolph's. A few proclaimed, as Patrick Henry did, that
they would work with all their power "to retrieve the loss of liberty and
remove the defects of that system in a constitutional way."[119] Madison
himself, however, was far from finished with his effort to define a genuinely revolutionary, partly national, but also partly federal Union. The
skeptics therefore found a potent, partial ally in the Father of the Constitution, who would quickly join with Thomas Jefferson to lead most of
the former Antifederalists into a party dedicated to a strict interpretation
of the federal charter and a vision of the future much at odds with Hamilton's design for national splendor. First, however, there were promises
to keep and parchment outlines waiting to be filled.

CHAPTER NINE

Spanning the Abyss: Madison, the Bill of Rights, and the Inauguration of the Federal Republic

THE CONSTITUTION WAS INTENDED BY ITS FRAMERS to resolve specific problems, most of which had been intractable for years. Domestic creditors had not received the interest on their notes since early in the decade. The Confederation Congress had defaulted on a payment due to France and was approaching the exhaustion of its credit with Dutch bankers. Spain had closed the Mississippi River. Britain occupied a string of forts in the Northwest, which she refused to leave until the states met treaty obligations of their own. And although a weak recovery had started by the time the Constitution was approved, one recent study estimates that the per capita gross national product may still have been some 46 percent below the level reached by the beginning of the Revolutionary War.[1] In addition, the inauguration of a reconstructed government posed difficulties of its own. The Constitution left it to the first new Congress to create judicial and executive departments, to define the relationships between the governmental branches, and even to determine how the members of these branches would address each other in their messages and personal communications. As Madison observed in a July 5, 1789, letter to his father, the members of this Congress faced "a wilderness without a single footstep to guide us."[2]

More clearly, though, than any other member of this Congress, Madison believed that it must also meet another challenge, hardly less imposing than the rest. The triumph of the Constitution was conditional and incomplete. Two states were still outside the reconstructed Union. In many of the others, nearly half of the attentive citizenry had disapproved of the reform, and some of them were still determined to dilute it. Antifederalist anxieties were not restricted to concerns that this or that specific interest might be disadvantaged by the new regime. Rather, they extended to a very real and very potent apprehension that the fundamental objects of the Revolution were at risk. Half a nation needed to be reassured, and Madison's distinctive, self-selected role would be to guide this reconciliation. The effort is as worthy of remembrance as his central part in the adoption of the Constitution, and it was hardly less important to the document's success.

The centerpiece, of course, was Madison's decision to prepare the Bill of Rights, to which he has as sound a claim to principal paternity as he has to the initial resolutions at the Constitutional Convention. The strategy, however, encompassed much besides the effort to secure the first amendments, which itself is easily misjudged unless it is examined in the context of his broader goals. In the year between the victory at Richmond and the meeting of the First Federal Congress, Patrick Henry organized a dedicated effort to exclude Madison from Virginia's congressional delegation, hoping to construct a Congress that would recommend severe revisions of the Constitution or the convocation of a second federal convention. For Madison, the personal ordeal was so distasteful that a number of his allies in the struggle for reform, most of whom were less disposed to compromise with their opponents, believed that he was frightened into sponsoring the first amendments and, in no great time, into reversing the positions he had held since early in the decade.[3] Many recent analysts have followed these contemporary critics, although it is by no means clear that Madison's career was gravely threatened by the Antifederalist maneuvers or that a supposed preoccupation with his own political survival can account for his decisions. A fuller study of the context may suggest that the Virginia contests deepened his appreciation of the public mood and strengthened inclinations that, in any case, would have profoundly influenced his positions.

At the Constitutional Convention and throughout the struggle over the adoption of the Constitution, Madison had been distinctive for his effort to assure himself, as well as others, that the great reform would be consistent with the nation's revolutionary values. From the outset of the first new Congress, the same determination guided his distinctive strategies and conduct. The Bill of Rights, from this perspective, was undoubtedly intended to defuse demands for substantive reductions in the powers of the new regime. To Madison, however, this was far from the whole story. Proper in itself, the Bill of Rights was also central to a great campaign to give the lie to charges that the Federalists were less republican than their opponents, to seat the Constitution in the hearts and heads of the whole political nation, and to encourage and exemplify a style of leadership that would ensure that *all* of the specific measures of the new regime would foster national conciliation. Beginning with his first remarks in Congress, Madison deliberately set out to inculcate "a conscious responsibility for the destiny of republican liberty" and to persuade his colleagues to adopt "a system of legislation founded on the principles of an honest policy and directed by the spirit of diffusive patriotism."[4] From the semi-comic battle over titles, through the clashes over tariffs, and until the session closed, he conscientiously attempted to direct the reconstructed Congress toward a set of policies that would establish its republican credentials, demonstrate a scrupulous respect for charter limitations, adopt the highest principles of private ethics as a standard for the public, and maintain a rigorous regard for equity between the nation's several sections: a "patriotic" (or republican) consideration for the interests of the whole. The effort cost him some of the esteem with which his colleagues honored him at first, and it would lead in no great time to a collision with his higher-flying allies—but not before it proved almost as critical as Washington's prestige to the experiment's success. Madison became the bridge across which the opponents of the Constitution moved to its support, the leader of a party that would venerate the people's charter more profoundly than would many of its framers. In the process, he developed or revealed dimensions of his personality and vision that had barely been discerned by many of his allies in the struggle for reform, dimensions greatly underestimated to this day in studies which conclude with the adoption of the Constitution or which emphasize a great divide between his contributions to the making of the Constitution and the rest of his career.

Virginia ratified the Constitution on June 25, 1788. On the anniversary of Independence, Madison was at Mount Vernon, where he visited with Washington for several days before departing for New York and his position in the final session of the old Confederation Congress. Neither man expected their opponents in Virginia to submit without a fight, and Madison had barely reached New York before he was denouncing the "remarkable" form and "pestilent tendency" of that state's instrument of ratification.[5] New York had ratified the charter only "in full confidence" that its proposed amendments would receive an early consideration and under the assumption that the powers of the federal government would not be exercised in full until a second general convention could consider a revision of the plan. It had accompanied its ratification with a circular letter calling on the other states to join in requesting such a meeting.[6] Madison continued to believe that any such assemblage would "mutilate the system, particularly in the article of taxation."[7] Within the week, however, Edmund Randolph told him that the Old Dominion "*perhaps* ought, and probably [would] concur" with New York's action,[8] leading Madison to wonder if the New York letter would be "more injurious" than an absolute rejection would have been. Indeed, he wrote to Washington on August 24 that he was unable to account for local Federalists' concurrence in this project "on any other principle than the determination to purchase an immediate ratification in any form and at any price rather than disappoint the city of a chance for [hosting] the new Congress."[9]

The endless battle over the location of the federal government was one of two considerations that had hurried the Virginian back to Congress. Always an opponent of remaining in New York, he worried, too, that a decision for this city would provide another handle for Virginians who opposed the Constitution "on account of the eastern preponderancy in the federal system."[10] Accordingly, although the Confederation Congress was preparing legislation to inaugurate the new one, Madison focused almost single-mindedly on the maneuvers over its location. As before, his ultimate objective was to fix the government on the Potomac, where it would be convenient to (and more profoundly influenced by) the South and West. In the meantime, as he had for years, he favored Philadelphia as a temporary site, both because he calculated that a Philadelphia location would promote his ultimate objective and because a New York seat displayed "a shameful partiality to one extremity of the continent"—a partiality especially disturbing to Kentucky, where the Mississippi question had already generated deep suspicion of New England and New York, and where Spain was still attempting to seduce the westerners from their allegiance.[11]

The Mississippi was the second issue to which Madison devoted his particular attention, leaving it to Edward Carrington to handle most of the routine affairs between Virginia and the Congress. Along with a removal from New York, the founder saw a final resolution of the crisis prompted by the Jay-Gardoqui talks as critical to easing the anxieties with which so many southerners and westerners approached the launching of the new regime, whose early measures, he expected, would indeed be partial to the North and East.[12] Now, at last, he was successful in securing nearly everything he wished. In the middle of September, Congress passed two public resolutions: one denying that the federal government had ever been disposed to sacrifice its claim to an enjoyment of the Mississippi, and one declaring that the navigation of the river was a clear, essential right. To these, it added yet another, secret resolution ending the negotiation with Gardoqui and referring the dispute about the river to the new administration. This was very much the outcome Madison had advocated for a year; and putting secrecy aside, he rushed the news to his Virginia friends and to Kentuckian John Brown, who had engaged him in a confidential talk about the Spanish plotting in the West before returning to the district from his place in the Virginia delegation.[13]

Madison hoped that the resolutions on the Mississippi would assuage the anger over the congressional decision to remain in New York. In that, he wrote, the southern members had been forced to acquiesce in order to resolve an impasse.[14] Still, he did not hide his disappointment. A temporary seat anywhere south of the Delaware, he thought, would have secured a final residence on the Susquehanna or the Potomac. Now, he feared that central Pennsylvania was the best that could be hoped for, and the risk of stopping at the Delaware had been considerably increased. Worse, he thought it "truly mortifying that the outset of the new government should be immediately preceded by such a display of locality as portends the continuance of an evil which has dishonored the old," one which might be represented in the South as "a justification of all the antifederal arguments drawn from that danger."[15]

The news from home did not bode well for the transition. By the middle of October, when Congress lost its quorum and Madison prepared to depart, correspondents in Virginia were bombarding him with almost daily lamentations on the fall assembly session. In his absence, they complained, the Federalists were both outnumbered and outgeneraled; and Henry was directing a concerted effort to "impede or frustrate" the transition.[16] Warning Madison that even staunch supporters of the Constitution were considering a plan to join in New York's call for a convention,[17] allies asked for his advice on the proposal and for his ideas about a district or a statewide plan for the elections to the federal House.[18] Most of all, they wished to know his own desires concerning service in the Senate or the House, a subject on which he had been so reticent that even Joseph Jones and Edmund Randolph had to beg him for a line.[19]

By the middle of October, it would seem, Madison had done no more to clarify his wishes on the final subject than to talk with Edward Carrington—and then, perhaps, at Carrington's request—before the latter left New York to take his seat in the assembly. Judging from their later letters and from those to other friends, Madison authorized his colleague to convey his willingness to serve in either branch of Congress, but expressed so many reservations or so definite a preference for the lower house that even Carrington remained uncertain of his feelings.[20] Not until November 2 did he make these clear—in letters that did not arrive in time to influence the assembly's actions.[21] The delay is not to be accounted for by the exigencies of other business; he had written weeks before that Congress might not ever find another quorum. Neither was his reticence an effort to dissemble his positions; his letters, when they did arrive, were quite forthcoming. Still, Madison left his allies in the dark, and whether he intended to or not, that fact has much to teach about his character and culture.

By the middle of October, Washington and other Federalists were certain that their only chance to keep Virginia from sending two Antifederalist to the Senate was to enter Madison against the Antifederalist selections and to throw their second votes away. But in Virginia, a defeat in such a contest was regarded as a serious humiliation. Understanding that their candidate preferred the House, his backers carefully explained the situation and assured him that they would desist if he objected to the plan or if there seemed no prospect of success.[22] Yet Madison's continued silence left them helpless in the face of Henry's warnings that the hero of the late convention thought the Constitution perfect and would not support amendments. On November 8, Virginia's legislators cast 98 ballots for Richard Henry Lee, 86 for William Grayson, and 77 for Madison. Madison's inaction probably contributed, not only to his own defeat, but to the utter rout of Federalism in the session. On October 30, the House of Delegates had voted overwhelmingly to join New York in calling for a second federal convention.[23] Now, the legislature followed its decision on the Senate by deciding on a district plan for the elections to the lower house and by attaching a provision that required that candidates be residents within their districts for a year preceding the elections. This last provision was deliberately designed to render Madison incapable of standing in a district where he would have had no competition, and the district plan included Orange within a set of counties that had voted six to two against the Constitution.[24] As Randolph said, "Nothing [was] left undone which can tend to the subversion of the new government."[25]

How can we account for Madison's inaction? The letters of November 2, which were written just before he left New York and seven days before the ballot on the Senate, show that it was certainly not true that he would not support amendments. These letters demonstrate, in fact, that he had moved from his position at the state convention, where he said that he would *not oppose* amendments ("not because they are necessary but because they . . . may gratify some gentlemen's wishes"),[26] into positive support for action by the first new Congress.[27] As early as the middle of October, for that matter, Madison had turned his thoughts in earnest toward the contents of a bill of rights, although he did not hide his opposition to amendments that might damage the "foundation of the fabric."[28] In short, a full communication of his private sentiments could not have hurt and might have helped him in the state assembly.[29] But this may be exactly why he waited till too late to make his feelings known.

Madison was not a thin-skinned politician. Nevertheless, his skin was clearly thinnest when his honor was impugned or when he was accused of personal ambition. His delay in making his opinions clearer seems to have reflected a deliberate refusal to do anything at all that might have been interpreted as "running" for the Senate, even though this put his allies in a bind. Indeed, as he eventually explained to Randolph, he was willing "to afford any service that might be acceptable from me . . . to put the government into quiet and successful operation." He preferred the House of Representatives, he said, provided that the law would make it possible for his election to result "from the spontaneous suffrage" of the voters. Service there could not be imputed to personal ambition. Still, he would relinquish this desire if Federalists considered it essential to support him for the Senate. He was sure that he would lose. In fact, he had already said that he did not expect to be elected even to the House, since even that might call for steps that would betray "a solicitude which I do not feel or have the appearance of a spirit of electioneering, which I despise."[30] Obviously, Madison was hoping to be drafted. He yearned to be the object of an unsolicited demand, to be selected purely on the basis of his reputation and his record. More than that, he may have been attempting, as he had in 1777, to provide a personal example of how republican elections "ought" to be conducted.

It was a fleeting and romantic moment, prolonged by several weeks of trying to convince himself that he could winter in New York instead of in his Henrymandered district.[31] Already, though, his friends were pleading for him to return to Orange and take an active role in the election. James Monroe, warned Carrington, would soon declare himself a candidate for this position, and "you are upon no occasion of a public nature to expect favors from this gentleman."[32] The Antifederalists would spare no pains, Carrington and others added, to misrepresent his views and keep him out of Congress.[33] Grudgingly—and probably because he saw that he might well be blamed for his continuing inaction—Madison at last surrendered. Spending Christmas at Mount Vernon, he arrived at the family plantation just before the finish of the year.[34]

Distasteful though he found it, Madison became a capable campaigner once he put himself in harness, pursuing his "pretensions," he admitted, far beyond his earliest intentions.[35] As his backers recommended, he probably called personally on Baptist minister John Leland to enlist that sect's support, and he addressed an early letter to the Reverend George Eve, pastor of the Blue Run Church in Orange.[36] In this and in a flood of later letters, some of which were meant for publication, he candidly explained his sentiments about amendments:

> I freely own that I have never seen in the Constitution as it now stands those serious dangers which have alarmed many respectable citizens. Ac-

cordingly, whilst it remained unratified and it was necessary to unite the
states in some one plan, I opposed all previous alterations as calculated to
throw the states into dangerous contentions and to furnish the secret enemies of the Union with an opportunity of promoting its dissolution. Circumstances are now changed: The Constitution is established on the
ratifications of eleven states and a very great majority of the people of
America; and amendments, if pursued with a proper moderation and in a
proper mode, will be not only safe, but may serve the double purpose of
satisfying the minds of well-meaning opponents and of providing additional
guards in favor of liberty. Under this change of circumstances, it is my
sincere opinion that the Constitution ought to be revised, and that the first
Congress meeting under it ought to prepare and recommend to the states
for ratification the most satisfactory provisions for all essential rights, particularly the rights of conscience in the fullest latitude, the freedom of the
press, trials by jury, security against general warrants, etc. I think it will be
proper also to provide expressly in the Constitution for the periodical increase of the number of representatives until the amount shall be entirely
satisfactory, and to put the judiciary department into such a form as will
render vexatious appeals impossible. There are sundry other alterations
which are either eligible in themselves or, being at least safe, are recommended by the respect due to such as wish for them.[37]

It would be quicker and more certain, he continued, to amend the Constitution by this method than to wait until two-thirds of the states applied
for another convention, especially since several states would certainly reject a call for a convention yet would probably approve amendments by
the Congress. A convention, too, "meeting in the present ferment of parties and containing perhaps insidious characters from different parts of
America, would at least spread a general alarm and be but too likely to
turn everything into confusion."[38]

Madison assured his correspondents that he would feel "bound by the
strongest motives" to work for such amendments even if he personally
believed that no such alterations were to be desired. But actually, he
added, he had always thought the Constitution subject to improvement,
had been an advocate at Philadelphia for several of the changes now desired, and positively favored such amendments as would "either make it
better in itself or, without making it worse, will make it appear better to
those who now dislike it."[39] The principal exception, he admitted, was the
widespread sentiment for the deletion of the federal power of direct taxation. That power, he maintained, was absolutely necessary to assure that
"every state [would] bear its equitable share of the common burdens." A
requisition system had been shown to lead to partial and inequitable compliance. In time, it could result in "quarrels, wars, . . . disunion and a gen-

eral confusion." Direct taxation, he believed, would not be likely to be used unless emergencies required it. If they did, the only question would be whether taxes would be raised in all the states by federal action or in some states only by a requisition system, "whilst others unjustly withdraw their shoulders from the common burden." Moreover, if the federal government should be reduced to a reliance on the impost, Virginia and the South, which were particularly vulnerable to foreign threats, would also have to bear an unfair portion of the tax load.[40]

In the judgment of his allies, Madison's impressive letters (some of which were circulated privately, then lost) were indispensable to his success. In his own opinion, they were not enough to contradict the falsehoods circulating in the district: that he was rigidly opposed to any alterations of the Constitution, unconcerned about the Mississippi, even an opponent of religious freedom. Therefore, he abandoned his original determination to appear in public only in Orange County and attended public gatherings in Louisa and Culpeper as well. In the second half of January, he and James Monroe appeared together several times at courthouse gatherings and churches, managing the contest while maintaining their personal friendship.[41] All of this, he thought, was necessary to the outcome. "My absence would have left a room for the calumnies of antifederal partisans which would have defeated much better pretensions than mine. In Culpeper, which was the critical county, a continued attention was necessary to repel the multiplied falsehoods which circulated."[42] In the poll of February 2, in a district rigged against him, Madison received 1308 votes to Monroe's 972. He lost decisively in Spotsylvania and Amherst, but carried half the counties and 57 percent of the popular vote.[43]

By the end of February 1789, when he departed once again for Fredericksburg, Mount Vernon, and New York, Madison was notably more optimistic on the prospects for the first new Congress.[44] During their week together, February 22 through March 1, he and Washington reviewed the situation and discussed their mutual agenda. Washington, they knew, would be the unopposed selection of the first electoral college. At the general's request, Madison had drafted an inaugural address; and during the preceding fall, he and Hamilton and others in New York had reached agreement on a plan to back John Adams, the New England favorite, for the second-highest office (though not without reluctance and not without discussing ways to guarantee that Adams would get fewer votes than Washington).[45] As early as December, Madison had known that Congress would be overwhelmingly composed of friends of the new system.[46] In the aftermath of the elections, it was clear that seven of the ten Virginians chosen for the House had favored the adoption of the Constitution.[47] And finally,

although the Pennsylvania Antifederalists had met in Harrisburg to urge
amendments and a second federal convention, neither Pennsylvania nor
any of the other ratifying states had joined Virginia and New York in
issuing this call.[48]

None of which, however, altered Madison's (or Washington's) determination to "conciliate the well meaning of all parties and put our affairs
into an auspicious train."[49] No later than the middle of October, as the
movement for another Convention gathered force (and well before his
own election was in question), Madison had seen that quick congressional
approval of amendments would "quiet the fears of many" and supply
"those further guards for private rights which can do no harm to the
system."[50] The measures of the fall session of the Assembly, reinforced by
his ordeal within his district, had confirmed and deepened his support
for congressional action. Not only did he judge that public pledges of
support for such amendments had been necessary to his own election, he
had learned from countless face-to-face discussions in his counties that
anxieties about the new regime were not confined to several dozen hopelessly recalcitrant opponents of the Constitution; they were widely shared
among the body of the freemen.

Madison's political career was not profoundly threatened as he traveled to New York. He had come within five votes of being chosen for the
Senate by a state assembly dominated by his foes. He had secured election
to the House by an impressive margin and against a formidable opponent.
He would have been appointed to high office in the first administration
if Monroe had won the contest in his district. But Madison had always
been a fierce opponent of majority contempt for others' rights and wishes,
and he emerged from the election with a deepened sensitivity to the minority's desires. Therefore, from the moment when the House was called
to order, he intended to address specific problems with as much dispatch
as prudence would allow, but he intended also to address these problems
with a principled attention to minority concerns.

The House of Representatives achieved a quorum on April 1, 1789. Madison was in an unexampled place from which to influence all its measures.
Without exception, all of those whose national reputations rivaled or exceeded his had been elected to the Senate or anticipated appointments
in the other branches of the reconstructed system. In addition, Madison
was Washington's most influential confidant at the beginning of the new
administration, a principal adviser on appointments, presidential protocol, and the interpretation of the Constitution. In this unexampled situ-

ation, never replicated in the history of Congress, he would draft the president's inaugural address, the House of Representatives' response, the president's reply to that response, and even Washington's reply to the initial message from the Senate. Through it all, he would attempt deliberately to set the tone of dignified simplicity and presidential deference to the Congress that he regarded as appropriate for a republic.[51]

The consistency and reach of Madison's determination to define a set of guiding principles for Congress is unmistakable and striking. And among these fundamental guidelines, none were more important in his mind than the commitment to impartial, "patriotic," equal laws, together with the conscious sense of principal responsibility for liberty itself, which he would write of in the House reply to the inaugural address.[52] The first priority for Congress was to raise the steady revenues on which its other measures would depend, and as the president was being notified of his election, Madison proposed a set of resolutions looking toward an impost.[53] Months before, however, shortly after the Confederation Congress had again debated its location, he had privately announced a principle to which he would return repeatedly throughout these long deliberations: "A certain degree of impartiality, or the appearance of it, is necessary in the most despotic governments. In republics, this may be considered as the vital principle of the administration. And in a *federal* republic founded on local distinctions involving local jealousies, it ought to be attended to with a still more scrupulous exactness."[54]

Madison's original proposal for an impost was modeled on the congressional recommendations of 1783, which had already been approved by a majority of states. He hoped a quick agreement on this "temporary system" would permit taxation of the spring importations.[55] In fact, however, by the time that Congress had attained a quorum, it was probably too late to make this prospect realistic; and it was soon apparent that the northern members wanted to erect a more digested system, one with more specific duties and a more deliberate encouragement of native manufactures. As deliberations turned in this direction and continued into May, Madison worked steadily for a variety of ends; but he continued also, both by word and personal example, to encourage "mutual concessions," a consideration of "the general interests of the Union" as well as state and local objects, and the need to consciously define some basic principles of action.[56]

Meanwhile, in the midst of the deliberations on the tariff, Congress paused for Washington's inauguration and the first dispute between the Senate and the House. On May 9, expressing his delight that the proceedings on the impost had been relatively free from sectional collisions, Madison directed Jefferson's attention to the caption of the House of

Representatives' reply to Washington's address, which had included no
"degrading appendages of Excellency, Esquire," or the like.[57] On that very
day, however, a committee of the Senate, where the matter had preoccupied the members for a week, recommended that the president should
be addressed as His Highness the President of the United States and Protector of their Liberties. Madison was sorry, he reported now, that the
Senate "do not concur in the principle of dignified simplicity," to which
the House would "assuredly adhere." But Vice President Adams, he lamented, was a dedicated champion of elevated titles, and he was "seconded with all the force and urgency of natural temper by R[ichard]
H[enry] L[ee]!!!"[58]

On May 11, the House debated whether to appoint a committee to
confer with the Senate on the subject. As Fisher Ames remarked, "Not a
soul said a word *for* titles. But the zeal of [their opponents] could not
have risen higher in case of contradiction."[59] To calm the more outspoken
critics of the Senate,[60] Madison remarked that he did not believe that the
president would be dangerous to liberty "if you were to load him with all
the titles of Europe or Asia." But titles, he complained, were "odious"
and "ridiculous." "Not very reconcilable with the nature of our government or the genius of the people," they would in actuality "diminish the
true dignity and importance of a republic . . . [and] disgrace the manly
shoulders of our chief. . . . The more simple, the more republican we are
in our manners, the more rational dignity we acquire."[61] Appointed chairman of the House committee, which refused to agree with the Senate,
Madison had stronger feelings on this business than he stated on the floor,
where he was trying to encourage "due respect" for the other house and
good relationships between the branches. Writing Jefferson in cipher on
May 23, he admitted that the Senate's acquiescence in the simple "Mr.
President" had had to be extorted and that Lee and Adams had been
zealous for a project that would "have subjected the president to a severe
dilemma and given a deep wound to our infant government."[62]

Madison had not retreated from the preference for a strong executive
which he had come to at the Constitutional Convention. On May 19, after
the deliberations on the tariff reached a temporary resolution, he moved
for the establishment of three executive departments, whose heads would
be "nominated by the President and appointed by him, with the advice
and consent of the Senate—and removable by the President" alone.[63] The
language of his resolution led the House into its first extended argument
about interpretation of the Constitution, a matter which engaged his full
attention and compelled him, he admitted, to a more minute examination
of the charter than he had ever undertaken. When William Loughton
Smith (S.C.) suggested that the Constitution's silence on the subject made

impeachment the only lawful method of removing executive officials, Madison replied that this construction would give them all a good behavior tenure. Impeachment, as he saw it, might be necessary to remove an officer *against* the president's desires, and thus had been inserted "as a supplemental security" for the public. But it was "absolutely necessary" for the president alone to have the power to remove subordinate officials. Nothing else could render him responsible for the executive's affairs.[64] Neither was the framer in agreement with his old Virginia colleague, Theodorick Bland, that the requirement of concurrence by the Senate in the appointment of executive officials implied a Senate role in their removal. This interpretation, too, however plausible on first consideration, was "incompatible" with the pervading principle "that there should be the highest possible degree of responsibility in all the executive officers" and especially in the president himself. "Congress may establish officers by law; therefore, most certainly, it is in the discretion of the legislature to say upon what terms the office should be held."[65]

On second thought, however, Madison was not so certain that his first opinion had been right. He did not waver, to be sure, from his insistence that the Constitution sought to make the chief executive as independent and responsible as safety would permit (or from his arguments that this would be the weaker branch of government and had been more effectively protected from "ambitious or designing" chiefs than any such authority on earth).[66] Still, in a speech he delivered on June 16, he now acknowledged that a closer study of the Constitution had convinced him that his first ideas had been imperfect. Madison's original proposal had assumed that where the Constitution offered no specific guidance, the legislature could decide the question on its merits. A reconsideration had suggested that the best construction should consider all "the great departments" in the constitutional relationship they bore to one another. On this principle, he now concluded, the House of Representatives had no authority to qualify the constitutional decision to confide the legislative, executive, and judicial powers to separate branches. The Constitution had itself, of course, already qualified the natural executive power "of appointing, overseeing, and controlling those who execute the laws" by associating the Senate in the power of appointment. But Congress lacked a constitutional authority to extend this qualification by requiring the concurrence of the Senate in removals. A provision that the power of removal rested with the president alone was not a matter of discretion; it was "nothing more than explanatory of the meaning of the Constitution."[67]

During this debate, some congressmen suggested that the meaning of the Constitution ought to be determined by the courts. Madison sharply disagreed. "It is incontrovertably of as much importance to this branch of the government as to any other," he maintained on June 17, "that the Constitution shall be preserved entire." In the ordinary course of governmental operations, it was true, "the exposition of the laws and Constitution" would of course devolve upon the courts.

> But I beg to know upon what principle it can be contended that any one department draws from the Constitution greater powers than another in marking out the limits of the powers of the several departments. The Constitution is the charter of the people to the government; it specifies certain great powers as absolutely granted and marks out the departments to exercise them. If the constitutional boundary of either be brought into question, I do not see that any one of these independent departments has more right than another to declare their sentiments on that point. . . . In all [governmental] systems there are points which must be adjusted by the departments themselves, to which no one of them is competent. If it cannot be determined in this way, there is no resource left but the will of the community, to be collected in some mode to be provided by the Constitution or one dictated by the necessity of the case.

Although, as will be seen, he recognized a valuable and theoretically essential role for the judiciary in reviewing legislation, Madison was never willing to concede that the judicary's rulings could ultimately override the views of other branches. In modern language, he was clearly a proponent of judicial review, but he was never a proponent of defining this authority in a manner that placed supremacy in the judiciary's hands.[68]

Whether these arguments advanced a "strict" or a "broad" construction of the Constitution is difficult to say. It may be more important to remark the earnestness with which he wanted Congress to consider issues of this sort, his argument that sound constructions must consider the pervading principles or "spirit" of the charter as a whole, and—most especially—his frank acknowledgment that even he was subject to mistakes.[69] The question was decided as he wished; but it was little less important, in his own opinion, that the matter was deliberated with the care that it deserved. This decision, he explained, would

> become the permanent exposition of the Constitution; and on a permanent exposition of the Constitution will depend the genius and character of the whole government. It will depend, perhaps, on this decision whether the government shall retain that equilibrium which the Constitution intended, or take a direction toward aristocracy or anarchy among the members.

"I feel great anxiety," Madison said—and it was clearly an anxiety he wanted everyone to share—when

> called upon to give a decision . . . that may affect the fundamental princi-
> ples of the government and liberty itself. But all that I can do [and all that
> anyone could do] is to weigh well everything advanced on both sides, with
> the purest desire to find out the true meaning of the Constitution and to
> be guided by that and an attachment to the true spirit of liberty, whose
> influence I believe strongly predominates here.[70]

To Madison, this episode suggests, congressional interpretation of the Constitution was never to be merely instrumental to the ends that Congress wanted to pursue. And on this issue, too—as in the arguments concerning titles or the tariff—Madison appealed explicitly for sensitivity to the impressions to be made on the opponents of the Constitution. The Senate, he maintained, possessed "that proportion of aristocratic power which the Constitution no doubt thought wise to be established in the system, but which some have strongly objected against"—and which he himself did not believe should be increased beyond that measure.[71]

Concern for opposition sensitivities, of course, had kept the matter of amendments at the front of his mind since the beginning of the session. Together with a proud insistence on the great degree to which his principles of equity, equality, and magnanimity had actually prevailed in the proceedings to this point—"virtue" or "disinterestedness" were other terms for the "diffusive patriotism" Madison desired—his letters to Virginia had been filled from the beginning of the session with assurances that constitutional amendments would be passed.[72] Public reassurances had been inserted in the president's address, the House of Representatives' reply to the inaugural address, and Madison's announcement on May 4 that he would introduce amendments on May 25. The press of other business forced him to accept postponement when the twenty-fifth arrived, but he was rigidly determined not to let the session pass without proposing alterations that would make the Constitution "as acceptable to the whole people of the United States as it has been . . . to a majority of them," amendments that would prove that the supporters of the Constitution "were as sincerely devoted to liberty and a republican government" as any of its opponents.[73] With this in mind, he interrupted other business on June 8 to introduce some nineteen propositions: a bill of rights and several other alterations or additions. Since other matters still preoccupied the House—differences between its own and Senate versions of the impost bill, creation of executive departments, and the Senate's plan of a judiciary act—Madison did not insist on action at the moment. His resolutions were referred to a select committee on July 26 and did not come before the House until mid-August. At that point, however, he insisted that despite the urgency of other business, a large proportion of the people were "also anxious to secure those rights which they are apprehensive are endangered." Considering the confidence that had been placed in Congress when the Constitution was adopted, he considered it "incumbent" on the representatives "in point of candor and good faith, as well as policy" to "pursue the subject to effect."[74]

The standard story of the framing of the Bill of Rights may be familiar to most readers. Madison, this says, considered the persistent clamor for addition of a bill to be the lynchpin of the opposition coalition. Remove it, he perceived, and the supporters of the Constitution would "extinguish opposition to the system, or at least [would] break the force of it by detaching the deluded opponents [of the Constitution] from their designing leaders," who were still determined to impede or weaken the reform.[75] Accordingly, he carefully extracted from the changes recommended by the state conventions only those that he considered harmless, proposing a concession that would leave the powers and the fundamental structure of the federal government essentially untouched. Then, against the opposition of the Antifederalists in Congress, which was rendered all the more annoying by significant resistance from the Federalists themselves, he pleaded and persisted till the work was done. Every element of the completed bill was drawn from Madison's initial resolutions. It would not have been approved if he had not been present. And it succeeded brilliantly in meeting his objectives. It fractured the opponents of the Constitution, crushed the possibility of substantive amendments, and restored the author's popularity at home.[76]

All of this is true. Most of it, in fact, was candidly acknowledged by the sponsor of the first amendments in his speeches to the House. The problem with the standard story, insofar as one exists, is that it has been served so commonly in such a heavy sauce of modern disillusionment with politicians that much of the authentic flavor has been lost. This seems to me unquestionably the case when what is stressed most strongly is the point that may need emphasizing least: Madison's supposed alarm about his standing in Virginia, which had never been that seriously at risk. It seems the case, more subtly but more commonly, when nearly all the emphasis is placed on Madison's initial doubts about the wisdom and efficacy of libertarian amendments and his fixed determination to exclude amendments that would change the structure or reduce the powers of the new regime. Both of these concerns were present and important, but neither should be emphasized so heavily that we are left with the impression, as is frequently the case, that the Virginian acted from expediency alone:

that he was privately quite skeptical about attaching these amendments, found the project "nauseous" or galling, and decided to complete it only as a way of crushing the demand for more substantial changes.[77] For Madison, the first amendments were by no means mere "whip-syllabub," as one of his opponents said: "frothy and full of wind, formed only to please the palate," or a tub thrown out by sailors to amuse the whale and gain safe passage for the ship.[78] A close examination of Madison's thinking shows that while he did have reservations, he had also privately concluded that the Bill of Rights was proper in itself. The reasons ran much deeper than can possibly be captured in a cynical, reductionist account. Indeed, when they are placed within the context of the principles and strategy that he had advocated since the opening of Congress, the taste of his distinctive statesmanship emerges with a clarity that can improve our understanding of his course throughout the founding.

Writing Thomas Jefferson in mid-October 1788, Madison declared that he had "always been in favor of a bill of rights, provided it be so framed as not to imply powers not meant to be included in the enumeration."[79] This was as disingenuous, the evidence suggests, as he ever was about a previous political position. At the Constitutional Convention, the states unanimously defeated Mason's motion to prepare a bill of rights, and this could not have been the case if Madison had voted for it.[80] At the Virginia state convention, though he said that "he would be the last to oppose" such amendments, he also argued that "a solemn declaration of our essential rights" was both unnecessary and potentially pernicious.[81] For the months between the two conventions and for some time after the Virginia meeting, Madison's surviving papers are completely silent on the subject. As he said, this was a time when the demand for such a bill was so entangled with the possibility of a conditional ratification of the Constitution (or with the movement for a second federal convention) that it was necessary to deny that *any* alterations were required. Nevertheless, it seems quite certain that until the fall of 1788, Madison agreed with many other Federalists that a reservation of essential rights was inappropriate in a federal Constitution and could, indeed, be positively dangerous to many of the liberties that its proponents wanted to protect.

At the Constitutional Convention, Mason's motion to prepare a bill of rights was overwhelmed without significant discussion. Roger Sherman simply noted that the declarations of the states were not to be repealed by the new Constitution, "and being in force are sufficient."[82] There was nothing cavalier in this remark, and nothing in the quick rejection of the motion to suggest that members did not care about the rights in question. When Sherman said that it could not be necessary to prepare a federal declaration, he was speaking to a gathering that had been laboring for months to frame the Constitution. No one, then or since, has understood more clearly that the members had been working from the start to frame a government of delegated and enumerated powers—a government, that is, quite different from the governments of Europe or even of the several states, which were assumed to have a plenary authority to act, in any area at all, unless a written reservation or the natural rights of man imposed a prohibition. On this understanding, to insist on a federal bill of rights was simply to mistake the fundamental nature of the government they were creating. In fact, it was to make an error that was anything but friendly to the natural rights that everybody wanted to protect. For if the federal government were understood to have *no* powers other than the ones the Constitution granted, then it had *no* lawful right to enter into any other province. It was forbidden by its very nature to encroach on nearly all that vast domain where human rights are exercised and threatened; and all of that preserve—the province of the states—was therefore safer, on this understanding, than could ever be the case as a result of any effort to define it. For who could ever make a comprehensive list of all the liberties that were entitled to protection?[83] And if something should be inadvertently omitted, might that not imply a federal authority to act on matters that were meant to be beyond the federal sphere?

Though none of this was said at the convention, Federalists began to spell the implications out as soon as they encountered opposition.[84] In a widely published speech, delivered in the State House yard at Philadelphia on October 6, 1787, James Wilson developed the distinction between the federal Constitution, in which "everything which is not given is reserved," and the constitutions of the states, in which "everything which is not reserved is given." It would have been "superfluous and absurd," Wilson reasoned, "to have stipulated with a federal body of our own creation that we should enjoy those privileges of which we are not divested." Moreover, such a declaration "might have been construed to imply that some degree of power was given, since we undertook to define its extent."[85] Hamilton expanded on these arguments in *Federalist* no. 84, which also pointed out that there were numerous specific guarantees of rights in the body of the Constitution.[86] Madison was plainly influenced by the same considerations (and by both of these important texts). Thus he told his state convention that it was "unnecessary" to attach a bill of rights, since "everything not granted is reserved," and that it would be "dangerous" to frame a bill if the enumeration was imperfect, since omissions might be taken to imply a grant of federal powers that had never been intended.[87]

Antifederalists were not persuaded. Neither was the minister to France. On the morning after getting Madison's detailed report on the proceedings of the Constitutional Convention, Jefferson had answered with a lengthy letter praising most of the convention's work, but vigorously objecting to provisions he disliked. "A Bill of Rights," he wrote, "is what the people are entitled to against every government on earth, general or particular, and what no just government should refuse or rest on inference." Jefferson had seen James Wilson's speech and understood that the convention's plan proposed a limited regime. Still, he pointed out, the great convention had itself seen fit to write explicit guarantees of several rights into the body of the Constitution—a prohibition of religious tests for office, of ex-post-facto laws, and such. He wanted similar protections for the freedom of the press and freedom of religious conscience.[88] Accordingly, when he received the news that nine states had approved the Constitution, he was at his desk again to tell his old collaborator that he still believed that voices North to South were calling for additional protections. He understood the danger from omissions or a flawed enumeration, which was Madison's most serious concern, but he believed that this could be surmounted by declaring prohibitions to be absolute in cases where there seemed a difficulty in agreeing on legitimate exceptions— powers to create monopolies or standing armies for example.[89] In any case, he later added, the supporters of a bill of rights were "too respectable not to be entitled to some sacrifice of opinion," especially when most of the opponents of the Constitution would be satisfied with this addition.[90]

Jefferson did not elaborate his reasoning in full, but Madison could readily supply the missing steps as he had heard them from the Constitution's other critics. The Constitution, they observed, contained a clause declaring it the supreme law of the land. In case of conflict, it would clearly override state bills of rights. Moreover, in addition to its delegated powers, Congress was to have authority to pass such other laws as might be "necessary and proper" to carry its enumerated powers into action. In judging what was necessary, it might well decide that freedom of the press or other fundamental liberties would have to be infringed.[91] Thus, when he received the letters from his friend, Madison was prompted to explain his thinking more completely than he had in any of his papers to this time.

Except for the remark that he had always been in favor of a declaration, Madison's reply to Jefferson was candid. "At the same time," he continued, "I have never thought the omission a material defect, nor been anxious to supply it even by *subsequent* amendment for any other reason than that it is anxiously desired by others." In the first place, Madison explained, he thought the rights in question were protected by the grant of only limited authority to Congress, "though not in the extent argued by Mr. Wilson." Second, he was deeply doubtful that "a positive declaration of some of the most essential rights could . . . be obtained in the requisite latitude. I am sure that the rights of conscience in particular, if submitted to public definition, would be narrowed much more" than he or Jefferson would wish. Moreover, he had seen "the inefficacy" of bills of rights at just those times and on those points where they were most to be desired. "Repeated violations of these parchment barriers have been committed by overbearing majorities in every state." In Virginia, he reminded Jefferson, despite the bill of rights' provision for religious freedom, a general assessment would undoubtedly have passed if the majority of citizens had backed it. "If a majority of the people were now of one sect, the measure would still take place and on narrower ground than was then proposed," despite the passage in the meantime of the Statute for Religious Freedom. In America, in short, "power lies in the majority of the community, and the invasion of private rights is *chiefly* to be apprehended, not from acts of government contrary to the sense of its constituents, but from acts in which the government is the mere instrument of the major number of constituents." A bill of rights would not control a fixed, tyrannical majority of voters. "Wherever there is an interest and power to do wrong, wrong will generally be done, and not less readily by a powerful and interested party than by a powerful and interested prince."

Madison did not agree with Jefferson that "absolute restrictions" ought to be imposed "in cases that are doubtful." Emergencies would override the plainest charter prohibitions. If Spain or Britain, for example, should send an army to the neighborhood, a parchment prohibition of a peacetime army would at once be overruled. "No written prohibitions on earth" could prevent a measure if necessity and overwhelming public pressure should demand it, and "repeated violations" of such absolute restrictions would destroy the value of a bill of rights in "ordinary" cases. Madison unquestionably believed, as he had said so often, that private rights could be protected most securely, not by parchment declarations, but by the multiplicity of interests in a large republic and by constitutional devices that would check the passions of the moment with the cooler, more mature reflections of the system's other branches.[92]

And yet, although he found the arguments against a bill of rights persuasive, Madison did not consider them conclusive. Like Jefferson, he thought that the proponents of a bill of rights were too respectable and far too numerous to be ignored. To ease the anxious minds of men whose judgment he respected—men like Jefferson himself—was an appropriate republican objective. In addition, he observed, a bill of rights would have at least two further uses. First, he reasoned, "the political truths declared in that solemn manner [would] acquire by degrees the character of fundamental maxims of free government." As they became "incorporated with the national sentiment," these principles would work to "counteract the impulses of interest and passion" in the minds of the majority itself. Second, even though the rights in question would usually be threatened by an "interested majority" of people, there might still be times when the evil might issue from the usurpations of governing officials. At those times,

> a bill of rights will be a good ground for an appeal to the sense of the community. Perhaps, too, there may be a certain degree of danger that a succession of artful and ambitious rulers may by gradual and well-timed advances finally erect an independent government on the subversion of liberty. Should this danger exist at all, it is prudent to guard against it, especially when the precaution can do no injury.[93]

On June 8, when he presented his amendments to the House, Madison incorporated all the arguments elaborated in his private letters, together with the most persuasive Antifederalist appeals for "additional guards for liberty." To these, he added yet another argument, which Jefferson had offered in a letter of March 15: the legal check on governmental usurpations that a bill of rights would put into the hands of federal judges.[94] Once these changes were incorporated in the fundamental law, "independent tribunals of justice will consider themselves in a peculiar manner the guardians of those rights; they will be an impenetrable bulwark against every assumption of power in the legislative and executive" branches.[95] In this speech, as in his private letters, Madison did not disguise his hope that the adoption of his propositions would appease opponents of the Constitution and demonstrate that its supporters "were as sincerely devoted to liberty and a republican government as those who charged them with wishing . . . to lay the foundations of an aristocracy or despotism."[96] He was careful to assure the House that he had not included anything that would dilute essential powers, anything that he did not regard as proper on its merits, or anything that seemed unlikely to receive approval from the states. Obviously, there was nothing underhanded in these tactics, nor were these the only grounds on which he thought the House should act.

Madison apologized repeatedly for taking time from other business to deliberate a bill of rights, which helps explain why some of his contemporaries thought that he was tepid in his own commitment to the project.[97] He also spoke repeatedly about his promise to his district, which encouraged others to believe that he was courting popularity with voters.[98]

Nevertheless, these critics gravely underestimated an extraordinary man, an error which has been repeated all too often in historical discussions of his motives. Several of the other Federalists in Congress certainly believed that Madison was asking them to sacrifice their own opinions to the views of the opponents of the Constitution. Their resentment of concessions they considered both unnecessary and improper prompted much of the resistance to his motions, which was reinforced by sheer impatience to get on with other business.[99] But despite his early reservations, this was not how Madison himself was thinking of the project. In his own conception, he was not surrendering his private judgment to opponents of the Constitution who could be distracted and confused by basically cosmetic changes, nor was this what he was asking other Federalists to do.[100] On the contrary, what he asked in his remarks proposing the amendments will reward a very close consideration, for there is little in his life that tells us more about his thought or takes us closer to the concept of republican statesmanship that he had advocated and attempted to exemplify since the beginning of the session.

"A great number of our constituents . . . are dissatisfied," Madison said,

> among whom are many [who are] respectable for their talents, their patriotism, and . . . the jealousy they have for their liberty. . . . We ought not to disregard their inclination, but, on principles of amity and moderation, conform to their wishes and expressly declare the great rights of mankind secured under this Constitution. The acquiescence which our fellow citizens show under the government calls upon us for a like return of moderation.

Not only was it wise to reconcile the many who were "much inclined to join their support to the cause of federalism if they were satisfied in this one point." Not only was it well to seek reunion with the two nonratifying states. It was important in itself "to extinguish from the bosom of every member of the community any apprehension that there are those among his countrymen who wish to deprive them of the liberty for which they valiantly fought and honorably bled." Most of those who opposed the Constitution, Madison repeated, disliked it because they thought their rights unsafe, "*nor ought we to consider them safe* while a great number of our fellow citizens think these securities necessary."[101] "If we can make the Constitution better in the opinion of those who are opposed to it, without weakening its frame or abridging its usefulness in the judgment of those who are attached to it, we act the part of wise and liberal men."[102]

In many of his greatest speeches, Madison's habitual procedure was to summarize the arguments and options that had been developed in the course of a debate, to analyze their weaknesses and strengths, and thus to recapitulate for others the considerations that had led him to his own conclusions.[103] His mind was like a finely calibrated scale. It felt the weight of arguments on both sides of an issue, measured them with care, and tipped in one direction or the other. Like the scale, moreover, when the balance started tilting, it dropped decisively in that direction. Not infrequently, the arguments on the opposing side slid over and were blended with their opposites into a compound that was new. In addition, Madison was genuinely capable of thinking that the well-considered judgments of the collectivity could be superior to the conclusions of his own unaided reason. In the weeks between the federal convention and the time when he embarked on his defense of the completed Constitution, he decided that the finished charter was superior in most respects to the proposals he had drafted in his closet, a better plan than he had judged it at the moment of its signing. In *The Federalist*, accordingly, he freely used the arguments that his opponents had advanced at the convention. Something similar occurred between the state convention and the drafting of the Bill of Rights. Madison decided that the arguments in favor of a bill were stronger than the arguments against it—clearly so if the amendments could be drafted (by himself) in such a manner that the most apparent dangers could be skirted. And finally, though not the least, Madison, as always, was a *revolutionary* statesman, genuinely dedicated to a special concept of how decisions should be made in a republic. He believed that a republic ultimately rests on mutual respect among its citizens and on a recognition on the part of all that they are the constituents of a community of mutually regarding equals, participators in a polity that asks them to be conscious that they are, at once, the rulers and the ruled.[104] Legislators were by no means an exception. Not only did their duty tell them not to disregard the wishes and ideas of many valued brethren. It urged them to exemplify the mutual respect and the awareness of the differentiated whole which would be all the more essential in a federal system of republics.

If Madison had had his way entirely, the Bill of Rights would have been different in significant respects from the amendments that were finally approved. The alterations would have been incorporated in the body of the Constitution, not tacked onto its end. Madison believed that it would be more logical to interweave amendments with the text: that this would make the charter more accessible to ordinary understandings, and possibly that it would render the amendments as authoritative as the rest.[105] Roger Sherman, on the other hand, insisted that the Constitution, as originally approved, had been the highest sovereign action of the people and should not be alloyed with amendments based on the lesser authority of Congress and the states.[106] Sherman's motion to append the changes rather than incorporate them in the text was defeated when he first proposed it; but, as Madison lamented, the plan of interweaving the amendments proved a victim, in the end, "to *a few* who knew their concurrence to be necessary to the dispatch if not the success of the business."[107]

If Madison had had his way, the Constitution would have opened with a declaration

> that all power is originally vested in and consequently derived from the people.
>
> That government is instituted and ought to be exercised for the benefit of the people; which consists in the enjoyment of life and liberty, with the right of acquiring and using property, and generally of pursuing and obtaining happiness and safety.
>
> That the people have an indubitable, unalienable, and indefeasible right to reform and change their government whenever it be found adverse or inadequate to the purposes of its institution.[108]

Adoption of this language would have meant, of course, that it would never have been doubted that the fundamental principles of the Declaration of Independence (or of the Virginia Declaration of Rights, from which it was taken) are part of the Federal Constitution, along with the specific liberties which it protects. But Madison conceded in his June 8 speech that it might not be "absolutely necessary" to insert these "truths" at the beginning of the Constitution,[109] and others were determined to restrict the alterations to as few as their proponents could accept. The select committee which reported on July 28 substituted a single sentence in place of Madison's initial declaration, and even that was dropped when it did not receive approval from two-thirds of the House.[110] Another clause explicitly enunciating the implicit constitutional principle of separation of the three great branches was deleted by the Senate.[111]

Again, if Congress (and the states) had thoroughly indulged its sponsor, the Bill of Rights would have contained from the beginning a provision that did not become a part of constitutional law until the twentieth century—and then by way of the judiciary's construction of the First and Fourteenth Amendments: "No *state* shall violate the equal rights of conscience, or the freedom of the press, or the trial by jury in criminal cases."[112] This proposal to extend the First Amendment's guarantees to cover state as well as federal measures, which Madison regarded as "the most valuable . . . on the whole list,"[113] passed the House of Representatives in 1789, but was defeated in the Senate. The amendments passed that year and ratified in 1791 did not include additional securities against state or local legislation.

The Senate's alterations and deletions sharply tested Madison's good temper.[114] Even in the House, the tedious, extended process was a trial. After overcoming the initial opposition to considering a bill at all, Madison was forced to struggle with resentful Federalists, who were determined that the changes would be few and sparsely worded, as well as with the dozen Antifederalists in Congress, who worked repeatedly to add amendments he opposed, then turned to sheer obstructionism and delay.[115] As his original proposals were compacted into twelve amendments, some were lost and others suffered some dilution.[116] As he feared, it proved impossible to guarantee the most essential rights in all the amplitude that he preferred. He was unable to secure the liberties of conscience and the press against the possibility of state infringements. He was unable, for that matter, even to secure as broad and firm a guarantee of freedom of religion at the federal level as he would have liked. Madison's original proposal would have read: "The civil rights of none shall be abridged on account of religious belief or worship, nor shall any national religion be established, nor shall the full and equal rights of conscience be in any manner or on any pretext infringed."[117] The Senate weakened this to "Congress shall make no law establishing articles of faith or a mode of worship, or prohibiting the free exercise of religion."[118] Madison was forced to fight a final battle in the conference committee and the House in order to secure the language that was finally adopted, language that was nonetheless less sweeping than his first proposal and has led to countless modern arguments about the prohibition's meaning and extent: "Congress shall make no law respecting an establishment of religion, or prohibiting the free exercise thereof."[119]

Nevertheless, Congress did indulge its leading member very far indeed. With the exceptions of the article concerning state infringements and a measure to impose a monetary floor on appeals to the federal courts, not a single substantive proposal was defeated; and nothing was included in the finished bill that Madison had not originally proposed. The twelve amendments offered to the states, for all of the stylistic alterations, were very much the ones that he had drafted. Indeed, they represented his distinctive wishes more completely than is frequently suggested by repeated, casual references to his extraction from the propositions of the state conventions only those that he considered safe. The two amendments not approved by three-fourths of the states—one intended to ensure enlargement of the lower house and one providing that the salaries of congressmen could not be changed without an intervening federal election—were measures he had advocated since the Constitutional Convention.[120] The defeated article concerning state infringements of essential rights was as much his own unique proposal as the federal negative on local acts, of which it was, in fact, an echo. The Ninth Amendment, which was recommended only by Virginia and New York, was Madison's attempt to obviate the possibility that an enumeration of essential rights could lead to claims that rights not listed lacked the same protection, and thus to claims for larger federal powers than were granted in the constitutional enumeration. The Tenth Amendment, which reaffirmed the understanding that "the powers not delegated to the United States by the Constitution, nor prohibited by it to the States, are reserved to the States respectively, or to the people," did not include the word "expressly."[121] Tabulations vary, but it seems apparent that Madison drew as deeply for his propositions on his own ideas and on the revolutionary charters of the states as on the recommendations of the state conventions. And although he quite deliberately excluded nearly all of the demands for structural reforms or substantive reductions of the delegated powers, he included constitutional protections for the overwhelming body of the state and private rights for which the state conventions were concerned.[122]

Small wonder that before the session ended, nearly all of Madison's Virginia correspondents were reporting general satisfaction with the House proceedings on amendments, titles, and much else. If all the session's business had been finished so entirely as he wished, Madison might not have been so deeply troubled by the measures of the second session of our first and longest Congress. As it was, however, this was not the case. Already, he had felt the stirrings of significant suspicions; and in no great time, he would conclude that his conception of the Constitution and the nation's needs, together with his principles of equity, morality, and harmony between the sections, could only be defended by a public war against many of his one-time allies in the struggle to secure a strong and lasting Union.

PART FOUR

Tender of the Fire

MADISON ABOUT 1792.
Portrait by Charles Wilson Peale.
The Thomas Gilcrease Institute of American
History and Art, Tulsa, Oklahoma.

CHAPTER TEN

The Great Divergence

IN 1789, JAMES MADISON WAS MORE RESPONSIBLE than any other individual (apart, perhaps, from Washington himself) for putting an effective central government in action. Determined to complete a Constitution
sound enough and strong enough to meet the nation's needs, but hardly
less determined to legitimize the charter in the minds of its opponents,
he initiated legislation to create executive departments, to ensure an independent revenue, and to secure the fundamental liberties that many
thought at risk. Throughout the first session of the First Federal Congress,
he was indisputably the "first man" of the House.[1] Through these months,
he also acted, in effect, as minister without portfolio in Washington's administration, "the bridge between the executive and the legislature," adviser to the president on protocol, appointments, and executive
deportment. Wielding an authority that may have equaled or exceeded
any that he would possess as president himself, he had his way on issues
ranging from a title for the head of state to which specific liberties should
be protected by the first amendments. He even proved remarkably successful in establishing the character or "tone" that seemed to him essential if the Union was to last.[2]

When Congress reassembled for its second session, Madison assumed
a very different stance—or so, at least, is the impression left by first appearances and by the overwhelming weight of modern scholarly opinion.
Although Washington continued to solicit his advice, the president could
now rely on Attorney General Edmund Randolph and the heads of the
executive departments: Hamilton at Treasury, Jefferson at State, and
Henry Knox at War.[3] Then, in January 1790, Hamilton delivered his Report on Public Credit, which Congress had requested in September. To
Hamilton's surprise, the leader of the House, with whom he had established such a close collaboration during the preceding years, opposed his

plan for managing the debt, bringing Congress to an impasse that provoked new doubts about the viability of all that they had sought. The
deadlock was resolved, with Jefferson's assistance, by the famous bargain
trading the assumption of state debts for the location of the federal capital
on the Potomac. But in 1791, Madison attacked Hamilton's plan for the
creation of a national bank. Before the year was over, he and Jefferson
were obviously working to construct a systematic opposition to administration programs. In March of 1792, Hamilton openly declared that he
would treat his former ally as a dangerous opponent, whose discontents
could end in the subversion of the government itself.[4]

Hamilton had cause to feel betrayed and reason for concern. From
their earliest acquaintance, in the old Confederation Congress, he and
Madison had joined repeatedly in efforts to secure a more effective federal
system. The bolder, younger man had been accustomed to defer to the
Virginian's talents as a legislative leader. He had taken his position at the
Treasury, he wrote, expecting that "a similarity of thinking" would ensure
continuing cooperation; "Aware of the intrinsic difficulties of the situation and of the powers of Mr. Madison, I do not believe I should have
accepted under a different supposition."

Hamilton had solid reasons to expect that Madison would use his skills
to guide the funding plan through Congress. In 1783, Madison had been
the first public figure to propose a federal assumption of state debts. His
message to the states in April of that year had forcefully condemned the
concept of discriminating between original and secondary holders of the
federal notes. In a private conversation at the Constitutional Convention,
Hamilton reported, Madison had once again endorsed assumption. In all
their talks, "down to the commencement of the new government," he
had never hinted at a change of mind.[5]

Hearing that his old collaborator was uneasy with his plan, Hamilton
approached him just before the House of Representatives initiated its debate on the report and called attention to his stance of 1783. Madison
explained that massive transfers of the debt from its original to secondary
holders had "essentially changed the state of the question" concerning
discrimination, which he now intended to support. He also said that he
had always planned on an assumption of state debts, to which he still did
not object in principle, as those debts had stood at the conclusion of the
war, not as they existed in the aftermath of varied efforts to retire them.

Hamilton was not persuaded by this explanation. Neither has it satisfied the numerous historians who have attempted to explain Madison's
conduct. An assumption of the state debts paid since the conclusion of
the peace, together with the obligations not yet met, would have increased
the federal burden so enormously (and so unnecessarily) that it might

have been impossible to carry. Moreover, transfers of the revolutionary debt had been continuous since it was first incurred. Why was it only now that Madison advocated different treatment for original and secondary holders?

Hamilton's befuddlement increased as Madison denounced the national bank and showed (in Hamilton's opinion) a "womanish attachment to France and a womanish resentment against Great Britain," which the secretary feared could end in outright warfare with the latter. Indeed, as Hamilton perceived it, "in almost all the questions great and small" that arose after the first session of Congress, Madison sided with those "disposed to narrow the federal authority." His opposition culminated in deliberate attempts to drive Hamilton from office.

As the other major author of *The Federalist*, Hamilton knew that Madison had long maintained (and recently and publicly insisted) that "the real danger in our system was the subversion of the national authority by the preponderancy of the state governments." After 1789, however, "all his measures [seemed to] have proceeded on an opposite supposition." Hamilton could not conceive how he and Madison, "whose politics had formerly so much the same point of departure," could have reasoned to such contradictory conclusions in so short a time. Insisting on a concord of opinion through the first session of Congress, he dismissed the possibility that he and Madison might differ on questions of fundamental principle; and although he thought that Jefferson's pernicious influence must have played some part, he knew that Madison's decision to oppose the funding plan had antedated Jefferson's arrival in New York.[6] Hamilton decided, in the end, that Madison had been "seduced by the expectation of popularity and possibly by the calculation of advantage to the state of Virginia." Wishing to retain the veneration he had earned from the creation of the Constitution, and prompted also by an insecure position in Virginia, he had given in, at first, to popular demands. Then, as he endured repeated checks, his principles reversed. The nationalist of the 1780s turned into a champion of strict construction and states' rights. The friend of order was transformed into the idol of the American Jacobins. Madison became so used to "sounding the alarm with great affected solemnity at encroachments meditated on the rights of the states," to "holding up the bugbear of a faction in the government having designs unfriendly to liberty," that he eventually came to believe it. In time, he managed to convince himself that notions he had "sported to influence others" were actually true, that there was "some dreadful combination against state government and republicanism."

Hamilton's analysis is plausible and searching. It credits Madison's probity and good intentions. It rests on facts that no one can deny. As late as August 1789, Madison believed that state encroachments on the powers of the federal government would be most likely to endanger constitutional reform. By 1792, his fears were on the other side. Thus it hardly seems surprising that Hamilton's views have deeply influenced nearly every subsequent discussion. Even recent writers, though they differ widely in assessments of his motives, overwhelmingly agree that Madison reversed his course as swiftly and as thoroughly as Hamilton maintained, perhaps for reasons similar to those that Hamilton suggested.[7]

But Hamilton and Madison, as I have shown, had never really shared "the same point of departure"; and Madison's positions in the years through 1789 were not what many modern analysts have taken them to be. Hamilton misunderstood his colleague, and sharing some of Hamilton's assumptions, later analysts have often shared in his misjudgment. How, he asked, did Madison, the "nationalist" of the 1780s, become the Jeffersonian proponent of states' rights? How, historians have added, could the "father of the Constitution" have also written the Virginia Resolutions of 1798? These questions ask for information that was critical to Hamilton himself and has continued to be critical for everyone who wants to understand the shaping of the federal system and its ultimate collapse into a civil war. But posed in such a manner, queries of this sort incorporate the bias with which Hamilton began. They presuppose that a broad construction of the Constitution had been general among the Federalists of 1788, that Madison's resistance to Hamilton's own conception of the scope of federal powers *must* have meant a change of attitude about the document itself, and that the balance of authority between the central government and the states was unmistakably the most important issue of these years. The questions *posit* a polarity between Madison's objectives during the 1780s and the 1790s, between his original understanding of the Constitution and his stand in 1793, that was in fact quite foreign to his thought.[8]

Madison, as has been shown, had never been a "nationalist" in Hamilton's conception of that term. Even as he led the nation through the framing and ratification of the Constitution, he had also shown a lively fear of distant, independent rulers, a fear he had displayed repeatedly during the 1780s. Moreover, from the ratification contest through the nullification crisis, which came upon the country during his retirement, Madison consistently identified the new regime as an unprecedented compound, neither wholly national nor purely federal in its nature or intentions. Created by the bodies politic of the several united states, the Constitution, as he understood it, made the central government supreme within its sphere *and* strictly limited that sphere to matters that could not be managed by the states, whose peoples were the ultimate authority on its correct interpretation.[9] During the ratification contest, as in 1793, Madison desired a well-constructed, partly federal republic—not, like Hamilton, because he thought that nothing more could be obtained, but (more like many *Anti*federalists of 1788) because he thought that nothing else would prove consistent with the Revolution. In the 1780s as in the 1790s, Hamilton's most cherished object was to build a modern nation-state. Madison's fundamental purpose was to nurture and defend a revolutionary order of society and politics, which he regarded as profoundly inconsistent with the policies that many economic nationalists intended to pursue.

The key to the solution of the puzzle posed by Madison's supposed reversal is to realize, to start, that most of this "reversal" is, in truth, a product of our own interpretive constructions. The positions commonly identified as Madison's positions of the 1780s are ones that he had never really held. Prevailing understandings of his purposes and stance from 1782 through 1789 do not insist as strongly as they should that Madison's concern about majority abuses was invariably accompanied by a profound commitment to effective popular control, that his determination to secure a more effective union was consistently combined with a sincere determination to confine the central government within effective bounds, that he had always been inclined to strict construction of the federal charter, and—finally—that his distinctive mode of thought was so conditioned by its roots in the Virginia piedmont that he never wanted to create a great "commercial" republic.[10] If, however, some of these interpretive mistakes can be corrected, if we revise the usual conception of Madison's views of 1788, then we can see how much of what he thought and did during the early 1790s proceeds rather than departs from his vision of the 1780s. Indeed, with proper caution, it may then be possible to use the policies and writings of the early 1790s to illuminate his thinking in the years when he contributed most brilliantly to the creation of the federal system.

Madison needed little help from Antifederalists to sense the perils of "consolidation." His understanding of the nation's politics had been conditioned by his years in the Confederation Congress, where majorities were often jealous of and hostile to his state. As a former member of that Congress and as leader of the Federalists in the Virginia state convention, Madison was deeply conscious of the differences and animosities between the nations's regions. These, he was convinced, would have to be accommodated if the Union was to last, which helps explain why he was so concerned in 1789 to urge a spirit of disinterested attention to the needs of every region. And these, it would appear, are where historians must look for the beginnings of his break with many of the other advocates of constitutional reform.

As early as the crisis that accompanied the peace, Madison had shown significant discomfort with the views of the American admirers of the British system of administration and finance. His own developing conception of a sound political economy was more indebted to the eighteenth-century critics of this system. Nevertheless, his alienation from the other Federalists of 1788 did not originate with the Report on Public Credit. It did not even focus, at the start, on Hamilton himself. Instead, it seems entirely likely that an old disquietude about the attitudes of many of his allies had developed, just below the surface, even as they drew together in support of constitutional reform. Every major landmark on the path to constitutional revision was a landmark, too, in Madison's uneasiness about the disposition of the North and East: the Jay-Gardoqui crisis, the monarchical revival, growing talk of separate regional confederations, and the anti-western, antidemocratic sentiments of several members of the Constitutional Convention. Madison may even have been troubled by the Federalist resistance to a bill of rights.[11] On balance, to be sure, these underlying apprehensions were alleviated, even overmatched, by intersectional cooperation in the movement for reform, by Madison's determination not to be parochial himself, and by his great success in setting the directions of the infant federal system. Certainly, however, some of these anxieties were present, and some of them were heightened in the first few months of Washington's administration. When Hamilton presented his Report on Public Credit, Madison was more content than not about the course of the experiment thus far. But twice in the preceding session his anxieties had flamed into real anger, and on both of these occasions the eruption was provoked by what he saw as the unwillingness of northern Federalists to hold to the conciliating, harmonizing, "patriotic" conduct he considered indispensable to the experiment's success. Against this background, Hamilton's proposals on the debt compelled him to resist, not because he saw them from the first as indicators of a grand and unacceptable ambition, but because he saw them in their context as immoral, inconsistent with the spirit of a federal republic, and part of a disturbing trend toward an unjust and dangerous domination of the Union by New England. Only gradually would he begin to think of funding and assumption as foundations for a more elaborate (and deeply sinister) design.

On the first day of business of the First Federal Congress, in the resolutions looking toward an impost (April 8, 1789), Madison proposed discriminatory duties on the ships of nations having no commercial treaty with the United States.[12] It was a striking testimony to an object he had had in mind throughout the course of constitutional reform (and would continue to pursue until the War of 1812).[13] The Constitution, he insisted in a speech delivered on April 25, had been "brought about" by a determination to require the European nations "to pay us that respect which they have neglected on account of our former imbecility." After the conclusion of the peace, finding that the British, in particular, intended to do everything they could "to discourage our commercial operations," the several states had independently attempted "to counteract her nefarious schemes; but finding their separate exertions ineffectual, with an united voice they called for a new arrangement" capable of forcing "that reciprocity which justice demands."[14] Now, in order to secure "a speedy rescue of our trade," he wished "to teach those nations who have declined to enter into commercial treaties with us, that we have the power to extend or withhold advantages as their conduct shall deserve."[15]

As Congress turned from Madison's proposal of a temporary impost toward a system of specific duties, some of which would favor native manufactures, the Virginian carefully explained the underlying principles and calculations that had guided him for years. A national commercial system, he believed, must start from "principles of mutual concession," from consideration of "the general interests of the Union" as well as state and local wishes, and from quite explicit statements of the views "on which we mutually act." In theory, he explained, he was a "friend to a very free system of commerce": "Commercial shackles are generally unjust, oppressive, and impolitic—it is also a truth that if industry and labor are left to take their own course, they will generally be directed to those objects which are the most productive, and this in a more certain and direct manner than the wisdom of the most enlightened legislature could point out." And yet, if the United States did not retaliate against the Europeans, its ships would be excluded altogether from their ports. Moreover, "by encouraging the means of transporting our productions with facility, we encourage the raising them"; and he believed it proper "to consider the means of encouraging the great staple of America, I mean agriculture," which deserved "the manifest preference . . . over every other object of emolument in this country." Certain manufactures, he admitted, had been established with the aid of local regulations, and these "ought not to be allowed to perish" because of the new Constitution; "it would be cruel" to cause the suffering that would result. Some congressmen had argued, also, "that each nation should have within itself the means of defense independent of foreign supplies." Although there was "some truth in this remark," he was persuaded "that the reasoning on this subject has been carried too far." Accordingly, he thought the House should

concentrate on raising revenue and demonstrating its determination to
retaliate against the Europeans, not on premature attempts to unravel the
"intricate questions" raised by the desire to favor native manufactures.[16]

Although the temperament of Congress forced him to abandon his
initial hope that temporary legislation could be put in place in time to
tax the spring importations, Madison did not abandon his insistence on
these basic principles of action. Seeking equity between the sections, he
was willing to accept a tax on salt, which might weigh heaviest on the
poor, the backcountry, and the South, provided that the system as a whole
distributed the burden fairly and in some proportion to ability to pay.[17]
In order to secure such equity, he urged an eight-cent duty on molasses,
which would make allowance for a native manufacture "of considerable
importance," but would also make New England pay a fair proportion of
the duties, taxing her distilleries of rum without resorting to an excise.[18]
At the same time, he opposed a drawback of the duties on the export of
the finished product, most of which was shipped to Africa as part of a
trade that "ought to be reprobated instead of encouraged."[19] And he
resisted every effort, by southerners and northerners alike, to remove discriminatory duties on the ships of nations that had not concluded treaties.
These higher duties, he was well aware, would bear most heavily on southern planters, but, as he put it on April 21, "an acquisition of maritime
strength [was] essential to the country"—and especially to portions "most
exposed to the operations of a depredatory war." If greater sacrifices were
required by such discriminatory duties, the South would be "peculiarly
rewarded for it in the hour of danger," since the duties would encourage
American shipping as well as trade with America's allies.[20] Even small discriminations, he insisted on April 25, would transmit a beneficial message
to the British *and* to states which had relinquished their commercial powers "under an impression that a more efficient government would effectually support their views."[21]

Madison was willing, he suggested, to propose a plan that would delay
the imposition of discriminatory duties until Americans could increase
their tonnage. This would make it easier for those who currently relied
on foreign shipping. On the other hand, he roundly disagreed with those
who feared reprisals by the British. That nation, he insisted on May 4, had
"bound us in commercial manacles and very nearly defeated the object
of our independence"; and he was "not afraid" of a commercial confrontation. "Her interests can be wounded almost mortally, while ours are
invulnerable."[22] British regulations, he had long believed, excluded U.S.
ships from their "most natural and valuable markets" and helped perpetuate Great Britain's virtual monopoly of the states' external commerce.
To breach this system, to free the nation's trade to "flow *directly* to the

countries making the exchange," to give native ships their "due share in the transportation," and to establish a political economy appropriate for a republic, it was necessary to encourage nations friendlier to the United States and to compel the British toward a reconsideration. He had no doubt that it would work. American supplies were "necessary to the existence" of Britain's West Indian colonies, and American markets were essential to their value. "The returns are either superfluities or poisons" (mostly sugar, molasses, and slaves).

> In the direct trade with Great Britain, the consequences [of commercial confrontation] ought to be equally dreaded by her. The raw and bulky exports of the United States employ her shipping, contribute to her revenue, enter into her manufactures, and enrich her merchants, who stand between the United States and the consuming nations of Europe. A suspension of the intercourse would suspend all these advantages, force the trade into rival channels from which it might not return, and . . . hasten the establishment of manufactures here, which would so far cut off the market forever. On the other side, the United States would suffer but little. The manufactures of Great Britain, as far as desirable, would find their way through other channels, and if the price were a little augmented it would only diminish an excessive consumption. They could do almost wholly without such supplies, and better without than with many of them. In one important view the contest would be particularly in [America's] favor. The articles of luxury, a privation of which would be salutary to them, being the work of the indigent [of Britain], may be regarded as necessaries to the manufacturing party.[23]

When the commercial resolutions came before the House from the Committee of the Whole, Madison was satisfied that different sectional desires had been "adjusted as easily as could be well expected."[24] A Massachusetts effort to reduce the six-cent duty on molasses had severely tried his temper. The figure was already two cents lower than he wished. "Why these apprehensions for one part of the Union more than the other? Are the northern people made of finer clay? . . . Are they the chosen few? Are all others to be oppressed with accumulated burdens and they to take their course easy and unrestrained?"[25] Happily, his plea for "justice and impartiality" had beaten back this effort. In the end, the representatives approved discrimination and reduced the six-cent duty on molasses by a single penny.[26] As was true with his amendment to protect religious freedom in the states, Madison was not defeated in the House. He was defeated by the Senate, which halved the lower duty on molasses and dispensed entirely with the plan for differential duties on the ships of nations that had not concluded treaties with the Union.[27]

Madison was disappointed, even irritated, by the fate of his commercial propositions. The Impost Act did not achieve the equity he had envisioned. The lower duty on molasses, a result of "persevering opposition" from the eastern states,[28] reduced their contribution and increased the share of federal taxes that would be collected from the South, which would have paid a higher portion of a tax on foreign imports even if the higher duty on molasses had been kept. The failure of discrimination was an even harder blow for Madison, who had argued that the Constitution had been "instituted for the purpose of uniting the states in the vindication of their commercial interests" and thereby easing the distresses that were fundamentally responsible for such a large proportion of the nation's ills.[29] Nevertheless, the failure of discrimination was a complicated story. Northerners and southerners had both resisted higher duties.[30] Opposition in the Senate had apparently united the determined foes of any legislation of this sort with those who wanted *stronger* measures than the House proposed.[31] For all these reasons—which, in mid-July, were reinforced by his attempt to reassure the critics of the Constitution, establish smooth relationships between the Senate and the House, and inculcate a spirit of harmonious consideration for the needs of every section—Madison did not condemn the Impost Act or his opponents. Though less than perfect, he assured one correspondent, the impost showed that the supporters of the Constitution "did not err in supposing it to be safe in allowing a majority to decide."[32]

Such certainty did not survive the session. On the contrary, the old suspicion of the North and East, which had erupted briefly in the argument about the duty on molasses, was aggravated over the succeeding weeks until, at last, it got the better of his famous disposition. The outburst literally produced a national sensation as the press reported far and wide that Madison had told the House on September 3 that if a prophet had appeared in the Virginia state convention "and brought the declarations and proceedings of this day into their view, ... Virginia might not have been a part of the Union at this moment."[33]

A great deal has been made of this embittered reference to the prophet and of a succeeding speech in which Madison spoke of the United States as "a confederacy of states" and candidly acknowledged that he saw "a certain degree of force" in Antifederalist objections that the country was too large to be administered as a republic.[34] A great deal should be made of his undoubted anger, for the outburst was provoked by measures and proceedings that endangered several of his dearest objects and ideals. A great deal can be learned from it about the texture of his vision, although it is by no means true that he was wrenched immediately into a localistic stance and toward a theory of the Union that was radically at odds with his positions of the previous two years.[35]

The trigger for the founder's outburst was a preconcerted move by representatives from Pennsylvania, New England, and New York to keep the federal government in New York City for the next three years and then to move it to a permanent location on the Susquehanna River.[36] On September 3, when Benjamin Goodhue of Massachusetts introduced this motion and remarked that it had been agreed on by "the Eastern members, with the members from New York," Virginia's Richard Bland Lee proposed a preamble consistent with an earlier decision that the final residence should be as nearly central as communications with the ocean and the western country would permit. To violate this principle, Lee argued, would fulfill predictions "that partial measures would be pursued and that one part of the Union would be depressed and trampled on to benefit and exalt the other."[37] Lee's motion was defeated 24 to 17, and Madison was unsuccessful with a motion with a similar intent.[38] At this point, believing that a fixed majority was bent on ramming the decision through, Madison sarcastically observed that Goodhue had been frank enough "to tell us that measures have been preconcerted out of doors and that the point was determined, that more than half of the territory of the United States and near half of its inhabitants have been disposed of, not only without their consent, but without their knowledge." "After this," he hoped, the gentleman from Massachusetts might "extend his candor so much farther as to show" how his proposal would accord with the preliminary resolution that the capital should be constructed near the center of the nation's territory, wealth, and population, "that we may reconcile this fate to our own minds and submit to it with some degree of complaisancy."[39]

Madison insisted that a Susquehanna site (near York in modern central Pennsylvania) could not be as convenient to the West and the Atlantic as a seat on the Potomac, and he pledged to prove the point with charts and maps if given time to do so. In response, New York's John Laurance angrily denied that northern members had combined into a special-interest coalition and reminded Madison that he had said in course of the proceedings on the Tonnage Act that much of the Virginia opposition to the Constitution might have been alleviated if the "moderate and equal" policies of Congress could have been foreseen. Laurance's remarks (and possibly the attitude of one who had opposed him step by step in the deliberations on the impost) prompted Madison's admission that he had, indeed, made such a declaration, but was equally convinced that if Virginians had foreseen "the declarations and proceedings of this day," the

Constitution would have been defeated in their state convention.[40] And when another member took exception to his accusations of "a want of candor," Madison explained that he objected most of all to "the *manner* in which the business was conducted. . . . A majority ought to govern, yet they have no authority to . . . debar us the right of free debate." He wanted time for a discussion that could not be finished in a single day, and he objected to addressing "a determined and silent majority."[41]

The House gave Madison the time he asked, and on September 4, a major speech developed some of the considerations that had roused his ire.

> No government, he said, not even the most despotic, could, beyond a certain point, violate that idea of justice and equal right which prevailed in the mind of the community. In republican governments, justice and equality form the basis of the system. . . . In a federal republic, . . . it is even more necessary that a sacred regard should be paid to these considerations.

The reasons were straightforward. In a federal republic, he maintained, the local governments were certain to possess a "keen sense" of the "local distinctions" and "jealousies" inherent in the system, together with the power to "support and insist upon equitable demands." No issue could be judged more easily or certainly by these communities than a location for the permanent seat of government, and there was none "of which they will judge with more jealousy." If the residence was placed in an eccentric spot and representatives or private citizens from different states were given an "unequal" access, the House would

> violate the principle of equality where it ought most carefully to be ascertained and wound the feelings of the component parts of the community which can be least injured with impunity. . . . Those who are most adjacent to the seat of legislation will always possess advantages over others. An earlier knowledge of the laws, a greater influence in enacting them, better opportunities for anticipating them, and a thousand other circumstances [including greater access to the wealth that would inevitably concenter in this place] will give a superiority to those who are thus situated.[42]

Madison was most concerned to warn his colleagues not to risk the loyalty of citizens beyond the mountains by suggesting that they were to be "united with their Atlantic brethren on any other principle than that of equality and justice."

> It is impossible to reflect a moment on the possible severance of that branch of the Union without seeing the mischiefs which such an event

must create. . . . We shall speedily behold an astonishing mass of people on the western waters. Whether this great mass shall form a permanent part of the confederacy or whether it shall be separated into an alien, a jealous, and a hostile people, may depend on the system of measures that is shortly to be taken. The difference, he observed, between considering them in the light of fellow citizens, bound to us by a common affection, obeying common laws, pursuing a common good, and considering them in the other light, presents one of the most interesting questions that can occupy an American mind: Instead of peace and friendship, we shall have rivalship and enmity; instead of being a great people, invulnerable on all sides, and without the necessity of those military establishments which other nations require, we shall be driven into the same expensive and dangerous means of defense: We shall be obliged to lay burdens on the people to support establishments which, sooner or later, may prove fatal to their liberties. It is incumbent on us, he said, if we wished to act the part of magnanimous legislators, or patriotic citizens, to consider well, when we are about to take a step of such vast importance, that it be directed by the views he had described; we must consider what is just, what is equal, and what is satisfactory.[43]

On all these principles, he argued, it was plain that the Potomac (perhaps near Williamsport or Hancock, Maryland, well to the northwest of modern Washington, D.C.) offered a superior location.[44] A quick glance at any map of the United States would show that this was closer to the geographical center than a site on the Susquehanna, easier to access from the West or the Atlantic, and if not closer to the center of the nation's population in 1789, certainly closer to the center toward which the population was continually advancing.[45]

It may be tempting to dismiss this speech as brilliant special pleading (as, indeed, both Madison's opponents and some later analysts would do). A seat on the Potomac, after all, had been a cherished object for Virginians from the years when Madison had served in the Confederation Congress. A site on the Potomac would certainly serve Virginia's interests more directly than one on the Susquehanna would promote those of New England, whose spokesmen bitterly resented Madison's complaints about maneuvers out of doors and said repeatedly that they had made their bargain with the Pennsylvanians only when they learned that bargaining had long been under way between the Pennsylvanians and the South.[46] Some historians have argued that Madison had not only been involved in out-of-doors negotiations of his own, but that he also acted to protect a personal investment in a townsite at the falls of the Potomac.[47] But even if the whole of this were true—and there is reason to be skeptical about both claims—a cynical dismissal of this speech could shut the door to the important insights it affords. At minimum, it seems important to remark that Madison insisted that a site on the Potomac was essential, not because it would be farther south, but because it would be farther west and easier for westerners to reach.[48] The westerners were so much on his mind that he was privately prepared, should other options be exhausted, to accept the Susquehanna "as the least of the [remaining] evils."[49] And whoever had initiated the negotiations out of doors, Madison was unmistakably infuriated by an effort that appeared to him an underhanded, even unrepublican attempt to press a temporary sectional advantage in the face of vital principles of equity and at the risk of literally endangering the Union.[50]

It is unnecessary to insist again on the centrality of a continuing connection with the West to all of Madison's ambitions for the nation, perhaps unnecessary to insist again on his intense concern to ground the reconstructed government on principles of equity, conciliation, and a scrupulous respect for the intrinsic nature of a partly federal and thoroughly republican regime. But it is absolutely critical to place the conflict sparked by Goodhue's motion in the context of Madison's current information from Virginia and Kentucky. Madison had every reason to believe that the allegiance of the westerners was hanging by a thread and that the location of the seat of government could be decisive for the future of the Union.

On March 8, 1789, a month before the opening of Congress, Madison had written Washington that a communication from Arthur St. Clair, governor of the Northwest Territory, confirmed their information that a former loyalist, John Connolly, was stirring trouble in Kentucky, that other efforts were proceeding to create a colony of westerners on Spanish territory at New Madrid, and that Madison's colleague from Kentucky, Congressman John Brown, believed that the Kentuckians could be enticed by Spain as easily as they had been allured to the Kentucky district from the East.[51] Two weeks later, Madison sent Washington a copy of a handbill that the organizer of the Spanish project at New Madrid had been circulating in Pennsylvania and New Jersey.[52] Sending one to Jefferson as well, he told the minister to France that this promoter had the sanction of Gardoqui for a project meant to make the navigation of the Mississippi "bait for the defection of the western people." Some Kentucky leaders, he observed, were known to be supporting this idea. The outcome would depend on "the measures of the new government."[53]

The measures of the infant government were little help, and news from the Kentucky district heightened Madison's alarm. George Nicholas, who had moved there after the Virginia state convention, reported on May 8 that district leaders (including Brown himself) denied that they were working toward a separation from the Union; but it was widely "given out" that if Kentucky would become an independent state, "Spain would grant her the free use of the river and many other commercial advantages." Meanwhile, Colonel Connolly was offering assistance from the British if a separation should occur. Nicholas believed that the majority of people in the district wanted only separate statehood within the United States. Indeed, the right steps by the federal government, he thought— procurement of the navigation of the Mississippi and defense against the Northwest tribes—could make the new regime "more popular here than in any part of America." Nevertheless, he finished, Kentuckians were nearly ready to "live under any government that would meet their needs." "You know my attachment to the Union, but I declare freely to you if I am disappointed in my expectations from the justice and policy of the new government, I shall be ready to join in any other mode for obtaining our rights."[54]

When Madison received this letter, in the second half of June, he was anticipating quick approval of Kentucky statehood. He assured his old lieutenant that as long as Washington was president there could be no renewal of the danger to the Mississippi, "nor any defect of attention to the western interests in general."[55] The legislature proved him wrong. By the beginning of September, when Goodhue introduced his motion on the permanent and temporary seats, Congress had done nothing to fulfill the westerners' desires. The Senate had severely cut a House appropriation for negotiations with the western tribes, focused these on the negotiations with the Creeks, and left the troubles on Kentucky's borders much as they had stood.[56] Statehood had been stalled by disagreements over the conditions of Kentucky's separation from Virginia.[57] The Mississippi River was still closed. Acutely conscious of these errors of omission, Madison was deeply fearful that an act which many westerners might take as a deliberate affront could push them past endurance. In content and in context, Goodhue's motion seemed to him a deadly danger to the Union—not only for its probable effects on the allegiance of Kentucky, but also for the lesson it might teach to hundreds of uncertain citizens throughout the South and West, whose fear of northern domination had accounted for so much of the resistance to the Constitution. On all these counts—and they were lengthened and compounded in his mind by his opponents' manner of proceeding—he saw the whole affair as conduct unbecoming leaders of a federal republic.[58]

Before the session closed, the capable Virginian, who could be a legislative bulldog on important issues, managed to defeat the northern coalition. Despite his powerful performance of September 4, Lee's motion to replace the Susquehanna with a site on the Potomac was defeated 29 to 21. Goodhue's motion passed. The northern phalanx held together through eight roll calls in the House, and on September 22 forwarded a bill for action by the Senate. There, however, its support fell apart. The Pennsylvania delegation had been torn from the beginning by internal enmities between the members from Philadelphia and those from the western portion of the state, and Madison and his supporters had succeeded in attaching to the bill a clause requiring Pennsylvania to remove obstructions to the navigation of the Susquehanna (which would have favored rural trade with Baltimore at Philadelphia's expense). In the Senate, Robert Morris, who had constantly intrigued for a location on the Delaware instead of on the Susquehanna, managed to amend the bill to substitute a site surrounding Germantown as the eventual location. When the amended bill came back, Madison maintained that it amounted to a different act and should not be considered.[59] When the House approved it anyway, he managed (in a preconcerted tactic of his own) to win approval for a minor alteration, which sent it back to the Senate once again.[60] There, as he expected, the New York senators switched sides and joined with southerners to table further action. The postponement left the government in New York City—without the three-year limit of the tabled bill.[61]

Nevertheless, from Madison's perspective, much pernicious mischief had been done. At the conclusion of the session, he had not abandoned hope that an arrangement with the Pennsylvanians might still secure a seat on the Potomac, but he also saw a fixed "antipathy" among New Englanders to a residence so far to the southwest, which would repeatedly produce new arguments against it. Some of the northeasterners, he thought, were acting on the supposition that a separation from the westerners was inevitable, and they were likely to persist in policies that could undoubtedly produce it. "Extremely alarmed for the western country" and realizing that his time was running out, he thought it could become his "duty" to accept the Susquehanna as the least offensive place from which a workable selection could be made, the only way to parry plans "which would be fatal to the harmony if not to the existence of the Union."[62]

By this time, however, Madison had spent substantial portions of the ample fund of national prestige that he had carried with him into Congress—all of it, he thought, in efforts to secure a very fragile interregional and popular commitment to the Constitution. His insistence on the Bill of Rights had angered several members, and many of the most resistant took his whole campaign for principle and reconciliation as a demonstration of timidity and eagerness for popular applause.[63] The bitter fight about the residence had damaged him severely in the minds of many northeastern members. On September 13, an ally—John Dawson—wrote from Philadelphia that he was quite reliably informed that there were several people in New York who claimed that all was peaceful on the subject of amendments until Madison brought it up, who linked that effort with the residence dispute, and who had "entered into a combination" to "catch at any possible trifle to injure you if possible in the public estimation."[64]

By this time, moreover, Madison himself was almost equally embittered by the inclinations of a number of his colleagues. While he had advocated moderation, equity for every region, and a statesmanlike attention to the reasonable concerns of the opponents of the Constitution, they, it seemed, had been contemptuous of southern feelings, western interests, and the Antifederalists' demands. More than once, they had pursued a narrow, sectional advantage to the detriment of national harmony and needs. Already, Madison believed, the reconstructed government was favoring the North and East, which was precisely what the westerners and southerners had feared. On the residence question, at least, this tendency had been arrested for the moment.[65] Most of Madison's objectives for the session had been gained. But all of them, he feared, could be profoundly threatened if the federal tilting should resume. In combination with his views about the nature and foundations of a sound republic (and in combination, also, with his firm opinion that the Constitution would be judged according to its fruits), this worry would determine his response to Hamilton's report.[66]

Including the arrears of interest, which had not been paid for years, the state and federal governments owed roughly $80 million when Congress reassembled for its second session, mostly to domestic creditors who held the notes and other promises that had financed the Revolution.[67] Provision for this debt was indispensable if the capacity to borrow was to be restored. Simply put, the first Report on Public Credit, which Hamilton submitted to the House on January 14, 1790, recommended that the federal government assume responsibility for most of the remaining obligations of the states, as well as those of Congress, and agree to pay the whole, at full face value, to the current holders of its notes. The old certificates would be replaced by new ones paying lower interest. In exchange, the government would pledge its revenues to steady payment of that interest. With the interest payments guaranteed, the bonds would hold their value on the private money market, the nation's public credit would be instantly restored, and payment of the principal could be postponed until it was convenient for the government to act. In fact, as a security for creditors

against the possibility of early calls, Hamilton proposed to limit the redemption of the debt to one percent per year. The annual profits from
the postal service, estimated at $100,000, would be put into a sinking fund
and used from time to time to purchase the securities on private markets.[68]

A solid system of finance had carried tiny Britain to the pinnacle of
international prestige, and for a decade now, the new republic's secretary
of the treasury had taken Britain as an archetype of national success. Like
Robert Morris, whose proposals he had backed in the Confederation Congress, Hamilton intended to equip the infant Union with a funding system
modeled closely on Great Britain's. But even more consistently than Morris, Hamilton conceived of funding as the groundwork for a vastly more
elaborate design. A Hobbesian or Machiavellian in his conception of the
world, the secretary faced toward the Atlantic and envisioned an arena of
competing empires into which America must enter much like any other
state. In time, as he conceived it, the United States could take a brilliant
part in this arena, and he meant to earn immortal fame as founder of its
greatness. But to have this kind of future, he believed, America must first
possess the economic and financial preconditions for successful competition. In the meantime, it must conscientiously avoid a confrontation with
Great Britain, the single nation (with its naval power) which could
threaten the United States most dangerously in war or (through investments in the new republic's economic growth) assist it most impressively
toward greatness. Early in the new administration, Hamilton established
a connection with Great Britain's ministers to the United States and used
these private channels to assure that good relationships would be maintained.[69] Meanwhile, taking British institutions as a model and conceiving
of the Constitution as an instrument that would permit a vigorous administration to construct the economic and financial props of national greatness, he set about to lay the groundwork for a modern national state, a
nation capable in time of rivaling the European empires on the Europeans' terms.[70]

Hamilton's design for national greatness may have been complete in
its essentials when he made his first report. Certainly, his funding and
assumption program was intended from the first to further major economic and political goals as well as narrowly financial ones. Like Robert
Morris, Hamilton believed that proper management could turn the public
debt into a positive advantage for the country. Indeed, of all the nationalists of 1783, the young New Yorker had possessed the clearest vision of
a nation integrated on a British model and financially and economically
equipped for national greatness.[71] Now, he meant to put that vision into
practice. Federal funding of the state as well as national obligations could
accomplish much besides the reestablishment of public credit. On the one

side, it could tie the economic interests of a vital segment of America's elite to the success of national institutions and create a counterbalance to the local loyalties that Hamilton had long regarded as the greatest danger to the Union: "If all the public creditors receive their dues from one source, their interests will be the same. And having the same interests, they will unite in support of the fiscal arrangements of government."[72] On the other side, the funding program could become the principal foundation for the nation's future role in global competition. Even as it reestablished the ability to borrow and attached the monied interests to the central government's success, funding would invigorate—the modern word is "monetize"—the public debt, transforming governmental paper into liquid capital that could be multiplied by using the certificates to back creation of a national bank. The bonds and banknotes could be used, in turn, to foster manufacturing and commerce, which would serve as pillars for the nation's economic independence. In effect, by simply pledging that specific revenues would regularly pay the interest on its bonds, the nation could anticipate—and in the very process could ensure—its future greatness. By leaning on descendants who would benefit from its achievements and by drawing capital investments from abroad, it would be capable of rising by its bootstraps.[73]

The trouble with this scheme, which Hamilton unfolded gradually in a succession of reports, was that it favored certain men and certain regions more immediately than others. More than that, it deeply threatened other founders' visions of the sort of nation the United States should be. Both difficulties were immediately apparent. Although the whole of Hamilton's design would not be evident before his great Report on Manufactures, which was not delivered till the fall of 1791, the secretary said enough in 1790 to trouble several members of the Congress. And, of course, the similarities between his program and the British system of finance aroused the same concerns about a replication of the evils of the Modern Whig regime that had confounded Morris in the struggle of 1783.[74]

On February 8, the House of Representatives decided on a point by point consideration of Hamilton's plan. On February 9, James Jackson of Georgia, who had aleady blasted the "immoral," "avaricious" speculation sparked by the report, initiated the deliberations with a heated speech in which he questioned whether "a permanent funded debt" was ever beneficial to a country. Jackson favored heavy taxes on the current generation over any plan that would impose an endless burden on "the honest, hard-working part of the community," whose taxes would indefinitely "promote the ease and luxury of men of wealth."[75] In many cases, members knew, the current holders of the debt had purchased their certificates for fractions of their value, often from disbanding revolutionary soldiers who had sold the government's uncertain promises for ready cash. Over time, the bonds had gravitated disproportionately into the hands of monied interests in the North and East. To pay them to their present holders at their full face value would entail a major shift of wealth from South to North, from West to East, and from the body of the people to a few rich men whose fortunes would expand dramatically as a result of federal largesse. This prospect stirred immediate anxieties about a British system of corrupting links between the federal treasury and special-interest factions, and revulsion from that prospect was compounded by a rush of greedy speculators (some of them in Congress) to the further reaches of the Union, where they hoped to take advantage of the uninformed.[76] Discussion quickly focused on alternatives that might avoid full payment of the debt or might discriminate between original and secondary holders.[77] Aedanus Burke proposed discrimination and depreciation of the debt at the close of business on February 10, but withdrew the motion when debates resumed on February 11. At this juncture, Madison rose.

Madison rejected every scheme for a depreciation of the debt. The government had promised specie payment (and 6 percent, not 4 percent, in interest): "No logic, no magic . . . can diminish the force of the obligation." The only question, he believed, could be to whom the debt was fairly owed. Here, he recognized the rightful claims of secondary holders. As their advocates had said, the purchasers had done a service for the former owners and had taken a substantial risk in confidence that the confederacy would one day keep its promise. As holders of the public promise, they possessed "an undeniable demand on the public faith," on top of which "the best foundation" for the nation's public credit was indeed "adherence to [its] literal engagements," as Hamilton was recommending. Nevertheless, the original holders had an even more compelling claim. "The value stipulated and expected" when their notes were put into their hands had never been delivered by the public. Instead, the public's inability to pay had forced them to assign their notes, for ready money, for a little as a fifth or even as an eighth of their nominal value. To make the revolutionary soldiers in particular the only victims of the government's default—and then to make them pay new taxes to fulfill the claims "of those who have gained in the contrary proportion"—was "an idea at which human nature recoiled." The case was "so extraordinary," Madison concluded, that "the ordinary maxims" simply must not be applied. The only fair solution was to pay the secondary holders the highest price that had prevailed on private markets and to "let the residue belong to the original sufferers." This would not do "perfect justice," but it would redeem the public faith, permit a liberal compensation for the secondary holders, and "assuage the pain" of those to whom the govern-

ment was really most indebted. If there were any court on earth to force
a nation to do right, the United States would be compelled" to reach
an equitable solution on these lines.[78]

Supporters of the secretary's plan were stunned by Madison's proposal,
much as most historians have been. Elias Boudinot immediately replied
that the Virginian's motion did more credit to his heart than to his head.
For government to overturn the former owners' free decisions to assign
their notes was hardly justice by his definition, besides which it was doubtful that the records would permit the government to discover who the
original creditors were.[79] As others moved to Madison's support, a host of
one-time allies strengthened Boudinot's complaint. Theodore Sedgwick
pointed out that the Virginian's plan would "strip one class of citizens,
who have acquired property by the known and established rules of law,
under the specious pretense of doing justice to another"—and at a cost
of $1,600,000 more per year than Hamilton's proposal.[80] Over the suc-
ceeding days, Wadsworth, Laurance, Boudinot, and Ames repeatedly attacked his motion, objecting first to its unworkability and devastating
consequences for the nation's public credit, but insisting too that it was
wholly inconsistent with good faith. Assignability, they argued, had been
part of the initial contract. Proceeding on that basis, secondary holders
had assumed a risk, employed no fraud, and given value for certificates
received.[81]

Madison could only say that this was not "an ordinary case in law,"
but one that had to be decided "on the great and fundamental principles
of justice," to which the heart was truly the best guide. The government
was fundamentally responsible for the predicament of its disbanding soldiers, and Madison could not "admit that America ought to erect the
monuments of her gratitude, not to those who saved her liberties, but to
those who had enriched themselves in her funds." "The injustice" had
been "flagrant" and "enormous," making its "redress a great national
object." "A government ought to redress the wrongs sustained by its default."[82]

Still, the critics made a devastating case—so telling, for that matter,
that historians have been as skeptical about the framer's motives as most
of his contemparies were.[83] Although the transfer of the debt had started
early in the 1780s, Madison had never hinted that he would support discrimination. For him to do so, many thought, was a "perfidious desertion"
of his principles of public conduct, marking him as an "apostate" from
the maxims he had long supported.[84] And, indeed, these critics made a
point that we should understand in all its force and depth. Opponents of
his plan did not just say that it was costly, probably unworkable, and deeply
threatening to the republic's credibility with foreign and domestic lend-

ers. They saw it as a form of thievery, as more dishonest than the measure Madison opposed. And there is no denying that in point of simple fact, discrimination would have been as bald a governmental interference in existing private contracts as any of the local legislation Madison had frequently condemned. It would, quite literally, have taken property from some and given it to others. It would have been more redistributive in its intent and operation than Rhode Island's law requiring creditors to take repayment in the state's inflated paper. But for these very reasons, I would think, it seems implausible that Madison was acting from expediency alone: that this was really a maneuver to recoup his damaged standing in Virginia, to defeat assumption, or to curry favor with the rabble out of doors.[85] Something deeper was at work; and if we hope to grasp it, we are best advised to take him at his word and put his reasoning in context. Only thus can we recover his assumptions.

Madison's contemporary papers throw no light on his decision to support discrimination. They do not even show that he had made this choice before returning to New York. But this is quite consistent with his late-life recollections. Here, he wrote that his decision to support discrimination grew from "the enormous gain of the [secondary] holders, particularly out of soldiers' certificates, and [from] the sacrifice of these, to whom the public faith had not been fulfilled." In 1783, when he condemned the concept of discrimination, "the case of this class of creditors was less in view. . . . Until, indeed, the subject came close into view and the sacrifice of the soldiers was brought home to reflection, he had not sufficiently scanned and felt the magnitude of the evil." Therefore, he did not propose discrimination in November 1789, when he replied to Hamilton's request for his advice on managing the debt.[86] Instead, the thought "grew rapidly on him on his return to Congress as the subject unfolded itself and the outrageous speculation on the floating paper pressed on the attention." Even congressmen did not restrain themselves from purchasing certificates through brokers at the same time that their actions were transmuting those certificates "into the value of the precious metals."[87]

We think of Madison most often (and correctly) as an intellectual in public life, but Madison was not the coldly realistic theorist and calculating politician who emerges from some texts. He was not only a republican idealist, he was a dedicated moralist who was repeatedly revolted by "injustice": by policies that robbed the poor to benefit the rich no less—or even more—than policies that robbed the creditor to benefit his debtor. And Madison's revulsion knew no bounds when government itself or governmental "servants" of the people were the beneficiaries of injustice, especially when the specific policy at issue seemed profoundly incompat-

ible with his immediate objectives and his underlying vision of a sound
republic.

Madison was certainly as dedicated as Hamilton was to setting government on solid institutional foundations. Their strategies for doing so, however, were poles apart. Hamilton intended, over time, to arm the infant
government with most of the appendages of a successful European state.
Since early in the 1780s, he had hoped to overcome endemic localism,
which he always saw as the outstanding danger to the Union, by detaching
vital portions of the nation's leadership from their connections with the
states and binding them, by solid ties of interest, to the central government's success. Although he plainly hoped that national prosperity and
strength would benefit all segments of the population, his immediate concern was with the state rather than the citizens of whom the state is composed. "The premiere state-builder in a generation of state-builders,"[88]
he planned to replicate Great Britain's path toward national integration;
and he showed as little of the old concern about the civic virtue of the
people as did any statesman of his time.

Madison, by contrast, understood the Constitution as an instrument
by which America could long avoid the European institutions Hamilton
associated with a modern state. His politics had always been affected more
than some contemporaries saw (and more than most historians have seen)
by early revolutionary condemnations of the British system of finance and
by a preference for a social order characterized by honest industry, frugality, and simple manners. Under any circumstances, he believed, a
funded debt was a misfortune; it transferred wealth from the productive
body of the people to an idle few who lived on the treasury at popular
expense and undermined the relative equality appropriate for a republic.
Therefore, he had always held "the principle that a public debt is a public
curse and, in a republican government, a greater one than in any other."[89]
And he had always been revolted both by speculative greed and by the
exploitation of a public trust for personal advantage.[90]

Under current circumstances there were other, equally compelling reasons to resist both funding and assumption in the shapes in which they
were initially proposed. In 1790, as in 1789, Madison considered it essential to define a course that would conciliate the opposition and consolidate approval of the Constitution. Unlike Hamilton, he did not think that
this could be accomplished by obliterating, rather than accommodating,
local loyalties and interests or by separating the pecuniary interests of a
segment of the leadership from the prevailing inclinations of the people.
During the preceding session, he had advocated equity between the sections, conscious demonstrations of congressional awareness of the popular

and federal foundations of the new regime, and a determined effort to
secure the people's loyalty by making private standards of morality a
touchstone for the public. During the preceding session, he had grown
increasingly concerned about the eastern tilt of federal measures and its
probable effects on the remainder of the country. Mulling Hamilton's
proposals in the midst of raging speculation, Madison regarded them—
in their effects, though not as yet in their intentions—as profoundly inconsistent with republican morality, with harmony between the sections,
and with the economic underpinnings of a sound republic. Unwilling to
support depreciation, yet convinced that there was "something wrong,
radically and morally and politically wrong, in a system which transfers
the reward from those who paid the most valuable of all considerations
to those who scarcely paid any consideration at all"—experiencing an
almost physical revulsion from the thought that those to whom the country owed the most would "lose 7/8 of their dues and those who have no
particular merit toward their country . . . [would] gain 7 or 8 times as
much as they advanced"—he intervened with a proposal meant to rectify
a radical injustice while protecting public credit by repaying to the penny
everything the public owed.[91] Boudinot was right, in part, to think that
his emotions got the better of his head. His plan for a discrimination
would have blasted the ability to borrow. It damaged him severely in the
eyes of many of the Federalists in Congress. Nevertheless, his intellect was
on the same side as his feelings in this matter. It was hardly inconsistent
to believe that the injustices of local legislation had endangered the republican experiment and paved the way for constitutional reform, but also
to believe that loyalty could not be won by flagrant federal wrongs or by
a program that would benefit some states while risking the allegiance of
others. Historians may reasonably conclude that on the question of discrimination—perhaps on several issues of the early 1790s—Hamilton's
ideas were better calculated than his own to foster national prosperity and
to promote the nation's long-term interests. But whatever one believes
about this matter, it is crucial to acknowledge that, for Madison, prosperity
and rapid economic growth were not the only—not, indeed, the most
important—points to be considered.

On February 22, Madison was overwhelmingly defeated on his resolution
for discrimination.[92] Attention turned immediately to the assumption of
state debts, which split the Congress much more evenly and sharply. In
theory, states could neither gain nor lose from an assumption if the measure was connected closely with a settlement of state and federal accounts,

which was already under way. After the commissioners determined which expenses of the War for Independence had been undertaken in the common effort, how much debt had been retired, and what proportion of their quotas every state had paid, each state would either owe a balance or receive a refund from the Union. If too much debt had been assumed as a result of Hamilton's proposal, the excess would be added to the balance due to the Confederation; if more than its proportion had been paid, the surplus would be reimbursed. Nevertheless, until a final settlement occurred, assumption would relieve the states with large outstanding debts at the expense of those that had retired a larger portion of their obligations. Moreover, if the final settlement should be defeated or delayed or if the federal commissioners refused to credit claims for which the records were imperfect, states that had redeemed the largest portion of their debts or states that had the poorest records (often as a consequence of war) would end up paying more than their fair share. Therefore, Massachusetts and South Carolina, with large outstanding debts, were fervently in favor of assumption, supported by Connecticut and New Jersey. Maryland, Virginia, Georgia, and North Carolina, with smaller debts and poorer revolutionary records, were solidly opposed, the more so after the commissioners rejected some of their preliminary claims. The delegations from New York and Pennsylvania were internally divided, with several of the Pennsylvanians hoping to connect the matter with a favorable decision on the seat of government, for which they would intrigue throughout the long debate.[93]

Advocates of the assumption dominated the deliberations on February 23. Like Hamilton, they argued that the debts had been incurred in a collective effort and that making them a common burden would assure more rationality and fewer conflicts between the central government and the states. Madison did not involve himself in the debate until the end of business on the twenty-fourth, when only Michael Jenifer Stone of Maryland had spoken for the other side at length, objecting both to the inequity of the proposal and to its consolidating features.[94]

Madison's opinion was unsettled. In principle, he said, he favored a proposal that would settle the accounts and do "full justice" in a very complicated case, yet he did not believe that this could be accomplished by the current resolution. He therefore moved to link assumption with a measure crediting the states for debts already paid, and he condemned suggestions by its advocates that they considered the assumption "a condition" of the funding program as a whole.[95] Speaking only briefly over the succeeding days, he seemed to indicate that he would back assumption if, but only if, it could be rendered fairer to Virginia and its neighbors. Groping toward a motion that would meet this end, he settled on a resolution to assume the debts as they had stood at the conclusion of the peace. States that had retired the largest portion of their obligations would be credited for these and treated much like individuals who held the balance of the notes.[96]

Madison insisted that the only purpose of his resolution was to free assumption from "the evils" that might otherwise defeat it. His proposal would be fairer to the states whose efforts had been greatest and would not result in such a massive flow of revenues "from the distant states to the center of the Union." It would protect Virginia even if a final settlement should never happen on the liberal principles he urged.[97]

This seems a fair description of his motives. All the surviving evidence suggests that Madison was overwhelmingly concerned, at the beginning, with the equity of Hamilton's proposal, that he might indeed have voted for it if he had been able to amend it to assure fair treatment for Virginia.[98] It is true, as both opponents and supporters of assumption pointed out, that his amendment was as curious in some respects as his attempt to lessen the inequities of funding. Although he questioned whether Congress should assume the obligations of the states at all when it was hardly certain that the strictly federal obligations could be met, his own proposal would have *raised* the cost of the assumption by a third, increased the load of federal taxes, and secured more equal treatment of the states by forcing citizens to pay a second time for debts that had already been retired.[99] Yet nearly everyone was judging the assumption by its consequences for his state, Madison had always been a capable defender of his state's essential interests, and equity between the states had been a guiding principle for him since the adoption of the Constitution. By this time, moreover, Madison's Virginia correspondents were beginning to denounce assumption with a single voice, and he himself was growing more and more concerned that measure after measure seemed to benefit New England at the price of growing disaffection in the South and West.[100]

State interests, nonetheless, were only one dimension of the problem. By March 1, when Madison presented his proposal to assume the debts as they had stood in 1783, the argument had broadened into a debate about the wisdom of any form of assumption. Equity aside, some members wondered how the federal government could handle the additional expense. Only, it was clear, by levying internal taxes and prolonging the retirement of the debt, both of which would tend to increase federal power at the states' expense.[101] In this direction, many warned, lay just the unacceptable consolidation of authority which many Antifederalists had feared.[102] As always, Madison was sensitive to these concerns. Again, he found himself in a predicament not very different from the ones he had faced during the congressional debates of 1783 or even at the Constitutional Convention: caught between and learning from the members on both sides. And now, as in the controversy over Robert Morris's appeal for general funds, he found that his suspicion of the easterners, his dedication to a system only partly national in nature, and his underlying views about the fabric of a sound republic ultimately overweighed his interest in the greater rationality and greater federal vigor promised by assumption. The longer the debate continued and the more the advocates of the assumption hinted that they might oppose the funding bill itself unless assumption was included, the more resistant he became.

The argument about assumption stretched from February 23 through March and into April, with opponents gaining strength as congressmen arrived to represent North Carolina, which had ratified the Constitution in November 1789. Madison was mostly silent from the failure of his motion of March 1 through early April, when assumption was defeated 31 to 29 in the Committee of the Whole.[103] He did not speak at length until the twenty-second, when Roger Sherman moved to reinsert it. By then, his doubts about "the merits of the plan" had clearly overbalanced the "advantages" he still conceded.[104]

In the speech of April 22, his longest and most careful on the issue, Madison rejected claims that constitutional reform had made the states incapable of paying their remaining debts. He calculated that the eastern states, both individually and as a group, would pay a smaller portion of the federal taxes authorized thus far than would been their portion if the requisition system had continued. Neither did he think, despite the pleas of its proponents, that policy required a measure that was disapproved by four-fifths of the people. Assumption would increase existing "local jealousies" by drawing money to the center of the Union and by draining specie overseas to pay the foreigners who would acquire a large proportion of the notes. It would "enormously increase, . . . perhaps perpetuate" the "evil" of a public debt, because the federal government could not discharge the obligations as conveniently or quickly if it acted on its own as might be done by acting jointly with the states. Assumption would compel Virginia, which was due a reimbursement, to continue its advances till a final settlement occurred. It would oblige Virginia's citizens to pay an excise—the very tax to which they most objected.[105] In sum, it seemed increasingly unlikely that assumption could be carried into execution "without departing from every principle by which we ought to be guided." He knew that its defeat would "disappoint the citizens of Massachusetts," but its passage would entail a clear "injustice to a majority of the states." Accordingly, he recommended to the "gentlemen" who urged it with such fervor, "not so much for our sakes as their own. . . . no longer to assume a preeminence over us in the nationality of their motives" and to "forbear" their "frequent" warnings that unless assumption carried, the federal debt would also go without provision, "nay, that if the state debts are not assumed, the Union will be endangered."[106]

But, in fact, the Union *was* endangered. Sherman's motion to revive assumption was defeated. On April 26, by a roll-call vote of 32 to 18, the House decided to prepare a funding bill without provision for assumption. When this came in and Elbridge Gerry moved again to reinsert assumption, it was once again defeated. A bill without assumption was completed at the end of May and, on June 2, sent over to the Senate.[107] There, supporters of assumption had a bare majority for reinserting the provision, but assumptionists who wanted a removal from New York refused to act without a previous decision on the seat of government, which had embroiled the Senate in another bitter deadlock.[108] With tempers and anxieties increasing day by day, the stage was set for the encounter which extracted Congress from its impasse and avoided an adjournment in confusion, perhaps with drastic consequences for the fragile new regime. As Thomas Jefferson recalled it, a despondent and disheveled Hamilton approached him on the street as both were going to the president's for business. Hamilton appealed to him to intercede with southern friends to rescue the assumption. Failure of the measure, Hamilton maintained, could wreck the country's credit, force his resignation, and result in a withdrawal of New England from the Union. Barely settled into his position in the new administration, but recognizing that the sectional dispute had generated "most extreme ill humor," Jefferson invited Hamilton and Madison to dinner.[109]

According to the host, Hamilton and Madison appeared, and Jefferson encouraged them to reach an understanding "which might enable us to get along." Before they finished, Madison agreed that if assumption could be brought before the House again by way of an amendment from the Senate, "that tho' he would not vote for it, nor entirely withdraw his opposition, yet he should not be strenuous, but leave it to its fate." To soothe the southern states, this bitter pill would be accompanied by the establishment of the permanent seat of government on the Potomac, which southerners had struggled for for years. Madison would speak to Alexander White and Richard Bland Lee, whose districts lay on the Potomac, about accepting the assumption on these terms. Hamilton would work through Robert Morris for a bargain with the Pennsylvanians for a move to Philadelphia until the site on the Potomac was prepared.

Jefferson's account was almost certainly imperfect. The dinner-table bargain must have had at least as much to do with modifying the provisions of assumption as with trading it for the Potomac.[110] Hamilton's exertions were required, not only with the calculating Morris, but in order to dissuade the senators from Massachusetts and New York from interfering with the congressmen from Pennsylvania and Virginia, who seem already to have reached a separate resolution of the residence dispute.[111] Still, the host was right about essentials. Though we will never penetrate to every aspect of the intricate maneuvers (and Madison's specific role remains a subject for dispute), the basic facts about the compromise are clear. With Massachusetts helping to defeat alternative arrangements, the Senate passed a bill to move to Philadelphia and on to the Potomac. The House debated it on July 6 and 7, with Madison resisting every effort to amend it. As soon as it was signed, the Senate hurried through a final reading of the funding bill, reinserted a revised provision for assumption, and returned it to the House, where Jackson's motion to delete assumption was defeated 32 to 29. Two Marylanders, Daniel Carroll and George Gale, switched their votes along with White and Lee. Madison participated only briefly in the unrecorded arguments of July 22–26, but even though assumption had been modified so that Virginia would receive exactly what she paid, he voted with the opposition to the end.[112]

We cannot know what Madison was thinking as the second session closed. Like Jefferson, he seems to have concluded, as he told Monroe, that supporters of assumption "were determined to risk everything rather than suffer that finally to fail."[113] Perhaps he would have found a way to let the measure pass if there had never been a dinner-table bargain, for his dedication to the Union clearly overrode most of his other wishes at this time.[114] As it was, he managed to secure revisions that eliminated the financial hardship for his state and gained the residence as well: an object he had long considered vital to the West and South as well as to Virginia. Thus, the philosophical composure of a letter to his father must have been a real dimension of his thoughts. Many voted for assumption, he explained, believing it "a lesser evil than to risk" the consequences of rejection. It was now "incumbent on us all to make the best of what is done," and this should be the easier because, "in a pecuniary light, the assumption is no longer of much consequence to Virginia, the sum allotted to her being about her proportion of the whole, and rather exceeding her present debt."[115]

Nevertheless, as he admitted in his letters to his father and Monroe, Madison had not been able to "concur" with those who changed their votes on the assumption or even to "forbear" from "urging" his continuing objections.[116] It would have been embarrassing, of course, for him to simply drop his opposition after pressing it so far. And yet, if I am right, this hardly seems a comprehensive explanation of his motives. Rather, his initial doubts had swollen in the course of the deliberations until he finally opposed the policy itself, not merely the inequities of Hamilton's original proposal. Thus, he still described assumption as an "evil." He still regarded the financial program as a whole as radically unjust and inconsistent with the moral and political foundations of a sound republic. Once again, moreover, he had pressed his program of commercial pressure on the British, only to be stalled by the familiar coalition of the northern treasury supporters and South Carolina planters.[117] If Madison had been disturbed in 1789 about the sectional inequities of many federal measures, he had more and broader reasons to be troubled as the second session closed. Advantage-taking by New England seemed to be combining with an admiration of the British system of finance to turn the federal vessel to a course profoundly different from the heading he preferred.

This seemed undoubtedly the case to many of his closest correspondents. For many in Virginia and throughout the country, Hamilton's financial program might as well have been designed to reignite the potent criticisms of the British system of administration and finance that had profoundly shaped the early Revolution.[118] Months before, as Congress turned from funding to assumption, Benjamin Rush, the Philadelphia physician and reformer, had described the funding plan as little short of "highway robbery." Rush believed that the defeat of Madison's proposal to discriminate between original and secondary holders would "leave a stain upon our country which no time nor declamation can ever wipe away." Worse than that, the funding program would "lay the foundation of an aristocracy in our country, . . . change the property of nine-tenths of the freeholders . . . and be a lasting monument of the efficacy of idleness, speculation, and fraud above industry, economy, and integrity in obtaining wealth and independence." In seven years, the doctor wailed, the funding program would "introduce among us all the corruptions of the British funding system." It would show the world "that revolutions . . . are the rage of *many* for the benefit of a *few*."[119]

The feelings Rush expressed were common in Virginia. Over the succeeding months, Madison opened letter after letter showing that the old critique of British practices and institutions was reviving and assuming a configuration that, in no great time, would place the rising opposition to the Treasury and its supporters on the ground of fundamental maxims of the Revolution. Walter Jones confessed

no small abatement of ardor in the expectations I had formed of the new government, because I apprehend that a certain description of men in power have vicious views of government; that they, with strong auxiliary

numbers, have views equally vicious in finance; and that both are in combination with a predominating interest in a certain quarter of the Union
which is in opposition to the great agricultural interest of the states at large.

Jones condemned the institution of "a system of ruinous taxation and a
monied interest that seems utterly incongruous to the present condition
of society among us." Even in Britain, where society was different, "the
ruinous tendency of her national debt and its consequences has ever been
maintained by the most impartial and enlightened writers and speakers
on the subject."

> Indeed, sir, unless I am deluded in the extreme, there are men and meas-
> ures blended in the composition of the government of the Union that
> should put us much on our guard. I earnestly hope that every attempt to
> undermine the respectability of the state governments may be defeated,
> for if experience should evince that the component parts of the union are
> too heterogeneous to be kept together but by the artificial force and *influ-
> ence* of government, those of the states would be potent instruments [for
> effecting a reunion and a cure]. . . . I should, therefore, ever oppose the
> introduction of those artificial modes of administration and influence in
> the executive departments of government which are engendered in the
> inveterate corruption and complex interests and relations, internal and
> external, of the old European governments.[120]

George Lee Turberville was even more explicit. Knowing Hamilton, he
wrote—his powers, disposition, and reputation—Turberville could not
avoid a

> tremble at the thoughts of his being at the head of such an enormous sum
> as 86 millions of dollars—and the annual revenues of the Union. The
> number of dependents on him necessary to manage the great department
> of revenue, the multitude who will be interested in the funds (in opposi-
> tion, too, to the landed interest of the U.S.) all of whom will in some
> measure be dependent—or at any rate attached to the principal officer of
> the revenue—I profess creates with me apprehensions.[121]

Such apprehensions were to be responsible, before the year was finished,
for a memorial that irritated Hamilton into his earliest surviving comment
on the opposition to his plans. Protesting funding and assumption, the
Virginia legislature saw

> a striking resemblance between this system and that which was introduced
> into England at the Revolution [of 1689]: a system which has perpetuated

upon that nation an enormous debt, and has moreover insinuated into the hands of the executive an unbounded influence, which pervading every branch of the government, bears down all opposition and daily threatens the destruction of every thing that appertains to English liberty. . . .

To erect and concentrate and perpetuate a large monied interest is a measure which . . . must, in the course of human events, produce one or other of two evils—the prostration of agriculture at the feet of commerce, or a change in the present form of federal government fatal to the existence of American liberty.[122]

It is by no means clear that Madison was thinking in this pattern at the end of August 1790, when he and Jefferson departed for a pleasant journey through Annapolis and past Mount Vernon to their piedmont homes.[123] His speeches on the funding and assumption bills had mentioned points that do suggest the influence of the same inheritance of thought, and he was more familiar than his correspondents were with the disturbing statements made by Hamilton and others at and since the Constitutional Convention. Still, Madison had always been inclined to make allowances for merely theoretical positions (especially, perhaps, with Hamilton himself); and even in the heat of the congressional disputes, he seldom let himself forget his larger purpose of establishing a good relationship between the governmental branches and consolidating popular approval of the Constitution. A few days after the defeat of his proposal to discriminate between original and secondary holders, he had assured one correspondent (Edmund Pendleton) that the funding program was "in general well disgested . . . and supported by very able reasoning."[124] When Elbridge Gerry quarreled with a motion to direct the secretary of the treasury to report on revenues required to pay for the assumption, Madison declared that he would "be the last" to favor such a motion if it "carried with it any imputation that [Hamilton] was deficient in abilities or in industry," for such an "imputation would be flagrantly unjust."[125] In his April 22 speech on the assumption, Madison acknowledged that the plan "would not have originated in the quarter which proposed it" unless it had "at least plausible recommendations" in its favor.[126] Both privately and publicly, from the beginning of the session to its close, he limited his criticisms to the equity and policy of funding and assumption, never criticizing Hamilton's intentions or condemning his proposals as a whole.[127] Much can be inferred—and confidently so—from the specific character of his objections. But not until the third and final session of this Congress did his underlying worries get the better of his hopes, surge into the forefront of his thought, and come together in his mind to force conclusions similar to those already reached by several of his correspondents. The catalyst was Hamilton's proposal to create a national bank.

A national bank had been a centerpiece of Hamilton's political economy since early in the 1780s.[128] Now, he argued that a semipublic corporation, modeled on the Bank of England, could complete the funding program by facilitating a variety of fiscal operations: receiving federal taxes, holding federal funds, and serving as a ready source of short-term federal loans. Even more important, as Hamilton conceived it, a national bank could serve two larger ends. Capitalized at $10 million—four times the capital of America's three existing banks, a sum exceeding all the country's coin, and an amount sufficient to permit some regulation of the country's other lenders—the Bank of the United States would seal the union of the government's resources with the capital of private men of wealth, which was the lynchpin of the secretary's economic and political ambitions. It would complete the process of attaching monied men to the success of the financial institutions.[129] At the same time, it would concentrate the capital required for rapid economic growth, which was the secretary's second great objective. The government would own one-fifth of the corporation's stock (purchased by a loan from the new bank itself) and would appoint a fourth of its directors. The remaining stock (and the remainder of the board) would be in private hands, paid for in four installments: one-fourth in specie; three-fourths in government bonds. In exchange for its public services, the bank would hold an exclusive charter, assuring it substantial profits both from private loans and from the interest payments on the public's bonds. Starting with only $500,000 in specie, the institution would be capable, quite safely, of extending its commitments to the limits of its total capitalization. Its notes to borrowers, which were to be receivable for taxes and payable in specie on demand, would be a valuable resource for merchants. Circulating through the country, they would also—for the first time in its history—provide the nation with an ample, stable substitute for cash.[130]

Hamilton submitted his report proposing the creation of the bank on December 14, 1790, shortly after proposing an excise tax to pay for the assumption of state debts.[131] The measure cleared the Senate easily, in much the form he had introduced it.[132] The Senate bill came down on January 21, passed quickly through its first two readings, and came before the House on February 1, where a proposal to commit it for discussion and amendments was defeated 34 to 23.[133] At this late juncture, speaking with uncommon energy and heat, Madison delivered an oration that required the whole of the succeeding day.[134]

He opened with some brief remarks on the advantages and disadvantages of banking, as well as on the details of Hamilton's plan. He argued, first, that the advantages of banks, to merchants and the government alike, could be obtained more fully from a number of such institutions, properly distributed throughout the country, than from a single national institution. He also argued that the Senate bill was not as good a bargain for the public as the nation might have asked, and not entirely fair to all who might be interested in purchasing the stock.[135] Madison had long had major doubts about the wisdom of creating corporations. Later in the course of the deliberations, he "dilated on the great and extensive influence that incorporated societies had on public affairs in Europe: They are a powerful machine, which have always been found competent to effect objects on principles in a great measure independent of the people."[136] In making these remarks, however, he did not intend to say that the decision on the bill should be delivered strictly on its merits. For Congress, he insisted, was utterly without authority to pass it, an "impression" which was all the stronger in his mind because he well recalled that an authority to charter corporations was specifically rejected by the Constitutional Convention.[137]

Madison by no means rested his opinion of the bank on the actions or intentions of the Constitutional Convention, which he would never think the most authoritative source for the construction of the charter.[138] Rather, much as he had done in the debates about removal of executive officials, he insisted on considering the charter as a whole. The Constitution, he observed on February 2, 1791, was "not a general grant, out of which particular powers are excepted—it is a grant of particular powers only, leaving the general mass in other hands. So it had been understood by its friends and its foes, and so it was to be interpreted."[139] When the meaning of the document was clear, the consequences had to be admitted; but "in controverted cases, the meaning of the parties to the instrument"—the people who had ratified it in their several state conventions— was the most authoritative guide. In no event, moreover, could the Constitution be constructed in a manner "that destroys the very character of the government" it creates. A power claimed to be implicit in the Constitution was to be accepted or rejected by considering "its incidentality to an express authority," its intrinsic importance, and "the probability or improbability of its being left to construction."[140]

"Reviewing the Constitution with an eye to these positions," Madison maintained that "it was not possible to discover in it the power to incorporate a Bank." The "general welfare" clause, which had been copied

from the Articles of Confederation, was limited to acts "laying taxes" for
the purposes described. These "general purposes themselves were limited
and explained by the particular enumeration subjoined." To understand
the terms in any sense legitimating the incorporation of a bank, "would
give to Congress an unlimited power" and destroy the effect of the particular enumeration, together with the reservation of remaining powers
to the states.[141]

The bill at hand was not a borrowing of money, not an exercise of any
power listed in the constitutional enumeration, and not a levying of taxes
for the objects listed in the body of the Constitution. The sole remaining
source for an authority to pass it was the clause empowering the Congress
to enact such laws as might be "necessary and proper" to carry its delegated powers into effect; and "Whatever meaning this clause may have,
none can be admitted that would give an unlimited discretion to Congress." At minimum, a measure that would come within the meaning of
this clause would have to be limited "to means *necessary* to the *end* and
incident to the *nature* of the specified powers." The "necessary and proper
clause" was "in fact merely declaratory of what would have resulted by
unavoidable implication, as the appropriate and, as it were, technical
means of executing those powers. In this sense it had been explained by
the friends of the Constitution and ratified by the state conventions." To
construe it as permitting *any* means that might conduce to execution of
a delegated power, as suggested in the preamble to the bank bill, would
destroy "the essential characteristic of a government . . . composed of limited and enumerated powers." "Mark the reasoning on which the validity
of the bill depends," Madison protested:

> To borrow money is made the *end* and the accumulation of capitals *implied*
> as the *means*. The accumulation of capitals is then the *end* and a bank
> *implied* as the *means*. The bank is then the *end* and a charter of incorpo-
> ration, a monopoly, capital punishment, etc. *implied* as the *means*.
>
> If implications thus remote and multiplied can be linked together, a
> chain may be formed that will reach every object of legislation, every object
> within the whole compass of political economy.[142]

The power of incorporation, Madison insisted, could never be considered
merely "an accessory or subaltern power to be deduced by implication as
a means of executing another power; it was in its nature a distinct, an
independent and substantive prerogative, which not being enumerated in
the Constitution could never have been meant to be included."[143]

In conclusion, Madison reverted to the general principles with which
he had begun. When defenders of the Constitution were confronted with

demands for the addition of a bill of rights, they had replied that powers
not confided to the federal government were retained by the states or the
people "and that those given were not to be extended by remote implications." They had insisted that "the terms necessary and proper gave no
additional powers." The explanatory declarations and proposed amendments of the ratifying states were based upon the same assumptions, and
the Ninth and Tenth Amendments had confirmed this understanding.

> With all this evidence of the sense in which the Constitution was under-
> stood and adopted, will it not be said, if the bill should pass, that its adop-
> tion was brought about by one set of arguments and that it is now
> administered under the influence of another set; and this reproach will
> have the keener sting because it is applicable to so many individuals con-
> cerned in both the adoption and administration.

The bank bill was a "usurpation," Madison maintained. It would establish
precedents for an interpretation "leveling all the barriers which limit the
powers of the general government" and destroying "the main characteristic of the Constitution." It was "condemned by the exposition of the
friends of the Constitution, whilst depending before the public; was condemned by the apparent intention of the parties which ratified the Constitution"; was condemned by the Ninth and Tenth Amendments; "and
he hoped it would receive its final condemnation by the vote of this
house."[144]

Madison's denunciation of the bank, the fullest explication of the Constitution since the 1789 debate on the power to remove executive officials,
proved the opening barrage in an extended war between the advocates of
strict and broad constructions. Although the House of Representatives
approved the bill,[145] the president was troubled by his old adviser's stand
and asked his cabinet for their opinions. Madison's position was elaborated and endorsed by Jefferson and Randolph, with the former going
notably beyond his friend toward a complete rejection of the doctrine of
implicit powers.[146] Washington retained the bill until the final moment,
talked to Madison on more than one occasion, and asked him to prepare
a veto.[147] Hamilton, however, answered the Virginians in a brilliant brief
that would become the great foundation for the liberal interpretation of
the Constitution: "If the end be clearly comprehended within any of the
specified powers, and if the measure have an obvious relation to that end
and is not forbidden by any particular provision of the Constitution, it
may safely be deemed to come within the compass of the national authority."[148] On February 25, Washington signed the bank bill into law.

From then until the present, Madison's denunciation of the bank has

seemed the most surprising episode of his career. Congressional opponents scoffed at his position. "Full of casuistry and sophistry," said Fisher
Ames, who held the floor for a rebuttal all day long on February 3, the
constitutional objections were in truth a flimsy cover for an opposition
based on other grounds; even Madison's supporters "laughed" at his construction.[149] A minority of modern analysts concur with Ames and other
critics in attributing the framer's stand to southern fears that the creation
of the bank would impede the transfer of the government from Philadelphia to the Potomac.[150] In the Senate, southerners attempted unsuccessfully to limit the duration of the charter to the date appointed for this
move. Madison himself objected to the twenty-year duration, which would
keep the institution in existence in Philadelphia until 1811. In 1792,
moreover, William Loughton Smith maintained that the Virginia representatives had pressed the Pennsylvanians to accept a ten-year limit and
had threatened to oppose the bill in toto if its advocates insisted on a
longer term. "Had Pennsylvania acceded to the proposition, which the
writer knows was made, . . . the great constitutional artillery of the General
would have been reserved for some other occasion."[151]

Madison insisted that this charge was "false," and sympathetic analysts
have noted that the evidence that Madison and other southerners were
moved primarily by this concern consists almost entirely of the accusations
of their foes.[152] Led by his biographers, the friendly critics have advanced
a different explanation. Already troubled by the many ways in which Hamilton's program favored the Northeast, benefited the financial interests,
and created a corrupted corps of treasury supporters in the Congress,
Madison could not abide another huge bonanza for this crew or a construction of the Constitution that would free the predators from constitutional restraints.[153] Nevertheless, with very few exceptions, sympathetic
analysts have been as firm as Madison's detractors in interpreting his
speech as marking the decisive moment in a radical reversal of the attitudes he had displayed throughout the 1780s. Irving Brant may have expressed it in the most compelling fashion. Faced with an intractable
majority, the framer seized the best remaining ground. "The issue came
to him at the one spot—bank incorporation—where he had a record of
strict construction, contrasting sharply with his generally broad concept
of federal power. By conviction and compulsion he chose the narrow path
on this issue, and by that action was driven into lasting adherence to it."[154]

To Brant and to the overpowering majority of modern scholars, Madison's attack on broad construction of the Constitution was a quarrel with
himself. The doctrine of implied federal powers, Brant maintained, was
Madison's own invention, first advanced in the Confederation Congress,
then deliberately preserved when he prepared the Tenth Amendment,

and at least implicitly assumed in Madison's support since 1789 for federal
assistance for a purely scientific expedition to explore the longitudinal
deviations of the compass. Hamilton's opinion on the national bank,
Brant pointed out, deliberately paraphrased the argument of Madison's
Federalist no. 44.[155]

And yet if anything can fairly be declared to be conclusive, surely this
is so of the decisive evidence that Madison had *always* stood for scrupulous
respect for national charters—even for the Articles of Confederation. Relatively strict construction of these charters was his rule, not an occasional
exception, from his entry into the Confederation Congress through the
Constitutional Convention (where he moved for an extension of the list
of federal powers so that little would be left to implication) to his condemnation of the arguments deployed to justify the bank. Even in the
latter, to be sure, he plainly said that powers *could* result from necessary
implications. Neither then nor later did he ever go as far as Jefferson
toward tying Congress down in an impossibly restrictive understanding of
its limits. Like Jefferson, however, Madison was conscientiously and quite
consistently respectful of the fundamental law, and he was probably more
conscious than was Jefferson himself of the capacity of precedent to turn
the Constitution into something vastly different from the instrument the
people had approved. The arguments developed in the speech of 1791
had been prefigured countless times through the preceding decade and
on more than one occasion since the Constitution was approved. They
differed only in their language from the warnings he would issue through
the next ten years. If forced constructions of the Constitution were accepted by the government and public,

> every power that can be deduced from them will be deduced and exercised
> sooner or later by those who may have an interest in doing so. The char-
> acter of human nature gives this salutary warning to every sober and re-
> flecting mind. And the history of government in all its forms and in every
> period of time ratifies the danger. A people, therefore, who are so happy
> as to possess the inestimable blessing of a free and defined constitution
> cannot be too watchful against the introduction nor too critical in tracing
> the consequences of new principles and new constructions that may re-
> move the landmarks of power.[156]

"If this licentiousness in constructive perversions of the Constitution
[should] continue," he would write in 1800, "we shall soon have to look
into our code of laws and not the charter of the people for the form as
well as the powers of our government. Indeed, such an unbridled spirit

of construction as has gone forth in sundry instances would bid defiance
to any possible parchment securities against usurpation.''[157]

Again, however, Madison's consistency is not the most important point,
and not the most instructive benefit of questioning the predominant opinion. Deeper insights come from seeing what has been distorted or entirely
hidden by the dominant interpretation. First, as has been mentioned, the
prevailing view confuses what was actually a partisan interpretation of the
Constitution with the facts about its evolution. It suggests, as Hamilton or
Ames suggested, that when Madison diverged from other leading advocates of constitutional reform, he—not they—was *by that fact* departing
from the Federalist position, changing his opinion, and advancing a construction that would trouble and divide the nation through the Civil War
and well into the modern battles over civil rights and other national reforms. The movement for a stronger union, the retention of that movement's name by the Federalists of the 1790s, the rulings of the Marshall
Court, and many other events and contingencies have privileged the Hamiltonian interpretation of the Constitution. But, surely, Madison's insistence that the Hamiltonians were pushing a construction that the
Federalists of 1788 had most decidedly disclaimed was fully as consistent
with the facts as their own contention that the opposition leader was re-
treating from his previous position. Different men may well have held
contrasting private suppositions at the moment when the Constitution was
approved, but the supporters of the Constitution had unquestionably reassured its critics that they need not fear the charter's sweeping clauses.

All these points have further implications. In the first place, it is hardly
likely that Madison or any of the founders had attempted a complete and
rigorous consideration of exactly what the Constitution would permit until
the bank bill raised the question and provoked the effort to define the
limits of congressional discretion. At that point, it was apparent that the
Constitution was unclear; and careful reading of his speech of February
2 shows that Madison was quite aware that neither strict nor broad construction of its language (as those terms would later be defined) was actually—much less inherently—correct. Certain legislative powers *were*
implied, as Madison explicitly conceded, but it also certain that constructive powers had to have *some* limit if the government was really to be
limited at all. The meaning of the Constitution was contested ground. It
had been argued over from the start. It would be argued over in the
future. And for all of their impressive foresight, even those who framed
it did not know from the beginning quite what it implied. Madison had
more than once confessed his own uncertainty and advocated a collective
and impartial effort ''to find out,'' as in the argument about the power
to remove executive officials.[158] Like other mortals, he and other framers

were compelled to come to terms with the provisions of the Constitution, to consider these in all their implications, only as developments gave rise to new and different questions. This was just what he was trying to accomplish in his speech when he maintained that the power to create a corporation could not safely be considered merely as a means to ends undoubtedly entrusted to the Congress.

When he did so, nonetheless, conflicting suppositions and contrasting understandings of the goals of constitutional reform erupted in a bitter party battle. For, in truth, the Federalists of 1788 had never been united on the ultimate objectives of reform. Hamilton and Madison, the most important spokesmen for the movement, were Federalists in very different senses of that term. For Hamilton, the Constitution was an instrument permitting vigorous administration, and a sound administration was to be the agency for winning citizens away from their attachment to the states and for consolidating power by degrees until the Constitution actually became as national as required (although it might be well to note than even Hamilton was hardly a consolidationist by European or by modern standards). Madison, by contrast, was committed to a system only partly national in nature: to a government that could effectively conduct the business of the Union, but would stay within the limits necessary to preserve the liberty that union was intended to protect. Month by month, the differences among the Federalists of 1788 had come to be increasingly apparent. With the bank bill, they exploded.

Madison's biographers are right to stress his growing discontent with Hamilton's financial program. Both regional and deeply theoretical considerations contributed to his alarm. The national bank, like funding and assumption, benefited mainly monied and commercial interests in the North and East. Indeed, the holders of securities, whose fortunes had ballooned with funding and assumption, were encouraged to increase their wealth again by trading their securities for bank stock, which could hardly fail to earn substantial profits. With the institution of the bank, which made it obvious that Hamilton was recreating the familiar (and corrupting) British system of finance, the monied interests in and out of Congress were to be united, as opponents saw it, in a single corporation obligated to the Treasury, dependent on the federal government for its success, and capable of exercising potent influence through its loans to private citizens and government officials. Like the English oppositionists before him, like his correspondents in Virginia, Madison concluded that the nation's liberty was seriously at risk.[159]

Strict construction of the Constitution, nonetheless, was always more to Madison than a convenient strategy for mounting a resistance to a program he opposed. To see his constitutional constructions simply as a

means to other ends, as mostly or entirely instrumental, gravely underes-
timates the depth of his commitment to the constitutional division of authority between the central government and the states, as well as to a
higher-law interpretation of the Constitution. Madison had *always* been
opposed to shifting *too much* power to the federal level, in largest part
because he had always feared that this would shift too much authority to
rulers least responsive to the people. No less important, he *genuinely* understood the Constitution as the *people's* law, which was to be revered and
not remolded by their servants. And finally, he was—to depths that we
today are barely able to imagine—an eighteenth-century gentleman of
honor. In his condemnation of the bank, as in his speeches on the Bill
of Rights, he called upon the gentlemen around him to be conscious that
their honor was at stake. It was dishonorable to break a solemn promise:
to secure the Constitution by portraying it as one thing, then proceed as
though it were another; to turn the victory of 1788 into an underhanded
trick. Doing so, moreover, could profoundly threaten its survival, for the
Union rested on essential equity among its different sections, on the
grounding of the government in popular consent, and on the people's
firm conviction of its worth. Hamilton's financial measures *were* deliberately contrived to separate the interests of the capitalists and merchants
from prevailing, localistic inclinations and attachments. But allegiance to
the Constitution, Madison believed, was not to be secured by bribing a
minority with federal largesse. The few who would indeed be bound by
ties of personal advantage would comprise, in actuality, a special-interest
faction, neither national enough nor well enough respected in the new
United States to integrate it on a British model.[160] To combat them, Madison would educate and mobilize the many. With the signing of the bank
bill, he decided to arouse a popular resistance to a scheme that he was
coming to perceive as a concerted effort to subvert the people's Constitution and to undermine the liberty that he had meant that Constitution
to preserve.

CHAPTER ELEVEN

Opposition Leader

THE FINAL SESSION OF THE FIRST FEDERAL CONGRESS ended on March 4, 1791. Eight months elapsed before the meeting of the Second. During the adjournment, Madison was freer from his ordinary cares than he had been in all the years since the Annapolis Convention. He stayed in Philadelphia throughout the early spring, enjoying Jefferson's French meals, riding out into the country with his friend, and spreading out his books and papers for a "little task" that he had lacked the leisure to complete. Late in April, he departed for New York, hoping to fulfill an old desire to travel through New England. Jefferson came up on May 19, and on the twenty-first the two Virginians headed up the Hudson and Lake George to Lake Champlain, across to Bennington, Vermont, down the Connecticut Valley to Long Island Sound, and back across the island to the city. Jefferson hurried on to Philadelphia to catch up on his work. Madison continued in New York, still hoping to arrange a tour through Massachusetts. A bout of bilious fever and an inability to match his schedule with the plans of other friends defeated this intention, but he was able to join Jefferson again at the beginning of September. From Philadelphia, they traveled home through Georgetown, where they paused to meet with the commissioners of the new federal district, then back through Georgetown once again for the October meeting of the Second Congress.[1]

Weeks of welcome exercise and stimulating travel left the congressman invigorated and refreshed. Jefferson believed that he had never seen him in such rosy health as when they separated in New York. Nevertheless, the interlude between the First and Second Congresses was not a period of undistracted pleasure. It also marked, quite unmistakably, the great divide between the two Virginians and the Federalists who kept that name during the party conflict of the 1790s. By the middle of the summer of 1791, Madison and Jefferson were ready to combine persistent governmental opposition to their foes with a deliberate attempt to foster popular resistance. By the time the Second Congress met, Madison was thoroughly prepared, not only to direct a dedicated legislative opposition, but to take a major hand in arousing the voters to the dangers of the Hamiltonian design, a scheme he now regarded as a fundamental danger to the Revolution. In the process, he would both develop and explain the vision that had guided him throughout the previous five years. His understanding of the character and purposes of constitutional reform would settle into the configurations that would shape the rest of his career.

Though it is difficult to reconstruct the frame of mind in which Madison and Jefferson had approached the final session of the First Federal Congress, it is not so hard to capture their opinions at its close. The excise and the bank had been the only major legislation. The former, coming early in the session, Madison had swallowed with distaste, admitting that an excise was in many ways the most objectionable of taxes, but seeing no alternative if Congress was to pay for the assumption without resorting to a tax on lands.[2] The national bank, however, coming later in the session, was absolutely more than he could down. Hamilton's financial program had disturbed him from the start, not only by its individual and sectional inequities, but also by the way in which it bound some individuals and interests—speculating congressmen as well as favored citizens and states—to an administrator whose pervasive influence was becoming clearer day by day. The bank not only threatened to cement the bond between the secretary and the interests that had benefited from his plans—and thus to reconstruct a hated British system of administration. It also rested on a posture toward the Constitution which was just what Antifederalists had feared, which changed the people's charter by an act of governmental usurpation, and which threatened to remove a powerful restraint on the ability of Hamilton and his supporters to pursue designs that seemed to Madison more ominous with every passing month.

The final point was not a small consideration. Between the passage of the excise and acceptance of the bank, developments had turned Madison's uneasiness into outright alarm. Disgruntlement with the advantage-taking and inequities surrounding the financial program had been deepened, then transmuted, by disputes that stretched across an ever wider range of public issues. Before the session closed, Madison was questioning the ultimate intentions of his foes, and his conclusions forced the critical decisions of the summer.

Commercial policy was once again a leading subject of contention.

Through both of the preceding sessions, Madison had pressed his plan to force the British to relax their navigation laws. On May 10, 1790, shortly after rejecting assumption, the second session of the House of Representatives had gone into Committee of the Whole on a proposal to increase the tonnage duty on foreign vessels and to impose a 10 percent surcharge on ships arriving from ports where U.S. vessels were excluded.[3] William Loughton Smith immediately objected to imposing extra burdens on the South "for the exclusive benefit of the Eastern States," and Madison jumped in to argue for a plan that would specifically discriminate against the British, not against the French and other foreigners as well.[4] On May 14, he introduced a resolution that would set specific dates, first for raising tonnage duties on the ships of nations having no commercial treaty with the Union, then for barring vessels of this sort from carrying off any nonmanufactured U.S. goods.[5] To those who feared commercial confrontation with the British, he answered as he had in 1789 that this would be like war between the country and the town: "The farmer can live better without the shopkeeper than the shopkeeper without the farmer." "America had nothing to fear from Great Britain," he insisted, which would not, in any case, risk the very existence of her West Indian colonies, together with enormous hardships for her merchants, manufacturers, and seamen, rather than accept reciprocal arrangements. America must either act to force a reciprocity or leave her commerce to be regulated by others, and if the South should bear a larger portion of the burden, southerners would have sufficient compensation in the increase of the nation's maritime resources, which would be a valuable recourse in war.[6]

In 1790 as in 1789, Madison's proposals to discriminate against the British were defeated by a coalition of deep southerners and northern treasury supporters. If Madison had changed his mind on funding and assumption, Hamilton had long since dropped his own support for commercial retaliation.[7] Ninety percent of the revenues required to finance the funding program would come from duties on foreign imports. Ninety percent of imported manufactures came from Britain. From 1790 forward, the secretary of the treasury would be a vigilant and vigorous opponent of any legislation that could interrupt the flow of British goods.[8]

Hamilton's determined opposition was an obvious and major influence in defeating Madison again in 1791. On this occasion, Madison and Jefferson, with Washington's support, concerted a deliberate campaign for pushing the insistence on commercial reciprocity that Federalists and Antifederalists alike had thought would be an early consequence of the approval of the Constitution. At the beginning of the session, Madison inserted in the president's address a passage calling on the legislature to "render our commerce and agriculture less dependent on foreign bottoms," then drafted a reply in which the House agreed about the need to relieve American commerce "from the injurious dependence on the navigation of other nations."[9] In January, Washington submitted to the Senate Jefferson's report on French remonstrances against the tonnage acts—the first in a succession of reports in which the secretary of state blamed the British for the lack of progress in commercial talks as well as in negotiations on fulfillment of the terms of peace, contrasted French and British policies toward the United States, recommended measures that would grant concessions to the French as a return for their commercial favors, and cautioned that the British seemed determined on "mounting their navigation on the ruins of ours," a policy that could "only be opposed by counter-regulations on our part."[10] The report on French remonstrances was referred to a Senate committee, whose Hamiltonian majority sat on it until the last days of the session, then rejected Jefferson's proposals. But shortly after Jefferson's report on the failure of Gouverneur Morris's mission to England, a House committee on which Madison was serving introduced a measure modeled on the British navigation acts and meant to force a reciprocity from Britain. Again, the Hamiltonians resisted, warning of the danger of commercial warfare and appealing for delay until a British minister arrived. The issue was debated warmly on February 23 and 24, but with the session coming to a close, the advocates of counterregulations could secure no more than an agreement to refer the matter back to Jefferson again for an additional report.[11]

All of Jefferson's biographers agree that the disputes about commercial policy, which raged throughout the winter in the offices of the administration, marked the opening of the direct collisions between Jefferson and Hamilton that would explode in their confrontation over the question of the bank.[12] By April, Jefferson was telling James Monroe that treasury supporters would continue to submit to British domination of the country's trade in order to protect the fiscal system. They would also take advantage of "every rag of an Indian depredation" in order to promote a standing army and perpetuate the debt. "We are ruined, Sir," he wailed, "if we do not overrule the principles that 'the more we owe, the more prosperous we shall be,'" that if the debt should ever be paid off, "'we should incur another by any means,' . . . etc., etc."[13] It does not require a bold imagination to suspect that Jefferson was saying much the same to Madison (or Madison was saying much the same to him).

By this time, moreover—just as they were starting to discern a disciplined, persistent coalition dedicated to protecting and extending the advantages conferred by Hamilton's financial program—Jefferson and Madison were coming to be equally alarmed about the sentiments expressed in the *Gazette of the United States* and in the higher social circles in the city. Two days after Madison's denunciation of the bank—the date does not seem incidental—Jefferson expressed his hope that a new revolutionary government would soon be firmly established in France. On this, he told George Mason on February 4, would depend the fate of liberty in Europe. Indeed, the firm establishment of liberty in France might even be required

> to stay up our own [new government] and to prevent it from falling back to that kind of halfway house, the English constitution. It cannot be denied that we have among us a sect who believe [the English constitution] to contain whatever is perfect in human institutions; that the members of this sect have, many of them, names and offices which stand high in the estimation of our countrymen. . . . The only corrective of what is amiss in our present government will be the augmentation of the numbers in the lower house, so as to get a more agricultural representation, which may put that interest above that of the stock-jobbers.[14]

A few weeks later, Jefferson would tell another correspondent that it was the country's great good fortune that "our chief executive magistrate is purely and zealously republican. We cannot expect all his successors to be so, and therefore should avail ourselves of the present day to establish principles and examples which may fence us against future heresies preached now, to be practiced hereafter."[15]

The preaching Jefferson referred to is identifiable without conjecture, as are certain of the "names and offices" he numbered in this "sect." Over the preceding year, John Fenno's semiweekly newspaper, the only one of Philadelphia's twelve to have pretensions to a national circulation, had been publishing a lengthy series titled "Discourses on Davila." Although the series was unsigned, the whole political establishment believed that these prolix and winding commentaries on an obscure history of the French religious wars were written by Vice President John Adams; and among some readers, puzzlement and even anger greeted every new installment. The author seemed not only to prefer the British constitution to the unicameral experiment now under way in France, he seemed to actually commend the British mixed regime as better than any government derived entirely from elections.[16]

"Davila" was, in fact, Adams's continuation of an international debate that he had opened in 1787 with his *Defence of the Constitutions of Government of the United States*. The country's second-highest magistrate was an adherent to the neoclassical conception of a government in which the many and the few would each control one legislative house and would be refereed and balanced by a single chief executive, who must be wholly independent of them both. Horrified by what he saw as French contempt for the universal lessons of history (and worried that the radical ideas of Condorcet, Turgot, and others might infect the new United States), he mounted an impassioned, deeply learned argument for the superiority of balanced constitutions. First in the *Defence* and then, more stridently, in the "Discourses on Davila," Adams argued that the French might hope that abolition of hereditary privilege and the consolidation of authority in a single national assembly would assure that merit, not heredity, would rule, but they would find that riches, beauty, birth, and taste are more admired (or easier to recognize) than talent—that, indeed, "the chance of having wisdom and integrity in a senator by hereditary descent would be far better" than the chance of finding these by popular election.[17]

> The rich and the poor, the laborious and the idle, the learned and the ignorant, are distinctions as old as the creation and as extensive as the globe, distinctions which no art or policy, no degree of virtue or philosophy can every wholly destroy. . . . These parties will be represented in the legislature and must be balanced, or one will oppress the other. There will never probably be found any other mode of establishing such an equilibrium than by constituting the representation of each an independent branch of the legislature and an independent executive authority, such as that in our government, to be a third branch and a mediator or an arbitrator between them.[18]

As in the *Defence*, so also in his commentaries on Davila, Adams was convinced that natural aristocrats would rule unless they were confined or ostracized within a single legislative house, "that three branches of power have an unalterable foundation in nature, that they exist in every society natural and artificial, and that if all of them are not acknowledged in any constitution of government it will be found to be imperfect, unstable, and soon enslaved."[19]

Adams never understood the outrage and abuse that greeted the "Discourses," although it was foreshadowed in the critical reception given the *Defence*.[20] But Adams's adherence to a theory that assimilated the American and British constitutions was repulsive to republicans, who thought that the United States had made a world-historical departure from tradition. More than that, the critics had substantial reasons for believing that the commentator on Davila actually *preferred* the British constitution and meant to recommend it to Americans as well as to the intellectuals in France. Not only did he say that equal laws and ostracism of the aristocracy required "some signs or other of distinction and degree," he seemed to set such stringent standards for independence in a head of state that it was hard to see how these could possibly be satisfied by means of an elective process once George Washington was gone.[21] The final essay said that men had "tried all possible experiments of elections of governors and senates, but . . . found so much diversity of opinion and sentiment among them, so much emulation in every heart, so many rivalries among the principal men, such division, confusions and miseries, that they had almost unanimously been convinced that hereditary succession was attended with fewer evils than frequent elections."[22] No wonder Jefferson believed that Adams had abandoned his republican convictions. No wonder Jefferson referred to the *Gazette of the United States*, in which the publication of "Davila" was accompanied by unrelenting praise of Hamilton's achievements, as "a paper of pure Toryism, disseminating the doctrine of monarchy, aristocracy, and the exclusion of the influence of the people."[23] No wonder that on February 28, three days after Washington approved the national bank, the secretary of state offered an appointment as a part-time clerk in his department to an editor who might be willing to create a national paper of a very different stripe.[24]

But a position for Philip Freneau, who was working at the *Daily Advertiser* in New York, did not begin as Jefferson's idea. It was suggested to him by Madison, the poet's Princeton classmate, who may have been reminded of an earlier attempt to find an office for Freneau by yet another schoolmate, "Lighthorse Harry" Lee.[25] Exactly how the ball was carried from that point—which of the Virginians introduced the concept of a second national paper—is impossible to say. But Madison, at least, had known from the beginning that Freneau was thinking of establishing a paper of his own; and Jefferson's initial letter to the poet made it clear that the position as a translator "gives so little to do as not to interfere with any other calling the person may choose." Beginning with this letter, both of the Virginians were committed to establishing a counterweight to the *Gazette of the United States*; and Madison, not Jefferson, assumed the leading role.[26]

Freneau initially declined Jefferson's offer, explaining that he had been trying for some time to establish a gazette in rural New Jersey and was now on the verge of success.[27] But Madison was soon in touch, in person, with his college friend. Shortly after reaching New York City for the break between the sessions, he reported back to Jefferson that he had seen Freneau, explained the limited duties in the State Department, argued the superior advantages of Philadelphia as a location for his paper, and given him a note to take to Jefferson himself.[28] Freneau did not show up in Philadelphia, and Jefferson expressed regret.[29] Madison was not so easily dissuaded. When Jefferson arrived for their adventure to the lakes,

Madison arranged a breakfast with Freneau at which the two Virginians were sufficiently persuasive to secure a tentative agreement. They may have pressed quite hard. They would have had good reason, for Jefferson had left a furor in his wake.

Part One of Thomas Paine's *The Rights of Man* was published in London in March 1791. When it arrived in Philadelphia, John Beckley, the Virginia clerk of the House of Representatives, lent a copy to Madison, who passed it on to Jefferson before departing for New York. As Beckley had requested, Jefferson sent it in turn to Jonathan Bayard Smith, whose son was planning an American edition of Paine's defense of Lockean contractualism, republican government, and written constitutions against the challenge of Edmund Burke's *Reflections on the Revolution in France*. "To take off a little of the dryness" of the note explaining the enclosure, Jefferson remarked that he was "pleased to find . . . that something is at length to be publicly said against the heresies which have sprung up among us. I have no doubt our citizens will rally a second time to the standard of Common Sense." To Jefferson's "astonishment," the printer issued the American edition on May 3—with a preface quoting these very remarks.[30]

Jefferson was mortified to see his words in print. "I had in view, certainly, the doctrines of Davila," he explained to Madison, "but certainly never meant to step into a public newspaper with that in my mouth." In consequence, his friendship with John Adams was endangered. "Col. Hamilton and [British agent] Col. Beckwith are open mouthed against me . . . as likely to give offense to the court of London. H[amilton] adds further that it marks my opposition to the government. Thus endeavoring to turn on the government itself those censures I meant for the enemies of the government, to wit those who want to change it into a monarchy."

Madison expressed surprise that "British partisans" were using Jefferson's remarks against him: "The sensibility of H[amilton] and B[eckwith] to the indignity to the British Court is truly ridiculous."[31] But Madison, who had instinctively disliked John Adams long before they met, could hardly sympathize with Jefferson's distress about disruption of an ancient friendship.[32] "Mr. Adams can least of all complain. Under a mock defense of the republican constitutions of this country, he attacked them with all the force he possessed, and this in a book with his name to it whilst he was a representative of his country at a foreign court." Even as vice president, said Madison to Jefferson, "his pen has constantly been at work in the same cause; and though his name has not been prefixed to his antirepublican discourses," his authorship was clear. "Surely if it be innocent and decent in one servant of the public thus to write attacks against its

government, it cannot be very criminal or indecent in another to patron-
ize a written defense of the principles on which that government is
founded."[33]

While Madison and Jefferson were traveling through New York and on
into New England, the controversy started by the note on Paine spread
rapidly throughout the country. On June 8, the *Columbian Centinel* in Boston published the first of eleven letters by "Publicola," which everybody
thought was Adams's rejoinder (though they were actually written by his
son).[34] The reaction was immediate and loud. Dozens of responses to
"Publicola" appeared in newspapers throughout the country during the
summer of 1791, condemning the vice president's supposed apostasy from
republican principles.[35] Madison, who was ensconced in New York City as
the fury reached its crest (and finally succeeding in the long negotiation
with Freneau), could not surpress his wry amusement over Adams's discomfort.[36] Neither could he check his outrage over the disgusting scene
that opened with the offering of rights to purchase shares in the Bank of
the United States.[37] "The plan of the institution gives a moral certainty
of gain to the subscribers with scarce a physical possibility of loss," he
wrote to Jefferson. "The subscriptions are consequently a mere scramble
for so much public plunder, which will be engrossed by those already
loaded with the spoils of indi[vi]duals." It was becoming ever clearer, he
protested, "in what proportions the public debt lies in the country—What
sort of hands hold it, and by whom the people of the U.S. are to be
governed. Of all the shameful circumstances of this business, it is among
the greatest to see the members of the legislature who were most active
in pushing this job openly grasping its emoluments."[38]

By August, Madison was writing Jefferson again to warn him that

> packet boats and expresses are again sent from this place to the Southern
> States to buy up the paper of all sorts which has risen in the market here.
> These and other abuses make it a problem whether the system of the old
> paper under a bad government or of the new under a good one be charge-
> able with the greater substantial injustice. The true difference seems to be
> that by the former the few were the victims to the many, by the latter the
> many to the few.

Which, of course, was anything but an improvement. Indeed, the troubled
champion of constitutional reform concluded this denunciation with a
metaphor that ranks among the most suggestive in his writings. "My imagination," he remarked, "will not attempt to set bounds to the daring
depravity of the times. The stockjobbers will become the pretorian band
of the government—at once its tools and its tyrant; bribed by its largesses,

and overawing it by clamors and combinations." Though not, he did not need to add, without his adamant resistance.[39]

Meeting in October in the aftermath of the extended furor over Adams, Jefferson, and Paine—and just a week before Freneau launched his *National Gazette*—the Second Federal Congress differed greatly from the First. Its initial session saw the first contemporary comments on coherent legislative parties.[40] It witnessed Hamilton's elaboration of his vision for the future in the great Report on Manufactures. On the other side, it did not close before the president was treated to a livid condemnation of Hamilton's designs. When Washington expressed a fear that Jefferson's decision to retire, if Jefferson persisted, would result in public discontent, Jefferson responded that the "single source" of public discontent was in the Treasury Department. "A system had there been contrived for deluging the states with paper money, . . . for withdrawing our citizens from [useful] pursuits . . . to occupy themselves and their capitals in a species of gambling destructive of morality, and which had introduced its poison into the government itself." Some congressmen had profited from the financial bills while they were pending, Jefferson maintained. From that point forward, they had "lent all the energy of their talents and instrumentality of their offices to the establishment and enlargment of this system," while supporting such constructions of the Constitution "as made it a very different thing from what the people thought they had submitted to."[41]

Six weeks later, in the House of Representatives, a young Virginia congressman identified the end toward which these speculating congressmen seemed clearly to be working. All representative governments, said William Branch Giles, displayed a natural tendency to degenerate from republicanism toward monarchy, principally because of the unequal distribution of wealth among the people. But Hamilton's financial program had accelerated this degeneration by enriching the minority who had acquired the public debt and binding them into a single interest. This created, in opposition to the agricultural and republican majority of the country, "a great monied interest . . . who, having embarked their fortunes with the government, would go all lengths with its administration whether right or wrong." Giles "saw systems introduced to carve out of the common rights of one part of the community privileges, monopolies, exclusive rights, etc. for the benefit of another with no other view . . . but to create nursuries of immediate dependents upon the government whose interest will always stimulate them to support its measures however iniquitous and tyrannical." Measures to defeat this system, Giles maintained, would decide whether America "would preserve the simplicity, chastity, and purity of her native . . . republicanism . . . or will prostitute herself to the venal and borrowed artifices and corruptions of a stale and pampered monarchy."[42]

Madison agreed entirely with these friends. On March 30, 1792, Benjamin Rush recorded in his commonplace book that he had spent an evening with Madison in his room at Mrs. House's boardinghouse. The conversation focused on the "evils introduced into our country by the funded debt." Madison said "that he could at all times discover a sympathy between the speeches and the pockets of all those members of Congress who held certificates."[43] Then, when Washington requested Madison's advice about his own determination to retire, the congressman did not disguise his close agreement with his allies on the issue now at stake.

When Washington explained that the rising "spirit of party"—within the government and even within his own administration—was a leading reason for his eagerness to leave, Madison replied that no development could argue more persausively for yet "another sacrifice" from the only man who might unite all parties until "the character of the government" could be decided. In one of the emerging parties, Madison conceded, "there might be a few who, retaining their original disaffection to the government, might still wish to destroy it, but . . . they would lose their weight with their associates by betraying any such hostile purposes." Similarly, "although it was pretty certain that the other [party] were in general unfriendly to republican government and probably aimed at a gradual approximation of ours to a mixed monarchy, yet the public sentiment was . . . so rapidly manifesting itself, that the party could not long . . . retain a dangerous influence." Washington's continued leadership for only one more term could "give such a tone and firmness to the government as would secure it against danger from either of these descriptions of enemies." No probable successor, Madison maintained, could expect the same results. If Jefferson could somehow be persuaded to relinquish his "extreme repugnance to public life . . . , local prejudices in the northern states," along with Pennsylvania's continuing resistance to the move to the Potomac, would probably defeat him. "With respect to Mr. Adams, his monarchical principles, which he had not concealed, . . . had produced such a settled dislike among republicans everywhere, and particularly in the southern states, that he seemed to be out of the question." And finally, John Jay, who was "believed to entertain the same obnoxious principles with Mr. Adams," was "held in peculiar distrust and disesteem" among "the western people," who considered him "their most dangerous enemy."[44] In the course of the discussion, Madison revealed quite unmistakably that, like his friends, he had concluded that the imitation of the British system of administration would be pushed until it undermined the government itself.[45]

The first session of the Second Congress saw little in the way of major legislation. Attention focused on enlarging and apportioning the House according to the recently completed census, on the failure of Arthur St. Clair's expedition against the western tribes, and on a further assumption of state debts. Nevertheless, both the first and the last of these issues touched vitally on the concerns that Jefferson and Madison were privately expressing to the great commander. In the arguments about apportioning the House, the advocates of a 1:30,000 ratio of representatives to population—the fullest representation possible under the Constitution—advanced a systematic condemnation of the replication in the new United States of the corrupting practices that had subordinated Parliament to the executive in Britain. Like Jefferson and Madison, Giles and others made it clear that they considered ownership of public bonds or bank stock incompatible with legislative independence. Like Jefferson, they were convinced that such corruption had to be combated by enlarging the House of Representatives and overwhelming its stockjobbers and bank directors with genuine representatives of the agricultural interest.[46] Similarly, the opponents of additional assumptions of state debts resisted both the new inequities involved and the perpetuation of the fund on which the influence of the Treasury depended.[47] Opposition sentiment was moving strongly toward the measures of the second session, when Giles would introduce his resolutions censuring the secretary of the treasury's administration of the national finances and Jefferson and Madison would favor constitutional amendments to exclude the treasury dependents from Congress.[48]

During these debates, as Hamilton conceded in his lengthy letter analyzing the Virginians' opposition to his programs, Madison was usually content to let his allies take the lead and make the major speeches. This was not the case, however, when he saw additional attempts to push beyond the limitations of the Constitution, to enlarge executive prerogatives, or even (in an imitation of the practices of monarchies) to put the image of the president on coins.[49] Overhanging every other issue of the session in his mind, were the constitutional and other questions raised by Hamilton's Report on Manufactures. Sending this to Henry Lee, Madison asked the volatile ex-cavalryman what he thought of Hamilton's employment of the general welfare clause to justify the use of bounties as a means of encouraging native productions. "The federal government," he noted, "has been hitherto limited to the specified powers by the greatest champions for latitude in expounding those powers. If not only the *means* but the *objects* are unlimited, the parchment had better be thrown into the fire at once.''[50]

When Lee replied with a fierce condemnation of Hamilton's system of "rivetting on these states" schemes "imitative of the base principles and wicked measures" of European monarchies, schemes encouraging the manufacturing and monied interests at the expense of virtuous ploughmen,[51] Madison drew back to reassure his friend that things were not as bad as they would have been if the Constitution had been defeated. Still, he added,

> With respect to the general spirit of the administration, you already know how far my ideas square with yours. You know also how extremely offensive some particular measures have been; and I will frankly own (though the remark is for yourself alone at present) that if they should be followed by the usurpations of power recommended in the Report on Manufactures, I shall consider the fundamental and characteristic principle of the government as subverted. It will no longer be a government possessing special powers taken from the general mass, but one possessing the general mass with special powers reserved out of it. And this change will take place in defiance of the true and universal construction, and of the sense in which the instrument is known to have been proposed, advocated, and ratified. Whether the people of this country will submit to a Constitution not established by themselves but imposed on them by their rulers is a problem to be solved by the event alone.[52]

From the beginning of session, Madison had been attempting everything he could to influence this event. The salience of constitutional concerns in his infrequent interventions in debates had been impossible to miss. Then, on February 6, he swept in like a hawk to strike at arguments that bounties were a constitutional exercise of the power to promote the general welfare, elaborating the contentions of his letters to Edmund Pendleton and Lee. Should this construction be accepted, he complained, it would "convert the government from one limited as hitherto supposed . . . into a government without any limits at all. . . . Everything, from the highest object of state legislation down to the most minute object of police would be thrown under the power of Congress," for almost any purpose "would admit the application of money and might be called, if Congress pleased, provisions for the general welfare."[53]

As Drew McCoy has written, the Report on Manufactures was Hamilton's response to Madison's (and Jefferson's) campaign for commercial discrimination.[54] The capstone of the great succession of reports in which the secretary of the treasury unfolded his ambitious vision for the nation,

it also marked the culmination of a disagreement that had been developing since the conclusion of the peace: a disagreement in which Madison
and Hamilton (though neither was aware of all of the opinions of the
other) had emerged as probably the most effective spokesmen for conflicting understandings of the purposes of constitutional reform.[55]

Confronted with the crisis of the middle 1780s, Madison had become
convinced that constitutional reform was necessary to combat the European regulations that impeded oceanic trade, depressed the national
economy, and led to legislation that endangered the republican commitment or encouraged economic changes dangerous for a republic. Hamilton, by contrast, had come to be increasingly committed to intensive
economic change. For him, the sound solution to the problems of the
farmers was to build a large internal market for their goods. Economic
self-sufficiency, in any case, was indispensable to national greatness. In
addition, whereas Madison and Jefferson believed that the United States
could force the British toward a world of freer trade, Hamilton believed
that a developed state would triumph in an economic confrontation with
a less-developed rival. In the meantime, the financial system, which supported all his other plans, could be disastrously affected by obstruction of
the flow of British imports. Therefore, the Report on Manufactures systematically addressed the reservations of agrarian opponents, explained
the universal benefits of economic growth, insisted on the constitutionality
of federal encouragement of native manufactures, and recommended federal bounties as the most effectual incentive. Madison was not mistaken
to conclude that Hamilton's political economy was hardly less consistent
with his own ambitions for the nation than the secretary's systems of administration and finance. If added to the funding program and the bank,
the plan for manufactures could tighten and extend the links between
the federal executive and factions bound to its desires by multiple pecuniary favors. It could entrench a dangerous construction of the Constitution. It could push the country toward a set of social circumstances
incompatible with its republican ideals—which seemed, increasingly, exactly what some Federalists intended. Thus, as capstone of a systematic
program to remold the infant government into a shape that would subvert
the Revolution, the Report on Manufactures was, to Madison, the trigger
and the context for a great campaign to rouse the people to defend the
revolutionary order they and the Convention had intended to complete.

In the process that transformed disputes among the leaders of the new
republic into open party war, few developments were more portentous

than the founding of the *National Gazette*. Freneau initiated publication of
the semiweekly paper on October 31, 1791, about a month before Hamilton submitted the Report on Manufactures. For most of the remainder
of the year, while he was building circulation, the editor maintained a
basically nonpartisan position. By winter, this disguise was wearing thin;
and in the spring, the paper carried a crescendo of attacks on the financial
system and the motives of its author and supporters. Aided by Freneau
and choosing pseudonyms that would remind their readers of the heroes
of the classical or British oppositions to destroyers of republics, "Caius,"
"Brutus," "Sidney," and their friends constructed a coherent ideology
explaining their resistance to administration programs and appealing to
the public for support. Hamilton was only slightly off his mark when he
initiated public warfare with his foes by striking at Freneau's position as
a clerk in Jefferson's department: "The editor of the *National Gazette* re-
ceives a salary from government. *Quere*—Whether this salary is paid him
for *translations* or for *publications* the design of which is to vilify those to
whom the voice of the people has committed the administration of public
affairs."[56] The *National Gazette* was certainly the leading vehicle for the
development and national dissemination of a powerful, coherent ideology
of opposition, and there is every reason to believe that it was acting as the
organ of a rapidly emerging party.[57]

"Party," to be sure, is not the proper term for what the opposition
leaders thought they were creating. Neither did Freneau conduct his paper under anyone's direction; he and his contributors were working as an
undirected team with shared objectives and a common set of mental tools.
Still, as had been true from the beginning, Freneau's relationship with
Madison was close—a good deal closer than the one with his employer.
Just how close is open to conjecture. The absence of a written record
means that we can only wonder whether the one-time classmates discussed
a strategy for the gazette or if Madison enlisted some of the anonymous
contributors to the Republican campaign. All we know for certain is that
Madison himself wrote nineteen essays for the paper. These proceeded,
much as did the paper as a whole, from nonspecific pieces laying down a
groundwork for direct attacks to hammerblows against the Hamiltonian
design. Interwoven with the series signed by "Brutus," "Sidney," and the
like, along with scores of squibs and columns by Freneau, the unsigned
essays made a major contribution to the opposition's effort to define itself
and carry its position to the public, which was a vital step in the formation
of a popular political party. Moreover, although the essays for the *National
Gazette* have not been studied with the diligence reserved for Madison's
writings and speeches of 1787 and 1788, they merit similar attention.[58]
They represent, at once, an effort to explain the author's earlier positions

and another major landmark in the evolution of his thought. Like his acts and speeches in the First Federal Congress, they did not repudiate or even contradict *The Federalist* or speeches in the federal and state conventions. Rather, they illuminated the assumptions of preceding years as those, in turn, throw needed light on them. Not, indeed, until the contributions to *The Federalist* and to the *National Gazette* are seen as parts of one evolving corpus—not until the sets of essays have been read together, each within its context and as each explains the other—can we grasp Madison's vision as a whole.[59]

The publication order of the essays for Freneau's gazette is something of a puzzle. They do not comprise a series but a set of little pieces, each essentially complete and none referring to the others. Although seventeen were published during the first session of the Second Congress (and the final two before the second session gathered in the fall), they do not appear to have been written in direct relationship to what was happening in Congress at that point or to the press of current national events (apart from the appearance of the Report on Manufactures). There is evidence that several of the essays, mostly those appearing early in the set, were fragments of a lengthy, systematic treatise that Madison had been considering as early as the spring of 1791, when he declined to take a room at Jefferson's because he had assigned himself a "little task" for which he had his books and papers spread about him.[60] If this was so, however, Madison did not adopt the systematic ordering of contents of the notebook he was using for that project and would draw upon for drafts of several essays. That notebook, published in his papers as "Notes for the *National Gazette* Essays,"[61] moves in philosophical progression from the influence of the size of a nation on government through the influences of the stage of society, public opinion, education, religion, and slavery, toward a consideration of the government and political economy of the United States. The essays, on the other hand, begin with general reflections on political economy, interrupted by the essay "Consolidation," and move from there into a scattershot of three quite different pieces introducing themes that were to be returned to for direct attacks on Hamilton's designs: "Public Opinion," "Government," and "Charters." After these, Madison alternated more and more direct attacks on Hamiltonian finance with stronger and stronger condemnations of admiration of the British constitution, bringing these distinctive lines of argument together only in the last three essays. If something more was meant to be implicit in this order, it has yet to be described.

More evident, I think, are the political and intellectual concerns that Madison was trying to address. Both, it seems, had welled up in his mind during the spring and summer of 1791, following his third defeat on commercial discrimination, shortly after the creation of the bank, and probably about the same time as he recommended a position for Freneau. Both concerns solidified during the furor over Jefferson and Paine and as he watched the greedy scramble for the "public plunder" represented by the bank stock. He may well have promised to contribute something to the paper in the course of the negotiations with Freneau. He may have made a firm decision only in the fall, prompted both by the arrival of a British minister to the United States and by the imminence of the Report on Manufactures, in which Hamilton revealed the full dimensions of his own contrasting views.[62] At either point, he would have had the same political objective: to arouse a public that appeared disturbingly complacent in the face of tendencies and programs that he now believed might be deliberately counterrevolutionary in intent. Politically, he meant to bring his own variety of Federalists together with the body of the old opponents of the Constitution to compose a vigilant, awakened, and "republican" resistance to these schemes, much as he had always sought to bring these groups together in the Congress. Intellectually—for Madison was never simply a polemicist or propagandist—the task he put upon his table was a good deal more complex.

The Constitution, it was now apparent, was in practice more ambiguous than he had once expected it to be. In operation, it did not define for everyone, as clearly as it did for him, that "middle ground" which he had sought throughout the later 1780s: the vital "mean" between state sovereignty and an excessive concentration of authority in distant, unresponsive hands. To Madison himself, the grounds for a correct interpretation of the Constitution seemed apparent. Since 1789, he had repeatedly suggested that the arguments surrounding the adoption of the charter had defined its fundamental character and meaning. A national covenant had been completed when supporters of the Constitution answered its opponents with specific promises and explanations. Although important matters of detail were yet be determined by contingencies and practice, the basic lines of the division of authority between the general government and states, together with the lines between the branches of the general government itself, had been identified in national deliberations and were clear enough to hold. The lines would prove defensible, his numbers of *The Federalist* had said, because all parts of all these governments would be responsive to a common master, who would keep them all within the boundaries that national discussion had defined.

In fact, however, even the adoption of the first amendments had by no means settled the essential meaning of the Constitution. Neither had it settled underlying disagreements over the essential character and needs of the compound republic outlined in the Constitution. To Madison's extreme embarrassment—and, once again, we must not underestimate the force of his conviction that his own and national honor were at stake— the direst prophecies about the dangers of the Constitution's sweeping clauses were already coming true. The federal division of responsibilities, together with the lines between the branches of the central government itself, were both increasingly endangered. The general government was not responding to the common master: the agricultural majority that he had solemnly assured Virginia Antifederalists would guarantee the safety of the South and the West and, with them, the perpetuation of the Union and the cause of liberty itself. Therefore, the advantages and—more especially—the vulnerabilities of large, compound republics would have to be rethought. Why were things not working as he had hoped? What was the solution? The assumptions that had underpinned *The Federalist* would have to be examined and explained more thoroughly than he had needed to pursue them in that work. The practicable sphere of a republic, the people's role therein, and the conditions necessary if the people were to play that role would all require additional consideration.

The centrality of these concerns in Madison's own thinking is suggested by the notebook that he drew on for several of the essays. We cannot be absolutely sure that he began this notebook in the spring of 1791, that he was thinking of composing an extended work on the American republic, or even that the notes all date to any single time. Nevertheless, the "Notes on Government," as Colleen Sheehan calls them, do seem more suggestive of the worries of the spring than of the winter of 1791–92, when the essays finally appeared. They do appear to have been organized as a beginning toward a systematic exploration of the social, educational, and economic circumstances that support or threaten free regimes. And Madison left ample space between his jottings for further entries and ideas.

Several of the themes that lend coherence to the essays are prefigured in these notes. In both, Madison held to his idea that an extension of the sphere is an appropriate, republican corrective for the vices most endemic to republics: the necessary cure for instability and popular abuses. But even in his earlier developments of this idea, Madison had recognized, although he had not stressed, that an enlargment of the size of a republic carries with it an inherent risk of governmental "independence" from the people. The rulers of a large republic would be distanced from the voters, less familiar with their needs, and better situated to escape entirely from dependence on their will. Therefore, Madison as "Publius" had said, the rulers of the federal republic had been given only those essential powers, few and carefully defined, that could be safely trusted to their hands. Along with checks and balances within the central government

itself, the federal structure was a necessary surety against the risk of unresponsive rule.

By 1791, however, all of these securities seemed threatened. All of
them together seemed unequal to their task. The reasons had been growing clearer year by year. Madison had always known that none of these
securities was automatic or sufficient, either singly or when linked with all
the others. Useful, even necessary, as they were, the constitutional divisions of political authority depended on the voters, who had to be alert
enough and well enough informed to jerk them taut whenever government officials took advantage of the slack. This, of course, the people and
the states had seemed, if anything, entirely too prepared to do through
most of the preceding decade. In 1788, as one perceptive scholar has
observed, a vigorous and active public was the least of Federalist concerns;
Madison and others had been able to *assume* effective and continuing
involvement.[63] By 1791, however, everything seemed to have changed. The
tiny central government touched lightly on the lives of ordinary people,
who sometimes lacked the information to remain abreast of federal decisions even when they had an interest in the central government's affairs.
With the adoption of the Constitution, old assumptions had been rendered problematic, unanticipated difficulties had emerged, and many of
the preconditions for a healthy public life had come to seem endangered.
The creation of the *National Gazette* was an initial step toward a corrective.
Now, the paper would be used to explicate the danger and encourage
popular employment of the leash.

"Population and Emigration," the first of Madison's essays, opens with
the observation that humans, like other animals, have a natural capacity
to reproduce beyond their current numbers and even beyond the limits
of subsistence.[64] But what may seem at first, quick glance to be the ru-
minations of a natural philosopher, turns out to be an argument with a
decidedly political intent: one that may have been connected with the
spring defeat on commercial discrimination as well as with the imminence
of the Report on Manufactures in the fall. Madison maintains that sound
morality (since vices flourish best in thickly settled places), an increase in
the happiness and numbers of the species, and even the productions of
the lands from which the emigrants depart are all facilitated by a liberal
policy concerning emigration.[65] In the conclusion, he observes that although the body of the essay might appear to have slight application to
the situation of the new United States, it might at least "prevent mistaken
and narrow ideas on an important subject." Followed quickly by "Dependent Territories," which condemned monopolistic exploitation of the
colonies established by a mother state—like slavery, exploitative policies
encouraged "pride, luxury, and vanity on one side; on the other, vice and

servility or hatred and revolt"—"Population and Emigration" was intended to allay concerns that westward emigration would depopulate
"Connecticut, Rhode Island, or New Jersey" and retard the development
of native manufactures.[66] Madison's perduring dedication to the westward
movement and to equal treatment for emerging western states, together
with his running battle with "illiberal" attitudes in Congress, were evident
in the conclusion of the piece. And in conjunction with the two-part essay
"Money," written mostly in 1780 but suggesting that the value of a paper
currency (or of certificates of debt?) must fall unless there seems a certainty of its eventual redemption, "Population" and "Dependent Territories" cleared a path for more direct attacks on Hamilton's political
economy.[67]

Meanwhile, between "Population and Emigration" and "Dependent
Territories," Madison had introduced another unifying theme for several
later essays. "Consolidation," published on December 3, is critical to the
continuing debate about how Madison may have shifted his position in
the years surrounding the adoption of the Constitution. Scholars who believe that Madison had been an eager centralizer in the years before the
Constitutional Convention or that *Federalist* no. 10 was an unqualified endorsement of a large republic have pointed to "Consolidation" as an
obvious retreat, complete with second thoughts about the virtues of a
multiplicity of interests. In this essay, Madison maintained that "a consolidation of the states into one government" (or even an increasing concentration of responsibilities in federal hands) would necessarily produce
two dangerous effects. First, because a single legislature could never over-
see the multifarious concerns traditionally confided to the states, consolidation would inevitably demand such concentration of authority in the
executive department as would force a choice between abandoning a single chief executive or accepting such an increase in the "splendor" and
"prerogatives" of this official as would move the nation toward a king.
Second, an excessive concentration of authority would render it impossible to gather or to call into effect the genuine opinions of the people,
which were currently conveyed through many "local organs" of opinion.
In such a situation, the impossibility of acting with effect could lead to
"universal silence" and indifference in the people. And without effective
popular control, "which is essential to a faithful discharge of its trust,"
the legislature too would quickly be released to follow a "*self-directed course,*
which, it must be owned, is the natural propensity of every government."[68]

Almost as though to answer those who have interpreted the tenth *Federalist* as an argument for *multiplying* the variety of interests in a state (or
who have argued that its author wanted to confine the people's role to
choosing their officials), "Consolidation" argues that a certain "unifor-

mity" of "sentiments" and "interests" is essential to permit accommo-
dative legislation and to make unnecessary the accumulation of "new and
dangerous prerogatives" in the executive department: "The less the supposed difference of interests and the greater the concord and confidence
throughout the great body of the people, . . . the more seasonably can they
interpose a common manifestation of their sentiments, the more certainly
will they take alarm at usurpation or oppression, and the more effectually
will they *consolidate* their defense of public liberty." "Consolidation" was
a plea for unity between the friends of state authority and all "who may
be more inclined to contemplate the people of America in the light of
one nation"—unity in order to resist the centralizers, but also to eradicate
"local prejudices and mistaken rivalships" and thus to "erect over the
whole one paramount empire of reason, benevolence, and brotherly affection." Reminding us again that Madison conceived of clashing interests
as an evil, though an unavoidable and even useful evil, the essay raised a
standard to which all who feared the consequences of the Hamiltonian
design could rally in defense of the compound republic. It advocated both
the healing stance between the Antifederalists and higher-flying Federalists that Madison had taken at the outset of the first new Congress *and*
his call for a fraternal, "patriotic" consideration of the needs of all.

With essay number 6, Madison was ready for his scattershot of pieces
introducing his most serious concerns. "Public Opinion" drew even more
extensively than "Consolidation" on sections 1 and 3 of his notebook,
pursuing his concerns about the proper size of a republic, the people's
role therein, and the consequences of excessive centralization. "The
larger a country," Madison observed, the harder it would be for the public's true opinion to be ascertained. But once this true opinion was "pre-
sumed" (or even "counterfeited"), that opinion would be even more
effective than it was in smaller states. The larger the country, the more
insignificant each individual would feel—a fact "unfavorable to liberty"
and powerfully supporting the authority of any government that could
pretend to follow this "real sovereign" of every free regime. Accordingly,
"Whatever facilitates a general intercourse of sentiments, as good roads,
domestic commerce, a free press, and particularly a *circulation of newpapers
through the entire body of the people* and *representatives going from and returning
among every part of them,* is equivalent to a contraction of territorial limits,
and is favorable to liberty where these may be too extensive."[69] Though
Madison had not retreated from the view that an extension of the sphere
of a republic was a valuable corrective for majority abuses, he was still
determined to define that "middle ground" for which he had been
searching for some years: the "mean" between too little central power

and too much, between too unrestrained a following of the majority's immediate demands and power not responsive to majorities at all.

"Government" (December 31) reiterated Madison's insistence that aristocracy or monarchy were poorly suited to extensive states despite the greater tendency of larger states to favor the hereditary forms: "A representative republic chooses the wisdom of which hereditary aristocracy has the chance, whilst it excludes the oppression of that form. And a confederated republic attains the force of monarchy whilst it equally avoids the ignorance of a good prince and the oppression of a bad one." Nevertheless, in order to secure this system, Madison observed, "every good citizen" would have to be "at once a sentinel over the rights of the people, over the authorities of the confederal government, and over both the rights and the authorities of the intermediate governments."[70]

The implications were driven home in "Charters" (January 18, 1792). In Europe, this began, "charters of liberty have been granted by power. America has set the example, and France has followed it, of charters of power granted by liberty. This revolution in the practice of the world may, with an honest praise, be pronounced the most triumphant epoch of its history"; and in proportion to the unexampled value of this revolution "ought to be the vigilance" with which these charters should be guarded by the people and respected by those citizens who hold the "public trust." Americans, who originated this epochal revolution and established a complex division of authority between the central government and the states, will be peculiarly judged by their success "in defending liberty against power, and power against licentiousness." "How devoutly," then, it was to be desired that an enlightened public would attach itself to "these political scriptures" and defend them "with a holy zeal." To Madison, a written constitution "authenticated by . . . the only earthly source" of legitimate political authority—the people acting in their highest sovereign role—was not only "superior in obligation to all other" compacts. It was literally "sacred." It was to be, not just respected, but revered.[71]

With "Charters," Madison completed his foundation for increasingly direct attacks on his political opponents. Building on concessions he had made (but had not emphasized) in 1787 and 1788, he had articulated his concerns about the vulnerabilities of large republics, which he had always known would have to be combated both by rigorous defense of constitutional divisions of authority and by a statesmanlike attention to the means of spreading national information and facilitating the development of an involved and educated public (a process that appeared, at once, more problematic and more urgent by 1792). "Parties" (January 23) made a nice transition to his main attack. Here, in what I take as a direct rebuttal of a popular misreading of *Federalist* no. 10, Madison condemned financial schemes that added "artificial" to the "natural" differences among the people. Parties, he repeated, are an unavoidable result of different interests, which every civilized society will have. They are nonetheless an "evil," and the object of enlightened statesmen ought to be to "combat the evil":

> 1. By establishing a political equality among all. 2. By withholding *unnecessary* opportunities from a few to increase the inequality of property by an immoderate, and especially an unmerited, accumulation of riches. 3. By the silent operation of laws which, without violating the rights of property, reduce extreme wealth towards a state of mediocrity and raise extreme indigence towards a state of comfort. 4. By abstaining from measures which operate differently on different interests, and particularly such as favor one interest at the expense of another. 5. By making one party a check on the other so far as the existence of parties cannot be prevented, nor their views accommmodated.

"In all political societies," Madison still believed, "different interests and parties arise out of the nature of things, and the great art of politicians lies in making them checks and balances to each other." Nevertheless, "from the expedience in politics of making natural parties mutual checks on each other, to infer the propriety of creating artificial parties, in order to form them into mutual checks, is not less absurd than it would be in ethics to say that new vices ought to be promoted, where they would counteract each other, because this use may be made of existing vices." The latter policy—and Hamilton's financial program plainly looms between the lines—is not, said Madison, the way of reason or the wish of the defenders of republics. And a *multiplication* of parties was not what Madison had recommended in 1787 and 1788, any more than he had meant to justify a large republic on the grounds that it would frustrate the desires of a *non*factious majority of the people.[72]

With the groundwork thus prepared, Madison was ready for his main attack. Here, in alternating sets of essays—one objecting to the policies, the other to the unrepublican opinions of his foes—he laid down what amounted to a walking cannonade against the sentiments and programs of the Federalists of 1792, concluding with a thundering barrage accusing his opponents of deliberately attempting to subvert the Constitution and transform the new republic into a second Britain.

Madison had been aware for years that some of the supporters of the Constitution openly admired the British system and that many of them thought (or even actually hoped) that the United States would someday adopt a mixed regime. At the Constitutional Convention, Hamilton had openly confessed his skepticism that a representative democracy would do.[73] John Adams was (in Madison's opinion) a public advocate of the superiority of British institutions who had tirelessly employed his office and his pen in a campaign for titles, much as Hamilton had worked consistently for greater federal power, especially for its executive officials. Thus, in four of his remaining essays, Madison attempted to demolish the opinion that property was safer in a government with only one elective branch or that Great Britain was in any sense a proper model for the new United States.

"The boasted equilibrium" of Britain's constitution, he maintained in "British Government," was not a consequence of institutional arrangements but of popular opinion in that country—in so far as Britain really had (or had historically possessed) a governmental equilibrium at all.[74] Madison reminded those who were inclined to praise the British system or to imitate the policies of British statesmen of the Lockean foundations of the Revolution. "As a man is said to have a right to his property, he may be equally said to have a property in his rights": in his opinions and their free communication; in the practice and profession of his faith; in "the free use of his faculties and free choice of the objects on which to employ them"; and, in short, in "everything to which a man may attach a value . . . and which leaves to everyone else the like advantage." Government was "instituted to protect property of every sort," not merely property defined as one's material possessions. No government was worth admiring which did not "impartially secure to every man whatever is his own." And judged by these criteria, he made it clear, neither the British government nor British economic practices were worthy "pattern[s]" for Americans to follow. However well these guarded individuals' material possessions, the British system also violated in a myriad of ways "the property which individuals have in their opinions, their religion, their persons, and their faculties." Through its mercantilist economic system and its grinding and invasive taxes, the British system even violated "that sacred property which Heaven, in decreeing man to earn his bread by the sweat of his brow, kindly reserved to him in [also permitting] the small repose that could be spared from the supply of his necessities" for leisure and relief from his fatigues.[75]

To Madison, Great Britain was, in truth, a model for little except corruption. In one of his cleverest essays, "Spirit of Governments," he proposed to replace Montesquieu's famous categorization of governments into those depending on fear, honor, or virtue with one distinguishing between those governments which rested on "a permanent military force," those which derived their energy "from the will of the society" and operated by appealing to its understanding and interests, and those which operated "by corrupt influence." In writing of the latter, he was unmistakably referring both to England and to Hamiltonian attempts to replicate the British system of administration and finance. This was a government

> substituting the motive of private interest in place of public duty; converting its pecuniary dispensations into bounties to favorites or bribes to opponents; accommodating its measures to the avidity of a part of the nation instead of the benefit of the whole: in a word, enlisting an army of interested partisans whose tongues, whose pens, whose intrigues, and whose active combinations, by supplying the [place of] the terror of the sword, may support a real domination of the few under an apparent liberty of the many.[76]

"Spirit of Governments" followed the essay "Universal Peace," which condemned the modern practice of financing wars by means of perpetual funded debts,[77] and was immediately succeeded by Madison's most direct replies to the Report on Manufactures. Nothing in the set is more revealing than this latter group of essays of the vision that had guided him throughout the founding of the federal republic.

"Republican Distribution of Citizens" (March 3, 1792) suggested that "a perfect theory on this subject," although not enforceable by legislation, could at least provide a warning against "experiments by power." The distribution most appropriate for a republic, Madison opined, would be the one "which would most favor health, virtue, intelligence, and competency in the greatest number of citizens." The life of the "husbandman" was "preeminently suited" to them all. Intelligence could be as well developed in the country as in any walk of life. "The extremes both of want and of waste have other abodes," as do insanity and crime; "tis not the country that peoples either the Bridewells or the Bedlams. These mansions of wretchedness are tenanted from the distresses and vices of overgrown cities."[78]

If the farmer's life was most ideally suited for a citizen of a republic, the sailor's life was least: monotonous and stultifying, poor and constantly exposed to every scene of vice.[79] Between these two extremes were all who worked the raw materials and agricultural productions of the earth, to which there might be added lawyers, merchants, and the members of the various professions. The numbers of the latter would adjust themselves according to demand. As to the former, it was happy for humanity—and for America especially—that so many of the most essential manufactures could be "prepared in every family," often on the farm. "The regular branches of manufacturing and mechanical industry," Madison believed, should be promoted or discouraged according to the kind of life they would promote. "Whatever is least favorable to vigor of body, to the faculties of the mind or the utilities of life, instead of being forced or fostered by public authority, ought to be seen with regret as long as occupations more friendly to human happiness lie vacant." Madison was not, as has been noted, an unbending enemy of every form of governmental aid for necessary manufactures. In his determined quest for reciprocity from Britain, he acted as a dedicated champion of native shippers. But when it came to higher manufactures or to favoring the mercantile pursuits at the expense of better modes of life, to pushing their emergence prematurely, or—especially—to forcing their emergence at the price of equal rights and other people's dedication to the Union, Madison was wholly Jeffersonian in his reaction.[80]

The line to be regarded by a sound republican administration—the line that Hamilton was crossing—he clarified in "Fashion." In Britain, Madison remarked, the Prince of Wales had lately been petitioned to return to wearing buckled shoes. A sudden preference for shoestrings and slippers had destroyed the jobs of twenty thousand people. "The most precarious of all occupations," Madison concluded, were those "depending on mere fashion"; and of all the occupations, those were "least desirable in a free state which produce the most servile dependence of one class of citizens on another." The contrast between America and Britain could not be more instructive on this point (whether one considered the advisability of economic confrontation with the British or the wisdom of encouraging the higher manufactures). In America, the great majority of citizens were occupied in tilling their own soil, supplying labor necessary for the cultivation of the land, or "in supplying wants" that satisfied real needs. This ensured a comfortable subsistence for the working poor. More than that, the "independent situation" and "reciprocity of dependence" among such citizens encouraged "manly sentiments" and inspired "a dignified sense of social rights." In proportion as a nation consists of individuals who depend for their livelihoods on external commerce or luxury productions, "it is dependent on the consumption and caprice of other nations," and is, Madison believed, poorly suited to sustain a sound republic.[81]

Madison considered the government of the United States humankind's most admirable political achievement. In his essay "Government of the United States," he insisted that if it could be sustained, it might well prove "the best legacy ever left by lawgivers to their country and the best lesson ever given to the world by its benefactors." Other nations, though with less success, had separated the great departments of government and divided the legislative power between two separate houses: "a first principle of [all] free governments." To these contrivances, however, the United States had added written constitutions and a form of government derived entirely from elections.

> The political system of the United States claims still higher praise. The power delegated by the people is first divided between the general government and the state governments, each of which is then subdivided into legislative, executive, and judiciary departments. And as in a single government these departments are to be kept separate and safe by a defensive armor for each, so, it is to be hoped, do the two governments possess each the means of preventing or correcting unconstitutional encroachments of the other.[82]

But all of this was fragile. All of it had preconditions—facts that Madison had recognized (if not so clearly) but had had no cause to dwell on five years before. If it was hard enough to maintain the division of powers between the branches of a single government, he now conceded, it would be harder still to maintain the one between the general government and the states. And yet, however difficult it was, maintenance of this division was a task that "must by no means be abandoned," for to do so would entail a choice between disunion and consolidation, "both of them bad, but the latter the worst, since it is the high road to monarchy, than which nothing worse, in the eye of republicans, could result from the anarchy implied by the former." Every patriot, in Madison's opinion, had to be involved in explicating and defending the constitutional boundaries between the central government and the states, in urging moderation in the policies of both, and in abstaining from such policies as might sustain existing jealousies or generate still greater ones. Every patriot should understand that

> In bestowing the eulogies due to the partitions and internal checks of power, it ought not the less to be remembered that they are neither the sole nor the chief palladium of constitutional liberty. The people who are the authors of this blessing, must also be its guardians. Their eyes must be ever ready to mark, their voice to pronounce, and their arm to repel or repair aggressions on the authority of their constitutions: the highest authority next to their own, because the immediate work of their own, and the most sacred part of their property, as recognizing and recording the title to every other.

And every patriot, of course, should recognize how incompatible was all of this with Federalist opinion, Hamiltonian finance, and Hamiltonian administration.

From the beginning of his essays, Madison had been appealing to the genuine supporters of the Constitution, Federalists and Antifederalists alike, to come together to defend the people's charter and the social and political conditions under which the great republican experiment could thrive. On March 31, with all the anger that had swelled in him when his opponents claimed to be more federal than he, he closed the essays written while the Second Congress was in session by asking who were truly the supporters of the Union. Not, he answered, those who multiplied its enemies by "pampering the spirit of speculation" and accumulating debts (and with those debts the sources of corruption and new taxes). Not, he added, those who labored by their forced constructions of the Constitution "to pervert the limited government of the Union into a government of unlimited discretion, contrary to the will and subversive of the authority of the people." Not those who advocated monarchy, betrayed a preference for hereditary power, or espoused "a system of measures more accommodated to the depraved examples of those hereditary forms than to the true genius of our own." The real supporters of the Union were the citizens who recognized that "the authority of the people" was the Union's "sole foundation," liberty its end, and a "limited and republican system of government the means provided by that authority for the attainment of that end." The real friends of the Union were those who saw a public debt as injurious to the people and "baneful to the virtue of the government," who would resist its increase, and who would stand as "enemies to every public measure that might smooth the way to hereditary government." The real supporters of the Union were the citizens and statesmen who cherished the compound republic as the only structure capable of winning popular allegiance and consistent with the revolutionary principles that continental union was intended to protect.[83]

When Madison returned to Philadelphia at the beginning of November 1792, he returned as legislative leader of a governmental faction that was quickly evolving into a full-fledged party. Here and there, congressional campaigns were being fought with party weapons, and although Washington himself was unopposed, the Republicans were trying to unseat John Adams.[84] During the recess of Congress, Hamilton had opened his attack on Jefferson and Jefferson's connection with the *National Gazette*. Madison and James Monroe had started a defense of Jefferson against his rival's unrelenting accusations in the press.[85] Treated to the spectacle of public war between the two great ministers of state, people everywhere were mobilizing in support of the conflicting parties.[86] And in his next-to-last essay for the *National Gazette*, Madison had made his most direct attempt to influence the campaign.

"A Candid State of Parties," published on September 22, 1792, brought together nearly all the themes developed in the spring. It was a powerful appeal to Federalists and former Antifederalists to recognize the wiles of crafty men who would divide "those who never differed as to the end to be pursued, and may no longer differ as to the means." Although the original supporters of the Constitution did, "no doubt," include some men "who were openly or secretly attached to monarchy and aristocracy, and hoped to make the Constitution a cradle for these hereditary establishments," the great majority of Federalists "were unquestionably friends to republican liberty." Similarly, although a few of the opponents of the Constitution might have been exceptions, "the great body were certainly well affected to the Union and to good government." In any case, the essay argued, this division "was terminated by the regular and effectual establishment of the federal government in 1788." It had already been replaced by a division that arose "out of the administration" of the new federal system. And only one of these new parties, "being the weaker in point of numbers," had an interest in strengthening itself with men of monied influence and weakening its opponents "by reviving exploded parties and taking advantage of all prejudices, local, political, and occupational, that may prevent or disturb a general coalition of sentiments."

One of these new parties, Madison maintained,

> consists of those who, from particular interest, from natural temper, or from the habits of life, are more partial to the opulent than to the other classes of society; and having debauched themselves into a persuasion that mankind are incapable of governing themselves, it follows with them, of course, that government can be carried on only by the pageantry of rank, the influence of money and emoluments, and the terror of military force. Men of those sentiments must naturally wish to point the measures of government less to the interest of the many than of a few, and less to the reason of the many than to their weaknesses, hoping perhaps . . . that by giving such a turn to the administration, the government itself may by degrees be narrowed into fewer hands and approximated to an hereditary form.

The other party was composed of those who hated hereditary power "as an insult to the reason and an outrage to the rights of man," who took offense at every measure that did not appeal "to the understanding and to the general interest of the community," who believed that men were "capable of governing themselves," and who would stand against every measure "that is not strictly conformable to the principles and conducive to the preservation of republican government." Unlike their opponents, "the Republican party, as it may be termed," was "conscious that the mass of people in every part of the Union, in every state, and of every occuption must at bottom be with them, both in interest and sentiment." It was thus the only party interested in "burying all antecedent questions" and "banishing every other distinction than that between enemies and friends to republican government," in seeing that the federal government would be administered "in the spirit and form approved by the great body of the people."[87]

The second session of the Second Congress was a theater for party war. Anticipating victory in the elections to the newly reapportioned House, Republicans intended to delay important business until the Third Congress met. In the meantime, Madison continued to oppose the practice of requesting cabinet officers to come in person for reports to Congress, a British habit which "involved a conclusion in respect to the principles of the government which, at an earlier day, would have been revolted from.[88] He quarreled with an effort to instruct the secretary of the treasury to report a plan for reducing the debt, insisting that the House should exercise deliberative functions on its own and that the secretary of the treasury already had an undue influence on the body.[89] He also stubbornly opposed a plan to use $2,000,000 marked for the repayment of a loan from France to pay, instead, the whole sum borrowed from the national bank at its creation. Only the first of ten installments on the latter loan was actually due, and Madison was deeply angered by a proposition to employ resources that were desperately needed for "the cause of liberty" abroad to benefit the speculators and the bank.[90]

During the debates about the use of this two million, Madison and others called repeatedly for explanation of the money that was lying in the Treasury without a clear accounting to the House. Republicans suspected that the secretary was involved in some financial trick and possibly in sheer mismanagement of the accounts. Virginia's Giles eventually succeeded in compelling a report, and the result provided the dramatic highlight of the session. Working day and night, Hamilton delivered everything the House had asked for by February 13, 1793. Madison was made the chairman of the House committee which examined the reports and recommended that selected documents be published.[91] As he wrote to Edmund Pendleton on February 23, the documents appeared to show that there had been "at least a very blamable irregularity" in Hamilton's procedures,[92] which had mixed together monies authorized by separate loans and brought to the United States a sum intended for repayment of the foreign debt. Madison appears to have preferred to drop the matter with the publication of these excerpts, which would have left the secretary dangling until the Third Congress convened. But Jefferson, who saw an opportunity to pay his rival back for his campaign of public vilification, had different ideas. On February 27, Giles proposed nine resolutions censuring Hamilton's conduct and attempting to compel his resignation.[93]

Madison supported Giles's Resolutions, which Jefferson had drafted. On March 1, he was one of only five congressmen who voted for them all.[94] But they were not his project. On the contrary, he seems to have believed that it was a strategic error to initiate this effort so late in the congressional session, and he was not surprised when it was overwhelmingly defeated.[95] Like Jefferson, he probably attributed the loss to the fundholders and bank directors in the House.[96] Like Jefferson, however, he also hoped that the next Congress would sink the treasury dependents in a flood of genuine representatives of the people,[97] and he was perfectly delighted by the news that Louis XVI had been deposed and a republic proclaimed in France. Throughout the session, the Republicans had watched the situation on the French frontiers in high anxiety about the fate of liberty in Europe, which they already thought would have enormous consequences for its fate in the United States.[98] Hardly had the session closed before the news arrived that France had also gone to war with Britain, development that would dramatically transform the political dispute at home.

Madison, however, had already set the course that he would hold to, with explainable and minor deviations, through the rest of his career. In December, in his final essay for the *National Gazette*, he had again defined its compass. Presenting his convictions in the form of a dialogue between a Republican and an Anti-republican, he left us with a lesson that should caution everyone who has been tempted to misjudge his fears and objects at the founding. "Who Are the Best Keepers of the People's Liberties?" the essay asked. "The people themselves," says the Republican. The Anti-republican may think that "the people are stupid, suspicious, licentious," that when they have established a good government, "they should think of nothing but obedience, leaving the care of their liberties to their wiser rulers." But the Republican believes that although "the people may betray themselves," it does not follow that they should surrender, blindfold, "to those who have an interest in betraying them. Rather, conclude that the people ought to be enlightened, to be awakened, to be united, that after

establishing a government they should watch over it, as well as obey it."
It was, said Madison, "a perversion of the natural order . . . to make *power*
the primary and central object of the social system, and *liberty* but its sat-
ellite."[99] How could scholars have concluded that he ever wanted the reverse, that he was ever anything except a tender of the fire?

CHAPTER TWELVE

Retrospect and Prospect

FROM THE PROGRESSIVE ERA TO OUR OWN, polemicists and scholars have disputed the intentions of the founders; and as modern scholarship has put him in his place as first among the framers of the Constitution, first among the writers and tacticians who secured its ratification, first among the congressmen who put a working federal government into effect, and first (once Jefferson's imposing shadow was removed) in organizing the resistance that eventually became the nation's oldest political party, Madison has naturally become a major focus for these disputations. Despite two hundred years of change, Americans prefer to stress the continuity of their political regime and thus to look back to the years surrounding the adoption of the Constitution for the principles behind it. There are still political advantages in an appeal to the authority of Madison or Jefferson or other "Founding Fathers," still a strong temptation to enlist them in a cause. And there is still an inclination, as there was in Charles Beard's day, to blame them for the evils thought to be endemic in the system. Indeed, as modern social critics have increasingly associated the "empowerment" of disadvantaged groups with how we understand and write about the past, as some of them have set about deliberately to reconstruct this understanding from the point of view of people who were once ignored, the inclination to condemn the founders may have risen to the point that it is stronger now than during Beard's own time. Progressives blasted the creators of a system that protected property at the expense of other rights and seemed to stand between the people and reform. Modern critics add that it protected slavery, permitted the extermination of the natives, and excluded women from political participation.

Scholars are the products of their time, and the canons of their disciplines do not invariably prevent them from transporting current arguments into their studies of the past. Moreover, there is surely some validity in asking what the founders might have thought about this issue or that. Madison and his contemporaries certainly believed that they were reasoning from universal principles and grappling with concerns of lasting relevance to any people dedicated to the rule of the majority, but dedicated also to the rights of individuals or groups who may not be a part of that majority on some or all occasions. In addition, the professionals whose disciplines are most concerned about the Founding do not carry with them only the contemporary worries and commitments that are brought to it by every reader of their works. They also bring their disciplines' professionally generated topics for dispute. Historians must ultimately fit the Founding into their interpretations of the larger stream of which it was a part—most commonly, in recent years, into professional analyses of the relationship between political developments and social change in the age of the democratic revolutions. Political theorists, by definition and profession, share in the historians' concern about the sources of the founders' thought. They also search for core assumptions and beliefs that may have universal import, and they do so in the light of a continuing professional dispute about the nature of modernity itself. Madison has therefore been entangled in professional as well as in political debates. In the Progressive era (and continuing, to some degree, today), he was ensnarled in a professional dispute about "the spirit of the Constitution" as contrasted with "the spirit of the Declaration of Independence." In the 1950s (and to some degree today), he was enlisted in the pluralist reply to Marx. Recent scholarship has added or returned to other knotty questions. Was Madison a democrat? Was he fundamentally a "liberal" or mostly a "republican" in the configurations of his thinking? Was his thinking wholly "modern?" Did he value order and the rights of property too highly? Did he chain us to ideas and institutions that are choking us today?

A modicum of common sense could help untangle several of these snarls. Without denying that the Madisons (and Hamiltons) have much to say to their descendants—indeed, I think that we ignore them or condemn them only at a cost—it needs to be remembered that the revolutionary generation neither planned nor hoped for what we have become, that they are only distantly and very partially responsible for what we like or hate about America today. If we and they do actually share some values and ideals, it is worth our while to study how they reasoned, for many in that generation thought about the fundamentals with uncommon clarity and to a depth that few today have plumbed. But there were other fundamentals, we should note, that most of that impressive generation quite deliberately evaded or that may have been beyond the limits of their great imaginations. Ours were not their worries. Some of theirs are little relevant today. And always, they approached their own concerns with mental tools that were significantly different from our own. Accordingly, perhaps exactly in proportion as we can in fact learn much of value from their generation, it is worth our while to start by hearing what they said, which is impossible to do without a thorough reconstruction of the circumstances under which they acted, wrote, or spoke. Madison was sometimes right and sometimes wrong, and individuals today are all entitled to their own (informed) opinions concerning when he was correct, misguided, or irrelevant to our concerns. First, however, let us hear from Madison himself and not from some theatrical concoction of our own political debates or of our current, doubtless fleeting scholarly conventions.

The Madison who speaks to us today through modern secondary studies is in largest part a creature of our own interpretive conventions. It is not James Madison we hear, but through thick earmuffs, a dramatic, distant character who echoes back imperfectly the fears or aspirations of a later time. The eighteenth-century gentleman whose most particular contempt was saved for the projectors, jobbers, and promoters of his day speaks powerfully, to one time, as the theorist of bourgeois counterrevolution. To another, he appears the spokesman (villainous or admirable, according to the writer's own convictions) for the modern "commercial" republic, which is pretty much what he profoundly hoped America would *not* become. The man who thought he was devoting his career to vindicating liberty—by which *he* meant a system based entirely on the people and responsive to their well-considered will—is summarized as having *meant* that ordinary people ought to have as small a part in governing as democratic notions would permit, so that the propertied might long protect themselves against the prospect of redistribution. The constant champion of charters and the ablest advocate that the United States has ever seen of an extended, but compound, republic is recast as a New Dealer who retreated from and then dissembled his original desire to centralize the system. The living figure who attempted desperately to *get around* a choice between two partially conflicting conceptions of human freedom, who tried to set a standard of disinterested public service, and who urged affectionate consideration for the interests of the other citizens who were embarked in the collective effort, is represented as a theorist who moved the nation from its classical republican to modern liberal foundations and assured it that a calm pursuit by everyone of their particular self-interests would suffice for modern times—if only, by mechanical contrivances, ambition could be made to counteract ambition.

The present author does not claim immunity from modern times or current scholarly conventions and contentions. But it is clear that many of the arguments surrounding Madison and many of the so-called inconsistencies or puzzles that sustain conflicting misinterpretations are the products of our own concerns, not his. Madison seems inconsistent or misguided, in substantial part, because he does not fit the patterns we ourselves impose upon the past. We presume that a consistent thinker would have done this thing or that. Madison did not. And we do not consider whether it is really *our* assumptions, not his own, that turn the facts into a problem.

This seems to me most clearly so with the prevailing understanding of the framer's thinking and objectives during the years before the Constitutional Convention. From Beard until the present, modern scholarship has focused overwhelmingly on Madison's (or the conservative elite's) unquestionable anxiety about the situation in the states, discounting or debunking his (or their) anxieties about the problems of the Union as a union. Insights have undoubtedly resulted from the modern fascination with the social sources of political contentions. But we have also come to be too ready to accept the language of the leading modern student of the new American republic:

> The defects of the Confederation . . . do not account for the elite's expression of crisis, nor do they explain the ambitious nature of the nationalists' Virginia Plan. . . . The nationalists' aims and the Virginia Plan went way beyond what the weaknesses of the Articles demanded. Granting Congress the authority to raise revenue, to regulate trade, to pay off its debts, and deal effectively in international affairs did not require the total scrapping of the Articles and the creation of an extraordinarily powerful and distant government, the like of which was virtually inconceivable to Americans a decade earlier.[1]

Elite concern about an "excess of democracy" does help explain the Federalists' sense of crisis. The Virginia Plan *was* aimed to overcome this crisis and is less than fully comprehensible unless we take these fears into account. Nevertheless, it was precisely the contention of the author of that plan that the debilities of the existing federal system were *insoluble* within the framework of the old Confederation. That conviction, not his very real concern about the mutability, injustices, and multiplicity of local laws, was the initial spark that led to his proposals for reform. Those proposals were unquestionably intended to attack the other malady as well. But sometimes, we might say, a crisis of the Union is exactly that—intrinsically and fundamentally political and governmental in its nature, not simply a reflection of an underlying argument between competing social groups.

At issue here is much besides an effort to recapture the exact progression of the founder's thoughts. For Madison insisted that the single greatest *source* of the majority abuses in the states was the Confederation's inability to handle its commercial problems and establish the conditions under which the Revolution could succeed. On top of that, he was about as worried by the evidence of a monarchical revival and of serious consideration of division of the Union as he was about majority injustice and the poorly balanced constitutions of the states, since he was certain that disintegration of the Union would lead to the destruction of the nation's liberal republics. Those republics—in the plural—he was altogether dedicated to preserving.

The Virginia Plan, as we have seen, was not a wholly national solution to the crises Madison intended to address. Madison was not a nationalist in many of the usual implications of that word—much less an advocate of multipling interests in an extended, "commercial" republic. He did not become an advocate of a consolidated, rather than a partly federal, republic because he always thought that concentrated central power would conflict with genuine dependence on the people; and we will never understand his purposes and thinking if we regularly emphasize his fear of state majorities at the expense of recognizing the centrality of his commitment to a truly popular regime.

Two tendencies of modern scholarship seem most to blame for current misinterpretations of the framers's purposes and contributions. One of these is the unshakable insistence on the absolute centrality of *Federalist* no. 10 to understanding Madison's intentions and assumptions, accompanied by chronic misinterpretations of this essay. The other, which is often closely linked with these misreadings, is a nearly universal disregard of the confederal dimensions of his thinking. Living in the modern great republic, we today are seldom more than slightly or conventionally concerned about the constitutional division of responsibilities between the central government and the states. Our constructions of the Constitution are mostly instrumental. We think almost exclusively about the rights and needs of citizens of the United States and feel uncomfortable when it is brought to our attention that the punishments for crimes and many other matters vary markedly from state to state. To come to grips with Madison, however, it is absolutely indispensable to notice how completely federalist assumptions permeated every aspect of his thought. It will not do to give a passing nod to these assumptions: to acknowledge them sincerely, but proceed to read his words as though they had been written for the largely unitary system of today. It is essential to remind ourselves at nearly every point that it is only when we fit these federal assumptions back into the fabric of his thought, only when we understand these concepts as an underlying, truly central feature of his thinking, that the shape of his distinctive vision can emerge. Taking federalism seriously, approaching Madison as an impressive spokesman for the large, *compound* republic, will inevitably alter nearly everything we hear.

This is obviously true if we are trying to interpret Madison's apparent shift of course soon after the Constitution was adopted or to understand his methods of constructing the federal charter. But it is also true—and every bit as vital—if we hope to understand his thoughts about the people's role in an enlarged republic. In 1788, Madison undoubtedly anticipated that the greatest dangers to the Union and the Revolution would result from state attachments, state encroachments, and majority abuses. He discounted, even as he recognized, the possibility of federal encroachments. He also underestimated—though, again, he certainly acknowledged—how difficult it soon would seem to keep the people actively engaged in federal concerns and thus to keep the government from favoring minorities at their expense. But when we clearly understand how much of what he disagreed with in the new administration's course was what he thought the federal government was never meant to be involved in (or the opposite of policies that nearly everyone believed that it had been created to pursue), his shift of course—concerning popular involvement *and* concerning local rights—will seem a good deal less abrupt and less substantial than his enemies believed. Modern scholarship has privileged the Hamiltonian interpretation of the Constitution, although the Federalists of 1788 were not a single-minded movement.[2] Nevertheless, from Madison's perspective—and perhaps on a dispassionate consideration of the facts—Madison was absolutely right to say that he "deserted Colonel Hamilton, or rather Colonel H. deserted me . . . from his wishing to . . . administer the Government . . . into what he thought it ought to be, while, on my part, I endeavored to make it conform to the Constitution as understood by the Convention that produced and recommended it and particularly by the state conventions that *adopted* it."[3] Doubtless, Madison confused the people's understanding with his own; but doubtless, also, we ourselves will certainly mistake James Madison if we do not perceive how earnestly he took the Constitution as the people's act, accepted federal features of the system as essential to preserve the Revolution, and intended to assure that federal officials would remain responsive to the people's will.

Madison was not, of course, a democrat by current definitions of that word. His concept of the people usually excluded large proportions of the population.[4] In addition, he decidedly did not believe that the immediate and unenlightened inclinations of majorities of people should be put into effect without resistance. But this was not because he valued order and protection for the rights of property above all else, although he was in fact quite deeply dedicated to protecting both these things. It was because he knew that *every* kind of right could be endangered by majorities of people, especially when heated passions were involved. He may have been, for modern tastes, a markedly conservative defender of republican self-government. This is quite apparent if we weigh him on a modern scale. But we should not forget that what he was committed to conserving were the most profoundly revolutionary institutions and convictions of his time.

Madison's commitment to the people's rule may not have been as eloquent, as unreserved, or as incautious as Jefferson's or Thomas Paine's or that of some of his opponents in the ratification struggle (who, however, were resisting a proposal that would place substantial federal powers, for the first time, in the hands of the immediate representatives of the voters). His was not the sort of democratic faith attractive to the radical imagination, in his own time or in ours. For all of this, however, Madison was very much a democrat by eighteenth-century standards—and even by some tests that many of the most self-righteous modern democrats would fail. Like Jefferson, who used this term, while Madison did not, he clearly hoped that "natural aristocrats" would rule, not any Dick or Jane who might as well be chosen by blind chance. (Most founders were "elitists" in this sense.) But "natural aristocracy," the two Virginians thought, should rest exclusively on merit and the people's recognition, not on wealth, or birth, or formal educational attainments. Moreover, the "aristocrats" who led should never, as they saw it, cease attending to the people's needs and will. Madison was certainly as firm if not as eloquent a spokesman for political equality as either Jefferson or Paine, and this does not exhaust the senses in which he was thoroughly entitled to this label. However much he feared an unrestrained, self-interested, and passionate majority of people, Madison was also adamant that once the proper checks had been imposed and passing passions had been cooled, the will of the majority must rule.[5] Our century has blamed him for his fears or praised him for his wisdom. It could just as justifiably have asked if he was really hopelessly romantic. For, in truth, how many of our own contemporaries share his faith that the majority of ordinary people can and should be trusted once their will has been matured—even with constructing or remodeling the fundamental law? How many modern democrats believe, with Madison, that fundamental liberties of both the private and the public sort are safer with the people than they are with an elite of federal officers and judges?

Americans (whatever others may believe) prefer to see themselves as a pragmatic people: realistic and contemptuous of speculative theory. The Constitutional Convention has been celebrated by admirers for its practical solution to the problems of its day. It has been blamed by others for

its heartless bargaining among a set of men who reasoned more from
their experience and current needs than from the noblest aspirations of
their theory. Similarly, Madison has seemed to some a realistic hero of
the Founding: the sober man of prudence who detoxified the democratic
Revolution. To others, he has seemed the coldly realistic champion of
property and private rights who led the way to the emasculation of the
democratic promise. His contemporaries often saw him in completely different terms: as an impractical, infatuated stickler for the merely theoretic;
as a man of honest heart and probably unrivaled knowledge who, for all
his brilliance, had too little understanding of the world.

Contemporaries were at least as right as many modern analysts have
been when moderns praise or blame this founder as the realistic hero of
his time: a man who took humanity for what it really is and reconstructed
both political ideas and national institutions to allow for mankind's selfishness and warts. For Madison can just as fairly be described, as Paine or
Jefferson have been, as first to last the theorist—and not infrequently the
ideologist—of the party of the Revolution. That Revolution, in his own
conception, was at once entirely liberal and perfectly republican in nature.
His fundamental, self-selected role was to assure that its enduring contribution would be both: first, to solve the problems of the Union and correct the errors of the early Revolution, then to be the bridge across which
Federalists and Antifederalists alike could transit from the thinking of the
early Revolution to a federal republic that would still encompass early
revolutionary aspirations and assumptions. To this end, he helped create
a Constitution that would offer more security against majority infringements of the rights that governments were instituted to protect, but one
that was intended not the less to also guarantee both popular control and
the establishment of social, economic, and political conditions under
which self-government could last. Once the Constitution went into effect,
he set about deliberately to understand the kind of covenant it represented and to show by teaching and example how the spirit of that compact could be cherished and improved, to make the conduct of the
government consistent with the purposes for which it had been formed.
When, instead of a diffusive, patriotic, and republican concern for every
portion of the Union, a spirit of advantage-taking marked the measures
of the infant Congress, when the new administration set a course that
seemed to favor a minority at popular expense and at the risk of massive
disaffection from the Union, and when measures and elite opinion both
appeared to threaten the republican and partly federal foundations of the
charter, he appealed again directly to the people. He did not reverse his
course. Rather, the majority of modern analysts has poorly understood his
wishes, stands, and contributions in the years before the federal govern-

ment began its operations. The strict constructionism, the concern about the economic, cultural, and moral underpinnings of a healthy public life, and even the insistence on states' rights that culminated in the Virginia Resolutions of 1798 were always integral components of his vision.

Madison, of course, did not stop thinking at the end of 1792. Events continued to unfold, and a reflective statesman is a leader who attempts to grapple with contingencies in terms of a coherent understanding of the current situation, a commitment to a worthy set of goals, and the capacity to modify his course as new developments require without abandoning his underlying vision. Madison would serve another quarter century before retiring. After 1817, he would continue for another twenty years to write about the Founding and involve himself occasionally in national disputes. As always, he sometimes won and sometimes lost, and sometimes made some serious mistakes. The country that he died in, not considering America today, was not the country he had struggled to create. History, on balance, judges him a mixed success as president and party leader.

By 1793, however, Madison's conception of the Constitution had assumed the basic shape that would endure, with only minor deviations and refinements, through the rest of his career. By 1793, he had already outlined the domestic and commercial policies that the Republicans would follow through the War of 1812.[6] He had identified the central problematic of the years in opposition. He had initiated an attempt to solve this fundamental problem.

In *Federalist* no. 10, Madison had given only passing notice to the problem of a faction that "consists of less than a majority of people." From this, he said, "relief is supplied by the republican principle, which enables the majority to defeat its sinister views." A faction with minority support might "clog the administration," might even "convulse the society," but it would be "unable to execute and mask its violence under the forms of the Constitution."[7]

Experience taught different lessons. The danger posed by a minority with sinister designs—a faction fully capable of masking its intentions under cover of the Constitution—could be harder to defeat than number 10 suggested. The difficulty, in a large, diffuse republic—noted in *The Federalist*, but not developed there—was that the same conditions that impeded the formation of a dangerous majority could also make it harder for a sound majority to coalesce, to recognize its strength, and to develop and enforce the public will. Popular engagement could not be assumed. Instead, majority opinion had to be elicited or formed, the people mobilized and energized to make their will effective. The *National Gazette* was founded for this purpose, and Madison employed it to this end. Throughout the 1790s, he would search for other methods of developing majority opinion and ensuring its effectual expression in the intervals between elections. Organized so as to emphasize this theme, the story of the later 1790s offers a concluding lesson in his thoughts about the people's part in shaping national policy as well as in his inability to solve the riddle of a limited and partly federal regime.

In April 1793, the context of the early party quarrel was profoundly changed by news of war between Great Britain and the infant French Republic. As the greatest trading neutral of the time, the United States could not avoid entanglement in what would rapidly become a worldwide war between the giants of the age, each of which intended to deny its enemy the benefits of neutral commerce. Neither could Americans escape emotional involvement in the conflict. Republican idealism and the memory of French assistance in the War for Independence generated potent sympathies, on one side, for the French Republic. On the other, many sympathized with England: the motherland of libertarian ideas, the most effective barrier to French expansion, and by far the most important trading partner of the new United States.

On April 22, after sharp debates within the Washington administration, the executive proclaimed that the United States intended to pursue a "friendly and impartial" conduct toward the warring powers. Madison, who had departed for Virginia shortly after the adjournment of the Second Congress, followed the reaction in the press and moved in tandem with the discontent of much articulate opinion. With many of his countrymen, he had followed the developments in France with admiration tempered by occasional alarm. The torch of liberty, which the United States had lit, could either pass through France to light all of Europe or it could be extinguished by the coalition of aristocrats and kings, who might decide to turn their energies against America if they could first defeat the champions of liberty abroad. The Jeffersonian Republicans already saw themselves as champions of liberty at home, defenders of the revolutionary cause against those who would betray it. Few of them desired direct involvement in the European war, although the revolutionary treaty of alliance did contain a clause by which America agreed to guarantee the French West Indies. Many, nonetheless, considered strict neutrality between republicans and kings to be desertion from the cause, and many were prepared to see their Federalist opponents reaching out for an alliance with the European despots, perhaps in time for a reunion with the English fountainhead of Hamiltonian ideas.[8]

Thousands of Americans turned out to see the French Republic's first ambassador to the United States, "Citizen" Edmond Genet, who came ashore at Charleston and conducted a triumphal tour to Philadelphia in

the spring of 1793 while Jefferson and Hamilton were arguing the implications of the treaty of alliance.[9] In May, the press erupted in a furious
debate about Washington's decision for neutrality. A score of democratic-
republican societies sprang up in every portion of the country, filled with
"citizens" determined to support the French and to assert the people's
rights at home.[10] Hundreds donned the French cockade, while other hundreds grew increasingly alarmed about the violence in France, the confiscations of aristocratic property, attacks upon the Church, and the
enthusiasm of so many of their countrymen for French examples and
successes.

Madison, of course, was always slow to criticize George Washington.
He may have been the more reluctant, in this case, when Jefferson expressed his own support for a "fair neutrality" even though he knew that
the executive's "cold caution" toward the French would be "a disagreeable pill to our friends."[11] Nevertheless, when Jefferson reported that
Hamilton had argued that the change of government in France was
grounds for abrogation of the treaty of alliance, Madison agreed with
Jefferson that "the attempt to shuffle off the treaty altogether" was
"equally contemptible" for "its meanness and folly."[12] And by June 13,
he was informing Jefferson that he had been unable to respond convincingly to sensible Virginians who were picking up objections to the proclamation from the papers: to such a firm insistence on a strict neutrality
despite the obligations of the treaty; to the impartiality enjoined upon the
people despite "their moral obligations"; and, especially, to the administration's declaration of the "disposition" of the nation when decisions
for war or peace were "essentially and exclusively" vested in the legislative
branch.[13] Three days later, having read another set of papers from the
north, he had decided that "the proclamation was in truth a most unfortunate error. It wounds the national honor by seeming to disregard the
stipulated duties to France. It wounds the popular feelings by a seeming
indifference to the cause of liberty. And it seems to violate the forms and
spirit of the Constitution by making the executive" the organ of decisions
that belonged to other branches.[14]

By the beginning of July, the landscape had been radically transformed. Misled by the enthusiasm for his country, Genet encouraged violations of neutrality and set himself on a collision course with the
administration. In his *Letters of Pacificus*, Hamilton had opened an infuri-
ating, yet effective, effort to defend the president's authority to issue the
proclamation.[15] The combined effects of the ambassador's misconduct
and the secretary's pen were markedly affecting popular opinion. "Never
in my opinion was so calamitous an appointment made as that of the
present minister of F[rance]," Jefferson complained to Madison. More-

over, no one answered Hamilton, "and his doctrine will therefore be taken for confessed. For god's sake, my dear Sir, take up your pen, select the most striking heresies, and cut him to pieces in the face of the public. There is nobody else who can and will enter the lists with him."[16]

Madison consented, in a work whose tone he later judged "of no advantage either to the subject or to the author."[17] His letters of "Helvidius," published in the Philadelphia *Gazette of the United States* between August 24 and September 18, 1793, took issue less with Washington's pronouncement than with Hamilton's attempts to justify the proclamation with a liberal construction of the scope of the executive prerogative. Hamilton's construction of the Constitution, Madison insisted, was modeled on the practices and theory of monarchical Britain. It was "pregnant with inferences and consequences against which no ramparts in the Constitution could defend the public liberty, or scarcely the forms of republican government." In proportion as it came to be accepted, enormous powers would inevitably be claimed by those who had an interest. "A people, therefore, who are so happy as to possess the inestimable blessing of a free and defined constitution, cannot be too watchful against the introduction nor too critical in tracing the consequences of new principles and new constructions that may remove the landmarks of power."[18]

The letters of "Helvidius" were not sufficient to arrest the drift of popular opinion (or, as Madison perceived the situation, to prevent the misinterpretation of the people's feelings likely to be fostered by resolutions such as those adopted by a Richmond meeting on August 17). While "Helvidius" was still in process, he complained to Jefferson about "the language of the towns." "The Anglican Party," he charged, was using the misconduct of Genet to lead the people "from their honorable connection with [France] into the arms and ultimately into the government of G[reat] B[ritain]." To counteract this business, he explained, he and James Monroe had drafted model resolutions for consideration in the counties, where "the real sentiments of the people"—of "the agricultural, which is the commanding part of the society"—could be collected by their leaders.[19] "Vast efforts are making by a combination of princes and nobles to crush an example that may open the eyes of all mankind to their national and political rights," the resolutions said. Attempts were likewise being made "to alienate the good will of the people of America from the cause of liberty and republican government in France," to weaken their attachment to their own free governments, to connect them with Great Britain, and thereby to assimilate the American system to "the form and spirit of the British monarchy."[20] County meetings might expose the counterfeiting of the people's sentiments in resolutions coming from the cities. Or if county meetings proved incapable of energizing country people, who

were otherwise too uninformed and "too inert" to speak, "the state legislatures, and the federal also if possible," would have to be "induced to
take the matter up in its true point of view."[21]

The major effort to employ the *federal* legislature to correct the country's course unfolded in the first session of the Third Congress, aided at
the start, but then eventually defeated, by increasing British seizures of
U.S. merchant ships. On December 16, 1793, two weeks before retiring
as secretary of state, Jefferson submitted his "Report on the Privileges and
Restrictions on the Commerce of the United States with Foreign Countries," which had been ready for a year but had been held while he ne-
gotiated with George Hammond.[22] Armed with Jefferson's comparison of
French and British regulations, Madison presented seven resolutions
aimed to institute his policy of commercial retaliation.[23] Developments
defeated him again. By early March, the British had seized 250 U.S. ships
engaged in commerce with the French West Indies. The Republicans in
Congress moved behind a bill to institute nonintercourse with Britain and
a measure to sequester British debts. The Federalists preferred a final
effort to negotiate with Britain, linked with measures to bolster the national defenses. John Adams cast the vote defeating nonintercourse in the
Senate. On April 16, Washington nominated Chief Justice John Jay to
make a final effort at a diplomatic resolution of the crisis.[24]

In the summer of 1794, while Jay was still in England, popular resistance to the excise tax erupted in an armed rebellion. Madison and most
Republicans, who were severely damaged by the rioting in western Pennsylvania, condemned resistance to the laws and backed the use of the
militia to suppress the insurrection.[25] Nevertheless, when Congress reassembled, Madison, who was increasingly concerned to find effective ways
to foster the development and free expression of the people's views, was
shocked by Washington's address, which charged that "certain self-created
societies"—the democratic-republican clubs—had fomented the Whiskey
Rebellion. Appointed chairman of the committee to prepare the House
of Representatives' response, he drafted a reply that would have passed
over the president's remark in silence, although he privately considered
it "perhaps the greatest error of [Washington's] political life": nothing
less than an "attack on the most sacred principle of our Constitution and
of republicanism."[26] The Federalists, however, were determined to employ
the president's prestige to damage their party rivals. Indeed, as Madison
described it in his letters to his friends, the effort by the Federalists to
echo Washington's remark was "a most dangerous game . . . against Republicanism."[27] The object was "to connect the democratic societies with
the odium of the insurrection—to connect the Republicans in Congress
with those societies—to put the President ostensibly at the head of the

other party in opposition to both, and by these means to prolong" the delusion of New England and influence the elections in Virginia.[28] To avert these dangers, Madison was willing to confront the president himself.

Speaking on November 27, Madison confessed that he had wanted to avoid a discussion so delicate in its relationship to the chief magistrate. He nevertheless insisted "that an action innocent in the eye of the law"— the resolutions and activities of the democratic clubs—"could not be the object of censure to a legislative body." "Opinions are not the objects of legislation." An "indiscriminate censure" of the popular societies would constitute a punishment for their opinions: "a vote of attainder." But by the nature of republican government, "the censorial power is in the people over the government, and not in the government over the people." The House (and, by implication, Washington himself) had no right to say "that institutions confessedly not illegal, were subjects of legislative censure."[29]

The democratic-republican societies were among the many "local organs" of opinion that Madison had been insisting were essential to the formulation and expression of the public will. To condemn them, he believed, was to attack "the essential and constitutional rights of the citizens."[30] It had to be discerned, he wrote Monroe,

> that no two principles can be either more indefensible in reason or more dangerous in practice—than that 1. arbitrary denunciations may punish what the law permits, and what the legislature had no right, by law, to prohibit—and that 2. the government may stifle all censures whatever on its misdoings; for it if be itself the judge it will never allow any censures to be just, and if it can suppress censures flowing from one lawful source it may [also suppress] those flowing from any other—from the press and from individuals as well as from societies, etc.[31]

Madison's defense of the societies was a deliberate attempt to cut off at its roots a doctrine that would flower later in the decade: "the doctrine ... that, in a republic, the people ought to consider the whole of their political duty as discharged when they have chosen their representatives," should presume that their elected officers cannot possess an interest different from their own, and thus should place "unlimited confidence" in their rulers. "In no case," Madison insisted, "ought the eyes of the people to be shut on the conduct of those entrusted with power, nor their tongues tied from a just wholesome censure on it, any more than from merited commendations."[32]

At the moment, to be sure, Madison did not imagine that within four years, the people's right to criticize their government would be subjected to a much more formidable attack. In defending the societies, he was returning to his maxim that the distant implications of a measure had to be resisted when the danger first appeared, much as patriots had once opposed the implications of the stamp tax. Within the year, however, Washington would sign Jay's Treaty with the British; and Madison would see that treaty as a proof that a minority of plotters, having insulated Washington from sound advice and from the sentiments and interests of the people, were bent on an eventual alliance with the British as a means of pressing their conspiracy against the Constitution. From that point forward, he was more and more inclined to use the legislatures of the states, as well as public meetings, Congress, and the press, as instruments for shaping and enforcing popular opinion.

The Treaty of Amity and Commerce between the United States and Britain, concluded in November 1794, was one of the least attractive in American history. In exchange for a British agreement to evacuate their posts in the American Northwest and to admit small American vessels to the direct trade with the British West Indies (on terms that were to be rejected by the Senate), the United States abandoned its position on the rights of neutral shippers, granted Britain most-favored-nation status in its ports, and forswore the imposition of discriminatory duties on the British. Boundary disputes, American claims for British spoliations, and British claims against American debtors were referred to joint commissions. British impressment of American sailors and American claims for slaves carried away by the British at the conclusion of the war went unmentioned in the treaty. Although historians are generally convinced that Jay obtained the best agreement circumstances would permit,[33] the first American reactions were decidedly adverse. Washington withheld the treaty until the meeting of a special session of the Senate, which ratified it by a single vote on June 24, 1795. He then withheld his own approval for almost two months while gatherings throughout the country urged him not to sign.[34] Hamilton was driven from the platform in New York when he attempted to defend the treaty. Jay was burned in effigy, threatened with impeachment, and physically attacked.[35]

Madison shared the general sense of outrage, which was deepened by the threat that France would take offense at the provisions that would benefit Great Britain in the middle of a war. "After yielding terms which would have been scorned by this country in the moment of its greatest embarrassments," he wrote, Jay had added to "the ruinous bargain with [Britain] a disqualification to make a good one with any other" nation, since the United States would be precluded from offering to any other country privileges that the British would not automatically enjoy. In addition, the abandonment of commercial discrimination disarmed the Union of its most effective weapon for coercing reciprocity from Britain. Indeed, from one end to the other, Jay's Treaty had to be regarded as a demonstration that the party which approved it was "a British party, systematically aiming at an exclusive connection with the British government and ready to sacrifice to that object as well the dearest interests of our commerce as the most sacred dictates of national honor."[36]

When Madison advanced these comments, early in August 1795, he hoped the public outcry would prevent the president from signing. By August 25, however, he had read the president's dismissive answers to addresses from public meetings in Boston and Richmond, and Washington's approval of the treaty was affecting popular opinion. Hamilton, by then, had started an anonymous defense of the agreement, and Jefferson and others were again appealing for an answer.[37] Rather than debate Hamilton again, Madison decided to employ the tested instrument of popular petitions to elicit action from the Virginia state assembly. Assuming that the Senate's suspension of Article 12 of the treaty would require approval by the British, after which the document would have to go before the Senate yet again, he drafted a petition urging the Virginia legislature to condemn the pact "in virtue of their constitutional right of appointing Senators."[38] Remarking that the president's responses to the meetings in Boston and Richmond had "virtually refused to view the representations of the people as a source of information worthy of his consideration" and had "rendered all further representations and applications to him upon the subject absurd and nugatory," the petition argued that it was essential "that the people should boldly exercise their right of addressing their objections to all other constituted authorities within the United States who possess any agency" that might "prevent the final ratification . . . of an instrument which is deemed fatal to the interests, the happiness, and perhaps finally to the liberty and independence of the United States."[39]

As Madison had feared, however, George III accepted the conditional ratification of the treaty, and Washington proclaimed it in effect on February 29, 1796, without resubmitting it to the Senate. This put the anti-treaty forces in the House of Representatives in an impossible position, although approval by the House would be required to authorize appropriations necessary to support the joint commissions and fulfill the treaty's terms. Madison preferred to address the treaty in the House reply to Washington's annual message, delivered early in December 1795. He deferred, he later said, to those who preferred to take it up separately, only to find that his allies were less forward than he had expected and that the situation was enormously "perplexing."[40] The president had headed off an early confrontation by agreeing in his speech to lay the treaty before the House once the king's response was known. Through January, Madison resisted plans to call for information, fearing that attempts to bring the matter on before the treaty was presented would embroil the House with Washington and crack the antitreaty coalition. When the treaty was proclaimed and Edward Livingston proposed to call for Jay's instructions and for other documents relating to the matter, so that the House could determine the constitutionality of the agreement and the extent of its own powers regarding its implementation, Madison still considered this a risky proposition.[41] Nevertheless, he was surprised when Washington refused the call for papers, and most authorities believe that he prepared the resolutions of April 6, which reasserted the constitutional powers of the House.[42]

Madison's speeches on Jay's Treaty rank among his most elaborate and agonized attempts to understand the spirit and provisions of the Constitution. During the debates on whether to request the papers, Madison delivered an address in which he tacitly admitted that consideration by the House of a refusal to provide the funding necessary for the treaty raised perplexing questions. "Taken literally and without limit," he observed, the treaty-making powers of the president and Senate clearly clashed with those specifically delegated to the Congress as a whole: to regulate commerce, to declare war, to raise armies, and so on. In cases of this sort, the servants of the people were obliged to undertake a close consideration of the constitutional division of authority and to discover a construction that "would best reconcile the several parts of the instrument with each other, and be most consistent with its general spirit and object."

No construction, Madison confessed, was altogether free from serious objections. Yet, surely, none could be admitted that would free the president and Senate, acting through their power to conclude a treaty, to decide on war or peace, to raise an army, or to do the other things undoubtedly entrusted to the Congress as a whole.

> The powers given up by the people for the purposes of government had been divided into two great classes. One of these formed the state governments, the other the federal government. The powers of the [federal] government had been further divided into three great departments; and the legislative department again subdivided into two independent branches. Around each of these portions of power were seen also exceptions and qualifications, as additional guards against the abuses to which power is liable. With a view to this policy of the Constitution, it could not be unreasonable, if the clauses under discussion were thought doubtful, to lean toward a construction that would limit and control the treaty-making power, rather than toward one that would make it omnipotent.

The Constitution declared treaties to be supreme over the laws and constitutions of the states, but not over the Constitution and laws of the fed
eral government itself. On these grounds, Madison's own opinion was that
the treaty power "required at the same time the legislative sanction and
cooperation in those cases where the Constitution had given express and
specific powers to the legislature." In such cases, the legislature should
certainly "exercise its authority with discretion," but it must still be able
to deliberate and reason; it must still possess a will of its own.[43]

Congressional opponents pounced on Madison's admission that his
own interpretation was not "perfectly free from difficulties," berating him
again for reversing his stands of 1787 and 1788. His situation was the
more perplexing—and the more embarrassing—when Washington refused the call for papers partly on the grounds that a proposal at the
Constitutional Convention to require that treaties be confirmed by laws
had been specifically rejected, which, of course, reminded everyone of
Madison's position on the national bank.[44] The charge of inconsistency
was not unfair. Neither were objections that his argument, in practice,
could involve the House repeatedly in matters not confided to it by the
Constitution. On the other hand, these charges hardly answered what was
certainly a powerful interpretation of the charter, and the charge of inconsistency assumed (as many modern analysts have done) that Madison
had seen from the beginning all the implications of the charter, knew
how it should be constructed, and was twisting now to find an avenue that
would permit him to accomplish what he wished. In fact, however, Madison had more than once insisted that a sound interpretation of the Constitution could be difficult to find, and he had more than once insisted
that the understandings of the Constitutional Convention—if these could
even be recovered—were not the most authoritative guide to the interpretation of the charter. Like the national bank, the treaty raised a question that had not, until that time, come clearly into view; and neither
Madison nor his opponents were unquestionably correct in their constructions. Madison had worried systematically about a sound, coherent understanding of the Constitution from the moment when the government
began. He had thought his way toward a coherent view more systematically
than most. But he was still attempting, as he said, to find a doctrine that
would give significance "to every part of the Constitution," would be
"most consistent with its general spirit," and would be "most likely in
practice to promote the . . . public good."

When Washington refused the call for papers and the House began
debating a proposal to insist on the constitutionality of its request and to
refuse appropriations for treaty provisions that encroached on its powers

over commerce, Madison was thoroughly prepared to answer Washington's objections and defend his own position. It was surprising, he maintained, that such "peculiar stress" should have been placed on information from the Constitutional Convention. When he himself had used such information as an argument against the bank, he was rebuked by its proponents, and there was not a single instance since "in which the sense of the Convention had been required or admitted as material in any constitutional question."[45]

> Whatever veneration might be entertained for the body of men who formed our Constitution, the sense of that body could never be regarded as the oracular guide in expounding the Constitution. As the instrument came from them, it was nothing more than the draft of a plan, nothing but a dead letter, until life and validity were breathed into it by the voice of the people, speaking through the several state conventions. If we were to look, therefore, for the meaning of the instrument, beyond the face of the instrument, we must look for it not in the general convention, which proposed, but in the state conventions, which accepted and ratified the Constitution.

Looking to these sources, it was clear in his opinion that the treaty power was "a limited power." None of the state conventions had supposed that powers over commerce, war and peace, and even the disbursement of the public funds could be assumed, in practice, by the Senate and executive alone.[46]

The House of Representatives approved the reassertion of its rights by a margin of twenty-two votes, and Madison condemned the treaty's substance in a major speech of April 15.[47] By this time, however, public sentiments were shifting, a petitioning campaign was under way in favor of the treaty, and Republicans in Congress were having second thoughts, fearing that the Senate might refuse appropriations for the treaties with the Northwest Tribes, the Spanish, and the Algerines, all of which had just been funded, if the House defeated funding for the pact with Britain. With Madison condemning the defections by his allies (and probably regretting his resistance to considering the matter early in the year), appropriations for Jay's Treaty passed the House on April 30 by a margin of 51 to 48. It was a heavy blow.[48] It sealed his earlier decision to retire from Congress.[49] And it led directly to the kind of crisis he particularly feared, in course of which he would pursue his search for methods of protecting limited, responsive government—and thus the cause of liberty itself—to its most dangerous and controversial extreme.

In the presidential election at the end of 1796, John Adams defeated

Thomas Jefferson by a margin of three electoral votes. But Washington had left the hapless Adams with a crisis. Damaged and offended by Jay's Treaty, the French Directory announced that they would treat American vessels "in the same manner as they suffer the English to treat them." Seizures followed, and the new president responded, much as Washington had done in 1794, by recommending both negotiations and increased appropriations for defense. Adams chose John Marshall of Virginia and Elbridge Gerry of Massachusetts to join Charles C. Pinckney, whom the French had refused to accept, for a mission to resolve the crisis. The negotiations stalled when unofficial agents of the French foreign minister—referred to in American dispatches as X, Y, and Z—informed the American commissioners that nothing could be done until they paid a bribe to Talleyrand and agreed to a large American loan to the Republic.

In April 1798, goaded by Republicans in Congress, Adams released the papers revealing the XYZ Affair. Patriotic fury of an unexampled nature swept the states from end to end; and on the crest of this hysteria, which swelled into a widespread fear of treasonable plots between the French and their Republican supporters, the Federalists embarked on a naval war with France. They also seized the opportunity to launch a program of repression consciously intended to destroy domestic opposition to their programs. French and Irish immigrants supported the Republicans and favored France in its collision with Great Britain. In June and July, in the Alien Acts, Congress extended to fourteen years the period of residence required for naturalization and gave the president the power summarily to deport any alien whose residence he deemed a threat to the United States. Then, in a direct blow to the opposition, Congress passed the Sedition Act, making it a criminal offense to incite opposition to the laws or to "write, print, utter, or publish . . . any false, scandalous, and malicious writing . . . against the government of the United States, or either house of the Congress of the United States, or the President of the United States with intent to defame them or to bring them . . . into disrepute."[51]

Enforced by a partisan judiciary, the Alien and Sedition Acts unleashed a bloodless reign of terror on the country. Under the Sedition Act (or under the common law of seditious libel), every important Republican newspaper in the country was attacked. William Duane of the Philadelphia *Aurora* (which had replaced the *National Gazette* as the leading Republican organ when the latter failed financially in 1793), Thomas Adams of the *Independent Chronicle* in Boston, and Republican pamphleteers such as Thomas Cooper and James Thompson Callender all faced prosecution. The *Time Piece* and the *Argus*, the only Republican newspapers in New York City, were forced out of business. Matthew Lyon of Vermont, a Republican congressman, was imprisoned for a publication incident to his reelection campaign in 1798. Men were prosecuted under the Sedition Act for offenses as diverse and as trivial as circulating a petition for its repeal, erecting a liberty pole, or expressing a drunken wish that a cannonball had struck the president in his behind.

At first, Republicans were seriously disheartened by the drastic shift of popular opinion. At the peak of the patriotic fever, during the summer of 1798, several congressmen went home and left the Federalist majority to work its will. Jefferson and others who remained in Philadelphia were trailed by self-appointed spies, who hoped for proof of the leaders' French connections. In the elections of 1798, the Federalists made substantial gains, and some Virginians talked about secession or preparing to defend themselves against the larger federal army. To Republicans, the Quasi-War with France, the Alien and Sedition Laws, and a measure authorizing the enlistment of a provisional army of 50,000 men, which could be mobilized in the event of an invasion, seemed abundant proof that the conspiracy against the nation's liberties had burst into the open.[52] Yet neither Jefferson nor Madison lost faith in their ability to bring the people to their senses.[53]

While Albert Gallatin and Edward Livingston opposed the crisis laws in Congress, insisting that the legislation was a flagrant violation of the First Amendment and a potent danger to the people's underlying right to change their government through free elections, Jefferson (who had, of course, become vice president under the terms of the original Constitution) determined to arouse the states against the challenge to the Constitution.[54] He found a willing ally in his closest friend, who had been following developments from his retirement and who likewise understood the Constitution as a compact among the sovereign peoples of the several states.[55] Virginia had a long tradition of protesting federal measures, beginning with the General Assembly's 1790 remonstrance against the funding and assumption plan. Madison had tried to organize a legislative condemnation of Jay's Treaty in 1795. In 1797, he had aided Jefferson in drafting a petition prompted by a federal presentment of Congressman Samuel Jordan Cabell for the congressman's attacks on the government in circular letters to his constituents.[56]

In 1798, the problem for the two Virginia leaders was apparent: how to check a federal government whose branches seemed united in a program that Republicans regarded as a patent violation of express provisions of the Constitution, a bald assumption of usurped authority, and a direct attack on "that right of freely examining public characters and measures, and of free communication among the people thereon, which has ever been justly deemed the only effectual guardian of every other right"—

indeed, the fundamental right which underpinned elective government itself [57] Their answer was to use Virginia and Kentucky to spearhead the resistance. Each prepared a set of legislative resolutions condemning the Alien and Sedition Laws. Jefferson sent his to John Breckinridge of Kentucky. Madison sent his to John Taylor of Caroline, Virginia's agricultural thinker and the Republican party's most influential pamphleteer. On November 16, 1798, Kentucky's legislature resolved that "whensoever the General Government assumes undelegated powers, its acts are unauthoritative, void, and of no force." On December 24, Virginia voted a similar condemnation and, like Kentucky, called on the other states to join the protest.

The authorship of the Kentucky and Virginia Resolutions was a secret closely held until John Taylor mentioned Madison in print in 1809. Little has survived about the details of their drafting. The two Republicans undoubtedly discussed the outlines of a plan when Jefferson stopped by the Madison plantation on his annual return from Philadelphia at the beginning of July. Madison returned the visit with a trip to Monticello near the middle of October, by which time the senior partner's draft had been sent to Kentucky.[58] On November 17, Jefferson sent his friend a copy of this draft and probably enclosed a copy of the Kentucky Resolutions as actually enacted, on which he carefully noted variations from his draft.[59] Madison then proceeded on his own.

Commentators on the resolutions have conventionally emphasized—indeed, they may have overemphasized—the younger partner's greater caution. Jefferson had started from the premise that the several states did not unite "on the principle of unlimited submission to their General Government," that "the government created by this compact was not made the exclusive or final judge of the extent of the powers delegated to itself," and that the parties to the compact each retained "an equal right to judge for itself, as well of infractions as of the mode and measure of redress." Act by act, his draft of the Kentucky Resolutions listed legislation in which Congress had assumed authority not delegated by the Constitution, often in the face of the explicit language of the Bill of Rights. Calling each of these examples "altogether void and of no force," it argued that in all such cases "every state has a natural right . . . to nullify of their own authority all assumptions of power by others within their limits." Urging other states to join in these opinions—"they alone being parties to the compact and solely authorized to judge the last resort of the powers exercised under it, Congress being not a party but merely the creature of the compact"—Jefferson concluded by appealing also for concurrence in adopting "measures of their own for providing that neither these acts, nor any others of the General Government not plainly and intentionally authorized by the Constitution, shall be exercised within their respective territories."[60]

The legislators of Kentucky (or, more likely, Breckinridge himself) deleted Jefferson's suggestion that the rightful remedy for federal usurpations was a "nullification" of such acts by each state acting on its own to prevent their operation within its respective bounds. Rather than suggesting individual, although concerted, measures of this sort, Kentucky was content to ask its sisters to unite in declarations that the acts were "void and of no force" and in "requesting their repeal" at the succeeding session of the Congress. Madison was similarly cautious in his draft of resolutions for Virginia, which also called on the other states to concur in declaring that the acts in question were "unconstitutional," but which did not add that they were "not law, but utterly null, void, and of no force or effect." Madison, indeed, was possibly, although not certainly, responsible for checking an attempt by Jefferson to have the latter phrase inserted in his text.[61] In consequence, years later, Madison would have good ground for his insistence that he never said that any single state could constitutionally impede the operation of a federal law.[62] Even as he wrote the resolutions, he probably already saw the problem he would bring to Jefferson's attention while they waited for the legislature's action:

> Have you ever considered thoroughly the distinction between the power of the *State* and that of the *Legislature* on questions relating to the federal pact? On the supposition that the former is clearly the ultimate judge of infractions, it does not follow that the latter is the legitimate organ, especially as a convention was the organ by which the compact was made. This was a reason of great weight for using general expressions that would leave to other states a choice of the modes possible of concurring in the substance [of the Resolutions] and would shield the General Assembly against the charge of usurpation in the very act of protesting the usurpations of Congress.[63]

For all of this, however, Madison had not avoided language that confused the several senses in which "state" was commonly employed, and it is not as certain as the standard commentaries argue—or as Madison himself would argue in the Report of 1800—that he meant the resolutions simply as a declaration of opinion and a means of stimulating popular action.[64] After an expression of Virginia's "warm attachment to the Union," the Assembly did "peremptorily declare"

> that it views the powers of the federal government as resulting from the compact to which the states are parties; as limited by the plain sense and

intention of the instrument constituting that compact; as no farther valid than they are authorised by the grants enumerated in that compact, and that in case of a deliberate, palpable, and dangerous exercise of other powers not granted by the said compact, the states who are the parties thereto have the right, and are in duty bound, to interpose for arresting the progress of the evil, and for maintaining *within their respective limits,* the authorities, rights, and liberties appertaining to them.[65]

Like Jefferson's, Madison's draft attacked specific violations of amendments to the Constitution, together with the federal government's attempts

to enlarge its powers by forced constructions of the constitutional charter . . . so as to destroy the meaning and effect of the particular enumeration which necessarily explains and limits the general phrases; and so as to consolidate the states by degrees into one sovereignty, the obvious tendency and inevitable consequence of which would be to transform the present republican system of the United States into an absolute, or at best a mixed monarchy.

Like Jefferson, Madison called on the states, not only to concur in declaring these usurpations unconstitutional, but also in declaring "that the necessary and proper measures will be taken by each for cooperating with this state in maintaining unimpaired the authorities, rights, and liberties reserved to the states respectively, or to the people."[66] As Jefferson had said while they were planning their attack, the fundamental object was to win the other states' cooperation in condemning the repressive laws and in affirming basic principles "so as to hold to that ground in future and leave the matter in such a train as that we may not be committed absolutely to push the matter to extremities, and may yet be free to push as far as events will render prudent."[67]

Madison would soon—and many times—regret his carelessness or lack of foresight in the preparation of these resolutions. When seven other states condemned Kentucky's and Virginia's declarations, pointing out that local interventions in the federal sphere could raise again the devil that had wrecked the old Confederation, Madison reentered the Virginia legislature to defend and to refine his language (without, of course, admitting that the language was his own). As he and Jefferson discussed this measure, he rejected Jefferson's suggestion that Virginia and Kentucky should declare that they were "not at all disposed to make every measure of error or wrong a cause of scission," that they would "wait with patience till those passions and delusions shall have passed over which the federal government have artfully and successfully excited to cover its own abuses," but that they were nonetheless determined "to sever ourselves from that union we so much value rather than give up the rights of self-government which we have reserved and in which alone we see liberty, safety, and happiness."[68] Nevertheless, although he admitted that the language used in 1798 had been "inaccurate and inconsistent,"[69] Madison did not retract the logic of state interposition; and far from temporizing his denunciation of the measures and intentions of his Federalist opponents, he indicted them again in terms that justified his politics since the ratification of the Constitution. "Nowhere in American political literature," write Adrienne Koch and Harry Ammon, "does there exist a more careful, precise and mature reiteration of the principles of republican self-government" than in Madison's report on state responses to the Virginia Resolutions. "Nowhere is it clearer that the intermediate existence of state governments between the people and the 'General Government,'" was indispensable, as Madison conceived it, to the preservation of the large republic.[70]

The Report of 1800 was a clause by clause elaboration and defense of the Virginia (and Kentucky) Resolutions.[71] Reaffirming his contention that the Constitution was created by a compact of the states, Madison conceded "that the term 'states' is sometimes used in a vague sense, and sometimes in different senses, according to the subject to which it is applied." Sometimes it refers to territories, sometimes to the governments of these, and sometimes to "the people composing those political societies in their highest sovereign capacity." But in this final sense, at least, he thought it undeniable that "states" were parties to the compact, as it was also undeniable that compacts had to be interpreted according to the plain intentions of the parties. On these grounds, he found the logic unimpeachable which said "that where resort can be had to no tribunal superior to the authority of the parties, the parties themselves must be the rightful judges in the last resort, whether the bargain made has been pursued or violated." A decision that it had been violated, to be sure, was not to be imposed "either in a hasty manner or on doubtful or inferior occasions," but for just these reasons the Assembly had objected only to "a *deliberate, palpable,* and *dangerous* breach of the Constitution": to legislation and constructions "*dangerous* to the great purposes for which the Constitution was established."[72] And in cases of this sort, unless the parties to the compact could legitimately interpose—at least so far as to arrest the evil, to maintain their rights, and to preserve the Constitution—"there would be an end to all relief from usurped power ... as well as a plain denial of the fundamental principle on which our independence itself was declared."[73]

It was true, of course, that other states objected that the parties to the compact *had* created a superior tribunal to decide on disagreements of this sort: the Constitution made the *courts* the agencies of last resort in constitutional disputes. But what was the recourse, asked Madison, when the judiciary sanctioned federal usurpations? The judiciary was, indeed, the branch of last resort "in relation to the authorities of the other departments of the government," but it was not the last resort "in relation to the right of the parties to the constitutional compact, from which the judicial as well as the other departments hold their delegated trusts. On any other hypothesis, the delegation of judicial power would annul the authority delegating it."[74] "The authority of constitutions over governments, and of the sovereignty of the people over constitutions, are truths which are at all times necessary to be kept in mind; and at no time perhaps more necessary than at the present."[75]

Having reaffirmed that the Constitution is a compact, Madison proceeded to elaborate the Resolutions' condemnation of the crisis laws and of the constitutional constructions of the Federalist administration. Usurpations by construction, he insisted, had begun as early as the law establishing the national bank. From then until the present, both the general-welfare clause and the necessary-and-proper clause had been employed repeatedly to justify assumptions of authority not clearly granted by the Constitution and not intended by the parties to the compact. Madison elaborated his contention that constructions of this sort could gradually destroy the meaning and effect of the enumeration, and repeated arguments developed in the *National Gazette* that concentration of authority in federal hands would necessarily entail a vast enlargement of executive authority and the eventual replacement of elections by hereditary rule.[76] Turning next to the repressive laws of 1798, he argued at great length that the Alien and the Sedition Acts fundamentally subverted the basic maxims of the Constitution. The former exercised a power nowhere granted by the Constitution, vested the executive with legislative and judicial powers, and transgressed the Tenth Amendment. The Sedition Act was worse. Not only did it exercise a power never granted, it exercised a power "expressly and positively forbidden" by the First Amendment: a power "leveled against that right of freely examining public characters and measures, and of free communication thereon," which was essential to elective government itself.[77]

Madison's defense of First Amendment freedoms became a landmark in the libertarian tradition.[78] Federalists had argued that the First Amendment's guarantee of freedom of the press did not prevent the government from punishing seditious libels, only from prohibiting their publication— even that the common law of crimes had been adopted with the Constitution and might have been enforced without restraint if the Sedition Act had not provided new protections. Madison had always thoroughly condemned this last "pretension," and he seized on the occasion to present his fullest argument that British common law had never been adopted as "a law of the United States." Were it otherwise, he reasoned, the authority of Congress would be coextensive with the subjects of that law, which was to say with every possible topic of legislation; the concept of the Constitution as a grant of limited authority would be completely overturned.[79]

The argument that freedom of the press extended only to a prohibition of preventing publications (or censorship defined as prior restraint) could never, Madison insisted, be accepted as "the American idea of it." In the United States, in contrast to Great Britain, every branch of government was limited and based on free elections. Accordingly, the states themselves had generally accepted some abuses of the freedom of the press in order to protect the processes of free elections, and they had plainly meant the First Amendment "as a positive denial to Congress of any power whatever on the subject." In republics, Madison suggested, it was right and proper that officials who did not discharge their trusts "should be brought into contempt or disrepute," that such officials *should* "incur the hatred of the people." To argue that the federal act would punish only *false* opinions was a sham, since arguments and inferences could never, by their nature, be subjected to the tests required to prove a fact in court. The Sedition Act was obviously crafted to protect the current officeholders from the people's censures and contempt. But free elections were "the essence of a free and responsible government," and free elections were impossible unless the people could examine and discuss "the comparative merits and demerits of the candidates" for office. Therefore, the Virginia Resolutions had been right to say that free examination and discussion of public men and measures was "the only effectual guardian of every other right."[80]

In declaring the Sedition Act and other federal measures a transgression of the Constitution, Virginia, Madison insisted, was within its lawful bounds; and it remained within those bounds when it expressed its confidence that other states would join in taking proper measures to maintain the rights reserved to them or to the people. If the other states had joined Virginia in such declarations, these and protests flowing more directly from the people would have been sufficient to arrest the danger they protested. Other means might also have been used—petitions to the Congress, instructions to their senators to move amendments to the Constitution, or an exercise of the authority of three-fourths of the states to call for a convention—although the General Assembly did not choose "to point out to the other states a choice among the farther measures" of resistance. If the Federalists of 1788 had thought it proper to support approval of a stronger federal system by emphatically appealing "to the intermediate existence of the state governments between the people and that government, to the vigilance with which they would descry the first symptoms of usurpation, and to the promptitude with which they would sound the alarm to the public," it was proper now for states to interpose against a train of evils that could wreck the Constitution and the Union.[81]

The Virginia Resolutions, even as refined by the Report of 1800, would return, of course, to haunt their author to his grave, as John Calhoun and his associates employed them to elaborate a doctrine that the aging champion of Union thoroughly condemned. Although it rested on an accurate historical account of how the charter had been put into effect, the logic of the compact theory of the Constitution could be extended far too easily, as nullifiers were to show, to the conclusions that the draft of the Kentucky Resolutions actually drew: that any of the parties to the compact could legitimately judge a federal act to be a violation of the terms on which it had assented to the Constitution and, accordingly, not law, but an assertion of an illegitimate authority that might be justifiably resisted. Moreover, as secessionists would one day show, the argument that plenary conventions of the sovereign people, not the ordinary legislatures of the states, had ratified the Constitution was by no means an insuperable impediment to state attempts to break the federal union.

During his retirement, Madison was not defeated by the nullifiers' logic. As an advocate of the compound republic—of a system neither wholly national *nor* merely federal in its history or its logic—he could plausibly maintain that single parties to the compact had no right to tell the other parties what the compact meant, much less to break it by a unilateral decision. Madison's distinctive concept of a covenant among the sovereign peoples of the several states was more complex than Jefferson's and fully equal to the task of answering Calhoun.[02] And yet, though he denied that any single party to the compact was entitled by the Constitution to reject a federal act, he always recognized that any sovereign people did retain the natural right of revolution. It was a fine distinction. It did not prevent secession. It was not an unimpeachable solution to the riddle that had ruined the British empire: how to keep the central government within the boundaries defined by natural rights, by "constitutional" prescription, and by powers vested in the other agencies of a complex regime without destroying the federal union.[83] *Governmental* sovereignty could *not* in practice be divided on a line that would not shift and could be recognized distinctly by an honest and dispassionate examination of the circumstances under which the compact had been made. No agency—not legislatures, federal courts, or even state conventions—could be universally acknowledged as a final judge without encountering one problem or another.

Madison, in truth, did not resolve a number of apparent tensions, ambiguities, or contradictions in his thought. His confidence in the security afforded by the multiplicity of interests in a large, compound republic always coexisted, somehow, with the old belief that liberty depended on an agricultural majority of people—not because he was unable to conceive of farmers as an interest, but perhaps because he could identify the farmers so entirely with the population that he did not see how all them could come together in the differentiated Union of his day as anything except a people with a vast variety of interests, faiths, and habits. Again, he never found a really satisfying answer to the problem posed for his republican convictions by his certainty that, over time, the land would fill, the nation would be forced to turn to complicated manufactures, and the country would be faced with what a Marxist might describe as the unavoidable proletarianization of the masses—that history would ineluctably produce majorities whose way of life would be profoundly inconsistent with their freedoms. Drew McCoy has pointed out that after the conclusion of the War of 1812, Madison acknowledged that the growth of higher manufacturing was unavoidable in light of the development of other sources for the raw materials that Europeans needed, hoping that a large republic grounded on an educated people would be able, nonetheless, to manage the transition to a higher economic stage. This hope, however—like his self-deluding hope that slavery could be ended by diffusion—was a triumph of his faith and not, in truth, a genuine solution to the problem he descried.

Yet faith, for Madison, was really what his life and thought were premised on from the beginning. As Koch and Ammon long ago observed, the strategy of 1798 was not developed for the sake of states as states, but for the sake of the republican and liberal ideals that were the essence of the Revolution. The legislatures of Virginia and Kentucky were employed, as Madison explained, as "intermediate, local authorities" which existed partly as "so many bodies of observation" on the actions of the general government and as authoritative vehicles for the collection and expression of the public will.[84] In this respect, their protests clearly operated much as he and Jefferson intended, despite the negative responses of their sisters. Assisted by the higher taxes levied to finance the Quasi-War, by Adams's decision to resolve the clash with France, and by the Federalists' continuing insistence on repression, the Republicans were overwhelmingly triumphant in the national elections at the end of 1800. The victory in the congressional as well as in the presidential contests cleared the way for a retraction of the general government into the sphere that Jefferson and Madison believed had been intended by the people. And as long as they presided over its executive department, its policies would be the ones that Jefferson enunciated in his first inaugural address:

> A wise and frugal government which shall restrain men from injuring one another, shall leave them otherwise free to regulate their own pursuits of industry and improvement, and shall not take from the mouth of labor the bread it has earned. . . .
>
> Peace, commerce, and honest friendship with all nations; entangling alliances with none.
>
> The support of the state governments in all their rights as the most competent administrations for our domestic concerns and the surest bulwarks against anti- republican tendencies. . . .
>
> A well disciplined militia, our best reliance in peace and for the first moments of war, till regulars may relieve them. . . .
>
> Economy in public expense, that labor may be lightly burdened.
>
> The honest payment of our debts and sacred preservation of the public faith.[85]

As Jefferson's most trusted aid and then as his successor, Madison would tend the sacred fire on much the same conditions, keeping liberty aflame and keeping federal power—even during wartime—comfortably within the circle of its light.

The Personalities of "Publius"

IN 1788—BEFORE, NOT AFTER, HE AND HAMILTON COLLIDED—
Madison disclaimed responsibility for some of the positions taken by his
partner in their great collaboration.[1] In a late-life memorandum, he remarked again that neither he nor Hamilton had wished to sanction all
the other's views, and partly for that reason had dispensed with their initial practice of reading each other's essays before they went to press.[2] If
my interpretation of the course of their relationship is sound, the 1788
remark reflected a significant uneasiness with Hamilton that had been
building intermittently in Madison since 1783. The late-life comment, too,
was probably an honest recollection of the genuine discomfort he had felt
while *The Federalist* was being written. Madison's unwillingness to be identified with all of Hamilton's opinions is of obvious importance to our
understanding of his thought and to the long debate about the nature of
The Federalist itself. Nowhere, though, did Madison specify his reasons.

One possibility stands out. In essays 23–28 and 34, Hamilton engaged
in a direct exchange with "Brutus" on the federal power to maintain a
peacetime army and on the relationship between the Union's military
needs and the unlimited federal power of taxation.[3] "Brutus" did not
advocate the total prohibition of a peacetime (or "standing") army. He
did insist, however, that the federal power to maintain a peacetime force
(and to monopolize the revenue resources necessary to support it) ought
to be proportioned to the threats the country would actually face. Defensive wars, he made it clear, were the only kind that he expected the United
States to fight; and he could see slight probability of any sudden attack
that the state militias would not be able to parry until a wartime army
could be raised. From first to last, by contrast, Hamilton defended an
unlimited authority to raise a peacetime army and to levy the taxes necessary to support it, "because it is impossible to foresee or to define the

extent and variety of national exigencies" (*Federalist* 23:147). Long a leading spokesman for the view that the United States must have a permanent, though small, professional establishment to garrison its posts and serve as the expandable foundation for a wartime force,[4] Hamilton was not content to offer a compelling argument along these lines. He proceeded to denounce the idea that the militia could conduct a war successfully "against a regular and disciplined army"—"War, like most other things, is a science to be acquired and perfected by diligence, by perseverance, by time, and by practice"—and he suggested that professionals would have to be on hand *before* their presence was required by war *or* by domestic insurrection (25:161–62). He also condemned "the novel and absurd experiment . . . of tying up the hands of government from offensive wars founded upon reasons of state" (34:211).

Madison agreed with Hamilton that the convention could not prudently have limited the federal power to raise and maintain a peacetime army: "The means of security can only be regulated by the means and danger of attack" (41:270). Indeed, he opened his discussion of this power by referring readers back to Hamilton's extended treatment of the subject: "The answer to these questions has been too far anticipated in another place to admit an extensive discussion" (ibid). Obviously, Madison could have simply dropped the subject at this point, which is exactly what he did when he discussed the federal power over commerce (42: 281). Instead, he seized on the occasion to deliver an admonishment that even "Brutus" might have envied: "The liberties of Europe . . . have with few exceptions been the price of her military establishments. A standing force, therefore, is a dangerous at the same time that it may be a necessary provision. On the smallest scale it has its inconveniences. On an extensive scale its consequences may be fatal. On any scale it is an object of laudable circumspection and precaution" (41:271).

It is true, of course, that Hamilton himself admitted that a standing army on a European scale would pose a danger. He even argued (much as Madison had argued at the Constitutional Convention) that the Union was essential to prevent this danger (8:44–50). These concessions are a clear example of the mutual influence of the authors and of our ability to find a general consistency throughout the series. On the other hand, we also have to be aware that the collaborators and their countrymen were sensitive to nuances of thought that can elude an age whose principal preoccupations are quite different. To the revolutionary generation, standing armies were a subject that provoked intense emotions; and I find it hard to doubt, when the relevant essays of "Publius" and "Brutus" are considered in the sequence in which they appeared, that Madison was consciously attempting to revise and moderate the overall impression

Hamilton had left. On standing armies, as the body of this book should show, Madison's essential sympathies had always been as close to those of "Brutus" as they were to his coauthor's.

That Madison was troubled partly by Hamilton's stand on peacetime armies might be argued on another ground, although this ground is far less certain. If we can fairly read his late-life memorandum to suggest that there was *some specific point* at which "it was found most agreeable to each not to give a positive sanction to all the doctrines and sentiments of the other," the possibility that essays 23–26 may mark that point will seem the stronger when we recollect that Hamilton and Madison were evidently still reviewing one another's essays as Madison prepared his numbers on ancient and modern confederacies. Numbers 18–20 are the only ones about which it is known that either author gave the other some materials to use.

Sensible conjecture can suggest, although it cannot prove, that there were several topics on which Hamilton might well have made the other Publius uneasy. Notwithstanding Hamilton's denials that it did have this effect, Madison may well have seen his doctrine of judicial review (78: 524–26 and 81:542–46) as implying "a superiority of the judiciary to the legislative power" in the construction of the Constitution (78:524). This was undeniably a prospect that worried him at the time.[5] Again, he could have understood some passages in *Federalist* no. 27 to imply that the central government *should* intrude increasingly and comprehensively into "matters of internal concern" (27:173–74). And it is even likelier that he was troubled by some passages in *Federalist* no. 11. Hamilton's grand vision of the projection of American might to win ascendency in the western hemisphere, to "teach [the Europeans] moderation," and to "dictate the terms of connection between the old and the new world" (11:173–74) was fundamentally at odds with Madison's ways of thought.

Specific passages and comments, though, may not have been the only or the most important source of Madison's unwillingness to be identified with Hamilton's positions. The body of the essays written by each man do undeniably (if sometimes subtly) illustrate the underlying differences in their agendas, principles, and hopes. As Gottfried Dietze expressed it, Madison regarded the completed Constitution as the product of a federal compact that invigorated the existing Union. He repeatedly insisted that the powers of the reconstructed government were few and carefully defined, and he repeatedly displayed a clear respect for the remaining state preserves. Hamilton's essays were significantly different in their tenor: "state-inimical" where Madison's were "state-friendly," "ardent" in their nationalism where his colleague's were "reluctant."[6] Dietze detected much the same divergence that Douglass Adair did: "Where Hamilton saw the corporate spirit of the several states as poisonous to the union, Madison was aware that the preservation of the state governments could serve the cause of both liberty and union."[7] Madison, it has been said, was fundamentally preoccupied with balances of power: between the central government and the states as well as between the parts of the central government itself.[8] Hamilton, by contrast, did not entirely hide his private preference for an entire subordination of the states or for a further concentration of the powers of the central government itself in the executive and judiciary branches. As Isaac Kramnick writes, Hamilton was "the premier state-builder in a generation of state-builders"; his conception of the national state was recognizably more European in its flavor.[9] Madison's conception of a sound republic was influenced overwhelmingly by eighteenth-century British opposition thinking ("Country" or "Old Whig"). Hamilton was influenced much more fundamentally by "Modern Whig" opinion.

Which, of course, is not to side with one against the other. Here, as in the text throughout, my object is to understand the founders, not to judge them. The passages in Chapter 7 which insist that Madison's positions in *The Federalist* were generally consistent with his private views, whereas Hamilton's were less so, are not exceptions to this rule.[10] These passages are not intended to suggest that Madison was fundamentally more honest than his colleague. Indeed, my own opinion, as I may have hinted, is that the candid Hamilton was usually the more forthcoming of the two, often with disastrous consequences for his own career. Madison was not dishonest either, but he *was* less open—so noncombative, cautious, and reserved that Hamilton may always have been wrong in his assumption that his own affection for his partner was repaid.

I realize, of course, that every scholar runs a risk of sympathizing too completely with his subject. Some may judge that I have not escaped this pitfall in suggesting that Madison's contributions to *The Federalist* were remarkably consistent with his private opinions, whereas many analysts have plausibly maintained that they are not reliable indications of his private feelings at all. Since this point is more than merely incidental to my disagreements with prevailing views, it, too, may need additional discussion.

Madison unquestionably suffered serious defeats at the Constitutional Convention, especially on the apportionment of the senate and the federal veto on state laws. The finished document, as has been shown, differed quite significantly from his original proposals. To these facts, two others are commonly added to suggest that he was privately quite discontented with the Constitution and, therefore, that *The Federalist* cannot be used dependably as a guide to his real opinions: (1) his reports to Jefferson of September 6 and October 24, 1787, the latter written only thirty days before he started to compose his contributions to the classic; and (2) Jefferson's remark of November 18, 1788, that "in some parts [of *The Federalist*] it is discoverable that the author means only to say what may be best said in defense of opinions in which he did not concur."[11] Madison's September 6 report to Jefferson predicted that the plan would "neither effectually answer its national object nor prevent the local mischiefs which everywhere excite disgusts against the state governments." His letter of October 24 incorporated a lengthy defense of a federal negative on state laws and suggested that, without this power, the system still involved "the evil of imperia in imperio."

My rebuttal of this argument suggests, to start, that Madison's opinions changed *as he was working on the series*—a possibility that ought to seem entirely likely to anyone who has completed a major piece of writing, and one for which the evidence must obviously come from the positions Madison took *after* February 1788, not from letters written prior to *Federalist* no. 10. That evidence, I think, powerfully supports the view that the writing of *The Federalist* left Madison convinced that the Constitution was a better document than he had thought a month before he started writing. The best example may be the concept of the federal veto on local legislation. I do not recall a single instance after October 1787 in which he still defended this provision, though its excision from the Constitution was unquestionably the foremost reason for the discontents expressed in his letters to Jefferson. If I am right, however, the exhaustive reconsideration prompted by his writing of *The Federalist* should have shown him that the federal veto was a bad (and certainly an unacceptable) idea.

Approached from this perspective, Jefferson's remark that he could find some cases in which "Publius" defended clauses with which he had not agreed seems better evidence *for* the consistency between Madison's private and public views than for the opposite conclusion. And, in fact, my own analysis assumes that whenever Madison continued to dislike provisions of the Constitution, this dislike is readily apparent. The clearest instance was his argument for equal voting in the Senate (62:416–17). State equality, he wrote, is not "without some reason," given the partly federal character of the system, but "it is superfluous to try by the standards of theory" a provision that was "evidently the result of compromise." This clause, he said, "would be more rational if any interests common to [the small states] and distinct from those of [the large] would otherwise be exposed to peculiar danger." Still, the clause might prove "more convenient in practice than it appears to many in contemplation." Notice, too, that Madison does not merely say that state appointment of the Senate was "most congenial with the public opinion"; he adds that this provision has "the double advantage of favoring a select appointment and of giving to the state governments such an agency in the formation of the federal government as must secure the authority of the former, and may form a convenient link between the two systems." Madison was candid in admitting that the differences between the large and the small states compelled the convention "to sacrifice theoretical propriety to the force of extraneous considerations" and give the small states an equal vote (37:237). But on the matter of a role for states as states, he seems to have accepted opinions he had previously rejected.

As the text insists, *The Federalist* was not a full and finished exposition of Madison's political philosophy. It simply did not enter into many major subjects, including some on which the two collaborators were most unquestionably divided. Still, I challenge skeptics to identify a single case in which the Virginian clearly dissembled his private opinions in these essays. My own first thought was that he might have done so when defending the small size of the House of Representatives (numbers 55–56), a clause about which he continued to be privately concerned. Reexamination proved that this was not a genuine exception. "The smallness of the number, *as a temporary regulation*," is not "dangerous to the public liberty," he wrote (55:375, my italics). Indeed, he frankly says that if he did not think the numbers of representatives would increase with population, "I should admit the objection to have very great weight indeed" (ibid.).

As the labored opening of number 54 suggests, Madison was patently uneasy when his clause-by-clause discussion reached the provision for a representation of three-fifths of the slaves, although this was a clause that he had favored during the convention. Thus, he stated the objections fairly, candidly confessed their strength, and made the strongest case he could for this concession to the South, admitting that it "may appear to be a little strained." Similarly, he admitted that "it were doubtless to be wished" that the Constitution had included a power to act immediately against the international slave trade. Still, he wrote, it was "a great point gained in favor of humanity that a period of twenty years may terminate forever within these states a traffic which has so long and so loudly upbraided the barbarism of modern policy" (42:281–82).

The closest thing I can discover to a genuine exception to the rule that Madison's positions in the classic were not at odds with his private opinions is a passage in *Federalist* no. 45 (312–13). Here, Madison acknowledged that the new government would "possess and may exercise the power of collecting internal as well as external taxes," but then suggested that the power would probably "not be resorted to except for supplemental purposes of revenue, that an option will then be given to the states to supply their quotas by previous collections of their own, and that the eventual collection under the immediate authority of the Union will generally be made by the officers and according to the rules appointed by the several states.'' But even the suggestion that the federal government might authorize a state collection of internal federal taxes may have represented his genuine expectations *at the moment*. This was just what Congress had suggested in its recommendations of 1783, and Madison was not a prophet. He could see quite far, but even he could not anticipate in every instance exactly how the new regime would work. Indeed, if he had actually foreseen how Hamilton and others would interpret and employ the Constitution, the Virginia delegation to the Constitutional Convention might have had a third non-signer.

Notes

DHFFC	*Documentary History of the First Federal Congress of the United States of America, March 4, 1789-March 3, 1791*, ed. Linda Grant Depauw et al. Baltimore: Johns Hopkins University Press, 1972–.
DHFFE	*The Documentary History of the First Federal Elections, 1788–1789*, ed. Gordon DenBoer et al. Madison: University of Wisconsin Press, 1984.
DHRC	*The Documentary History of the Ratification of the Constitution*, ed. Merrill Jensen et al. Madison: State Historical Society of Wisconsin, 1976–.
Federalist	*The Federalist*, ed. with intro. and notes by Jacob E. Cooke. Cleveland: World, 1961. Cited by essay number and page.
JCC	*Journals of the Continental Congress, 1774–1789*, ed. Gaillard Hunt. 34 vols. Washington: Government Printing Office, 1904–1937.
LJM	*Letters and Other Writings of James Madison*, ed. William C. Rives and Philip R. Fendall. 4 vols. Philadelphia, 1865.
LMCC	*Letters of Members of the Continental Congress*, ed. Edmund C. Burnett. 8 vols. Washington: Carnegie Institution, 1921–1936.
PAH	*The Papers of Alexander Hamilton*, ed. Harold C. Syrett and Jacob E. Cooke. 26 vols. New York: Columbia University Press, 1961–1979.
PJM	*The Papers of James Madison*, ed. William T. Hutchinson et al. Chicago and Charlottesville: University of Chicago Press and University Press of Virginia, 1962–.
PTJ	*The Papers of Thomas Jefferson*, ed. Julian P. Boyd et al. Princeton: Princeton University Press, 1950–.
RFC	*The Records of the Federal Convention of 1787*, ed. Max Farrand. Revised edition. 4 vols. New Haven: Yale University Press, 1937.
WJM	*The Writings of James Madison*, ed. Gaillard Hunt. 9 vols. New York: G. P. Putnam's Sons, 1900–1910.
WTJ	*The Works of Thomas Jefferson*, ed. Paul Leicester Ford. 12 vols. New York: G. P. Putnam's Sons, 1904.

Biographies

Brant	Brant, Irving. *James Madison.* 6 vols. Indianapolis, Ind., 1941–61.
Ketcham	Ketcham, Ralph. *James Madison: A Biography.* New York, 1971.
Rakove	Rakove, Jack N. *James Madison and the Creation of the American Republic.* Library of American Biography. Glenview, Ill., 1990.
Schultz	Schultz, Harold S. *James Madison.* New York, 1970.

THE MADISONIAN MADISON: AN INTRODUCTION

1. JM to William Cogswell, March 10, 1834, *RFC* 3:533.

2. A point well made in Harold S. Schultz, "James Madison: Father of the Constitution?" *QJLC* 37 (1980): 215–22.

3. I am referring, of course, to the biographies by Irving Brant, Ralph Ketcham, Harold S. Schultz, and Jack N. Rakove, cited in full on page 404. These are hereafter cited by author's last name, volume if appropriate, and page number.

4. Book-length studies of Madison's political thought include Edward McNall Burns, *James Madison: Philosopher of the Constitution* (New Brunswick, N.J., 1938); Neal Riemer, *James Madison: Creating the American Constitution* (Washington, D.C., 1986); Robert J. Morgan, *James Madison on the Constitution and the Bill of Rights* (New York, 1988); Jennifer Nedelsky, *Private Property and the Limits of American Constitutionalism: The Madisonian Framework and Its Legacy* (Chicago, 1990); William Lee Miller, *The Business of May Next: James Madison and the Founding* (Charlottesville, Va., 1992); and Richard K. Matthews, *"If Men Were Angels": James Madison and the Heartless Empire of Reason* (Lawrence, Kans., 1994). The best is Drew R. McCoy, *The Last of the Fathers: James Madison and the Republican Legacy* (Cambridge, 1989), which focuses on the retirement years.

5. The influence of the remarkable flowering of books since 1988 (or of my own articles as listed in the acknowledgments) is as yet hard to judge. Often markedly at odds with one another, these works, in any case, are only the latest and most comprehensive of the scores of studies that comprise the body of Madison scholarship. Some, although by no means all, of the recent studies cited in note 4 do challenge one or more aspects of the "prevailing views." All except McCoy's (and Miller's more popular and derivative study) remain, in my opinion, within the general framework I discuss.

6. See my article "The Hamiltonian Madison: A Reconsideration," *VMHB* 92 (1984): 3–28.

7. Ketcham 314–15.

8. Marvin Meyers, "Beyond the Sum of the Differences," in *The Mind of the Founder: Sources of the Political Thought of James Madison* (Indianapolis, Ind., 1973).

9. Brant 2:110–11; vol. 3, chap. 10; and 3:180–81, 332–33.

10. John Zvesper, "The Madisonian Systems," *Western Political Quarterly* 37 (1984): 236.

11. Charles A. Beard, *An Economic Interpretation of the Constitution of the United States* (1913; New York, 1960). See also Merrill Jensen, *The Articles of Confederation: An Interpretation of the Social-Constitutional History of the American Revolution, 1774–1781* (Madison, Wis., 1940) and *The New Nation: A History of the United States during the Confederation, 1781–1789* (New York, 1950).

12. Gordon S. Wood, *The Creation of the American Republic, 1776–1787* (Chapel Hill, N.C., 1969), 513.

13. Wood, *Creation of the American Republic*, is the fullest and most influential discussion of the sources and development of Federalist thinking. The conservative

character of much of that thinking is reemphasized in Wood's more recent *Radicalism of the American Revolution* (New York, 1991).

14. Chapter 15 of Jack N. Rakove, *The Beginnings of National Politics: An Interpretive History of the Continental Congress* (New York, 1979), and chapter 5. of his *James Madison and the Creation of the American Republic* are particularly effective on the critical importance of Madison's linkage of the crisis of the Union with the problems in the states.

15. John Agresto, "'A System without a Precedent'—James Madison and the Revolution in Republican Liberty," *South Atlantic Quarterly* 82 (1983), 129–44, is a tidy presentation of these views. Their great pioneer, however, was the late Martin Diamond, whose essays are now collected in *As Far as Republican Principles Will Admit: Essays by Martin Diamond*, ed. William A. Schambra (Washington, D.C., 1992).

16. In addition to Diamond, Wood, and other works already cited, see J. G. A. Pocock, *The Machiavellian Moment: Florentine Political Thought and the Atlantic Republican Tradition* (Princeton, N.J., 1975), 519–26.

17. As in the interview with N. P. Trist, September 27, 1834, *RFC* 3:533–34.

18. See especially JM to N. P. Trist, December 1831, *WJM* 9:471–77.

19. On these points, Diamond's influential essays, which contributed so critically to the challenge to Progressive views, have been a starting point for new mistakes. With Irving Brant and Douglass Adair, Diamond played a vital part in reasserting Madison's profound commitment to the principles of the Declaration of Independence, but Diamond seldom looked beyond *The Federalist* or into Madison's thinking in the early 1780s. Partly as a consequence, his writings, like those of Brant, have also played a major role in the general underestimation of Madison's dedication to a system only partly national in nature and in the nearly universal tendency to make *Federalist* no. 10, which Diamond misread, so much the centerpiece of Madison's thought. For Diamond's challenge to Progressive views, see especially "Democracy and *The Federalist*: A Reconsideration of the Framers' Intent," *APSR* 53 (1959): 52–68. For the positions I dispute, see Diamond, "*The Federalist's* View of Federalism," in *Essays in Federalism*, ed. George C.S. Benson et al. (Claremont, Calif., 1961), 21–64, and Jean Yarbrough, "Rethinking '*The Federalist's* View of Federalism,'" *Publius* 15 (1985): 31–53, and "Madison and Modern Federalism," in *How Federal Is the Constitution?*, ed. Robert A. Goldwin and William A. Schambra (Washington, D.C., 1987), 84–108. An excellent critique of Diamond, developed independently of my analysis in Chapter 7, is Alan Gibson, "The Commercial Republic and the Pluralist Critique of Marxism: An Analysis of Martin Diamond's Interpretation of *Federalist* 10," *Polity* 25 (1993): 497–527.

20. In this paragraph, I use the language made familiar by an extended scholarly debate over the "republican" and "liberal" dimensions of revolutionary thinking. I am conscious that the terminology and framework of this argument can be as much a hindrance as a help toward understanding those who managed to combine both modern liberal and neoclassical (republican) ideas coherently. My object here is to recover Madison's perspective, not to force him into ours. In the language of our own debates, however, I consider Madison a key exemplar of the

revolutionary blend of modern liberal and old republican traditions. Among his most important contributions was his role in the transmission of this revolutionary blend to later generations.

CHAPTER ONE. JAMES MADISON AND THE NATIONALISTS

1. Thomas Rodney Diary, *LMCC* 6:20

2. Brant 1:360–65.

3. This paraphrases the biased, but accurate, assessment in the *Autobiography of Thomas Jefferson*, ed. Dumas Malone (New York, n.d.), 58.

4. Brant 2:418, 301.

5. E. James Ferguson, "The Nationalists of 1781–1783 and the Economic Interpretation of the Constitution," *JAH* 56 (1969): 241–61. Among the subsequent biographers, Rakove is a clear exception. For agreement with Brant, see Ketcham 126–34; also see Merrill D. Peterson, ed., *James Madison: A Biography in His Own Words* (New York, 1974), 51, 69–71. Important monographs identifying Madison with a group of nationalistic reformers include Merrill Jensen, *The New Nation: A History of the United States during the Confederation, 1781–1789* (New York, 1950); E. James Ferguson, *The Power of the Purse: A History of American Public Finance, 1776–1790* (Chapel Hill, N.C., 1961); H. James Henderson, *Party Politics in the Continental Congress* (New York, 1974); and Joseph L. Davis, *Sectionalism in American Politics, 1774–1787* (Madison, Wis., 1977).

6. It is not sufficient to concede, as several influential authors do, that there were differences between Madison and the nationalists from the Middle States. The force of the caveat is usually obscured by the vagueness of the concession. For example, in *Power of the Purse*, 158–60, Ferguson writes that Madison "was not in the inner councils of the Morris group," at least during the Newburgh affair. Yet Ferguson, with Brant, describes Madison as "an unwavering Nationalist," a phrase he usually defines in terms of Morris's objectives. The reader may fairly infer that what distinguished Madison from the inner group was that he was "less intransigent" in his insistence on a common program (166). Other authors make no distinction at all between Madison and the Morrisites, sometimes with disturbing consequences. For a recent example, see James H. Hutson, "Country, Court, and Constitution: Antifederalism and the Historians," *WMQ* 38 (1981): 337–68.

7. Charles Royster, *A Revolutionary People at War: The Continental Army and American Character, 1775–1783* (Chapel Hill, N.C., 1979), 299–300; Edmund Cody Burnett, *The Continental Congress* (New York, 1941), 401–3; Jack N. Rakove, *The Beginnings of National Politics: An Interpretive History of the Continental Congress* (New York, 1979), 255–74; E. Wayne Carp, *To Starve the Army at Pleasure: Continental Army Administration and American Political Culture, 1775–1783* (Chapel Hill, N.C., 1984), chap. 7.

8. JM to TJ, March 27, 1780, *PJM* 2:6. For the convenience of modern readers, I have modernized spelling, capitalization, and punctuation when I was certain that this would not alter the writer's meaning. Abbreviations in quoted passages have normally been expanded.

9. As Ketcham notes, 101.

10. See, especially, JM to ER, May 20, 1783, *PJM* 7:59. Also helpful here is Stanley Elkins and Eric McKitrick, "The Founding Fathers: Young Men of the Revolution," *Political Science Quarterly* 76 (1961): 181–216.

11. See the sources cited in notes 5 and 7, together with *JCC*, vols. 16–17, and *LMCC*, vol. 5.

12. JM to TJ, May 6, 1780, *PJM* 2:19–20.

13. JM to John Page, May 8, 1780, *PJM* 2:21-22; to TJ, June 2, 1780, *PJM* 2:37–38; and to Joseph Jones, October 24, 1780, *PJM* 2:145–46. Madison and Jones were usually in close accord concerning congressional measures, and Madison may have been privy to Jones's correspondence with George Washington. On May 31, Washington wrote Jones: "Certain I am unless Congress speak in a more decisive tone, unless they are invested with powers by the several states competent to the great purposes of war, or assume them as matter of right . . . our cause is lost." On June 19, Jones replied that "Congress have been gradually surrendering or throwing upon the several states the exercise of powers they should have retained. . . . . This body never had or at least . . . have [seldom] exercised powers adequate to the purpose of war, and such as they had have been . . . frittered away to the states." See *LMCC* 5:226–27, and the secondary works cited in note 3.

14. JM to Edmund Pendleton, September 12, 1780, *PJM* 2:81–82.

15. JM to Edmund Pendleton, November 7, 1780, *PJM* 2:166. For additional hints of his persistent hope that problems could be solved within the present structures, see JM to TJ, May 6, 1780, *PJM* 2:19-20, and to John Page (?), May 8, 1780, *PJM* 2:21.

16. JM, "Resolutions Respecting Vermont Lands," September 16, 1780, *PJM* 2:87–88. On September 19, 1780, Madison wrote Jones that he believed a decision should be made "on principles that will effectually discountenance the erection of new governments without the sanction of proper authority" (*PJM* 2:90). Jones's reply confirms the impression that the Virginians, who were faced with a weak secession movement in Kentucky, had this matter much in view: "Such excrescences should be taken off on their first appearance. . . . We know not what may be the consequences if Congress shall countenance by precedent the dismembering of states" (*PJM* 2:106).

17. *JCC* 18:916. For the issue of the western lands to this point see Thomas Perkins Abernethy, *Western Lands and the American Revolution* (New York, 1937), chap. 19, and Peter Onuf, "Toward Federalism: Virginia, Congress, and the Western Lands," *WMQ* 34 (1977): 353–74. Onuf's insistence that a resolution of this issue was, for many Virginians, a prerequisite for support of stronger federal powers has been especially helpful.

18. JM to Jones, October 17, 1780, *PJM* 2:136–37.

19. For now, Madison insisted that Virginia could still accomplish the exclusion of the companies simply by attaching to its act of cession a condition voiding private claims, perhaps even a provision that "no private claims be complied with" in the cessions of any state (ibid.). See also JM to Jones, September 19, 1780, *PJM* 2:89–90.

20. Jones to JM, October 9, 1780, *PJM* 2:120–21; JM to Jones, October 24, 1780, *PJM* 2:145; Brant 2:77–79.

21. Quoted in Brant 2:14.

22. JM to John Jay, October 17, 1780, *PJM* 2:127–35.

23. JM to Jones, November 25, 1780, *PJM* 2:203. See also JM to Jones, December 5, 1780, *PJM* 2:224.

24. Virginia Delegates to TJ, December 13, 1780, *PJM* 2:241–42.

25. Thomas Burke to William Bingham, February 6, 1781, *LMCC* 5:562–63.

26. "I have always conceived the several ministerial departments of Congress to be provisions for aiding their counsels as well as executing their resolutions" (JM to James Monroe, March 21, 1785, *PJM* 8:255–56).

27. Madison "used every stratagem to expand" congressional authority, moving to give Congress power to prohibit trade with Britain, to permit impressment of supplies, etc. (Ketcham 114). This accords closely with the longer discussion in Brant, vol. 2, chap. 8: Madison believed in "easy discovery of implied powers where none were expressly stated" (110). Defeated in his move for a coercive power, he drove "to the same end by specific legislation based on implied powers" (111). "Forced by necessity, Congress adopted one specific measure after another which Madison put before it, based on implications of power" (118).

28. *JCC* 19:110–13.

29. JM, "Motion on Impost," February 3, 1781, *PJM* 2:303–4.

30. JM, "Proposed Amendment of Articles of Confederation," March 12, 1781, *PJM* 3:17–19.

31. JM to TJ, April 16, 1781, *PJM* 3:71–72.

32. Ibid.

33. Most eloquently in the 1785 "Memorial and Remonstrance against Religious Assessments," which I discuss in Chapter 3 and is printed in *PJM* 8:295–306.

34. The single issue on which Madison might fairly be accused of torturing the charter saw him argue, while he was working frantically to rush assistance to Virginia, that five states should be sufficient to form a congressional quorum for ordinary business. See Thomas Rodney Diary, March 5, 1781, *LMCC* 6:8.

35. JM to Pendleton, January 8, 1781, *PJM* 4:22–23. See also Virginia Delegates to Gov. Benjamin Harrison, *PJM* 4:19.

36. *PJM* 3:133; *JCC*, vols. 20–21; Brant 2:137–40, 143–46.

37. JM to Pendleton, August 14, 1781, *PJM* 3:224.

38. See Virginia Delegates to Gov. Thomas Nelson, October 9, 16, 23, 1781, *PJM* 3:281–82, 286–88, 293; Abernethy, *Western Lands*, chap. 19. See also Madison's draft of a protest against the proceedings of the new committee, whose report was not acted on until 1782, in *PJM* 3:284–85.

39. Randolph to Nelson, November 7, 1781, *LMCC* 6:259–60.

40. JM to TJ, November 18, 1781, *PJM* 3:307–8.

41. JM to Pendleton, January 22, 1782, *PJM* 4:38–39. Madison complained that with every indication of approaching hostilities between the Vermonters and the authorities of New Hampshire and New York, it might be necessary to accept congressional intervention despite the constitutional and practical arguments

against it. Before the Articles were ratified, he had urged congressional intervention to defend the jurisdictions of these states. Now that the Articles contained a
clause establishing a different procedure for resolving territorial disputes between
states, he condemned it, saying, "It is very unhappy that such plausible pretexts,
if not necessary occasions, of assuming power should occur. Nothing is more distressing to those who have a due respect for the constitutional modifications of
power than to be obliged to decide on them."

42. JM to Pendleton, April 23, 1782, *PJM* 4:178; JM to ER, May 1, 1782, *PJM*
4:196–97. See also Madison's memorandum, "Observations Relating to the Influence of Vermont and the Territorial Claims on the Politics of Congress," May 1,
1782, *PJM* 4:200–203.

43. JM to Arthur Lee, May 7, 1782, *PJM* 4:217–18.

44. JM to ER, May 7, 1782, *PJM* 4:220.

45. JM to Pendleton, November 27, 1781, *PJM* 3:317. See, similarly, JM to TJ,
November 18, 1781, *PJM* 3:308: Virginia "ought to be as fully impressed with the
necessity of the Union during the war as of its probable dissolution after it." Brant
and the editors of *PJM* are on very shaky ground in suggesting that Madison
coauthored Randolph's "Facts and Observations" on America's western claims,
inserting in this document the argument for a federal title to the western lands.
In every instance Madison denounced this doctrine, though he was willing to see
it used for foreign consumption. The "Facts and Observations" (*JCC* 23:481–521),
delivered to Congress on August 18, 1782, suggested to the peace commissioners
that if the arguments derived from state titles seemed an insufficient defense of
the western claims, they might argue that the vacant lands had devolved from the
crown to the United States collectively. In a letter to Randolph reporting the congressional proceedings (*PJM* 5:87), Madison, who repeatedly referred to the document as "your report," called this argument an "expedient" meant to bring the
landed and landless states together on the matter. On the same day, during a
debate on whether Congress should hear petitions from Kentuckians desiring independence, Madison said: "As to the supposition that the right of the crown
devolved on the U.S., it was so extravagant that it could not enter into the thoughts
of any man," which remark occasioned a "storm of dissent" from the landless
states (Charles Thomson's Notes on Debates, *JCC* 23:83–84).

46. Henderson, *Party Politics,* 249.

47. Ibid., 250–51, and chap. 10. The "Old Revolutionaries" included Samuel
Adams, Elbridge Gerry, and other members who had served since before Independence.

48. Ibid., 288–89. Indeed, if I read Henderson correctly, his reason for placing
the Virginia bloc in this coalition is the link between Randolph, Jones, and some
of its marginal members and the Pennsylvania-Maryland bloc, which was the core
of the "Middle-Southern Coalition." This, of course, has little to do with Madison's
own position, which might fairly be characterized as eccentric. Henderson sees the
"Middle-Southern Coalition" of 1781 as opposed to a "New England Group"
more on matters of foreign policy than on domestic issues, yet Madison often
found his closest allies in the arguments over peace terms among the Mas-

sachusetts men, who were willing to defend Virginia's western claims in exchange for Virginia's support for American access to the Newfoundland fisheries.

49. Ibid., 295.

50. The evidence is scanty because Madison did not yet save all of his incoming correspondence and did not make copies of outgoing letters. We must depend primarily on letters he recovered late in life from Pendleton, Jefferson, Randolph, and Jones. He corresponded with his two congressional colleagues when they traveled to Virginia but himself made no such visits, establishing an unexampled record of attention to congressional duties.

51. JM to ER, July 23, 1782, *PJM* 4:435; "Comments on Instructions to Peace Commissioners," *PJM* 4:436–38.

52. JM to ER, June 4, 1782, *PJM* 4:313. Lee's opinion of Madison is also worth remarking: "Without being a public knave himself, he has always been a supporter of public knaves, . . . duped by . . . the rapacious Morris and the intriguing Marbois." See Lee to Thomas Lee Shippen, April 25, 1790, quoted in Brant 2:199.

53. For additional defenses of state preserves or attempts to determine the "constitutional" boundaries between the central government and states, see *PJM* 4:195–96, 298, 367–71, 391–94, 410–12, and 444–45.

54. JM, "Notes on Debates," November 14, 1782, *PJM* 5:273–74 (hereafter cited as "Notes"); JM to ER, September 10 and November 5, 1782, *PJM* 5:115–16, 242–43. By December 5, Congress was again considering whether to threaten the recalcitrant Vermonters with federal coercion. Significantly, Madison moved to alter the proposed resolution in order to base congressional interposition on acts of New Hampshire and New York as well as on the need to preserve the peace of the Confederation. Following defeat of his amendment, he voted for the original resolution, but this is yet another case where he was hesitant about assuming powers not clearly granted to Congress. See *PJM* 5:367–71.

55. For the evolution of Morris's proposals and early congressional action, see the sources cited in notes 5 and 7, together with Clarence L. VerSteeg, *Robert Morris: Revolutionary Financier* (New York, 1954), chap. 5 and 123–29. Morris's report of July 29, recommending a land tax, a poll tax, and an excise, is in *JCC* 22:429–46.

56. JM, "Report on Payment of New Jersey Troops," *PJM* 5:173–77.

57. "Notes," December 4, 1782, *PJM* 5:363–64.

58. On the latter issue, his defense of local interests conflicted with his support for Morris. Morris's advice, "in rigid adherence to his maxims of public faith," as Madison put it, was that state surpluses of the old continentals be credited at the official rate of 40 to 1. The eastern states particularly had retired great quantities at far lower rates. Madison opposed ratios of 40 to 1, 75 to 1, 100, and even 150 to 1. See "Notes," November 26, 1782, *PJM* 5:321–22, and JM to ER, December 3, 1782, *PJM* 5:356–57.

59. For the events of December 24, see ER to JM, December 13, 1782, *PJM* 5:401, and "Notes," *PJM* 5:441–42.

60. VerSteeg, *Robert Morris*, 166–77, 185–87, quotation at 169.

61. Ibid., 171.

62. With Madison now keeping his "Notes on Debates," the single most important source for the crisis of 1783, it is possible to reconstruct a day-by-day account. My discussion rests primarily on these and on *JCC*, vol. 24.

63. Deliberations on a method of assessing lands, a necessary starting point for any adjustment of state accounts under the provisions of the Articles, can be followed in "Notes" from January 9 to January 28, when the issue merged into the larger question of general revenues. As a guardian of southern interests, Madison differed with Morris and his supporters on details. He called Hamilton's proposal that Congress assign uniform rates to various types of lands "totally inadmissable" to the thinly populated South. He also opposed Wilson's suggestion for a formula combining reported population with returns of quantities of granted lands.

64. "Notes," January 24, 1783, *PJM* 6:120.

65. JM to ER, January 22, 1783, *PJM* 6:55.

66. "Notes," January 28, 1783, *PJM* 6:143–47.

67. "Notes," February 4, 1783, *PJM* 6:187.

68. *JCC* 24:137. Madison condemned the plan as contrary to the Articles because it required a return of population as part of the formula for making an assessment. See *PJM* 6:256, 195–98, 209, 213, 215–16, and 247.

69. "Notes," February 18, 1783, *PJM* 6:251.

70. "Notes," January 28, 1783, *PJM* 6:143.

71. Ibid. Entered by Madison as a long footnote to his record of Hamilton's speech.

72. See also Nathaniel Gorham's remarks in Congress, in "Notes," February 18, 1783, *PJM* 6:249–50, together with the famous letter of February 7 in which Governeur Morris told General Henry Knox: "If you will permit me a metaphor from your own profession, after you have carried the post, the public creditors will garrison it for you" (*LMCC* 7:34n–35n).

73. JM to ER, February 13, 1783, *PJM* 6:232–33.

74. FitzSimons and Williamson both said openly that they hoped the army would not disband. Williamson added, "If force should be necessary to excite justice, the sooner force were applied the better" ("Notes," February 19, 1783, *PJM* 6:260–61).

75. Ibid., 259–61.

76. "Notes," February 20, 1783, *PJM* 6:265–266.

77. The precise nature of the relationship between the army radicals and the nationalists and public creditors supporting Morris is unknown. Interpretations range from Henderson's suggestion that Hamilton and Gouverneur Morris, who was Robert's assistant at the treasury, made "hesitant and uncoordinated efforts to encourage continuing verbal protests from the army" (*Party Politics*, 332–35) through an argument that Hamilton and both Morrises conspired to provoke a coup d'etat by the group around Horatio Gates and then to alert Washington in time to squelch it. For the latter see Richard H. Kohn, *Eagle and Sword: The Federalists and the Creation of the Military Establishment in America, 1783–1802* (New York, 1975), chap. 2, and C. Edward Skeen, "The Newburgh Conspiracy Reconsidered," with a Rebuttal by Richard H. Kohn, *WMQ* 31(1974): 273–98. I suspect that a

declaration of intention not to disband was more than Hamilton or Robert Morris wanted from the army, but it is clear that Morris's supporters urged the army to look to Congress rather than the states for satisfaction of its demands and that they used the agitation at camp to generate an atmosphere of crisis in Philadelphia. All authorities agree that Madison was not involved in contacts with the army.

78. "Notes," February 21, 1783, *PJM* 6:270–272.

79. Ibid., 290–92.

80. Ibid., 375.

81. Brant 2: chap. 15; Ferguson, *Power of the Purse*, chap. 8, in which Madison's authorship of the recommendations of April 18 is not even mentioned.

82. Madison's sketch of February 26 appears as a long footnote in his "Notes of the Debates." The "Report on Restoring Public Credit" as reported from the select committee of Madison, Hamilton, Gorham, FitzSimons, and Rutledge (March 6) is printed in *PJM* 6:311–14. The committee altered Madison's original proposals so that only the impost and the additional state appropriations would be linked. Congress struck his call for an assumption of state debts and disjoined the other elements of the plan. After the assumption of state debts had been removed, Madison decided against further attempts to rejoin its several parts. He feared that the completed plan had "no bait for Virginia," yet hoped that "a respect for justice, good faith, and national honor" would secure the state's approval (JM to TJ, May 20, 1783, *PJM* 6:481).

83. "Notes," *PJM* 6:297–98. This was in response to Mercer's charge that commutation tended "in common with the funding of other debts to establish and perpetuate a monied interest" that "would gain the ascendance of the landed interest . . . and by their example and influence become dangerous to our republican constitutions."

84. "Notes," February 21, 1783, *PJM* 6:272.

85. JM to TJ, May 6, 1780, *PJM* 2:19–20, quoted on p. 17 above.

86. Morris, Report of July 29, 1782, *JCC* 22:435–37.

87. Morris to John Jay, July 13, 1781, quoted in Ferguson, *Power of the Purse*, 123–24; Morris, report of July 29, 1782, *JCC* 22:432.

88. See, especially, Hamilton's letters to an unknown recipient (n.d.), *PAH* 2: 234–51; to James Duane, September 3, 1780, *PAH* 2:418; and to Robert Morris, April 30, 1781, *PAH* 2:604–35; along with the conclusion of "The Continentalist," *PAH* 2:234–51, 400, 418, 604-35, 3:99–106.

89. Morris, who overplayed his hand and angered nearly everyone in Congress by publishing his threatened resignation, still preferred a tariff to an impost, objected to the twenty-five-year limitation of the latter, and continued to insist on congressional appointment of collectors as well as on the need to add a land tax, house tax, and an excise. For congressional response to Morris's publication of his letter, together with continuing attempts by Hamilton and Wilson to secure the superintendent's objectives, see "Notes," March 11, 1783, and March 20, 1783, *PJM* 2:322–25, 370–72, along with JM to ER, March 11, 1783, *PJM* 2:326. On April 22 Madison wrote to Jefferson that only Rhode Island had voted against his amended plan, although New York's vote was divided and lost "by the rigid ad-

herence of Mr. Hamilton to a plan which he supposed more perfect" (*PJM* 2:481). For Hamilton's objections, see his letter to George Clinton, May 4, 1783, *PAH* 3: 354–55.

90. Ferguson was first to see that the Morris nationalists understood and wished to replicate "the role of funded debt and national bank in stabilizing the regime founded in Britain after the revolution of 1689" (*Power of the Purse*, 289–90 and passim). As historians have continued to explore the character of the eighteenth-century British regime and the thinking of the "modern Whigs" or English "court"—terms that Ferguson did not employ— the implications of this desire have emerged more clearly. For a preliminary exploration of the course of "court" thinking in America, see Lance Banning, *The Jeffersonian Persuasion: Evolution of a Party Ideology* (Ithaca, N.Y., 1978), 126–40 and passim. Since then, a host of useful contributions have appeared: Drew R. McCoy, *The Elusive Republic: Political Economy in Jeffersonian America* (Chapel Hill, N.C., 1980); John M. Murrin, "The Great Inversion, or Court versus Country: A Comparison of the Revolution Settlements in England (1688–1721) and America (1776–1816)," in *Three British Revolutions: 1641, 1688, 1776*, ed. J. G. A. Pocock (Princeton, N.J., 1980), 368–453; J. G. A. Pocock, "1776: The Revolution against Parliament," in Pocock, *Three British Revolutions*, 265–88; and Ralph Ketcham, *Presidents above Party: The First American Presidency, 1789–1829* (Chapel Hill, N.C., 1984), 31–38 and chap. 10. The nearly simultaneous, unsuccessful movement to establish a professional peacetime army, in which Hamilton was also a central figure, is a subject for Kohn, *Eagle and Sword*, and Lawrence Delbert Cress, *Citizens in Arms: The Army and Militia in American Society to the War of 1812* (Chapel Hill, N.C., 1982), 78–93. Also helpful on the plans for managing the debt is Janet A. Riesman, "Money, Credit, and Federalist Political Economy," in *Beyond Confederation: Origins of the Constitution and American National Identity*, ed. Richard Beeman, Stephen Botein, and Edward C. Carter II (Chapel Hill, N.C., 1987), 128–61.

91. "Notes," February 21, 1783, *PJM* 6:272. Four days later, Madison repeated this language in a letter to Randolph (*PJM* 6:286–87). Note also that in listing the probable reactions of the several states to his plan for compromise, he thought that Virginia would approve a general revenue "as tending to secure her the protection of the Confederacy against the maritime superiority of the eastern states" (*PJM* 6:291).

92. Madison's fullest and most fervent explanations of the inseparable connection he perceived between the Union and the republican revolution would come in his speech of June 29, 1787, to the Constitutional Convention (*RFC* 1: 464–65) and in *The Federalist* no. 41. The development of this argument between 1783 and the Convention will be traced below.

93. Madison probably saw or heard about the letter to Joseph Jones in which Washington suggested that the first Newburgh Address was written in Philadelphia and that the agitation at camp was ultimately attributable to Robert or, more likely, Gouverneur Morris. In his "Notes" for March 17 (*PJM* 6:348), he remarked that from "private letters from the army and other circumstances there appeared good

ground for suspecting that the civil creditors were intriguing in order to inflame the army" and secure congressional approval of general funds.

94. *PJM* 6:488–94, quotation at 489.

95. In his "Address to the States" Madison admitted that the new financial plan was fully consistent neither with a strict regard for public credit nor with a conventional distrust of central power. In a letter to Edmund Randolph (May 20, 1783, *PJM* 7:59) he also noted that the plan departed from the principles of the Confederation. He was not entirely happy with this fact, but argued that "unless those who oppose the plan can substitute some other equally consistent with public justice and honor and more conformable to the doctrines of the Confederation, all those who love justice and aim at the public good will be advocates."

96. Hamilton drafted a congressional resolution calling for a federal convention shortly before he retired from Congress, then decided that there was too little support to introduce it (*PAH* 3:420–26). VerSteeg and Rakove disagree with Ferguson as to whether Morris also hoped for a structural transformation of the system.

97. Hamilton mentioned his desire for a convention in a debate of April 1 ("Notes," *PJM* 6:425). Stephen Higginson, who favored the idea, told Henry Knox in 1787 that he had "pressed upon Mr. Madison and others the idea of a special convention. . . . But they were as much opposed to this idea as I was to the measures they were then pursuing to effect, as they said, the same thing" (*LMCC* 7: 123n).

98. Ferguson, *Power of the Purse*, 292.

99. The literature on British opposition thinking is extensive, but see, as a beginning, J.G.A. Pocock, "Machiavelli, Harrington, and English Political Ideologies in the Eighteenth Century," *WMQ* 22 (1965): 549–63; and *The Machiavellian Moment: Florentine Political Thought and the Atlantic Republican Tradition* (Princeton: N.J., 1975); Isaac Kramnick, *Bolingbroke and His Circle: The Politics of Nostalgia in the Age of Walpole* (Cambridge, Mass., 1968); and Roger Durrell Parker, "The Gospel of Opposition" (Ph.D. diss., Wayne State University, 1975).

100. P.G.M. Dickson, *The Financial Revolution in England: A Study in the Development of Public Credit, 1688–1756* (New York, 1967); John Brewer, *The Sinews of Power: War, Money, and the English State, 1688–1783* (New York, 1989).

101. Its stabilizing role is a central theme for J. H. Plumb, *The Growth of Political Stability in England, 1675–1725* (London, 1967). Pocock adds that, just as the parliamentary system maintained unity between the government and the landed gentry, the financial system linked the government with the commercial and financial segments of the elite (*Three British Revolutions*, 270–71).

102. [John Trenchard and Thomas Gordon], *Cato's Letters, or Essays on Liberty, Civil and Religious, and other Important Subjects*, 4 vols., 3d ed. (London, 1733); J[ames] B[urgh], *Political Disquisitions, or an Inquiry into Public Errors, Defects, and Abuses*, 3 vols. (London, 1774–75). Tory spokesmen, led by Viscount Bolingbroke, were more inclined to express the landed gentry's discontent with rising commerce in itself.

103. J.G.A. Pocock, ed., *The Political Works of James Harrington* (Cambridge, 1977),

and Pocock, "Machiavelli, Harrington, and English Political Ideologies." Contrast, however, Paul A. Rahe, *Republics Ancient and Modern: Classical Republicanism and the American Revolution* (Chapel Hill, N.C., 1992), which is the most impressive argument that early-modern English thought was consciously inimical to truly classical ideas and thus should not be characterized as "civic humanist," "classical republican," or even "neoclassical" at all. I will address such issues later. For now, it may suffice to say that though I recognize Rahe's book as an illuminating treatment of the differences between ancient and modern republicanism, Rahe seems to me to go too far toward denying the influence of classical ideas on Harrington and other English writers, though he does not dispute the major influence of the English opposition writers (or of truly classical ideas) on American opinion. See, further, the powerful summary of some of Rahe's main themes in "Antiquity Surpassed: The Repudiation of Classical Republicanism," in *Republicanism, Liberty, and Commercial Society, 1649–1776*, ed. David Wooton (Stanford, Calif., 1994), 233–69; and compare his interpretation with the alternative being pioneered in works such as Alan Houston, *Algernon Sidney* (Princeton, N.J., 1991); Michael P. Zuckert, *Natural Rights and the New Republicanism* (Princeton, N.J., 1994), and Jerome Huyler, *Locke in America: The Moral Philosophy of the Founding Era* (Lawrence, Kans., 1994).

104. The masterworks on the enormous influence of this thinking on the early Revolution are Bernard Bailyn, *The Ideological Origins of the American Revolution* (Cambridge, Mass., 1967), and Gordon S. Wood, *The Creation of the American Republic, 1776–1787* (Chapel Hill, N.C., 1969). Robert Shalhope's articles, "Toward a Republican Synthesis: The Emergence of an Understanding of Republicanism in American Historiography," *WMQ* 29 (1972): 49–80, and "Republicanism and Early American Historiography," *WMQ* 39 (1982): 334–56, provide an introduction to the rapidly growing literature. For some of the most recent contributions, see Peter S. Onuf, "Reflections on the Founding: Constitutional Historiography in Bicentennial Perspective," *WMQ* 46 (1989): 341–75.

105. See note 83. For the perceptions of Morris's opponents, in addition to remarks already quoted, see Stephen Higginson to Samuel Adams, May 20, 1783, *LMCC* 7:167: "There are those also among us who wish to keep up a large [military] force, to have large garrisons, to increase the navy, to have a large diplomatic corps, to give large salaries to all our servants. Their professed view is to strengthen the hands of government, to make us respectable in Europe, and I believe they might add to divide among themselves and their friends every place of honor and profit." Madison questioned the constitutional authority of Congress to maintain a peacetime army and favored a small, inexpensive diplomatic corps (*PJM* 7:159, 5:298).

106. They were more at odds than any of them realized because Madison did not elaborate his opposition to a "perpetual" debt whereas Hamilton and Morris both developed their ideas more fully in private correspondence or anonymous newspaper pieces than they did in congressional speeches or reports. In addition, although Ferguson was right to note that nearly all the elements of Hamilton's financial program were anticipated in Morris's plans, the superintendent's pro-

posals of the spring of 1783, tailored to a current crisis, were not as obvious an imitation of the British system of finance as Hamilton's would one day be.

107. JM, "Address to the States," *PJM* 6:494.

108. I have postponed a full discussion of Madison's republican convictions to Chapter 3, for there was never an occasion during or before his years in Congress for him to explain them at length. He implied much, however, in the stands already covered, and this may be the clearer if we note a few additional occasions on which his assumptions did peek through. Early in his service, when Joseph Jones informed him that Virginia's legislature was considering an enlistment bounty in the form of slaves, Madison asked if it would not be better just to liberate the slaves and turn them into soldiers. "It would certainly," he wrote, "be more consonant to the principles of liberty, which ought never to be lost sight of in a contest for liberty" (November 28, 1780, *PJM* 2:209). His own determination to keep these principles in view was often quite explicit when resisting excessive centralization. But the early revolutionary fabric of his thinking—a phrase I define later—seems apparent in a host of lesser instances: his scathing contempt for Benedict Arnold's "thirst for pelf" (*PJM* 2:123) or for the "sordid attachment to gain" which led some Americans to participate in illegal trade with the British (4:352); his close approaches to condemning Jefferson's withdrawals from public life (5:170); his support for simplicity and economy on the part of the foreign establishment (5:298); and his hostility toward speculation in Virginia soldiers' warrants (7:308). As was true in the debates on Morris's financial plan, he could occasionally imply volumes in a sentence. This was so, for example, when he informed Randolph that the Dutch ambassador, expected any day, had ordered "*six* elegant horses . . . for his coach," together with "one of the best houses in the most fashionable part of this city. Wherever commerce prevails there will be an inequality of wealth, and wherever the latter does a simplicity of manners must decline" (September 30, 1983, *PJM* 7:363). Madison's commitment to republican simplicity was apparent even in his dress.

CHAPTER TWO. THE CRISIS OF CONFEDERATION GOVERNMENT

1. On September 17 and October 8, 1783, two essays appeared in the *Pennsylvania Journal* over the signature "The North American." Irving Brant drew valuable support for his portrait of Madison as a radical nationalist by arguing that he wrote these essays and that only here did he reveal the true direction of his thinking, proposing that the state and federal constitutions be revised in order to transfer sovereignty to the central government and render the states subordinate units. See "Two Neglected Madison Letters," ed. Irving Brant, *WMQ* 3 (1946): 569–87. The attribution of these letters to Madison has since been generally rejected (e.g., *PJM* 7:319–46), but it is not so often realized how critical this attribution was to Brant's interpretation of Madison or how greatly Brant exaggerated the radical nationalism of the "North American" himself, whoever he may have been.

2. The emphasis on disenchantment with conditions in the states as the essential impetus to sweeping constitutional reform is as clear in Gordon S. Wood, *The Creation of the American Republic, 1776–1787* (Chapel Hill, N.C., 1969), as it was in Beard, *An Economic Interpretation of the Constitution of the United States* (New York, 1913). There are signs that this is changing in the aftermath of works such as Jack N. Rakove, *The Beginnings of National Politics: An Interpretive History of the Continental Congress* (New York, 1979), and Peter S. Onuf, *The Origins of the Federal Republic: Jurisdictional Controversies in the United States, 1775–1787* (Philadelphia, 1983). See, for example, "*The Creation of the American Republic, 1776–1787*: A Symposium of Views and Reviews," *WMQ* 44 (1987): 549–640. Nevertheless, the assumption retains nearly axiomatic status. It is fundamental, in my understanding, even in Rakove's own writings on Madison.

3. The reference to "calumnies" on republican government is from Rufus King's record of Madison's speech to the Constitutional Convention, June 4, 1787, *RFC* 1:108. The longer quotation is from Madison's preface to his own notes of these debates, *RFC* 3:542–43. In the latter, I believe, Madison recaptured his opinions on retirement from the Congress more precisely than most later analysts have. "The radical infirmity of the Articles of Confederation," he wrote, "was the dependence of Congress on the voluntary and simultaneous compliance with its requisitions by so many independent communities, each consulting more or less its particular interests and convenience and distrusting the compliance of the others." Once the continental presses had been stopped, "the war was merely kept alive and brought to a successful conclusion by such foreign aids and temporary expedients as could be applied, a hope prevailing with many and a wish with all that a state of peace and the sources of prosperity opened by it would give to the Confederacy in practice the efficiency which had been inferred from its theory." Peace, however, "brought no cure for the public embarrassments," and Madison seems clearly to suggest that it was only at this point that he concluded that the "theory" was itself defective.

4. Through the remainder of the spring, Congress was primarily concerned with the details of peace: indemnifying army officers against civilian claims for damages connected with their duties, instructing Washington about the northwest posts, and debating what to do about the slaves retained by the British in violation of the treaty. Madison's "Notes on the Debates" were now quite brief, even on the subjects that had always been of central interest. See also *JCC*, vol. 25.

5. See Madison's "Notes" for June 19–26, 1783, *PJM* 7:165, 167, 176–78, and Kenneth R. Bowling, "New Light on the Philadelphia Mutiny of 1783: Federal-State Confrontation at the Close of the War for Independence," *PMHB* 101 (1977): 419–50.

6. JM to TJ, August 11, 1783, September 20, 1783, *PJM* 7:268, 352. The romance with Kitty Floyd is fully detailed in Brant, vol. 2, chap. 18. Madison calculated that his eligibility for service would end under the provisions of the Articles on October 31, 1783, the conclusion of his third full year in Congress.

7. For Madison on the seat of government, see JM to ER, July 8, July 28, and October 13, 1783, *PJM* 7:216, 256–57, 373–375, and his "Notes on Congress' Residence," *PJM* 7:216, 236-57, 373-75, 378–80. The residency issue is briefly

discussed in Laurence Delbert Cress, "Whither Columbia? Congressional Residence and the Politics of the New Nation, 1776 to 1787," *WMQ* 32 (1975): 581–600, but see especially Kenneth R. Bowling, *The Creation of Washington, D.C.: The Idea and Location of the American Capital* (Fairfax, Va., 1991).

8. "Notes," June 10 and 20, 1783, *PJM* 7:125–26, 167–68; letters of these months to Jefferson, Randolph, and Jones; Thomas Perkins Abernethy, *Western Lands and the American Revolution* (New York, 1937), 270–73; and Peter Onuf, "Toward Federalism: Virginia, Congress, and the Western Lands," *WMQ* 34 (1977): 353–74.

9. JM to ER, June 24, 1783, *PJM* 7:191–92.

10. JM to TJ, December 10, 1783, *PJM* 7:401–3, quotation on 401. For Mason's problematic stand on federal issues, see his draft of instructions to Fairfax County delegates to the Virginia assembly, May 30, 1783, in *The Papers of George Mason, 1725–1792*, ed. Robert A. Rutland (Chapel Hill, N.C., 1970), 2:779–83. Madison and Jefferson both dated their acquaintanceship to their common service in the Virginia Assembly in 1776. This had deepened in 1779 and 1780, when Madison served briefly on the Council of State during Jefferson's tenure as governor, but there was an obvious change in the texture of their correspondence, reflecting their closer bond, at the time of the Floyd romance. Jefferson had come to Philadelphia late in December 1782 to prepare for service as a peace commissioner. He left for Baltimore on January 26, expecting to sail on a French frigate. When his diplomatic mission was suspended by news of the preliminary peace, he returned to Philadelphia on February 26, stayed until April 12, and returned for service in Congress on October 29.

11. JM to ER, May 20, 1783, *PJM* 7:59–62. Compare JM to TJ, May 13, 1783, *PJM* 7:39.

12. JM to ER, August 30, 1783, *PJM* 7:295–96.

13. JM to ER, September 13, 1783, *PJM* 7:314–15.

14. On December 9, 1783, the Virginia legislature empowered Congress to counteract restrictions on American trade and asked the other states to do the same. On April 30, 1784, Congress asked the states for power to prohibit foreign imports for a period of fifteen years. The growing movement for a federal power over commerce can conveniently be followed in the first volume of George Bancroft, *History of the Formation of the Constitution of the United States of America*, 2 vols. (New York, 1882), where it is seen as giving "the immediate impulse to a more perfect constitution" (1:146). See also the convenient summary of British restrictions and American responses in Frederick W. Marks III, *Independence on Trial: Foreign Affairs and the Making of the Constitution* (Baton Rouge, La., 1973), chap. 2.

15. JM to TJ, December 10, 1783, *PJM* 7:401.

16. JM to TJ, March 18, 1786, *PJM* 8:502.

17. Drew R. McCoy, *The Elusive Republic: Political Economy in Jeffersonian America* (Chapel Hill, N.C., 1980), especially chap. 3.

18. PH to JM, April 17, 1784, *PJM* 8:18. For Madison's reputation and the "great hopes" that assembly members had from such a "general," see the letters to Jefferson from William Short, Randolph, and Eliza House Trist, *PTJ* 7:257, 260, 97. For Virginia politics, I have relied primarily on the biographies of leading

politicians, Norman K. Risjord, *Chesapeake Politics, 1781–1800* (New York, 1978), and Gordon Roy DenBoer, "The House of Delegates and the Evolution of Political Parties in Virginia, 1782–1792" (Ph.D. diss., University of Wisconsin, 1972). See also Alan Schaffer, "Virginia's 'Critical Period,'" in *The Old Dominion: Essays for Thomas Perkins Abernathy*, ed. Darrett B. Rutman (Charlottesville, Va., 1964), 152–70.

19. For Henry, see Robert Douthat Meade, *Patrick Henry*, 2 vols. (Philadelphia, 1957–69); Richard R. Beeman, *Patrick Henry: A Biography* (New York, 1974); and Henry Mayer, *A Son of Thunder: Patrick Henry and the American Republic* (New York, 1986).

20. JM to TJ, April 25, 1784, *PJM* 8:20.

21. See the report from Council of State member William Short to Jefferson, *PTJ* 7:257. Although historians have long since ceased to think of Madison as simply Jefferson's lieutenant, there is still a lingering temptation to assimilate their views. Thus, many secondary sources still suggest that Madison shared Jefferson's hostility toward Henry, though Madison's papers show that this was far from true in 1784. Risjord and DenBoer both maintain that after Madison's return, the House of Delegates tended increasingly to polarize into a creditor-oriented, nationalistic faction headed by Madison and a debtor-oriented, antinationalistic coalition headed by Henry. DenBoer notes, however, that this configuration did not solidify until late in 1786 (see "House of Delegates," chaps. 2–3), and I see little evidence for conflict on these lines until 1787 and 1788. As I maintain in Chapter 3, a clash between Madison and Henry developed slowly, with disagreements on a range of social issues coming quicker than a split on federal and financial matters. For evidence that Madison thought of Henry as a friend of federal measures through much of 1786, see JM to GW, December 7, 1786, *PJM* 9:200.

22. Brant, vol.2, chap. 20, is a superb discussion of the spring assembly session. See also *PJM*, vol. 8, for May and June 1784, and Madison's lengthy report on the session to Jefferson, in *PJM* 8:92–95.

23. For the fall session, I have depended primarily on Madison's post-session report to Jefferson, January 9, 1785, *PJM* 8:222–33, JM to James Monroe, January 8, 1785, *PJM* 8:221; and the legislative drafts and other correspondence printed in *PJM* 8:122–217. Brant's discussion of the fall session (2:343–60, 365–66) is not as clear or full as for the spring.

24. ER to TJ, *PTJ* 7:260–61; JM to TJ, July 3 and August 20, 1784, *PJM* 8:93, 102–3. In the latter, Madison noted that, by inadvertence, the completed bill, scheduled to take effect on June 10, 1786, placed Virginia citizens on a better footing than those of other states, "contrary to the Confederation." For a full discussion of the bill and Madison's thinking, see Drew R. McCoy, "The Virginia Port Bill of 1784," *VMHB* 83 (1975): 288–303, and Robert B. Bittner, "Economic Independence and the Virginia Port Bill of 1784," in *Virginia in the American Revolution*, ed. Richard A. Rutyna and Peter C. Stewart (Norfolk, Va., 1977), 73–92.

25. The resolution is printed in *PJM* 8:89–90. For its background, see the letters between Madison and Jefferson in *PJM* 8:10–11, 20, 24. Though appointed one of the commissioners, Madison was never notified of the arrangements for the conference and did not attend the meeting.

26. GW to JM, November 28 and December 28, 1784, *PJM* 8:159, 203–5; JM to GW, January 1 and 9, 1785, *PJM* 8:208–9, 234–35; JM to TJ, January 9, 1785, *PJM* 8:223–25. Washington had written Madison in June to suggest the legislature's aid for Thomas Paine, initiating a relationship in which Madison would often serve as legislative manager for the general.

27. JM to TJ, January 9, 1785, *PJM* 8:226.

28. Edmund Cody Burnett, *The Continental Congress* (New York, 1941), 606–10.

29. JM to TJ, September 7, 1784, *PJM* 8:114.

30. Mercer to JM, November 26, 1784, *PJM* 8:152.

31. R. H. Lee to JM, November 26, 1784, *PJM* 8:151.

32. JM to R. H. Lee, *PJM* 8:201. If Madison wrote to Mercer on the subject, the letter has been lost with most of his outgoing correspondence from these months. Even the reply to Lee is from a rare file copy.

33. JM to Monroe, April 12, 1785, *PJM* 8:260–261.

34. For the condition of Congress and the proceedings concerning trade, see Burnett, *Continental Congress,* chap. 32, and Rakove, *Beginnings of National Politics,* 337–59. The standard study of federal finance is E. James Ferguson, *The Power of the Purse: A History of American Public Finance, 1776–1790* (Chapel Hill, N.C., 1961). For the postwar depression, see Curtis P. Nettles, *The Emergence of a National Economy, 1775–1815* (New York, 1962), 48–63. State attempts to counter British restrictions (and their frustration by neighboring states) are conveniently summarized in Bancroft, *History of the Formation,* vol. 1, book 2, chap. 4; Nettles, *Emergence,* 72–75; and Marks, *Independence on Trial,* 80–82. See, more fully, Cathy D. Matson and Peter S. Onuf, *A Union of Interests: Political and Economic Thought in Revolutionary America* (Lawrence, Kans., 1990), chaps. 2–3. In the most notorious examples of noncooperation, Massachusetts felt compelled to suspend her retaliatory acts in July 1786 because Connecticut had declined to go along with other northeastern states, and Pennsylvania's measures were defeated when its neighbors actually lowered their own import duties.

35. JM to Monroe, June 21, 1785, *PJM* 8:307–8. Compare JM to R. H. Lee, July 7, 1785, *PJM* 8:315. See also JM to TJ, August 20, 1785, *PJM* 8:344–45, where Madison also explained his hope that the Port Bill would speed a specialization of merchants into importers and retailers and thereby make it more difficult for consumers to purchase luxuries on long-term credit.

36. JM to Monroe, August 7, 1785, *PJM* 8:333–36.

37. Information on the trip is scanty. He left Orange on August 24 or 25, spent about three weeks in Philadelphia, and would have traveled on into New England if Monroe had been able to join him. Instead, he visited briefly in New York, then hurried back to Richmond by way of Philadelphia and Mason's Gunston Hall. See the letters between Madison and Monroe in *PJM* 8:319, 331–32, 341, and 490–491, suggesting that the two may have already started looking toward their speculation in Mohawk Valley lands. For the trip of 1784, on which Madison fell in with the Marquis de Lafayette and accompanied him to Fort Stanwix, see *PJM* 8:112–21, and Brant vol. 2, chap. 21.

38. JM to TJ, October 3, 1785, *PJM* 8:373–75.

39. Ibid. For Jefferson's decided approval of these congressional powers see

his letter of February 8, 1786, *PJM* 8:486: "The politics of Europe render it indispensably necessary that with respect to everything external we be one nation only, firmly hooped together. Interior government is what each state should keep to itself."

40. JM to Monroe, December 30, 1785, *PJM* 8:465–66; and JM to TJ, January 22, 1786, *PJM* 8:477.

41. JM to GW, December 9, 1785, *PJM* 8:439–40; JM to TJ, January 22, 1786, *PJM* 8:478.

42. The outline for the speech is in *PJM* 8:431–32. For its background, see his letter to GW, November 11, 1785, *PJM* 8:404, and the editorial notes and legislative drafts in *PJM* 8:406–10, 413–15.

43. JM to GW, December 9, 1785, *PJM* 8:438–39.

44. JM to TJ, January 22, 1786, *PJM* 8:476–77.

45. JM to Monroe, January 22, 1786, *PJM* 8:483.

46. "Preface to Debates in the Convention," *RFC* 3:544.

47. Seizing on the passage cited from *RFC* 3:544 and on a letter to Noah Webster of October 12, 1804, Irving Brant maintained that Madison was both the instigator and the secret draftsman of Tyler's resolution (2:381–82, 384). Noting Madison's preference for a grant to Congress and disliking Brant's dependence on these late-life writings—in contemporary letters Madison consistently referred to "Tyler's" resolution—Julian P. Boyd powerfully disputed both of these claims. See the editorial note in *PTJ* 9:204–8. The editors of *PJM* agree with Boyd, although they also note that New England delegates in Congress thought of the Annapolis Convention as Madison's project (8:470–71; 9:115–19). My account attempts to reconcile the arguments and evidence on both sides of this disagreement. Madison never claimed that he had *drafted* Tyler's resolution, but the late-life writings do suggest that Tyler moved in close cooperation with the leading spokesmen for the grant to Congress, and Madison's contemporary letters are consistent with the probability that he played a central role, at least, in reviving the motion. The absence of an unambiguous contemporary claim to this effect means nothing. Madison *never* claimed responsibility for legislative actions, writing rather of the actions of the "friends" of a specific measure even when there is no doubt that his was certainly the central role. He did not deviate from this objective manner of reporting even when informing Jefferson of the successful effort to enact the Statute for Religious Freedom.

48. By March of 1786, Madison knew that many states had appointed delegates, saw a better prospect for success, and hoped that such expedients could be "repeated . . . as the public mind becomes prepared for further remedies" (JM to TJ and to Monroe, *PJM* 8:503, 505). But he was of two minds about the prospects for the meeting through September, and it is inappropriate to seize on any single statement as conclusive evidence that he was following a consistent plan throughout, much less that he was aiming at an early point for a plenary convention. It is sensible, I think, to recognize that Madison knew from the beginning that he could not know what Tyler's resolution might produce. Envisioning a range of possibilities and options, his basic strategy was to respond to the developments that were unfolding month by month.

49. Countless passages from his contemporary letters unmistakably assume continuation of the present federal system. See, for example, JM to CW, December 9, 1785, *PJM* 8:439: "The difficulty now found in obtaining a unanimous concurrence of the states in any measure whatever must continually increase with every increase of their number." Compare JM to Lafayette, March 20, 1785, *PJM* 8:252, which I discuss more fully below. The only passage in which Madison indicated any other thought was in the August letter to Monroe.

50. For intervening difficulties, see, however, Peter S. Onuf, *Statehood and Union: A History of the Northwest Ordinance* (Bloomington, Ind., 1987).

51. My discussion of Madison and the West is deeply indebted to Drew R. McCoy, "James Madison and Visions of American Nationality in the Confederation Period: A Regional Perspective," in *Beyond Confederation: Origins of the Constitution and American National Identity*, ed. Richard Beeman, Stephen Botein, and Edward C. Carter II (Chapel Hill, N.C., 1987), 226–58.

52. *PJM*, vol. 8, is filled with evidence of Madison's excellent information from Kentucky (e.g., 267, 286), and it is likely that his correspondence with Kentuckians was a great deal broader than surviving letters would suggest. In addition, Montpelier was a frequent stopping place for travelers to and from the western country. Madison's father and brothers bought over 16,000 acres of Kentucky lands between May 9, 1780, and March 5, 1781. Family purchases, in which Madison at some point acquired a small, unknown share, continued into the 1790s, but the family never profited significantly from these speculations. For the family's finances during the middle 1780s, see Brant 2:306–7, 324, 363, and Ketcham 144–49. Throughout the period I discuss, Madison was essentially dependent on his salary from public office and occasional assistance from his father.

53. JM to Lafayette, March 20, 1785, *PJM* 8:251.

54. See Chapter 1 and, for the Mississippi more particularly, *PJM* 2:202–4, 224, 241–42, 302–3, and 3:261–62.

55. Madison's clearest statement of his policy concerning Kentucky is in the letter to R. H. Lee, July 7, 1785, *PJM* 8:314. See also, the legislative drafts and letters from Caleb Wallace in *PJM* 8:320–23, 377, 441–42, and 450–53.

56. Their journey to Fort Stanwix is entertainingly recounted in Brant, vol. 2, chap. 21.

57. JM to TJ, September 7, 1784, *PJM* 8:113–14. In New York, as promised, Lafayette showed Madison a letter he had written to his foreign minister about the problem. See JM to TJ, September 15, 1784, *PJM* 8:115.

58. JM to TJ, August 20, 1784, *PJM* 8:104–8.

59. See also the editorial notes in *PTJ* 7:408, 410, where Boyd suggests that Madison had reason to believe that Jefferson had been indifferent to the issue of navigation rights on the Mississippi.

60. JM to Lafayette, March 20, 1785, *PJM* 8:250–53. Useful background is in JM to TJ, March 20, 1785, *PJM* 8:268–69.

61. JM to Lafayette, March 20, 1785, *PJM* 8:251.

62. This litany is all but universal in the writings and conversations of political scientists on *Federalist* no. 10. It can be traced to the enormously influential essays of Martin Diamond, which I discuss more thoroughly in Chapter 7.

63. Most explicitly, moreover, in the passages deleted from the letter to Jefferson and written before his chance encounter with Lafayette. Madison did not intend these thoughts for French consumption only.

64. For the 1780s debate on manufacturing, see McCoy, *Elusive Republic*, chaps. 4–5, especially 121–31. For the pro-developmental position and its power in the movement for federal reform, the fullest discussion is Matson and Onuf, *Union of Interests*, chaps. 2, 4, 5.

65. The literature on Scottish economic thought is growing with a speed that may recall the interest in American republicanism in the 1970s. A useful introduction to the new concerns is *Wealth and Virtue: The Shaping of Political Economy in the Scottish Enlightenment*, ed. Istvan Hont and Michael Ignatieff (Cambridge, 1983). See also Albert D. Hirschman, *The Passions and the Interests: Political Arguments for Capitalism before Its Triumph* (Princeton, N.J., 1977), and Joyce O. Appleby, *Economic Thought and Ideology in Seventeenth-Century England* (Princeton, N.J., 1978).

66. Adam Smith, *An Inquiry into the Nature and Causes of the Wealth of Nations*, ed. Edwin Canan, Modern Library Edition (New York, 1937), 734–40. As Forrest McDonald remarks, however, "Smith devoted almost all of book 4 of the *Wealth of Nations* to a massive repudiation . . . of the mercantile system": to policies designed, as Smith described it, "to enrich a great nation rather by trade and manufactures than by the improvement and cultivation of land, rather by the industry of the towns than by that of the country" (*Novus Ordo Seclorum: The Intellectual Origins of the Constitution* [Lawrence, Kans., 1985], 125, together with Smith, 591). To Smith, as to the French physiocrats, agriculture was the most productive form of labor, manufacturing was second, commerce third; and nations were mistaken to invest extensively in less productive enterprises when the more productive ones were not yet fully exploited (346–48). McCoy, *Elusive Republic*, 19–21, 35–40, includes a superb discussion of Smith's ambivalence and of that of Scottish thought in general. The problematic consequences of intensive change were more particularly a theme of Adam Ferguson, *An Essay on the History of Civil Society* (1767). For its axiomatic character in early revolutionary thinking, sample the extensive secondary literature cited in Robert Shalhope, "Republicanism and Early American Historiography," *WMQ* 29 (1972):49–80, or Lance Banning, "Jeffersonian Ideology Revisited: Liberal and Classical Ideas in the New American Republic," *WMQ* 43 (1986): 3–19.

67. Query 19 of *Notes on the State of Virginia*, written in 1781–82 and carefully read by Madison no later than the early fall of 1785 (*PJM* 8:415–16).

68. I discuss the *National Gazette* essays, "Republican Distribution of Citizens" (March 3) and "Fashion" (March 20, 1792), reprinted in *PJM* 14:244–46, 257–59, more fully in Chapter 11.

69. TJ to JM, October 28, 1785, *PJM* 8:285–88.

70. JM to TJ, June 19, 1786, *PJM* 9:76–77. Discussing this exchange, McCoy remarks the striking contrast between Madison's analysis and that of Thomas Malthus. See "Jefferson and Madison on Malthus: Population Growth in Jeffersonian Political Economy," *VMHB* 88 (1980): 259–76.

71. In light of recent scholarly disputes, it is important to insist that there was

nothing backward-looking or nostalgic in this vision. See Joyce Appleby, "Commercial Farming and the 'Agrarian Myth' in the Early Republic," *JAH* 68 (1982): 833–49, and "What Is Still American in the Political Philosophy of Thomas Jefferson?" *WMQ* 39 (1982): 287–309; also see Banning, "Jeffersonian Ideology Revisited."

72. For the March discussions, see *LMCC* 8:xxxvi.

73. JM to Monroe, May 13, 1786, *PJM* 9:55.

74. Madison's rising sense of urgency and growing inclination to believe that the Annapolis Convention was now the most appropriate beginning toward reform can be followed in his letters to Monroe and Jefferson in *PJM* 8:498, 8:502–3, 8:505–6, and 9:50. "The efforts for bringing about a correction through the medium of Congress have miscarried," he wrote Monroe. "Let a convention then be tried. If it succeeds in the first instance it can be repeated. . . . The assembly here would refer nothing to Congress" (*PJM* 8:505).

75. JM to Monroe, April 9, 1786, *PJM* 9:25.

76. I have relied especially on the excellent discussions in H. James Henderson, *Party Politics in the Continental Congress* (New York, 1974), 387–94; Burnett, *Continental Congress*, 654–59; Marks, *Independence on Trial*, 24–45; and Richard B. Morris, *The Forging of the Union, 1781–1789*, New American Nation Series (New York, 1987), 233–44. The fullest discussion of the negotiations with Spain is still Samuel Flagg Bemis, *Pinckney's Treaty: America's Advantage from Europe's Distress, 1783–1800*, rev. ed. (New Haven, Conn., 1960), chaps. 2–4.

77. Henderson, *Party Politics*, is the fullest demonstration. See also Joseph L. Davis, *Sectionalism in American Politics, 1774–1787* (Madison, Wis., 1977).

78. See, for example, Charles Thomson's report of the speech of Rufus King, August 16, 1786, in *LMCC* 8:429.

79. Theodore Sedgwick to Caleb Strong, August 6, 1786, quoted in Burnett, *Continental Congress*, 657. A recent, full, and interesting discussion of the widespread talk of separate regional confederations can be found in Matson and Onuf, *Union of Interests*, 82–90.

80. Thomson's "Minutes of Proceedings," August 16, 1786, *LMCC* 8:427–28.

81. Ibid., 429, 438. See also Charles Pinckney's speech of August 16 in *JCC* 31:935–48.

82. The point is powerfully developed in McCoy, "Visions of American Nationality."

83. Monroe to Henry, August 12, 1786, *LMCC* 8:422–25.

84. JM to Monroe, June 21, 1786, *PJM* 9:82–83.

85. Chaired by Charles Pinckney of South Carolina and appointed in July, the grand committee recommended seven substantial amendments to the Articles of Confederation, including federal powers to regulate trade and to levy an impost and penalties for failure to meet requisitions. This report of August 4, the most ambitious plan for federal reform ever proposed in Congress, was sidetracked by the Jay-Gardoqui conflict and never formally discussed. It is available in *JCC* 31:494–97.

86. Surviving correspondence leaves no doubt, however, that Monroe and

Grayson consulted with him freely. I am struck, moreover, by apparent echoes in Pinckney's speech of August 16 (see *JCC* 31:935–48) of Madison's letter to Monroe, especially by Pinckney's parallel to Madison's reference to a barter of the rights of one part of the empire to the interests of another "in time of profound peace."

87. JM to TJ, August 12, 1786, *PJM* 9:95–97.

88. JM to Monroe, August 12, 1786, *PJM* 9:90.

89. Monroe to JM, August 11, 1786, *PJM* 9:91–92. On August 15 (*PJM* 9:107), Madison replied that he had not seen Arthur St. Clair and did not know him well enough for such a conversation. He had discussed the matter "freely" with James Wilson, who understood that Jay's proposal could defeat the objects of the Annapolis Convention, but he could not determine Wilson's ultimate position. In Annapolis, as Monroe desired, he would also talk to Abraham Clark of New Jersey and Thomas Stone of Maryland. Like Monroe, he saw the middle states as "swing votes" on the issue and was seizing every opportunity to bend their leaders to his side.

90. Monroe to JM, August 14, 1786, *PJM* 9:104.

91. JM to Monroe, August 17, 1786, *PJM* 9:107–8. The Virginia motion (*LMCC* 8:440–42) is another illustration of the general assumption that the Mississippi was the natural route for western exports but (before the steamboat) not necessarily for western imports. The compromise concocted by Monroe and Grayson was skillfully contrived for joining those Virginians who were less than eager for an open Mississippi with Madison and others who would champion the navigation even if the Mississippi rivaled the Potomac. Though Madison wrote that the proposal "would be beneficial and even pleasing" to the citizens who would be most immediately affected, there is room to wonder whether he objected only on strategic grounds.

92. *PJM* 9:109. Delaware was the only state unrepresented during the crisis.

93. *PJM* 9:113–14. The Virginia delegates had argued all along that seven states were constitutionally inadequate to write what were, in practice, new instructions. Madison agreed: "If the affirmative vote of seven states should be pursued, it will add the insult of trick to the injury of the thing itself" (*PJM* 9:121). Nevertheless, Jay did pursue his talks, and his supporters added further insult to their triumph with a procedural ruling that prevented the resumption of congressional discussions until the spring of 1787, by which time Madison was once again a member and taking the leading role.

94. JM to Monroe, September 11, 1786, *PJM* 9:121.

95. Marks, *Independence on Trial*, chap. 1, is a convenient summary.

96. Ferguson, *Power of the Purse*, 234–35 and chap. 11. In 1787, Congress defaulted entirely on a repayment of principal due to France.

97. See *JCC* 30:7–10, 62–63, 70–76, 93–94, 102–8, and 364.

98. JM to TJ, March 18, 1786, *PJM* 8:502.

99. Ibid.

100. JM to Monroe, October 5, 1786, *PJM* 9:140–41.

101. JM to TJ, March 18, 1786, *PJM* 8:502.

102. His bill is in *PJM* 9:119–20.

103. JM to (brother) Ambrose Madison, September 8, 1786, *PJM* 9:120–21.

104. Ibid. and JM to Monroe, September 11, 1786, *PJM* 9:121–22. Present were Madison, Randolph, and St. George Tucker from Virginia; William C. Houston, Abraham Clark, and James Schureman from New Jersey; John Dickinson, George Read, and Richard Bassett from Delaware; Tench Coxe from Pennsylvania; and Hamilton and Egbert Benson from New York.

105. The full address of September 14 is available in *PAH* 3:686–90.

106. Contemporary information on the Annapolis Convention is extraordinarily scanty, which may explain the paucity and brevity of secondary studies (e.g., Burnett, *Continental Congress,* 665–68; Morris, *Forging of the Union,* 253–57). Only by conjecture can a scholar get significantly beyond the facts reported in the address itself. Attribution of the draft to Hamilton, who is also widely suspected of having instigated the recommendation, is essentially dependent on Madison's recollections in a letter to Noah Webster of October 12, 1804 (*WJM* 7:165), a letter also stating that he had a dim impression that the formal recommendation originated with Abraham Clark. Madison's knowledge that he would be joining the Monroes as soon as the convention had concluded, together with his frantic schedule after his arrival in Virginia, may explain why there is no report on the convention in his papers from the period right after its adjournment. Delegations from New Hampshire and Massachusetts were en route to the convention when the members acted, and some New Englanders were deeply suspicious of current southern talk about a plenipotentiary convention. These facts have sometimes been remarked in order to suggest that the convention members acted hastily in order to accomplish something of a nationalistic coup. It is not, in fact, impossible that in the aftermath of Jay-Gardoqui, Madison and the others—all of whom were mid-states continentalists by some contemporary reckonings—were less than eager for the New England delegations to arrive. But it does not seem clear that anyone was certain that the Yankees would appear before some other members would be forced to leave, and their arrival still would not have made a quorum of the states. As it was, the members did not act until the Thursday of the second week of the convention, and it seems more likely that they acted out of desperation than with any certainty that their proposal would succeed.

107. The writings of Jack Rakove are especially impressive on the novelty and critical importance of Madison's linkage of the problems of the Union and the problems in the states. See his *Beginnings of National Politics,* 389–96, and "From One Agenda to Another: The Condition of American Federalism, 1783–1787," in *The American Revolution: Its Character and Limits,* ed. Jack P. Greene, (New York, 1987), 80–103. My discussion differs from Rakove's and from the body of preceding literature in stressing Madison's tendency to *trace* the local problems to the inability of the Confederation to improve the economic situation. Madison was fully as concerned about the vicious local consequences of a weak Confederation as he was about the problems for the Union caused by narrow-minded legislatures in the states.

CHAPTER THREE. THE CRISIS OF REPUBLICAN CONVICTIONS

1. I borrow the title of Pauline Maier, *From Resistance to Revolution: Colonial Radicals and the Development of American Opposition to Britain, 1765–1776* (New York, 1972).

2. "James Madison's Autobiography," ed. Douglass Adair, *WMQ* 2 (1945): 198. For Madison's education and the atmosphere at Princeton, see Brant, vol. 1, chaps. 4–5; Ketcham, chaps. 2–3; John Witherspoon, *Lectures on Moral Philosophy*, ed. Varnum Lansing Collins (Princeton, N.J., 1912); Dennis F. Thompson, "The Education of a Founding Father: The Reading List for John Witherspoon's Course in Political Theory, as Taken by James Madison," *Political Theory* 4 (1976): 523–29; and *PJM* 1:3–69. Specific references to the details of his early involvement in the Revolution are from *PJM* 1:135, 153, 163.

3. The literature of this debate is now enormous. For an introduction, see the substance and citations of my articles, "Jeffersonian Ideology Revisited: Liberal and Classical Ideas in the New American Republic," *WMQ* 43 (1986): 3–19; "Some Second Thoughts on Virtue and the Course of Revolutionary Thinking," in *Conceptual Change and the Constitution*, ed. Terence Ball and J.G.A. Pocock (Lawrence, Kans., 1988), 194–212; and "The Republican Interpretation: Retrospect and Prospect," in *The Republican Synthesis Revisited: Essays in Honor of George Athan Billias*, ed. Milton M. Klein et al. (Worcester, Mass., 1992), 91–117. Also see the other essays in *Republican Synthesis Revisited*, as well as Joyce Appleby, "Republicanism in Old and New Contexts," *WMQ* 43 (1986): 20–34; James T. Kloppenberg, "The Virtues of Liberalism: Christianity, Republicanism, and Ethics in Early American Political Discourse," *JAH* 74 (1987): 9–33; Isaac Kramnick, "The 'Great National Discussion': The Discourse of Politics in 1787," *WMQ* 45 (1988): 3–32; and Daniel T. Rodgers, "Republicanism: The Career of a Concept," *JAH* 79 (1992): 11–38. Since the middle 1980s, I have argued that this whole debate is largely misconceived, that nearly all Americans were both "republicans" and "liberals" from the beginning of the Revolution to its end and did not see the sort of clash between these two distinguishable bodies of ideas that has been posited by many modern scholars. In the middle 1990s, scholarship in general may be coming round to this position. Many recent writers speak of "liberal republicanism," as I do in this book, and some argue that we ought to drop these terms completely. At this point, this last solution would be premature—because the long debate is not yet over, because so much of the existing scholarship is cast in just these terms, and because some writers insist that "liberal republicans" were, by definition, incoherent and confused. In order to address these problems, I accept the risk of getting tangled in the current terminological confusion. My object, though, is to explain concretely—over several chapters—the content of Madison's republican (or early revolutionary) commitments, which were strongly influenced by the British opposition writers and the sorts of dangers they described, and then to show how these commitments interplayed with his liberal (or modern and contractarian) convictions. It should be obvious that I have no intention of denying that Madison was a liberal, *providing* that we do not use this term—as several writers have—to mean that he was thoroughly at ease with the emerging world of acquis-

itive, individualistic, "bourgeois" democracy. It will be clear as well that by "republican," I do not mean that Madison was ever literally classical in the sense that Paul A. Rahe or most political theorists would define that term. Although I do believe that early revolutionary thought was partly neoclassical in lineage, my "Second Thoughts on Virtue" and "The Republican Interpretation" both discuss the difficulties introduced into the scholarly debate by references to British opposition thought as "classical republican" in nature (in my own earliest writings as well as in those by others).

4. This was a major theme of "Progressive" historiography, pressed most forcefully perhaps in Merrill Jensen, *The Articles of Confederation: An Interpretation of the Social-Constitutional History of the American Revolution, 1774–1781* (Madison, Wis., 1940) and *The New Nation: A History of the United States during the Confederation, 1781–1789* (New York, 1950).

5. JM to Rev. Thomas Martin, August 10, 1769, *PJM* 1:42–43; Pauline Maier, "John Wilkes and American Disillusionment with Britain," *WMQ* 20 (1963): 373–95.

6. JM to James Madison Sr., September 30, 1769, July 23, 1770, *PJM* 1:45–46, 49–50.

7. For the movement of radical opinion, see Maier, *From Resistance to Revolution*. For Madison's movement with it, see his letters to college classmate (and future attorney general) William Bradford, together with the "Address to Captain Patrick Henry" of May 9, 1775, in *PJM*, vol. 1. The quotation and other specifics are at *PJM* 1:105, 115, 121, 129, 135, and 147.

8. The spirit of the early Revolution may never have been captured better than it was in the pioneering classics of the current, "republican" interpretation: Bernard Bailyn, *The Ideological Origins of the American Revolution* (Cambridge, Mass., 1967); Gordon S. Wood, *The Creation of the American Republic, 1776–1787* (Chapel Hill, N.C., 1969), part 1; Maier, *From Resistance to Revolution*; and other titles mentioned in Robert E. Shalhope, "Toward a Republican Synthesis: The Emergence of an Understanding of Republicanism in American Historiography," *WMQ* 29 (1972): 49–80.

9. JM to Bradford, November 9, 1772, *PJM* 1:75. Madison also corresponded with other former classmates, especially Hugh Henry Brackenridge and Philip Freneau, but little survives from these years except the letters Bradford copied into a notebook. See the editorial note in *PJM* 1:71–72, and references at 83, 86, and 89.

10. JM to Bradford, November 9, 1772, *PJM* 1:75.

11. For fun at the expense of the enthusiasts, see JM to Bradford, April 1, 1774, *PJM* 1:111–12: "The world needs to be peopled, but I should be sorry it should be peopled with bastards as my old friend [and schoolmate Thaddeus] Dod . . . seems[s] to incline. . . . I hope his religion, like that of some enthusiasts, was not of such a nature as to fan the amorous fire." But note, as well, his remark that "the specious arguments of infidels have established the faith of enquiring Christians" (115).

12. JM to Bradford, September 25, 1773, *PJM* 1:96. See, further, *PJM* 1:51–60, 101.

13. Brant believed that Madison moved from a rational Christianity toward Deism as he aged (1:114–15, 118, and chap. 5). I agree with Ralph Ketcham ("James Madison and Religion—A New Hypothesis," *Journal of the Presbyterian Historical Society* 38 [1960]: 65–90) that the evidence permits no firm conclusions about the nature of his convictions after he entered public life, though there is reason to believe that he continued to accept a rational Christianity at least into the middle 1780s.

14. For plainness, simplicity, and hostility to social ceremony, see JM to Bradford, April 28, 1773 and January 20, 1775, *PJM* 1:83, 136. The many writings of Rhys Isaac offer a superb discussion of the resonance between dissenting and republican ethics, both of which challenged the prideful, boisterous, and gambling ways of the more raucous gentry: "Evangelical Revolt: The Nature of the Baptists' Challenge to the Traditional Order in Virginia, 1765 to 1775," *WMQ* 31 (1974): 345–68; "Preachers and Patriots: Popular Culture and the Revolution in Virginia," in *The American Revolution: Explorations in the History of American Radicalism*, ed. Alfred F. Young (DeKalb, Ill., 1976), 125–56; and *The Transformation of Virginia, 1740–1790* (Chapel Hill, N.C., 1982).

15. On frivolity, see JM to Bradford, November 9, 1772, *PJM* 1:74–76. For his persisting fear of the threat posed to patriotism by need and greed, see *PJM* 1: 152, and note 108 to Chapter 1.

16. JM to Bradford, September 25, 1773, *PJM* 1:96.

17. "James Madison's Autobiography," 198.

18. Ibid., 199, and JM to Bradford, November 9, 1772, *PJM* 1:75.

19. JM to Bradford, November 25, 1773, and January 24, 1774, *PJM* 1:96, 105. On July 26, 1785 (*PJM* 8:328), as he began to consider speculating in land in the Mohawk Valley, Madison wrote to Randolph: "My wish is if possible to provide a decent and independent subsistence without encountering the difficulties which I foresee in [the law]. Another of my wishes is to depend as little as possible on the labor of slaves." In 1774 and 1775, however, his only references to slavery expressed a fear that Britain might provoke an insurrection (*PJM* 1:129–30, 155).

20. The Princeton University Library holds a four-page manuscript in Madison's late-life hand, probably his earliest draft of an autobiographical sketch ("Memorandum first Sept. 1816 to Mr. Delaplaine at his request," de Coppell collection, p. 238). This memorandum says that he was prevented from entering the army by "his feeble health and a constitutional liability to sudden attacks, somewhat resembling epilepsy and suspending the intellectual functions. These continued through his life, with prolonged intervals." Brant and Ketcham both suggest that this was the same problem that had troubled him from his final months at Princeton, and Brant believed that the illness was functional in nature, existing "only in his mind" (1:134). I am not convinced on either count. The same sketch seems to blame the early disability on too much study and too little sleep during his final year at Princeton, and the letters to Bradford do not suggest an epileptiform disorder. There may have been two separate or connected problems, neither of which has yet been diagnosed. But it is certain that the situation had improved sufficiently by the spring of 1774 to permit a pleasure trip to Albany, followed by intensive preparations for involvement in the war.

21. JM to Bradford, December 1, 1773, *PJM* 1:101. Madison was particularly interested in acquiring Joseph Priestley's *Essay on the First Principles of Government; and on the Nature of Political, Civil, and Religious Liberty,* Josiah Tucker's *Apology for the Present Church of England . . .* , and Philip Furneaux's *Essay on Toleration.* See *PJM* 1: 101, 160, and notes.

22. JM to Bradford, January 24, 1774, *PJM* 1:105.

23. JM to Bradford, April 1, 1774, *PJM* 1:112–13.

24. JM to Bradford, January 24, 1774, *PJM* 1:106.

25. JM to Bradford, November 26, 1774, *PJM* 1:129.

26. JM to Bradford, January 20, 1775, *PJM* 1:135. The mobilization in the aftermath of the Coercive Acts and the activities of the local committees are effectively described in David Ammerman, *In the Common Cause: American Response to the Coercive Acts of 1774* (New York, 1975).

27. JM to Bradford, June 19, 1775, *PJM* 1:153.

28. Ibid., 141.

29. JM to Bradford, July 28, 1775, *PJM* 1:161. For the Orange militia, see Charles D. Lowery, *James Barbour, A Jeffersonian Republican* (University, Ala., 1984), 4.

30. The identification of the cause with "liberty and property" is in JM to Bradford, January 24, 1774, *PJM* 1:105. Note also his conviction that "the union, virtue, and love of liberty at present prevailing throughout the colonies is such that it would be as little in the power of our treacherous friends as of our avowed enemies to put the yoke upon us" (June 19, 1775, *PJM* 1:152).

31. References to slavery are extremely rare in Madison's papers from the period before the Constitutional Convention. During the 1780s, he often handled family business on his trips outside the county, but he was evidently not expected to assume an active role in management of the plantation, which he did not inherit until 1801. His activities and feelings in his later years, for which the evidence is more extensive, are examined fully and with great sensitivity in Drew R. McCoy, *The Last of the Fathers: James Madison and the Republican Legacy* (Cambridge, 1989), chap. 7. See also, however, the powerful indictment of Madison and Jefferson in Paul A. Rahe, *Republics Ancient and Modern: Classical Republicanism and the American Revolution* (Chapel Hill, N.C., 1992), especially 648–50, 691–98: "To stop a nonexistent [Federalist] conspiracy against the republic, they acquiesced in the tyranny exercised by the white southern majority over the region's black minority" (696).

32. The statistics are from Lowery, *James Barbour,* 4–5. Still useful for the politics of late-colonial Virginia is Charles S. Sydnor, *Gentlemen Freeholders: Political Practices in Washington's Virginia* (Chapel Hill, N.C., 1952), but see the brilliant discussion of both the persistence and disintegration of deference in prerevolutionary America in Gordon S. Wood, *The Radicalism of the American Revolution* (New York, 1991). For the relationship between Virginia representatives and voters and the frequency of the phrase "father of his country," see also Isaac, *Transformation of Virginia,* especially 131–32, 251–52. For the character of life within the family, Madison's letters to his brothers and his father, the latter always addressed "Honored Sir" and closed with affection (see, especially, *PJM* 1:232–33, 315–20) can

be read in light of Daniel Blake Smith, *Inside the Great House: Planter Family Life in Eighteenth-Century Chesapeake Society* (Ithaca, N.Y., 1980).

33. Serious confusions have been introduced into the scholarly debates about the "classical" or "modern" features of revolutionary thinking by ignoring this fact. See my "Second Thoughts on Virtue," and, more broadly, the works of Paul A. Rahe.

34. JM, "Who Are the Best Keepers of the People's Liberties?" *PJM* 14:426–27. This last of Madison's essays for the *National Gazette*, which appeared on December 20, 1792, came as close as any of his writings to conveying his republican convictions in a phrase.

35. Exertions were apparently required to save the Baptists from imprisonment in Orange as well as to secure their freedom in Culpeper County. Madison's intervention, he recalled, "though a mere duty prescribed by his conscience, obtained for him a lasting place in the favor of that particular sect" ("James Madison's Autobiography," 198–99). In 1776, with Thomas Barbour and James Taylor, the county's previous representatives, both in the army, Madison and William Moore were easily elected. All four men were members of the committee of safety. All were neighbors with ties of blood, marriage, or close association (Brant 1:198).

36. John Locke, *Epistola de Tolerantia/A Letter on Toleration*, ed. Raymond Klibanskey and J. W. Gough (Oxford, 1968). Locke's list of four opinions not entitled to toleration (131–35) was aimed primarily against atheists and Catholics but extended to any "doctrines incompatible with human society" or to any church that refused to teach the principle of toleration. Madison was certainly familiar with the *Letter*, which was one of Witherspoon's favorite texts. See James H. Nichols, "John Witherspoon on Church and State," *Journal of Presbyterian History* 42 (1964): 166–74.

37. *PJM* 1:173–75. For the proceedings in convention I have followed Brant, vol. 1, chap. 12; Thomas E. Buckley, *Church and State in Revolutionary Virginia, 1776–1787* (Charlottesville, Va., 1977), 15–19; and the editorial note at *PJM* 1:170–71. Helpful for the broader context is Thomas J. Curry, *The First Freedoms: Church and State in America to the Passage of the First Amendment* (New York, 1986).

38. Locke rejected toleration for sects opposed to equal liberty. Madison's phrase sought stricter limits on state action. He may have been influenced in writing his second amendment by Priestley, who pointed to the inconsistency between Locke's premises and conclusions and urged the magistrate to interfere only in case of "manifest and urgent necessity." See *The Theological and Miscellaneous Works of Joseph Priestley*, ed. J. T. Rutt (1771; New York, 1972), 22:33.

39. It has often been suggested that Madison would certainly have seen the liberal provision for religious freedom in Jefferson's draft of a constitution, which arrived in time to influence the drafting committee. Jefferson's phrasing would also have guaranteed freedom rather than mere toleration. Yet Jefferson's phrasing did not look unambiguously toward disestablishment, nor did it place the rights of conscience on as fair a ground as Madison's. "All persons shall have full and free liberty of religious opinion," Jefferson wrote, "nor shall any be compelled to frequent or maintain any religious institution" (*PTJ* 1:363). Madison would cer-

tainly have recognized that Locke defended freedom of religious *opinion* and went on to justify restrictions on the grounds that *conduct* was a legitimate concern of the civil authority. Free "exercise," a term already present in the committee's draft, afforded broader protection, and Madison's remarkable phrasing of the exception—"unless the preservation of equal liberty and the *existence* of the state are manifestly endangered"—seems a carefully considered response to Locke's support for civil action whenever religious beliefs appeared to threaten the moral foundations of political society.

40. "He never once narrowed his objective and never ceased to think of the dangers that lurked in small deviations" from the principle of separation (Irving Brant, "Madison: On the Separation of Church and State," *WMQ* 8 [1951]: 24). See also William Lee Miller, *The First Liberty: Religion and the American Republic* (New York, 1986), part two, "The Vocation of Jemmy Madison," and Robert S. Alley, ed., *James Madison on Religious Liberty* (Buffalo, N.Y., 1985), which includes excerpts from Madison's writings and several helpful essays.

41. For the fall assembly session, see Buckley, *Church and State*, 21–36; *PTJ* 1: 525–58; Brant 1:296–304; and the editorial note in *PJM* 1:186.

42. *PTJ* 2:305–665, includes all 126 bills of the revision, together with a lengthy headnote on its preparation, contents, and legislative history. The statute is at 545–53. An excellent bicentennial appreciation is *The Virginia Statute for Religious Freedom: Its Evolution and Consequences in American History*, ed. Merrill D. Peterson and Robert C. Vaughan (Cambridge, 1988).

43. Buckley, *Church and State*, chap. 2. The 1779 bill creating a Christian establishment is reprinted by Buckley as appendix 1.

44. "James Madison's Autobiography," 199–200; "Popular Elections," in James Madison, "Detached Memoranda," ed. Elizabeth Fleet, *WMQ* 3 (1946): 562–63; Brant 1:306–8. Madison's frequent retelling of this story—always without blaming the voters—suggests that he was hurt more deeply than his humor may suggest. His supporters petitioned that Charles Porter's election be set aside as based on bribery and corruption, but the petition was rejected for lack of proof.

45. "Grave of useful talents" is from JM to TJ, March 16, 1784, *PJM* 8:9. Since many of the wartime records were destroyed, relatively little can be said about his service on the eight-man council, which assisted and advised the governor in his essentially administrative duties. See, however, Brant 1:315 and chaps. 16–17; Emory G. Evans, "Executive Leadership in Virginia, 1776–1781: Henry, Jefferson, and Nelson," in *Sovereign States in an Age of Uncertainty*, ed. Ronald Hoffman and Peter J. Albert (Charlottesville, Va., 1981), 185–225. Evans makes a persuasive case that all three governors were capable and effective, and it needs to be remembered that almost all of Madison's service was with Henry. Jefferson was elected governor in June 1779; Madison went home in July and returned for only a few weeks before his election to Congress.

46. See TJ to JM, June 17, 1783, *PJM* 7:156–57, which enclosed Jefferson's proposals for a revised constitution (*PTJ* 6:278–84, 294–308).

47. JM to TJ, May 15 and July 3, 1784, *PJM* 8:34, 93, together with the outline for a speech supporting constitutional revision in *PJM* 8:77–78.

48. Madison reported on the session at length in a letter to Jefferson of July

3, 1784, from which the quotations are taken (*PJM* 8:92–95). For the terms and background of the incorporation bill, see Buckley, *Church and State*, 81–88. Madison told his father that the bill was "wholly inadmissable" in this original version (*PJM* 8:217), but the letter to Jefferson shows that he was most disturbed by the degree to which it would have freed the clergy from lay supervision. He does not appear to have objected in 1784 to giving the Episcopalians title to their present holdings, although the dissenters repeatedly opposed this transfer of state property to one denomination. He did object, however, to vesting title in a purely clerical body and to a church's unrestrained capacity to increase its holdings. Madison's fullest condemnation of the latter power can be found in his "Detached Memoranda," 556–58.

49. Again I have depended primarily on Madison's postsession report to Jefferson on January 9, 1785 (*PJM* 8:222–33), together with legislative drafts and other correspondence printed in *PJM* 8:122–217. Brant's discussion of the fall session at 2:343–60 and 365–66 is not as clear or complete as for the spring.

50. The text of this bill, too, is conveniently available in appendix I of Buckley's *Church and State*, which offers a fine discussion of the implications of Virginia's actions as well as an excellent history of the path to the Virginia settlement. Also helpful for placing Virginia's struggle over a general assessment in the national context are William G. McLoughlin, "The Role of Religion in the Revolution: Liberty of Conscience and Cultural Cohesion in the New Nation," in *Essays on the American Revolution*, ed. Stephen G. Kurtz and James H. Hutson, (Chapel Hill, N.C., 1973), 197–255, and Stephen Botein, "Religious Dimensions of the Early American State," in *Beyond Confederation: Origins of the Constitution and American National Identity*, ed. Richard Beeman, Stephen Botein, and Edward C. Carter II (Chapel Hill, N.C., 1987), 315–30.

51. The preface to the bill of 1784 summarized this view rather eloquently: "Whereas the general diffusion of Christian knowledge hath a natural tendency to correct the morals of men, restrain their vices, and preserve the peace of society, which cannot be effected without a competent provision for learned teachers, . . . and it is judged that such provision may be made by the legislature, without counteracting the liberal principle heretofore adopted and intended to be preserved by abolishing all distinctions of preeminence among the different societies or communities of Christians;

Be it therefore enacted . . ."

52. JM to James Monroe, November 27, 1784, *PJM* 8:157–58. See also *PJM* 8: 172, 175.

53. Both quotations are from JM to Monroe of April 12, 1785, *PJM* 8:261, but they seem a fair expression of Madison's reaction from the first. For the background of the petition and Presbyterian lobbying in the assembly, see Buckley, *Church and State*, 92–99. The Presbyterian clergy was by no means united on this change of course, and several Shenandoah Valley congregations petitioned against both the assessment and the incorporation bill before the session ended.

54. JM to TJ, January 9, 1785, *PJM* 8:228–29. It is not clear which features of the incorporation act Madison still found objectionable. Partly in response to the objections that he shared with the dissenters, the revised bill was very different

from the one drafted in the spring. Rather than incorporating the clergy alone, it made each parish vestry and clergyman a corporate body with control over parish property, which could not exceed the value of L800 per year. A convention composed of the clergyman and one layman from each parish would become the governing body of the church, which could not appoint or remove a minister without vestry approval. Thus, the clerical independence and the indefinite power to acquire property, which had been the strongest of Madison objections in the spring, were both removed. Indeed, Madison reported that the legislature had actually intended the Episcopal convention to be composed of the clergyman and *two* laymen from each parish, but that an unnoticed error had crept into the bill, which he hoped would prove "a standing lesson to [the laity] of the danger of referring religious matters to the legislature" (JM to James Madison Sr., January 6, 1785, *PJM* 8:217; Buckley, *Church and State*, 106–7).

55. *PJM* 8:197–99.

56. Buckley, *Church and State*, 109–10, which includes a map of the vote.

57. George Nicholas to JM, May 22, 1785, *PJM* 8:264–65. After 1784, the assembly met only in the fall.

58. *PJM* 8:298–306. One recent author calculates that Madison's opinions, expressed most fully in this classic, have been cited in at least forty federal and fifty-five state cases concerning church and state since 1878. See Donald L. Drakeman, "Religion and the Republic: James Madison and the First Amendment," *Journal of Church and State* 25 (1983): 427–45.

59. See his letter to Monroe of May 29, 1785, written at about the same time (*PJM* 8:286): "It gives me great pleasure to observe" that Congress has expunged the clause in the land-sales bill that would have set aside portions of land for support of the majority's religion. "How a regulation so unjust in itself, so foreign to the authority of Congress, so hurtful to the sale of public land, and smelling so strongly of an antiquated bigotry could have received the countenance of a committee is truly matter of astonishment."

60. All authorities suggest the debt to Locke, on whom successive generations of English Protestant dissenters had built a more and more complete defense of total toleration. The Memorial is also fairly and traditionally considered an elaboration of the principles of Jefferson's bill, which also showed Locke's influence. A good, recent discussion of their similarities to and differences from Locke is Sanford Kessler, "Locke's Influence on Jefferson's 'Bill for Establishing Religious Freedom,'" *Journal of Church and State* 25 (1983): 231–52.

61. *PJM* 8:299.

62. Ibid., 299–300.

63. Ibid., 300. Madison returned time after time in later writings to the example of revolutionary resistance to first encroachments, especially to the three-penny duty on tea. A sensitivity to the power of precedent to alter a constitution entirely in time was another distinguishing characteristic of his thought. The Virginia Resolutions of 1798 and the "Letters of Helvidius" both made the danger of precedents a major theme.

64. Ibid., 300–301.

65. Ibid., 301.

66. Ibid., 301–03.

67. Ibid., 304.

68. The Memorial was obviously written from a Christian point of view. Admittedly, this may have been a tactical consideration, but it was not a *necessary* tactic in this situation. I am convinced that Madison consistently adopted tactics that did not dissemble his private views, that there was very little of the propagandist in his makeup. The Memorial is thus my major reason for concluding that his thinking still had room for the authority of revelation at least as late as 1785.

69. "Additional Memoranda," 560–62.

70. Editorial note, *PJM* 8:295–98.

71. Buckley, *Church and State,* chap. 4, is an excellent discussion of developments between the sessions.

72. Buckley, *Church and State,* 144–52, and the editorial note in *PJM* 8:297–98. Madison's Memorial obtained approximately 1700 signatures. Although decidedly most influential in the long term, it was by no means the most widely subscribed at the time. Twenty-nine petitions, signed by nearly 5000, followed a different, still-anonymous, antideistic draft, which may have been the work of the Baptists. Twenty-one followed the Presbyterian memorial of August 25. There can be no doubt, as Madison was well aware, that overwhelming opposition from the dissenters was principally responsible for crushing the assessment. For more on the dissenters and their petitions, see Rhys Isaac, "'The Rage of Malice of the Old Serpent Devil': The Dissenters and the Making and Remaking of the Virginia Statute for Religious Freedom," in Peterson and Vaughan, *Virginia Statute for Religious Freedom,* 139–69.

73. See note 41.

74. The finished bill, with the deletions in italics and helpful editorial notes, is in *PTJ* 2:545–53. The best account of its passage is Buckley, *Church and State,* 157–63. In the Delegates, the move to substitute Article 16 for Jefferson's preamble was defeated on December 16, 38 to 66. After failure of a motion to postpone the final reading, it carried the House the following day, 74 to 20.

75. JM to TJ, January 22, 1786, *PJM* 8:474.

76. Archibald Stuart to John Breckenridge, December 7, 1785, quoted in *PJM* 8:446 n. 3.

77. Again I have relied primarily on the end-of-session report to Jefferson, progress reports to Washington and Monroe, drafts of legislation, and editorial notes in *PJM* 8:389–484.

78. JM to Monroe, January 22, 1786, *PJM* 8:483.

79. JM to Monroe, December 9, 1785, *PJM* 8:437.

80. JM to TJ, January 22, 1786, *PJM* 8:477.

81. *PJM* 8:473.

82. Stuart to Breckenridge, January 26, 1786, *PJM* 8:446 n. 3.

83. See above, pp. 56–57.

84. JM to TJ, January 22, 1786, *PJM* 8:475. Supplemental legislation needed to initiate the plan for circuit courts was defeated 63 to 49, and only a suspension

of the act could save it from repeal. Opposed by much of the bench and bar, the assize bill never actually went into effect.

85. *PJM* 8:477.

86. *PJM* 8:299.

87. For Madison's profound hostility to paper money see, further, his letter to Jefferson of August 12, 1786, and his speech in the House of Delegates of November 1, 1786, *PJM* 9:94–95, 156–60. In the latter, he condemned paper money as an "unjust," "antifederal," and "unconstitutional" interference with private contracts. He argued that it would encourage "luxury," "extravagance," and the "unfavorable balance of trade." Above all, perhaps, he thought it had a tendency to enrich "collectors and sharpers," to vitiate morals, to reverse the "end of government, which is to reward [the] best [men or conduct] and punish [the] worst," and to "disgrace republican government in the eyes of mankind."

88. JM, "Vices of the Political System of the United States," *PJM* 9:353–54 (hereafter cited as "Vices").

89. JM, "Observations on Jefferson's Draft of a Constitution for Virginia," 1788, *PJM* 11:287–88.

90. JM, speech of June 4 (Rufus King's notes) and speech of June 6 (JM's notes), *RFC* 1:108.

91. The revolutionary state constitutions can be found in *The Federal and State Constitutions, Colonial Charters, and Other Organic Laws*, ed. Francis Newton Thorpe, 7 vols. (Washington, D.C., 1909). Their provisions are discussed most fully in Willi Paul Adams, *The First American Constitutions: Republican Ideology and the Making of the State Constitutions in the Revolutionary Era*, trans. Rita Kimber and Robert Kimber (Chapel Hill, N.C., 1980), and in Donald S. Lutz, *Popular Consent and Popular Control: Whig Political Theory in the Early State Constitutions* (Baton Rouge, La., 1980). The indispensable authority for constitutional thinking in the 1780s is Wood, *Creation of the American Republic*, however, I differ in significant respects from Wood, not least by suggesting that the revolutionaries were departing from traditional ideas about the balanced constitution and enduring differences between the many and the few more slowly and less radically than he implies. For a fuller explanation of these differences with Wood, see my "Second Thoughts on Virtue" and "The Problem of Power: Parties, Aristocracy, and Democracy in Revolutionary Thought," in *The American Revolution: Its Character and Limits*, ed. Jack P. Greene (New York, 1987), 104–23.

92. The transforming effects of an individualistic, natural-rights philosophy is a major theme for Wood and for Bailyn, *Ideological Origins*, the works that have become the starting point for the prevailing view.

93. The argument that Britain's "boasted constitution" was in fact composed of such discordant elements that it could function only when the ministry corrupted its "republican materials" was most effectively developed in *Common Sense*. See *The Complete Writings of Thomas Paine*, ed. Philip S. Foner (New York, 1945), 1: 6–9 and below. A superb discussion of the pamphlet is Bernard Bailyn, "Common Sense," in *Fundamental Testaments of the American Revolution*, Library of Congress Symposia on the American Revolution, no. 2 (Washington, D.C., 1973), 7–22.

94. *Federalist* 10:57.

95. JM, speech opposing paper money, November 1, 1786, *PJM* 9:158–59, and "Vices" *PJM* 9:353–54.

96. JM to Monroe, October 5, 1786, *PJM* 9:141.

97. *Federalist* 51:351–52. The phrasing is anticipated in JM to TJ, October 24, 1787, *PJM* 10:214.

98. JM to TJ, August 20, 1785, *PJM* 8:345.

99. JM to GW, November 8, 1786, *PJM* 9:166; Bill Providing for Delegates to the Convention, *PJM* 9:163–64.

100. See the letters between Madison and Washington of November 8 and 18, 1786; December 12 and 16, 1786; and January 12, 1787, in *PJM* 9:166, 170–71, 199, 215–16, 224. By this time, their friendship has grown close enough that both men closed with affection and Madison always stopped by Mount Vernon on his travels to and from the North. He worked to help the general find a way around his earlier refusal to attend a meeting of the Cincinnati, which was scheduled in Philadelphia at the same time as the convention, but he was nearly as reluctant as the older man himself to see him risk his great prestige until it was apparent that the meeting might succeed. See, also, JM to ER, April 15, 1787, *PJM* 9:378.

101. JM to GW, November 1, 1786, *PJM* 9:155, and JM to James Madison Sr., November 1, 1786, *PJM* 9:154. Informing his father of the congressional proceedings, Madison wrote that, if pursued, the Jay-Gardoqui project "will not fail to alienate the western country and confirm the animosity and jealousy already subsisting between the Atlantic states."

102. JM to GW, December 7, 1786, *PJM* 9:200. Note also the fears expressed in Edmund Pendleton to JM, December 9, 1786, *PJM* 9: 202–3.

103. The resolutions, which passed the House unanimously on November 29 in response to a memorial from the Kentucky members, are in *PJM* 9:182–83. It is generally agreed that Madison drafted them Certainly, the argument and language closely paralleled the phrases of his letters, condemning "a sacrifice of the rights of any one part [of the union] to the supposed or real interests of another part" as a "direct contravention of the end for which the federal government was instituted" and as "provoking the just resentments and reproaches of our western brethren."

104. JM to Pendleton, January 9, 1787, and JM to GW, December 24, 1786, *PJM* 9: 244, 224–25.

105. JM to TJ, December 4, 1786, *PJM* 9:189. See also JM to James Madison Sr., December 12, 1786, *PJM* 9:205–6: "Such an interposition of the law in private contracts is not to be vindicated on any legislative principle within my knowledge" and is subject to "the strongest objections which prevailed against paper money."

106. JM to James Madison Sr., November 1, 1786, and the speech against paper money, November 1, 1786, *PJM* 9:154, 156–59.

107. As late as December 18, 1786 (see *PJM* 9:218), Edward Carrington was writing from New York that he believed that Massachusetts would not attend.

108. JM to Pendleton, January 9, 1787, *PJM* 9:243. See also JM to GW, December 24, 1786, *PJM* 9:225. Before the session closed, Madison had written to his father and to Washington that he had "acquiesced" in an act making tobacco

receivable for taxes, calling this departure from strict principles "a prudential compliance with the clamors within doors and without" (*PJM* 9:178, 200). On December 4, 1786, he told Jefferson that this "indulgence to the people" was the only instance in which "the general principles of finance have been departed from." But he also complained that "the fruits of the impolitic measures taken at the last session with regard to taxes are bitterly tasted now. Our treasury is empty, no supplies have gone to the federal treasury, and our internal embarrassments torment us exceedingly" (*PJM* 9: 190). Contrary to Madison's expectations, the port bill was not repealed, and there was further progress on the revision of the laws. But he had not felt able to raise the question of the British debts.

109. *PJM* 9:154. Lee's letter of October 19, 1786 (*PJM* 9:144), referring to "authentic information" in the hands of Congress, had estimated that the five "seditious counties" in western Massachusetts contained 40,000 of the state's 75,000 men between sixteen and sixty.

110. GW to JM, November 5, 1786, *PJM* 9:161.

111. William Grayson to JM, November 22, 1786, *PJM* 9:174.

112. JM to George Muter, January 7, 1787, *PJM* 9:231. The truth about the insurrection was, of course, quite different. The fullest, most recent account is David P. Szatmary, *Shays' Rebellion: The Making of an Agrarian Insurrection* (Amherst, Mass., 1980). Also still useful is Robert J. Taylor, *Western Massachusetts in the Revolution* (Providence, R.I., 1954).

113. Virginia Delegates to Gov. Randolph, February 12, 1787, *PJM* 9:266. The legislature adjourned on January 11; Madison hurried to Orange, stayed for just two days, and reached New York on February 9.

114. JM to Muter, January 7, 1787, *PJM* 9:231.

115. Ibid.

116. Madison's letters from New York during February and March reported widespread suspicions of a growth of promonarchy sentiments in New England and even among the section's delegates in Congress. More on these, to which he plainly gave some credence, in Chapter 4. But see, particularly, JM to GW, February 21, 1787, and his "Notes" of the same date, *PJM* 9:286, 291–92.

117. Edmund Cody Burnett, *The Continental Congress* (New York, 1941), 672.

118. "Notes," *PJM* 9:276–79. By March 28, King was able to inform Congress that the situation had improved sufficiently to stop the enlistments. Madison continued to be anxious, nonetheless, until the eve of his departure for the Philadelphia convention.

119. ER to JM, March 1, 7, and 15, 1787, *PJM* 9:301, 303, 312–13.

120. See the account and explanation in his "Notes," February 21, 1787, *PJM* 9:290–92.

121. "Notes" April 10 and 11, 1787, with JM to ER, April 18, 1787, *PJM* 9:372, 375, 379–80.

122. See, for example, letters from John Campbell, February 21, 1787, and from ER, March 1, 1787, *PJM* 9:287, 301.

123. Madison recorded these visits at length in his "Notes" for March 13 and 29, 1787, *PJM* 9:309–11, 337–39. He tried to bluff Gardoqui, but it is clear that, by this time, he was afraid that the closing of the Mississippi would lead the west-

erners eventually to "set up for themselves . . . [and] slide like Vermont insensibly into a communication and latent connection with their British neighbors" (JM to GW, March 18, 1787, *PJM* 9:316, and JM to TJ, March 19, 1787, *PJM* 9:319).

124. ER to JM, March 1, 1787, *PJM* 9:301. Both men always attributed Henry's refusal to attend the Constitutional Convention to the Jay-Gardoqui project.

125. "Notes," March 20 and April 2, 1787, *PJM* 9:340–41, 368.

126. JM to ER, April 15, 1787, and "Notes," April 18, 1787, *PJM* 9: 380, 389–90.

127. JM to TJ, April 23, 1787, *PJM* 9:400.

128. "Notes," April 23–26, 1787, *PJM* 9:400–407.

129. JM to ER, February 25, 1787, *PJM* 9:299.

130. JM to Pendleton, February 24, 1787, *PJM* 9:294–95.

131. JM to Eliza House Trist, February 10, 1787, *PJM* 9:259.

132. JM to ER, April 15, 1787, *PJM* 9:379.

CHAPTER FOUR. THE VIRGINIA PLAN

1. The most comprehensive scholarly studies of the framing of the Constitution are Charles Warren, *The Making of the Constitution* (Boston, 1928), and Clinton Rossiter, *1787: The Grand Convention* (New York, 1966). Catherine Drinker Bowen, *Miracle at Philadelphia: The Story of the Constitutional Convention, May to September 1787* (Boston, 1966), and Christopher Collier and James Lincoln Collier, *Decision in Philadelphia: The Constitutional Convention of 1787* (New York, 1986), are the best of the more popular accounts. Among shorter studies, the most instructive on the complexity of the convention's divisions is Forrest McDonald, *Novus Ordo Seclorum: The Intellectual Origins of the Constitution* (Lawrence, Kans., 1985), chaps. 6–8. The fullest computer-assisted examination is Calvin C. Jillson, *Constitution Making: Conflict and Consensus in the Federal Convention of 1787* (New York, 1988).

2. Consider John P. Roche, "The Founding Fathers: A Reform Caucus in Action," *APSR* 55 (1961): 799–816, which sees "no over-arching principles" at work in the convention, or Merrill Jensen, *The Making of the Constitution* (Princeton, N.J., 1964), which suggests a sharper ideological polarization than was present.

3. As in Calvin C. Jillson, "Constitution-Making: Alignment and Realignment in the Federal Convention of 1787," *APSR* 75 (1981): 598–612, though Jillson's studies supersede all quantitative analyses that do not consider changes over time.

4. As in Calvin C. Jillson and Cecil L. Eubanks, "The Political Structure of Constitution Making: The Federal Convention of 1787," *American Journal of Political Science* 28 (1984), 435–58, or in Jillson, *Constitution Making*, which suggest that *either* differences of principle *or* differences of interest account for coalitional configurations at specific points in the convention. I believe that both kinds of differences were always constantly at work.

5. Helpful for their insistence on the collective mission of the convention and for their realization that the process of compromise was more than a matter of trucking and bargaining are Herbert J. Storing, "The Constitutional Convention: Toward a More Perfect Union," in *American Political Thought: The Philosophic Dimen-*

sion of American Statesmanship, ed. Morton J. Frisch and Richard G. Stevens (New York, 1971), 51–00, and David C. Smith, *The Convention and the Constitution: The Political Ideas of the Founding Fathers* (New York, 1965).

6. *RFC* 3:455. See also 497, 517, 521, and 537. Unless otherwise indicated, quotations are from Madison's notes of the debates.

7. *RFC* 1:20–22.

8. The weaker New Jersey Plan nevertheless included a provision for coercion of delinquent states, a power to regulate trade, and powers to impose a stamp tax, postal duties, and an impost (*RFC* 1:242–45). A large majority of states had ratified amendments to the Articles approving an impost and a partial federal authority to regulate trade.

9. *RFC* 1:48.

10. *RFC* 1:134.

11. For the preparation of the resolutions, see *RFC* 1:18, 3:23, 3:409, 3:525, and passim. The Virginia Plan provided for rotation of the members of the lower house, but not the senate; Madison's preconvention letters had recommended the reverse. Other minor differences will be discussed below, but I can find no evidence that Madison opposed any of the resolutions or that the Virginia Plan either advanced significantly beyond or (except in the matter of a federal negative on local legislation) retreated significantly from his precaucus desires.

12. "Notes on Ancient and Modern Confederacies," *PJM* 9:3–24. During his retirement, Madison remembered writing these *after* his appointment to the Constitutional Convention ("James Madison's Autobiography," ed. Douglass Adair, *WMQ* 2[1945]: 201–2). Irving Brant 2:465, Ketcham 183–85, and the editors of *PJM* all date them to the spring of 1786, the latest time at which they could have been prepared with all his books around him at his home. The question might best be considered unresolved. In either case, however, this research was certainly his *first* step toward a systematic analysis of current ills, which is a point of real importance.

13. JM to TJ March 19, 1787, *PJM* 9:318–19; to ER, April 8, 1787, *PJM* 9:368–71; and to GW, April 16, 1787, *PJM* 9:382–85.

14. *PJM* 9:345–58. In estimating Madison's initial influence on the convention it is useful to bear in mind that this memorandum, which was a polished piece of writing, may have been read by several members. It is headed by a note that a copy was made by Daniel Carroll, a Maryland delegate, and sent by permission to Charles Carroll of Carrollton.

15. In "The Political Ideology of the Founders," in *Toward a More Perfect Union: Six Essays on the Constitution,* ed. Neil L. York (Provo, Utah, 1988), 10, Gordon Wood restates a point that has been emphasized by modern scholarship for years: "Many Americans . . . wanted a firmer union." Yet they knew "that the principal weaknesses of the Confederation and the strengthening of the union could be solved without totally scrapping the Articles of Confederation and creating a radically powerful national government, the like of which had not been even conceived of ten years earlier." Madison and the convention therefore recommended radical reform because "the oppressive behavior of the state legislatures . . . was uppermost in the[ir] minds." I seek to show that Madison's stand was actually

quite different: that he repeatedly denied that the Confederation's weaknesses were curable within the framework of the Articles, that he was led to this conclusion by consideration of the structure of the Union rather than the problems of the states, and that he did not want "a radically powerful national government." My argument is also usefully contrasted on these points with Jack N. Rakove, "The Great Compromise: Ideas, Interests, and the Politics of Constitution Making," *WMQ* 44 (1987): 424–57, and *James Madison and the Creation of the American Republic.* Though Rakove criticizes Wood's *Creation of the American Republic* for its relative neglect of federal problems, I do not believe the insight has been pressed far enough. Indeed, in all the literature on Madison's initial thinking and on the Virginia Resolutions, two articles by Michael P. Zuckert are the only writings that approach a sound appreciation: "Federalism and the Founding: Toward a Reinterpretation of the Constitutional Convention," *Review of Politics* 48 (1986): 166–210, and "A System without a Precedent: Federalism in the American Constitution," in *The Framing and Ratification of the Constitution*, ed. Leonard W. Levy and Dennis J. Mahoney (New York, 1987), 132–50.

16. JM to TJ, March 19, 1787, *PJM* 9:318, and to ER, April 8, 1787, *PJM* 9:370.

17. To TJ, *PJM* 9:318.

18. Revenue requisitions are "a law to the states," as state acts are laws to individuals (JM, speech in the Confederation Congress, February 21, 1783, *PJM* 6:271).

19. "Vices," *PJM* 9:351.

20. *RFC* 2:92–93. For early formulations of these thoughts, see Madison's letters to Jefferson (*PJM* 9:318), Randolph (*PJM* 9:370), and Washington (*PJM* 9:385). For a recent study of the background of this concept (which culminates, however, in a challengeable discussion of Madison himself), see Edmund S. Morgan, *Inventing the People: The Rise of Popular Sovereignty in England and America* (New York, 1988).

21. JM to TJ, March 19, 1787, *PJM* 9:318. See also JM to ER, April 8, 1787, *PJM* 9:369.

22. See, especially, Charles F. Hobson, "The Negative on State Laws: James Madison, the Constitution, and the Crisis of Republican Government," *WMQ* 36 (1979): 215–35, though Hobson now believes that this article pressed the argument too far.

23. Compare the articles by Michael Zuckert cited in note 15.

24. Moreover, it was in this context, in the letter to Randolph (April 8, 1787, *PJM* 9:369), that Madison remarked that an effectual reform must make the states "subordinately useful." Frequently cited as evidence of his consolidationist sentiments at this point, the remark was in fact merely an incident in his attempt to conceptualize the federal problem.

25. Ibid., 370. Compare JM to GW, April 16, 1787, *PJM* 9:383: the negative is "the least possible encroachment on the state jurisdictions." The distinction between "positive" powers and "this defensive power" begins in JM to TJ, March 19, 1787, *PJM* 9:318.

26. TJ to JM, June 20, 1787, *PJM* 10:64.

27. The unanswerability of Madison's analysis became most striking in the brief debate preceding the convention's decision to adhere to the Virginia Plan in preference to the New Jersey Resolutions (*RFC* 1:241–333). As Rakove remarks, opponents of the Virginia Plan did not even try to counter the insistence on the insufficiency of a purely federal system, focusing instead on practical and legal obstacles to a more fundamental reform ("Great Compromise," 441–47).

28. "I hold it for a fundamental point that an individual independence of the states is utterly irreconcileable with the idea of an aggregate sovereignty. I think at the same time that a consolidation of the states into one simple republic is not less unattainable than it would be inexpedient. Let it be tried then whether any middle ground can be taken which will at once support a due supremacy of the national authority, and leave in force the local authorities so far as they can be subordinately useful" (JM to ER, April 8, 1787, *PJM* 9:369). The reference to "middle ground" reappears in the letter to GW, April 16, 1787, *PJM* 9:383.

29. JM to GW, April 16, 1787, *PJM* 9:385, which then went on to indicate a hope that the necessity for force might be "precluded" by means of the federal negative. "Or perhaps some defined objects of [internal] taxation might be submitted, along with commerce, to the general authority." The obvious presumption here is that the general government will still resort to requisitions.

30. See Gordon S. Wood, *The Creation of the American Republic, 1776–1787* (Chapel Hill, N.C., 1969), 525. See also Zuckert, "Federalism and the Founding," which insists that the Virginia Plan envisioned "national means to federal ends" (180) and also that Madison's desires—the Virginia Plan plus a universal federal negative—would clearly have intermixed a "national" mode of operation with a "federal" one more thoroughly than did the Virginia Resolutions themselves. The problem of sovereignty in a system that divided powers between a central and provincial government—the problem that had wrecked the British empire—was enormously complex. In addition to Wood, *Creation of the American Republic,* and Morgan, *Inventing the People,* see Jack P. Greene, *Peripheries and Center: Constitutional Development in the Extended Polities of the British Empire and the United States, 1607–1788,* Richard B. Russell Lectures, no. 2 (Athens, Ga., 1986). But two key points, pursued below, might be anticipated at this point: (1) the concept that *ultimate* sovereignty rested in the people did not obviate the need to address the question of *governmental* sovereignty even after the Constitution was in force; and (2) Madison did not, in the convention or later, achieve a "resolution" of the interlocking questions concerning sovereignty by conceiving of it as vested in a single American people. Contrary to Morgan, Madison consistently conceived of sovereignty as vested in the peoples of the several states. Passages already quoted clearly implied that only the people of Virginia (for example), not the people of the United States, could alter the Virginia constitution and compel its government to submit to central commands. Accordingly, the finished Constitution was to go into effect only among the ratifying states.

31. This paraphrases *Federalist* no. 41 and Madison's speech in the Convention on June 29. But Madison's association of Virginia's vulnerability, collapse of the Confederation, and an end of republican liberty was apparent, as has been shown,

as early as February 21, 1783 (*PJM* 6:272), and well developed by the time of his speech in the Virginia legislature in November 1785 (*PJM* 7:431–32). Candid references to the South's special vulnerability are in the speeches of August 29 and 16, *RFC* 2:452, 306–7.

32. JM to TJ, March 19, 1787, *PJM* 9:318.

33. The fullest, most suggestive recent treatments of the rising talk of separate confederations are Cathy D. Matson and Peter S. Onuf, *A Union of Interests: Political and Economic Thought in Revolutionary America* (Lawrence, Kans., 1990), chap. 5, and Peter S. Onuf, "Constitutional Politics: States, Sections, and the National Interest," in York, *Toward a More Perfect Union*, 29–57.

34. See Madison's letters to Randolph, Washington, and Jefferson of February 15 and 18, 1787, March 11 and 19, 1787, and April 16, 1787 at *PJM* 9:270, 272, 307, 315, 321, and 386. For the severity and consequences of the legislature's reaction, see Richard D. Brown, "Shays' Rebellion and the Ratification of the Federal Constitution in Massachusetts," in *Beyond Confederation: Origins of the Constitution and American National Identity,* ed. Richard Beeman, Stephen Botein, and Edward C. Carter II (Chapel Hill, N.C., 1987), 113–27.

35. ER's letters of March 1, 7, and 15, 1787, at *PJM* 9:301, 303, and 312–13.

36. Dawson to JM, April 15, 1787, *PJM* 9:381. On June 12, after the Convention had begun, Dawson added that arsonists had burned the courthouse in King William County in order to destroy the county records (*PJM* 10:470). Meanwhile, Governor Randolph was receiving regular reports of jailbreaks, threats against the courts, and other antitax or antidebt commotions in Virginia.

37. Preface to JM's notes of the debates in the Convention, *RFC* 3:548–49.

38. *PJM* 9:290–292.

39. JM to GW, February 21, 1787, *PJM* 9:286.

40. GW to JM, March 31, 1787, *PJM* 9:342–43.

41. JM to TJ, March 19, 1787, *PJM* 9:318.

42. "Notes," February 21, 1787, *PJM* 9:292.

43. JM to Edmund Pendleton, February 24, 1787, *PJM* 9:295.

44. JM to ER, February 24, 1787, *PJM* 9:299. After he arrived in Philadelphia, Madison was further troubled by the quick applause for the first volume of John Adams's *Defence of the Constitutions of Government of the United States of America,* which he evidently read while waiting for the Constitutional Convention to assemble. "Many of the remarks in it ... are unfriendly to republicanism," he complained to Jefferson, and—especially in New England—would encourage the revival of "the predilections of this country for the British constitution" (June 6, 1787, *PJM* 10:29–30).

45. On separate confederations, see note 33. Though badly dated, the fullest exploration of the other question is Louise Burnham Dunbar, *A Study of "Monarchical" Tendencies in the United States, from 1776 to 1801,* University of Illinois Studies in the Social Sciences 10, no. 1 (Urbana, Ill., 1922). Madison never named the influential New Englanders, in Congress and without, whom he suspected of monarchical opinions.

46. JM to ER, April 8, 1787, *PJM* 9:369, 371. His emphasis.

47. This is a principal theme of Wood's *Creation of the American Republic*, especially chap. 10.

48. The opposite is often said—or clearly implied by Wood. But none of Madison's surviving papers, to my knowledge, can be quoted to support the view that he believed that a failure of public virtue was endangering the Revolution or that public virtue was insufficent to support a republican regime. My article "Second Thoughts on Virtue" (cited in full at Chapter 3, note 3) is a systematic consideration of this revolutionary concept.

49. JM to TJ, March 19, 1787, *PJM* 9:318.

50. "The first step to be taken is, I think, a change in the principle of representation. According to the present form of the Union, an equality of suffrage, if not just toward the larger members of it, is at least safe to them, as the liberty they exercise of rejecting or executing the acts of Congress is uncontrollable by the nominal sovereignty of Congress. Under a system which would operate without the intervention of the states, the case would be materially altered. A vote from Delaware would have the same effect as one from Massachusetts or Virginia" (JM to ER, April 8, 1787, *PJM* 9:369–70). The letters to Jefferson and Washington also state that the reform must start with this change.

51. All three of the preconvention letters insist on a division of the powers currently exercised by the single-chamber Congress. The letters to Randoloph and Washington suggest a lower house elected by the state legislatures *or* by the people at large. But if Madison was really undecided at this point, he was committed firmly to a popular election by the opening of the convention. Jefferson't first response to the completed Constitution is also instructive on the point: a lower house elected by the people would be "very illy qualified to legislate for the Union, for foreign nations, etc., yet this evil does not weigh against the good of preserving inviolate the fundamental principle that the people are not to be taxed but by representatives chosen immediately by themselves" (TJ to JM, December 20, 1787, *JPM* 10:336).

52. JM to GW, April 16, 1787, *PJM* 9:384. And *note well* that Madison's reference to a "dispassionate umpire" over contending interests applies specifically and *solely* to a federal referee over contentions within individual states, that he does not envision a federal legislature capable of dispassionately supervising *national* conflicts of interest. "Vices of the Political System," which he wrote at about the same time, but which is phrased in such a way that it is not so obvious that he had the federal veto in mind as the means by which the large republic "meliorates the administration of a small," has been repeatedly misread as evidence that he hoped to create a neutral sovereign over national interests and factions: "The great desideratum in government is such a modification of the sovereignty as will render it sufficiently neutral between the different interests and factions to control one part of the society from invading the rights of another, and at the same time sufficiently controlled itself from setting up an interest adverse to that of the whole society" (*PJM* 9:357).

53. "Vices," *PJM* 9:354–57.

54. Charles Pinckney's plan may have also incorporated such a power. If it did,

however, this is very probably because Madison had mentioned it to Pinckney and to others in New York. See William Grayson to William Short, April 16, 1787, *LMCC* 8:581. For the complicated question of the contents of Pinckney's plan, see *RFC*, vol. 3, appendix D, and Brant 3:28–29. Certainly, the federal veto struck TJ and others as a novel and surprising thought. In the convention on June 8, Gerry said that the idea "has never been suggested or conceived among the people. No speculative projector . . . has in any pamphlet or newspaper thrown out the idea." Wilson responded that "however novel it might appear, the principle of it . . . is right" (*RFC* 1:165).

55. "Vices," *PJM* 9:354.

56. Ibid., 353–54.

57. JM, speech of June 6, *RFC* 1:134–36. Compare the phrasing in "Vices," *PJM* 9:355.

58. JM, speech of June 6, *RFC* 1:135–36. See also his speech of June 26, *RFC* 1:421–23. Madison and others usually referred to "republics" rather than "democracies," but this was his own phrasing. The distinction between the two became more common after he made it a strategy of *The Federalist.*

59. "Vices," *PJM* 9:351.

60. See the discussion at pp. 98–101.

61. "Vices," *PJM* 9:355–56; JM, speech of June 6, 1787, *RFC* 1:135; *Federalist* 10:58; JM to TJ, October 24, 1787, *PJM* 10:214.

62. *Federalist* 10:56.

63. JM to TJ, October 17, 1788, *PJM* 9:297–98. JM's emphasis.

64. *Federalist* 51:351–52. The phrasing is anticipated in JM to TJ, October 24, 1787, *PJM* 10:214.

65. Numerous perceptive scholars have observed that his defense of large republics as a remedy for democratic faction thus emerged originally as a corollary and defense of his proposal of a universal federal veto. See, especially, Hobson, "Negative on State Laws," and John Zvesper, "The Madisonian Systems," *Western Political Quarterly* 37 (1984): 236–56.

66. See TJ to JM, June 17, 1783, *PJM* 7:156–57, which enclosed Jefferson's proposals for revision (*PTJ* 6:278–84, 294–308). The two men certainly discussed the matter at length during their weeks together at the seat of Congress. See *PJM* 7:401, 426.

67. JM to TJ, May 15, 1784, and July 3, 1784, *PJM* 8:34, 93.

68. *PJM* 8:77–78.

69. Here, as elsewhere, the essential history is Wood, *Creation of the American Republic,* especially chaps. 7–8. For Jefferson's thinking see, further, Query 13 of *Notes on the State of Virginia.*

70. JM to Caleb Wallace, August 23, 1785, *PJM* 8:350–57. For the Kentuckians' requests see *PJM* 8:218–19, 320–23. The "Memorial against Assessments," as I have shown, incorporated Madison's most eloquent discussions of the origins and limits of governmental power, of the natural equality of men, and of the possibility that even the majority could exceed its rightful limits.

71. Quotations at *PJM* 8:352, 355.

72. "I have made up no final opinion whether the first magistrate should be

chosen by the legislature or the people at large or whether the power should be vested in one man assisted by a council or in a council of which the president shall be only primus inter pares." If elected frequently or by the people, the executive could be indefinitely reeligible for reelection. If chosen for a longer term, "a temporary or perpetual" ineligibility "may not be amiss" (*PJM* 8:351, 354–55). Virginia's governor was really first among the equals on the council. He could serve three annual terms and then would not be eligible again until three years had passed. Jefferson decidedly preferred a longer term and an ineligibility for reelection.

73. *PJM* 8:350–51.

74. See further his 1788 "Observations on Jefferson's Draft of a Constitution for Virginia" (*PJM* 11:281–94). Neither the federal nor the state constitutions, this remarked, made provision for a disagreement between the three great branches on the constitutionality of laws. Thus, a final decision might be left, by default, to the courts, which would have to make the last decision to enforce or refuse to enforce the disputed legislation. "This makes the judiciary department paramount in fact to the legislature, which was never intended and can never be proper" (293). Madison, as we shall see, certainly accepted judicial review of federal as well as state legislation, but he also consistently maintained that the judiciary did not possess an ultimate power to overrule the executive or legislative, which possessed coequal powers to decide on the constitutionality of legislation.

75. *PJM* 8:351, 355.

76. See Jefferson's similar complaint in Query 13 of *Notes on the State of Virginia*: "The Senate is, by its constitution, too homogeneous with the House of Delegates. Being chosen by the same electors at the same time and out of the same subjects, the choice falls of course on men of the same description. The purpose of establishing different houses of legislature is to introduce the influence of different interests or different principles. Thus in Great Britain it is said their constitution relies on the House of Commons for honesty and the Lords for wisdom, which would be a rational reliance if honesty were to be bought with money and if wisdom were hereditary. In some of the American states, the delegates and senators are so chosen that the first represent the persons and the second the property of the state. But with us, wealth and wisdom have equal chance for admission into both houses. We do not, therefore, derive from the separation of our legislature into two houses those benefits which a proper complication of principles are capable of producing and those which alone can compensate the evils which may be produced by their dissensions."

77. *PJM* 8:351, 354.

78. The November 1788 "Observations on Jefferson's Draft," also written in response to the Kentuckians' request for his advice, must be used with caution when reconstructing the ideas of 1787, for Madison's thinking and proposals changed significantly as a result of the federal convention. Still, this document's fuller justification of the differential suffrage, which attracted Madison throughout his life, is probably a fair reflection of the thoughts already present in 1785: "A freehold or equivalent of a certain value may be

annexed to the right of voting for senators and the right left more at large in the election of the other house. . . . [This] reconciles and secures the two cardinal objects of government: the rights of persons and the rights of property. . . . Give a defensive share to each and each will be secure." Early in the Revolution, he explained, personal rights were emphasized, and it was thought that property rights would automatically be protected as part of the former. Experience had since suggested that "in all populous countries, the smaller part only can be interested in preserving the rights of property." These, therefore, had to be secured while the majority itself was propertied. If they were not, the majority would eventually combine against the propertied and serve the ends of ambition, as "their poverty and dependence will render them the mercenary instruments of wealth" (*JPM* 8:287–88). Two observations should be added for a full appreciation of these suggestions: every state in 1785 restricted the franchise to those who were considered to have an independent will of their own; and in Virginia, Madison's proposal would have *widened* the present franchise. The only Virginians who had the right to vote at all were those who would elect his senate for Kentucky.

79. *PJM* 8:354.

80. JM to Edmund Pendleton, February 24, 1787, *PJM* 9:295.

CHAPTER FIVE. TO PERPETUATE THE UNION

1. See the sketch by Georgia delegate William Pierce, *RFC* 3:94: "Every person seems to acknowledge his greatness. He blends together the profound politician with the scholar. In the management of every great question he evidently took the lead in the convention. . . . He always comes forward the best informed man of any point in debate. The affairs of the United States he perhaps has the most correct knowledge of of any man in the Union."

2. Two of many excellent attempts to measure Madison's contributions against those of his colleagues are particularly helpful on this point: Clinton Rossiter, *1787: The Grand Convention* (New York, 1966), 247–52; and Harold S. Schultz, "James Madison: Father of the Constitution?" *QJLC* 37 (1980): 215–22.

3. The most extreme example of the emphasis on his defeats and disappointments is Forrest McDonald, *Novus Ordo Seclorum: The Intellectual Origins of the Constitution* (Lawrence Kans., 1985), especially 205–9, to which new attention has been drawn by Richard K. Matthews, *"If Men Were Angels": James Madison and the Heartless Empire of Reason* (Lawrence, Kans., 1994). McDonald constructs a "Madisonian constitution" from the Virginia Plan and from specific motions Madison spoke or voted on during the convention, finds that he was on the losing side in forty of seventy-one cases, and uses the findings to debunk "the myth that he was the Father of the Constitution." But even Madison's biographers tend to stress his disappointment at the conclusion of the convention and to warn against confusing the views expressed in *The Federalist* with his private opinions (e.g., Rakove, 71).

4. See Madison's numbers of *The Federalist* and Gorden S. Wood, *The Creation of the American Republic, 1776–1787* (Chapel Hill, N.C., 1969), chaps. 13, 15.

5. JM to TJ, June 6, 1787, *PJM* 10:163–64.

6. "Vices," *PJM* 9:352.

7. JM to GW, April 16, 1787, *PJM* 9:385.

8. As late as his speech of June 28, (*RFC* 1:449), Madison remarked that there were several instances in which the present central government acted directly on the individual members of society, making the Confederation less purely "federal" than certain members claimed.

9. *RFC* 1:54. Except where otherwise noted, quotations are from Madison's notes of the debates.

10. Madison entered a footnote describing this meeting in his record of proceedings for May 28 (*RFC* 1:10–11).

11. Among the rules adopted on May 28, the most important was the rule of secrecy, which freed the delegates from outside pressures and made it easier for them to change their minds as a result of the discussions. They abided with astounding faithfulness by this decision, some of them for years after the convention had adjourned. This means, however, that the letters written while the meeting was in session are of little use for understanding what was happening within the statehouse or outside its walls. All accounts of the convention rest essentially, as mine does, on the members' notes on the debates. On the integrity of these— and Madison's in particular—see the editorial note in *PJM* 10:6–10, and especially James H. Hutson, "The Creation of the Constitution: The Integrity of the Documentary Record," *Texas Law Review* 65 (1986): 1–39. I agree on most of the essential points with Hutson but am not as cynical as he about the usefulness of even Robert Yates's notes. Unlike some other analysts, I also work from an impression, based on a careful study of the record, that a minimum of backstage management occurred, that Madison or other record keepers tell us of occasional exceptions because these were, in fact, just that. This impression does not flow from a naive assumption that the members were "above" maneuvers of this sort. It comes from a conclusion that the politicians of the 1780s usually abided by a principled conviction that their business should be done within the hall.

12. See Madison's preconvention letters to Jefferson, Randolph, and Washington at *PJM* 9:318–19, 368–71, and 382–85.

13. The title of chapter 9 of Rossiter, *1787*.

14. May 30, *RFC* 1:37. Read was on the ground quite early, knew that this proposal would be made, and had himself written these instructions (Read to John Dickinson, May 21 and January 17, 1787, *RFC* 3: 24–26, 575–76). In the course of their preconvention caucus, according to Madison's notes, the Virginians squelched a Pennsylvania suggestion that they should move immediately to deprive the small states of equal votes in the convention (*RFC* 1:10–11).

15. May 30, *RFC* 1:34.

16. On May 31, Roger Sherman objected that "the people . . . should have as little to do as may be about the government. They want information and are constantly liable to be misled." Gerry followed with his condemnation of an "excess of democracy" (*RFC* 1:48).

17. *RFC* 1:53.

18. May 30, *RFC* 1:35–36. The Virginians knew that their proposals would

revive the ancient arguments between the North and South over methods of assessing lands and counting slaves. The language of the original resolution was surely intended to demand proportional representation while postponing the inevitable battles over what "proportional" would mean. For reasons I can only guess at, Madison must have decided that the language was more likely to provoke an early conflict than to postpone it. Certainly, it had long been his own opinion that population was the fairest test of wealth, and he had been responsible for including in the congressional recommendations of 1783 an amendment that would have based federal requisitions on population (counting slaves as three-fifths of whites) instead of on the value of lands. (Note also that a resolution apportioning representation to contributions is another indication that the delegates still assumed that requisitions would be required occasionally.)

19. Ibid., 35.

20. For Madison on the veto, see his brief remarks of June 4, *RFC* 1:99–100. From the beginning of proceedings, Wilson proved the meeting's most persistent and effective advocate of fully independent, fully countervailing branches and, accordingly, of popular election of the executive and senate. The Virginia Plan, in his opinion, made too many links between the branches of the federal government and between the general government and states. Thus, I do not mean to assimilate his views with Madison's. "Democratic nationalist" is merely a convenient label at this point for leaders of the push for structural reform, leaders who believed that an effective central government demanded popular election of at least one house.

21. *RFC* 1:179. Charles Warren, *The Making of the Constitution* (Boston, 1928), 216–17, quickly shows the grounds for small-state fears. The earliest plan for apportionment of the Senate would have given the three largest states 13 of 28 members. By current estimates, they had a population of 1,350,000; the other ten states had 1,710,000. By the census of 1790, the states of Massachusetts, New York, Pennsylvania, and Virginia had a white population of 1,750,000; all the rest had 1,390,000. After this census, the House of Representatives was reapportioned to give these four states 56 members, the rest 47. Territorial comparisons are even more stunning. Virginia, North Carolina, and Georgia—none of which had ceded their enormous claims to territory south of the Ohio—encompassed 340,000 square miles; all the other states encompassed 167,000.

22. *RFC* 1:180.

23. See, particularly, the speeches of Dickinson, Sherman, and George Mason on June 6 and 7, *RFC* 1:133, 136–37, 155, together with Dickinson's "Letters of Fabius," *RFC* 3:304. Recent scholarship has clearly recognized the substantive importance of Dickinson's insistence that a federal role for states as states was more than just a matter of protecting smaller states against potential domination by the large ones. See Michael P. Zuckert, "Federalism and the Founding: Toward a, Reinterpretation of the Constitutional Convention," *Review of Politics* 48 (1986): 199–207; McDonald, *Novus Ordo Seclorum*, 212–15, 230–33, 260, 277; and James H. Hutson, "John Dickinson at the Federal Constitutional Convention," *WMQ* 40 (1983): 256–82.

24. June 1, *RFC* 1:69.

25. June 6, *RFC* 1:134.

26. June 7, *RFC* 1:151–52, 154. If the smallest states were given at least one member, a senate based on proportional representation would have to have numbered more than fifty members.

27. *RFC* 1:164. Here, again, Madison called the negative "the mildest expedient" necessary to defend national supremacy, prevent disputes between the states, and protect "the weaker party" from majority oppressions.

28. See, for example, his speech of July 17, *RFC* 2:27–28. For his position at the end of the convention and his fullest explanation of the federal veto, see JM to TJ, October 24, 1787, *PJM* 10:205–20.

29. June 6, *RFC* 1:134. See also Madison's speech of June 19, *RFC* 1:318.

30. Madison recorded Randolph and Mason voting against extension of the negative (*RFC* 1:168). I think it certain that the two eventual non signers were responsible for the limitation of the power in the resolutions of May 29.

31. *RFC* 1:242.

32. June 12, *RFC* 1:215.

33. These were the concessions made by William Pierce and George Mason to the arguments of Dickinson and Sherman (June 6, *RFC* 1:137; June 7, *RFC* 1: 155).

34. The fragmentary records on the drafting of the plan are gathered in *RFC*, vol. 3, appendix E. For the mixed motives of its framers, see Madison's note, *RFC* 1:242, and Joseph Reese Strayer, ed., *The Delegate from New York or Proceedings of the Federal Convention of 1787 from the Notes of John Lansing, Jr.* (Princeton, N.J., 1939), 70–71. The latter plainly indicate that members from the smaller states were not tenacious in defending the New Jersey Plan because it granted powers to the central government on which the small-state delegates were not agreed. The real issue was representation, Lansing said, and most of the small-state delegates preferred to battle on this ground rather than debate the merits of the two sets of resolutions. Lansing's notes of his motion and speech of June 20 say that he made this clear.

35. Hamilton did not submit this plan as a proposal. He read it, he declared, to illustrate his own ideas and to suggest amendments he would probably submit if the convention stuck with the Virginia Resolutions. The remark that the Virginia Plan was "pork still" is from Yates's notes, but Madison later agreed that Hamilton had used the phrase.

36. For portions of this speech, Madison may well have drawn almost verbatim from his "Vices of the Political System." He clearly did so in the passage of his notes referring to the Massachusetts insurrection and the need for an authority to intervene in case of similar commotions in the future: "According to republican theory, indeed, right and power, being both vested in the majority, are held to be synonymous. According to fact and experience, a minority may in an appeal to force be an overmatch for the majority. 1. If the minority happen to include all such as possess the skill and habits of military life, with such as possess the great pecuniary resources, one-third may conquer the remaining two-thirds. 2. One-third of those who participate in the choice of rulers may be rendered a majority by the

accession of those whose poverty disqualifies them from a suffrage, and who for obvious reasons may be more ready to join the standard of sedition than that of the established government. 3. Where slavery exists, the republican theory becomes still more fallacious." Compare this passage, *RFC* 1:318, with *PJM* 9:350–51.

37. For Hamilton and Madison on sectional divisions, see *RFC* 1:466, 447. Johnson's remark June 29, is at *RFC* 1:461. For Mason's admission, see *RFC* 1:407.

38. The first clear signal of a breach in the large-state coalition came on June 25. Although it seldom happens, this is one occasion on which Madison's notes are quite imperfect. His record of Charles Pinckney's speech—the brash young nabob's most impressive of the meeting—simply breaks off in the middle with a note that Pinckney did not furnish the remainder. Lansing's notes (p. 81) reveal that Pinckney finished by proposing that the states might be classed in such a way that they would get from one to five votes in the Senate. Yates's notes suggest that Nathaniel Gorham of Massachusetts was up next to announce that he was also willing to adopt some compromise by which the large states would not be represented according to their total populations, "perhaps on the plan Mr. Pinckney has suggested." The convention then ignored both Pinckney and Gorham, but their proposals clearly signaled that the large-state delegates were bending.

39. *RFC* 1:468–69.

40. June 30, *RFC* 1:482.

41. June 28, *RFC* 1:446.

42. June 30, *RFC* 1:486–87. The rule he had been thinking of would have counted the southern slaves for purposes of representation in one house of the legislature but not in the other. But this, he added, would not be fair because the meeting planned on giving greater powers to the Senate than to the lower house.

43. June 28, *RFC* 1:447.

44. This paragraph is an amalgam of the speeches of June 29 and 30 and July 14. Quotations are at *RFC* 1:464, 476, 490, and 2:9–10.

45. This quotation is from Yates's notes of his speech of June 30, *RFC* 1:500. Madison's reporting style seems often to have drained some of the heat from such exchanges.

46. From Madison's notes, *RFC* 1:492.

47. In the Georgia delegation, William Houstoun voted with the large states. Abraham Baldwin, who had recently moved to Georgia and was a native of Connecticut, voted with the small.

48. Indeed, Randolph and Mason made it clear from the beginning that they saw this clause as an integral part of the compromise. The subsequent decision to permit the senate to amend money bills, together with the North-South compromise permitting a majority to make commercial regulations, would be the leading reasons for their eventual decisions not to sign.

49. See especially Madison's speech of July 5, *RFC* 1:527.

50. June 28, *RFC* 1:447.

51. Although I do not agree with it in whole, the sketch of Madison in Stanley Elkins and Eric McKitrick, *The Age of Federalism: The Early American Republic, 1788–1800* (New York, 1993), is one of a very few that do not mistake his character and

temper. "James Madison was not really a compromiser. He was a revolutionary; his ideological presuppositions, deep down, were immovable; despite all appearances to the contrary, he was one of the most stubborn and willful men of his time" (79).

52. By the terms of the committee report of July 10, the states from Maryland south—the states, not incidentally, that had opposed the Jay-Gardoqui treaty—would only be outnumbered 36 to 29 in the first lower house; and everyone assumed that population was moving rapidly into the South and West. Randolph's motion for a periodic census to adjust apportionment to the movement of population was resisted most ferociously by Gouverneur Morris, who was explicit in his fear of southern and western domination.

53. July 5, *RFC* 1:533.

54. July 14, *RFC* 2:8–9.

55. Earlier on July 14, *RFC* 2:5.

56. Main speech of July 14, *RFC* 2:8. If the government *was* to be partly national and partly federal, he said, the proper compromise would have the states vote equally in cases where the central government would act on states and proportionally in cases where it would act on the people.

57. July 5, *RFC* 1:527–529.

58. July 17, *RFC* 2:19–20. On July 10, Randolph had communicated to Madison a plan intended to conciliate the small states by granting an equal vote in the Senate on certain specific matters and by incorporating other provisions that would have given all the states additional assurances for the protection of their specific interests (*RFC* 3:55–56). Madison hinted in his speech of July 14 that some such arrangement might be proper if the convention was bent on a partly national, partly federal system. Madison's declared position on this point, together with the language of his record of the large-state caucus, is the basis for my guess that he preferred to return to the convention and confront the small states with an ultimatum demanding an alternative compromise along the lines of Randolph's proposal.

59. JM to TJ, September 6, 1787, *PJM* 10:163–64.

60. Brant, 3:chaps. 1–12, is the fullest and most influential study of Madison's course at the convention. There and in his condensation of the larger study, *The Fourth President: A Life of James Madison* (Indianapolis, 1970), 170–74, Brant maintains that the Connecticut Compromise "affected at once his attitude toward federal powers," determining him to favor an enumeration over a broad grant of legislative authority and initiating the reversal that would mark the 1790s. Ketcham endorses this interpretation, which is certainly the dominant opinion: "Madison's nationalism . . . reached its peak during the weeks when it seemed likely representation would be according to population"; after the large-state caucus, he "became more cautious about the powers granted to the general government" (215).

61. This view is forcefully and gracefully presented in Jean Yarbrough, "Madison and Modern Federalism," in *How Federal Is the Constitution?*, ed. Robert A. Goldwin and William A. Schambra (Washington, D.C., 1987), 84–108: "Had Madison's original proposals succeeded, the Constitution would have established a basically consolidated national government in which the states were no more than admin-

istrative agencies, stripped of all vestiges of sovereignty" (86). See, further, Yarbrough, "Rethinking '*The Federalist*'s View of Federalism,'" *Publius* 15 (1985): 31–53, where this interpretation is traced to the highly influential essays of Martin Diamond, especially "The Federalist's View of Federalism," in *Essays in Federalism,* ed. George C. S. Benson et al. (Claremont, Calf., 1961), 21–64, and "What the Framers Meant by Federalism," in *A Nation of States,* ed. Robert A. Goldwin (Chicago, 1963), 24–41. For thirty years, especially among political theorists, Diamond's views have been as influential for discussions of Madison's founding vision as have Brant's, and Diamond differed from Brant primarily by putting even greater stress on Madison's consolidationism during the convention and even in *The Federalist,* dating his "reversal" to the period after 1789.

62. JM to Andrew Stevenson, March 25, 1826, *RFC* 3:473–74. See also JM to N. P. Trist, December 1831, in *WJM* 9:474–75.

63. JM to Robert S. Garnett, February 11, 1824, *WJM* 9:176–77; JM to John Tyler, 1833, *RFC* 3:526–29.

64. Merrill Jensen, *The Making of the American Constitution* (Princeton, N.J., 1964), treated this as a "basic issue from the outset" in the arguments between "nationalists" and "federalists" at the convention (48, 66–67, 72–73, 80). Several other authors also see a substantive dispute: Warren, *Making of the Constitution,* 163–64, 314–15, 388–89, 548–49; Rossiter, *1787,* 208–9, 250; perhaps McDonald, *Novus Ordo Seclorum,* 238, 267. Brant and Ketcham both assume that Madison preferred a broad grant before July 16, then retreated to an enumeration.

65. JM to TJ, October 24, 1787, *PJM* 10:208.

66. *RFC* 1:53–54. Connecticut was divided on the vote: Sherman was in favor; Ellsworth, opposed.

67. How strong Madison's preference for an enumeration was may be suggested by a passage in his letter to Caleb Wallace, August 23, 1785, *PJM* 8:351. Here, in his advice about a constitution for a *state,* he wrote: "If it were possible it would be well to define the extent of the legislative power, but the nature of it seems in many respects to be indefinite. It is very practicable, however, to enumerate the essential exceptions."

68. Several other members kept records of the day's proceedings. Only one, Pierce Butler, mentioned this debate—in notes that offer *stronger* confirmation of my reading than Madison's own report (*RFC* 1:59–60). Butler says that Sherman opened the debate with an objection that the clause was "too indefinitely expressed—and yet it would be hard to define all the powers by detail." Madison, as Butler has it, then observed that "it was necessary to adopt some general principles" instead of "wandering from one thing to another." George Wythe and Rufus King both followed by suggesting that the meeting should define some general principles before proceeding to details. "Mr. Randolph was of the opinion that it would be impossible to define the powers . . . just at this time." And immediately before the final comments by Madison, Wilson said that he did not believe that an enumeration was possible at all. Wilson's comment tends, of course, to make it even clearer that Madison was playing a mediating role and trying to get past the matter without an extended debate. Butler's own report of Madison's last remarks can be interpreted two different ways: "Mr. Madison said he had

brought with him a strong prepossession for the defining of the limits and powers of the federal legislature, but he brought with him some doubts about the practicability of doing it:—at present he was convinced it could not be done." I interpret this as insisting only that an enumeration could not be done *at present.* If Madison had agreed with Wilson that an enumeration could not be done at all, he would have had no reason to discuss his prepossession in its favor. On this matter, Zuckert, "Federalism and the Founding," 177–79, challenges the prevailing view on similar grounds.

69. *RFC* 2:17, 25–27.

70. See *RFC* 2:324–25, 615–16.

71. *Federalist* 41:270. See also *Federalist* 42:280.

72. *Federalist* 45:314; Jonathan Elliot, ed., *The Debates in the Several State Conventions on the Adoption of the Federal Constitution,* 2d ed., 5 vols. (Philadelphia: J. B. Lippencott, 1901), 3:259.

73. John P. Roche, "The Founding Fathers: A Reform Caucus in Action," *APSR* 55 (1971):28. See also Jensen, *Making of the American Constitution,* 51: "The extreme nationalists, such as James Madison, James Wilson, Alexander Hamilton, and Gouverneur Morris, wanted to subject the states absolutely to a national government. Their ideal, perhaps, was the abolition of the states, but at the very least they wanted to reduce them to mere administrative districts."

74. Speeches of June 26 and June 30, *RFC* 1:463, 490.

75. *RFC* 1:355.

76. *RFC* 1:356–58.

77. For just how "fatal" he thought the latter could prove, the speech of June 29 may profitably be read in close conjunction with this one of a week before.

78. *RFC* 1:449.

CHAPTER SIX. TO REDEEM THE REPUBLICAN NAME

1. All of Madison's biographers and several other authors recognize and sometimes even emphasize his republican commitments: Brant; Ketcham; Schultz; Rakove; Martin Diamond, "Democracy and *The Federalist:* A Reconsideration of the Framers' Intent," *APSR* 53 (1959): 52–68; Robert J. Morgan, "Madison's Analysis of the Sources of Political Authority," *APSR* 75 (1981): 613–25, and, *James Madison on the Constitution and the Bill of Rights* (New York, 1988); and Neal Riemer, "The Republicanism of James Madison," *Political Science Quarterly* 69 (1954): 45–64, and *James Madison: Creating the American Constitution* (Washington, D.C., 1986). Among these writers, though, Brant and Diamond were also highly influential in establishing interpretations I dispute. In my opinion, only Riemer and Michael P. Zuckert approach a proper emphasis on the limits of Madison's nationalism. Neither is concerned with his distinctively Virginian point of view, and neither detects the changes of mind that he experienced in the course of the convention.

2. *RFC* 2:17.

3. July 7, 1787, *RFC* 1:551. Brant and others have interpreted this comment as foreshadowing a sharp reversal of his course.

4. July 17 and September 12, *RFC* 2:27–28, 589.

5. August 16 and 21, *RFC* 2:306–7, 361.

6. August 29, 8, and 13, *RFC* 2:451–52, 224, 276–77.

7. In this sense I think Madison was quite correct to say that "candor discovers no ground for the charge that the Resolutions [of May 29] contemplated a government . . . more national than that in which they terminated" (JM to Tyler, 1833, *RFC* 3:529). For the contrary view, see the sources cited in notes 60 and 61 of Chapter 5.

8. This accords with Schultz, 67–68, 73–74. Calvin C. Jillson's repeated insistence in *Constitution Making: Conflict and Consensus in the Federal Convention of 1787* (New York, 1988) that voting alignments changed when the convention moved from "higher level" questions to questions about the distribution of power among states and sections is also helpful on this point.

9. His most important speeches on the uses of a senate came on July 7 (*RFC* 1:151–52) and June 29 (*RFC* 1:421–23). See also June 12, 1787, *RFC* 1:218.

10. *RFC* 1:88, 90, 92, 101, 107–8; 4:15–20.

11. *RFC* 1:66–67, 70, 74.

12. Though King and Pierce agree that Madison favored a single executive with a council whose advice would not be absolutely binding, their accounts are contradictory on other points. Pierce says that Madison opposed ineligibility for a second term (*RFC* 1:74). King says that he urged "7 years and an exclusion for ever after—or during good behavior" (71). A good-behavior term hardly seems consistent with King's own account of Madison's fear of an elective monarch or with other things we know about Madison's positions, but King and Pierce at least agree in reinforcing the conjecture that he voted with his colleagues against executive reeligibility. His advice to Caleb Wallace on a constitution for Kentucky had also recommended "a temporary or perpetual" ineligibility for reelection if the executive was to serve a lengthy term (*PJM* 8:354–55).

13. The quotation is added from his speech of July 21 (*RFC* 1:74).

14. See Madison's speech of July 19, *RFC* 2:56–57, where he favored popular election over legislative choice. Wilson had consistently condemned provisions in the resolutions of May 29 that made the lower house responsible for the election of the other branches. He was certainly the meeting's foremost early advocate of independently derived and fully countervailing branches. No other member, I believe, influenced Madison more.

15. July 21, *RFC* 2:80–81.

16. *RFC* 2:392.

17. At the end of the convention, he still called the senate "the great anchor of the government" (JM to TJ, October 24, *PJM* 10:209). The decisions for a six-year term, per capita voting, and federal payment of salaries, all of which made the senators more independent of the states, undoubtedly contributed to his conviction that the upper house might still embody the principles he wanted in such a body.

18. September 7, *RFC* 2:540.

19. Ibid., 542.

20. September 12, *RFC* 2:587.

21. The powers and mode of appointment of the executive dominated the convention's proceedings from July 17 to July 25. The members reaffirmed election by the legislature, struck the clause confining the executive to a single term, agreed that this would probably result in an improper link between the branches, moved to an election by the local legislatures, and then moved back again to an election by the Congress. By July 24, as Gerry put it, they seemed "entirely at a loss." Madison reviewed the problem on July 25. Election by the legislature, he explained, might introduce intrigues and render the executive incapable of acting as a check on legislative usurpations—plainly so if he were eligible for reelection. Election by the local legislatures or the state executives might introduce the influence of the very bodies whose "pernicious influence" he still hoped to check. Two alternatives remained: election by electors chosen by the people, which had been suggested on July 19 by King and Paterson, but handily defeated; or direct election by the people, which he himself now favored but which seemed to put the small states and the South (with its large, nonvoting slave population) at a major disadvantage. On July 26, the meeting returned full circle to the original decision for election by the legislature for a single term, but almost no one was now content with this provision. The Committee on Unfinished Business (or on Postponed Parts) untangled these knots at the beginning of September by drawing on the discussions of July. Their report recommended an electoral college, creation of a vice president, and so on. Dickinson, who served on the committee, later recalled that it was Madison who sketched out its recommendations on the mode of election (Dickinson to George Logan, January 16, 1802, *RFC* 5:300–301).

22. JM to TJ, October 24, *PJM* 10:210.

23. See, particularly, *Federalist*, nos. 39, 45, 62.

24. *DHRC* 9:997, 10:1295.

25. Particularly good on this point is Gordon S. Wood, *The Creation of the American Republic, 1776–1787* (Chapel Hill, N.C., 1969), 526–32.

26. See, especially, Martin Diamond, "*The Federalist*'s View of Federalism," in *Essays in Federalism,* ed. George C. S. Benson et al. (Claremont, Calif., 1961).

27. Extraordinary caution is required in making the suggestion that Madison's reconciliation to a partly federal system may have started during the convention as a consequence of his uneasiness with the position of his higher-flying allies. I am well aware that he never said as much and, therefore, that we lack the one specific piece of evidence required to prove the point beyond dispute. Nevertheless, I found suggestive a remark in a letter from Edmund Randolph: "I confess to you without reserve that I feel great distrust of some of those who will certainly be influential agents in the [new] government and whom I suspect to be capable of making a wicked use of its defects. . . . I reverence Hamilton, because he was honest and open in his views," but "the management in some stages of the convention created a disgustful apprehension of the views of some particular characters" (ER to JM, September 3, 1788, *PJM* 11:246–47). To my knowledge, Madison made no contemporary statement of this sort. Neither did he make a later statement to exactly this purport, although he did occasionally approach it. (See, for example, "A Candid State of Parties," *National Gazette*, September 22, 1792, in *PJM* 14:371: Among the Federalists "there were, no doubt, some who were openly

or secretly attached to monarchy and aristocracy; and hoped to make the Constitution a cradle for these hereditary establishments.'') Statements from the early 1790s must, of course, be suspect, since Madison was in a party war with some of his allies of 1787 by that time. On the other hand, the absence of a clear contemporary confirmation of these feelings may be less surprising than at first appears, for why should Madison have armed the doubters, either during the convention or as he was trying to secure adoption of the plan? The speculative nature of my claim would be more troublesome, as well, if I intended to make more of the suggestion than I do. Madison's reconciliation to a partly federal system seems itself beyond dispute. The object here is simply to suggest that during the convention, as in 1783, he felt some early stirrings of concerns that were to quicken in the years immediately ahead and lead to the position he defended through the rest of his career—stirrings that were poorly organized as yet and less alarming to his consciousness than many other things, but which forced themselves to his attention after 1789. The extent of his discomfort during the convention is impossible to weigh. Its presence, I believe, can nonetheless be shown; and, if correct, the speculation may be worth pursuing.

28. A modern biography is John J. Reardon, *Edmund Randolph: A Biography* (New York, 1975).

29. Robert A. Rutland, *George Mason: Reluctant Statesman* (Williamsburg, Va., 1961); Helen Hill Miller, *George Mason: Gentleman Revolutionary* (Chapel Hill, N.C., 1975).

30. See Randolph's speech of May 29, introducing the Virginia Plan and arguing that nothing less than a complete reconstitution of the central government could meet the nation's needs, along with Mason's early effort to distinguish a "national" government from one purely "federal" (*RFC* 1:18-23, 34).

31. See, for example, Mason's defenses of popular election of the lower house on June 6 and June 21, their joint defense of a provision requiring an oath from state officers to support the federal constitution and federal laws, Randolph's comparison of the Virginia and New Jersey Plans on June 16, and Mason's speech of June 20 on the powers of the convention and the impracticability of Paterson's proposals (*RFC* 1:133-34, 359, 203, 255-56, 338-40).

32. Both men accepted the convention's central compromise with deep reluctance and only on condition that the upper house should be denied a role in framing money bills. See Madison's explanatory note of July 5 and Mason's remarks of July 6, together with Randolph's alternative proposal for conciliating the smaller states (*RFC* 1:526, 544; 3:55-56).

33. The complicated maneuvers on these subjects occupied the delegates from July 9 through July 14, the days immediately preceeding the critical vote on the upper house.

34. *RFC* 1:578-79.

35. August 29, *RFC* 1:451.

36. Ibid., 452-53.

37. August 31, *RFC* 1:479. On the same date, Mason prepared a list of changes he considered necessary and solicited the Marylanders' aid in securing them. These included more explicit definition of the powers of the national government,

a two-thirds rather than three-fourths vote to override a presidential veto, a two-thirds requirement for navigation laws, a money-bill clause, a prohibition of "perpetual" taxes, and executive ineligibility for a second term. See *RFC* 4:56–57.

38. *RFC* 2:537.

39. *RFC* 2:560–561, 563–64.

40. Motion and speech of September 15, *RFC* 2:631. Here, of course, Mason was asking for the same concession that the Carolinians and Georgians had been granted on the slave trade.

41. September 12, *RFC* 2:587–588.

42. Mason's pamphlet is available in *RFC* 2:637–40; *DHRC* 13:348–51; and *The Papers of George Mason, 1725–1792,* ed. Robert A. Rutland (Chapel Hill, N.C., 1970), 3:991–93. For Lee's agreement, see Lee to Mason, October 10, 1787, in *Papers of George Mason,* 3:996–99.

43. Mason, "Objections to the Constitution of Government formed by the Convention," *DHRC* 13:348–51.

44. For Madison's and Mason's views of each other—even in the aftermath of the ratification dispute—see the touching exchange between Mason and Jefferson in *Papers of George Mason,* 3:1224.

45. See, especially, Madison's speeches of June 28 and 30, *RFC* 1:446–49, 486–87.

46. Madison did not enter significantly into the occasional, sharp exchanges over slavery, but he did condemn it in passing. For example, in the great speech of June 6 he observed, "We have seen the mere distinction of color made in the most enlightened period of time the most oppressive dominion ever exercised by man over man" (*RFC* 1:135). Also, on August 25, he was the only member to speak against C. C. Pinckney's motion to extend the prohibition on interference with the slave trade from 1800 to 1808: "Twenty years will produce all the mischief that can be apprehended from the liberty to import slaves. So long a term will be more dishonorable to the national character than to say nothing about it in the Constitution." He then joined Sherman in objecting to some wording on grounds that it would be "wrong to admit in the Constitution the idea that there could be a property in men" (*RFC* 2:415, 417).

47. This paraphrases a remark of June 30, *RFC* 1:486.

48. With most recent students of the convention, I have concluded that slavery itself, although the subject of some bitter words, seldom generated serious, prolonged divisions at the meeting. Most northern delegates were unprepared to challenge the insistence of Georgia and the Carolinas that they would not concur in a unanimous recommendation unless their basic demands were met. The three-fifths formula, familiar from the old Confederation, got the meeting past a number of potential difficulties with relative ease; the old idea that there was an important three-fifths compromise is now universally rejected (see Howard A. Ohline, "Republicanism and Slavery: Origins of the Three-Fifths Clause in the United States Constitution," *WMQ* 28 [1971]: 563–84). Finally, delegates from every section understood that neither the present government of the Union nor any conceivable new one could possess the practical power to act effectively against the institution in the South. The direct confrontations of the nineteenth century should not be

projected onto these years, when most politicians were more concerned with the sectional clash of economic interests. For a recent argument that slavery *was* a central subject of division, see, however, Paul Finkelman, "Slavery and the Constitutional Convention: Making a Covenant with Death," in *Beyond Confederation: Origins of the Constitution and American National Identity*, ed. Richard Beeman, Stephen Botein, and Edward C. Carter II (Chapel Hill, N.C., 1987), 226–58.

49. Proceedings of September 7 and 8, *RFC* 2:540–41, 547–49.

50. Speeches of August 16 and 21, *RFC* 2:306–7, 361.

51. August 21, *RFC* 2:363. The convention did forbid state export taxes.

52. See his speech of August 29, *RFC* 2:451–52, and, more fully, Drew R. McCoy, "James Madison and Visions of American Nationality in the Confederation Period: A Regional Perspective," in Beeman, Botein, and Carter, *Beyond Confederation*, 226–58.

53. August 29, *RFC* 2:452.

54. JM to William Bradford, November 26, 1774, *PJM* 1:129–30.

55. JM to Bradford, June 19, 1775, *RFC* 1:153.

56. See especially his speech of June 29, *RFC* 1:464–65, and *Federalist*, no. 41. But Madison's association of southern weaknesses, collapse of the Confederation, and an end of republican liberty went back at least as far, as has been shown, as February 21, 1783 (*PJM* 6:272).

57. The commotions typified by Shays's Rebellion and reported from Virginia as the Great Convention met were also a reminder that Virginia might require the Union's help—not, perhaps, at any moment, but as landless whites and slaves became a larger portion of its population. This helps explain the insistence in Madison's "Vices" (*PJM* 9:350–51), repeated in his speech of June 19 (*RFC* 1: 318), that might and right (or might and the majority of voters) could not be automatically assumed to go together in republics.

58. August 29, *RFC* 2:452

59. Mason has been celebrated by a range of modern scholars as among the meeting's foremost spokesmen for the people's rule. This is not invalid. Neither is the universal view that Madison was the most distinctive advocate of the advantages of a plurality of interests. Both descriptions, nevertheless, can be misleading—plainly so if they are pressed in a way that suggests that either Virginian was less liberal or less republican than the other. Whereas Madison opted firmly for a popular election of the executive, Mason warned that "it would be as unnatural to refer the choice of a proper character for chief magistrate to the people as it would be to refer a trial of colors to a blind man" (July 17, *RFC* 2:31; compare July 26, *RFC* 2:119). On July 26, Mason moved to insert a landed property qualification for members of the legislature. Madison moved to strike it, arguing that men who had acquired their land on credit often "got into the legislatures with a view of promoting an unjust protection against their creditors" and thus were more responsible than any other group for unjust local legislation. A large landed qualification, he argued, "would exclude the proper representatives" of the commercial and manufacturing classes, whose "interests and rights . . . should be duly represented and understood in the public councils." He preferred property qualifications for the franchise if any were to be imposed at all—and then would seek a

standard that would distinguish "real and ostensible" property (*RFC* 2:123–24). Later on, however, Mason forcefully objected to a freehold franchise: "Every man having evidence of attachment to and common interest with the society [perhaps including every father] ought to share in all its rights and privileges" (August 7, *RFC* 2:203). Madison, by contrast, was powerfully attracted to a freehold limitation. The critical differences between the two Virginians, which will be pursued in Chapter 8, were not about the fundamental precepts of the Revolution and not about the need for federal and even state reforms. They disagreed most fundamentally about whether the majority, in practice, *would* actually control the new central government and—not a separate question—over whether the constitutional division of authority between the central government and states could be maintained.

60. See, for example, Robert A. Dahl, *A Preface to Democratic Theory* (Chicago, 1956), chap. 1, "Madisonian Democracy," and James MacGregor Burns, *The Deadlock of Democracy: Four-Party Politics in America* (Englewood Cliffs, N.J., 1963).

61. King's notes on the speech of June 7, *RFC* 1:158. Compare Lansing's record of a remark by Madison on June 26 in *The Delegate from New York or Proceedings of the Federal Convention of 1787 from the Notes of John Lansing, Jr.*, ed. Joseph Reese Strayer (Princeton, N.J., 1939), 84: "The Senate ought to represent the opulent minority."

62. June 26, *RFC* 1:422.

63. June 12, *RFC* 1:218.

64. June 26, *RFC* 1:423.

65. JM to J. G. Jackson, December 27, 1821, *RFC* 3:449–50.

66. June 26, *RFC* 1:422–23.

67. August 7, *RFC* 2:203–4.

68. *RFC* 2:204 n. 17.

69. The other quotations are from his second, longer note on the speech of August 7, probably written in 1821 (*RFC* 3:450–51). Here, although he again defended his concept of a differential suffrage for the two branches of the state legislatures, he finally concluded: "If the only alternative be between an equal and universal right of suffrage for each branch of the government and a confinement of the *entire* right to a part of the citizens, it is better that those having the greater interest at stake, namely that of property and persons both, should be deprived of half their share in the government than that those having the lesser interest, that of personal rights only, should be deprived of the whole" (454–55).

70. Though there are many points at which I sharply disagree with the interpretation, there is much of value on the centrality of Madison's concern for property rights—in 1787 and in the distant future—in Jennifer Nedelsky, *Private Property and the Limits of American Constitutionalism: The Madisonian Framework and Its Legacy* (Chicago, 1990). Where Nedelsky is badly wrong, in my opinion, is in her argument that, for Madison, "political rights had no intrinsic value," that they were mere means to the protection of civil rights, especially those of property (5). Nedelsky concedes that Madison himself "never treated [property] as a priority in principle," but argues that he did "in practice and emphasis" accord the rights of property priority over the rights of the people to political participation and control (16). By suggesting that he saw "the people" (not factious majorities of

people) as the problem (see, for example, 205), that he hoped "to design a government that could permanently frustrate the majority's ongoing" desire to interfere with property rights or to redistribute wealth (32), and that he neglected the relationship between economic and political power (144), Nedelsky conflates Madison's vision with the Constitution as modified by the Marshall Court, judicial review, and nineteenth-century liberalism, which is her real (and probably a worthy) target. These difficulties are compounded by ignoring the role of federalism in Madison's thinking. Many of the same problems characterize Richard K. Matthews, *"If Men Were Angels": James Madison and the Heartless Empire of Reason* (Lawrence, Kans., 1994). A very quick rebuttal would only need to note that no one who accorded a higher priority to property rights than to the people's right to rule could possibly have taken the position Madison took in the 1790 argument about the funding of the revolutionary debt, which I discuss in Chapter 10.

71. "The legislative vortex," July 17, *RFC,* 2:35.

72. July 21, *RFC* 2:74.

73. September 12, *RFC* 2:586–87.

74. August 14, *RFC* 2:291.

75. September 5, *RFC* 2:514.

76. July 17, *RFC* 2:35.

77. May 31, *RFC* 1:49–50.

78. July 10, *RFC* 1:568.

79. *RFC* 2:553.

80. Hamilton grasped this point immediately when he first heard Madison's great speech in the convention on enlarging the sphere. "The assembly, when chosen, will meet in one room if they are drawn from half the globe," he jotted, and "paper money is capable of giving a general impulse" (that is, of creating a majority faction among the people and thus in the national legislature [*RFC* 1: 146]).

81. See, especially, "Vices," *PJM* 9:354. Riemer, "Republicanism of James Madison," and Morgan, "Madison's Analysis," are particularly valuable for their clear recognition of Madison's literal fear of counterrevolution and for their insistence that his fear of an unresponsive or "independent" government was fully equal to his fear of factious majorities.

82. Madison is easily misjudged unless we realize that he consistently assumed that his republican credentials were so widely recognized that there was little need for him to flaunt them. An instructive episode occurred in the convention on July 17, when Dr. James McClurg, in order to object to the executive's eligibility for reelection, moved a tenure during good behavior. Randolph had chosen this young physician as Patrick Henry's substitute in the Virginia delegation at Madison's particular suggestion, and Madison rushed in immediately to save the novice's face. He was not, he said, "apprehensive of being thought to favor any step toward monarchy" when he suggested that a "respect for the mover" entitled the motion to a fair hearing "until a less objectionable expedient should be applied for guarding against a dangerous union of the legislative and executive departments" (*RFC* 2:33–35). Ironically, this speech has often been incautiously interpreted as evidence that Madison *favored* a good-behavior term.

83. See, again, his speech of August 29, *RFC* 2:451–52, and, more broadly, McCoy, "Visions of American Nationality."

84. *RFC* 1:584.

85. August 7, *RFC* 2:203.

86. Morris's speech of July 2, *RFC* 1:511–14, is a quick introduction to the extent of his cynicism and his support for power independent of the people. Nedelsky also offers an instructive comparison of Morris's ideas with those of Madison and Wilson.

87. In addition to examples cited in the other notes, see remarks of August 7 and 10, *RFC* 2:203–4, 249–50.

88. This is so patently the case that one analyst has argued that internal checks and balances were intended *exclusively* as restraints on the rulers: George W. Carey, "Separation of Powers and the Madisonian Model: A Reply to the Critics," *APSR* 72 (1978), 151–64.

89. August 10, *RFC* 2:250.

90. For additional assertions that the legislators' special interests could be the problem, see the speeches of July 26 and August 7, *RFC* 2:123–24, 203–4.

91. A passage in *Federalist* 39:251 is sometimes said to contradict the latter point: A republic is best defined as "a government which derives all its powers directly or indirectly from the great body of the people and is administered by persons holding their offices during pleasure, for a limited period, or during good behavior." But Madison was obviously compelled to make allowance for the good-behavior tenure of the judges. The next sentence says, "It is *essential* to such a government that it be derived from the great body of the society, not from an inconsiderable proportion or a favored class of it." And five days before, he had written: "The genius of republican liberty seems to demand . . . not only that all power should be derived from the people, but that those entrusted with it should be kept in dependence on the people by a short duration of their appointments; and that, even during this short period, the trust should be placed not in a few, but in a number of hands" (*Federalist* 37:234).

92. *RFC* 1:464–65.

93. Ibid., 467. On September 14 (*RFC* 2:617), Madison supported a clause intended to "discountenance" armies in time of peace, as these were "allowed on all hands to be an evil."

94. *RFC* 1:424

95. JM to TJ, October 24, 1787, *PJM* 10:207–16, quotation at 209. Seventeen pages in manuscript, this was by far his longest as well as his most immediate private report on the new Constitution, and it contains his fullest defense of the federal negative on state laws. "It may be said," he noted, "that the judicial authority under our new system will keep the states within their proper limits and supply the place of a negative on their laws. The answer is that it is more convenient to prevent the passage of a law than to declare it void after it is passed . . . [and also] that a state which would violate the legislative rights of the Union would not be very ready to obey a judicial decree in support of them," entailing a resort to force. Neither were the prohibitions against paper money and interferences with private contracts likely to provide sufficient protection for private rights. "In-

justice may be effected by such an infinitude of legislative expedients that where the disposition exists, it can only be controlled by some provision which reaches all cases whatsoever" (211–12).

CHAPTER SEVEN: "THE PRACTICABLE SPHERE OF A REPUBLIC"

1. Edward Carrington to JM, September 23, 1787, *PJM* 10:172; JM to James Madison, Sr., September 30, 1787, *PJM* 10:178; Edmund Cody Burnett, *The Continental Congress* (New York, 1941), 694–700.

2. The congressional proceedings on the Constitution are printed and ably discussed in *DHRC* 13:229–42. See also JM to GW, September 30, 1787, *PJM* 10: 179–81.

3. See JM to James Madison Sr., September 30, 1787, *PJM* 10:178; to ER, October 7, 1787, *PJM* 10:186; to GW, October 14, 1787, *PJM* 10:194; and to TJ, October 24, 1787, *PJM* 10:217.

4. As early as September 27, for example, Tench Coxe sent Madison the first two numbers of his series, "An American Citizen," suggesting that he might confer with Hamilton about the usefulness of having them reprinted in newspapers in New York and Virginia (*PJM* 10:175). Through Joseph Jones, Madison arranged for their reprinting in the *Virginia Independent Chronicle* (*PJM* 10:227–28). Steven R. Boyd, *The Politics of Opposition: Antifederalists and the Acceptance of the Constitution* (Millwood, N.Y., 1979), is excellent for the organizational efforts on both sides. The standard narrative of the ratification contest is Robert Allen Rutland, *The Ordeal of the Constitution: The Antifederalists and the Ratification Struggle of 1787–1788* (Norman, Okla., 1966).

5. JM to GW, October 18, 1787, *PJM* 10:197.

6. JM to ER, October 21, 1787, *PJM* 10:199 and note 4. The first of the sixteen letters of "Brutus" appeared in the *New York Journal* on October 18, 1787. The authorship is still in doubt. See *DHRC* 13:411–12.

7. JM to Ambrose Madison, November 8, 1787, *PJM* 10:244.

8. The essential facts about the origins and publication of *The Federalist* are conveniently summarized in *DHRC* 13:486–90, and in the editor's introduction to the variform edition of the papers, which I cite by number and page throughout: *The Federalist*, ed. Jacob E. Cooke (Cleveland, Conn., 1961), xi–xiv. My conclusions accord closely with theirs and with Douglass Adair, "The Authorship of the Disputed Federalist Papers," in *Fame and the Founding Fathers: Essays by Douglass Adair*, ed. Trevor Colbourn (New York, 1974), 55–60.

9. The papers of Hamilton and Jay say nothing about the planning of the series. The evidence that Morris was approached and "warmly pressed by Hamilton" rests entirely on a letter from Morris to W. H. Wells, February 24, 1815, in *The Life of Gouverneur Morris*, ed. Jared Sparks (Boston, 1832), 3:339. This, however, seems entirely likely; although Morris represented Pennsylvania at the Constitutional Convention, he was a native of New York as well as an admirer of Hamilton. Madison's contemporary letters, together with a late-life memorandum (in James Madison, "Detached Memoranda," ed. Elizabeth Fleet, *WMQ* 3 [1946]: 564–65),

provide our only other information. None of these materials reveal exactly when Madison was told about the series, when Duer's essays were rejected, or whether Madison recommended Rufus King as an additional collaborator before or after he himself was asked to join. (Hamilton, the memorandum says, did not consider King's talents "as altogether of the sort required." Duer's essays were published separately over the signature "Philo-Publius.")

10. Burnett, *Continental Congress*, 700–701.

11. JM to Ambrose Madison, November 8, 1787, *PJM* 10:244; JM to ER, November 18, 1787, *PJM* 10:252.

12. JM to GW, November 18, 1787, *PJM* 10:254. Madison enclosed the first seven numbers of *The Federalist* and asked Washington to arrange for their reprinting in Virginia. "I will not conceal *from you*," he wrote, "that I am likely to have such a *degree* of connection with the publication here as to afford a restraint of delicacy from interesting myself directly in the republication elsewhere."

13. Thus, he told Washington that three authors were involved; "A fourth may possibly bear a part" (*PJM* 10:254). And on December 2, he told Randolph that he was in on the project "for a few numbers" (*PJM* 10:290). The reference to a fourth collaborator may refer to Duer, to King, or simply to a hope that someone could be found. But, certainly, it seems unlikely that Madison had hurried back from Philadelphia for reasons unconnected with the project, was immediately approached, and had involved himself to this extent within a day of his return. Coxe and other correspondents certainly assumed that Madison was in frequent contact with Hamilton after the adjournment of the Constitutional Convention. Thus, it is entirely possible that he was thoroughly informed about the series from a very early point, though there is overwhelming evidence for a belated plea for his participation. My guess is that Hamilton approached him just before he left New York, perhaps when it was clear that Morris could not be persuaded and that Jay was having trouble with his health.

14. For the circulation and reception of the series, see *DHRC* 13:490–94. Much of it did not appear in time to influence the decisions in the states that acted first, and relatively little of the series was reprinted by the newspapers outside New York. But numbers 1 through 36 were published as a book in March; and the remaining numbers, published a second volume on May 28, were circulated widely in their newspaper version, completed by April 2. There is ample evidence that they were widely read and widely drawn on for arguments by delegates to the later state conventions, which were usually more evenly divided.

15. JM to TJ, August 11, 1788, *PJM* 11:227.

16. Madison, "Detached Memoranda," 565. This late-life recollection, by itself, would certainly be suspect. But it does accord with the contemporary comment cited in note 15.

17. Jefferson immediately described *The Federalist* as "the best commentary on the principles of government which ever was written" (to JM, November 18, 1788, *PJM* 11:353). For some other contemporary reactions, see *DHRC* 13:492–94. A sampling of the later praise can be found in Isaac Kramnick's introduction to his recent edition for Penguin Classics: *The Federalist Papers* (Harmondsworth, U.K., 1987), 11, 14, 75–76.

18. See, especially, Adair, "Authorship"; Alpheus Thomas Mason, "The Federalist—A Split Personality," *AHR* 57 (1952): 625–43; and Gottfried Dietze, *The Federalist: A Classic on Federalism and Free Government* (Baltimore, 1960), 150–51, 260–64, 267–71.

19. These would include George W. Carey, "Publius—A Split Personality?" *Review of Politics* 46 (1984): 5–22, and *The Federalist: Design for a Constitutional Republic* (Urbana, Ill., 1989); David F. Epstein, *The Political Theory of "The Federalist"* (Chicago, 1984); Albert Furtwangler, *The Authority of Publius: A Reading of the Federalist Papers* (Ithaca, N.Y., 1984); Garry Wills, *Explaining America: The Federalist* (New York, 1981); Charles R. Kesler, ed., *Saving the Revolution: The Federalist Papers and the American Founding* (New York, 1987); and Edward Millican, *One United People: The Federalist Papers and the National Idea* (Lexington, Ky., 1990). Among earlier authorities, Martin Diamond, Herbert Storing, and Clinton Rossiter were also disinclined to emphasize the differences between the authors.

20. The course of this controversy is conveniently reviewed—and a substantial contribution made—in Cooke's edition, *Federalist*, xix-xxx. Other landmarks in its apparent resolution are Adair, "Authorship," and Frederick Mosteller and David L. Wallace, *Inference and Disputed Authorship: "The Federalist"* (Reading, Mass., 1964). Since the middle 1960s, there have been few dissenters from the view that Madison wrote the numbers in dispute: 18–20, 49–58, and 62–63.

21. The crucial document here is an undated, private memorandum written shortly after the adjournment of the Constitutional Convention: "Conjectures About the New Constitution," *PAH* 4:275–77. But AH exercised such caution in the published papers that Jefferson plainly thought that Madison had written the overwhelming burden. See TJ to JM, November 18, 1788, *PJM* 11:353.

22. Both of these assertions call for fuller proofs than can be offered in a footnote. Neither is sufficiently important for a long digression in the text. See the appendix.

23. June 16, 1787, *RFC* 1:253.

24. JM, Speech on Jay's Treaty, April 6, 1796, *PJM* 16:296. Compare *Federalist* 40:264: The Constitution "is to be of no more consequence than the paper on which it is written unless it be stamped with the approbation of those to whom it is addressed."

25. JM to Thomas Ritchie, September 15, 1821, *LJM* 3:228. Compare JM to N. P. Trist, *WJM* 9:477.

26. See James H. Hutson, "The Creation of the Constitution: The Integrity of the Documentary Record," *Texas Law Review* 65 (1986): 1–39.

27. Another powerful explanation of the difficulty—even the absurdity—of trying to identify some single moment or text as Madison's authoritative, original understanding of the meaning of the Constitution is Jack N. Rakove, "The Madisonian Moment," *University of Chicago Law Review* 65 (1988): 473–505. As Rakove says, "The quest for the historical Madison . . . requires relating the familiar arguments of *The Federalist* to the more complex body of ideas and concerns from which they emerged and of which they were only a partial expression" (475).

28. This possibility is also discussed in the appendix.

29. JM to J. G. Jackson, December 27, 1821, *RFC* 3:450.

30. Although I strongly disagree with many of its other arguments, Furtwangler, *Authority of Publius,* is excellent for its insistence that *The Federalist* was a product of "two strong minds, each still growing in its own comprehension of the Constitution" (147).

31. JM to ER, October 21, 1787, *PJM* 10:199.

32. In numbers 3–5, Jay had argued the necessity of union for securing the United States against foreign threats. In numbers 6–8, Hamilton had argued its necessity for preventing interstate disputes. In number 9, Hamilton had summarized the standard arguments for the advantages of a confederacy in defeating faction or sedition in a single member.

33. *Federalist* 10:56–65.

34. For Montesquieu, see especially, book 8, chap. 16, of *The Spirit of the Laws,* trans. Thomas Nugent (New York, 1966), 120: "It is natural for a republic to have only a small territory; otherwise it cannot long subsist. . . . In an extensive republic the public good is sacrificed to a thousand private views. . . . In a small one, the interest of the public is more obvious, better understood, and more within the reach of every citizen; abuses have less extent, and, of course, are less protected."

35. Since Douglass Adair's "'That Politics May Be Reduced to a Science': David Hume, James Madison, and the Tenth *Federalist,*" *Huntington Library Quarterly* 20 (1957): 343–60, reprinted in Calbourn, *Fame and the Founding Fathers,* 93–106, it has been widely recognized that JM drew specifically on Hume's political essays for his discussion of the character of factions and his argument for the superiority of large republics. Compare the language and train of reasoning in "Vices," *PJM* 9:355–56, and *Federalist* 10:60–62 to passages in Hume's "Of the Independency of Parliament," "Of Parties in General," and "Idea of a Perfect Commonwealth," in *Essays: Moral, Political, and Literary,* ed. Eugene F. Miller (Indianapolis, 1985), 43, 55–56, 528. More recently, however, there has also been a gathering agreement that Hume's influence can be greatly exaggerated and distorted. Excellent recent discussions include Theodore Draper, "Hume and Madison: The Secrets of Federalist Paper No. 10," *Encounter* 58 (1982): 34–47; Epstein, *Political Theory,* 101–3; Edmund S. Morgan, "Safety in Numbers: Madison, Hume, and the Tenth *Federalist,*" *Huntington Library Quarterly* 49 (1986): 95–112; and Drew R. McCoy, *The Last of the Fathers: James Madison and the Republican Legacy* (Cambridge, 1989), 42–44, 48–51. These writers all agree—and this is critical for proper judgment of Madison's intentions as well as of his originality—that the concept of extending the sphere of popularly elected representative government to incorporate a multiplicity of interests bore only "a superficial resemblance" to Hume's analysis of the advantages of large republics (Morgan, "Safety in Numbers," 102). Madison drew most clearly on Hume for a typology of faction and for arguments that factions will not be restrained by a regard for public good, for honor, or for religion. Madison may have found the opening premise of his argument that large republics would restrain the violence of factions in Hume's remark (perhaps suggested, in turn, by Harrington's *Oceana*) that "the force of popular tides and currents" would be less "sensible" in large republics, making it "very difficult, either by intrigues, prejudice, or passion, to hurry them into any measures against the public interest" ("Idea of a Perfect Commonwealth," 528). But Hume's analysis of factions was

not explicitly concerned with majority violations of private rights, nor did Hume discuss the multiplicity of factions in the modern state. The burden of Madison's analysis was therefore quite distinctive, as was his conception of the proper structure of the large republic.

36. Hamilton had introduced this distinction in *Federalist* 9:50–52, quoting Montesquieu effectively on the advantages of a confederation for solving the problem of the size of republics.

37. The traditional, alternative solution to the problem of the many and the few—"creating a will in the community independent of the majority"—is condemned in *Federalist* 51:351. And indeed, from this time forward, Madison mounted an increasing effort to contrast "unmixed" republics with liberal regimes such as the British, which incorporated both elective and hereditary parts. I think it worth some serious consideration whether his employment of this terminology is yet another indication of his underlying worry over comments made at the convention. Hamilton's own outline for his lengthy speech of June 18 seems clearly to suggest that Hamilton meant to argue that the British government was superior to that of any of the states precisely because it incorporated a "permanent will" distinct from the will of the democratic many. Lansing, Yates, and King all took extensive notes on this great speech. Their versions all confirm that Madison's longer one was accurate in its suggestion that Hamilton's central argument was that a viable corrective for the nation's ills would have to move as close to the incorporation of the principle of permanence inherent in the British lords and king as could be reconciled with an elective system. See *RFC* 1:282–311.

38. Among the most effective are Rakove, "Madisonian Moment"; Neal Riemer, "The Republicanism of James Madison," *Political Science Quarterly* 69 (1954): 45–64; John Zvesper, "The Madisonian Systems," *Western Political Quarterly* 37 (1984): 236–56; and Robert J. Morgan, "Madison's Analysis of the Sources of Political Authority," *APSR* 75 (1981): 613–25.

39. Martin Diamond, "Democracy and *The Federalist*: A Reconsideration of the Framers' Intent," *APSR* 53 (1959): 52–68; "The Federalist's View of Federalism," in *Essays in Federalism*, ed. George C.S. Beman et al. (Claremont, Calif., 1961), 21–64; and "The Federalist, 1787–1788," in *The History of Political Philosophy*, ed. Leo Strauss and Joseph Cropsey (Chicago, 1972), 631–51—all now available in *As Far as Republican Principles Will Admit*. Although they were not his last or only words, these essays—and especially the first two—are unquestionably the works most widely cited and of most enduring influence on historians as well as political scientists. Although I sharply criticize some of their major themes, I also acknowledge their lasting value. As Irving Brant was principally responsible for removing Madison from Jefferson's imposing shadow and restoring him to his appropriate stature among the founders, Diamond was similarly responsible for reasserting Madison's commitment to republicanism and for clarifying many aspects of the founding generation's thought. His influence on this book is as profound as Brant's.

40. For the reputation and interpretation of the essay through the 1940s, see Douglass Adair, "The Tenth Federalist Revisited," in Colbourn, *Fame and the Founding Fathers*, 75–92. Together, Adair and Diamond severely challenged the Progressive understanding pioneered in Charles Beard's *Economic Interpretation of the*

Constitution of the United States (New York, 1913) and laid the most important groundwork for more recent interpretations.

41. Robert A. Dahl, *A Preface to Democratic Theory* (Chicago, 1956), chap. 1, "Madisonian Democracy." But Dahl was only one of many to interpret the essay in this way. See Paul F. Bourke, "The Pluralist Reading of James Madison's Tenth *Federalist,*" *Perspectives in American History* 9 (1975): 271–95.

42. Daniel Walker Howe, "The Political Psychology of *The Federalist,*" *WMQ* 44 (1987): 504, 502. Millican, *One United People,* 120–21, also puts the matter nicely.

43. Zvesper's "Madisonian Systems," for example, offers a superb discussion of the origins and limits of the argument for an extension of the sphere, but nonetheless proceeds to make that argument the crux of Madison's position in 1787. Even Rakove, in my judgment, falls into this trap.

44. JM to TJ, October 24, 1787, *PJM* 10:207: "It was generally agreed that the objects of the Union could not be secured by any system founded on the principle of a confederation of sovereign states. . . . Hence was embraced the alternative of a government which . . . should operate without their intervention on the individuals composing them; and hence the change in the principle and proportion of representation."

45. Diamond, "Democracy and *The Federalist,*" 66–68.

46. See note 39 and Jean Yarbrough, "Rethinking '*The Federalist*'s View of Federalism,' " *Publius* 15 (1985): 31–53. Millican, *One United People,* can be read as a recent, book-length elaboration of Diamond's argument that both Madison and Hamilton were democratic consolidationists who barely disguised their desire for a progressive centralization.

47. See above, pp. 98-102.

48. *Federalist* 10:62.

49. Although this reading of the essay emerges most fully in Wills's *Explaining America,* Madison's wish for an improved and less responsive representation is also a major theme for interpreting the essay and the Federalist movement in Gordon S. Wood, *The Creation of the American Republic 1776–1787* (Chapel Hill, N.C., 1969), chap. 12, especially 505, and in many other sources as well. On this "impartial representation" or "disinterested umpire" interpretation, see Alan Gibson, "Impartial Representation and the Extended Republic: Towards a Comprehensive and Balanced Reading of the Tenth *Federalist* Paper," *History of Political Thought* 12 (1991): 263–304.

50. *Federalist* 10:63.

51. See, for example, *Federalist* 46:318–19.

52. Injustice could also be checked, of course—though not by the variety of interests—if the representatives continually resisted their constituents' demands or transcended specific local interests entirely. But it *is* the multiplicity of interests that Madison clearly stresses, and putting *Federalist* no. 46 aside, in number 10 he observes: "The regulation of these various and interfering interests forms the principal task of modern legislation, and involves the spirt of party and faction in the necessary and ordinary operations of government. . . . What are many of the most important acts of legislation, but so many judicial determinations . . . ; and what are the different classes of legislators, but advocates and parties to the causes which

they determine? . . . It is in vain to say that enlightened statesmen will be able to adjust these clashing interests, and render them all subservient to the public good. Enlightened statesmen will not always be at the helm: Nor, in many cases, can such an adjustment be made at all without taking into view indirect and remote considerations, which will rarely prevail over . . . immediate interest."

53. Zvesper's excellent discussion of the evolution of the concept of an extension of the sphere of government, "Madisonian Systems," 248–49, is absolutely accurate in its insistence that Madison developed the idea that large republics offered more security for private rights in order to explain why a republican central government could be trusted with the *negative* responsibility of overseeing local quarrels, but that he then employed it in *The Federalist* to advocate a Constitution under which the federal Congress was *not* to exercise a federal veto on state laws. What Zvesper does not see, however, is that Madison *still* employed the idea for limited and fundamentally negative purposes in *Federalist* no. 10 itself. When this is recognized, Zvesper may be more correct than he believed when he said that "Madison did not place as much weight on this argument as most commentators have supposed" (240).

54. JM to TJ, October 24, 1787, *PJM* 10:214. Yet many commentators also generalize too broadly from this letter, failing to remark that Madison *never* argued that the national legislators would be capable of acting as impartial referees over clashing interests at the national level—or even, for that matter, over quarrels in a single state once the convention had removed the federal veto from the plan. (See, quite vividly, for example, Gordon S. Wood, *The Radicalism of the American Revolution* [New York, 1991], 253–55). But *all* of Madison's references to "modify[ing] the sovereignty" to make it "neutral between different parts of the society" (*PJM* 10:214) refer to modifying the sovereignty of *single states* by means of the federal veto.

55. "Vices," *PJM* 9:354–57. And note well *Federalist* 62:421: Election of the rulers by the people is a slight advantage if the laws are so voluminous or incoherent that "no man who knows what the law is today can guess what it will be tomorrow"; instability gives an "unreasonable advantage . . . to the sagacious, the enterprising, and the moneyed few over the industrious and uninformed mass of the people. Every new regulation concerning commerce or revenue . . . presents a new harvest to those who watch the change."

56. *Federalist* 10:62–63.

57. JM to TJ, October 24, 1787, *PJM* 10:214.

58. *Federalist* 51:349. See also "Vices," *PJM* 9:357.

59. *Federalist* 51:353.

60. *Federalist* 10:63

61. It is neglected even in Gibson, "Impartial Representation," and Carey's superb discussion of *Federalist* No. 10 in *The Federalist: Design for a Constitutional Republic*, 9–44—in which Carey forcefully insists that this essay is a discussion of the problem of faction—is followed by an argument that federalism "was largely tangential to [the authors'] synthesis and not . . . vital to the preservation of liberty" (xxxviii).

62. The best and fullest appreciation of *The Federalist*'s position on this sub-

ject—one which clearly sees that the separation of federal powers *and* a proper division of responsibilities between the central government and the states was fully as important to Madison as an extension of the sphere—is Vincent Ostrom, *The Political Theory of a Compound Republic: Designing the American Experiment*, 2d ed. (Lincoln, Nebr., 1987), especially 105.

63. JM, "Parties," *National Gazette*, January 23, 1792, *PJM* 14:197–98. See also "Consolidation," *National Gazette*, December 3, 1791, *PJM* 14:138–39.

64. Commerce was Hamilton's topic, especially in numbers 11 and 12. The most vivid contrasts between the farmer-soldiers of antiquity and modern Americans (*Federalist*, 8:47), the most unqualified praise of commerce as "the most useful as well as the most productive source of national wealth" (12:73), and the most effusive celebrations of the "unequalled spirit of enterprise" of American merchants and seamen (11:69) are all in Hamilton's essays.

65. "A landed interest, a manufacturing interest, a mercantile interest, a monied interest, with many lesser interests, grow up of necessity in civilized nations and divide them into different classes" (*Federalist* 10:59). Similarly, in the letter to Jefferson of October 24, 1787 (*PJM* 10:212–13), Madison contrasts "civilized societies," which are characterized by heterogeneity, with the homogeneity of "the savage state." But he never compares "commercial societies" to noncommercial ones.

66. Indeed, it is instructive to notice how clearly Diamond constructed the conception of Madison as an advocate of multiplying interests in a large "commercial" republic by citing Hamilton's essays! For an excellent longer critique of Diamond's interpretation, see Alan Gibson, "The Commercial Republic and the Pluralist Critique of Marxism: An Analysis of Martin Diamond's Interpretation of *Federalist* 10," *Polity* 25 (1993): 497–528. Another able summary of Diamond's position and its influence is Charles R. Kesler, "*Federalist* 10 and American Republicanism," in Kesler, *Saving the Revolution*, 14–16.

67. Read in isolation, *Federalist* no. 10, especially 58–59, may readily suggest that Madison held a Hobbesian view of human nature. For the widespread influence of this error and a valuable corrective, see Joseph F. Kobylka and Bradley Kent Carter, "Madison, *The Federalist*, and the Constitutional Order: Human Nature and Institutional Structure," *Polity* 20 (1987): 190–208.

68. *Federalist* 57:386.

69. "You ask me why I agreed to the Constitution . . . ? I answer, because I thought it safe to the liberties of the people, and the best that could be obtained from the jarring interests of states and the miscellaneous opinions of politicians; and because experience has proved that the real danger to America and to liberty lies in the defect of *energy* and *stability* in the present establishments of the United States. . . . In your closet at Paris and with the evils resulting from too much government all over Europe fully in your view, it is natural for you to run into criticisms dictated by an extreme on that side. Perhaps in your situation I should think and feel as you do. In mine I am sure you would think and feel as I do" (JM to Philip Mazzei, October 8, 1788, *PJM* 11:278).

70. *Federalist* 51:351.

71. Ibid., 51:352.

72. This paraphrases Dietze, *Federalist,* 330. See also (among many others) Diamond, "Democracy and *The Federalist,*" 62, and Jennifer Nedelsky, *Private Property and the Limits of American Constitutionalism: The Madisonian Framework and Its Legacy* (Chicago, 1990), chap. 2, especially 16, 37–38.

73. Passages from numbers 10, 14 and 51 are often cited to this effect.

74. I am dating here from Wood's *Creation of the American Republic* (1969), though Wood's discussion of the end of classical politics was strongly influenced by Diamond and other earlier writers (and Wood's own position seems significantly different in his recent writings). My distinction between "freedom from" and "freedom to" owes much to Hannah Arendt, *On Revolution* (New York, 1963), and J. H. Hexter, "Republic, Virtue, Liberty, and the Political Universe of J.G.A. Pocock," in *On Historians* (Cambridge, Mass., 1979), 255–303, although it could be followed back to Benjamin Constant.

75. I have contributed to this debate and anticipated the following discussion in a succession of articles and essays: "Jeffersonian Ideology Revisited: Liberal and Classical Ideas in the New American Republic," *WMQ* 43 (1986): 3–19; "Some Second Thoughts on Virtue and the Course of Revolutionary Thinking," in *Conceptual Change and the Constitution,* ed. Terence Ball and J.G.A. Pocock (Lawrence, Kans., 1988), 194–212; "Quid Transit? Paradigms and Process in the Transformation of Republican Ideas," *Reviews in American History* 17 (1989): 199–204; and "The Republican Interpretation: Retrospect and Prospect," in *The Republican Synthesis Revisited: Essays in Honor of George Athan Billias,* ed. Milton M. Klein et al. (Worcester, Mass., 1992), 91–117. For evidence of the emerging agreement that republican and liberal ideas were both extremely influential and that neither should be seen as having gained a clear ascendency during the 1780s or 1790s, see also Joyce Appleby, "Republicanism in Old and New Contexts," *WMQ* 43 (1986): 20–34; James T. Kloppenberg, "The Virtues of Liberalism: Christianity, Republicanism, and Ethics in Early American Political Discourse," *JAH* 74 (1987): 9–33; and Isaac Kramnick, "The 'Great National Discussion': The Discourse of Politics in 1787," *WMQ* 45 (1988): 3–32.

76. For this reason, arguments since 1969 have sometimes taken on an interdisciplinary flavor. On this point see Peter S. Onuf, "Reflections on the Founding: Constitutional Historiography in Bicentennial Perspective," *WMQ* 46 (1989): 341–75.

77. See the discussion of his "Memmorial and Remonstrance against Religious Assessments" in Chapter 3. Consider also his essay "Property" (*National Gazette,* March 27, 1792, *PJM* 14:266–68), which seems to me consistent with the intensively analyzed passage from *Federalist* 10:58. Here, as in the later essay, Madison took great care to make it clear that "the first object of government" is to protect "the diversity in the faculties of men from which the rights of property originate," not simply to protect property more narrowly defined.

78. Montesquieu, *Spirit of the Laws,* 23.

79. The fullest argument that "Publius" was making no such choice is Epstein, *Political Theory.* See especially 110, 195, and the introduction. The fullest recent presentation of the standard, opposing view is Nedelsky, *Private Property*—a work, not incidentally, that almost totally neglects the federal dimensions of Madison's

thinking. Paul A. Rahe, whose masterful *Republics Ancient and Modern: Classical Republicanism and the American Revolution* (Chapel Hill, N.C., 1992) is incomparably the fullest argument for the anticlassical and modern character of the British republican tradition, nevertheless sees clearly that Madison and other founders valued both sorts of freedom.

80. J.G.A. Pocock, *Virtue, Commerce, and History: Essays on Political Thought and History, Chiefly in the Eighteenth Century* (Cambridge, 1985), 271; Jean Yarbrough, "Madison and Modern Federalism," in *How Federal Is the Constitution*, ed. Robert A. Goldwin and William A. Schambra (Washington, D.C., 1987), 84–108; and Howe, "Political Psychology," 505–7.

81. *Federalist* 14:84, 88–89.

82. *Federalist* 55:374, although I by no means agree with the implications seen in this remark by Richard K. Matthews, *"If Men Were Angels": James Madison and the Heartless Empire of Reason*(Lawrence, Kans., 1994).

83. For further explanation, see my "Second Thoughts on Virtue."

84. Montesqueiu was clearly one of those "celebrated authors" who, "being subjects either of an absolute or limited monarchy, . . . have endeavored to heighten the advantages or palliate the evils of those forms" by comparing them with "the turbulent democracies of ancient Greece" and then ascribing to all republics "observations applicable to a democracy only" (*Federalist* 14:84).

85. For Paul A. Rahe, whose *Republics Ancient and Modern* is the most authoritative discussion of the differences between the two traditions, ancient (or truly classical) republicanism aimed ultimately and essentially at the creation or preservation of a polity and way of life that instills self-sacrificing moral virtue in its citizens and prepares them for their direct, immediate role in both political and military affairs. Moderns, Rahe insists, deliberately rejected both the ancient way of life and the classical assumption that citizens were capable of reasoning together about the just and the good. Accordingly, Rahe finds it inappropriate to refer to the American revolutionaries as heirs to a "classical republican," "civic humanist," or even "neoclassical" tradition. And indeed, if we accept Rahe's definitions, it is hard to doubt that he is mostly right: the British republican tradition (Old Whig, Country, oppositionist, commonwealth, neo-Harringtonian, or whatever we might call it) was never truly classical in nature. But I am not entirely in accord with Rahe's interpretation, which still appears to polarize what the revolutionaries and their sources managed to combine, and I have not accepted his constricted definition of what was classical and what was not. For Rahe, a concern with political architecture—with institutional devices for securing good government more than for moral education—is, by definition, modern. To me, by contrast, the British republican tradition seems to have begun when Harrington and others began to think in terms of a governmental mixture of the powers and virtues of the one, the few, and the many, then proceeded over time to worry about the conditions that could threaten or preserve this governmental balance and the public virtue on which it was taken to depend. "Virtue," to be sure, was not defined by these early modern thinkers as Montesquieu or the ancients defined it. But the concept of mixed government was clearly classical in lineage, and a huge proportion of the worries that identified the eighteenth-century opposition radiated outward

from this concept. In an effort to avoid confusion and to take advantage of Rahe's insights, I refer to the British tradition as *neo*classical and (except when describing the scholarly debate) avoid the terms "classical republican" and "civic humanist." But "neoclassical," as I employ the term, refers to eighteenth-century thinking that I take as combining a modern liberal insistence on security for natural rights with a revival and modification of classical concerns about balanced governments and their foundations. Rahe and I are mostly in agreement on the character of Madison's thinking and in our common insistence that most American revolutionaries were liberal republicans throughout the Founding era. Where he argues, though, that the Americans did not imbibe their confidence in reason and their commitment to popular self-governance from modern republican sources, but perhaps directly from the classics, I counter that these were also present in their eighteenth-century British sources.

86. The soundness of this summary of Hamilton's speech of June 18 should be judged by reading all the records, beginning with Hamilton's own outline. All are available in *RFC* 1:282–311. For Hamilton's insistence that despite his doubts, he was emotionally committed to a perfectly republican system, see *RFC* 1:424, or AH to Edward Carrington, May 26, 1792, *PAH* 11:443. Even Jefferson's "Anas" recorded Hamilton as remarking on August 13, 1791, that if the Constitution should not succeed, "there are still other and other stages of improvement which . . . may be tried and ought to be tried before we give up the republican form altogether, for that mind must be really depraved which would not prefer the equality of political rights which is the foundation of pure republicanism."

87. Among the grounds for doubt, two documents stand out. The first is his late-life note on the suffrage (*RFC* 3:450–55), in which he wrote that if the only choice should lie between universal suffrage and protecting property rights by confining the suffrage to property holders, he would opt for universal suffrage. The other is the letter to Thomas Richie of December 18, 1825 (*LJM* 3:506–7) in which he wrote that if despite a multiplicity of safeguards, the majority should still abuse its legitimate powers, "the appeal can only be made to the recollections, the reason, and the conciliatory spirit of the majority of the people against their own errors, with a persevering hope of success and an eventual acquiesence in disappointment, unless indeed oppression should reach an extremity overruling all other considerations." Later comments of this sort are not, of course, convincing evidence of his position at the Founding, but I am not aware of any statements—before 1788 or later—which unmistakably suggest that Madison would have chosen protection for private rights over democracy or majority control. The closest exception I can think of (if it really was) was his willingness to restrict the suffrage to freeholders in *one* branch of a state legislature.

88. Contrast, particularly, Matthews, *"If Men Were Angels."*

89. Madison, "Detached Memoranda," 565.

90. *Federalist* 20:128–29. Numbers 18–20 reviewed the Amphictyonic and Achaean leagues of classical Greece, the Holy Roman (or Germanic) Empire, Poland, Switzerland, and the Netherlands. These numbers are the only ones conventionally attributed to Madison with Hamilton's assistance. Although there is little evidence that Hamilton's materials had much effect on the finished essays, Madi-

son said that Hamilton gave him a brief draft on the subject after discovering that he was "engaged in [it] with larger materials." See Cooke's edition of *The Federalist,* 616–18.

91. *Federalist* 39:250.

92. *Federalist* 14:86.

93. *Federalist* 37:233–34.

94. *Federalist* 39:251. On these grounds, he refused to grant the name to Holland, Venice, Poland, or England.

95. These were the provisions emphasized by Diamond in his famous challenge to the Progressive argument that the Constitution was less democratic than the Articles of Confederation.

96. *Federalist* 57:384, 387.

97. Ibid., 384.

98. Ibid., 384–87, including: "If this [vigilant and manly] spirit shall ever be so far debased as to tolerate a law not obligatory on the legislature as well as on the people, the people will be prepared to tolerate anything but liberty."

99. *Federalist* 55:378.

100. "Standing on as different foundations . . ." is from *Federalist* 55:377. The other quotations are from 51:349. Although it overestimates the role he assigned to the judiciary in the process, an excellent discussion of Madison's thinking on the subject is William Kristol, "The Problem of the Separation of Powers: *Federalist* 47–51," in Kesler, *Saving the Revolution,* 100–130. Kristol insists that Madison saw the system of checks and balances both as a needed restraint on majorities and as a protection against ambitious rulers. It was, he argues, precisely the principle that Madison thought could reconcile good government with government by consent.

101. *Federalist* 47:324.

102. Ibid., 323–24. Objections along exactly these lines were pouring in from some of Madison's closest allies in Virginia. See, particularly, the letters from the Reverend James Madison, October 29, 1787, and from Joseph Jones, October 29, 1787, *PJM* 10:183–85, 227–29.

103. *Federalist* 47:324–26.

104. *Federalist* 48:332.

105. Ibid., 333.

106. *Federalist* 51:348–49. In the intervening numbers, 49 and 50, Madison agreed with Jefferson that an appeal to the people, their common master, was the ultimate recourse in unresolvable collisions between the branches, but he insisted that this "road" should be reserved for "great and extraordinary occasions." "Frequent appeals would in great measure deprive the government of that veneration which time bestows on everything, and without which perhaps the wisest and freest governments would not possess the requisite stability. . . . In a nation of philosophers this consideration ought to be disregarded. A reverence for the laws would be sufficiently inculcated by the voice of an enlightened reason. But a nation of philosophers is as little to be expected as the philosophical race of kings wished for by Plato. And in every other nation, the most rational government will not find it superfluous to have the prejudices of the community on its side" (49:340).

107. *Federalist* 48:333.

108. *Federalist* 51:350.

109. Ibid., 351.

110. *Federalist* 63:428–29.

111. *Federalist*, numbers 62–63, quotations at 418, 416, 429.

112. *Federalist* 58:396.

113. Ibid. Note, however, that numbers 55–57 of *The Federalist* had been concerned throughout to answer worries (which the author shared) that the House of Representatives would be too small to truly reflect the people's interests and desires. Madison admitted that if he did not believe that the numbers of the lower house would be increased from time to time, this criticism would have "very great weight indeed" (55:375). But in the current circumstances, he insisted—and especially considering the division of authority between the central government and the states—he was "unable to conceive that there are at this time, or can be in any short time, in the United States any sixty-five or an hundred men capable of recommending themselves to the choice of the people at large who would either desire or dare within the short space of two years to betray the solemn trust committed to them" (55:376).

114. *Federalist* 58:396. See, more broadly, numbers 48–50.

115. *Federalist* 62:416–17.

116. My summary of this distinction paraphrases its ablest proponent: Herbert J. Storing, *What the Anti-Federalists Were FOR: The Political Thought of the Opponents of the Constitution* (Chicago, 1981), especially 41. But Martin Diamond, Merrill Jensen, and many others employed a similar distinction.

117. *Federalist* no. 14, reading p. 86 in the context developed in the essay's preceeding pages.

118. *Federalist* no. 39 was the ratification contest's most precise discussion of the partly "national" and partly "federal" characteristics of the "composite" system. Madison used both words essentially as they had been employed at the convention. He found the system federal, not national, in the mode of its creation: rising from the assent of the people "not as individuals composing one entire nation, but as composing the distinct and independent states to which they respectively belong" (39:254). In the manner of its operation—on the people individually and not "on the political bodies composing the confederacy"—the central government was mostly national in nature; but it was not so in the extent of its powers. The jurisdiction of the general government extended "to certain enumerated objects only," and the states were "no more subject within their respective sphere to the general authority than the general authority is subject to theirs within its own sphere" (256). Finally, in structure, the general government combined a national House of Representatives with a federal Senate and a president who would be chosen in a manner that mixed both forms.

119. Wood, *Creation of the American Republic*, especially chap. 9, remains an unsurpassed discussion of the Federalists' concept of sovereignty and of the important role this played in the ratification contest. Wood's argument is conveniently summarized in "The Political Ideology of the Founders," in *Toward a More Perfect Union: Six Essays on the Constitution*, ed. Neil L. York (Provo, Utah, 1988), 20–25.

120. *Federalist* 44:308.

121. *Federalist* 45:308–11.

122. Ibid., 311–14. Of particular interest in this series of connected essays are Madison's explanations of the "sweeping clauses" of the Constitution. In vol. 3, chap. 10 of his biography, Irving Brant constructed a remarkably flimsy but highly influential argument that the "general welfare" clause was a deliberate and substantive grant of power maneuvered into the text by Madison, Wilson, and others as the Committee on Postponed Parts completed its work. Garry Wills and others have followed Brant as well in arguing that Madison's numbers of *The Federalist* employed the "necessary and proper" clause to advance a doctrine of broad construction and implied powers, which Hamilton would build on in the 1790s. This seems to me a quite remarkable example of lifting a passage out of context. If the Constitution had contained no necessary and proper cause, says the passage most often cited (e.g., Brant 3:180–81), the central government would still have possessed "all the particular powers requisite as means of executing the general powers . . . by unavoidable implication. No axiom is more clearly established in law or in reason than that wherever the end is required, the means are authorized; wherever a general power to do a thing is given, every particular power necessary for doing it is included" (*Federalist* 44:304–5). Certainly, Hamilton used similar language in his defense of the national bank; but it is equally certain that the whole object of *Federalist* no. 44 was to show that this clause was *not* a grant of extensive additional powers, just as the object of 41:277–78 was to show that the general welfare clause was not a grant of power at all. Madison's numbers of *The Federalist* are peppered with defenses of specific powers on grounds that these would obviate "necessary usurpations of power, every precedent of which is a germ of unnecessary and multiplied repetitions" (41:270; compare 42:280, 43:297).

123. *Federalist* 46:315–21.

124. *Federalist* 41:268–69.

125. I have interlined and expanded *Federalist* 51:351.

126. JM to Archibald Stuart, October 30, 1787, *PJM* 10:232. *Federalist* no. 1, which poses the question "whether societies of men are really capable or not of establishing good government from reflection and choice, or whether they are forever destined to depend for their political constitutions on accident and force," was published on October 27.

127. *Federalist* 37:238. In line with my interpretive premises and my conclusion that we have almost no evidence concerning his mature religious views, I do not reject the possibility that Madison meant it literally when he suggested to Jefferson that "the degree of concord which ultimately prevailed" at the convention could not be considered "as less than a miracle" (October 24, 1787, *PJM* 10:208).

128. *Federalist* 38:246.

129. *Federalist* 14:83, 86. Compare *Federalist* 45:308–9.

CHAPTER EIGHT. THE VIRGINIA RATIFYING CONVENTION

1. The only other absences of note were Richard Henry Lee, who disliked the Richmond climate, and his brother Arthur, who withdrew from the elections in favor of another Antifederalist candidate.

2. For initial estimates by leaders on both sides, see JM to GW, June 4, 1788,

PJM 10:400; Robert A. Rutland, ed., *The Papers of George Mason, 1725–1792* (Chapel Hill, N.C., 1970), 3:1040, 1044–46; and William Wirt Henry, *Patrick Henry: Life, Correspondence, and Speeches* (1891; New York, 1969), 2:342–43.

3. Rutland, *Papers of George Mason,* 3:1000–1001; *DHRC* 8:23–25.

4. ER to JM, October 29, 1787, *PJM* 10:229. Randolph did not publish his letter to the speaker of Virginia's House of Delegates (dated October 10, but not sent) until December 27, 1787. Versions are available in *RFC* 3:123–27; and *DHRC* 8:260–75.

5. The General Assembly's proceedings on the Constitution are summarized and excerpted in *DHRC* 8:57–59, 110–20, and 183–93. Volumes 8–10 of this magnificent collection include virtually all of the relevant primary sources on the contest in the state: local publications, private letters, official records, and reports of public meetings. For additional evidence of the early enthusiasm, see *DHRC* 8:20–24, 80, 85–86, 91–93, and 96–97, together with *PJM* 10:181–82, 198, 312.

6. In addition to *DHRC* for the fall of 1787, see the letters from Monroe, Archibald Stuart, Randolph, James McClurg, and Henry Lee in *PJM* 10:193, 202–3, 229–230, 233–34, 290–92, and 295–96.

7. JM to Ambrose Madison, November 8, 1787, *PJM* 10:244.

8. JM to GW, February 20, 1788, *PJM* 10:526–27.

9. Letters from Lawrence Taliaferro, December 16, 1787, *PJM* 10:328–29; Henry Lee, December 20, 1787, *PJM* 10:339–40; James Madison Sr., January 30, 1788, *PJM* 10: 446; William Moore, January 31, 1788; *PJM* 10:454–55; James Gordon Jr., February 17, 1788, *PJM* 10:515–16; and John Dawson, February 17, 1788, *PJM* 10: 517–18.

10. *PJM* 10:6 n. 2 and 542 n. 4. Tradition insists (and I tend to believe) that he also stopped between Fredericksburg and Orange for a talk with John Leland, leader of the Virginia Baptists. His father had warned that the Baptists were "generally opposed," and Joseph Spencer had particularly recommended a talk with Leland (February 28, 1788, *PJM* 10:541).

11. JM to Eliza House Trist(?), March 25, 1788, *PJM* 11:5–6.

12. Madison led the poll with 202 votes, Gordon got 187, and Antifederalists Thomas Barbour and Charles Porter received 56 and 34. Materials concerning the election in Orange are conveniently gathered in *DHRC* 9:595–606.

13. For the nature and closeness of the popular division, see Norman K. Risjord, *Chesapeake Politics, 1781–1800* (New York, 1978), 293–317, and "Virginians and the Constitution: A Multivarient Analysis," *WMQ* 31 (1974): 613–32; Norman K. Risjord and Gordon DenBoer, "The Evolution of Political Parties in Virginia, 1782–1800," *JAH* 60 (1974): 961–84; Robert E. Thomas, "The Virginia Convention of 1788: A Criticism of Beard's *An Economic Interpretation of the Constitution,*" *JSH* 19 (1953): 63–72; Jackson Turner Main, *Political Parties before the Constitution* (Chapel Hill, N.C., 1973), chap. 9; and Forrest McDonald, *We the People: The Economic Origins of the Constitution* (Chicago, 1958), 255–83. Volume 8 of *DHRC* includes a superb map of the final division.

14. JM to TJ, December 9, 1787, *PJM* 10:311–13; Jon Kukla, "A Spectrum of Sentiments: Virginia's Federalists, Antifederalists, and 'Federalists Who Are for Amendments,' 1787–1788," *VMHB* 96 (1988): 277–96.

15. For Madison's concern about the Kentuckians, see JM to George Nicholas, April 8, 1788, *PJM* 9:12, and to John Brown, April 9, 1788, *PJM* 9:16–17.

16. The letters to Kentucky have not survived. Their central arguments, however, can be found in JM to George Nicholas, May 17, 1788, *PJM* 11:45–50.

17. ER to JM, February 29, 1788, *PJM* 9:542–43, and JM to ER, April 10, 1788, *PJM* 11:18–19. The earlier letters are in *PJM* 10:182, 185–86, 199–200, 229–31, 252–53, 346–47, and 354–56.

18. ER to JM, April 17, 1788, *PJM* 11:25–26.

19. JM to John Brown, May 27, 1788, *PJM* 11:60.

20. King to JM, January 20 and 27, 1788, *PJM* 10:400, 436–37.

21. JM to GW, June 4, 1788, *PJM* 11:77; to Tench Coxe, June 11, 1788, *PJM* 11:102; and—on Henry—to TJ, December 9, 1787, *PJM* 10:312.

22. TJ to William Carmichael, December 15, 1787, *DHRC* 8:241.

23. See JM to AH, June 22, 1788, *PJM* 11:166: "I have thought it prudent to withhold by a studied fairness in every step on the side of the Constitution every pretext for rash experiments." The best short narratives of the convention include Gordon S. DenBoer, "The House of Delegates and the Evolution of Political Parties in Virginia, 1782–1792" (Ph.D. diss., University of Wisconsin, 1972), chap. 6; David John Mays, *Edmund Pendleton, 1721–1803: A Biography* (Cambridge, Mass., 1952), 2:217–72; and Jackson Turner Main, *The Antifederalists: Critics of the Constitution, 1781–1788* (Chicago, 1961), 223–33. The fullest is still Hugh Blair Grigsby, *History of the Virginia Federal Convention of 1788* . . . , 2 vols., Virginia Historical Society, *Collections* 9–10 (Richmond, 1890–91).

24. *DHRC* 9:931–36. The Virginia ratifying convention is the only public meeting of the revolutionary years for which we have a close approximation of a word-by-word account. We owe this record to an enterprising Petersburg attorney, David Robertson, who took shorthand notes and published the proceedings later in the year. Robertson's report is reprinted in Jonathan Elliot, ed., *The Debates in the Several State Conventions* . . . , vol. 3, and in *DHRC*, vols. 9–10. James H. Hutson, "The Creation of the Constitution: The Integrity of the Documentary Record," *Texas Law Review* 65 (1986): 23–24, cautions that Robertson's reporting was a good deal less reliable than we might wish, but I am not convinced that it was quite so undependable as Hutson implies. On this matter, see also the editorial note in *DHRC* 9:904–6.

25. This summarizes parts of Henry's first two speeches in the convention, June 4 and 5, 1788, *DHRC* 9:929–31, 951.

26. *DHRC* 9:952.

27. William Grayson, *DHRC* 9:1167.

28. *DHRC* 9:967.

29. *DHRC* 9:954.

30. *DHRC* 9:951–52.

31. *DHRC* 9:954–55, 959, 953, 959.

32. Antifederalist writings are collected in Herbert J. Storing, ed., *The Complete Anti-Federalist*, 7 vols. (Chicago, 1981). The most important secondary studies are the general introduction to Storing's collection, available separately as *What the Anti-Federalists Were FOR: The Political Thought of the Opponents of the Constitution* (Chi-

cago, 1981); Main, *Antifederalists*; and the introduction to *The Antifederalists*, ed. Cecelia M. Kenyon (Indianapolis, 1966). For additional recent writings, see James H. Hutson, "Country, Court, and Constitution: Antifederalism and the Historians," *WMQ* 38 (1981): 337–68.

33. *DHRC* 9:951.

34. I dicuss The Bill of Rights in Chapter 9.

35. *DHRC* 9:1072, 10:1477.

36. *DHRC* 9:1067.

37. *DHRC* 9:1170.

38. *DHRC* 9:936–37.

39. *DHRC* 9:1068.

40. *DHRC* 9:937–38.

41. *Letters from the Federal Farmer to the Republican,* ed. Walter Hartwell Bennett (University, Ala., 1978), 10, 14, 22. See also, more largely, 47–52. Bennett writes that the evidence for the traditional attribution of these letters to Richard Henry Lee, "while strong, hardly seems sufficient to justify continuing this attribution" (xx). The attribution was disputed to my satisfaction in Gordon S. Wood, "The Authorship of the *Letters from the Federal Farmer,*" *WMQ* 31 (1974): 299–308. A plausible but not compelling alternative attribution has recently been suggested in Robert H. Webking, "Melancton Smith and the *Letters from the Federal Farmer,*" *WMQ* 44 (1987): 510–28.

42. Mason, "Objections to the Proposed Federal Constitution," *DHRC* 13:348–51.

43. *DHRC* 9:1169–70.

44. *DHRC* 9:1072.

45. Amos Singletary in Jonathan Elliot, ed., *the Debates in the Several State Conventions on the Adoption of the Federal Constitution,* 2d ed., 5 vols. (Philadelphia: J. B. Lippincott, 1901), 2:102.

46. *DHRC* 9:1160.

47. *DHRC* 9:931.

48. The landmark studies were Charles A. Beard, *An Economic Interpretation of the Constitution of the United States* (New York, 1913), and Merrill Jensen, *The Articles of Confederation: An Interpretation of the Social-Constitutional History of the American Revolution, 1774–1781* (Madison, Wis., 1940), and *The New Nation: A History of the United States during the Confederation, 1781–1789* (New York, 1950).

49. Gordon S. Wood, *The Creation of the American Republic, 1776–1787* (Chapel Hill, N.C., 1969), 513–14.

50. See especially E. James Ferguson, *The Power of the Purse: A History of American Public Finance, 1776–1790* (Chapel Hill, N.C., 1961), and "The Nationalists of 1781–1783 and the Economic Interpretation of the Constitution," *JAH* 56 (1969): 241–61; and Richard H. Kohn, *Eagle and Sword: The Federalists and the Creation of the Military Establishment in America, 1783–1802* (New York, 1975).

51. Neither here nor later, readers should be clear, do I maintain that Henry and his allies were simply right about the motives of even the highest-flying advocates of constitutional reform. But it is critical to understand that Antifederalist

concerns were wholly rational and even justified to some degree if we are first to comprehend Madison's achievement, then to identify his own position.

52. *DHRC* 9:1094.

53. Mason insisted that many members of the convention *had* desired consolidation, but that Madison had "expressed himself against it" in a private conversation and that he had never heard any Virginia delegate advocate a unitary system. Madison "declared himself satisfied," and Mason finished his speech (*DHRC* 10: 1401–2). Hugh Blair Grigsby, whose *History of the Virginia Federal Convention* was based in part on oral information, was being overly dramatic when he wrote that Madison "demanded reparation in a tone that menaced an immediate call to the field" (90), but there can be no doubt that Madison sharply resented the remark. Madison was universally described as a man of remarkably "sweet" manners, who never lost his temper, but he was capable of flashes of hard anger—and an uncharacteristic breach of parliamentary decorum—when he thought himself accused of consolidationism or when someone seemed to doubt his commitment to republicanism.

54. *DHRC* 9:997.

55. *DHRC* 10:1295.

56. *DHRC* 9:996.

57. *DHRC* 10:1295. Madison's most elaborate explanations of the partly federal, partly national derivation and structure of the new system—and of the guarantees against a further consolidation—came in his speeches of June 6 and 11, *DHRC* 9:995–98, 1150–52; and especially *The Federalist*, numbers 39, 45, 46, 51, 62.

58. "The genius of republican liberty" demands "not only that all power should be derived from the people, but that those entrusted with it should be kept in dependence on the people" (*Federalist* 37:233–34).

59. JM to TJ, March 19, 1787, *PJM* 9:318. See also his reference in the state convention (*DHRC* 9:996) to the necessity of "submitting to the inconvenience" of greater federal power.

60. *Federalist* 10:63. But there are any number of indications that Madison assumed that federal representatives *would* reflect their constituents' will, which was a logical necessity for his argument that the large republic would defeat factious majorities. Among the clearest are *Federalist* 46:318–19, 51:353, and especially 57:384–87.

61. *DHRC* 9:992.

62. *DHRC* 10:1283. My emphases.

63. *DHRC* 10:1417.

64. See also *Federalist* 57:384–87. As I argue in my article "Some Second Thoughts on Virtue and the Course of Revolutionary Thinking," in *Conceptual Change and the Constitution,* ed. Terence Ball and J.G.A. Pocock (Lawrence, Kans., 1988), 194–212, Madison was not suggesting here that a republic has to rest on the heroic, absolutely selfless, truly classic virtue that Montesquieu described. He was, however, calling for the very kind of virtue that the eighteenth-century British opposition and the early Revolution had demanded.

65. *DHRC* 10:1283.

66. *DHRC* 9:1028ff.

67. *DHRC* 9:1034–35.

68. *DHRC* 9:1028.

69. Madison's earliest sketch of a reform (to TJ, March 19, 1787, *PJM* 9:318–19) suggested that an independent federal taxing power would require a reconstitution of Congress on the basis of proportional representation. Jefferson approved the power and likewise insisted that the reform must "preserve inviolate the fundamental principle that the people are not to be taxed but by representatives chosen immediately by themselves" (10:336).

70. JM, speech of June 29, *RFC* 1:464–65.

71. *Federalist* 41:273–74. Compare *DHRC* 10:1269, 1272–73, where Madison agreed with Mason that a standing army "is one of the greatest mischiefs that can possibly happen" and defended federal powers over the militia as "the most effectual way" to make a professional force "unnecessary."

72. *DHRC* 10:1287.

73. *DHRC* 9:990.

74. Wood, *Creation of the American Republic*, 523–24.

75. Ibid., 562, 615.

76. Though necessary to the book's larger purpose (and not misleading on the Federalists' positions), an exclusive focus on Madison may leave a misleading impression of the meeting's first few days, when "theoretical" considerations dominated the discussion. From first to last, a handful of speakers carried almost all the burden for both sides. Speaking almost every day and often rising several times, Henry was a genuine colossus for the opposition, though he was very capably assisted by Mason and William Grayson. The Federalists distributed the weight more evenly at first, with Randolph, Madison, Henry Lee, George Nicholas, and Edmund Pendleton all speaking often. Monroe and Marshall entered the lists more briefly and infrequently for the opposing camps, though both were quite effective when they did. Madison truly dominated the convention only after it renewed its resolution to proceed in terms of a clause-by-clause discussion.

77. See note 53.

78. See above, pp. 173-77.

79. See JM to ER, January 10, 1788, *PJM* 10:355; Edward Carrington to JM, February 10, 1788, *PJM* 10:494; George Nicholas to JM, April 5, 1788, *PJM* 11:9; and JM to TJ, April 22, 1788, *PJM* 11:28. Henry's sparse surviving correspondence does not clearly confirm the contemporary attribution of his alienation to his anger over the congressional proceedings of 1786, but none of his biographers has doubted that contemporaries were correct about the sources of his discontent.

80. Compare the June 13 letters to King and Washington, the June 16 letter to Hamilton, or the June 18 letters to King and Tench Coxe with the June 4 letters to Washington and Coxe, *PJM* 11:77, 102, 133–34, 144, 151–52.

81. June 7, 1788, *DHRC* 9:1039.

82. Madison's illness forced him to be absent on June 5 and probably on June 9. On June 11, he told Coxe that "for several days preceding yesterday [I] was

confined to my room with a bilious attack. I am now able to resume my seat in the convention, though am extremely feeble" (*PJM* 11:102). In fact, he does not seem to have recovered entirely before the convention adjourned. This illness, together with his naturally weak voice, helps account for the recorder's occasional complaints that he could not be clearly heard.

83. Grayson, speech of June 11, 1788, *DHRC* 9:1171. This speech is the single best source for Grayson's distinctive view of the Constitution as "too weak for a consolidated and too strong for a confederated government."

84. Ibid.

85. *DHRC* 10:1186. See also Mason's eloquent initial speech (*DHRC* 9:936–40) in which he warned that a concurrent power of direct taxation would entail a competition that the central government would certainly win and that the federal taxes would be levied "by those who have neither knowledge of our situation, nor a common interest with us, nor a fellow-feeling." Note, too, that Monroe's rather restrained opposition to the Constitution also focused on the power of direct taxation and the likelihood of a competition for revenues that would destroy the states (*DHRC* 9:1103–15).

86. Mason, speech of June 11, 1788, *DHRC* 9:1156–59. Mason did not belabor the obvious: poll taxes might include a levy on slaves; and southerners, including Madison in 1783, had always fiercely and successfully resisted a tax on acreages of land, whereas New Englanders had always blocked a tax on assessed values. For Henry's and Grayson's agreement with Madison that the population of the South would soon exceed that of New England, see Elliot 3:57, 292.

87. PH, speech of June 24, 1788, *DHRC* 10:1476–77.

88. Henry's remarks came late in the convention, when the Antifederalists plainly feared defeat, and he did not envision a civil war over slavery but a national response to manpower shortages such as those experienced during the War for Independence. *DHRC* incorporates essentially all of the surviving publications from and private correspondence about the ratification contest in Virginia. Fear of direct federal action against slavery made no significant appearance either here or in convention speeches. See also Madison's brusque demolition of such concerns (*DHRC* 10:1503).

89. Gingsby, *History of the Virginia Federal Convention,* 1:230–33. And see JM to Rufus King, June 13, 1788, *PJM* 11:133: "The Mississippi, the Indiana claim, with some other local matters are made a great handle of, particularly out of doors, where the chief mischief is effected." It now appears that Kentucky votes "will turn the scale, and there is perhaps more to fear than to hope from that quarter. ... The event is as ticklish as can be conceived."

90. *DHRC* 10:1229. Privately, Lee had been the only Virginia congressman willing to accept Jay's proposal. Though he had sided with the rest of the delegation in public, his personal views cost him his seat at the next election.

91. *DHRC* 10:1229–39. Quotation from Monroe, *DHRC* 10:1235. For more on Monroe's reaction to the Constitution, which was so mixed that Madison counted him a Federalist until shortly before the convention met, see his draft of a letter to constituents in *DHRC* 9:944–77.

NOTES TO PAGES 256–60

92. *DHRC* 10:1239.

93. *DHRC* 10:1239. Compare Madison's speech of June 12, 1788, *DHRC* 10: 1208 and Nicholas, *DHRC* 9:1131.

94. *DHRC* 10:1240–41. See also June 12, *DHRC* 10:1208–9 where Madison insists that New Jersey, Connecticut, Delaware, and New Hampshire should not be seen as carrying states—much the same analysis he had advanced at Philadelphia.

95. *DHRC* 10:1242. Madison did not suggest that Washington would doubtless win the first presidential election, but he knew that this would naturally occur to all his hearers. He did say, truthfully, that if he were at liberty to mention all the circumstances in his knowledge, he could convince the house that "this project will never be revived in Congress." On the superior security of the Mississippi under a stronger regime see also the June 10 speeches of Nicholas and Marshall.

96. Patricia Watlington, *The Partisan Spirit: Kentucky Politics, 1779–1792* (New York, 1972), 149–56, argues that the Kentucky delegation had an Antifederalist majority of 11 to 3 at the beginning of the meeting and voted 10 to 3 (with one member absent) against ratification. The counties in present-day West Virginia sent four delegates, all of whom were probably Federalists from the beginning.

97. Among the amendments recommended by the convention were a two-thirds vote in Congress for passage of commercial regulations, a requirement of two-thirds of the whole Senate for passage of commercial treaties, a requirement of three-fourths of the whole number of *both* houses for ratification of treaties ceding territories or navigation claims, and a provision that would make it possible for states to raise their share of direct taxes in advance of federal collection.

98. *DHRC* 9:1072, 10:1477.

99. PH, speech of June 24, *DHRC* 10:1479–81. Compare Grayson, *DHRC* 10: 1496–98. Edward Carrington conveyed an important truth before the convention when he told Madison that Henry would try to force amendments no matter how many states had previously ratified, believing "that the other states cannot do without us" (*PJM* 10:383).

100. *DHRC* 10:1283, 9:996.

101. *DHRC* 9:992, 10:1417.

102. ER, *DHRC* 9:973.

103. JM, June 24, *DHRC* 10:1500–1501.

104. *DHRC* 9:987.

105. *DHRC* 10:1481–82.

106. *DHRC* 10:1487–88. "This country," in context, means Virginia.

107. ER, speech of June 6, *DHRC* 9:976–83. Recall, additionally, Madison's defense of the federal power to intervene in cases of internal disorder in *Federalist* 43:294: "Force and right," he insisted, could not be assumed to be always "on the same side in republican governments." A minority (as had seemed possible in Massachusetts) might have such a superiority of "pecuniary resources, of military talents and experience, or of secret succors from foreign powers" as to prevail. Or slaves (a word he avoided) might tip the balance in a time of violence to whichever party they aligned with.

108. *DHRC* 9:988, 983. Defending the power of direct taxation as indispensable in time of war, Madison also "beg[ged the] gentlemen to consider" that "the

southern states are most exposed" (speech of June 11, *DHRC* 9:1145, repeated, *DHRC* 10:1502). Contrast Henry's insistence that Virginia could defend itself, if necessary, against the whole weight of the rest of the Union or any foreign threat (*DHRC* 9:962, 1039–44, 1050–54).

109. See, especially, *DHRC* 9:1081–83. In his *History of the Virginia Federal Convention*, 165, Grigsby says that in the evening after this exchange Colonel William Cabell called on Randolph as a friend of Henry, but that the convention was relieved to learn the next morning that a reconciliation had been achieved without a recourse to the field. I doubt that there was any serious consideration of a duel— this was the eighteenth, not the nineteenth, century—but Randolph *had* used language that one gentleman did not use to another.

110. *DHRC* 9:932–33, 10:1537.

111. *DHRC* 9:971, 973.

112. *DHRC* 10:1537, 9:972.

113. The recommended amendments are in *DHRC* 10:1551–56. The declaration of rights (in twenty parts) was approved without a roll call. Madison characterized "several" of the substantive amendments as "highly objectionable" (to GW, June 27, 1788, *PJM* 11:182). With ratification secured, however, many Federalists were willing to approve all of the opposition's recommendations. A motion to strike the amendments permitting a state to raise its own quota of direct taxes in advance of federal collections was defeated 85 to 65. The recommendatory amendments were then approved without a division (*DHRC* 10:1556–58).

114. The most extensive and quantitatively sophisticated argument to the contrary concedes that differences of wealth, occupation, education, and the like "account for only a tiny portion of a delegate's voting behavior" (Risjord, *Chesapeake Politics*, 316). This discussion builds on Risjord, "Virginians and the Constitution"; Risjord and DenBoer, "Evolution of Political Parties in Virginia"; DenBoer, "House of Delegates"; and Main, *Political Parties before the Constitution*. All find a slight, though significant, correlation between support for the Constitution and wealth, continental military service, higher education, and the like. Contrast Thomas, "Virginia Convention of 1788," and McDonald, *We the People*, 268, which insists that economic and occupational differences fell into "no meaningful pattern whatever" and that the property holdings of delegates on opposite sides "were virtually identical except that more small farmers from the interior supported ratification than opposed it."

115. Of course, some delegates or voters may have made decisions for reasons that were not discussed in the debates at Richmond and were very seldom mentioned in public writings or private correspondence. The evidence for this is slight, but since there are interpreters inclined to emphasize the hidden motives, other issues bear a mention. Randolph once attributed much of the opposition to a fear that the new government would force a payment of the British debts. Madison twice ascribed some of the opposition to a fear of a revival of the Indiana Company claim, and, on October 17, told Jefferson that "the articles relative to treaties, to paper money, and to contracts created more enemies than all the errors in the system ... put together" (*PJM* 10:230, 11:18, 133).

116. In the convention even Henry frequently admitted the necessity for

change. His letter to R. H. Lee, November 15, 1788, is the only evidence I know of that he may have given a passing thought to a separate regional confederation. This letter does appear to hint that if the first Congress should deny "substantial amendments," North Carolina and Virginia's Southside might create a separate government under which he might seek shelter. See Henry, *Patrick Henry*, 2:428–30.

117. Thus Madison consistently supported direct federal taxation partly because he reasoned that an exclusive reliance on import taxes would overburden the South. See especially his speech of June 11 in *DHRC* 9:1142–46, together with his letter to George Thompson, January 29, 1789, in *PJM* 11:436–37.

118. For Patrick Henry on Madison, see Spencer Roane to William Wirt, in Henry, *Patrick Henry*, 2:517–18.

119. *DHRC* 10:1537. Madison correctly feared that Henry's plan would be "to engage two-thirds of the legislatures in the task of undoing the work; or to get a Congress appointed in the first instance that will commit suicide" (to GW, June 23, 1788, *PJM* 11:168).

CHAPTER NINE. SPANNING THE ABYSS

1. John J. McCusker and Russell R. Menard, *The Economy of British America, 1606–1789: Needs and Opportunities for Study* (Chapel Hill, N.C., 1985), 373–74.

2. *PJM* 12:278.

3. "Poor Madison got so cursedly frightened in Virginia that I believe he has dreamed of amendments ever since" (Robert Morris to Francis Hopkinson, August 15, 1789, in *Creating the Bill of Rights: The Documentary Record from the First Federal Congress*, ed. Helen E. Veit, Kenneth R. Bowling, and Charlene Bangs Bickford [Baltimore, 1991], 278). In this collection also compare Morris to Richard Peters, August 24, 1789, and Theodore Sedgwick to Benjamin Lincoln, July 19, 1789, 288 and 263.

4. Madison's reply for the House of Representatives to Washington's inaugural address, May 5, 1789, *PJM* 12:133.

5. JM to TJ, August 10, 1788, *PJM* 11:226–27, and JM to GW, August 11, 1788, *PJM* 11:230.

6. Veit, Bowling, and Bickford, *Creating the Bill of Rights*, 24.

7. See JM to ER, August 22, 1788, and, more fully, JM to TJ, August 23, 1788, and JM to GW, August 24, 1788, *PJM*, 11:237–242. The quotation is from the letter to Jefferson at *PJM* 11:238.

8. ER to JM, August 13, 1788, *PJM* 11:231–32. In November, Randolph followed through on this letter's forewarning that he would resign the governorship to reenter the assembly, where he would not resist a second convention but would work to leave its members free from instructions on direct taxation and other matters.

9. *PJM* 11:240.

10. JM to ER, August 2, 1788, *PJM* 11:215.

11. JM to TJ, August 23, 1788, *PJM* 11:239. See, further, the letters to Randolph (August 11 and 22, *PJM* 11:228, 237–38), Washington (August 11 and 24,

PJM 11:229, 240–242), and Jefferson (August 23, *PJM* 11:238–40). In the August 11 letter to Randolph, Madison calculated that the states north and east of New York (counting Rhode Island) would have seventeen representatives and eight senators, while those to its south and west would send forty-two representatives and sixteen senators; the city was three hundred miles from the easternmost metropolis of the Union and at least four times that far from the southernmost.

12. JM to GW, August 24, 1788, *PJM* 11:241.

13. JM to TJ, September 21, 1788, *PJM* 11:257; to ER, September 24, 1788, *PJM* 11:263; and to John Brown, September 26, 1788, *PJM* 11:266–67.

14. JM to ER, September 14, 1788, *PJM* 11:253.

15. JM to GW, August 24, 1788, *PJM* 11:241, together with JM to ER, September 14, 1788, *PJM* 11:253, and JM to GW, September 14, 1788, *PJM* 11:255.

16. GW to JM, September 23, 1788, *PJM* 11:262.

17. George Lee Turberville to JM, October 20, 1788, *PJM* 11:309.

18. Ibid.; also Francis Corbin to JM, October 21, 1788, *PJM* 11:310–11.

19. Joseph Jones to JM, October 20, 1788, *PJM* 11:208; ER to JM, October 23, 1788, *PJM* 11:314.

20. Edward Carrington to JM, October 24, 1788, *PJM* 11:315. See also JM to ER, October 19, 1788, *PJM* 11:305.

21. JM to ER, November 2, 1788, *PJM* 11:329–30, and JM to Turberville, November 2, 1788, *PJM* 11:330–32.

22. Carrington to JM, October 19, 1788, *PJM* 11:305–6; ER to JM, November 5, 1788, *PJM* 11: 335–36. Virtually all surviving information on the Virginia elections and their background is available in *DHFFE.*

23. Francis Corbin's substitute motion calling on Congress to prepare a bill of rights and other changes was defeated 39 to 85.

24. See the reports from Carrington on November 9 and 15, Randolph on November 10, and Turberville on November 10, 13, and 16 (*PJM* 11:336–38, 338–39, 340–41, 343–44, 345–46, 346–47). Carrington and Turberville both assured Madison that in the Senate contest, sixty-three legislators had voted exclusively for him. Turberville's letter, written before the passage of the residence requirement and remarking that the author had "not even heard of a letter to any of your correspondents here," also sketched a plan to elect Madison from a safe, Tidewater district. On November 13, a house motion to strike the requirement of twelve months' residence in the district failed 32 to 80 (*DHFFE* 2:287–88).

25. ER to JM, November 10, 1788, *PJM* 11:339.

26. See the long speech of June 24, 1788, and his closing remarks of this date, in *PJM* 11:177 and *DHRC* 10:1507, 1504.

27. JM to Turberville, November 2, 1788, *PJM* 11:330–32: "I am not of the number, if there be any such, who think the Constitution lately adopted a faultless work. On the contrary, there are amendments which I wished it to have received before it issued from the place in which it was formed. These amendments I still think ought to be made," although a second general convention is not the safest or even the most effective way "for getting to the object."

28. JM to TJ, October 17, 1788, *PJM* 11:297–300; JM to Turberville, November 2, 1788, *PJM* 11:331.

29. His allies plainly thought so. When his letter to Turberville arrived in Rich-

mond, they proposed to quote it in a pamphlet meant to counteract the opposition's charges that the Federalists would not support amendments. Madison refused permission. See Carrington to JM, November 15, 1788, *PJM* 11:345–46; Turberville to JM, November 16, 1788, *PJM* 11:346–47; and Richard Bland Lee to JM, November 17, 1788, *PJM* 11:348. Madison also answered Corbin's request for his advice about a statewide or district plan for the elections to the lower house. The absence of this letter or of any other on this subject is a heavy loss, since Corbin's answer to the missing letter (*PJM* 11:341–42) tells us little about its contents. There are tantalizing hints in other sources that Madison may have favored or at least anticipated statewide elections, which was the plan adopted by Connecticut, New Hampshire, New Jersey, and Pennsylvania and would have been consistent with his view that large electoral districts would favor the selection of men of elevated views and reputation (see JM to ER, October 17, 1788, *PJM* 11: 305, and Carrington to JM, November 9, 1788, *PJM* 11:336). Yet Corbin's answer probably suggests that Madison warned *against* the statewide plan, which would have opened Federalists to doubts about their democratic bona fides and would not have been consistent with his hope that representatives would faithfully reflect the interests of their districts or with his expectation that the reconstructed Congress would contain more agricultural and inland members. Pulled in both of these directions, Madison may have felt a genuine ambivalence about the matter. When he reported to Jefferson that Pennsylvania had decided on the plan for representatives at large, he remarked that this decision would be "favorable to merit. It is, however, liable to some popular objections urged against the tendency of the new system" and seemed unlikely to be imitated in Virginia. "It is perhaps to be desired that various modes should be tried, as by that means only the best mode can be ascertained" (October 8, 1788, *PJM* 11:276).

30. JM to ER, November 2, 1788, *PJM* 11:329–30; JM to ER, October 17, 1788, *PJM* 11:305.

31. JM to ER, November 23, 1788, *PJM* 11:362–63.

32. Carrington to JM, November 18, 1788, *PJM* 11:352.

33. Carrington to JM, November 26, 1789, *PJM* 11:369; R. B. Lee to JM, November 25, 1789, *PJM* 11:368; Burgess Ball to JM, December 8, 1789, *PJM* 11: 385–86.

34. Chronology, *PJM* 11:xxv.

35. JM to GW, January 14, 1789, *PJM* 11:418.

36. Burgess Ball to JM, December 8, 1788, *PJM* 11:385–86; George Nicholas to JM, January 2, 1789, *PJM* 11:406–8; JM to George Eve, January 2, 1789, *PJM* 11:404–5. For Eve's and Leland's exertions on his behalf, see Benjamin Johnson to JM, January 19, 1789, *PJM* 11:423–24, and John Leland to JM, approx. January 15, 1789, *PJM* 11:442–43. See also the anonymous appeal to religious voters in the Fredericksburg *Virginia Herald* of January 15, 1789 (*DHFFE*, 2:336–37), which reminded them of Madison's services to religious freedom.

37. JM to George Eve, January 2, 1789, *PJM* 11:404–5.

38. Ibid., 405.

39. JM to Thomas Mann Randolph, January 13, 1789, *PJM* 11:416 (published in the *Virginia Independent Chronicle*, January 28, 1789). Compare "To a Resident

of Spotslyvania County," January 27, 1789, *PJM* 11:428–29 (published in the Fredericksburg *Virginia Herald,* January 29, 1789).

40. JM to George Thompson, January 29, 1789, *PJM* 11:433–37 (published in the Baltimore *Maryland Journal,* March 31, 1789).

41. George Nicholas to JM, January 2, 1789, *PJM* 11:406–8; JM to GW, January 14, 1789, *PJM* 11:418; David Jameson Jr. to JM, January 14, 1789, *PJM* 11:419; and Edward Stevens to JM, January 31, 1789, *PJM* 11:438; Brant, vol. 3, chap. 18, especially 241–42.

42. JM to ER, March 1, 1789, *PJM* 11:453.

43. The results are printed in *PJM* 11:438–39 and in *DHFFE* 2:346, from the *Virginia Herald* of February 12, 1789.

44. Although he did remark that he saw "on the lists of representatives a very scanty proportion who will share in the drudgery of business. And I foresee contentions first between federal and antifederal parties and then between northern and southern parties" (JM to ER, March 1, 1789, *PJM* 11:453).

45. AH to JM, November 23, 1788, *PJM* 11:365–67; William Duer to JM, approx. November 25, 1788, *PJM* 11:367–68.

46. JM to TJ, December 8, 1788, *PJM* 11:381–83, and December 12, 1788, *PJM* 11:390.

47. Indeed, there were to be only ten Antifederalists among the fifty-five members of the first session of the House of Representatives. The two Virginians were the only ones elected to the Senate.

48. Steven R. Boyd, *The Politics of Opposition: Antifederalists and the Acceptance of the Constitution* (Millwood, N.Y., 1979), 134. See chap. 7 of this work generally for the fate of Antifederalism between approval of the Constitution and the meeting of the First Congress.

49. JM to TJ, December 12, 1788, *PJM* 11:390.

50. JM to Edmund Pendleton, October 20, 1788, *PJM* 11:307; and to TJ, October 17, 1788, *PJM* 11:297–300. Through much of 1788, the question of amendments was so thoroughly entangled with demands for a second convention that it is difficult to date Madison's decision to support them. A letter to Jefferson of August 23 (*PJM* 11:238–39) denounced an "early" convention. "A very short period of delay would produce the double advantage of diminishing the heat and increasing the light of all parties. A trial for one year will probably suggest more real amendments than all the antecedent speculations of our most sagacious politicians." This may suggest that Madison preferred to wait a year for action even by the Congress. By September 21, however, he may already have intended to include himself among opponents of a second convention who "prefer the other mode provided in the Constitution as most expedient at present for introducing those supplemental safeguards to liberty against which no objections can be raised and who would, moreover, approve of a convention for amending the frame of government itself as soon as time shall have somewhat corrected the feverish state of the public mind and trial have pointed its attention to the true defects of the system" (to TJ, *PJM* 11:257–58).

51. *PJM* 12:121–24, 132–33, 141–42, 166–67. The inaugural address was itself a fine example. On February 16, 1788, Washington sent Madison a draft by David

Humphreys which was seventy-three pages in manuscript and full of specific policy recommendations. This "strange production," as Madison referred to it years later, was scrapped in favor of the short and simple draft he delivered to Mount Vernon on his journey north. In the latter, apart from Washington's expression of his confidence "that the foundations of our national policy will be laid in the pure and immutable principles of private morality" and that the "equal eye" of Congress would "watch over this great assemblage of communities and interests," the only policy recommendation was advanced in language scrupulously respectful of the legislature's independence: "It will remain with your judgment to decide how far" the article providing for amendments should be used to answer the objections raised against the system or "the inquietude which has given birth to them." The president was sure "that whilst you carefully avoid every alteration which might endanger the benefits of an united and effective government, or which ought to await the future lessons of experience, a reverence for the characteristic rights of freemen and a regard for public harmony will sufficiently influence your deliberations on the question how far the former can be more impregnably fortified or the latter be safely and advantageously promoted" (*PJM* 12:123). See, further, the letters from Washington and the editorial notes in *PJM* 11:409, 437–38, and 446–47.

52. See note 4.

53. See April 8, 1789, *PJM* 12:64–66.

54. JM to Pendleton, October 20, 1788, *PJM* 11:306–7.

55. *PJM* 12:64–66, 68–73.

56. Ibid., 70.

57. JM to TJ, May 9, 1789, *PJM* 12:143.

58. JM to ER, May 10, 1789, *PJM* 12:148; James H. Hutson, "John Adams' Title Campaign," *New England Quarterly* 41 (1968), 30–39.

59. Ames to George Richards Minot, May 14, 1789, in *Works of Fisher Ames, with a Selection from His Speeches and Correspondence*, ed. Seth Ames (Boston, 1854), 1:36; *DHFFC* 10:582–86, 592–602.

60. Especially Thomas Tucker (S.C.), Aedanus Burke (S.C.), and John Page (Va.), although Richard Parker (Va.), George Clymer (Pa.), Richard Bland Lee (Va.), and others also spoke forcefully on the subject.

61. JM Remarks of May 11, 1789, *PJM* 12:155.

62. JM to TJ, May 23, 1789, *PJM* 12:182–83.

63. *DHFFC* 4:693–94.

64. *PJM* 12:170–71.

65. Ibid., 172–73. Interestingly, in *Federalist* no. 67, Hamilton had assumed that Senate concurrence would be necessary.

66. JM to ER, May 31, 1789, *PJM* 12:190; speech of June 16, *PJM* 12:226.

67. *PJM* 12:225–29.

68. Ibid., 232–39.

69. His tentative approach was also honestly acknowledged in his private letters, as when he explained to Randolph (June 17, 1789, *PJM* 12:229): "My present opinion is that the Senate is associated with the President by way of exception [from the latter's natural powers] and cannot therefore claim beyond the excep-

tion. This construction has its inconveniences, particularly in referring too much to a single discretion, but is checked by the elective character of the executive," by the impeachment powers, and much else.

70. JM, speech of June 17, 1789, *PJM* 12:232.

71. Ibid., 237. Compare the speech of May 19, 1789, *PJM* 12:174.

72. On the degree to which his guiding principles had actually prevailed, see JM to TJ, May 9, 1789, *PJM* 12:142. On "disinterestedness," "diffusive patriotism," or "virtue," see Gordon S. Wood, "Interests and Disinterestedness in the Making of the Constitution," in *Beyond Confederation: Origins of the Constitution and American National Identity*, ed. Richard Beeman, Stephen Botein, and Edward C. Carter II (Chapel Hill, N.C., 1987), 69–109, and Lance Banning, "Some Second Thoughts on Virtue and the Course of Revolutionary Thinking," in *Conceptual Change and the Constitution*, ed. Terence Ball and J.G.A. Pocock (Lawrence, Kans., 1988), 194–212. For reassurances about amendments, see JM to TJ, March 29, 1789, *PJM* 12: 38; JM to Pendleton, April 8, 1789, *PJM* 12:51; and JM to Governor Samuel Johnson of North Carolina, July 31, 1789, *PJM* 12:317.

73. JM, speech of June 8, 1789, *PJM* 12:198.

74. JM, speech of August 13, 1789, *PJM* 12:332.

75. JM to TJ, March 29, 1789, *PJM* 12:38.

76. There are many excellent studies of the Bill of Rights and several close examinations of Madison's special role and thinking, though my discussion of the "standard story" is an effort to convey my sense of the impression left by the even broader literature of which they are a part. The most respected general studies of the Bill and its background include Irving Brant, *The Bill of Rights: Its Origin and Meaning* (Indianapolis, 1965); Edward Dumbauld, *The Bill of Rights and What It Means Today* (Norman, Okla., 1957); Robert Allen Rutland, *The Birth of the Bill of Rights* (Chapel Hill, N.C., 1955); and Bernard Schwartz, *The Great Rights of Mankind: A History of the American Bill of Rights* (New York, 1977). The best recent study of the passage of the Bill through Congress is Kenneth R. Bowling, " 'A Tub to the Whale': The Founding Fathers and the Adoption of the Federal Bill of Rights," *JER* 8 (1988): 223–51. The most recent studies of Madison's role are Jack N. Rakove, "The Madisonian Theory of Rights," *William and Mary Law Review* 31 (1990): 245–66; Arthur E. Wilmarth Jr., "The Original Purpose of the Bill of Rights: James Madison and the Founders' Search for a Workable Balance between Federal and State Power," *American Criminal Law Review* 26 (1989): 1261–1321; and Paul Finkelman, "James Madison and the Bill of Rights: A Reluctant Paternity," *Supreme Court Review* (1990): 301–47.

77. For all their virtues, many of the finest studies are flawed in my opinion by one or more of these problems of emphasis. Bowling's "Tub to the Whale" and Finkelman's "Reluctant Paternity" suggest the problem in their titles. See also Rakove, " Madisonian Theory of Rights," 254, and "The Madisonian Moment," *University of Chicago Law Review* 65 (1988): 501. Wilmarth's emphasis on Madison's commitment to securing the rights of the states is a valuable corrective, as is Ralph Ketcham's insistence that Madison came to support a bill of rights on its merits (Ketcham 290–292, 303). I would also strongly second Robert Rutland's condemnation of the frequent references in the secondary literature to Madison's refer-

ence to the "nauseous project" of amendments in his letter to Richard Peters of August 19, 1789 (*PJM* 12:346). As Rutland points out in "The Trivialization of the Bill of Rights," *William and Mary Law Review* 31 (1990): 290–91, Madison was referring to a satirical poem in which Peters had compared the draftsmen to cooks brewing a disgusting soup. Yet Madison went on immediately to refuse to apologize for the project: "A constitutional provision in favor of essential rights is a thing not improper in itself and was always viewed in that light by myself. It may be less necessary in a republic than a monarchy and in a federal government than the former, but it is in some degree rational in every government, since in every government power may oppress and declarations on paper, though not an effectual restraint, are not without some influence" (353). The best recent argument that Madison was a genuine convert to the value of a bill of rights is Stuart Leibiger, "James Madison and Amendments to the Constitution, 1787–1789: 'Parchment Barriers,' " *JSH* 59 (1993): 441–68.

78. Aedanus Burke, August 15, 1789, in Veit, Bowling, and Bickford, *Creating the Bill of Rights*, 175. This volume, drawn from the files of the *DHFFC*, is by far the fullest and most convenient source for the congressional proceedings. It prints the House of Representatives' debates as they appear in the old *Annals of Congress*, which took them from Thomas Lloyd's *Congressional Register*, but adds alternative reports from other newspapers, letters to and from the members, and other useful sources. "Whip-syllabub" was a contemporary light dessert. The reference to the whale and the tub, which seems ubiquitous in the contemporary records, derived from Jonathan Swift's "Tale of a Tub."

79. JM to TJ, October 17, 1788, *PJM* 11:297.

80. See September 12, 1789, *RFC* 2:588. Mason, Randolph, Madison, Washington and John Blair were present on this date, and Mason and Randolph unquestionably supported a bill.

81. JM, speech of June 24, 1788, *DHRC* 10:1507, Elliot, 3:626–27.

82. *RFC* 2:588.

83. As Theodore Sedgwick complained, in course of the congressional debate on the right of the people to assemble, it was "trifling" and redundant to include protections for every "self-evident, unalienable right which the people possess." The Constitution might as well declare "that a man should have a right to wear his hat if he pleased, that he might get up when he pleased, and go to bed when he thought proper" (August 15, 1789, in Veit, Bowling, and Bickford, *Creating the Bill of Rights*, 159).

84. Indeed, as Alan Gibson reminded me, Madison may well have been the first to do so. When Richard Henry Lee objected in the Confederation Congress to the absence of a bill, he replied: "A bill of rights [is] unnecessary because the powers are enumerated and only extend to certain cases, and the people who are to agree to it are to establish this" ("Melancton Smith's Notes," *DHRC* 1:332–33, 335–36).

85. *DHRC* 13:339–40. See, further, Wilson's widely published speeches at the Pennsylvania state convention (December 1787), *DHRC* 2:382–83, 387–91, 469–71.

86. *Federalist* 84:575–81. Indeed, Irving Brant counted twenty-four elements of

a bill of rights in the original Constitution and thirty more in Madison's amendments.

87. I have quoted here from two speeches of June 24, 1788, available in *PJM* 11:175 and *DHRC* 10:1498–1505, 1507. In his congressional speech of June 8, 1789, the letter to Jefferson of October 17, 1788, and several other places, Madison called the argument about the danger from omissions the "most plausible" of the objections he had heard. As a consistent advocate of strict, though full, enumeration, he clearly found it weightiest in his own mind. His solution was the current Ninth Amendment, without which he would still have feared this possibility and might still have resisted an enumeration: "The enumeration in the Constitution of certain rights shall not be construed to deny or disparage others retained by the people." For the growing recent literature on this "forgotten" amendment, see "Symposium on Interpreting the Ninth Amendment," *Chicago-Kent Law Review* 64, no. 1 (1988), and *The Rights Retained by the People: The History and Meaning of the Ninth Amendment*, ed. Randy E. Barnett (Fairfax, Va., 1989).

88. TJ to JM, December 20, 1787, *PJM* 10:337. Madison did not receive this letter until the following July, after the adjournment of the state convention.

89. TJ to JM, July 31, 1788, *PJM* 11:212–13. Received by Madison on October 15, 1788.

90. TJ to JM, November 18, 1788, *PJM* 11:353–54.

91. Among the best Antifederalist arguments for a bill of rights were "Agrippa," numbers 15 and 16; "The Federal Farmer," numbers 4 and 16; and "Brutus," number 2.

92. Ralph A. Rossum, "*The Federalist's* Understanding of the Constitution as a Bill of Rights," in *Saving the Revolution: The Federalist Papers and the American Founding*, ed. Charles R. Kesler (New York, 1987), 219–233, is an excellent discussion of this subject, though Rossum also forcefully insists that Madison sponsored the amendments only as a way of conciliating the opposition and defending the Constitution.

93. JM to TJ, October 17, 1788, *PJM* 11:297–300.

94. TJ to JM, March 15, 1789, *PJM* 12:13. Received at the end of May.

95. Ibid., 207. This is the single matter on which Jefferson unquestionably exercised a quite specific influence on his friend. Most of Jefferson's letters did not reach Madison until after his decisions had been made. See notes 88, 89, and 94.

96. Ibid., 198.

97. See Pierce Butler to James Iredell, August 11, 1789, in Veit, Bowling, and Bickford, *Creating the Bill of Rights*, 274.

98. Fisher Ames to Thomas Dwight, June 11, 1789, in Veit, Bowling, and Bickford, *Creating the Bill of Rights*, 247. Madison, of course, saw his pledge to his district as a point of honor. "In many states the Constitution was adopted under a tacit compact in favor of some subsequent provisions on this head. In Virginia it would have been *certainly* rejected had no assurances been given by its advocates that such provisions would be pursued. I *feel* myself bound by this consideration" (JM to Richard Peters, August 19, 1789, *PJM* 12:347).

99. The introduction of amendments at this time, one Federalist complained,

"unhinges the public mind, gives an opening to the artful, unprincipled, and disaffected—who are waiting with burning impatience for an opportunity to embroil and embarrass public affairs" (John Fenno to Joseph Ward, July 5, 1789, in Veit, Bowling, and Bickford, *Creating the Bill of Rights*, 259). See also on 276 of the same collection "Pacificus [Noah Webster] to James Madison," published in the *New York Daily Advertiser* of August 17, 1789.

100. On August 15, replying to Burke's charge that his amendments were not "those solid and substantial amendments which the people expect," but mere "whip-syllabub" and a "tub to the whale," Madison insisted that they were exactly "those most strenuously required by the opponents of the Constitution," although they did not include such changes as would not receive approval and could put the rest in danger (Veit, Bowling, and Bickford, *Creating the Bill of Rights*, 176).

101. Ibid., 77–79; *PJM* 12:198–200. My emphasis.

102. Veit, Bowling, and Bickford, *Creating the Bill of Rights*, 86; *PJM* 12:209.

103. On this point, see Fisher Ames to George Richards Minot, May 29, 1789, *Works of Fisher Ames*, 1:49.

104. For more on this concept, see my "Second Thoughts on Virtue."

105. "I am not, however, very solicitious about the form, provided the business is but well completed" (Veit, Bowling, and Bickford, *Creating the Bill of Rights*, 118).

106. Roger Sherman, speech of August 13, 1789, in Veit, Bowling, and Bickford, *Creating the Bill of Rights*, 105, 108–9, 117–18, 125–26. In the same collection on 271, see also Sherman to Henry Gibbs, August 4, 1789. Sherman was strongly seconded in this argument by Samuel Livermore (N.H.), James Jackson (Ga.), Michael Jenifer Stone (Md.), and others.

107. JM to Alexander White, August 24, 1789, *PJM* 12:352. Rossum makes an interesting point about the congressional decision: "By placing the amendments at the tail of the Constitution, a significance has been given to the Bill of Rights that neither Madison nor the other members of Congress intended. Moreover, the unity of purpose and commitment to rights in both the Constitution and Bill of Rights has been obscured. . . . The Bill of Rights tail has come to wag the constitutional dog. . . . [and] the original Constitution [is] now regarded as a 'superfluity'" ("*The Federalist*'s Understanding," 232).

108. Veit, Bowling, and Bickford, *Creating the Bill of Rights*, 11–12; *PJM* 12:200.

109. Veit, Bowling, and Bickford, *Creating the Bill of Rights*, 81; *PJM* 12:203.

110. Veit, Bowling, and Bickford, *Creating the Bill of Rights*, 29, 198. No debate was recorded on the action of August 19.

111. "The powers delegated by this Constitution [are] appropriated to the departments to which they are respectively distributed, so that the legislative department shall never exercise the powers vested in the executive or judicial, nor the executive exercise the powers vested in the legislative or judicial, nor the judicial exercise the powers vested in the legislative or executive departments" (ibid., 14).

112. Ibid., 13.

113. Ibid., 188–89; *PJM* 12:344.

114. See JM to Pendleton, September 14, 1789, *PJM* 12:402; Fisher Ames to Caleb Strong, September 15, 1789, in Veit, Bowling, and Bickford, *Creating the Bill of Rights*, 297; and especially Paine Wingate to John Langdon, September 17, 1789:

"As to amendments to the Constitution, Madison says he had rather have none than those agreed to by the Senate" (ibid.). Most modern commentators have agreed with Roger Sherman, however, that abridgements by the Senate changed them "for the better" (ibid., 287).

115. Bowling, "Tub to the Whale." On the Antifederalists, who were often joined by Livermore and John Floyd (N.Y.), see also the longer discussion in Bowling, "Politics in the First Congress, 1789–1791" (Ph.D. diss., University of Wisconsin, 1968), chap. 5, together with the letters printed in Veit, Bowling, and Bickford, *Creating the Bill of Rights*, 280–81. The most helpful discussion of voting coalitions is Rudolph M. Bell, *Party and Faction in American Politics: The House of Representatives, 1789–1801* (Westport, Conn., 1973), 33–36, which accords closely with Bowling, "Politics in the First Congress," 136 n. 31 and chart 12.

116. Compare the language of the Ninth Amendment—"The enumeration in the Constitution of certain rights shall not be construed to deny or disparage others retained by the people"—to Madison's original wording: "The exceptions here or elsewhere in the Constitution made in favor of particular rights shall not be so construed as to diminish the just importance of other rights retained by the people, or as to enlarge the powers delegated by the Constitution, but either as actual limitations of such powers or as inserted merely for greater caution" (Veit, Bowling, and Bickford, *Creating the Bill of Rights*, 13).

117. Ibid., 12; *PJM* 12:201–2.

118. See Veit, Bowling, and Bickford, *Creating the Bill of Rights*, 38, 46.

119. The Senate changes and the resolution of the differences between the houses are economically reviewed in Bowling, "Tub to the Whale," 246. The Senate also struck provisions requiring criminal trials in "the vicinage" and placing monetary floors on appeals to federal courts, changes Madison saw as striking at some of "the most salutary articles" (to Pendleton, September 14, 1789, *PJM* 12: 402). The former deletion was eventually restored with "the vicinage" changed to "of the state and district."

120. The lower house was enlarged by statute after the first census. After nearly two hundred years (and a notorious example of just the sort of congressional conduct that Madison hoped to avoid), the other provision was finally ratified as the twenty-seventh amendment (1992).

121. Antifederalists twice moved to make it read, "The powers not expressly delegated," which was preferred by most of the state conventions and would have conformed to the Articles of Confederation. For the debates on these motions on August 18 and 21, during which Madison explained that the Virginia convention had defeated this proposal because it was impossible "to confine a government to the exercise of express powers . . . unless the Constitution descended to recount every minutiae," see Veit, Bowling, and Bickford, *Creating the Bill of Rights*, 197, 199.

122. All authorities agree that Madison used a compilation of the amendments proposed by seven state conventions (or the minorities thereof) to prepare his proposals: *The Ratifications of the New Federal Constitution, Together with the Amendments, Proposed by the Several States* (Richmond, 1788). He plainly drew most heavily, however, on the proposals of Virginia, which relied in turn on the Virginia Declaration

of Rights. Citing Dumbauld, *The Bill of Rights and What It Means Today*, Schwartz calculates that Madison proposed fourteen of the twenty-two protections recommended by four or more states and that all of his proposals except the just compensation clause of the Fifth Amendment can be found in the state recommendations (*The Great Rights of Mankind*, 157–59, 165). Bowling estimates that Madison offered all but seven or eight of the thirty "procedural" or rights-protecting clauses recommended by the conventions, but only five of the sixty-five "structural" proposals, which were at least as dear to many Antifederalists ("Politics in the First Congress," 122). Perhaps most helpful of all are tables 3.2 and 3.3 in Donald S. Lutz, *A Preface to American Political Theory* (Lawrence, Kans., 1992), which graphically convey the closer correlation with the state declarations of rights.

CHAPTER TEN. THE GREAT DIVERGENCE

1. "First man" is from a letter of Fisher Ames to George Richards Minot, in *Works of Fisher Ames, with a Selection from His Speeches and Correspondence*, ed. Seth Ames (Boston, 1854), 1:36. Ames was critical of Madison almost from the beginning and would grow more so as the first session proceeded—"very much Frenchified in his politics . . . too much of a book politician, and too timid in his politics"—but Madison absolutely dominates his letters to this friend.

2. The last two sentences paraphrase and modify the editorial remarks in *PJM* 12:121. Note also Ames's implicit confirmation: "There is less party spirit, less of the acrimony of pride when disappointed of success, less personality, less intrigue, cabal, management, or cunning than I ever saw in a public assembly" (to Minot, July 8–9, 1789, *Works of Fisher Ames*, 1:64).

3. When the first session adjourned, Madison stayed on in New York to copy his notes on the Constitutional Convention, hoping that Jefferson would arrive from France and travel with him to Virginia. When he was disappointed, he left behind a letter begging Jefferson to accept the appointment as secretary of state: "The President is anxious for your acceptance. . . . The Southern and Western Country have it particularly at heart" (October 18, 1789, *PJM* 12:433).

4. AH to Edward Carrington, May 26, 1792, *PAH* 11:426–45. The whole of the following summary of Hamilton's analysis is taken from this letter.

5. Hamilton neglected or forgot Madison's repeated criticisms of "prolonging" or "perpetuating" the public debt, which he included even in the recommendations that Hamilton had asked for as he worked toward his report (JM to AH, November 19, 1789, *PJM* 12:451).

6. Madison's discrimination proposal was defeated on February 22, 1790. Jefferson arrived on March 21.

7. "Madison had completely reversed his former position" on assumption and discrimination and offered a "dubious" explanation for doing so; his opposition to the plan was "probably a tactical maneuver . . . dictated by political expedience," a move to strengthen his position in Virginia and Virginia's position in national politics (E. James Ferguson, *The Power of the Purse: A History of American*

Public Finance, 1776–1790 [Chapel Hill, N.C., 1961], 297–99). Ferguson's is among the most persuasive presentations of an interpretation whose shadings range from the emphasis on Madison's self-interest and hypocrisy in Forrest McDonald, *Alexander Hamilton: A Biography* (New York, 1979), 175, 177–86, 199–201, to the sympathetic explanations of Madison's biographers. Hamilton and Madison, the latter suggest, "disagreed from the outset on social and economic matters. This disagreement grew until it produced a change in Madison's political and constitutional views" (Brant 2:217). Madison shifted "his views of the powers that could be safely consigned to the federal government in order to *preserve* consistency on the vastly more important matter of republican freedom" (Ketcham 314–15).

8. For more on the biases of Irving Brant, whose study is the fountainhead of recent interpretations, see my article, "The Hamiltonian Madison: A Reconsideration," *VMHB* 92 (1984): 10–11.

9. Edward McNall Burns, *James Madison: Philosopher of the Constitution* (New Brunswick, N.J., 1938), 178–79 and passim, offers the best brief discussion of the general compatibility of Madison's position in the Virginia Resolutions and in *The Federalist*.

10. The most comprehensive recent history of the 1790s, Stanley Elkins and Eric McKitrick, *The Age of Federalism: The Early American Republic, 1788–1800* (New York, 1993), forcefully insists on seeing Madison as a Virginian and on recognizing the enormous difference between his own and Hamilton's ideas about the economic underpinnings of a sound republic. It follows Brant, however, in portraying Madison as a determined nationalist through 1789 and in insisting on the unity of his and Hamilton's positions in this respect (79–92, 100–105, 113). With many others, Elkins and McKitrick also see a strict construction of the Constitution as merely instrumental to Madison's more fundamental ends, and place the tenth *Federalist* at the center of his thought (233–34). This understanding of his positions during the 1780s leads, in my opinion, to a narrow and unsatisfactory discussion of the clash of 1790 and is at the root of most of my differences with what is generally a fine and sensitive account.

11. Late in life, he did describe the opposition to his amendments as "ominous" (*LJM* 3:245), but there is little in his papers of 1789 to confirm that he felt this at the time. One exception may be a sentence in his letter to Jefferson of February 4, 1790 (*PJM* 13:21): "The evils suffered and feared from weakness in government and licentiousness in the people have turned the attention more toward the means of strengthening the former than of narrowing its extent in the minds of the latter." Another may be found in a letter to Philip Mazzei of December 10, 1788 (*PJM* 11:389): "Philosophers on the old continent in their zeal against tyranny would rush into anarchy: as the horrors of superstition rush them into atheism. Here perhaps the inconveniences of relaxed government have reconciled too many to the opposite extreme."

12. JM, speech of April 8, 1789, *PJM* 12:66.

13. See especially Drew R. McCoy, *The Elusive Republic: Political Economy in Jeffersonian America* (Chapel Hill, N.C., 1980).

14. JM, speech of April 25, 1789, *PJM* 12:110.

15. Speeches of April 8 and 25, 1789, *PJM* 12:66, 109.

16. Speech of April 9, 1789, *PJM* 12:69–73. See also the outline for this speech in *PJM* 12:68–69, and JM to Edmund Pendleton, April 19, 1789, *PJM* 12:89. Note that the latter more clearly condemned "the premature policy of stimulating manufactures." Madison was making *very* limited concessions to protectionist desires.

17. Speech of April 14, 1789, *PJM* 12:85–87.

18. *PJM* 12:80–81.

19. Speech of April 20, 1789, *PJM* 12:92–93. He also unsuccessfully opposed a differential duty favoring teas imported directly from China or India in American ships, seeing this long-distance trade in luxury articles as of little benefit to the United States (88).

20. *PJM* 12:102. See also *PJM* 12:97–98.

21. *PJM* 12:112. The argument for even small discriminations was offered in support of motions to favor imports of French brandies over imports of Jamaican (i.e., British) rum.

22. *PJM* 12:125–30. Compare the entry for April 25, 1789, *PJM* 12:112–13.

23. JM to TJ, June 30, 1789, *PJM* 12:269–70, summarizing the case made in Congress.

24. JM to Pendleton, April 19, 1789, *PJM* 12:89.

25. JM, speech of April 28, 1789, *PJM* 12:119.

26. See *PJM* 12:144–47, 163–65. Madison also successfully moved to add a clause limiting the duration of the impost bill, suggesting that, in principle, no revenue measure should be indefinite in its duration. This was yet another demonstration of his conscientious effort to proceed according to basic principles.

27. The legislative history of the Impost Act is in *DHFFC* 5:940–83. For the Tonnage Act, which was separated from the former on April 28, see *DHFFC* 6: 1947–56. A good, brief history is Curtis Nettles, *The Emergence of a National Economy, 1775–1815* (New York, 1962), 109–11. The House initially adhered to its position on discrimination by a single vote, but gave it up on July 1 after the Senate adhered to its position as well. A preference for American over *all* foreign shipping was never seriously at issue. The Tonnage Act imposed a duty of fifty cents per ton on foreign vessels and only six cents per ton (payable only once per year) on native vessels, giving the latter a monopoly of the coastal trade and significant advantages in trade overseas.

28. JM to George Nicholas, July 5, 1789, *PJM* 12:280–81.

29. JM to TJ, June 30, 1789, *PJM* 12:669.

30. On the final vote, in which the House agreed to concur with the Senate, New England and New York overwhelmingly opposed discriminatory duties, but they were joined by six of the seven representatives from Georgia and South Carolina and by nearly a third of the Virginia delegation.

31. See Madison's remarks to the House after serving on the conference committee, together with JM to TJ, June 30, 1789, *PJM* 12:236, 269. On June 17, the Senate appointed a committee that recommended on July 13 that the House prepare a plan of discrimination and retaliatory duties, but there was no further action during the session.

32. JM to George Nicholas, July 5, 1789, *PJM* 12:281.

33. *PJM* 12:372. The sensation was compounded by a misreporting of Madison's comments in the New York *Daily Advertiser* (republished in the *Pennsylvania Packet*), according to which he seemed to have condemned not only the day's proceedings but also "the persons who compose this House." See note 1, *PJM* 12: 396–97; Tench Coxe's request for an explanation of "the unknown causes of such high disapprobation," September 9, 1789, *PJM* 12: 394–96; John Dawson to JM, September 13, 1789, *PJM* 12:400; and Madison's only partly apologetic reply to Coxe, September 18, 1789, *PJM* 12:409–10.

34. Speech of September 4, 1789, *PJM* 12:373–74.

35. See Kenneth Russell Bowling, "Politics in the First Congress, 1789–1791" (Ph.D. diss., University of Wisconsin, 1968), 252–54, and "The Compromise of 1790" (paper delivered to the convention of the Organization of American Historians, Washington, D.C., March 22, 1990), 2–3.

36. For background, see Kenneth R. Bowling, *The Creation of Washington, D.C.: The Idea and Location of the American Capital* (Fairfax, Va., 1991), 128–29, 136–37, and Madison's letter to his absent colleague, Alexander White (August 24, 1789, *PJM* 12:353). Madison warned White that Thomas Scott of western Pennsylvania had given notice that he would bring on the subject of a permanent residence and asked White to judge whether he should return. "I suspect that the motion is the result of a preconcert of a pretty serious nature" between Pennsylvania, New England, and New York. On August 27, 1789, the Committee of the Whole approved Scott's motion that a permanent residence should be fixed "as near the center of wealth, population, and extent of territory" as would be consistent with convenient access to the Atlantic and the West.

37. *DHFFC* 11:1400–1401.

38. *DHFFC* 11:1405; *PJM* 12:369. Madison moved to strike out "wealth" from Scott's resolution of August 27 on grounds that "an equal facility to communicate with government is due to all ranks."

39. *DHFFC* 11:1423; *PJM* 12:370.

40. *DHFFC* 11:1426–32; *PJM* 12:371–72.

41. *DHFFC* 11:1432–33; *PJM* 12:372.

42. *PJM* 12:373–76.

43. Ibid., 377.

44. See the excellent editorial note in *PJM* 12:379–80, and the map in Bowling, "Politics in the First Congress," 159.

45. *PJM* 12:378–79: "If there be an event on which we may calculate with certainty, I take it that the center of population will continually advance in a southwestern direction." For the general contemporary agreement on this point, see Drew R. McCoy, "James Madison and Visions of American Nationality in the Confederation Period: A Regional Perspective," in *Beyond Confederation: Origins of the Constitution and American National Identity,* ed. Richard Beeman, Stephen Botein, and Edward C. Carter II (Chapel Hill, N.C., 1987), 226–58.

46. See Ames to Minot, *Works of Fisher Ames,* 1:71, and especially the exchanges of September 5, 1789 in *DHFFC* 11:1459–66. In the latter, in response to Madison's protests, Goodhue objected that southerners had forced the issue on the House at a time when the easterners were unready. Madison replied that south-

erners had not made the motion to take the question up, although they had supported it once made; "as in fact we find a predetermined majority ready to dispose of us, the sooner we know our destiny the better." This prompted Jeremiah Wadsworth (Conn.) to object again to "the reiteration" of complaints about a bargain. Like Ames and Goodue, Wadsworth insisted that New Englanders had been "the last" to enter into bargains, only after learning that the southerners were working toward a move to the Potomac. Madison replied that he would like to see everything known about the question put into writing; this would show that southerners "had not listened to a proposition until they had reason to think it necessary to prevent a sudden and improper decision."

47. On the Potomac speculation, the sources most frequently cited are Mc-Donald, *Alexander Hamilton*, 175, and Julian Boyd's editorial note, "Locating the Federal District," in *PTJ* 19:6-20. On October 29, 1788, Henry Lee offered Madison a part in his purchase of 500 acres of land at the great falls, on which Lee hoped to lay out a town (*PJM* 11:321-22). After consulting with Washington (334, 349-50), he expressed an interest, but said that since he had no funds, he would be able to participate only if the purchase could be made to pay its own obligations (November 30, 1789, *PJM* 11:371-72). Lee set out to make a deal that would permit them to escape the payment of overdue rent, assuming that, together with a speedy sale of lots, this would satisfy Madison's conditions (387-88). When this arrangement fell through, Lee wrote to Jefferson, with Madison's help, to offer Jefferson a share if he could find a European purchaser or lender (Lee to TJ, March 6, 1789, *PTJ* 14:619-21; Lee to JM, June 10, 1789, *PJM* 12:213; and JM to TJ, June 13, 1789, *PJM* 12:217). There the matter stood when Scott and Goodhue introduced their motions.

Jefferson was unsuccessful in attracting European interest and, by this time (although the news could not have reached New York), did not expect success (TJ to JM, August 28, 1789, *PJM* 12:364; TJ to Lee, September 11, 1789, *PTJ* 15:415-16). But Lee continued to pursue the project and, as late as April 1790, when the residence question was once again preoccupying Congress, to plead with Madison to stir himself to borrow money in New York (Lee to JM, March 4, 1790, and April 22, 1790, *PJM* 13:90-91, 157-59). Madison declined and probably had privately dismissed the project by this time (JM to Lee, April 13, 1790, *PJM* 13:148). After April 1790, nothing survives on the subject until August and December 1791, when Madison insisted on withdrawing from any interest Lee might still consider him to have in the project (see *PJM* 14:66, 144, 155, 185).

48. Second speech of September 4, 1789, *PJM* 12:381.

49. JM to Henry Lee, October 4, 1789, *PJM* 12:426. And Lee, of course, was just the man who had initiated the Potomac speculation.

50. It would be far more useful, if my reading is correct, to know the truth about the out-of-doors negotiations than to know if Madison ever really counted on the Great Falls speculation. As far as I can see, his conduct on the seat of government would not have differed in the least if he had had no interest whatsoever in Lee's projected town; both before and after Lee's appeals, he was a fierce proponent of the Potomac. If, by contrast, he had actually assumed a major part from the beginning in the out-of-doors maneuvers, his repeated condemnations

of this manner of proceeding were hypocritical in the extreme. Bowling's "Politics in the First Congress," 157–65, for years the fullest study of the question, concluded that the Pennsylvanians did first approach Virginia with a plan for Philadelphia and the Potomac, that northerners got wind of this, and that the Pennsylvanians then broke faith with the Virginians to secure the permanent location for themselves. Madison's ire, in this account, had more to do with broken bargains than with his dislike of out-of-doors dealing. More recently, however, this account has been supplanted by the fuller study in *Creation of Washington, D.C.*, chap. 5, where Bowling seems to conclude that the Pennsylvania-Eastern bargain did indeed come first (especially 128–29, 136–38). To my mind, even this account does not succeed entirely in unraveling this complicated business. But Madison's public protests were certainly consistent with his session-long insistence on an open, patriotic manner of proceeding, as well as with his explanation in a letter to Edmund Pendleton of September 14, 1789 (*PJM* 12:402–3). "Early in the session," this reported, "secret negotiations were set on foot" between the Pennsylvanians and a New York–New England coalition. Unable to agree, both parties "made advances to the southern members." Pennsylvania offered the Potomac in exchange for "temporary advantages," but as this "prospect became flattering, . . . a reunion was produced among the original parties." Madison did meet with a group of Pennsylvanians at their request on the evening of September 2, the night before Goodhue's motion. Arriving at the boarding house of Clymer and Fitzsimons, he talked to them downstairs. Rufus King and Goodhue, representing New York and Massachusetts, were already talking with the Pennsylvanians upstairs. See Bowling, *Creation of Washington, D.C.*, 138, and Brant 3:278–80.

51. *PJM* 12:6.

52. JM to GW, March 26, 1789, *PJM* 12:28–30. The handbill had been sent to him by Tench Coxe (20), who wrote another lengthy letter on April 21 suggesting that the danger should be handled by speedy reassurances about the Mississippi and a program of improvement that would link Kentucky with Atlantic ports.

53. JM to TJ, March 29, 1789, *PJM* 12:39.

54. *PJM* 12:138–41. See further, the letter from Henry Lee, who had just returned from a trip to the upper country and warned that western expectations were so fixed on a Potomac capital that "suggestions to the contrary fill every mind with passions. . . . Pray be careful," Lee appealed. Haste or "evident trick" would do great mischief (September 8, 1789, *PJM* 12:389–90). Compare also Adam Stephen to JM, September 12, 1789, *PJM* 12: 398–99.

55. JM to Nicholas, July 5, 1789, *PJM* 12:279–82 (quotation at 280), and JM to TJ, July 27, 1789, *PJM* 12:186.

56. Charlene Bangs Bickford and Kenneth R. Bowling, *Birth of the Nation: The First Federal Congress, 1789–1791* (Madison, Wis., 1989), 80–81.

57. Patricia Watlington, *The Partisan Spirit: Kentucky Politics, 1779–1792* (New York, 1972), chap. 4; Lowell H. Harrison, *Kentucky's Road to Statehood* (Lexington, Ky., 1992), chap. 4.

58. Even Coxe expressed a fear "that a phalanx that has been forming for two years by the states east of Jersey has manifested itself in such a way as to make us tremble upon all the great subjects—the seat of government—the judicial offi-

cers—the Treasury and the other great departments." The response of the "middle and southern states" to "such extensive and powerful combinations" could put the Union itself in danger (Coxe to JM, September 9, 1789, *PJM* 12:395).

59. Speech of September 26, 1789, *PJM* 12:422–23.

60. September 28, 1789, *PJM* 12:425. Madison's amendment provided that the laws of Pennsylvania would remain in force within the district until Congress provided otherwise.

61. Bowling, *Creation of Washington, D.C.*, 145–59. The legislative history of the residence bill is in *DHFFC* 6:1850–70.

62. JM to Henry Lee, October 4, 1789, *PJM* 12:425–27.

63. Ames's letters to Minot may be the most instructive illustration (*Works of Fisher*, 1:35–36, 39–40, 42, 47–49, 64), but see also the remarks cited in note 78 of Chapter 9.

64. John Dawson to JM, *PJM* 12:400.

65. Indeed, when Madison reached Virginia, he wrote Washington (himself a dedicated friend of the Potomac) that he had fallen in with Robert Morris on the way. A bitter foe of a continuation in New York, the Pennsylvania senator indicated his desire "to keep alive" the possibility of a Pennsylvania-Southern bargain. When Morris said that he was looking for a way to free himself from his engagements with New England and would then "speak seriously" to the South, Madison replied that Morris would have to speak "very seriously" indeed in light of Pennsylvania's recent conduct. Madison expected that the Pennsylvanians would renew their effort to bring New England and New York into a Susquehanna bargain. If that failed, they would approach the South, while the northeasterners would try a range of threats in order to defeat a Pennsylvania bargain with Virginia (November 20, 1789, *PJM* 12: 452–53).

66. McCoy, "Visions of American Nationality," sees Madison's anger on this matter in similar terms, as "the earliest phase of the disillusionment that would soon energize the Republican insurgency of the 1790s. Hamiltonianism subsequently appeared to him, and indeed to many southerners, as in large part the logical extension of the familiar eastern particularism of the 1780s" (253). See also Bowling, *Creation of Washington, D.C.*, 143.

67. The federal debt to U.S. citizens was roughly $28 million plus $13 million in accrued interest and another $2 million in unliquidated obligations such as the old Continental paper. The debt to foreign governments and bankers, about which there was no dispute, was roughly $12 million. The states owed approximately $25 million. See Ferguson, *Power of the Purse*, 329–30; McDonald, *Alexander Hamilton*, 168.

68. The Report on Public Credit is in *PAH* 6:69–107. The Funding Act as signed by George Washington on August 4, 1790, is in *DHFFC* 5:713–21. The fullest, clearest explanations of the intricacies and workings of the plan are in McDonald, *Alexander Hamilton*, chap. 8; Ferguson, *Power of the Purse*, 292–97, 329–30; and Donald F. Swanson, *The Origins of Hamilton's Fiscal Policies* (Gainesville, Fla., 1963). In the end, the government pledged all revenues in excess of $600,000 arising from the impost and tonnage duties to payment of the interest on the foreign debt, which was refinanced with new and cheaper loans. It then provided

for two new loans, one subscribable in the old certificates of federal debt and one subscribable in assumed state securities, for which the creditors would receive a variety of new certificates bearing varied rates of interest averaging four rather than six percent. Other revenues were pledged to payment of this interest. The sinking fund, which Hamilton used primarily to keep the price of the certificates near par (McDonald, *Alexander Hamilton*, 171), would be supplied mostly from the proceeds on the sale of western lands.

69. Hamilton's relationships with George Beckwith and George Hammond were not as sinister as they appear in Julian P. Boyd, *Number Seven: Alexander Hamilton's Secret Attempts to Control American Foreign Policy* (Princeton, N.J., 1964), but it is generally agreed that they occasionally torpedoed the administration's official stance in Anglo-American negotiations.

70. For Hamilton's grand vision, see John C. Miller, *Alexander Hamilton: Portrait in Paradox* (New York, 1959), 46–51 and passim; Gerald Stourzh, *Alexander Hamilton and the Idea of Republican Government* (Stanford, Calif., 1970), 70–75 and passim; McDonald, *Alexander Hamilton*; McCoy, *Elusive Republic*, 146–52; my own *Jeffersonian Persuasion: Evolution of a Party Ideology* (Ithaca, N.Y., 1978), 129–40; Jerald A. Combs, *The Jay Treaty: Political Battleground of the Founding Fathers* (Berkeley, Calif., 1970), chap. 3 and p. 47; and Elkins and McKitrick, *Age of Federalism*, 92–114 and passim.

71. See above, pp. 35-37, 39-41.

72. "If on the contrary there are distinct provisions . . . [t]hat union and concert of views among the creditors, which in every government is of great importance to their security and to that of public credit, will not only not exist, but will be likely to give place to mutual jealousy and opposition" (Report on Public Credit, *PAH* 6:80–81). See also the similar justification for the national bank in Hamilton's "Notes on the Advantages of a National Bank," which he prepared at Washington's request (8:223).

73. See the sources cited in notes 68 and 70.

74. For the opposition to Morris and its sources in British opposition and early revolutionary thought, see Chapter 1.

75. *Annals of Congress* 1:1132, 1179–82. Expanding this on February 10 (1214), Jackson said: "We learn from Blackstone that the reason for establishing a national debt was in order to . . . establish the new succession at the [Glorious] Revolution; because it was deemed expedient to create a new interest, called the moneyed interest, in favor of the Prince of Orange, in opposition to the landed interest. . . . I hope there is no such reason existing here."

76. Ferguson, *Power of the Purse*, 329–30, calculates that funding raised the market value of the federal debt from about $5 million in 1786 to nearly $42 million (including the arrears of interest) in 1791. Most of the speculation, he agrees, was in the final settlement certificates, totaling some $17 million, issued to disbanding soldiers in 1783. These had passed for as little as ten to fifteen cents on the dollar and were nearly all in the hands of secondary holders by 1790, at which time there may have been no more than 15,000 or 20,000 security holders in the nation (252–53, 255, 285, and chap. 12 more fully). Assumption multiplied the value of the state securities by similar proportions. For several months in 1789 and 1790,

North Carolina and South Carolina securities sold for ten to twenty cents on the dollar, Virginia securities at twenty to thirty cents. Sixty percent of Virginia's certificates and 90 percent of North Carolina's were in the hands of large secondary holders. See Whitney K. Bates, "Northern Speculators and Southern State Debts, 1790," *WMQ* 19 (1962): 32-34, 39.

77. In addition to a scale of depreciation, possibilities included making the certificates receivable for taxes or for sales of western lands. Jackson's allies included Thomas Scott of Pennsylvania, John Page of Virginia, and Thomas Tucker and Aedanus Burke of South Carolina. Boudinot, Ames, Sedgwick, Sherman, Laurance, and William Smith of South Carolina defended Hamilton's proposals and denied that they would create a permanent debt.

78. Speech of February 11, 1790, *PJM* 13:34-39; *Annals of Congress* 1:1233-37.

79. *Annals of Congress* 1:1238-39.

80. *Annals of Congress* 1:1349. In his speech of February 10, Madison acknowledged that his plan to pay the 6 percent originally agreed on would increase the burden. "I regret, as much as any member, the unavoidable weight and duration of the burdens to be imposed, having never been a proselyte to the doctrine that public debts are public benefits. I consider them, on the contrary, as evils which ought to be removed as fast as honor and justice will permit." But honor, he believed, compelled the government to pay the full amount that it had promised.

81. *Annals of Congress* 1:1247-1307, 1:1316-2:1298 (*sic*, in this edition, not yet superseded by publication of these debates in *DHFFC*, vols. 1 and 2 are paged consecutively, but vol. 2 accidentally reprints parts of vol. 1 without allowing for this; the reader must move from 1:1322 to 2:1277). Madison's supporters included Virginians Alexander White, Andrew Moore, and John Page, Jackson of Georgia, and Michael Jenifer Stone of Maryland.

82. JM, February 18, 1790, *Annals of Congress* 1:1307-16; *PJM* 13:48-50, 54. Madison also maintained that the problem of identifying the original creditors was resolvable, a matter on which Ferguson concurs (*Power of the Purse*, 301).

83. See note 7.

84. "Perfidious desertion" was Manasseh Cutler's characterization of Hamilton's feelings about Madison's discrimination scheme. Sedgwick called him "an apostate." Both are quoted in Ketcham 310-11. See, similarly, George Cabot to Benjamin Goodhue, May 5, 1790, Beverly Goodhue Papers, New York Historical Society Library; and Gouverneur Morris to Robert Morris, May 3, 1790, Gouverneur Morris Letterbook, Library of Congress (kindly supplied by Kenneth Bowling from the files of *DHFFC*).

85. Ferguson, *Power of the Purse*, 299, and McDonald, *Alexander Hamilton*, 173-81, both suggest that Madison's expensive plan may well have been contrived to block assumption, though Ferguson is also one of many who acknowledge that it is by no means clear that Madison intended to oppose assumption to the end (311). A desire to mend his fences in Virginia or to garner popular support has been the favorite explanation for his "switch" from the beginning, though Madison was not in fact in danger in Virginia and his correspondents in that state were hardly clamoring for a discrimination. Although most of them opposed assump-

tion, many of his closest friends disliked discrimination. See JM to Edward Carrington, March 14, 1791, *PJM* 13:103–5; Carrington to JM, March 27, 1790, *PJM* 13:124–27; and George Nicholas to JM, May 9, 1790, *PJM* 13:187.

86. On October 12, 1789, Hamilton asked Madison for his thoughts on the "*least* unpopular" additional taxes "and also as to any modifications of the public debt which could be made consistent with good faith, the interest of the public, and of its creditors." On November 19, 1789, writing from Orange, Madison recommended an excise on home distilleries, an increase in the duty on imported spirits, a land tax, and a stamp tax on proceedings in the federal courts. He had not "revolved" the other question carefully enough, he said, "to form any precise ideas," but he hoped that the domestic debt could be reduced by purchases on the private markets and by sales of western lands. This could have been slight help to Hamilton, who was receiving much more specific advice from other correspondents. But in light of the experience of 1783, Hamilton might well have taken Madison's final point as a serious caution: "I consider it as very desirable that the provision to be made should . . . put the debt in a manifest course of extinguishment. There are respectable opinions I know in favor of prolonging if not perpetuating it." But "general reasonings" aside, "such a policy is disrelished to a degree that will render heavier burdens for discharging the debt more acceptable than lighter ones not having that for their object."

87. "James Madison's Autobiography," ed. Douglass Adair, *WMQ* 2 (1945): 204–5. Brant 3:300–305 provides a vivid description of some of the most deplorable insider speculation. Some of this, he shows, was not spontaneous gambling, but "the work of international syndicates of European bankers and American politicians and financiers, operating in millions of dollars, with the second highest officer of the United States Treasury [William Duer] as organizer and manager" (304).

88. Isaac Kramnick, ed., *The Federalist Papers* (Harmondsworth, U.K., 1987), 67. See, more fully, 67–75 and Kramnick, "The 'Great National Discussion': The Discourse of Politics in 1787," *WMQ* 45 (1988): 23–32.

89. JM to Henry Lee, April 13, 1790, *PJM* 13:148. For Madison's repeated condemnations of a prolonged or permanent debt, see also pp. 34-37, 40-42; notes 69 and 70; and note 86. It is also well worth noting that Congress opened its debate on funding four days after Madison wrote his reply to Jefferson's famous letter announcing that the earth belongs to the living (see *PJM* 12:382–87, 13:18–21). I have decided to defer a full discussion of this instructive exchange to another work, but it is useful to recall that Jefferson's specific purpose was to argue that one generation could not legitimately saddle its debts on another and that Madison opened his reply by remarking that the point "suggests many interesting reflections to legislators, particularly when contracting and providing for public debts."

90. Although Madison joined Monroe in a small speculation in Mohawk Valley lands (and tried to find a way to take a part, without investing funds or personally soliciting a loan, in Henry Lee's Potomac speculation), his cold contempt for speculative use of public office by no means spared land jobbers. Recall his early blasts against the continental congressmen who pressed the Indiana Company's claims

in the Northwest or his remark in the Convention that some of the worst state abuses could be traced to individuals who purchased land on credit, then entered the legislatures to defraud their debtors. Among the very few exceptions to the rule that Madison never touted his achievements or integrity was a passage in his autobiography: "Whilst a member of the H. of Reps. he forbore to follow the example, to which he believes he was the sole exception, of receiving at the public expense the articles of stationery provided for the members, to which he thought he was no more entitled than to the supply of other wants incident to his station. To this resolution he adhered throughout, though without attracting any notice to it that might lead to a reflection on others. On his first entering public life, he had laid down strict rules for himself in pecuniary matters. One invariably observed was never to deal in public property, lands, debts, or money whilst a member of the body whose proceedings might influence these transactions" ("James Madison's Autobiography," 203).

91. JM to Edward Carrington, March 14, 1790, *PJM* 13:104, and JM to Edmund Pendleton, March 4, 1790, *PJM* 13:85–86. Compare JM to Benjamin Rush, March 7, 1790, *PJM* 13:93–94.

92. The vote was 36 to 13, and 9 of the 13 were fellow Virginians.

93. Again, I have relied primarily on Ferguson, *Power of the Purse*, especially 307–11, for the workings of and thinking on assumption. Bowling, "Politics in the First Congress," 217–20, is also helpful for the congressional division. Bowling, *Creation of Washington, D.C.*, chaps. 6–7, should be consulted on the residence dispute.

94. *Annals of Congress* 2:1308–42. The advocates were led by Laurance (N.Y.), Clymer (Pa.), FitzSimons (Pa.), Smith (S.C.), Gerry (Mass.), Ames (Mass.), and Burke (S.C.).

95. *PJM* 13:60–63.

96. *Annals of Congress* 2:1342–78, 1384–85; *PJM* 13:65–66. I use this language purposefully about remarks that were equivocal and difficult to fathom. For an alternative account, which starts from the conclusion that Madison opposed assumption from the first, see Elkins and McKitrick, *Age of Federalism*, 146–51.

97. *Annals of Congress* 2:1384–85; *PJM* 13:73–75: "Few states . . . will be willing to incur a load of debt, for which there is not a pressing necessity, and rely upon the final settlement of accounts to obtain redress."

98. Madison's correspondence fails to clarify his thinking on this matter, but Ferguson, *Power of the Purse*, 313, agrees with Brant and Ketcham that the equity of the proposal was Madison's first concern. Even Hamilton's assessment, summarized at the beginning of this chapter, says that Madison insisted in their talk before the opening of the debate that he was not opposed in principle to the assumption. See, further, JM to Edmund Pendleton, March 4, 1790, *PJM* 13:86, in which he calculated that under Hamilton's plan, Virginia would pay one-fifth of the cost of assumption and her citizens receive one-seventh or one-eight of the payments, whereas Massachusetts would pay one-seventh or one-eighth and receive no less than one-fifth. Compare JM to ER, March 14 and 21, 1790, *PJM* 13:106, 110.

99. See the remarks of Jackson, Ames, Gerry, and FitzSimons, *Annals of Congress* 2:1384–95.

100. Into early March, Madison's incoming correspondence had not been generally critical of assumption. By the middle of the month, it was. More than that, a number of his allies from the state convention were beginning to agree with Henry Lee: "This government which we both admired so much will I fear prove ruinous in its operation to our native state. . . . I had rather myself submit to all the hazards of war and risk the loss of everything dear to me in life than to live under the rule of a fixed insolent northern majority" (March 13, 1790, *PJM* 13: 102–3, and April 3, 1790, *PJM* 13:137). See the letters from Walter Jones (March 25, 1790), Edward Carrington (March 27 and April 7, 1790), George Lee Turberville (April 7, 1790), and George Nicholas (May 3, 1790), in *PJM* 13:118–121, 127, 142–45, and 187.

101. On March 2, the House ordered Hamilton to report on the revenues required by assumption (*Annals of Congress* 2:1395–1405). He complied on March 4, and the debate resumed on March 8 and 9 (1417–21).

102. See Jackson's speech of March 1, *Annals of Congress* 2:1378–82, and Henry Lee's letter of April 4, *PJM* 13:136–37: "[Patrick] Henry already is considered as a prophet; his predictions are daily verifying."

103. On March 2, just before his resolution was defeated 28 to 22, Madison did strongly support Alexander White's motion to require Hamilton to report on the taxes necessary to support assumption (*Annals of Congress* 2:1395–1408; *PJM* 13: 81). He also entered the debates briefly on March 10 and 11 to object to describing the certificates as "irredeemable" and to setting so long a term as thirty-five years for retiring the debt; he wished "to shorten the duration of the debt as much as possible" (*PJM* 13:99–101).

104. JM to Pendleton, March 4, 1790, *PJM* 13:86; speech of April 22, 1790, *PJM* 13:164.

105. An excise tax "gives arbitrary power to the collectors and exposes our citizens to vexatious searches. It opens a door to frauds and perjuries that tend equally to vitiate the morals of the people and to defeat the public revenues." Of all internal taxes, it was the most expensive to collect.

106. *PJM* 13:163–74. (An elaborate outline is at 159–63.) Note that here as in his earlier speeches and letters, Madison targeted his protests directly at New England, although the members from South Carolina were every bit as hot for the assumption.

107. *Annals of Congress* 2:1587–1616, 1619. The complete legislative history of the Funding Act is in *DHFFC* 5:713–937.

108. Bowling, *Creation of Washington, D.C.*, 173–80.

109. *PTJ* 17:205–8. Written after the creation of the national bank, probably in 1792, this memorandum (and a briefer comment in TJ to GW, September 9, 1792) is the only reference to the dinner in the surviving papers of the three participants. Jefferson had taken up his duties at the end of March. His letters through June 20, the date most commonly conjectured for the dinner, are consistent with the memorandum's claim that he believed assumption sectionally un-

just, but feared that its defeat would jeopardize the Union. See TJ to George Mason, June 13, 1790, to James Monroe, June 20, 1790, to T. M. Randolph, June 20, 1790, to George Gilmer, June 27, 1790, and to Edward Rutledge, July 4, 1790, *PTJ* 17:493, 536–38, 540–41, 601.

110. Jefferson's memorandum of 1792(?), which was the basis for the best accounts of the 1950s and 1960s (Brant 3:312–18; Dumas Malone, *Thomas Jefferson and His Times*, 6 vols. [Boston, 1951–81], 2:299–305; and Julian Boyd's editorial note, *PTJ* 17:163–83), is not inconsistent with this claim; but Jacob E. Cooke, "The Compromise of 1790," *WMQ* 27 (1970): 523–45, showed conclusively that it was incomplete. Assumption was significantly modified before its final passage, and Hamilton's role was different from Jefferson's depiction of it.

111. A previous arrangement between Pennsylvania and Virginia, first uncovered in Bowling's dissertation, was also suggested by Cooke. Subsequent studies agree, however, that Cooke went too far in suggesting that the dinner-table bargain was never really consummated and that the two measures passed separately as the result of independent bargains. Cooke underestimated Hamilton's influence on the Senate. See Kenneth R. Bowling, "Dinner at Jefferson's: A Note on Jacob E. Cooke's 'The Compromise of 1790,'" with a response by Cooke, *WMQ* 28 (1971): 629–48; Norman K. Risjord, "The Compromise of 1790: New Evidence on the Dinner Table Bargain," *WMQ* 33 (1976): 309–14; and Bowling, *Creation of Washington, D.C.*, 178–89.

112. *Annals of Congress* 2:1660–80; *PJM* 13:264–67, 283 n. 1; Bowling *Creation of Washington, D.C.*, 185–89, 193–95. See Ferguson, *Power of the Purse*, 321–24, for the modifications of assumption and of the related act concerning the settlement of state accounts, by means of which Virginia received at least her share.

Bowling (180–84) suggests that Madison and Jefferson, supported by the president behind the scenes, had taken the initiative in the attempts to link assumption with the residence before Jefferson's encounter with Hamilton. The evidence for this seems slight and fails entirely if, as Boyd believed (*PTJ* 17:170), Jefferson's meeting with Hamilton actually occurred on June 14 or 15 rather than on June 20. Certainly, the possibility that Madison had been working toward a residence-assumption bargain from the start, holding the assumption hostage to a site on the Potomac (McDonald, *Alexander Hamilton*, 173–75), is convincingly refuted by Boyd's note (*PTJ* 17:166–67), by Bowling (173–83), and by a raft of letters showing that, at least through May, Madison had slight hope that the Potomac could be chosen. The interesting unanswered questions have to do primarily with the specific actions taken by Madison and Jefferson. Most authorities believe that Jefferson was more involved in the maneuvering than his memorandum would suggest. Indeed, remarking that the only evidence in all of Madison's papers for a link between the residence and the assumption is a note of June 15(?) from Josiah Parker telling him that Pennsylvania's congressmen had declined a proposition (probably from Hamilton) to support assumption in exchange for both the permanent and temporary seats, the editors of *PJM* (13:243–46) conjecture that Madison may have done no more than talk to White and Lee about accepting a revised assumption. Like Cooke, they probably incline too far toward severing the pieces of the bargain. At least two of Madison's letters seem consistent with the possibility that bargaining was under way around the time of Jefferson's dinner. To Monroe, a staunch opponent of assumption under any terms, he wrote on June 17, 1790 (see *PTJ* 19: 240–47): "It is not improbable that the permanent seat may be coupled with the temporary one. The Potomac stands a bad chance, and yet it is not impossible. . . . The assumption still hangs over us. The negative of the measure has benumbed the whole revenue business. I suspect that it will yet be unavoidable to admit the evil in some qualified shape." To Pendleton (June 22, 1790, *PTJ* 13:252), he may have made a stronger hint: the assumption, "from the zeal and perseverance of its patrons, threatens a very unhappy issue to the session, unless some scheme of accommodation should be devised. The business of the seat of government is become a labyrinth for which the votes printed furnish no clue, and which it is impossible in a letter to explain to you. We are endeavoring to keep the pretensions of the Potomac in view, and to give to all the circumstances that occur a turn favorable to it. If any arrangement should be made that will answer our wishes, it will be the effect of a coincidence of causes as fortuitous as it will be propitious." Although Madison's letters do suggest "that he was an observor rather than a manipulator of events, . . . that he was as much in the dark about the fate of the two measures as were his correspondents in Virginia" (ed. note, *PTJ* 13:245), Madison had a habit of reporting in this way and an interest in conveying this impression, especially to correspondents like Monroe who thought that a residence-assumption bargain would be unwise. Malone believes that it was Jefferson, not Madison, who approached White and Lee (*Jefferson*, 2:301), but Madison had long seen the seat of government as crucial for Virginia and the West. He surely thought that it would counterbalance the assumption even in a monetary sense, especially for congressmen whose districts lay on the Potomac. Accordingly, I have slight doubt that he insisted on it as a quid pro quo and pointed out the benefits to the five Virginia and Maryland congressmen (four representatives and Senator Charles Carroll) who changed their votes.

113. JM to Monroe, July 4, 1790, *PJM* 13:262.

114. Brant believed he would have (3:318).

115. July 13, 1790, *PJM* 13:285. Compare JM to Monroe, July 24, 1790, *PJM* 13:282–83: "In its present form it will very little affect the interests of Virginia." If it should pass, "I shall wish it to be considered as an unavoidable evil, and *possibly* not the worse side of the dilemma."

116. The record of the final debate tells us only that Madison "spoke in favor of [Jackson's] motion to reject the assumption" (*PJM* 13:283 n. 1).

117. Madison's position varied little from his stand in 1789 and will be taken up again in Chapter 11. The legislative history may be followed in *DHFFC* 6:1968–73 and *Annals of Congress* 2:1557–81, 1653, 1655–56. It might be noted, though, that he surely knew by now that Hamilton was an active opponent of commercial discrimination despite the latter's position in *Federalist* no. 11. See the record of Hamilton's conversation with George Beckwith, October 1789, *PAH* 5:482–90.

118. The evolution of the old critique of "government by money" into a persuasive condemnation of Federalist governance was my central theme in *The Jeffersonian Persuasion*.

119. Rush to JM, February 27 and April 10, 1790, *PJM* 13:67–69, 145–46.

120. Jones to JM, March 25, 1790, *PJM* 13:118–21. Compare Henry Lee to JM, April 3, 1790, *PJM* 13:136–37.

121. George Lee Turberville to JM, April 7, 1790, *PJM* 13:143–45. Compare George Nicholas to JM, May 3, 1790, *PJM* 13:187: "A government that relies for support on its creditors and not on the affections of the people cannot be durable. And yet I find this one of the arguments relied on in favor of this system."

122. *American State Papers: Documents, Legislative and Executive, of the Congress of the United States,* 38 vols. (Washington, 1832–1961), 1:90–91, which I have compared to the text forthcoming in *DHFFC* as supplied by Kenneth Bowling. The remonstrance was the work of a committee of Patrick Henry, Henry Lee, and Francis Corbin (Harry Ammon, "The Formation of the Republican Party in Virginia, 1789–1796," *JSH* 19 [1953]: 291). It proceeded dramatically to prefigure the doctrine of state interposition developed in Madison's Virginia Resolutions of 1798: "As the guardians . . . of the rights and interests of their constituents, as sentinels placed by them over the ministers of the federal government to shield it from their encroachments, or at least to sound the alarm when it is threatened with invasion, they can never reconcile it to their consciences silently to acquiesce . . ."

123. Madison was not concerned to reach Virginia in time for the federal elections, in which he was unopposed. He simply enclosed an explanation in his letter to his father of August 14, 1790, asked that this be conveyed to "a friend in each county," and expected his brothers Ambrose and William to attend the polls in Louisa and Culpeper (*PJM* 13:292–94).

124. JM to Pendleton, March 4, 1790, *PJM* 13:85.

125. Speech of March 12, 1790, *PJM* 13:80.

126. *PJM* 13:164.

127. As late as April 13 (*PJM* 13:147–48), he wrote to Henry Lee: "I cannot feel all the despondency which you seem to give way to. . . . I think with you that the Report of the Secretary of the Treasury is faulty in many respects. . . . The novelty and difficulty of the task he had to execute form no small apology for his errors, and I am in hopes that in some instances they will be dimi[ni]shed if not remedied." Assumption "under some modifications would be favorable to the pecuniary interests of Virginia and not inconsistent with the general principles of justice," although it was not attainable in such a form.

128. See Chapter 1, note 88.

129. "An attentive consideration of the tendency of an institution immediately connected with the national government, which will interweave itself into the *monied* interest of every state, which will by its notes insinuate itself into every branch of industry, and will affect the interests of all classes of the community, ought to produce strong prepossessions in its favor in all who consider the firm establishment of the national government as necessary to the safety and happiness of the country and who . . . believe that it stands in need of additional props" (AH to GW, March 27, 1791, *PAH* 8:223).

130. The Report on the Bank is in *PAH* 7:305–42. See also McDonald, *Alexander Hamilton,* 192–95; John C. Miller, *The Federalist Era* (New York, 1960), 55–56.

131. Hamilton's report recommending an excise on wines, coffee, tea, and do-

mestic spirits (December 13, 1790, *PAH* 7:225-36) provoked some of the sharpest condemnations to date of the administration's measures, in the House of Repre sentatives as well as in the press. See the remarks of Jackson, Livermore, Gerry, and others in *Annals of Congress* 2:1924-27, and the newspaper quotations in Banning, *Jeffersonian Persuasion*, 147-48. Excise taxes were expensive to collect and dramatically extended the patronage available to the executive, requiring a horde of prying revenue officers whose potential influence on elections made this kind of tax traditionally offensive to English-speaking peoples. Madison "acknowledged that he felt the force of these objections. . . . Of all the various kinds of taxes, he admitted the excise to be the most disagreeable" and "would not agree to it . . . if any other scheme could be adopted." But Congress was obliged to pay for the assumption, imports were already taxed as heavily as they would bear, and the people were decidedly adverse to his own preference for a land tax. On these grounds, he voted for the measure. See his speeches of December 27, 1790, and January 6, 1791, and his letters to Ambrose Madison and Edmund Pendleton of January 2, 1791, in *PJM* 13:336, 349-51, 341-42, and 344.

132. The Senate bill chartered the bank for twenty years rather than during the duration of the debt and left the establishment of branches to the discretion of the directors. These were soon established in Boston, New York, Baltimore, Richmond, and Charleston.

133. House proceedings can be followed in *Annals of Congress* 2:1940-2012.

134. *PJM* 13:372-82.

135. Madison had taken notes on banks (the Bank of England in particular) sometime before this speech (*PJM* 13:364-69). He now suggested that the Bank of England had paid a higher price for its original, eleven-year charter than was asked of the American institution, and was also compelled to pay an even higher price for each renewal. His objections concerning equity—that only those near Philadelphia would be able to subscribe for stock, and only in six percent bonds— were redressed by a supplemental law of February 23. This set the date for the subscriptions back from April to July, made shares available in Boston, New York, Baltimore, and Charleston as well as in Philadelphia, and permitted payment in other denominations of bonds. See Madison's additional remarks on these points and on the ill-advised, twenty-year charter in his speech of February 8, 1791 (*PJM* 13:387), and in the veto message he drafted for Washington on February 21, 1791 (*PJM* 13:395).

136. JM, speech of February 8, 1791, *PJM* 13:384.

137. Indeed, it was Madison himself who had proposed this and other additions to the delegated powers in a motion of September 13, 1787 (*RFC* 2:324-25, 615-16). It is by no means clear, however, that the defeat of his motion amounted to a deliberate rejection of the authority to create corporations. On this matter, see pp 161-162 above, together with Benjamin K. Klubes, "The First Federal Congress and the First National Bank: A Case Study in Constitutional Interpretation," *JER* 10 (1990): 19-41.

138. See above, pp. 200-201.

139. Speech of February 2, 1791, *PJM* 13:374.

140. Ibid.

141. Ibid., 375. "The preamble to the Constitution," he added on February 8, "only states the objects of the confederation, and the subsequent clauses designate the express powers by which those objects are to be obtained" (384).

142. Ibid., 376–78.

143. Ibid., 379.

144. Ibid., 380–81. Other men, he added after several members had attacked his stand, might have consented to the Constitution on a different understanding, "but he considered the enlightened opinion and affection of the people the only solid basis for the support of the government" (February 8, 1791, *PJM* 13:386–87).

145. The division on the bill was sectional: 33 of the 39 votes in favor came from north of the Potomac, whereas 15 of the 20 votes opposed were from Virginia and the South (Miller, *Federalist Era*, 57 n. 6).

146. Jefferson's opinion, which is better known today than Madison's speeches (but was strictly private at the time), is in *PTJ* 19:275–80. For its background and dependence on Madison's speeches, see Malone, *Jefferson*, 2:337–42, and Merrill D. Peterson, *Thomas Jefferson and the New Nation* (London, 1970), 432–37.

147. Washington's "belief in the utility of the establishment and his disposition to favor a liberal construction of the national powers formed a bias on one side," Madison recalled. "On the other, he had witnessed what had passed in the convention which framed the Constitution, and he knew the tenor" of the ratifying debates. "He held several free conversations with me on the subject in which he listened favorably, as I thought, to my views of it, but certainly without committing himself in any manner whatever. Not long before the expiration of the ten days allowed for his decision, he desired me" to draft a veto. "I had inferred that he would not sign the bill" (" Detached Memoranda," ed. Elizabeth Fleet, *WMQ* 3 [1946]: 542).

148. *PAH* 8:62–134; quotation at 107.

149. Fisher Ames to Thomas Dwight, February 7, 1791, and to George Richards Minot, February 17, 1791, in *Works of Fisher Ames*, 1:94–96.

150. McDonald, *Alexander Hamilton*, 198–200; Bowling, *Creation of Washington, D.C.*, 215–19; and more fully, Kenneth R. Bowling, "The Bank Bill, the Capital City, and President Washington," *Capitol Studies* 1 (1972): 59–71.

151. William Loughton Smith, *The Politics and Views of a Certain Party Displayed* (1792), 17.

152. Sometime after November 1, 1792, when he arrived in Philadelphia for the meeting of the Second Congress, Madison prepared a rough draft of a rebuttal of Smith's pamphlet, which he saw correctly as "a continuation of the [newspaper] attack on republican principles" that Hamilton had recently launched (*PJM* 14:396–401). Smith often spoke for Hamilton in Congress and in the press, and the pamphlet's attack on the conduct of "the General" (Madison) and "the Generalissimo" (Jefferson) since the inauguration of the Constitution is so strongly reminiscent of Hamilton's letter to Edward Carrington with which this chapter began that Madison's sketch of a reply is the closest thing we have to a direct rebuttal of both. On the matter of the bank, Madison did not deny that certain unnamed Virginians had approached the Pennsylvanians in an attempt to limit the charter

to ten years. He did deny, however, that anyone suggested that the bank would be opposed on constitutional grounds only if the limitation was not accepted; the unconstitutionality of the Senate's bill was "uniformly asserted from the beginning to the end of the business," he insisted. He also denied that he had ever personally "considered the Bank as a real bar to the removal to the Potomac." He had, he said, feared that the twenty-year duration of the charter could have that appearance "and hence be used as an engine for turning the fears and hopes of particular states to party purposes"; but this was only one of his reasons for opposing the long duration (*PJM* 14:399–400). For Madison, it was a general principle that "monopolies . . . ought to be granted with caution and guarded with strictness against abuse." The Constitution, he believed, limited the federal right to grant monopolies to the two cases of copyrights and patents, and "perpetual monopolies of every sort"—even charters incorporating towns—were "forbidden not only by the genius of free government but by the imperfection of human foresight" (551–53). In his "Political Observations" of 1795 (*PJM* 15: 511–12) and his post-retirement memoranda as well as in the draft of the reply to Smith, Madison was also careful to remark that Hamilton's original proposal would have made the bank co-durable with the debt and that the charter was "not without difficulty" limited to a period of twenty years. "A more impolitic mode of regulating its duration . . . could not have been devised," since this would have given the bank "a direct and powerful interest in prolonging the public debt . . . and even promoting wars and wasteful and expensive establishments military as well as civil" (*PJM* 14:545).

153. Brant 3:331–32, and in his shorter work, *The Fourth President. A Life of James Madison* (Indianapolis, 1970), 251; Ketcham 321–22.

154. Brant 3:332. See, similarly, Elkins and McKitrick, *Age of Federalism*, 229–34: "Matters had reached the point where the Constitution was not really the highest ground after all. . . . [H]e could no longer feel bound even by his own previous version of the Constitution."

155. Brant 3:331–32. Compare Ketcham 322; Peterson, *James Madison*, 182; Miller, *Federalist Era*, 57; McDonald, *Alexander Hamilton*, 201; and Elkins and McKitrick, *Age of Federalism*, 231–32. Hamilton did paraphrase the language of *Federalist* no. 44, but Madison had used this language in an essay that unquestionably *denied* that the sweeping clauses granted additional powers. On this matter, see Chapter 7, note 120.

156. JM, "Helvidius" no. 4, September 14, 1793, *PJM* 15:106–7.

157. JM to TJ, March 15, 1800, *PJM* 16:373. Madison's denunciation of "constructive perversions" of the Constitution culminated, of course, in the fourth of the Virginia Resolutions of 1798: "Indications have appeared of a design to expound certain general phrases (which, having been copied from the very limited grant of powers in the former Articles of Confederation, were the less liable to be misconstrued) so as to destroy the meaning and effect of the particular enumeration which necessarily explains and limits the general phrases; and so as to consolidate the states by degrees into one sovereignty, the obvious tendency and inevitable result of which would be to transform the present republican system of the United States into an absolute or, at best, a mixed monarchy" (*PJM* 17:189).

Madison elaborated and defended this charge at length in his Report of 1800, *PJM* 17:312–16, which I discuss in Chapter 12.

158. See pp. 276-79.

159. In Madison's opinion—and to a notable degree in fact as well— many of his fears about the bank were rapidly confirmed. The opening of subscriptions for the stock, which was purchased overwhelmingly by foreigners and northeastern financiers, produced a speculative orgy in which rights purchased for $25 on July 4 rocketed to as much as $325 by August 10 and six percent bonds trading at 75 or 80 cents on the dollar reached $1.30 (McDonald, *Alexander Hamilton* 222–23). As early as September 2, 1793, Madison was warning Jefferson that John Marshall had recently obtained a loan from the bank or its associates: "I think it certain that he must have felt, in the moment of the purchase, an absolute dependence on the monied interest, which will explain him to everyone that reflects, in the active character he is assuming" (*PJM* 15:94). "Money in all its shapes is influence," Madison wrote in an essay of 1799. Anyone "dependent" on the bank for its "credits and favors" was "a kind of vassal, owing homage to his pecuniary superior, on pain of bankrupcy and ruin." Whenever bank directors had canvassed for votes or for subscriptions to public addresses and petitions, this influence had been seen ("Foreign Influence," *PJM* 15:219).

160. Seeing something of this sort, Elkins and McKitrick, who argue powerfully that most of the important policies of Washington's administration were, in fact, more realistic and better suited to the nation's needs than those of its opponents, nonetheless make two significant concessions. (1) Hamilton's system did unleash a gambling spirit, "an ungoverned weakness for the fast buck" and the "quick killings," which could well be seen as corrupting the morals of the people and which was not very compatible with the long-term commitments actually required for the development of manufactures; and (2) "The claim of a greatly restricted political class in England to elite status was for practical purposes uncontested." The Federalists might try to claim the status of a governing elite, but in America, such claims were "close to meaningless." The major prop for such pretensions became the Federalists' own image of themselves (*Age of Federalism*, 280–282, 713).

CHAPTER ELEVEN. OPPOSITION LEADER

1. JM to TJ, March 13, May 12, June 23, and July 10, 1791, *PJM* 13:405, 14: 23, 35–36, and 43; to Ambrose Madison, March 2 and April 11, 1791, *PJM* 13: 401–2, 14:5–6; and to Richard Bland Lee, April 17, 1791, *PJM* 14:5–6; Madison Chronology, *PJM* 13:xxvii; Brant 3:336–40.

2. JM, speech of December 27, 1790, *PJM* 13:336. See also JM to Ambrose Madison, January 2, 1791, *PJM* 13:341–42, and JM to Edmund Pendleton, January 2, 1791, *PJM* 13:344. Proceedings on a uniform militia bill, which failed to reach a third reading, were nevertheless suggestive for their broader implications. On December 16, 1790, Madison unsuccessfully moved to amend the bill so as to exempt members of Congress from militia service only when traveling to, attend-

ing, or returning from their sessions, arguing that it was an important general principle that framers of a law should be exempted from its operation only so far as it was absolutely necessary: "The greatest security for the preservation of liberty is for the government to have a sympathy with those on whom the laws act, and a real participation and communication of all their burdens and grievances" (*PJM* 13:323). He would also have exempted "persons conscientiously scrupulous of bearing arms" (328–31).

3. These resolutions were an answer to a petition from merchants of Portsmouth, reported on April 16 by a committee appointed on March 29. The course of legislative proceedings can be followed in *DHFFC* 6:1968–73 and *Annals of Congress* 2:1557–86, 1653–56.

4. *Annals of Congress* 2:1557, 1570–71; *PJM* 13:211–14.

5. *PJM* 13:216–19, together with his bill of May 17, at 13:219–20.

6. This combines portions of Madison's speeches of May 13 and 14 and June 25; quotations at *PJM* 13:213, 256. See, further, his notes on trade, *PJM* 13:198–211.

7. In *Federalist* no. 11, Hamilton had argued that the Constitution would permit the legislature to "oblige foreign countries to bid against each other for the privileges of our markets" and that the United States could force Great Britain to relax its regulations. It is possible, of course, that this was special pleading, but it is also possible that Hamilton favored retaliation at this point.

8. Curtis P. Nettles, *Emergence of a National Economy, 1775 to 1815* (New York, 1962), 231; John R. Nelson, Jr., *Liberty and Property: Political Economy and Policymaking in the New Nation, 1789–1812* (Baltimore, 1987), 10. Hamilton's activities against retaliatory legislation began in the fall of 1789 and intensified in 1790 and 1791. See British agent George Beckwith's report of a conversation with Hamilton in October 1789, *PAH* 5:482–90; Drew R. McCoy, *The Elusive Republic: Political Economy in Jeffersonian America* (Chapel Hill, N.C., 1980), 138–41, 146–47.

9. *PJM* 13:313, 317. Jackson, Smith, and Tucker objected to this passage in the House reply, which was nonetheless approved, as was another passage in which the House assured the president that it would "never lose sight of the policy of diminishing the public debt as fast as the increase of the public revenues will permit."

10. Jefferson reported on Gouverneur Morris's mission to England (written December 15, 1790, but submitted to the Senate on February 14, 1791, *PTJ* 18:301–3), on the French protests against the tonnage acts as violations of the treaty of 1778 (January 18, 1791, *PTJ* 18:565–70), on the Mediterranean trade, on problems with Algiers, on impressment, on the consular establishment, and on the whale and cod fisheries (February 1, 1791, *PTJ* 19:206–20). The quotation is from the last.

11. Whenever Jefferson and Madison were living only blocks apart, they had no need to write the letters on which we might otherwise rely. Moreover, House debates on the navigation bill, submitted on February 23, 1791, were not reported. Nevertheless, as Julian Boyd remarked, the sequence of events leaves little doubt that they were working hand-in-hand (ed. note, *PTJ* 19:546). Madison's biographers do not discuss these proceedings, but the story can be reconstructed from

the lengthy notes in *PTJ* 18:220–83 and 516–58, together with Dumas Malone, *Jefferson and His Time*, 6 vols. (Boston, 1951–81), 2:327–36; Merrill Peterson, "Thomas Jefferson and Commercial Policy, 1783–1793," *WMQ* 22 (1965): 601–6; and Peterson, *Thomas Jefferson and the New Nation* (London, 1970), 419–37.

Stanley Elkins and Eric McKitrick, *The Age of Federalism: The Early American Republic, 1788–1800* (New York, 1993), 68–74, 130–31, 209–11, 375–88, 431–39, and later, make a formidable and generally persuasive case that the Virginians' campaign for commercial discrimination was wildly unrealistic and based on very flawed assumptions: "Neither the state of French manufacturing, the mentality of the French bourgeoisie, nor the condition of the French economy as a whole could provide the least basis for theorizing that France . . . might become . . . a major commercial power" and replace Great Britain as the major trading partner for the new United States (70); Britain would surely have retaliated against discriminatory duties, and a shutting off of trade would have put three-fourths of American commerce at risk (compared to only a sixth of Britain's), undercut a solid financial plan, and called for heavy sacrifices at a time when prosperity was just reviving—all to secure the legal opening of West Indian markets, which were "already accessible informally" (131). Nevertheless, this argument appears to me a great deal more persuasive for the years after 1793 than it does for the years before the outbreak of the Franco-British wars. Once Britain came to be involved in a war to the finish with revolutionary and Napoleonic France, she probably would not have changed her course whatever the United States might do. Before that time, however, Jefferson and Madison at least had solid reasons for believing that a confrontation (or a creditable threat thereof) might well have forced concessions. It did, at least, persuade the British, whose policies *were* intended to damage American rivals (both before and after 1793), to appoint a minister to the United States. I am not convinced that Jefferson and Madison were acting out of anglophobia alone or that they were determined to apply discrimination whatever Britain's attitude might be.

12. For the movement of Jefferson's opinions, see Peterson, *Thomas Jefferson*, 432–37; Malone, *Jefferson*, 2:327–28, 337–42; and Boyd's editorial notes as cited in note 11.

13. TJ to Monroe, April 17, 1791, *PTJ* 20:236.

14. TJ to George Mason, February 4, 1791, *PTJ* 19:241–42.

15. TJ to James Innes, *PTJ* 19:543.

16. John Fenno established the *Gazette of the United States* in New York in 1789 and moved it to Philadelphia with the new government in 1790. The "Discourses on Davila" appeared between April 28, 1790, and April 27, 1791. All but the last and most controversial of the essays are in Charles Francis Adams, ed., *The Works of John Adams* (Boston, 1850–56), 6:221–403. For the final number, see Zoltan Haraszti, ed., "The 32nd Discourse on Davila," *WMQ* 11 (1954): 89–92.

17. "Davila" no. 6, in Adams, *Works of John Adams*, 6:249–50.

18. "Davila" no. 13, in Adams, *Works of John Adams*, 6:280. "Perhaps it may be said that in America we have no distinctions of ranks and therefore should not be liable to those divisions and discords which spring from them; but have we not laborers, yeomen, gentlemen, esquires, honorable gentlemen, and excellent gen-

tlemen? and are not these distinctions established by law? . . . We cannot alter the nature of men. . . . All that we can say in America is that legal distinctions, titles, powers, and privileges are not hereditary" (*Defence*, in Adams, *Works of John Adams*, 5:488).

19. The final quotation is from the *Defence*, in Adams, *Works of John Adams*, 4:579. See, further: "The rich, the well-born, and the able acquire an influence among the people that will soon be too much for simple honesty and plain sense. The most illustrious of them must, therefore, be separated from the mass and placed by themselves in a senate; this is, to all honest and useful intents, an ostracism. A member of a senate of immense wealth, the most respected birth, and transcendent abilities has no influence in the nation in comparison of what he would have in a single representative assembly" (4:290–91).

20. The best discussion of Adams's inability to adjust to the theoretical changes promoted by the Revolution and the Constitution is still chap. 14 of Gordon S. Wood, *The Creation of the American Republic, 1776–1787* (Chapel Hill, N.C., 1969), on which I drew for the shorter explanation in *The Jeffersonian Persuasion: Evolution of a Party Ideology* (Ithaca, N.Y., 1978), 94–100.

21. "Davila" no. 12, in Adams, *Works of John Adams*, 6:270. Adams's distinctive emphasis on the executive as the referee between the many and the few, accompanied by lavish praise of the independence of the king, was heavily influenced by Jean Louis De Lolme, "that ingenious Genevan to whom the English nation is indebted for a more intelligible explanation of their own constitution than any that has been ever published by their own" (396). See J. L. De Lolme, *The Constitution of England* (London, 1777).

22. Haraszti, "32nd Discourse," 90.

23. TJ to Thomas Mann Randolph Jr., May 15, 1791, *PTJ* 20:416.

24. TJ to Philip Freneau, May 15, 1791, *PTJ* 19:351. And this was only weeks before one of Jefferson's most famous recollections of heretical opinions. In the latter, Jefferson recalled a dinner in April 1791 at which John Adams had remarked that the British constitution, purged of its corruptions, would be the best government on earth. "Hamilton paused and said, 'purge it of its corruption and . . . it would be an impracticable government; as it stands at present, with all its supposed defects, it is the most perfect government which ever existed.'" "Hamilton," Jefferson concluded, "was not only a monarchist, but for a monarchy bottomed on corruption" (*WTJ* 1:167–83).

25. JM to ER, September 3, 1792, *PJM* 14:364; TJ to Freneau, February 28, 1791, *PTJ* 19:351.

26. Beginning with Hamilton, whose 1792 attack on the connection between Jefferson and the *National Gazette* will be discussed later in the chapter, commentators usually assumed that Jefferson took the lead in efforts to arouse the public. Jefferson's more obvious enthusiasm for a vital role for popular opinion, the old though now discredited idea that Madison was always Jefferson's lieutenant, and perhaps the happenstance that Jefferson's surviving letters from these weeks are more revealing of the progress of their views may all have bolstered this assumption. But dominant interpretations of Madison's attitude toward popular participation are almost as problematic as the concept that he followed Jefferson's lead,

as these developments may help to show. Even Jefferson's biographers would now insist that, through the argument about the bank, Madison was leading Jefferson more often than Jefferson was leading him; and much of the surviving evidence suggests that Madison, not Jefferson, may well have introduced the thought that something should be done to counteract the *Gazette of the United States*. For other narratives of these developments, most of which agree that the Virginians were intent upon establishing a paper from an early point in the negotations with Freneau, see the editorial note in *PTJ* 20:718–53; Peterson, *Thomas Jefferson*, 444–46; Brant 3:334–36; Ketcham 323–27; and Lewis Leary, *That Rascal Freneau: A Study in Literary Failure* (New Brunswick, N.J., 1941), chap. 8.

27. Freneau to TJ, March 5, 1791, *PTJ* 19:417. Jefferson soon wrote to Franklin's grandson, Benjamin Franklin Bache, wishing (with no success) that Bache would alter his Philadelphia daily to make it suitable for national distribution and provide "a purely republican vehicle of news . . . between the seat of government and all its parts" (April 22, 1791, *PTJ* 19:246).

28. JM to TJ, May 1, 1791, *PJM* 14:15: "The more I learn of his character, talents, and principles, the more I should regret his burying himself in the obscurity of N. Jersey. . . . There is not to be found in the whole catalogue of American printers a single name that can approach to a rivalship."

29. TJ to JM, May 9, 1791, *PJM* 14:18. "We have been trying to get another *weekly* or *halfweekly* paper set up . . . [to] furnish a whig vehicle of intelligence. We hoped at one time to have persuaded Freneau to set up here, but failed" (TJ to Thomas Mann Randolph Jr., May 15, 1791, *PTJ* 20:416).

30. Jefferson's correspondence on this matter is published as a set in *PTJ* 20: 290–312, with a helpful editorial note at 268–90. The other quotations, and those in the succeeding paragraph, are from TJ to JM, May 9, 1791, *PJM* 14:19.

31. JM to TJ, May 12, 1791, *PJM* 14:22.

32. Madison's instinctive dislike of Adams was apparent as early as 1783, when Adams was a peace commissioner and Madison was in Congress. See JM to TJ, February 11 and May 6, 1783, *PJM* 6:221, 7:18. Madison's congressional opponents were Adams's supporters, and in these letters, Madison condemned Adams's "prejudice against the French Court and his venom against Doctor Franklin," whom he much admired. But Madison was even more clearly repelled by the commissioner's vanity and pomposity. Jefferson was quite mistaken when he predicted that Madison would love his "friend" if ever he should meet him (*PJM* 9: 249).

33. JM to TJ, May 12, 1791, *PJM* :14:22–23. On first seeing the *Defence*, Madison had written Jefferson that he feared it would contribute "to revive the predilections of this country for the British constitution. Men of learning find nothing new in it. Men of taste many things to criticize" (June 6, 1787, *PJM* 10:29). By October 1788, he was telling TJ that "Adams has made himself obnoxious to many particularly in the Southern states by the political principles avowed in his book" (*PJM* 11:296). For just how obnoxious Adams seemed, see the letter to Madison from his cousin, Bishop James Madison, of June 11, 1787, *PJM* 10:44–45.

34. The Virginians did not learn that the junior Adams was the author until

much later in the summer. "Publicola" is reprinted in Worthington Chauncy Ford, ed., *The Writings of John Quincy Adams* (New York, 1913), 1:65–110.

35. See Banning, *Jeffersonian Persuasion*, 156–59.

36. See his series of letters to Jefferson in *PJM* 14:36–38, 46. On July 10, 1791, Madison reported that he had just heard that Freneau had abandoned the Philadelphia project (43). On July 24, he wrote that he had seen Freneau and, along with Henry Lee, had "pressed" the advantages of Philadelphia again; he would renew the effort in another conversation (52). Perhaps with Madison's and Lee's assistance, Freneau was finally able to make an arrangement with his New York bosses, Childs and Swain, under which they took a financial part in the concern but left him editorial freedom. See the interesting letter accepting Jefferson's offer (August 4, 1791, *PTJ* 20:754), after which both Madison and Jefferson made extensive efforts to secure subscriptions from Virginia.

37. For this frenzy, see Forrest McDonald, *Alexander Hamilton: A Biography* (New York, 1979), 222–23.

38. JM to TJ, July 10, 1791, *PJM* 14:43.

39. JM to TJ, August 8, *PJM* 14:69.

40. See Banning, *Jeffersonian Persuasion*, 161, and Noble E. Cunningham, *The Jeffersonian Republicans* (Chapel Hill, N.C., 1957), 22–23 and appendixes. The latter show that two-thirds of the time on major issues, Madison could count on the Virginia, North Carolina, and Georgia delegates, half of the Maryland contingent, Tredwell of New York, and Findley of Pennsylvania. Most of the New England delegates opposed him with equal consistency. The remaining half of the House aligned consistently with neither side.

41. "Memoranda of Conversations with the President," February 28 and 29, 1792, *PTJ* 23:186–87. Peterson, *Thomas Jefferson*, 463, identifies the following month as the first during which Jefferson began to speak of the "heats and tumults of conflicting parties" and to refer consistently to "we" and "they" in his correspondence.

42. William B. Giles, speech of April 9, 1792, *Annals of Congress*, Second Congress, 546–48. Compare his speech of November 14, 1791, also in *Annals of Congress*, Second Congress, 178. For Jefferson's pushing of the same interpretation in the face of Washington's protests that "there might be *desires* but he did not believe there were *designs* to change the form of government into a monarchy," see the memoranda for July 10, 1792, and October 1, 1792 (*WJT* 1:227–31, 233–37). In the former, Jefferson said "that the two great complaints were that the national debt was unnecessarily increased and that it had furnished the means of corrupting both branches of the legislature. That [Washington] must know and everybody knew there was a considerable squadron in both whose votes were devoted to the paper and stock-jobbing interest . . . [and] uniformly for every treasury measure," which they provided the votes to pass. "That therefore it was a cause of just uneasiness when we saw a legislature legislating for their own interests in opposition to those of the people." In the latter, Jefferson insisted that he knew Hamilton to be in favor of monarchy. "I had heard him say that this Constitution was a shilly shally thing of mere milk and water, which could not last and was only good as a

step to something better. That when we reflected that he had endeavored in the Convention to make an English constitution of it and, when failing in that, we saw all his measures tending to bring it to the same thing, it was natural for us to be jealous."

43. *PJM* 14:272 n. 1. The conversation occurred on the evening before publication of Madison's essay "The Union: Who Are its Real Friends?" It was followed on June 12 (*PJM* 14:318) by Madison's transmission to Jefferson of a list Jefferson had requested on June 4 (314–15) so that he could "enumerate names" to the president and "show him that I had not been speaking merely at random." Note also Madison's claim in his draft of a reply to Smith's *Politics and Views* that the 1790 proposal to discriminate between original and secondary holders of the debt would have passed if only "the disinterested part of the people of the U.S. had decided the question," perhaps if only "the *disinterested* part" of the House of Representatives had voted (November 4, 1792, *PJM* 14:398).

44. "Memorandum on a Discussion of the President's Retirement," May 5, 1792, *PJM* 14:299–304. See, further, Jefferson's famous letter to Washington of May 23, 1792 (*PTJ* 23:535–41), which also used an appeal against Washington's retirement as a launching pad for Jefferson's fullest explanation to the president of the grounds of opposition to the Hamiltonian program and which surely reflected Madison's as well as his own concerns. Indeed, it seems highly likely that Jefferson planned this letter in discussions with Madison before the latter's departure for Virginia—on the very day the letter was dated. Particularly striking are the similarities between the passages at 538 of the letter and Madison's earlier complaints about sectional favoritism and the fulfillment of Antifederalist prophecies: "Whenever Northern and Southern prejudices have come into conflict, the latter have been sacrificed and the former soothed; . . . the Antifederal champions are now strengthened in argument by the fulfillment of their predictions . . . by the Monarchical federalists themselves, who, having seen the new government merely as a stepping stone to monarchy, have themselves adopted the very constructions of the Constitution of which, when advocating its acceptance before the tribunal of the people, they declared it insusceptible."

45. For this conclusion, see especially JM, "A Candid State of Parties," September 26, 1792.

46. Banning, *Jeffersonian Persuasion*, 162–64. Madison spoke and voted consistently for the 1:30,000 ratio and provided some of the constitutional arguments that led to Washington's veto of the bill in which the House finally accepted the Senate's insistence on a 1:33,000 ratio with fractional representation of the people as a body. See, especially, *PJM* 14:171–72, 195, 198–99, 253, and 261.

47. For Madison's opposition to the additional assumption, attempts to require the funding of the remaining federal debt at the lowest market price, and efforts to speed the redemption of the debt, see *PJM* 14:275–76, 281.

48. On the final day of the second session the Senate tabled a motion by the Virginia senators for constitutional amendments restricting application of the general-welfare clause explicitly to the enumerated powers, denying Congress the power to grant charters of incorporation or monopoly, and excluding from Congress anyone concerned in the direction or management of any bank or monied

corporation. Sometime around March 3, 1792, Madison drafted, probably for newspaper publication, a piece reporting these amendments and suggesting, for "the purification of the legislature from the pecuniary influence so much complained of," the addition of another. This would have required each member of Congress, upon taking his seat, to disclose on oath the amount of his property in bank and public stocks and to swear that, during his term, "he will not purchase or deal in any such paper, or any public lands, or any other public property whatever" (*PJM* 14:470).

49. JM, speeches of December 7, 1791, and March 24, 1792, *PJM* 14:142–43, 262, 270.

50. JM to Henry Lee, January 1, 1792, *PJM* 14:180.

51. Lee to JM, January 8, 1792, *PJM* 14:183–85. The same date saw the publication of Madison's essay "Charters."

52. JM to Lee, January 21, 1792, *PJM* 14:193–94. Compare JM to Edmund Pendleton, same date, *PJM* 14:195–96: "If Congress can do whatever in their *discretion* can be *done by money* and will promote the *general welfare*, the government is no longer a limited one." And this even though that phrase was "copied from" the Articles of Confederation, "where it was always understood as nothing more than a general caption to the specified powers."

53. *PJM* 14:220–24. Compare Jefferson's denunciation of the same use of the general welfare clause in his conversation with Washington of February 29, 1792, which is quoted and discussed at note 41 above (*PTJ* 23:187).

54. McCoy, *Elusive Republic*, 150.

55. The report was submitted to the House on December 5, 1791. The final version is printed in *PAH* 10:230–340, with the argument from the general welfare clause opening at 302. Until it appeared, as will be recalled, the fullest developments of both men's views had been in private letters or anonymous newspaper series.

56. *Gazette of the United States*, July 25, 1792. This article was signed with the initials "T. L."

57. I detail the role of the *National Gazette* in the construction of an opposition ideology in *Jeffersonian Persuasion*, 167–172.

58. Brant, for example, offers little more than an annotated table of contents (3:346–48). Ketcham's discussion, although excellent, is also quite brief (327–30). The principal exception is the ongoing work of Colleen A. Sheehan, especially "Madison's Party Press Essays," *Interpretation: A Journal of Political Philosophy*, 3d ser., 17 (1990): 355–77, and "The Politics of Public Opinion: James Madison's 'Notes on Government,'" *WMQ* 49 (1992): 609–27.

59. The contrary position—that the essays for the *National Gazette* "repudiated many of the arguments of *The Federalist Papers*," that Madison here "assailed his previous position as Publius"—is argued in Douglas W. Jaenicke, "Madison v. Madison: The Party Essays v. The Federalist Papers," in *Reflections on the Constitution: The American Constitution after Two Hundred Years*, ed. Richard Maedment and John Zvesper (Manchester, U.K., 1989), 116–35.

60. This is Sheehan's argument in "Politics of Public Opinion" and in "James Madison's Plan for a Treatise on Government" (typescript), anticipated in William

B. Allen, "Justice and the General Good: *Federalist 51*," in *Saving the Revolution: The Federalist Papers and the American Founding*, ed. Charles R. Kesler (New York, 1987), 133–36. The editors of *PJM* (13:406 n. 1) suggest that the "little task" was a reworking of his notes from the federal convention, but he would not have needed his books as well as his papers for that.

61. *PJM* 14:157–68.

62. On October 30, 1791, Madison wrote that British minister George Hammond had been in town "some days" (*PJM* 14:90). Given his close relationship with Tench Coxe, who drafted much of the Report on Manufactures, he probably already had some notion of its basic lines.

63. Jean Yarbrough, "Republicanism Reconsidered: Some Thoughts on the Foundation and Preservation of the American Republic," *Review of Politics* 41 (1979): 61–95.

64. It was published on November 19, 1791, in the seventh issue of the *National Gazette* and is available in *PJM* 14:117–22. The drafts on which it was based, "Symmetry of Nature" and "Emigration," are in *PJM* 14:100–104, 113–16.

65. Indeed, "Symmetry of Nature" opens: "The planetary system . . . is regulated by fixed laws . . ."; and the topic of both the drafts and the essay seems related to the first section of the larger notebook: "Influence of the size of a nation on Government." It therefore seems conceivable—though this is pure conjecture—that the essay and its drafts, opening with this foundational phenomenon of nature, may well reflect Madison's abandoned efforts to find a beginning for a large and quite ambitious treatise. The table of contents for the larger notebook (100 pages of widely separated sections with ample room for additions to most) suggests a project reminiscent of, though surely not on the order of, Montesquieu's *Spirit of the Laws*.

66. JM, "Dependent Territories," December 12, 1791, closely based on an entry in the large notebook (*PJM* 14:164–65), was only recently attributed to Madison in Sheehan, "Madison's Party Press Essays," 356. It is now available in *PJM* 14:559–60.

67. JM, "Money," December 19 and 22, 1791, is in *PJM* 1:302–10. The question of additional assumptions of state debts, which Madison resisted partly on grounds that they would prolong or perpetuate the debt, would come before the House in March.

68. *PJM* 14:137–39.

69. JM, "Public Opinion" (*PJM* 14:178) was published on December 19, 1791, after the congressional debates on reapportioning and enlarging the House. Section 1 of the notebook (158–60) was titled "Influence of the size of a nation on Government"; section 3 (161–63), "Influence of public opinion on Government."

70. *PJM* 14:178–79, drawing on notebook sections 1 and 2, 158–61.

71. *PJM* 14:191–92.

72. *PJM* 14:197–98.

73. According to Jefferson, Hamilton had recently affirmed these doubts again in an unsuccessful effort to reassure his rival. During a conversation occasioned by the writings of John Adams, Hamilton "declared in substance": "I own it is my own opinion, tho' I do not publish it in Dan and Bersheba, that the present

government is not that which will answer the ends of society by giving stability and protection to its rights, and that it will probably be found expedient to go into the British form. However, since we have undertaken the experiment, I am for giving it a fair course, whatever my expectations may be." And indeed, Hamilton continued, the success so far had been far greater than he had expected. Moreover, "there are still other and other stages of improvement which, if the present does not succeed, may be tried and ought to be tried before we give up the republican form altogether, for that mind must be really depraved which would not prefer the equality of political rights which is the foundation of pure republicanism" ("Notes of a Conversation with Alexander Hamilton," August 13, 1791, *PTJ* 22:38).

74. JM, "British Government," January 28, 1792, *PJM* 14:201–2.

75. JM, "Property," March 27, 1792, *PJM* 14:266–68. Neither England nor the reflection of English political economy in the recent Report on Manufactures is mentioned in the essay directly. But no one could have mistaken the country Madison discussed, and reflective readers would surely have had slight trouble relating the condemnations of British economic and taxation policies to Hamilton's recent recommendations. Scholars will note that "Property" appeared after the attack on Hamilton's political economy in "Republican Distribution of Citizens" and in "Fashion," which clearly reflect Madison's fears about the road that Hamilton would travel.

76. JM, "Spirit of Governments," February 18, 1792, *PJM* 14:233–34—another source for Madison's mixed opinion of Montesquieu, who "was in politics not a Newton or a Locke, who established immortal systems, the one in matter, the other in mind. He was in his particular science what Bacon was in universal science: He lifted the veil from the venerable errors which enslaved opinion, and pointed the way to those luminous truths of which he had but a glimpse himself."

77. A full understanding of and commentary on "Universal Peace," January 31, 1792, *PJM* 14:206–9, would require an extended discussion beginning with the famous exchange occasioned by Jefferson's letter suggesting that "the earth belongs in usufruct to the living." I initiated such a discussion in the Merrill Jensen Lectures at the University of Wisconsin (October 1992; scheduled for separate publication in *Jefferson and Madison: Three Conversations from the Founding* [Madison, Wis., 1995]). Briefly, however, Madison built on Jefferson's argument that requiring each generation to pay for its own wars would put another leash on the dog of war to suggest that permanent peace might also require that the taxes to pay for wars "should include a due proportion of such as by their direct operation keep the people awake." The essay and associated texts are enormously instructive on the Jeffersonians' deep-seated hostility to accumulating and perpetuating public debts.

78. JM, "Republican Distribution," March 3, 1792, is in *PJM* 14:244–46. Bridewell was a London prison, Bedlam an asylum.

79. Note well the striking ambivalence about commerce in the concluding sentence of the paragraph on sailors: "How unfortunate that in the intercourse by which nations are enlightened and refined, and their means of safety extended, the immediate agents should be distinguished by the hardest condition of human-

ity." Madison acknowledges the civilizing benefits of trade, and yet the necessary implication of the passage is that a high proportion of a navigating nation will be miserable and quite unfit for a free public life.

80. This, of course, restates a central point of McCoy, *Elusive Republic*, which I also draw on for the paragraph that follows.

81. JM, "Fashion," March 20, 1792, *PJM* 14:257–59.

82. JM, "Government of the United States," February 4, 1792, *PJM* 14:217–18. And observe that in the "Notes" from which he drew (167), Madison referred to *Federalist* no. 51 and called this complex division of powers "the most characteristic trait in the Govt. of the U.S."

83. JM, "The Union: Who Are Its Real Friends?" *PJM* 14:274–75.

84. Madison took little part in this campaign before October 1 (see *PJM* 14: 373). By that time, Republicans in Pennsylvania and New York had focused their support on Governor George Clinton. The key Virginia leaders were not particularly happy with this choice. A former Antifederalist, Clinton had secured his reelection in New York only after his supporters voided ballots that would have given the governorship to John Jay. Nevertheless, the Virginians saw no other way to unify the opposition, especially since Clinton was enthusiastically supported by the former Antifederalists in their own state. Early in October, John Nicholson, Melancton Smith, and others got in touch with Madison and Monroe in an attempt to shift support to Aaron Burr. The two of them responded jointly, after a discussion, with a letter diplomatically squelching the idea (387). In the meantime, the New Yorkers and the Pennsylvanians met in Philadelphia and independently agreed to support Clinton and drop all thoughts of Burr (John Beckley to JM, October 17, 1792, *PJM* 14:383–85). On the campaign more generally, see Cunningham, *Jeffersonian Republicans.*

85. Hamilton's attack on Jefferson, opening with the "T.L." letter of July 25 and continuing under an array of different pseudonyms, can be followed in full in *PAH*, vols. 12–13. The fullest discussion of the riposte, which was planned at a meeting at Monticello in August, is Philip M. Marsh, *Monroe's Defense of Jefferson and Freneau against Hamilton* (Oxford, Ohio, 1948). Harry Ammon, *James Monroe: The Quest for National Identify* (New York, 1971), 93–95, suggests that Madison's contribution was largely confined to (all but the final paragraph of) number 3 of the "Vindication of Mr. Jefferson," which defended Jefferson's appointment of Freneau, was published in *Dunlaps' American Daily Advertiser* on October 20, 1792, and is available in *PJM* 14:387–92. But letters between Madison and Monroe strongly suggest that Madison also wrote nearly all of number 1, which answered Hamilton's accusations that Jefferson had opposed the Constitution by introducing a series of extracts from Jefferson's 1787–1788 letters to Madison ("a particular friend") and drove Hamilton from this ground. This appeared in Dunlap's paper on September 22, 1792, the same day that "A Candid State of Parties" appeared in the *National Gazette.* It is available in *PJM*, 14:368–70. Hamilton's attack and the Vindicator's replies then focused on Jefferson's conduct as minister to France, with Madison taking little if any part. Hamilton finally desisted when Monroe's final letter (December 31, 1792) closed with a veiled threat to reveal Hamilton's relationship with Maria Reynolds, which he had disclosed to Monroe and a few others as an

answer to charges that he had used Maria's husband as a confidential agent in improper speculations in the funds.

86. Shortly before the second session opened, William Loughton Smith had joined the fray with his *Politics and Views of a Certain Party Displayed* (1792), attacking Madison as well as Jefferson along the lines laid down in Hamilton's long letter to Edward Carrington. Madison drafted but decided against publishing a reply.

87. *PJM* 14:370–72.

88. Remarks of November 13, 1792, *PJM* 14:405–7.

89. *PJM* 14:413–17.

90. *PJM* 14:430–33. It should be recognized, however, that the Hamiltonian proposal would have lowered the government's interest costs.

91. *PJM* 14:450–51.

92. JM to Edmund Pendleton, February 23, 1793, *PJM* 14:452.

93. A standard, brief account is John C. Miller, *Alexander Hamilton: Portrait in Paradox* (New York, 1959), 327–32. A recent article stressing the full extent of Jefferson's involvement is Eugene R. Sheridan, "Thomas Jefferson and the Giles Resolutions," *WMQ* 49 (1992): 589–608. Sheridan and others have assumed that Madison was the conduit between Jefferson and Giles, but there is nothing in his papers to suggest this, and all of the historians have noted his apparent preference for a different manner of proceeding.

94. See, especially, his speech of March 1, 1793—his longest of the session—supporting the third resolution, which charged Hamilton with violating the Funding Act of 1790 (*PJM* 14:456–69). Again, Madison was most disturbed—apart from the apparent violation of the legislature's intent—that money positively due to France and desperately needed there was drawn instead to the United States, deposited in the bank, and then left there to be available for early repayment of the loan from that institution. Jefferson's draft is presented alongside the resolutions as actually introduced in *WTJ* 6:168–71. The proceedings in full are in *Annals of Congress* 3:899–963.

95. See JM to George Nicholas, March 15, 1793, *PJM* 14:472. Many congressmen feared that the resolutions might reflect on Washington. Moreover, Hamilton could reasonably be said to have been exercising a justifiable discretion in the public interest. See also the editorial note in *PAH* 13:532–41. All the resolutions were defeated by margins ranging upward from 33 to 15.

96. See Jefferson's memorandum for March 2, 1793, in *WTJ* 1:222–23.

97. See his remarks in the House that the next Congress would be more genuinely representative of the people (*PJM* 14:446, 448).

98. JM to George Nicholas, March 15, 1793, *PJM* 14:472, including: "We have every motive in America to pray for [French] success, not only from a general attachment to the liberties of mankind, but from a peculiar regard to our own. The symptoms of disaffection to Republi[can go]vernment have risen and subsided among us in such visible [co]rrespondence with the prosperous and adverse accounts from the French Revolution that a miscarriage of it would threaten us with the most serious dangers to our present forms and principles of our governments."

99. JM, "Who Are the Best Keepers . . . ?" December 20, 1792, *PJM* 14:426–27.

CHAPTER TWELVE. RETROSPECT AND PROSPECT

1. Gordon S. Wood, "Interests and Disinterestedness in the Making of the Constitution," in *Beyond Confederation: Origins of the Constitution and American National Identity*, ed. Richard Beeman, Stephen Botein, and Edward C. Carter II (Chapel Hill, N.C., 1987), 72.

2. Much modern scholarship has also adopted and revised the Antifederalist conception of the Constitution as a capitalistic or elitist plot.

3. Nicholas P. Trist's memorandum of a conversation with Madison of September 27, 1834, *RFC* 3:533–34.

4. Although it may be to his credit that his papers do not hold the misogynist or racist comments of his closest friend and ally. Shortly before his death in 1836, an interviewer asked him if he thought the negro was equal in natural capacities to the white. From his own observation, Madison replied, "their transformation from an almost brutal condition had been so great that he could not set a limit to their further improvement" (George Bancroft, *History of the Formation of the Constitution of the United States of America* [New York, 1882], 1:x).

5. Madison always recognized that even in a large republic—and even after all the structural and constitutional restraints have been applied—majority abuse may still occasionally occur. How can liberal republicans respond on such occasions? Perhaps his clearest answer came in his response to southerners who tried to build a constitutional defense against protective tariffs (which, unlike the crisis laws of 1798, he certainly believed to be within the letter and the spirit of the Constitution). "The appeal can only be made to the recollections, the reason, and the conciliating spirit of the majority of the people against their own errors, with a persevering hope of success and an eventual acquiescence in disappointment, unless, indeed, oppression should reach an extremity overruling all other considerations." There was always the right of revolution, but in a constitutional republic, there could be no constitutional appeal beyond the people in their highest sovereign role. JM to Thomas Ritchie, December 18, 1825, *LJM* 3:506–7.

6. A full discussion of his final thirty years is thus unnecessary for the task at hand and is the less required in light of McCoy's *Last of the Fathers: James Madison and the Republican Legacy* (Cambridge, 1989), which focuses on the neglected years of Madison's retirement and rounds out the interpretation of the Republican ascendancy pioneered in McCoy's *Elusive Republic: Political Economy in Jeffersonian America* (Chapel Hill, N.C. 1980) and in chapter 10 of my own *Jeffersonian Persuasion: Evolution of a Party Ideology* (Ithaca, N.Y., 1978).

7. *Federalist* 10:60.

8. For fuller explanation and citations, see my *Jeffersonian Persuasion*, 208–13.

9. Harry Ammon, *The Genet Mission* (New York, 1973).

10. Eugene Perry Link, *Democratic-Republican Societies, 1790–1800* (New York, 1942).

11. TJ to JM, April 28, 1793, *PJM* 15:10–11.

12. JM to TJ, May 8, 1793, *PJM* 15:12–13.

13. *PJM* 15:29.

14. *PJM* 15:33.

15. The seven letters of "Pacificus" appeared initially in the *Gazette of the United States* between June 29 and July 20, 1793. They were be followed by the shorter but more effective "Letters of Americanus" at the opening of 1794.

16. TJ to JM, July 7, 1793, *PJM* 15:43.

17. James Madison, "Detached Memoranda," ed. Elizabeth Fleet, *WMQ* 3 (1946): 567–68.

18. The quotations are from "Helvidius" numbers 2 and 4, *PJM* 14:80, 106–7, but the whole of number 2 decimates the logic of Hamilton's argument that the executive possesses something like a concurrent right with the legislature to determine whether treaty obligations compel war or peace. Number 1 (especially at *PJM* 14:68) had laid a groundwork for Madison's quarrel with Hamilton's "monarchical" reasoning by insisting that even Locke and Montesquieu were faulty guides to a consideration of the separation of powers: "Both of them" were "evidently warped by a regard to the particular government of England, to which one of them owed allegiance and the other professed an admiration bordering on idolatry."

The exchange between "Helvidius" and "Pacificus" may also be instructive for the light it throws on the inadequacy of conventional terminology—"strict" and "broad" constructions—to capture the dispute precisely. Madison specifically set out to rebut Hamilton's argument that the Senate's role in making treaties and the legislature's power to declare war are exceptions to the general grant of executive powers—and, as exceptions, are to be construed *strictly*. Madison reasons that the explicit grant of these powers to the legislature *implies* strict limitations on the power of the executive to interpret treaties or declare the disposition of the United States. Here, as on the issues raised by Jay's Treaty, Madison could be seen as advocating broad construction of the powers of the House, although his principal concern was certainly with the original understanding of the federal compact and with the instrinsic nature of republican government as he conceived it. Similarly, Hamilton was certainly a broad constructionist on questions of the reach of federal powers, as well as in his wish to define the role of the executive quite broadly. Although almost any terminology would risk misunderstanding, Madison might be described most aptly as an originalist and a republican advocate of a circumscribed role for the executive. This would keep us from forgetting that his "strict constructionism" never incorporated either a textual literalism or an absolute denial of a doctrine of implied powers. Thus "Helvidius" maintains that if the war and treaty-making powers are not, by nature, "purely legislative, they partake so much more of that than of any other quality" that constitutional logic must associate them principally with that department (69). His central, republican premise is that "those who are to *conduct a war* cannot in the nature of things be proper or safe judges whether *a war ought* to be *commenced, continued,* or *concluded*" (71).

19. JM to TJ, September 2, 1793, *PJM* 15:92–93. See also JM to TJ, September 1, 1793, *PJM* 15:87–88, with which he enclosed a copy of these resolutions for Archibald Stuart, who he hoped would introduce them to a meeting at Staunton. With the Federalists seeking to use Genet's quarrel with the executive to create animosities between the United States and France, to dissolve the treaty between

them, and to substitute a connection with Britain, it was the "duty of all good citizens," he wrote, "to deliberate on the best steps that can be taken for defeating the mischief." The best antidote would be "a true and authentic expression of the sense of the people," which would have to be collected "by the agency of temperate and respectable men who have the opportunity of meeting them. This is the more requisite in the country at large at present, as the voice of particular places . . . may otherwise be mistaken for that of the nation."

20. The resolutions are printed with a useful editorial note at *PJM* 15:76–80. Under Stuart's leadership, the Staunton meeting passed resolutions paraphrasing the draft, as did a meeting in Albemarle. A Caroline County meeting led by John Taylor and Edmund Pendleton also adopted the powerful concluding paragraph word for word. All were widely published. Madison prepared the draft while visiting Monroe to complete the editing of Taylor's *Enquiry into the Principles and Tendency of Certain Public Measures* (Philadelphia, 1793), which was another major landmark in the development of the Republican attack on Federalism and virtually an official expression of Republican principles and understandings at this time. For the contents and preparation of the later, see *Jeffersonian Persuasion*, 195–200.

21. JM to TJ, September 2, 1793, *PJM* 15:93.

22. For its background and an excellent analysis, see Merrill O. Peterson, *Thomas Jefferson and the New Nation*, 512–15, and "Thomas Jefferson and Commercial Policy, 1783–1793," *WMQ* 22 (1965): 584–610. For an account less flattering to Jefferson (or Madison), see Stanley Elkins and Eric McKitrick, *The Age of Federalism: The Early American Republic, 1788–1800* (New York, 1993), chap. 6.

23. The resolutions of January 3, 1794 are in *PJM* 15:167–69. Madison spoke at length in their defense on January 14 (182–201) and on January 30–31 (210–43), but he added little to the substance of his earlier arguments for discrimination against the British. Note, however, his response to arguments that the mercantile community opposed discrimination: "The body of merchants who carry on the American commerce is well known to be composed of so great a proportion of individuals who are either British subjects or trading on British capital or enjoying the profits of British consignments that the mercantile opinion here might not be an American opinion" (237). Elkins and McKitrick are quite right to stress the Virginians' instinctive dislike for many of the people actually engaged in the oceanic commerce they were trying to protect.

24. The editorial note on Madison in the Third Congress, *PJM* 15:145–52, is a good brief review of the session, as is John C. Miller, *The Federalist Era* (New York, 1960), 148–54. Little of Madison's outgoing correspondence survives from this session, but he reviewed it at length in his "Political Observations" of April 20, 1795 (*PJM* 15:511–34).

25. "The result of the insurrection ought to be a lesson to every part of the Union against disobedience to the laws. Examples of this kind are as favorable to the enemies of republican government as the event proves them to be dangerous to the authors" (JM to Hubbard Taylor, November 15, 1794, *PJM* 15:378).

26. JM to Monroe, December 4, 1794, *PJM* 15:406; JM to TJ, November 30, 1794, *PJM* 15:396. Madison's draft (November 24, 1794, *PJM* 15:386–87) expressed the House's concurrence in Washington's regret "that any part of our

fellow citizens should have shown themselves capable of an insurrection" that could be used by enemies of republican government as a "calumny against it," then noted that the body of the people had shown themselves as ready "to crush licentiousness as they have been to defeat usurpation."

27. JM to TJ, November 30, 1794, *PJM* 15:397.

28. JM to Monroe, December 4, 1794, *PJM* 15:406.

29. *PJM* 15:390–92. The House eventually inserted a compromise proposed by John Nicholas: "And we learn, with the greatest concern, that any misrepresentations whatever of the Government and its proceedings, either by individuals or combinations of men, should have been made and so far credited as to foment the flagrant outrage which has been committed on the laws." But Madison clearly saw the reply, together with Washington's unyielding response, as a Federalist victory.

30. JM to TJ, December 21, 1794, *PJM* 15:419. For Jefferson's angry agreement, see his reply of December 28, 1794, in *PJM* 15:426–28.

31. JM to Monroe, December 14, 1794, *PJM* 15:407. Compare JM to TJ, November 30, 1794, *PJM* 15:397–98: "If the people of America are so far degenerated already as not to see or to see with indifference that the citadel of their liberties is menaced by the precedent before their eyes, they require abler advocates than they now have to save them from the consequences."

32. JM, "Political Reflections," *PJM* 17:238–39. This appeared originally in the Philadelphia *Aurora* on February 23, 1799.

33. Jerald A. Combs, *The Jay Treaty* (Berkeley, Calif., 1970); Charles R. Ritcheson, *Aftermath of Revolution: British Policy toward the United States, 1783–1795* (Dallas, Tex., 1969), chap. 16; and Elkins and McKitrick, *Age of Federalism*, 406–14.

34. Washington delayed the signing in consequence of new reports of British seizures of American foodstuffs bound for France. He ultimately signed, in part, because the Federalists in the administration used intercepted letters from the French ambassador to suggest that Secretary of State Edmund Randolph, the principal opponent of acting before this matter was resolved, had been involved in improper communications with and solicitation of money from the French. Randolph's innocence has long been generally accepted. For new and disturbing light on Federalist motives and on Washington's own conduct in the matter, see Mary K. Bonsteel Tachau, "George Washington and the Reputation of Edmund Randolph," *JAH* 73 (1986): 15–34.

35. Miller, *Federalist Era*, 168–71.

36. JM to Robert R. Livingston, August 10, 1795, *PJM* 16:46–47. See, similarly, the letter to an unknown recipient (perhaps John Beckley) of August 23, 1795, in *PJM* 16:56–58. Again Madison complained bitterly to Livingston, who asked him to address the people and the president on the subject, that Hamilton and Jay had both urged the ratification of the Constitution on grounds that it would enable the United States "to extort what we justly claimed from G.B." Now, both would "voluntarily abandon" the power they had urged.

37. Hamilton initiated his letters of "Camillus" in the New York *Argus* on July 22. They eventually extended to thirty-eight installments, ten of which were written by Rufus King (*PAH*, vol. 18). Jefferson believed that both "Camillus" and Noah

Webster's "Letters of Curtius" were the work of Hamilton: "Hamilton is really a colossus to the antirepublican party. Without numbers, he is an host within himself. . . . When he comes forward, there is nobody but yourself who can meet him" (to JM, September 21, 1795, *PJM* 16:88).

38. See the excellent editorial note on the background and drafting of the petition, which was not earlier known to have been Madison's, in *PJM* 16:62–69. Madison's initial draft of the petition, which was revised at least three times is at *PJM* 16:69–77. The second revision may have been done in conjunction with an early October visit to Monticello, perhaps with some involvement by Jefferson.

39. The "Petition to the General Assembly of the Commonwealth of Virginia" as printed in the *Virginia Herald and Fredericksburg and Falmouth Advertiser* on October 30, 1795—from which it was picked up by the *Virginia Gazette*, the New York *Argus*, the *Aurora*, and other national papers—is in *PJM* 16:95–104; quotation at 95. The body of the petition, in five parts, is Madison's fullest attack on the treaty on substantive grounds: it compelled the United States to comply with the Treaty of Peace and to make compensation for previous delays without demanding similar compensation from Britain; it failed to protect American seamen from British impressment; it accepted the British practice of seizing provisions bound for places not actually blockaded; it broadened the definition of contraband to include naval stores; it abandoned the principle that free ships make free goods, although the treaties with France and Holland stipulated the reverse; and it took from Congress, by action of the president and Senate alone, the power to favor American over British shipping in its tonnage laws or to secure reciprocal agreements with other nations by peculiar commercial privileges. "A treaty thus unequal in its conditions, thus derogating from our national rights, thus insidious in some of its objects, and thus alarming in its operation to the dearest interests of the United States in their commerce and navigation" was (in the October version of the petition) "unworthy the voluntary acceptance of an independent people" (103). It was (in the November versions) "an abject sacrifice which ought to have been rejected with disdain in the most humiliating and adverse circumstances."

40. See JM to Monroe, December 20, 1795, and JM to TJ, December 27, 1795, *PJM* 16: 170, 173.

41. JM to TJ, March 6, 1796, *PJM* 16:247. Indeed, with Federalists suggesting that Livingston aimed to damage the administration or even to impeach Washington, the New York congressman agreed to except papers that might affect ongoing negotiations. Madison then moved unsuccessfully to extend the exception to any papers whose disclosure Washington judged to be against the national interest, insisting both on "delicacy to the other departments of government" and on the seriousness of the question whether the treaty power "supersedes the powers of the House of Representatives . . . so as to take to the executive all deliberative will and leave the House only an instrumental agency" (March 7, 1796, *PJM* 16:254).

42. See JM to TJ, April 4, 1796, *PJM* 16:286. This letter anticipated the substance of the resolutions introduced by Thomas Blount of North Carolina on April 6, which denied that the House was obliged to give its reasons for requesting the papers and insisted that "when a treaty must depend for its execution . . . on a law or laws to be passed by Congress . . . it is the constitutional right and duty of the

House of Representatives to deliberate on the expediency or inexpedience of carrying such treaty into effect." Miller, *Federalist Era*, 171–76, and the editorial note on "Madison in the Fourth Congress," *PJM* 16:143–49, offer excellent summaries of the proceedings and of Madison's stands, although the course of these debates and the stategies of both parties would certainly reward a fuller study. Elkins and McKitrick, *Age of Federalism*, 415–49, are particularly instructive for their insistence that public opinion, by this time, was swinging decisively in favor of the treaty.

43. Speech of March 10, 1796, *PJM* 17:255–63.

44. Fisher Ames to George Richards Minot, April 2, 1796, in *Works of Fisher Ames, with a Selection from His Speeches and Correspondence*, ed. Seth Ames (Boston, 1854), 1:191: Madison "is deeply implicated" by Washington's appeal to the proceedings of the Constitutional Convention. "Most persons think him irrecoverably disgraced."

45. For the accuracy of this claim, see H. Jefferson Powell, "The Original Understanding of Original Intent," *Harvard Law Review* 98 (1985): 885–948.

46. JM, speech of April 6, 1796, *PJM* 17:290–301, quotations at 294–96. Washington's message of March 30, refusing the House call for papers, did so partly on the grounds that a motion was made at the Convention "'that no treaty should be binding on the United States which was not ratified by a law'; and that the proposition was explicitly rejected"—an argument similar to the one that Madison had offered in opposition to the bank. But even in his "Detached Memoranda," written late in life, Madison insisted that Washington's citation of the Convention journal was erroneous. The vote of August 23, 1787, he argued, did not address the issue before the House in 1796: whether that body had "a legislative right to deliberate on the provisions depending on them for its execution" (i.e., on whether to vote the appropriations necessary to carry the treaty into effect). He repeated what he said in 1796 and on more than one occasion between 1790 and the current debate: "If the meaning of the Constitution" was to be discovered anywhere except in its text, "it was not in the General Convention, but the State Conventions. The former prepared it only; it was from the latter that it derived its validity and authority.... It is the sense of the nation . . . not the sense of the General Convention that is to be consulted" (543–44).

47. *PJM* 17:313–27. This, however, added little of critical importance to the position he had taken in his petition and letters.

48. And one that raises interesting questions about the degree to which Edward Livingston was right in his assessment of Madison's weaknesses as a party leader (and as president later on). Writing to his brother, Robert R. Livingston, on December 24, 1795, the freshman congressman from New York City said: "His greatest fault as a politician appears to me a want of decision and a disposition to magnify his adversaries' strengths. [He has] a habit of considering the objections to his own plans so long and so frequently that they acquire a real weight and influence his conduct. . . . He never determines to act until he is absolutely forced by the pressure of affairs and then regrets that he had neglected some better opportunity" (quoted in *PJM* 16:248 n. 5). Allowance should be made for Livingston's inexperience and slight acquaintance with Madison, for the intrinsic difficulties of the particular situation, and for the difficulty of gauging the mood of

a House that contained thirty-nine new members. Madison knew what he wanted on Jay's Treaty as on other things, and he could be as persevering as a bulldog when he had set his course. Nevertheless, as both a thinker and a political strategist, he did see matters in all their complexity—the flaws and weaknesses in his own position as well as the strengths of his opponents. Sometimes, as in his March 10 speech on the treaty, he could be so candid about this that he opened himself to derision. Moreover, he was not personally assertive, not inclined to whip people into line, and often more inclined to urge moderation than to spur the partisan spirit. On the treaty, as on other things, he preferred to gather the majority's sentiments and work from those, not to create a majority behind him. He was also capable of real uncertainty himself about the meaning of the Constitution. On top of this, Madison (and most Republicans) continually underestimated the extent to which Washington was coming to agree with their opponents and was personally responsible for strategies that would defeat their own best plans. On Jay's Treaty, nevertheless, Madison was soundly whipped, in a strategic sense, by Washington's timing of critical actions and by the president's great skill in using his unparalleled prestige to influence public opinion. A closer study of proceedings on the treaty would be most instructive on the political leadership of both these men.

49. See JM to TJ, May 1, 1796, *PJM* 16:343.

50. For the administration of John Adams, Stephen G. Kurtz, *The Presidency of John Adams: The Collapse of Federalism, 1795–1800* (Philadelphia, 1957), Manning J. Dauer, *The Adams Federalists* (Baltimore, 1953), and Ralph A. Brown, *The Presidency of John Adams* (Lawrence, Kans., 1975) should be added to sources previously cited. Alexander DeConde, *The Quasi-War: The Politics and Diplomacy of the Undeclared War with France, 1797–1801* (New York, 1966), remains the fullest source for the diplomacy I discuss herein. Although I accept Elkins and McKitrick's argument that French policy was driven more by French domestic politics than by real anger over the Anglo-American accord, it is also clear that the Directory was consciously attempting to assist their Republican sympathizers in the United States.

51. James Morton Smith, *Freedom's Fetters: The Alien and Sedition Laws and American Civil Liberties* (Ithaca, N.Y., 1956), and John C. Miller, *Crisis in Freedom: The Alien and Sedition Acts* (Boston, 1951).

52. TJ to JM, June 7, 1798, *PJM* 17:143.

53. See Jefferson's famous letter of June 1, 1798, warning John Taylor against secession, *WTJ* 8:430–33.

54. Adrienne Koch and Harry Ammon, "The Virginia and Kentucky Resolutions: An Episode in Jefferson's and Madison's Defense of Civil Liberties," *WMQ* 5 (1948): 145–76, remains the most authoritative study.

55. Recall, especially, Madison's *Federalist* 39:254: "The Constitution is to be founded on the assent and ratification of the people of America . . . not as individuals composing one entire nation; but as composing the distinct and independent states to which they respectively belong. . . . The act therefore establishing the Constitution will not be a *national* but a *federal* act. That it will be a federal and not a national act, . . . the act of the people as forming so many independent states, not as forming one aggregate nation, is obvious from this single consideration: that it is to result neither from the decision of a *majority* of the people of

the Union, nor from that of a *majority* of the states. It must result from the *unanimous* assent of the several states that are parties to it. . . . Were the people regarded in this transaction as forming one nation, the will of the majority of the whole people of the United States would bind the minority. . . . Each state in ratifying the Constitution is considered as a sovereign body independent of all others, and only to be bound by its own voluntary act." This passage, more clearly than any other, seems to invalidate Edmund Morgan's suggestion in *Inventing the People: The Rise of Popular Sovereignty in England and America* (New York, 1988) that Madison was calling in the sovereign people of the nation as a whole to overcome the sovereign states.

56. For this effort, which the two renewed as the resolutions of 1798 were being prepared, see Koch and Ammon, "Virginia and Kentucky Resolutions," 152–54, and *PJM* 17:33–37, 169–73.

57. The Virginia Resolutions of December 21, 1798, in *PJM* 17:189–90.

58. The detailed chronology in Koch and Ammon may be supplemented by the editorial note in *PJM* 17:185–88.

59. Koch and Ammon, "Virginia and Kentucky Resolutions," 159. The Kentucky Resolutions passed the state house of representatives on November 10, one week before Jefferson's letter, and were unanimously approved by the Kentucky senate three days later. As actually approved, they softened Jefferson's draft considerably. It is at least highly probable that Madison had seen the softened version by the time he wrote his own.

60. Jefferson's rough draft and fair copy of the resolutions are printed side by side, together with the resolutions as adopted, in *WTJ* 8:458–79.

61. After reading Madison's draft, Jefferson wrote Wilson Carey Nicholas, who carried the letter to John Taylor, that he still believed that the resolutions should invite the others states to join in declaring that the acts "were *ab initio*, null, void, and of no force or effect" (November 29, 1798, *WTJ* 8:483). Taylor introduced the resolutions with this phrase inserted, but moved to strike it out again before the vote of December 21. The editors of *PJM* point out that Madison was visiting relatives in Hanover County, near Richmond, during these proceedings, could have known about insertion of the phrase, and may have asked Taylor to delete it (17:187–88).

62. For Madison's late-life battle with the nullifiers over their use of the Virginia and Kentucky Resolutions, see the superb discussion in McCoy, *Last of the Fathers*, chap. 4. Here, Madison's central contention was that the right of the parties to the compact to act collectively as judges in the last (constitutional) resort of violations of the charter had to be distinguished from the claim that any party individually could constitutionally initiate suspension of a federal law. The latter doctrine, he maintained, would end in minority rule.

63. JM to TJ, December 29, 1798, *PJM* 17:191–92.

64. Report of 1800, *PJM* 17:348–49.

65. *PJM* 17:189. Partly by eliding the phrase italicized in my quotation, Koch and Ammon ("Virginia and Kentuck Resolutions," 161) leave the impression that Madison's resolutions were markedly different in their fundamental character from either Jefferson's draft or the Kentucky Resolutions as enacted. Here and in

her *Jefferson and Madison: The Great Collaboration* (New York, 1950), Koch emphatically insisted that Madison's commitment to the Union was more nearly "absolute" than Jefferson's. At minimum, however, we should recognize that there is logically no difference between declaring an act "unconstitutional" and declaring it to be "not law, but void and of no force or effect." In overruling legislatures, the courts do nullify their acts on just these grounds. The difference lies entirely in the words, which would appear more problematic only in the retrospective light that would be thrown on them by the "nullification" doctrine as expounded by Calhoun.

66. *PJM* 17:189–90. On the other hand, it is by no means clear even here that Madison was implying that any single state could constitutionally act on its own against a federal law. He still refers to states in the plural.

67. TJ to JM, November 17, 1789, *PJM* 17:175. Compare TJ to John Taylor, *WTJ* 8:458–59.

68. TJ to JM, August 23, 1799, *PJM* 17:257–58, suggesting a meeting at Monticello with Monroe and Wilson Carey Nicholas to coordinate responses by both states. This meeting did occur, though Nicholas was absent, the first weekend of September (ed. note, *PJM* 17:304). For Madison's success in tempering Jefferson's advice to the Kentuckians on the matter, see Koch and Ammon, "Virginia and Kentucky Resolutions," 167–69.

69. JM to TJ, January 4, 1800, *PJM* 17:302.

70. Koch and Ammon, "Virginia and Kentucky Resolutions," 173.

71. For its background, preparation, and passage through the legislature, see the editorial note in *PJM* 17:303–307. The report itself is printed at 307–51.

72. Madison could later say with justice that South Carolina's interposition against the protective tariff plainly failed this test.

73. *PJM* 17:308–11.

74. The language of this passage (*PJM* 17:311) was deliberately cautious, but taken out of context, it could still be read as making a larger concession than the author probably intended. It should be read in close conjunction with Madison's observations of October 1788 on Jefferson's draft of a constitution for Virginia. Here and in his speech in the First Congress on the power to remove executive officials, Madison observed that neither the federal nor the state constitutions made provision for a disagreement between the branches of a government on the constitutionality of laws. In consequence and by default, the decision could fall to the courts, which would have to agree or refuse to execute the law. "This makes the judiciary department paramount in fact to the legislature, which was never intended and can never be proper" (*PJM* 11:293). During his retirement, as he battled both the nullifiers and the Marshall Court, Madison argued that the federal courts were indeed the tribunals of next-to-last constitutional resort in arguments between the federal government and a single state, but not in arguments between the branches of the federal government itself. The states collectively, of course, always retained the ultimate authority to override the courts—by constitutional amendments or even by insisting on a constitutional convention.

75. *PJM* 17:312.

76. *PJM* 17:312–16.

77. *PJM* 17:317–45.

78. Leonard W. Levy, *Legacy of Oppression: Freedom of Speech and Press in Early American History* (Cambridge, Mass., 1960).

79. *PJM* 17:326–33.

80. Ibid., 336–45.

81. Ibid., 347–50.

82. In addition to McCoy, see Lacy K. Ford Jr., "Inventing the Concurrent Majority: Madison, Calhoun, and the Problem of Majoritarianism in American Political Thought," *JSH* 60 (1994): 19–58.

83. The issues raised by the Sedition Act and by the long succession of "abuses" in the years since 1791 were very like the ones James Otis and the other revolutionary pamphleteers had struggled with from 1764 until the Declaration of Independence. Like Otis, Jefferson, or even Locke, Madison insisted in the Resolutions of 1798 and in the Report of 1800 that only a long succession of tyrannical abuses could justify resistance. But such a long succession of abuses was exactly what the revolutionaries, the Republicans, and the secessionists of 1861 believed that they were faced with and exactly what Parliament, the Federalists, and the North denied.

84. "Political Reflections," February 23, 1799, *PJM* 17:247.

85. Jefferson's Inaugural Address, *WTJ* 9:197–98.

APPENDIX. THE PERSONALITIES OF "PUBLIUS"

1. JM to TJ, August 11, 1788, *PJM* 10:227.

2. James Madison, "Detached Memoranda," ed. Elizabeth Fleet, *WMQ* 3 (1946): 565.

3. The relevant numbers of "Brutus" are 6 through 8, *DHRC* 15:110–17, 234–40, 335–38.

4. See, especially, Richard H. Kohn, *Eagle and Sword: The Federalists and the Creation of the Military Establishment in America, 1783–1802* (New York, 1975).

5. "Observations on Jefferson's Draft of a Constitution for Virginia," October 15, 1788, *PJM* 11:293.

6. Gottfried Dietze, *The Federalist: A Classic on Federalism and Free Government* (Baltimore, 1960), 260–64, 269, 271.

7. Douglass Adair, "The Authorship of the Disputed Federalist Papers," in *Fame and the Founding Fathers: Essays by Douglass Adair*, ed. Trevor Colbourn (New York, 1974), 70.

8. See Alpeus Thomas Mason, "The Federalist—A Split Personality," *AHR* 57 (1952): 634–40.

9. Isaac Kramnick, ed., *The Federalist Papers* (Harmondsworth, U.K., 1987), 67. See, more fully, 67–75.

10. Two examples may suffice to illustrate the discrepancy between Hamilton's published and private opinions. In *The Federalist*, Hamilton was every bit as insistent as Madison that the states would be able to intervene effectively to check potential federal usurpations (see 28:179–80). No one, to my knowledge, believes that he

was genuinely comfortable with this idea. Hamilton also insisted that commercial retaliation against the British would be one of the first measures of the new government (11:67), a policy he roundly opposed from the outset (although it is just possible that he may not have opposed it in 1787). Madison attempted throughout his career to defend the Constitution as approved by the people (as he understood it). Hamilton always regarded the Constitution as milk and water, which a vigorous administration would have to shape into substantial stuff.

11. *PJM* 10:163–64, 207–16; 11:353.

Index